CULTURE,
RESOURCE,
and
ECONOMIC
ACTIVITY

PAUL F. GRIFFIN
AJMER SINGH
WAYNE RODGERS WHITE
RONALD L. CHATHAM

cartography and artwork by
JAY B. VANDERFORD

allyn and bacon, inc.
boston london sydney

CULTURE, RESOURCE, and ECONOMIC ACTIVITY

AN INTRODUCTION TO ECONOMIC GEOGRAPHY

second edition

752860

Cover photo courtesy of the Canadian Government Travel Bureau

The author and the publisher would like to express appreciation to the General Media
Corporation for the use of charts, graphs, and maps, and to the following for the use of
photos: Canadian Government Travel Bureau (p. 10), North Dakota Travel Division (p. 31),
Swedish Tourist Traffic Association (p. 65), The British Travel Association (p. 89), National
Aeronautics and Space Administration (p. 111), U.S. Soil and Conservation Service (p. 123),
U.S. Postal Service (p. 416), Florida Department of Commerce (p. 174), Imperial Oil (p. 189),
National Film Board (p. 202), Pacific Gas and Electric Company (p. 227), Bethlehem Steel
Corporation (pp. 246, 461), United States Steel (p. 262), Northrop Corporation (p. 282),
Humble Oil & Refining Company (p. 327), Atlanta Convention Bureau (pp. 359, 368), Arthur
Lavine (p. 396), Talbot Lovering (p. 406), Australian News and Information Bureau (p. 428),
Alberta, Canada, Department of Industry and Tourism (p. 444), Press-und Informationsamt
of Bonn (p. 475), A.T. & T. Photo Center (p. 491), and U.S. Department of Agriculture
(p. 139).

LIBRARY OF CONGRESS CATALOGING IN PUBLICATION DATA
Main entry under title:

Culture, resource, and economic activity.

Includes bibliographies and index.

1. Geography, Economic.   I.   Griffin, Paul Francis.
HF1027.C85   1976   330'.9   75-33221

ISBN 0-205-05021-2

CONTENTS

Preface x

INTRODUCTION   I
INTRODUCTION 2

1 GEOGRAPHY AND ECONOMIC ACTIVITY   3
economic activity 6;   economic geography 7;   references 8

2 CULTURAL FRAMEWORK OF RESOURCES AND
ECONOMIC ACTIVITY   10
culture and society 11;   overriding characteristics of culture,
society, and economic activity 11;   culture and resource 16;
wants 20;   exchange 21;   social choices and priorities 22;
making social choices 25;   analysis of resources and
economic activity 26;   references 26

VARIABLES IN ECONOMIC ACTIVITY   II
INTRODUCTION 30

3 MATERIALS–RESOURCE FRAMEWORK   31
limits on the supply of material resources 32;   land-based
resources 32;   energy resources 36;   minerals 44;   materials
crisis 47;   water resources 50;   ocean resources 50;   fresh
water resources 52;   pollution 56;   references 63

4 ECONOMIC FRAMEWORK   65
demand 66;   supply 69;   market 71;   substitution 76;
comparative advantage of location 77;   spatial dispersion and
efficiency 87;   references 88

5 SOCIOPOLITICAL FRAMEWORK   89
political factors 90;   social factors 97;   references 109

6   **TECHNOLOGICAL FRAMEWORK**   **111**
knowledge *112;*   skills *113;*   tools *114;*   technique *114;*
the process of technological change *115;*   technology and
economic activity *118;*   references *120*

PRIMARY ECONOMIC ACTIVITY
INTRODUCTION 122

7   **LOCATION THEORY OF PRIMARY ACTIVITIES**   **123**
the Von Thünen theory *124;*   spatial dynamics of agricultural
location *132;*   world agricultural regions *136;*   references *137*

8   **WORLD AGRICULTURAL SYSTEMS**   **139**
origin and dispersion *140;*   systems of agricultural production
142;   a hungry world: the challenge to agriculture *171;*
references *172*

9   **FISHING**   **174**
the food web *175;*   distribution and consumption *176;*   the
ocean's productivity *178;*   inland fishing *185;*   a look ahead
185;   references *188*

10   **FORESTS AND FOREST PRODUCTS**   **189**
forests *190;*   the natural environment of forests *190;*
location *191;*   classification of forests *192;*   volume *193;*
distribution *193;*   production *193;*   commercial products of
forests *194;*   nonwood forest products *197;*   international
trade *199;*   trends *200;*   references *201*

11   **MINING**   **202**
iron ore *203;*   ferroalloys *206;*   nonferrous metals *207;*
fossil fuels *209;*   natural gas *215;*   coal *216;*   nuclear fuels
223;   references *223*

SECONDARY ECONOMIC ACTIVITY
INTRODUCTION 226

12   **LOCATION THEORY OF SECONDARY
ECONOMIC ACTIVITY**   **227**
factors of industry location *228;*   current trends in major
location factors *235;*   theories of location of secondary
activities *238;*   references *244*

13 **MANUFACTURING SYSTEMS** **246**
eotechnic phase *247;* paleotechnic phase *249;* neotechnic phase *251;* general patterns of manufacturing activities *252;* factors modifying the operation of economic forces *258;* advantages brought by industry to a location *258;* manufacturing regions of the world *259;* references *260*

14 **MANUFACTURING: IRON AND STEEL AND LESSER INDUSTRIAL METALS** **262**
locational factors *263;* iron and steel industry *264;* lesser industrial metals *274;* references *280*

15 **METAL-FABRICATING INDUSTRIES** **282**
machine tools *283;* metal fabricating *284;* agricultural implements and farm machinery *287;* industrial machinery *289;* shipbuilding *292;* the automotive industry *297;* aerospace industry *303;* references *307*

16 **TEXTILE AND GARMENT INDUSTRIES** **309**
textiles *310;* garment manufacture *321;* economic outlook for textile and garment industries *325;* references *325*

17 **CHEMICAL INDUSTRIES** **327**
industrial chemicals *329;* agricultural chemicals *335;* petroleum-based chemicals *337;* economic outlook for chemical industries *340;* references *341*

18 **ELECTRICAL MACHINERY AND EQUIPMENT** **343**
electrical equipment *344;* electronics industry *347;* references *355*

TERTIARY ECONOMIC ACTIVITY **V**
INTRODUCTION 358

19 **LOCATION THEORY OF TERTIARY ECONOMIC ACTIVITY** **359**
central place theory *360;* references *366*

20 **SYSTEMS OF TERTIARY ECONOMIC ACTIVITIES** **368**
tertiarization of an economic system *369;* regional tertiary systems *373;* tertiary activities in central places *375;* references *379*

Contents

21 **TRANSPORTATION SERVICES**   **380**
theoretical considerations *381;*   waterways *383;*   railways
386;   motorways *389;*   airways *391;*   pipelines *393;*
references *395*

22 **MARKETING SERVICES**   **396**
functions of marketing *397;*   location of marketing activities
398;   wholesaling *400;*   retailing *400;*   marketing and
consumerism *402;*   references *405*

23 **MONEY, BANKING, AND FINANCIAL SERVICES**   **406**
money and its functions *407;*   federal reserve system *408;*
financial intermediaries *413;*   real estate services *414;*
references *414*

24 **GOVERNMENT SERVICES**   **416**
government participation in economic activity *418;*   U.S.
federal budget and economic activity *422;*   references *426*

25 **COMMUNICATION SERVICES**   **428**
theoretical considerations *429;*   a classification of
communication services *430;*   postal service *431;*   telegraph
services *432;*   telephone services *432;*   printing and
publishing *433;*   radio and television broadcasting *435;*
communications in the U.S. *435;*   references *442*

26 **RECREATION SERVICES**   **444**
demand for recreational services *445;*   international tourist
travel *446;*   recreational patterns abroad *450;*   Americans at
play *452*

POLICY AND PLANNING
INTRODUCTION   460

27 **REGIONAL PLANNING**   **461**
historical antecedents *462;*   regional development *463;*
planning process *464;*   planning approaches *467;*   state
planning *470;*   regional planning *471;*   local planning *473;*
references *473*

28 **MAN, ENVIRONMENT, AND ECONOMIC ACTIVITY**   **475**
concepts and characteristics of environment *476;*   environmental deterioration *477;*   causes of environmental

deterioration *480;*   solutions to environmental deterioration
483;   suggested programs *487;*   references *489*

29   **PROSPECTS   491**
the energy crisis *495;*   the other energy crisis *497;*
environmental pollution *497;*   references *498*

Index 501

PREFACE

This book is an introduction to economic geography in particular and to social science in general, reflecting an innovative approach and retention of well-established core materials. The text is designed to provide the reader with an analytical and meaningful understanding of the environment.

The seventies are a decade of notable changes in the focus of economic problems and policies to solve them. Almost all problems relating to food, energy, environment, unemployment, and inflation emerge from spatial differentiation in culture, political institutions, resources, and production. Economic geographers increasingly concern themselves with broader and more integrated approaches to understanding, analyzing, and solving these complex problems. Recognizing the need for such an approach, economic activities and related problems are presented through a model or systems approach that depicts man as a force influencing economic activities in the context of a space-time continuum.

The text is constructed around four interrelated frameworks—material, economic, sociopolitical, and technological—which are integrated into location theories of primary, secondary, and tertiary economic systems. Theory chapters are followed by substantive material, demonstrating practical application of theory.

We are indebted to all those who have supplied materials, ideas, and criticisms. Special thanks are owed to many colleagues who have contributed to the literature of economic geography and economics. We wish especially to thank reviewers of the revised manuscript for their scholarly criticisms and helpful suggestions from which we have benefitted greatly. Helpful comments from Fred Hirsch on the general organization of the book are gratefully acknowledged. We also wish to thank Alfred Kuhn and Irving Morrisett for offering many helpful suggestions on Part I, and Jay Vanderford who was responsible for selecting and compiling all of the maps, graphs, and drawings. Finally, we wish to thank our students, who serve as our patient critics.

Paul F. Griffin
Ajmer Singh
Wayne Rodgers White
Ronald L. Chatham

I

INTRODUCTION

CHAPTERS

1 Geography and Economic Activity
2 Cultural Framework of Resources and Economic Activity

introduction

Resources attain meaning if and when recognized as such by man. Their use and preservation are culturally defined. Because societies differ culturally, their perceptions of resources and human wants are relative. Cultural differentiation leads to variability in the kind and level of economic activities among geographical areas and among societies.

Economic activity emerges from a complex interplay of resources and culture. Resources and climatic environments exert major influences on the choice and level of economic activities. Culture, resources, and economic activities are dynamically interrelated. The cultural aspects of man play the commanding role in the choice and level of economic activities.

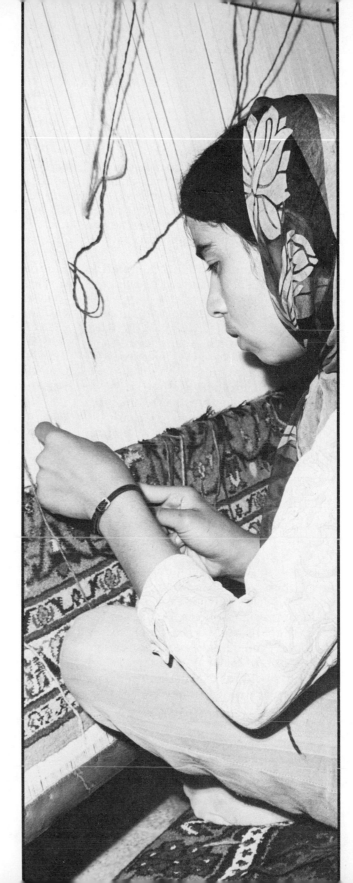

geography and
economic activity

1

1

The overriding objective of all sciences, whether physical or social, is to analyze, to interpret, and to understand the vast system on the earth's surface composed of man and his environment. Even before man developed analytical patterns that could be properly called science, we[1] have directly and indirectly attempted to increase our understanding of this system. The system is indeed vast, with many interrelated elements with a multitude of forms and functions. Often the system appears too complex for rational comprehension. However, by approaching the interrelated elements of the system with an analytical method, a sense of order, pattern, and regularity emerges.

Economic phenomena are basically a function of cultural milieu. Man's determination of economic activities begins with his perception and recognition of resources. One culture may consider certain parts of the environment as useful, or economic, resources, while another culture may consider them as wasteful. Besides the influences on the choice, variety, quantity, and quality of economic resources, cultural attributes direct what, how much, where, and when the goods and services are produced. Interaction of resources results in an array of goods and services that, to the economic geographer, assume certain spatial patterns and configurations.

These patterns may be analyzed with the aid of various frameworks—eco-

nomic, social, political, and technological. The frameworks, the choice of which is based on convenience and academic preferences for division of labor, provide tools to analyze the influence of culture on economic activities. To facilitate the understanding of the spatial patterns of economic activities, total production of goods and services may be classified on a functional basis as primary, secondary, tertiary, and quaternary production. Such a classification also permits the use of integrated models to show the convergence of the frameworks and to predict economic phenomena. Prediction can be verified by the detailed observation and analysis of the selected activities under each of these broad classifications. Some examples of integrative models are: the Von Thünen model of primary activities, the Weber and Lösch model for secondary activities, and Christaller's model for tertiary activities.

Understanding of economic activities may be enhanced by quantitative and statistical tools. These tools are implements cultural man uses to cause conscious and planned changes in the spatial patterns of resource use. A diagrammatic view of how cultural man acts as an overriding agent controlling economic phenomena is shown in Figure 1.

The theme and approach to economic geography described here is one of several practiced by the profession. We feel that this approach is superior because it emphasizes why certain activities are located where they are, rather than merely describing them. However, all approaches have four major, recurrent concepts. Generally, these are *man, environment, place,* and *relationship*. There are several ways in which these four concepts may be organized; however, the organization of these concepts will not necessarily indicate the major approach of geography.

In the four concepts associated with geography, you are part of man and, consequently, a part of the organization

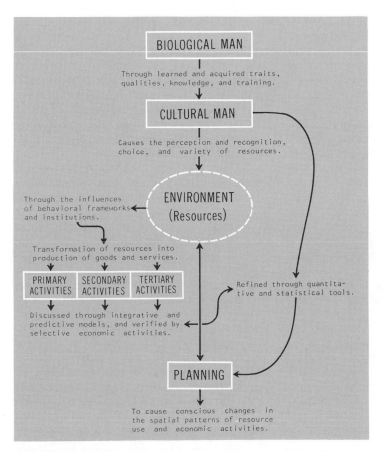

FIGURE 1–1 *Cultural Man as the Overriding Agent of Economic Phenomena*

of these concepts. Specifically, a proper manner of organizing them diagrammatically is:

Man is used generically and includes all men, women, and children. It refers to *cultural man*—man within the context of culture and society. *Biological man* is economically similar to unimproved land that has been protected from destruction by fire and erosion.

Environment is not limited to aspects of the physical environment (such as soil, water, landforms, vegetation), but more importantly encompasses all phenomena that are part of the environment by any group of men. For example, if we wish to examine coffee production in Brazil we must know something of the consuming habits of people in the United States, because Americans are part of the environment of the coffee producer. For reasons that will be developed later in this chapter, the environment of one group or society of men is not the same as another group's.

5

The concept of *relationships* is centrally located in the diagram because it is the essential and integrating element. It includes all processes, interactions, and events that take place between man and environment.

None of the four concepts is static. Man, environment, place, and relationships are constantly changing. The "place" occupied by the principles of the Industrial Revolution (mass production techniques, for example) is not the same "place" today as it was one hundred years ago or even last year. The "relationships" of the hunting-gathering Bushman are not the same today as ten years ago, and cultural man is not the same either. Not only do these concepts reflect change over time, but more important for the geographer, they change from place to place (across space) at the same time.

From this brief analysis, we may attempt a conceptualization of geography: Geography is the study of relationships between man and environment within the context of place. Thus we have added one other ingredient to this definition: "the study of." Mountains do not imply geography. Geography is a perspective from which some of the characteristics of man and environment are analyzed, and it can be used by a historian, political scientist, or student.

Economic geography stresses the set of man's activities that are generally referred to as economic.

ECONOMIC ACTIVITY

It is commonly assumed that man has social, political, economic, religious, and other types of activities and motivations. But what is an economic activity and how does it differ from other activities? Consider the following examples: Is casting a vote in an election a political activity, if the vote is cast for a candidate whose economic philosophy is in agreement with the voter? What if the election of the candidate results in the voter's acquiring a better job, a larger farm subsidy, or a government contract to construct a building? Clearly, in this situation voting is a political activity, but it was partly motivated by an economic consideration. How do we distinguish between the two? And, is the person who receives money for counting the ballots engaged in an economic or political activity?

Does the nationalization of foreign investments within a sovereign state constitute a political or economic act? If an entrepreneur decides not to invest in a particular manufacturing operation due to political instability in the area, is this an economic or political decision? Is the priest, rabbi, or minister who receives money to conduct religious services engaged in an economic or religious activity? In the United States, most weddings are performed by clergymen. May we then conclude that weddings are religious activities, even though some political entity must first issue a license?

Within the traditional Burmese village, the social beliefs and values associated with attaining a desirable "life after death" (a religious idea?) necessitated that one give all that was possible to another member of the village. (14) Indeed, many Burmese villagers would devote a great deal of labor to ventures such as hunting, gathering, agriculture, and manufacturing, solely to produce items to be given away. This cultural aspect had a significant influence on the production, distribution, and consumption of materials among the villagers. Did the processes of producing these items constitute economic or religious activities? Did the actual giving away of the materials constitute an economic, social, religious, or other activity?

The major points to emphasize are:

1. All activities are interdependent with other activities.

2. Whatever classification assigned to an activity, it is based on a person's prior experiences and ideas of what constitutes an economic, political, religious, etc., activity—which is not necessarily the same as what the people engaged in the activity think about it.

3. Any classification is arbitrary and selective; it is designed for and by the classifier.

What is an economic activity and how does it differ from other human activities? It is difficult to arrive at a satisfactory answer because all aspects of man's behavior are interdependent. Man's total activity, his behavioral patterns and entire way of life, is not a series of parts, but a whole. The terms "economic" and "political" refer to some aspect of human behavior; they do not describe something that stands alone, independent, and totally isolated from other aspects of human behavior. These concepts are only mentally contrived separations accomplished solely for the purpose of understanding human behavior. The manifestation of human behavior is not the result of a single motivation, nor can it be characterized by a single act, such as "politically motivated economic activity." The manifestation of behavior and motive are invariably results of man of complex interaction.

However, in attempting to examine the complexity of human behavior, we must devise some system of classification for purposes of analysis and communication. Even with the overriding problems and implications discussed above, we will here define one aspect of human behavior.

Economic activity is any manifestation of human behavior associated with the production, exchange, and/or consumption of goods and services.

The term *good* includes any material, i.e., tangible, object that man has ac-

quired for some use. Iron ore, automobiles, buttons, houses, shoes, hoes, slingshots, buildings, potatoes, and wheat are examples of goods. Service refers to the work done by one or several people for others. A teacher, for example, does not produce goods; he "produces" services, as does a lawyer, doctor, plumber, carpenter, taxi driver, or hairdresser. All of these workers use goods—maps, stethoscopes, wrenches, hammers, automobiles, and combs—as they perform their services.

Production refers to the process of making or creating a good or service. Man moves, changes the form of, and combines various types of matter to create goods. Man also provides ("produces") services.

Exchange is also a process, which refers to the obtaining of a good or service. It includes buying, selling, and bartering goods, as well as the transportation of goods and services from one place to another and the transfer of ownership of goods and services. The process of *consumption* includes the employment of goods and services to either produce or acquire other goods and services, as well as to satisfy a want or need. For example, an automobile is considered a consumer's good if it is used in the traditional manner of a typical American family. However, it is a producer's good when used by a taxi driver. In the first instance, we are assuming that the automobile will not be used for producing any other good or service. In the latter case, we are assuming that the owner will employ the automobile to produce a service of transporting people from place to place.

ECONOMIC GEOGRAPHY

Actually, economic geography is the study of economic activity. Since economic activity involves man's behavior, economic geography encompasses a study of the relationships between economic activity and environment within the context of a particular place.

Study would be greatly simplified if all economic activities, all environments, all places, and all relationships were exactly alike. However, such simplicity is not the case. In order to acquire some comprehension of economic activities it is necessary to analyze them as operational and homogeneous sets. The number of significant variables is quite large. However, if we can construct a mental approach that enables us to reduce the number of variables, then the task of analyzing economic activities becomes easier. This approach essentially involves the familiar process of factorizing and delineating common denominators by which relationships may become more apparent and perhaps more meaningful.

If there are common denominators, i.e., characteristics of economic activity that are present in all economic activities, analysis of common characteristics will enable us to better understand economic activity in general and specific economic activity as well. Are there, for example, characteristics common to the hunting-gathering Bushman, to you, to the people mining ore in northern Minnesota, and to the cattle rancher in Australia? Are there characteristics of industrial economic activities that are also present in pre-industrial societies? The resounding answers are yes, indeed!

The most important characteristic common to all economic activity is man who, in operating a set of elements, which may be referred to as resources, creates economic activity. Economic activity exists as a consequence of man's efforts to employ resources to achieve a set of objectives, a generalization that applies to all forms of economic activity. These efforts, however, are not random, but occur at specific places for specific reasons, although we may not be able to state all those reasons with specificity.

The efforts and reasons for economic activities are themselves consequences of other processes, particularly cultural processes. To begin our investigation of economic geography, therefore, it is logical to start with the integral and functional elements that are responsible for economic activity: culture and man's concept of resource.

references

1. Bredemeier, Harry C., and Getis, Judith, eds. *Environments, People, and Inequalities: Some Current Problems.* New York: John Wiley & Sons, 1973.

2. Bunge, William W. "The Geography of Human Survival." *Annals of the Association of American Geographers* 63 (September 1973):275–295.

3. Caldwell, Lynton Keith. *Environment: A Challenge For Modern Society.* Garden City, N.Y.: Natural History Press, 1970.

4. Ferguson, Charles E. *Economic Analysis.* Homewood, Ill.: Richard D. Irwin Co., 1974.

5. Finkelstein, Joseph. *Economists and Society: The Development of Economic Thought from Aquinas to Keynes.* New York: Harper & Row, 1973.

6. Galbraith, John K. *Economics and the Public Purpose.* Boston: Houghton Mifflin, 1973.

7. Gould, Peter. "Man Against His Environment: A Game Theoretic Framework." *Annals of the Association of American Geographers* 53 (September 1963): 290–297.

8. Hallowell, A. Irving. *Culture and Experience.* Philadelphia: University of Pennsylvania Press, 1955.

9. Hansen, Flemming. *Consumer Choice Behavior: A Cognitive Theory.* New York: Free Press, 1972.

10. Heilbroner, Robert L. *The Economic Problem.* Englewood Cliffs, N.J.: Prentice-Hall, 1970.

11. Hollander, Samuel. *The Economics of Adam Smith.* Toronto: University of Toronto Press, 1973.

12. Kaplan, David, and Manners, Robert A. *Culture Theory.* Englewood Cliffs, N.J.: Prentice-Hall, 1972.

13. Mead, Margaret. *Culture and Commitment: A Study of the Generation Gap.* New York: Natural History Press, 1970.

14. ———, ed. *Cultural Patterns and Technical Change.* New York: New American Library, 1955, p. 26.

15. Newman, James L. "The Use of the Term 'Hypothesis' in Geography." *Annals of the Association of American Geographers* 63 (March 1973):22–27.

16. Nieburg, Harold L. *Culture Storm: Politics and the Ritual Order.* New York: St. Martin's Press, 1973.

17. Odum, Harvard T. *Environment, Power, and Society.* New York: John Wiley & Sons, 1970.

18. Roscher, Wilhelm Georg F. *Principles of Political Economy.* New York: Arno Press, 1972.

19. Simmons, Peter J. *Choice and Demand.* New York: John Wiley & Sons, 1974.

20. Taaffe, Edward J. "The Spatial View in Context." *Annals of the Association of American Geographers* 64 (March 1974):1–16.

21. Wagner, Philip L. *Environments and Peoples.* Englewood Cliffs, N.J.: Prentice-Hall, 1972.

22. Waldron, Ingrid. *Environment and Population: Problems and Solutions.* New York: Holt, Rinehart and Winston, 1973.

cultural framework
of resources
and
economic activity

2

2

The components of a culture, especially its resources and economic activities, are internally and inextricably related. They possess certain ordinate features common to all societies. Discussion in this chapter will focus on features and concepts that are substantially common to all cultures, but whose manifestations vary from culture to culture.

CULTURE AND SOCIETY

Culture refers to the learned ways of living that people have created. More specifically, culture is the integrated system of learned behavioral traits of man that are not the result of genetic inheritance. Since we are presently concerned with all of mankind, we may generalize within a global context that there is only one culture. As a consequence of the variations perceived within this global culture, social scientists have contrived many divisions, each of which also is referred to as a culture. In this context, culture refers to the integrated system of learned behavior traits that are characteristic of the members of a society (*see* Figure 2–1).

A *trait* is a specific way of thinking, believing, or doing something and includes customs, habits, roles, values, language, religion, and tools. By definition, culture is not genetically or "naturally" induced, and therefore culture does not occur in nature and is not an attribute of other animals.[1] It is a result of social in-

vention and is maintained, promoted, and transmitted through communication and learning.

The concepts of society and culture are intimately interwoven and both are susceptible to a variety of interpretations. A culture is always borne by and is the reflection of a group; no one individual knows or manifests all the traits of his culture. A society is considered to be people, whereas a culture is not people but something that people have and do, i.e., learned behavior. An individual belongs to a society but not to a culture. More specifically, *society* may be defined as a group of people related by social and economic interdependence: they possess a conscious awareness of belonging together (*see* Figure 2–2).

OVERRIDING CHARACTERISTICS OF CULTURE, SOCIETY, AND ECONOMIC ACTIVITY

Whatever diversity is perceived among different societies, they all share several significant characteristics that include: being earth-bound, having spatial distributions, and spatial interactions. Societies also possess unique arrangements, functions, methods of preservation or maintenance, objectives, and change. In addition, each society has its own environment.[2]

EARTH-BOUNDNESS

All men, and hence all cultures, societies, and economic activities, are earth-bound. Man employs the elements of the physi-

---

[1] For many centuries man very jealously clung to the fact, which was based almost exclusively on teleological beliefs, that man alone possesses the ability to learn through communication. We have, however, discovered that many species of animals learn some of their behavior traits by communi-

cating and, according to the concept of culture, possess "culture." To distinguish between man's and other animals' learning via communication, the concept of protoculture was developed. Thus, we still consider ourselves as "separate" from animals.

[2] This list is not meant to be exhaustive. It is rather a set of general categories that includes characteristics such as kinship systems, property, housing, child care, etc.

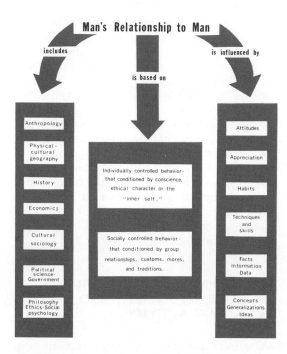

FIGURE 2–1 *The Meaning of Culture*

cal world to provide himself with the means and commodities for living. Of all the various elements that he uses, soil, ores, water, air, plants, and animals, only one—the sun—is not found at or near the surface of the earth. The continued existence of man is dependent on his involvement in a series of processes for the acquisition of goods, especially food, from the earth.

SPATIAL DISTRIBUTION

Culture is a result of the ability of human beings to communicate among themselves through the use of symbols. When people act and think in a similar fashion, they do so because they live, talk, and work together; learn from the same individuals or organizations; and talk about similar events, ideas, places, and people. Hence, they perceive similar meanings in

objects of the environment. Conversely, significant differences in learning, thinking, and acting are usually consequences of the absence of common symbols of communication and the absence of shared experiences. Since continual and habitual sharing of ideas is more likely to occur among people who occupy a common area, cultures are invariably spatially distributed. At particular times, common sets of behavior traits occupy distinct places on the earth's surface (see Figure 2–3).

A group of people sharing the same cultural traits may exist in a single isolated village in which all the members are in direct, daily, and prolonged contact with each other. Or a culture may be distributed over a much larger area within which people, ideas, and objects circulate relatively freely and continually. The size of the space in which a set of common traits is distributed results largely from the ability, which is especially dependent on the level of technology, and the desire of a society to extend its influence, or to interact spatially (see Figure 2–4).

SPATIAL INTERACTION

Societies must interact spatially with each other. The degree of intensity with which this spatial interaction can or does occur is a function of accessibility, which can be measured in a variety of ways, including distance, time, and/or cost relationships.

Spatial interaction, which may take the form of international wheat exchanges, rail and air connections, or telecommunications, invariably makes some identifiable impact on the participating societies. International wheat exchanges may result in diminished goods, higher prices, and subsequent increased replanting for the exporting society and in increased consumption for the importing

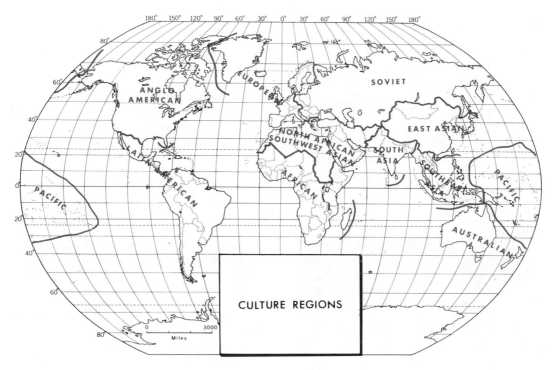

FIGURE 2–2

society. The interchange affects the intervening spaces by causing increased movements of trucks, trains, and ships.

Interaction within the space occupied by a society or within the spaces between societies arises from the distribution of social activities and economic processes. In turn, the initial distributions may be restructured in space, which results in new distributions and interactions.

In a larger and more general context, any form of behavior represents some form of spatial interaction; this is explored on a theoretical plane in Chapters 7, 13, and 20.

SOCIAL ARRANGEMENTS

This term refers to the ways in which a society arranges itself in the space it occupies. Generally, we may perceive two major arrangements: spatial and hierarchical.

Spatial Arrangement. As societies are spatially distributed over the earth's surface, so each society arranges its components within the confines of the area it occupies or controls. For example, areas occupied by most societies contain agricultural landscapes, in part composed of fields, fences, dwellings, transportation routes, and people. In American society, agricultural areas traditionally have been spatially arranged so that each farm family lives in a single-family dwelling, on a farm separated from other farms by fences, and connected with other farmers, merchants, and urban centers by roads.

In most large cities in the United States, slums are situated near the central city, whereas in most of the larger cities

13

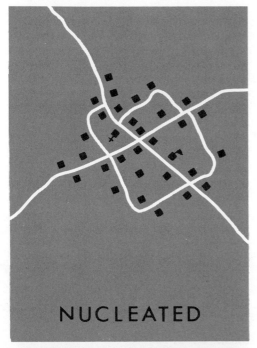

NUCLEATED

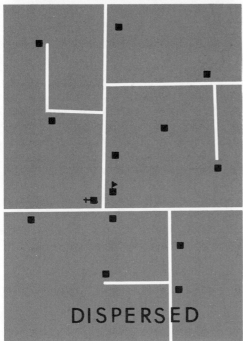

DISPERSED

FIGURE 2–3 *A Nucleated and a Dispersed Settlement*

of Latin America, slums occur near the fringes of the city. The difference in the arrangement of slums in relation to the central city is primarily a manifestation of the different ways that the cities have developed. Although all societies have contents that are spatially arranged, there is variation in the arrangement in different societies.

Hierarchical Arrangement. All societies arrange their activities into hierarchies. Almost invariably the survival of a society is given the highest priority and other activities, whether tangible or intangible, are ranked lower. Survival is applied here not to individuals within the society but to the basic values, concepts, and other contents that are deemed most important to the society as a whole. The highest point of the hierarchy of any society is maintenance of the basic set of values by which that society operates.

All major hierarchies in all societies are in part geared to promote the survival of society. Society principally sustains its values through hierarchical positions or structures, whether a village chieftain, dictator, religious leader, president, premier, or labor union. And, as individuals in a society belong to organizations within that society, they are also members of many hierarchies.

FUNCTIONAL ARRANGEMENTS

All elements of society serve particular functions. However, similar elements of two societies may have entirely dissimilar functions. For example, social scientists generally hold that agricultural activity for the peasant farmer of southern France represents a "way of life"—that agricultural efforts are actually an end in themselves. In the United States, however, most farmers view agricultural efforts as a means to increase their standard of living. Agriculture is viewed as a means toward an end. Just as similar contents

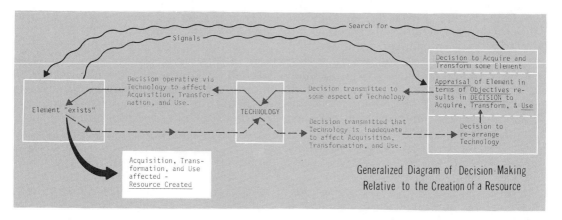

Generalized Diagram of Decision-Making
Relative to the Creation of a Resource

FIGURE 2–4

may have dissimilar functions, similar arrangements of contents in different societies may have dissimilar functions.

METHODS OF PRESERVATION

In attempting to ensure unity, solidarity, and the survival of essential traits of a culture, all societies have developed organizations or institutions whose functions include transmission of values to subsequent generations. Thus, a society ensures that its culture will remain relatively intact and change will be controlled. In many societies, the most important organization for such purposes is the family, extended family (clan), or tribe. Educational and religious organizations also reflect these purposes. Strictly in terms of preservation, the more obvious institutions, especially in sovereign states, are political and military organizations.

OBJECTIVES

Every society possesses certain overriding objectives that are of some significance to all of its members. These objectives include survival and transmission of essential cultural traits to subsequent generations. Societies also seek to ensure

that their contents and functions are arranged for the most beneficial use. "Most beneficial use" is not necessarily the same as "most economically productive use"; it is an objective contrived from the values of each individual society.

CHANGE

Each of these major characteristics tends to change as a result of the development of new thought patterns.[3] Generally, there are two principal processes by which change is effected in a society: by *invention* within the society of some idea or tool and by *diffusion* of an idea or tool from one society to another.

Invention of some item by a member of a society, however, does not necessarily mean that the other members will accept and use the invention. If, within the context of social values and past experiences, the invention is deemed undesirable, then the invention probably will be rejected. Consequently, the change that might have occurred does

[3] The characteristic of man being earth-bound, that is, requiring goods and services from the earth for sustenance, is presently being re-examined. Many scientists express the possibility of man being able to live in parts of the universe other than this planet.

15

not take place. Likewise, the social evaluation of an idea, whether invented within the society or introduced from another, may be totally or partly negative and hence may be wholly or partly rejected.

As an example of rejection, Moslem society generally has deemed swine to be unholy and unclean. As a consequence of this cultural idea, the swine are rejected and are notably absent from any economic activity (or any other behavior pattern) articulated by a dominantly Moslem society. In the United States, there are no dominant social values that exclude swine. The same object, swine, can be used as an example of acceptance and rejection; consequently, it is not the object that determines acceptance or rejection but the social values held about that object. This concept will be developed more fully in relation to resources.

Rates of change also have spatial arrangements. Change occurs faster or slower at different places among societies as well as at different places within the same society. Over the past several decades, change has occurred generally more quickly in northern Italy (especially the Po Basin) than in southern Italy and more quickly in southern California than in southern Appalachia.

As ideas are invented and diffused among societies, all of these characteristics tend to change. In addition to the changes outlined, there also may be changes in the spatial arrangements of entire societies as they migrate from one place to another.

CULTURE AND RESOURCE

There are many concepts associated with the term *resource*. Whatever the diversity, they all imply that resource involves the *use* of something.[4] Consequently, one

---

[4] One may also refer to the use by plants and animals of various foods, habitats, etc. Here, we are referring exclusively to use in terms of man.

may infer that resource presupposes the involvement of a person.

Assuming that resource involves the use of something and that use implies availability of a resource, either direct or indirect, then when similar things are available in different places, why do different societies "use" different things? Why, when many possible resources are present, do certain groups use certain things? Answers to these questions will shed light also on our understanding of some other characteristics of economic activities.

Part of the difficulty in understanding the variations of resource use among societies results from a misunderstanding of the term "resource." Traditional concepts that employ "natural resource" to refer to soil, rock, water, minerals, forests, and other physical elements, and "human resource" to refer to population and manmade objects, do not explain why, for example, some societies till the lateritic soils of the humid tropics, while others in immediately adjacent areas do not cultivate the soils at all. By examining the concept of resource within the context of its features that are common to all cultures, societies, and economic activities, we may be better able to answer these questions.

MAN AND NATURE

Let us assume that within the species *Homo sapiens* there are two levels of existence, which shall be referred to as man and MAN. The former represents *natural* man, literally stripped of all cultural traits—no thinking ability, no materials, religion, education, clothing, medical care, or other elements of culture. The term MAN refers to *Homo sapiens* as a cultural being.

Man is in a state of existence similar to that preceding the development of any cultural traits. He is totally natural and he needs and can obtain only naturally occurring elements for survival. The items man requires are:

1. Water to continue the biological processes within his body

2. Oxygen to maintain life through the biological processes

3. Land, because his body cannot perform well or survive long in an aquatic environment

4. Food to provide essential minerals and vitamins

5. Heat to maintain his bodily function, the minimum and maximum temperatures of which are relatively stable

6. Light, because his eyes do not function sufficiently well at night to ensure survival, especially against nocturnal animals

7. A form of internal immunity sufficiently high to protect bodily functions against disease and parasites

8. A member of the opposite sex to ensure survival of the species

The necessities of existence are indeed few. The quality or quantity of any of these need only be sufficient to maintain life. The type of food, be it snails, snakes, roots, seeds, or any other form of animal or plant life, is of no significance. Not only must these elements be present at all times, but they also must be capable of being obtained by man's own physical efforts. If food is too far from water, man will either starve or thirst to death, and the species will not survive. Within the area occupied by natural man, all the elements needed to sustain his existence exist in a natural context.

However, the existence of these elements within an area does not ensure that man will acquire and use them. The elements will remain inert and unused until operated on by man's articulating force. The most significant motivating force of man that will cause the naturally occurring elements to be used is instinct. Instinct is an inborn tendency to behave in a way characteristic of a species; it is a natural phenomenon contributed by

heredity and is not acquired. Without instinct, man would be unable to obtain and subsequently use the naturally occurring elements. Thus, within the natural state, instinct, which articulates other elements for sustenance and survival, is the single major resource employed by our man. Within this natural state, it is principally instinct that causes the manipulation of other elements so that they then become used.

All elements that man uses are referred to as *natural resources,* which occur in nature and are used in the context of and for natural processes. Within the concept of resource, each element of the environment is classified on the basis of its *use* or *function.* Elements that are not used by natural man are not called resources because we have assumed that any resource involves use.

However, natural man does not exist. All *Homo sapiens,* through the processes of invention and diffusion, have acquired cultural traits that were passed from one generation to another or from one place to another during the same generation. When these acquired attitudes and behavior patterns are directed and applied to naturally occurring elements of the environment, then those elements are used as a consequence of and for culturally generated purposes and hence are classified as *cultural resources.* With the development and use of cultural traits, instinct no longer was the dominant, energizing motivation.

Still, some basic questions are not completely answered. Why do different societies use the same or different resources in different ways?

THE PROCESS OF RESOURCE EMERGENCE

As mentioned previously, all human activities are earth-bound. On a global scale, all MEN share the same set of possible resources. In addition, the quantity,

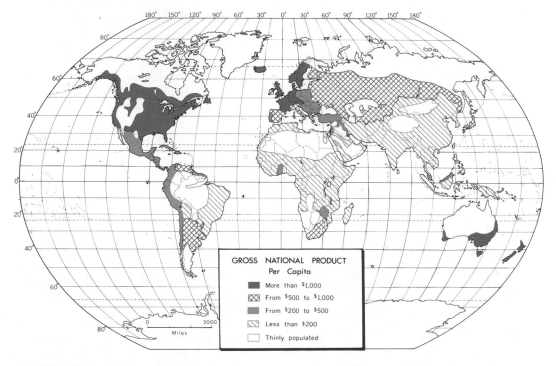

FIGURE 2–5

quality, and type of natural resources vary significantly. Each society has a distinct spatial distribution, as well as variation in its characteristics. These variations and distributions in part account for the differences in resources.

In general there is a relatively common process (*see* Figure 2–5) that occurs prior to the functioning of any element of the environment as a resource. First, the element must occur or exist. It can be naturally occurring, man-made, or even believed to exist without actually "existing." (The *belief* by the alchemists that base metals could be transmuted into gold, and a desire for the riches associated with perfecting this process, spurred them into research that subsequently led to the development of chemistry. The belief existed, but not the object of belief.

Second, MAN must recognize and appraise the element, and the appraisal must be positive. He must decide that use of the element is beneficial toward achieving his objectives. Third, he must possess the ability to acquire the element (technology). If acquisition cannot be effected, the element does not function directly as a resource. Fourth, the element is actually acquired and used.

MAJOR TYPES OF RESOURCES

All things that MAN uses are resources—iron ore, water, buildings, jet aircraft, and tankers, institutions and processes such as the family, tribe, sovereign state, government, religion, exchange arrangements, and so on.

One may argue about the inclusion of family, religion, government, technology, etc., in a list of resources. However, each of these, present in all societies, has specific uses or functions within a society. The political process and political institutions, for example, are frequently used as a means to direct the economic efforts of society. By offering tax incentives, special trading privileges, or access to state-owned land, the political framework assists in directing an economy. Political institutions are significant consumers of goods and services, as well as producers of services for the general welfare of the society. Religion and religious organizations also have a significant impact on many economic activities of a society. In many pre-industrial societies, religion is as pervasive an influence in economic behavior as is the political framework in an industrial society.

In order to facilitate more intensive analysis of this concept of resources, two broad sets may be created, one of which includes resources used specifically to organize and direct those in the other set. The former set, "frameworks," includes the sociopolitical, economic, and technological frameworks of a society. Each of these is discussed in detail in chapters 4, 5, and 6. The latter set includes those on which the former operate and organize in space: material, labor, and capital resources. They are discussed in the following paragraph.

Material Resources. Material resources include all naturally occurring man-transformed objects and processes that societies use in their economic activities.[5] These include timber, seeds, water, fish,

[5] Using a perspective other than environment, one may classify material resources as natural resources. Economists frequently refer to this class as "land," which includes everything under, in, and on the ground not made by man; however, only elements that have economic use are of practical importance.

minerals, rivers, etc.—all in the context of space.

Space is the most important concept here because it implies land as well as minerals and many other material resources. Also, control of space usually carries with it control of other resources associated with the particular space. However, in the United States control over space is sometimes vested at a social level. Control is not necessarily the same as ownership or vice-versa. Zoning ordinances, for example, represent social controls over privately owned land. In tribal societies, the village or tribal chieftains frequently dictate what shall be done with material resources. They, in effect, control the land, and the ownership, if such is recognized, is also vested in the same body.

Although naturally occurring objects that may function as material resources are limited, the perceived importance of the mass and location of material resources varies considerably.

Labor Resources. Labor per se does not refer to people, but to the expenditure of time and energy by people in the production of goods and services. Labor performed in a commercial activity generally results in remuneration; in a noncommercial or barter activity, the returns may be in the form of goods. In general, however, the labor resources of a society also may refer to the working force or the economically productive group.

The quantity of labor available to a society or an economic system is not fixed. It is principally a function of the size of the population, birth rate, death rate, migration, the percentage of the population in the working force, and the hours the society is willing to contribute to labor. The effectiveness of labor is a function of its quality and quantity. In any society, the aptitudes, education, skills, health, cooperativeness, ability, and willingness to assume responsibility and adapt to change vary widely.

The quality of a specific labor force is effectively measured only in terms of the activity it performs. For example, most of the labor force in the United States, however efficient it may be in an industrial society, would fail miserably in a pre-industrial society with shifting cultivation. With respect to this latter system, then, the U.S. labor force may be said to be of low quality.

Spatial distribution of labor resources also is variable, especially as wants change, necessitating changes in the forms of production and the type of labor. As the desire for labor in one area decreases and in another area increases, workers may respond by moving to the latter area. Here, labor can be considered spatially mobile as the demand for one type of worker ceases in one area and arises in another. If new people are trained in the area where the work is demanded, there will be no movement of people between areas, but an areal shift in demand.

Capital Resources. Capital resources include all resources created by the application of labor to material resources. The value of capital resources is derived from the value assigned to material resources; but it is principally a function of the value added to material resources by labor. Capital resources are then more valuable than material resources; however, without material resources, capital resources cannot be developed. Capital resources include items such as ploughs, railroads and locomotives, cranes, ships, fishing lines—in short, all items used in any form of production.

EFFECTIVENESS OF RESOURCES

Material and capital resources have discernible spatial variations, quantities, and qualities. Their effectiveness in any so-ciety can be evaluated by several criteria. For example, effectiveness can be evaluated on the basis of what a given society might be able to do with these resources. Almost invariably, however, members of one society tend to evaluate the characteristics of other societies on the basis of ethnocentric values.

The effectiveness of resources can be evaluated on the basis of what the ideal economic efficiency may be in a society; or, and perhaps most importantly, the effectiveness of one or all of these resources should be evaluated in terms of the values and needs of the society that uses the resource. A group commonly referred to as "backward" or "primitive," for example, may not want the goods and services associated with an industrial society; consequently, they will not organize their society to produce goods and services similar to those of an industrial society.

Materials that are present naturally and are directly usable by man are very meager. Nature, for example, does not provide housing, clothing, food, automobiles, iron ore, lead, steel, petroleum, lumber, glass, or aluminum; and the list can be extended almost indefinitely.[6]

WANTS

If man is to live an existence other than a natural one, he must transform naturally occurring resources by engaging in economic activity. Human wants are the mainspring of economic activity and their fulfillment is the end toward which all such activity is directed. In short:

> All economic activities of all societies
> are contrived for a common objective:
> to provide the goods and services

[6] These, as well as many other materials, do not occur either physically or chemically free in nature, but are rendered usable by mining, transporting, refining, hunting, agriculture, etc.

20

deemed desirable by all the people or a group of people in the society.

Goods and services are acquired through production and exchange and consumed to give satisfaction. Satisfaction has many connotations and includes innumerable motives that give rise to an activity—for example, the satisfaction derived by a person who owns an automobile; the satisfaction of a Zulu after catching a scorpion for dinner; the satisfaction of a businessman after successfully concluding a transaction; the satisfaction of a Chinese peasant when he gathers nightsoil from the village latrine; or the satisfaction of a student on graduating from college after having consumed goods (desks, chairs, maps, texts) and services (instructional and administrative) for four years.[7]

CHARACTERISTICS OF WANTS

Want, or the desire to be satisfied, has two major characteristics: it varies in time and space among all societies as well as within any society; and, on an aggregate level, the desire to be satisfied is insatiable. Wants arise as a consequence of natural bodily functions and from stimuli by invention or diffusion. By far, the most important needs result from the latter sources. Also, desire-satisfying processes frequently tend to create additional or new wants. The level of desire-satisfaction varies significantly from society to society and from time to time in all societies. In any society, a set of needs almost invariably tends to be greater than that which presently exists.[8]

[7] This consumption is generally perceived as an investment in the student because the purpose of education—to acquire knowledge and skills—enhances the productive capacity of the individual and also that of society.

[8] Measurements of economic levels, such as per capita income, gross product, net product, etc., do not measure needs. These indices, although

EXCHANGE

In general, all parts of all economic activities and all parts of space are to some degree specialized. Specialization refers to the division of effort and space into different units, each of which has its own function, which is determined by the needs and abilities of the society organizing and directing the effort and space.

Even in the most simple of forms, specialization implies, if not necessitates, exchange. The spear maker cannot eat his spears, nor can the bread maker defend himself with his product. If they want other goods, they must swap one good for another. This form of exchange is known as *barter*. If any regularity in the flow of goods and services is to be attained, then there must be an organization established to order not only production but also exchange. In time of scarcity, some system must exist for deciding priorities among consumers, as well as among goods and services.

In a small, isolated economy with little specialization, the organization, although complex, can be understood and participated in by all. However, in a highly specialized industrial economy the task of bringing producer and consumer together usually involves greater spaces and more people, and hence is much more complex.

Involved in producing this textbook, for example, were paper from lumbered forests; films and inks made at petrochemical plants; binding material manufactured with cotton at textile mills; printing presses made from iron ore and coal mines, iron smelters, and steel mills; rubber from rubber plantations, etc. Services related to this book were rend-

useful in some analyses of the performance of an activity, measure what has been accomplished, which is not necessarily the same as what was desired.

ered by a division of labor among the publisher, the printer, wholesalers, market analysts, advertising agencies, retailers, and finally the student.

In an exchange-oriented society, there may be as many or more people engaged in services as in goods production. A strike by railroad or print shop workers, a machinery failure, or lost orders or invoices may cause the production process to break down. If any part fails, failure may also occur in another part.

BARTER

Bartering is the exchange of one good or service for another, e.g., trading eggs for potatoes or skins for repair work on a canoe. About half the total population of the world does not fully participate in a barter economy. Societies that use barter as a means of exchange occupy more than half the entire inhabited land surface; their economy is closely associated with pre-industrial activities and a simple state of specialization.

A barter economy places several restrictions on a society and especially limits its involvement in international trade. Because agricultural goods, which predominate in a barter economy, are difficult to store, barter economies also have less ability to accumulate the kinds of goods necessary to develop more modern means of production. Hence, they cannot increase levels of consumption and/or exchange.

MONEY

Money is anything that serves as a medium of exchange which is acceptable to a society. The earliest forms of money were goods, such as cattle, honey, and salt. At various times and spaces, goods were significant in establishing what we now refer to as a money economy. The

word "salary," for example, is derived from the Latin word for "salt," which was a form of money frequently used to pay soldiers of the Roman Empire. Among the Navajo of Arizona and the Masai of East Africa, sheep and cattle, respectively, even now represent a medium of exchange (money), as well as social status.

Money per se has little economic value; the value of money lies in what it can buy. The same principle applies to gold or any precious metal. Money alone is not wealth. *Real wealth* is the existing resource stock and its susceptibility to social management.

SOCIAL CHOICES AND PRIORITIES

If all resources were present everywhere at all times and in quantities and qualities desired by all people, then the major choices of any individual or society would be associated primarily with the expenditure of time. However, resources are limited in time and space and wants are unlimited, so decisions about their "best" use must be made.[9] In making these decisions, there are certain specific questions that all societies must face and answer within the context of their own social values.

WHAT GOODS AND SERVICES?

Since the resources of any society, within a given time, are limited, it is not possible to satisfy all present wants. The decision about what shall be produced by the economy is primarily a problem of deciding which needs are most important and to what degree these needs should be satisfied. For example, should steel, presently available for production

[9] Resources are limited because a society's needs exceed what the reserves can provide at a given time and place.

of rails, automobiles, ships, guns, or for the construction of a university, be allocated equally toward producing all or a combination of these? Or should the steel or a portion thereof be sold and the returns used to purchase food or coal or some other good? If the decision is to use the steel for constructing one or a series of goods, other steel will not be available to produce other goods.

If the needs of society as a whole are to be satisfied, the decision-making process must be a social one. Each society must create a system of values that reflects the group priorities of needs, relative to the total range of goods and services that the society's economic activity can produce or acquire. The final decision about what shall be produced will be a reflection of what the society wants and is able to produce.

HOW WILL GOODS AND SERVICES BE PRODUCED?

Almost invariably, any society has a variety of choices about which methods to use in the production of goods and services. Societies with a scientific-industrial capability have a wider variety of choices than do those with a pre-industrial technology. For example, in an industrial society, iron can be produced by hand or by a variety of machine processes, including computer-assisted techniques. In a pre-industrial society, iron can be produced only by hand.

A society also must decide which process will produce the largest quantity, the highest quality, or the greatest variety of goods and services. The process that produces the largest quantity may not be the same one that turns out the highest quality goods. In most societies, a compromise is effected between quantity, quality, and variety of goods and services. Generally, as the quantity and/or variety of a good or service increases, there is a corresponding decrease in quality.

WHO WILL RECEIVE THE GOODS AND SERVICES?

There are many possibilities in deciding the distribution of goods and services among the members of a society once they are produced. One possibility is to allocate to each member or family the same amount. Another is to give each member or family a set of goods and services commensurate with the needs of the member or family. A third solution is to distribute the products according to the contribution each member makes to the process of production. Goods and services also may be allocated on the basis of some arbitrary dictates of a ruler or ruling elite. All of these methods of distribution are present in some form within any society; however, in some societies one method may be adopted more or less to the exclusion of the others (*see* Figure 2–6).

In addition to decisions associated with methods of distribution, a society also makes decisions about the distribution of specific products. Everyone has a place to live, but who lives in a house and who lives in an apartment? Who lives near his place of work and who does not? Who lives near the park and who lives near the refuse area? Who gets the T-bone steak and who gets the tongue and ears of the livestock? Who gets the stereo–TV console and who gets the radio?

In a money–exchange society, the total amount of goods and services acquired by an individual is partially a function of the individual's income and the amount he is willing to spend for various goods and services. Thus, the money income is in part a means of regulating the distribution of goods and services. By its willingness or unwillingness to spend its income for various goods and services, society also in part determines the income of people employed in specific activities.

23

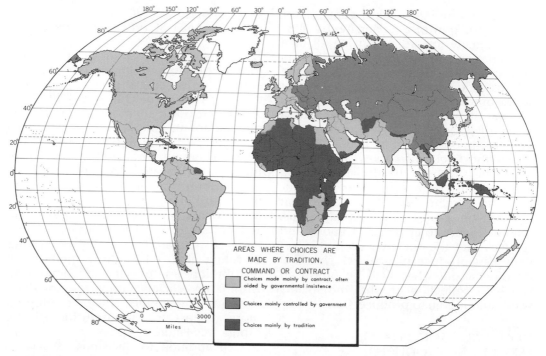

180° 150° 120° 90° 60° 30° 0° 30° 60° 90° 120° 150° 180°

AREAS WHERE CHOICES ARE
MADE BY TRADITION,
COMMAND OR CONTRACT

Choices made mainly by contract, often
aided by governmental insistence

Choices mainly controlled by government

Choices mainly by tradition

0   3000
Miles

FIGURE 2–6

HOW WILL PRODUCTIVE CAPACITY BE MAINTAINED AND IMPROVED?

Every society expects to maintain its productivity, and most desire to improve it. Maintenance includes keeping the productive power of economic activities intact so that production will not fall below the present level. Improvement refers to an increase in the type, quantity, quality, and variety of products, and an improvement in the techniques of production.

Material resources may be increased or changed by trial and error, scientific inquiry, and exchange with other societies. Labor resources can be increased by population rise and development of additional, or refinement of present, skills through education. Capital improvement must be accomplished by diverting some resources from consumption to use them to produce other goods. Improvements in production techniques result in a greater output of goods and services without an increase in the resources used in production.

Attempts to maintain the productivity of an activity commensurate with society's desires may not be fruitful, which may cause a society to introduce changes in an activity that will result in production more compatible with their wants. However, whatever changes are introduced generally will be made with a view to retaining as much of the traditional activity as possible. In some shifting agricultural societies, for example, newer food crops have been accepted to realize increased food production. However, although productivity may be increased manyfold by applying new

24

techniques to agriculture, the cultivators maintain the essence of their migratory economic activity. To shift to sedentary agriculture may be incompatible with tribal organization, division of labor, religion, land-tenure system, or some other social value deemed as important as increasing the production of food.

MAKING SOCIAL CHOICES

Each society develops, maintains, and promotes its own economic activities. Economic choices are determined by several factors that occur in a unique fashion within any society. These general factors are: tradition, command or central authority, and the voluntary arrangements between and among private parties, commonly called the market (see Figure 2–6).

TRADITION OR CUSTOM

Most societies choose which economic activities to pursue on the basis of tradition. In tradition-bound societies, what was decided and accomplished by the forebearers will be what is done now. Yesterday's decisions, however realized and whatever their results—unless they pose a threat to the existence of the society—are almost exclusively the basis of what is done today and tomorrow. Over a long period of time, the needs of society remain somewhat static. Material resources, labor resources, capital, technology, and entrepreneurship all remain relatively stable; hence economic activity and social characteristics continue almost unchanged.

COMMAND OR CENTRAL AUTHORITY

A central authority makes economic decisions, either democratically or despot-

ically, and then imposes them on society. A command, or central, authority usually is a characteristic of socialist and/or communist governments. A central authority benevolent toward all members of society will decide in the interest of the general public. More frequently, the central authority acts in the interest of a special class, usually itself. The Soviet Union is a classic example of this type of decision-making structure; almost all its major economic problems are resolved in the upper echelons of the party and government.

PRIVATE, VOLUNTARY ARRANGEMENTS

Members of a capitalist society are relatively free to act as individuals or as groups of individuals bound together voluntarily for mutual cooperation and action. An individual or groups of individuals, such as a family or corporation, produce what they desire, and live, work, and consume what their incomes allow. Their freedom of decision making is principally a function of the freedom the society allows and is limited primarily by their desire to negotiate with others for what they want. All negotiations or arrangements taken collectively are complex, and lest they become completely entangled and snarled must be regulated by law rather than by custom.

No society or economic activity relies strictly on a single method of decision making. All societies at various levels of the government hierarchy usually employ combinations of these three processes, emphasizing one and de-emphasizing others. The United States is a contemporary example of one society that employs a variety of controls over its economy. Although the dominant decision process has been, and still is, guided by voluntary arrangements, in the early 1970s the government attempted a command authority approach by instituting price and wage controls.

ANALYSIS OF RESOURCES AND ECONOMIC ACTIVITY

In this chapter we have identified the role of culture in organizing material resources involved in the production of goods and services. In modern societies goods and services are so numerous and widely scattered over space that geographers tend to analyze economic activities using two broad but inseparable approaches: systematic (or topical) and regional (or specific).

Systematic geography organizes geographical knowledge into categories, such as landforms, climate, etc.; it stresses study of "a particular group of features produced by one kind of process wherever these features may occur in the world."[10]

Regional geographical analysis studies geographic features that impart distinctive characteristics to specific areas of the earth. A region is a delineated location with some degree of homogeneity. Although the concept "region" is extensively discussed in the context of regional planning and policy making in chapter 29, it deserves a brief statement here. Definitions of region vary, depending upon the objectives and criteria chosen for delineation. Nevertheless any region basically involves four characteristics: contiguity of space; some degree of uniformity and homogeneity invoked by the chosen criteria; complementation and reciprocity of some activities in the region; and time which is meaningful and functional to the region. Students are accustomed to thinking of regions in terms of political boundaries. However, political boundary regions are not always suitable for studies requiring conditions of spatial homogeneity.

No special effort is made in this book to adhere to either the systematic or regional approach. Both approaches are integrated to yield to the requirements of the major theme and theoretical framework used to study man's economic activities.

references

1. Abler, Ronald; Adams, John S.; and Gould, Peter. *Spatial Organization: The Geographer's View of the World*. Englewood Cliffs, N.J.: Prentice-Hall, 1971.

2. Boyce, Ronald R. *The Bases of Economic Geography: An Essay on the Spatial Characteristics of Man's Economic Activities*. New York: Holt, Rinehart and Winston, 1974.

3. Choynicki, Zbryszko. "Prediction in Economic Geography." *Economic Geography* 46 (June 1970):213–222.

4. Clarkson, James D. "Ecology and Spatial Analysis." *Annals of the Association of American Geographers* 60 (December 1970):700–716.

5. Gould, Peter R. "A Man Against His Environment: A Game Theoretic Framework." *Annals of the Association of American Geographers* 53 (September 1963):290–297.

6. Griffin, Paul F. "A Cultural Geography." In *Methods of Geography Instruction*, edited by John W. Morris. Waltham, Mass.: Blaisdell Publishing Co., 1968.

7. Hoebel, E. Adamson. *Anthropology: The Study of Man*. 3rd ed. New York: McGraw-Hill Book Co., 1966.

8. Hudson, John C. *Geographical Diffusion Theory*. Evanston, Ill.: Northwestern Studies in Geography, 1972.

9. Hurst, Michael E. *A Geography of Economic Behavior*. North Scituate, Mass.: Duxbury Press, 1972.

10. Jaeger, Gertrude, and Selznick, Philip. "A Normative Theory of Culture."

---

[10] P. E. James, "American Geography at Mid-Century," *New View Points in Geography*. Twenty-Ninth Yearbook of the National Council of the Social Sciences (Washington, D.C.: The Council, 1959), p. 10.

American Sociological Review 29 (October 1964):653–669.

11.   Kaplan, David, and Manners, Robert A. *Culture Theory*. Englewood Cliffs, N.J.: Prentice-Hall, 1972.

12.   Lloyd, Peter E., and Dicken, Peter. *Location in Space: A Theoretical Approach to Economic Geography*. New York: Harper & Row, 1972.

13.   Logan, M. I. "The Spatial System and Planning Strategies in Developing Countries." *Geographical Review* 62 (April 1972): 229–244.

14.   Macinko, George. "Man and the Environment: A Sampling of the Literature." *Geographical Review* 63 (July 1973):378–391.

15.   Matley, Ian M. "Perception of Environment: The Case of the Airman." *The Professional Geographer* 24 (February 1972): 23–25.

16.   Paterson, John H. *Land, Work, and Resources: An Introduction to Economic Geography*. London: Edward Arnold, 1972.

17.   Pettit, George A. *Prisoners of Culture*. New York: Charles Scribner's Sons, 1970.

18.   Rostow, W. W. *The Stages of Economic Growth*. Cambridge: Cambridge University Press, 1960.

19.   Thomas, William L., ed. *Man's Role in Changing the Face of the Earth*. Chicago: University of Chicago Press, 1956.

20.   Wagner, Philip L. *Environments and Peoples*. Englewood Cliffs, N.J.: Prentice-Hall, 1972.

II

VARIABLES IN ECONOMIC ACTIVITY

CHAPTERS

3 Materials-Resource Framework
4 Economic Framework
5 Sociopolitical Framework
6 Technological Framework

introduction

Within all societies, numerous processes are implemented through a variety of interrelated frameworks. Framework is used here to refer to the arrangement or structure of parts that together constitute a major portion of a society. For example, the demand, supply, markets, buyers, sellers, producers, consumers, and resources are some of the parts that constitute the economic framework of every society. The way these parts are structured and the way that the structure is operated gives direction and control to the economic system.

In addition to the economic framework, every society has a political, social, and technological framework, each of which is composed of parts interrelated with all other parts and frameworks. The frameworks of a society are institutions that the society has created in order to give overall control and direction to its activities. Here, however, we are more interested in how these frameworks are reflected in the overall economic activities of the society, as opposed to some other social activities.

So interdependent are the parts and frameworks of a society we can only separate them conceptually for analysis. For example, in which part, or framework, does space belong? Obviously, it is a part of all frameworks, as are goods, services, resources, capital, and so on.

Part II will analyze each of these frameworks, indicating their relationships to each other and to the overall economic activities of society. Attention will be confined specifically to the parts of frameworks that are common to all societies. Whether or not members of a particular society recognize the importance of spatial array of material resources, market, supply, comparative advantage, political decision processes, etc., in the operation of their economy, these concepts are indeed operative.

materials-resource
framework

3

3

Problems associated with the importance and relative scarcity of resources have developed from a local social concern to include issues of adequacy of resources, their development and conservation, and alternative measures to meet human needs on a global scale. The significance of the relationship between economic activities and resources strongly suggests the need to understand their spatial distribution, form and quantities, and potential supplies—all of which have a strong bearing on where economic activities occur and develop.

LIMITS ON THE SUPPLY OF MATERIAL RESOURCES

Land constitutes slightly less than one-third (29.3 percent) of the surface of the earth, and water more than two-thirds (70.7 percent). Man has dominion over both the vast resources of the land, and the present and potentially abundant wealth of oceans. However, the land-based resources—for food, minerals, energy, water, and construction—have been and are being exploited many times more rapidly than those of the ocean. This is partly due to the relative cheapness of land-based activities under the prevailing technology. But, as population pressures impinge on the limits of land-based resources, increased exploitation of ocean-based resources becomes desirable, if not altogether feasible.[1]

[1] Besides the ocean, man has turned to atmospheric resources for making many products. Air, once considered useless for industrial purposes, now provides raw materials for the so-called gases industry, founded upon cryogenics. Revolutionary developments in the art of steel production, such as the Basic Oxygen Furnace (BOF) and other uses of products derived from air (nitrogen, argon,

The question of feasibility is a matter of technology and the relative scarcity of resources. In the past, man has responded to challenges by adapting or by discovering new means of meeting human demands. Although adaptations to the accomplishments of science and technology seem to be dramatically pitted against the increase of population, now running at 3 percent, or a doubling every twenty-four years in many developing areas, the exhaustibility of many resources is a naked fact.

LAND-BASED RESOURCES

Almost all of the earth's land surface has been explored by man, and the resources he has perceived are not only unevenly distributed but also are appropriated for diverse uses over space and time. A commonly used classification of resources is:

1. Land
2. Energy
3. Minerals
4. Water

Excluded from this list are the ice-covered wastes of Antarctica, many marshy and water-logged areas, and perhaps some parts of the deserts. These excluded items, however, are noneconomic resources only as long as present technology is insufficient to tap them and human demand for their use is nonexistent. With this thought in mind, some scholars regard noneconomic resources as potentially productive.

Of the approximately 14.9 billion square hectares (57.5 million square miles) that include continents, islands, and lakes and rivers, 55 million square miles (14.4 billion hectares) are land surface. After deduction is made for the ice-covered wastes of Antarctica, more than

hydrogen), have brought into existence in the United States approximately 500 manufacturing establishments engaged in the production of air-based products.

13 billion hectares remain. As shown in Table 3–1, approximately 1.5 billion hectares (10.9 percent) of this total is classified as arable land; 3.0 billion hectares (22.3 percent) is classified as meadows and pastures; 4.0 billion hectares (30.2 percent) is forest land; 0.4 billion hectares (1.6 percent) is classified as "unused but potentially productive"; and the remaining 4.5 billion hectares (35 percent) is wasteland and other.

Table 3–1 also shows the distribution of each resource category among the seven continents. Asia (excluding the USSR), with 57 percent of the world's population, has 43.7 percent of the world's arable cropland, whereas North America, with 6.2 percent of the world's population, possesses 12.2 percent of the world's arable cropland. Similar comparisons show a disproportionate distribution of people and land.

The land-use distribution pattern also varies considerably throughout the world. Table 3–1 shows this type of allocation for several areas. For example, India uses only 4.2 percent of its area for meadow or pasture, while approximately half of the area in both Australia and the United Kingdom is used for this purpose.

In the United States, about one-fifth of the surface land area is arable cropland; about one-third is forest land, meadows, and pasture; and approximately 21 percent is built upon, wasteland, or is used for other purposes. Approximately 80 percent of the surface is used for cropland, pasture, grazing, forestry; this includes "potentially productive" land.

The land-use pattern in the United States varies considerably by region. For example, more than 50 percent of the land in the northern Great Plains and the Corn Belt is used as cropland. Pasturing and grazing dominate in the mountain, southern Plains, and northern Plains regions. Forest is the dominant land use in the Southeast, the Mississippi Delta, the Northeast, and the Appalachian, Pacific, and Lake states regions.

Data indicate that land-use patterns have changed considerably over the past several years in the United States. From the 1880s to the 1940s, agricultural acreage showed an upward trend. During this period, acreage for farm crops more than doubled. From 1940 to 1970 farm crop acreage remained much the same, but farm output increased tremendously; this is attributed to the phenomenal increase in farm productivity, behind which lies a long list of improvements in the science of agriculture. Extensive mechanization, application of technical knowledge produced by land-grant colleges and universities, and changes in farm sizes and numbers are the basic factors responsible for higher U.S. farm productivity. Increases in cropland through reclamation—clearing, drainage, and irrigation—have been balanced by the abandonment or shifting of cropland for pasture and other uses. For example, between 1930 and 1950, 20 million acres of new cropland were brought into use by reclamation, but during the same period 24 million acres of cropland were shifted to pastures, woodland, and nonfarm uses.

Table 3–1 indicates that approximately 21 percent of the land area in the United States is either built upon, wasteland, or is used for other purposes. However, within this category, authentic information is scarce pertaining to further breakdown according to land use, i.e., buildings (residential, commercial, industrial, service), highways and roads, railroad rights-of-way, mining, airports, state and national parks, wildlife areas, national defense areas, powerline lanes, and the like. According to Frey, Kraus, and Dickason, the total area used for these purposes in 1964 was approximately 139.8 million acres out of the total land area of 1,904 million acres. The breakdown of this total is given in Table 3–2.

TABLE 3–1 Major Land Uses

	DISTRIBUTION OF WORLD POPULATION (1972)	TOTAL AREA (thousands of hectares)*	ARABLE CROPLAND, INCLUDING LAND UNDER PERMANENT CULTIVATION	PERMANENT MEADOWS AND PASTURE	FOREST LAND	OTHER LAND, INCLUDING UNUSED BUT POTENTIALLY PRODUCTIVE, AND WASTELAND
Continents/Regions						
Europe	12.4%	493,000	29.3	18.5%	28.6%	23.6
North America	6.2	1,934,000	12.2	13.9	38.7	35.2
Latin America	7.9	2,056,000	5.8	22.1	47.8	24.3
Near East	4.5	1,207,000	7.1	15.2	11.4	66.3
Far East	31.5	1,117,000	25.0	15.8	36.9	22.3
Africa	9.6	3,031,000	7.1	27.1	20.9	44.9
Oceania	.5	851,000	5.5	54.4	9.6	30.5
USSR	6.5	2,240,220	10.4	16.7	40.6	32.3
China	20.9	959,696	11.6	18.4	10.0	60.0
Selected Nations						
Australia	.3	768,681	5.8	58.6	4.5	31.1
Canada	.6	997,614	4.4	2.5	44.4	48.7
China	20.9	959,696	11.6	18.4	10.0	60.0
France	1.4	54,703	34.9	25.5	26.6	14.0
India	14.9	326,809	50.4	4.2	19.1	26.3
Japan	2.8	37,208	14.6	2.6	69.0	13.8
United Kingdom	1.5	24,479	29.6	47.5	8.0	14.9
United States (incl. Virgin Islands)	5.6	936,369	20.5	26.1	32.7	20.7
USSR	6.5	2,240,220	10.4	16.7	40.6	32.3
World Total		13,393,000	10.9	22.3	30.2	36.6

* Hectare is a metric measure of surface, equal to 10,000 square meters or 2,471 acres.

Source: Based on the *Statistical Yearbook, 1973* (New York: United Nations, 1974), pp. 67–73, and *Production Yearbook, 1972* (Rome: United Nations FAO, 1973), vol. 26, pp. 3–24.

**TABLE 3–2   Land Use in the United
States, 1964**

	MILLION ACRES	
Urban areas	29.3	20.9%
Highways and roads	21.2	15.2
Railroad rights-of-way	3.3	2.4
Airports	1.5	1.1
State and national parks	31.9	22.8
Wildlife areas	29.0	20.7
National defense areas	23.6	16.9
Total	139.8	100.0

Source: Frey, Krause, and Dickason, Major Uses of Land and Water in the U.S. with Special Reference to Agriculture, USDA, Agriculture Report 149, 1968, p. 26.

Generally speaking, nonagricultural uses of land resources have been heavily influenced by technology and by social objectives. Every use has also involved varying degrees of technology and a diversity of resources. For example, urban growth is a recent phenomenon resulting from great technological advancements. Table 3–3 shows the percent of the world's population living in cities during various years. It is obvious from this table that urbanization has gone ahead much

**TABLE 3–3   World's Population Living
in Cities**

	CITIES OF 20,000 OR MORE, BUT LESS THAN 100,000	CITIES OF 100,000 OR MORE
1800	2.4 %	1.7%
1850	4.3	2.3
1900	9.2	5.5
1950	20.9	13.1
1960	25.2	17.5
1970	38.04	

Source: Data from U.N. Report on the World Social Situation, Economic and Social Council, New York, 1957 (pp. 111–192) and during 1971 (pp. 153–155); U.N. World Survey of Rural and Urban Population Growth, Economic and Social Council, DDC. E/CN 9/187, March 8, 1965.

faster and reached proportions far greater during the past century and a half than at any previous time.

Structural and technological developments in the agricultural sector are partly responsible for the rapidity of urbanization. As farming becomes increasingly mechanized and business-like, fewer people are needed to produce food and fiber. Without technological developments, the land-use patterns of human settlement would most likely have been different. How far technology can influence land use is not known. Kingsley Davis (15) says that:

> if in addition to industrialized agriculture, food and fiber come to be increasingly produced by manufacturing processes using materials that utilize the sun's energy more efficiently than do plants, there is no technological reason why nearly all of mankind could not live in conurbations of large size.

Although the rate of urbanization in developed regions is decreasing, the rate of urbanization in the world as a whole is not slowing down because the urbanization gap between industrially developed and less developed regions is beginning to diminish. The percent of the world's population living in cities by regions from 1950 to 1970 appears in Table 3–4.

These developments are merely indicative of land-use patterns for nonagricultural purposes. Unfortunately, no authentic nonagricultural land-use data are presently available, except indirect measures, such as number of people and monetary worth of the commodities associated with nonagricultural land use; data for these measures, where available, may be used to derive land-use estimates. Varying regional or national measurement standards and nomenclature complicate the conversion of these measures into land-estimates. Not only

35

TABLE 3–4   World's Urban Population Living in Cities by Region, 1950–1970

	1950	1960	1970
Oceania	57.81%	63.84%	68.68%
North America	63.81	69.79	75.13
Europe (except USSR)	53.39	58.08	63.05
USSR	42.44	50.10	62.26
Latin America	40.34	47.51	54.43
Asia (except USSR and China)	18.47	22.97	26.50
China	11.02	16.55	23.54
Africa	13.80	17.71	21.84
World	28.23%	32.98%	38.04%

Source: Davis, Kingsley, *World Urbanization 1950–70*, vol. 1, Basic Data for Cities, Counties and Regions, Population Monograph Series No. 4, University of California, Berkeley, 1972, pp. 57–82. Reprinted by permission.

do measurement standards differ for a great number of commodities, they are also different for various commodities themselves.

ENERGY RESOURCES

The relation between economic progress and use of energy is universally recognized. Considerations of where and how energy is produced, transported, or distributed are the major topics treated here.

Energy value can be expressed by conversion into various common denominators, such as kilowatt-hours (kwh), calories, or British thermal units (Btu).[2] Converted energy data in the form of hard-coal-equivalent (h.c.e.) are readily available from United Nations sources,

so this measurement will be used in this text.[3]

Energy, the force behind all work, stems from both animate and inanimate sources. The so-called animate sources consist chiefly of man and animals; also included in this category are fuel woods and agricultural wastes, such as dung and dried stems, leaves, and roots. The inanimate sources include both the fossil and nonfossil energy resources. Fossil energy resources include coal, crude petroleum fuel and shale oils, gas, peat, and certain metals used in nuclear energy production. The nonfossil energy resources are water, wind, sun, and air. One-fifth of the world's supply of energy measured in h.c.e. is derived from animate sources, 65 percent of which is provided by fuel wood and agricultural wastes.

Energy has many meanings and di-

[2] Kwh is a unit of electrical energy or work equal to that done by one kilowatt acting for one hour. One kilowatt is equal to 1.34102 British horsepower, or the lifting of 21 short tons a foot per minute (equivalent to more than 55 Btu per minute). Btu is a unit of heat equal to 252 calories—the quantity of heat required to raise the temperature of one pound of water from 62° F to 63° F. A calorie is a unit of heat needed to raise the temperature of one gram of water one degree centigrade, called small calorie.

[3] Hard-coal-equivalent is a common denominator for various energy sources based on their calorific value; for example, one metric ton of coal briquette is equal to 0.67 metric ton of coal; one metric ton of crude petroleum and shale oil is equal to 1.3 metric tons of coal; 1,000 cubic meters of natural gas is equal to 1.33 metric tons of coal; and 1,000 kwh are equal to 0.125 metric ton of coal. Similarly, other sources have their conversion factors; one metric ton is 1,000 kilograms or 2,205 pounds.

verse manifestations, depending upon its source and the process required to convert it into work.[4] Table 3–5 shows that in 1972 the world's production of energy from coal, lignite, crude petroleum, natural gas, hydro and nuclear electricity, and peat was 7,566 million metric tons h.c.e. On a per-capita basis, this amounts to about 2,000 kilograms h.c.e.

The spatial variation in production and consumption of energy is highly significant. At one extreme, the United States, with just under 6 percent of the world's population (1972), produces 27.3 percent of the world's total energy and consumes about one-third of the world's total energy supplies. Toward the other end of the spectrum, India (not shown in the table), with almost 15 percent of the world's population, uses only less than 2 percent of the world's energy. This comparison is not entirely realistic because energy sources, such as wood, animal power, and dung, constitute a significant portion of all the energy used in India and many other developing regions. The Far East (excluding the People's Republic of China), harboring over 30 percent of the world's population, consumes only 9 percent of the world's commercial energy supplies. Table 3–6 shows that the relative importance of various energy sources has shifted strikingly over the past years.

Geothermal power is energy captured from the earth's heat. Although insignificant, it has a potential to provide added supplies of energy in the future. Electricity was first produced from geothermal steam in Larderello, Italy, in 1904, where a small dynamo powered five light bulbs. Today, geothermal power capacity worldwide is about 850,000 kilowatts. Italy still leads the world production with an installed capacity of 400,000 kilowatts.

The only producing field in the U.S. is The Geysers. Five years from now, its capacity is expected to more than quadruple to 850,000 kilowatts, and companies are still exploring potential geothermal fields in Nevada and California's Imperial Valley. New Zealand is far behind the U.S., with a capacity of 170,000 kilowatts. Mexico, Japan, and the USSR have small geothermal power plants, a new project has been started in the Philippines, and other countries are actively exploring geothermal resources.

During the past decade, U.S. oil companies and public utilities have become interested in geothermal steam as a possible supplement to present energy fuels. Scientists estimate that in the U.S. about 1.8 million acres of land are attractive for geothermal development and that the potential geothermal capacity ranges from 30 million to as much as 100 million kilowatts. By comparison, present installed electric-generating capacity from all sources is about 367 million kilowatts.

Development of geothermal power received encouragement in 1970 with the passage of the Geothermal Steam Act, a law that permits geothermal prospectors to lease federal lands. This is significant because most of the favorable geothermal areas are in the western third of the United States, where 47.7 percent of the land is federally owned. About 85 percent of Nevada, for example, is owned by the government.

Steam is not the only source of geothermal power. Experiments are being conducted on underground hot water in California's Imperial Valley. To date, commercial development has proved uneconomical because in places as much as 30 percent of the water contains highly corrosive solids. Some of these solids have economic value and might be extracted as a byproduct. In some dry areas,

[4] For detailed analysis of the nature and sources of energy, *see* Erich W. Zimmerman, *World Resources and Industries,* rev. ed. (New York: Harper & Row, 1951).

TABLE 3–5   Production and Consumption of Energy, 1972

	ENERGY (millions of metric tons of h.c.e)		WORLD TOTAL		POPULATION (millions)		PER CAPITA ENERGY[2] (kilograms h.c.e.)	
	PRODUCTION	CONSUMPTION[1]	PRODUCTION	CONSUMPTION	TOTAL	PERCENT	PRODUCTION	CONSUMPTION
North America	2322.47	2660.22	30.70%	35.90%	233	6.2 %	9968	11417
U.S.	2065.22	2424.79	27.30	32.73	211	5.6	9788	11492
Canada	257.25	235.01	3.40	3.17	22	.6	11693	10682
Latin America	407.85	284.50	5.39	3.84	300	7.9	1360	948
Western Europe (except USSR)	585.76	1435.75	7.74	19.38	363	9.6	1614	3955
Middle East	1224.77	95.42	16.19	1.29	111	3.0	11034	860
Asia (except Middle East, USSR, and China)	263.05	564.61	3.48	7.62	1245	33.0	211	454
Oceania	93.41	85.23	1.23	1.15	20	.5	4670	4262
Africa	441.42	133.95	5.83	1.81	364	9.6	1213	368
Eastern Europe (except USSR)	471.44	524.48	6.23	7.08	106	2.8	4448	4948
USSR	1312.46	1179.54	17.35	15.92	248	6.5	5292	4756
China	443.27	444.99	5.86	6.01	792	20.9	560	562
World total	7565.91	4708.68	100.00	100.00	3782	100.00	2000	1959

1 Bunkers supplied to foreign-going ships are excluded from consumption data.

2 Per-capita energy of metric tons of h.c.e. is converted into kilograms of h.c.e. @ one metric ton = 1,000 kilograms.

Source: Based on the *United Nations Statistical Yearbook, 1973* (New York: United Nations, 1974), pp. 347–50.

TABLE 3–6 Composition of Energy Use, 1953 and 1972

ENERGY SOURCE	NORTH AMERICA		WESTERN EUROPE		CENTRALLY PLANNED ECONOMIES[1]		OTHER REGIONS AND COUNTRIES OF THE WORLD		WORLD	
	1953	1972	1953	1972	1953	1972	1953	1972	1953	1972
Coal and Lignite	34.0%	18.8%	81.9%	26.2%	84.1%	57.7%	53.6%	24.9%	57.8%	32.5%
Crude Petroleum	38.5	43.2	14.9	57.8	13.3	24.4	39.4	61.4	27.8	43.4
Natural Gas	25.8	35.5	.6	12.3	2.1	16.8	3.7	10.4	12.6	21.6
Hydro and Nuclear Power	1.7	2.5	2.6	3.7	.5	1.1	3.3	3.3	1.8	2.5
Total (in million metric tons of h.c.e.)	1,295	2,660	638	1,436	631	2,149	303	1,164	2,867	7,409

1 Includes Eastern Europe, People's Republic of China, Mongolia, North Korea, North Vietnam, and USSR.

Source: United Nations Statistical Yearbook, 1973 (New York: United Nations), 1974, pp. 48–51.

the water can be used after the mineral matter is removed. As technology and economics permit, hot water utilization may provide a major advance in geothermal development.

According to the National Petroleum Council, in 1985 geothermal power is expected to provide from one-half of 1 percent to 2 percent of U.S. energy demands; this is about the same position nuclear power occupies today. In 1953, solid fuels (coal and lignite) supplied almost 58 percent of the world's commercial energy. By 1972, the solid-fuel fraction dropped to 33 percent. During the same period, the share supplied by liquid fuels (crude petroleum) increased from 28 to 43 percent. The biggest gain of all was in natural gas, which increased from 13 to 22 percent of the total. Although the portion supplied by hydropower and nuclear electric power increased substantially during this period, it continues to be a small fraction of the total of the world's commercial energy.

During these years, the United States led the way in the shift from solid to liquid and gaseous fuels and strongly influenced the world totals. Figure 3–1 shows that oil and natural gas supplied 77 percent of all the energy consumed in the United States. This figure will reduce to a projected 67 percent in 1980 as a result of the increased use of nuclear and hydropower. In Western Europe and the USSR, coal is still important. In the USSR, there is a moderate rise in the use of liquid fuels, and in Western Europe coal use has increased markedly.

The less developed and developing parts of the world depend on liquid fuels far more than do the developed regions. In 1972, liquid fuels represented about 61 percent of the total energy consumed by developing countries, compared to about 40 percent in 1953. Historically, developing countries have not followed a path of energy use similar to that experienced by developed countries—i.e.,

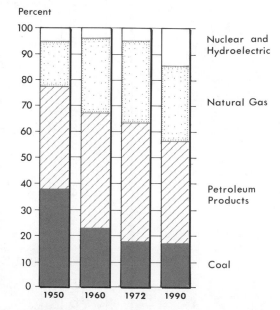

FIGURE 3–1 *Energy Sources of U.S.*

from coal to liquid fuels and from liquid fuels to hydroelectricity and natural gas. Developing countries are in line with the worldwide swing to liquid fuels and natural gas from coal. There are a number of reasons for this trend:

1. Oil can be transported much more cheaply than coal over long distances.

2. The known reserves of economically mineable coal are running low.

3. To meet increasing demands for energy, alternative ways of procuring it are being sought.

4. Both natural gas and liquid fuels provide greater energy per unit of weight.

ENERGY CRISIS

The question of the adequacy of energy resources has recently attracted widespread interest. The variables that enter into this appraisal are complex. The demand aspect considers future structural changes, type and level of economic activities, and consumer tastes and preferences. The supply aspect is controlled by "know-how," and the world's total energy resources are really not known. Under the present technology and cost limitations, the endowment is what is actually known to exist. Thus, the measure of the resource endowment is confined to resources that are known, exploitable now, or seem likely to be in the future.

Searl (21) estimates that between 1960 and 2000 the world will have consumed approximately 435 billion metric tons of h.c.e., which means that over a forty-year period the world's energy resources will be depleted at an annual rate of 2½ times that of 1960. Estimates developed by the U.S. Geological Survey indicate that a world total equivalent of 2,320 billion metric tons of recoverable coal are available for use in known deposits with seams fourteen or more inches thick and lying within 3,000 feet of the surface. (This estimate does not take into consideration allowances for discovery of new coal deposits.) If one subtracts the estimated consumption between 1960 and 2000 (435 billion metric tons h.c.e.) from 2,320, it still leaves 1,885 billion metric tons h.c.e., which is sufficient to satisfy the world's total demand for energy for almost another century beyond the year 2000 at the estimated annual level of consumption in the year 2000.

The world's potential resources of oil and natural gas, as estimated by responsible authorities—U.S. Geological Survey and the Shell Development Company—are between 535 and 1,620 billion metric tons h.c.e. The former figure is based on existing standards, and the latter includes deposits that are considered submarginal by today's standards and whose exploitation depends on future economic and technological improvements. These estimates are only indicators and are subject to substantial upward revisions. The increase in demand and price would justify the search for new deposits and the development of new technology.

Besides, vast potential resources of oil shale and oil-bearing tar sands have been discovered. Although the present contribution of hydro, nuclear, atomic, and solar power is very small, potential progress in these areas appears promising.

Finally, it is evident that the world's need for energy can be met with fossil fuels alone for at least two or more centuries. Nevertheless, as the costs of alternative energy-producing sources decline, they will effectively compete with and substitute for fossil fuels. When the world's resources of uranium, thorium, granite, and weightless and freight-free nuclear fuels are all taken into consideration, man can be said to have within reach an almost unlimited supply of energy.

Similar optimism was indicated in May 1973 by Joel Darmstadter and Milton F. Searl before the Senate Committee on Foreign Relations:

> The estimated U.S. resources of shale oil and crude oil are so large that it is unlikely that there will ever be a time at which the nation will not be able to develop substantial additional supplies of oil. It seems likely that long before the nation even comes close to exhausting either crude oil or shale oil resources, other sources of energy will have taken over the market. The nation may well leave large amounts of oil in the ground forever which would be recoverable at higher prices.[5]

The Potential Gas Committee, which represents the production, transmission, and distribution interests of the natural gas industry, estimates that at the end of

[5] Reported in bulletin of Resources for the Future, Inc., "Resources, Some Findings and Conjectures from Recent Research into Resource Development and Use," No. 43 (June 1973).

1970 there was nearly 1,200 trillion cubic feet of gas yet to be found "without a fundamental change in economics or technology." The U.S. Geological Survey does estimate the amount of natural gas originally in place—discovered and undiscovered—and its figures are much higher than those of the Potential Gas Committee, even when adjusted for recovery percentages and past discoveries. And, as was the case with crude oil, the estimated remaining resources of natural gas are far more than needed to support levels of production which might be desired through 1985. The problem lies with finding and developing the needed gas resources, not with their existence.

It is not necessary to go into any detail on coal resources. There is no question about their adequacy in the time period under consideration. There are, of course, questions about the ability to produce and consume this coal without undue damage to the environment, which is also true for natural gas and oil.

There is increasing evidence that we do not face as imminent a shortage of low-cost uranium as the Atomic Energy Commission[6] resource figures might lead one to believe. Thorium supply also appears to be abundant.

Assume a nation decides as a matter of policy that it wants to limit imports to only 20 percent of its oil and gas consumption in 1985, producing the rest domestically. This is a level of oil imports which the nation has historically found acceptable, but a higher level of gas imports than has prevailed in the past. Cumulative production of oil from 1973 to 1985, plus increases in reserves to support this production, will require about 70 billion additional barrels of oil re-

[6] The AEC was dissolved in 1974 by the Energy Reorganization Act under which the functions of the AEC were assigned to two agencies: the Nuclear Regulatory Commission (NRC) and the Energy Research and Development Administration (ERDA).

serves. This is clearly well within the previous conservative estimate of 300 billion barrels of oil that the nation could still produce. And this makes no allowance for extensive use of any of the 1,700 billion barrels of oil shale resources. As previously indicated, neither oil shale nor coal gasification is expected to play a large role before 1985.

In the case of natural gas, perhaps 450 trillion cubic feet may need to be added to reserves during the 1973 to 1985 period. This is only a little over one-third of the 1,200 trillion cubic feet that the Potential Gas Committee estimated.

The questions of how fast domestic output can be expanded or what the cost will be have not been dealt with, although many studies are exploring these questions. However, the following observation can be made: The National Petroleum Council study found in one of its supply cases that dependency on foreign oil and gas sources could be limited to approximately 20 percent in 1985. So far the preliminary indications from the authors' research do not contradict this conclusion.

In order to increase domestic energy production through 1985, we must expand output of crude oil, natural gas, and direct use of coal in power plants, along with scheduled expansion of nuclear power, rather than rely on new technologies. The resources are there. Price increases will be necessary; a policy of leasing federal lands is needed. Reasonable environmental standards can be maintained but ending the uncertainty about environmental requirements is important. Unless there is a crash effort by the government, oil shale and coal gasification are not likely to be major contributors by 1985, and the breeder reactor is not scheduled to contribute by then. It might be wise to direct a larger portion of the government's energy research and development to the possibility of using coal in an environmentally acceptable manner, to improve oil recovery, and possibly to advance drilling technology. These are the areas in which research and development could be a major asset within the next decade.

There is evidence of important oil and gas deposits in offshore areas beyond the established jurisdiction of the nation. Jurisdiction over these areas must be established, whether it comes under the United States or an international body, so that exploration and development can proceed with no more than normal business risk.

Action in resolving our energy policy is urgent. Decisions made next year instead of this year won't have much effect on short-term supply, but the principle of exponential growth applies to the longer term. If decisions are made this year, however hard that may be politically, domestic energy supply in 1985 may be 10 percent greater than if the decisions are made next year.

Despite optimistic statements by authoritative scholars, the issue of U.S. energy shortage is a genuine concern to Americans. In 1971, President Nixon sent a special message to Congress on U.S. energy problems. The major thrust of the message was the technological considerations influencing the supply of energy materials:

1. Stepped up federal support for development of the breeder reactor, including an increased share in the government's contribution to construction of a demonstration plant by 1980

2. Some expansion of currently modest federal assistance to make the conversion of coal into high-Btu gas commercially feasible

3. A signficant jump in funds for sulfur oxide control technology

4. A pledge of continued government assistance for a variety of research and development efforts, including coal liquification, magneto-hydrodynamic power cycles, and controlled thermonuclear fusion

Later in 1973 the Nixon administration abolished the oil quota and tariffs on imported oil; subject to a licensing fee, at least on amounts in excess of 1973 levels. New refineries were permitted to import 75 percent of their crude oil free of charge for five years, as a means of stimulating domestic refinery construction.

On the demand side, the 6 percent of the world's people who live in the United States have been increasing their energy demand almost 5 percent annually since the 1950s. This increase in demand has basically been due to two reasons: 1) historically, energy costs have fallen relative to the overall price level, and 2) during the late 1960s, U.S. household incomes increased at a faster rate than available supplies.

The demand for energy may be curbed by changing our production processes and consumption habits: more emphasis on air-tight buildings, better mass transportation, economical carboration by autos, and more efficient industrial processes and equipment.

The most commonly suggested solution of increasing prices to curb demand for energy has several social welfare implications. Some even contend that the demand for energy is relatively inelastic,[7] suggesting that the price mechanism is of limited value in curbing the demand for energy. Others contend that the long-run problem of energy demand may not reflect inelasticity because price increases make buyers more conscious of conserving energy. Energy has been so cheap for so long that, except for certain heavy industrial processes, no one has given much thought to using it efficiently. Price mechanisms could change this situation.

[7] The economic concept of inelasticity is discussed more fully in chapter 4. It basically means that consumers' responses to price increases are not enthusiastic and significant. This is especially true when the effective substitutes for energy are not easily available or economically feasible.

The solution of energy shortage via increased import of energy materials has numerous implications for U.S. balance of payments. For example, as Figure 3–2 shows, nearly two thirds of the world's proved oil reserves are located in Arab countries that import relatively few goods from the U.S. This imbalance tends to promote devaluation of the U.S. dollar; U.S. dollar devaluation, in turn, diminishes the revenue of other nations exporting oil to the U.S.

The principal oil-producing countries of North Africa, the Middle East, and the U.S. provide a case in point. Following two dollar devaluations in 1971 and 1973, U.S. oil importing companies had to sign a new agreement with oil-exporting nations boosting the price of crude oil by more than 30 cents a barrel. Because taxes and royalties paid to oil-exporting countries are based on posted prices, this agreement increased oil production costs, causing a rippling effect that ultimately reached the consumer in the form of higher prices. The question of importing energy resources deserves a careful and detailed analysis that explores ramifications for U.S. trade relations with other nations.

Figure 3–2 shows the Middle East as the largest single oil-producing region in the world, followed by North America, the USSR, several African countries, and a miscellaneous category which includes the major oil-producing countries of Venezuela and Indonesia. There is no certainty that the OPEC (Organization of Petroleum Exporting Countries) will continue to increase their oil output as they have in the past. The Arab–Israeli War of October 1973 resulted in reductions in production by most Arab exporters. Meanwhile, increases in the posted prices of crude oil achieved by the OPEC cartel have made it possible for the OPEC not to press for greater levels of production. Oil revenue flowing into the OPEC, which previously had been growing

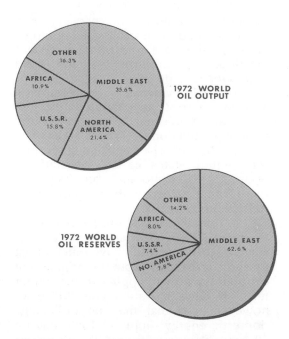

FIGURE 3–2 *World Oil Reserves and Production*

apace with increases in oil production, shot upward in 1974 because of price increases—from $1.00 at the start of the 1970s to $1.99 before the 1973 Arab–Israeli War to $3.44 at the end of 1973 to more than $10.00 at the end of 1974. The result was the greatest and swiftest transfer of wealth in all history: The 13 OPEC countries earned $112 billion from the rest of the world during 1974. The effects of this shift of money are manifold in terms of inflation, international balance of payments, and economic adjustments in the demand and supply of energy resources and, consequently, in the economic well-being of people.

MINERALS

Minerals are the basic source for energy fuels, chemicals, metals, and construction materials. Among the nonfuel, nonmetallic minerals, sulphur, salt, potash, lime, borates, phosphates, gypsum, asbestos, stones, and diamonds are the most common and widely extracted. Similarly, among the metallic minerals, the most important are iron ore, bauxite, manganese, chromite, copper, zinc, lead, nickel, tin, titanium, vanadium, molybdenum, tungsten, and cobalt. In addition, other metals are produced:

1. Primarily as by-products of processing other metals: antimony, aresenic trioxide, indium, platinum groups, cadminium, thallium, germanium, etc.
2. Primarily as by-products of mining other metals: hafnium, titanium, beryllium, columbium, and tantalum
3. Wholly or largely produced and processed independently: mercury, silicon, and strontium

Nonfuel minerals in various forms bear numerous and distinctive properties. For example, the general characteristics of acidity, alkalinity, solubility, and stability may be applied to chemicals; metals may possess the properties of strength, toughness, endurance, magnetism, conductivity, and the ability to withstand the influences of weather, weight, corrosion, and intense heat. By virtue of these properties, minerals provide the basic fabric of man's material progress. Time-series data on world economies indicate that the rising consumption of metallurgical and chemical products is positively correlated with per capita gross national product.

The industrially developed countries, which consume the major portion of the world's minerals, depend on the less developed countries for the bulk of their supply. For instance, the United States imports all its tin, more than 90 percent of its manganese, antimony, beryllium, and chromium ores, more than 85 percent of its nickel and bauxite, and 60 percent of its zinc and lead. The less developed societies, recognizing the re-

lationship between gross national product and the consumption of minerals by the developed societies, are venturing to capture benefits from their mineral wealth. Often, however, they face frustration in this endeavor because of the inability of their economies to effectively use these minerals.[8]

Behind demand and supply estimates lie certain assumptions and concepts, the understanding of which is important in the evaluation of mineral resources.

Grade. The grade or quality and the percent of metallic content of an ore often serve as a common criterion for the estimation of reserves at various locations.

Reserves. Mineral reserves are classified under at least three areas:

1. Known or proved reserves
2. Potential reserves
3. Ultimate or absolute reserves

Known or proved reserves are the amounts of ore (adjusted for grade) that are known to exist and are workable under the conditions of current technology. Potential reserves refer to the

[8] U.S. Joint Economic Committee, *Twenty Years After: An Appeal for the Renewal of International Economic Cooperation on a Grand Scale* (Washington, D.C.: U.S. Government Printing Office, 1966). The United States Subcommittee on International Exchange and Payments of the Joint Economic Committee, being aware of U.S. dependence on foreign mineral resources and the contemporay events in foreign countries associated with these minerals and other international trade considerations, prepared this report. The report is a thoughtful evaluation of the problem which was presented to Congress and the nations who trade with the United States. Using detailed analyses of demand and supply of minerals, the president's Materials Policy Commission expressed similar concerns during the early 1950s in *Resources for Freedom* (Washington, D.C.: U.S. Government Printing Office, 1952), Vol. II.

minerals that will be realized in the future with improved technology; materials that cannot be worked under present economic and technological constraints are termed potential minerals.

Ultimate reserves are commonly defined as the sum of past production, current proved reserves, and reserves that will be discovered in the future with the current conditions of cost and technology. All of these concepts depend upon inference based largely on geological surveys for their quantitative estimation; obviously systematically digging into even the first 100,000 feet of the earth's crust from pole to pole for precise quantitative estimation of minerals is an impossible task. For spatial evaluation of minerals, a common reserves criterion should be applied.

Substitution. Closely associated with the problem of estimating demand–supply relationships is the concept of substitution. Every ore that is mined for use occurs in a wide variety of conditions that collectively determine the demand supply of the ore. At one end of the spectrum are the conditions in which pure minerals are situated at the surface and located at the best possible site for transportation to markets. At the other end of the spectrum are ores of the lowest possible grade, with the highest percentage of deleterious impurities, at the greatest depth, in the poorest location, and with other disadvantages of winning the product from the ore. Each set of conditions reflects a cost which, in the absence of improved technology, rises as the resources approach depletion or exhaustion. The cost need not be a linear function of time and depletion.

Substitution plays an important role in the effort to make materials go further. For example, when high-quality iron ores of magnetite and hematite began to run out in the Lake Superior region, not only

were methods developed to use the lower grade taconite ores found in the same area, but also steel substitutes—aluminum, magnesium, titanium, structural concrete—and a variety of strong, durable plastics resistant to heat and cold began to replace steel in many industries. Steel alloys, which have a greater tensile strength with less weight, now are being substituted for conventional steel. The use of aluminum is common in the construction industry. Tens of thousands of tons of aluminum are being used in barges, bridges, truck trailers, railroad cars, and automobiles. Some even project that materials like plastics will replace steel, and steel will occupy the position held by plastics today.

New technologies not only are making substitutions practical, but they are also giving a new meaning to the serious concerns expressed immediately after World War II about the depletion of mineral resources. New devices and instruments to discover resources—areal cameras, air-borne magnetometers, scintilometers, electromagnetic induction devices—have doubled and tripled the world's known reserves of many materials.

It is difficult to obtain reliable reserves estimates because the economic and technological factors related to local phenomena determine whether material of a given grade is or is not an ore. A material might be entered in reserve columns but may never be economically feasible to mine. And future substitutions and structural changes in demand for an ore might change the whole picture.

Perhaps actual production of various ores can give an accurate indication of regional endowment and productivity. It is evident from Table 3–7 that:

1. Relatively few countries produce any significant share of the world's minerals. For example, only five countries account for over 50 percent of the total world output for every mineral listed.

    2. The United States, a major consumer of minerals, is greatly dependent on foreign resources for many of its mineral needs. The U.S. is the leading producer of eight of the twenty-four minerals. Of these eight, only three are virtual monopolies of the U.S.—molybdenum, nitrogen, and uranium.

    3. Although minerals are distributed in every continent except Antarctica, the developing nations and the USSR produce more base metals (copper, lead, zinc, and tin), light metals (bauxite), and ferroalloy metals (cobalt, manganese, nickel, and tungsten).

    Although Table 3–7 represents only crude mineral quantities, i.e., the ore content, it indicates a basic pattern of mineral resource distribution. Obviously, the columns related to consumption would change slightly when all kinds of production, and imports and exports of partially or fully refined material are considered.

MATERIALS CRISIS

Following the oil crisis precipitated by the OPEC cartel, some expressed fears that exporters of nonfuel minerals would take similar actions to raise prices. This concern gained some substance when Jamaica and other Caribbean countries increased prices on their bauxite exports. Although this concern has some validity, the following should also be considered: (1) Although the developing countries and the USSR produce more base and light metals and ferroalloys, the developed and free-market economies hold more than half the world's reserves of lead, zinc, chromium, molybdenum, titanium, and potash. These minerals could be mined at an accelerated rate. Centrally planned economies predominately have tungsten, vanadium, and land-based

magnesium, readily available from seawater. (2) The geographic and political diversity among producers and exporters of nonfuel minerals makes carteling less effective than it is in petroleum markets. The unifying political and cultural catalyst present in the Arab World is not as easy to find in countries producing most other minerals. Significant amounts of major materials are located in Canada, Australia, and Latin America, which are friendly to the U.S. (3) Many of these material-exporting countries are heavily involved with the importing countries in diversified trade patterns, and negotiations are most likely to result instead of unilateral action. The importing countries, considering the environmental factors, may favor transferring a growing share of processing to the raw material suppliers by long-term changes in the patterns of trade and foreign assistance policy, and thus may minimize the exporting countries' aspirations to form cartels. (4) Because materials suppliers depend heavily upon a continuing flow of foreign exchange earnings for both import procurement and budget support, they would not militate against risking production and export interruptions. (5) Given the prospects for economic conditions of the world during the 1970s, it seems unlikely that exporters will be interested in making further gains in prices, but rather they are likely to consolidate the gains achieved during the late 1960s. (6) Since substitutes for materials are becoming plentiful with expanding technology, the proliferation of cartels like the OPEC is not likely. (7) Sudden shortages in materials other than oil can be handled more easily because, compared to petroleum consumers, consumers of other materials are a moderate number. Consideration of these points seems to reflect that materials shortage and cartelizing is not as viable a threat to materials other than oil. However, long-

TABLE 3–7 Leading Countries in Mineral Production and U.S. Mineral Consumption, 1972

	PRODUCTION AS PERCENT OF WORLD TOTAL								TOTAL WORLD PRODUCTION†	U.S. PRODUCTION	U.S. CONSUMPTION‡ AS PERCENT OF WORLD PRODUCTION	U.S. PRODUCTION AS PERCENT OF U.S. CONSUMPTION
Antimony (ore content)	Rep.S.Af.	23%	China	19%	USSR	11%	Bolivia	10%	62,900 m.t.	1%	21.49%	3.27%
Asbestos (unmanufactured)	Canada	34	USSR	27	Rep.S.Af.	7	China	4	4,490,000 m.t.	3	19.80	16.28
Bauxite (crude and dried)	Australia	21	Jamaica	20	Surinam	10	USSR	7	65,800,000 m.t.	4	23.73	11.79
Chromium (ore content)	USSR	28	Rep.S.Af.	24	Turkey	13	India	5	2,770,000 m.t.	—	16.67	—
Cobalt (ore content)	Zaire	56	Canada	8	USSR	7	Cuba	6	23,265 m.t.	*	27.55	*
Copper (ore content: primary)	USSR	15	Zambia	11	Chile	11	Canada	10	6,780,000 m.t.	23	23.87	95.37
Gold (ore and base bullion)	Rep.S.Af.	76	USSR	14	Canada	4	Japan	2	1,195,000 m.t.	4	16.29	65.48
Iron (ore content)	USSR	26	Australia	9	Brazil	7	China	6	433,800,000 m.t.	11	16.77	61.35
Lead (ore content)	USSR	13	Australia	12	Canada	11	Mexico	5	3,410,000 m.t.	16	19.61	4.67
Manganese (35% or more)	Rep.S.Af.	31	USSR	16	Brazil	13	India	7	8,570,000 m.t.	*	10.21	*
Mercury	USSR	20	Spain	17	Italy	17	China	11	8,490 m.t.	3	18.92	13.77
Molybdenum (ore content)	Canada	14	USSR	10	Chile	7	China	2	79,450 m.t.	64	35.92	178.15
Nickel (ore content)	Canada	38	USSR	21	New Caled.	17	S. Rhodesia	12	614,300 m.t.	3	22.82	10.58
Nitrogen (contained N)	USSR	17	Japan	6	W. Germany	4	France	4	35,107,000 m.t.	24	21.00	112.82

TABLE 3-7 *Continued*

	PRODUCTION AS PERCENT OF WORLD TOTAL								TOTAL WORLD PRODUCTION†	U.S. PRO-DUC-TION	U.S. CON-SUMPTION‡ AS PERCENT OF WORLD PRO-DUCTION	U.S. PRO-DUCTION AS PER-CENT OF U.S. CON-SUMPTION
Phosphate Rock (rock and apatite)	USSR	23	Morocco	16	Tunisia	4	Nauru Is.	2	94,380,000 m.t.	41	24.44	163.27
Potash (K₂O equivalent)	USSR	27	Canada	18	W. Germany	14	E. Germany	12	20,490,000 m.t.	12	21.43	55.22
Silver (ore and base bullion)	Canada	17	Mexico	14	USSR	14	Peru	14	9,060 m.t.	13	52.63	24.57
Sulfur (elemental)	Canada	27	Poland	10	France	7	Mexico	3	26,214,000 m.t.	28	34.13	82.79
Tin (ore content)	Malaysia	39	Bolivia	16	Thailand	11	Indonesia	11	196,500 m.t.	*	14.53	*
Titanium (ilmenite concentrate)	Canada	26	Australia	22	Norway	19	Malaysia	5	3,253,530 m.t.	19	21.93	86.68
Tungsten (WO₃ content 60% base)	China	19	USSR	19	Thailand	7	N. Korea	6	46,810 m.t.	9	16.64	57.77
Uranium (U₃O₈ content)	Canada	20	Rep.S.Af.	16	France	16	Niger	1	19,185 m.t.	55	52.06	141.44
Vanadium (V₂O₅ content)	Rep.S.Af.	37	Finland	10	Norway	9	Namibia	5	11,770 m.t.	38	26.20	93.50
Zinc (ore content)	Canada	23	USSR	12	Australia	9	Peru	6	5,550,000 m.t.	8	11.90	65.24

* Less than 1 percent

† The weight measures in this column are metric ton (m.t.) kilograms (KG), and flasks. A metric ton is equal to 1,000 kilograms, 2,204 lbs., .984 long ton, or 1.1023 short tons. The short ton is equal to 2,000 lbs.

‡ The U.S. consumption was computed as the total U.S. production plus imports minus exports.

Source: Based on *United Nations Statistical Yearbook, 1973* (New York: United Nations, 1974), and *Minerals Yearbook 1972*, vol. I, *Metals, Minerals, and Fuels* (Washington, D.C.: U.S. Department of Interior, 1974).

range responses to material shortages involve other considerations.

WATER RESOURCES

Water is man's most abundant and most important mineral. Yet, ironically its spatial distribution and use are not properly understood. As a result, it is not uncommon to hear both concern about water shortage and assurances of an unlimited supply of water. The water shortage stems from:

    1. Our value system, which intractably holds water as a free gift from nature
    2. A limited use of market price to balance supply and demand
    3. The location of water away from economic and population centers
    4. Lack of knowledge or ability to use the available supply of water

In this section, water is evaluated and presented as a resource mineral in terms of its supply and demand patterns and problems of using the available supply.
    For analytical purposes, the total hydrosphere, i.e., the sum total of water found at the surface, in the ground, and in atmospheric vapors, is divided into four categories:

    1. Salt or sea water
    2. Ice-locked water
    3. Hydrologic cycle water
    4. Depth-locked underground water

The world's water supply, i.e., the total amount of water in the hydrosphere, is approximately 326,071,300 cubic miles (one cubic mile contains over 1,101 billion gallons). Over 99 percent of this is either salt water or is locked up as ice-caps in Greenland and Antarctica. Salt water alone constitutes about 97.2 percent of world's water supply. The remaining 1 percent is composed of water that

continually recirculates in the hydrologic cycle,[9] and that which has no direct relation to the hydrologic cycle, most of which lies at great depths not subject to replenishment, except through the long-run process of geological accumulation. Thus, for all practical purposes, when we think of water supply, we are concerned with the volume of flow through the hydrologic cycle and with that of oceans (see Figure 3–3).

OCEAN RESOURCES

Spatial analysis of oceans involves considerations of rights to exploitation by nations. The question of who owns the oceans includes many variables, such as seaward national boundaries, consideration of land-locked countries, criteria of ownership, and management of ocean resources. Discussion of these topics is beyond the scope here. It will take decades for the world to approximate the wealth hidden in the oceans; only then will the spatial variability of ocean resources be fully realized.
    Under existing arrangements, an individual nation's level of exploitation of ocean resources, which are mostly a common international property, is a combined result of the following factors:

    1. The sufficiency, quality, and feasibility of land-based resources
    2. Access and size of the continental shelf
    3. Technology suitable for handling ocean resources

[9] The hydrologic cycle is the process by which water moves from the atmosphere to the land to the sea and back to the atmosphere. Approximately 9 percent more water evaporates over the oceans than they receive as rain and snow, and more rain falls on the land than that which evaporates from it; thus the volume of water carried to the sea by glaciers, rivers, and coastal springs balances out, respectively, the differential excess and loss from the land and the ocean.

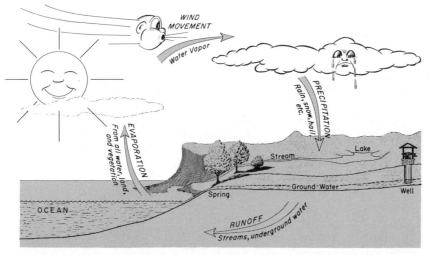

FIGURE 3–3 *Hydrologic Cycle*

4. Conditions of light and temperature for chemical processes and the growth of plankton[10]

5. Availability of funds for oceanographic research and development

Man has extracted food, energy, minerals, and pharmacological chemicals from the oceans. Perhaps the most important resource from the oceans is food, particularly protein. Fish meal concentrate recently approved by the United States Food and Drug Administration is an example of the potential that lies in the oceans. Man presently is harvesting over 60 million short tons of fish yearly from the oceans; this is only a tiny fraction of the estimated volume actually available. Moreover, it has been demonstrated that 50 tons of algae can be grown for chicken feed annually in a single surface acre of ocean water under proper climatic conditions.

The ocean is also being used as a source of power. From the waves, tides, currents, organic matter, and temperature differences, power is being harnessed. France, for example, has in partial operation a system of turbine generators that transforms the rise and fall of the tides into electrical power. When completed, the project will produce 544,000,000 kilowatt hours a year. Japan uses wave action for electric power at almost all its lighthouses, and test generators are under construction which will pipe wave energy to generating stations on land.

Since the first oil-drilling rigs went to sea in the 1940s, more than $3.5 billion have been invested. Today over 16 percent of the total world oil production comes from offshore wells and is expected to increase to 25 percent by 1975. In addition to oil and natural gas, numerous minerals have been found in the oceans, including magnesium, cobalt, copper, nickel, iron, tin, coal, silver, gold, sulphur, and diamonds. The United States, for instance, extracts 51,000 carats of diamonds per year from the sea, and it is estimated that there are 6 million tons of gold that can be removed from the ocean.

[10] The favorable conditions of sunlight and temperature encourage growth of plankton, the microscopic animal and plant life found floating or drifting in the oceans and in bodies of fresh water, which is used as food by fish.

The ocean is virtually one large chemical plant providing sources of new medical discoveries. Over 80 elements are present in ocean water. Currently man is extracting salt, magnesium, potassium, iodine, and bromine directly from sea water. Marine pharmacologists have extracted chemicals from water and marine organisms that kill pain, inhibit the growth of certain tumors, fight viruses, and stimulate the heart. In addition, the expanding demands for recreational use of the shore, inland waters, and ocean water for swimming, sport fishing, skin diving, boating, and surfing all point to the increasing value of ocean resources.

Finally, man's incessant desire for more water to satisfy his domestic and industrial demands most of which exists on the seacoast, points to the oceans for water. Over thirty processes have been developed for desalinating ocean water. The suitability of a particular method for a given location is a function of the amount of water in demand, the source and cost of energy, the degree of salinity, and other characteristics of the ocean water, storage facilities, and the disposability and market for the by-products extractable from brine. Distillation by the ion-exchange method using plastic membranes to purify ocean water has not yet been developed to the commercially feasible stage.

The most promising method of distillation now is multi-stage flash (MSF) distillation, the process used at the San Diego/Guantanamo plant at a cost of about $1 per 1,000 gallons.[11] Although the MSF process produces water with slightly less purity than the other methods—a close runnerup is a method called long-tube vertical (LTV) distillation—it is preferred by all three of the giant dual-purpose water and power plants under consideration: the Israeli–U.S. Mediterranean Seawater Desalination Project with an output of 32 to 40 million gallons a day (mgd) of fresh water and 175 to 200 megawatts[12] of power; Metropolitan Water District of Southern California and the U.S. Government Project to produce 150 mgd of fresh water and 1,800 megawatts of electricity from the Pacific Ocean; and the New York Project to produce 150 to 250 mgd.

These figures are indeed impressive when one compares them to current data. The two hundred plants of various sizes and types that desalinate water in the world today together produce only about 50 mgd of fresh water; approximately half of these plants use distillation processes. The largest is located in Aruba, an island off western Venezuela, with a capacity of 3.4 mgd and operating at three-quarters capacity.

The electrodialysis process of desalination has been applied to "sweeten" brackish water. Unlike distillation, which extracts pure water from saline water, leaving brine, electrodialysis takes salt particles from saline water, leaving potable water. The method of electrodialysis bears a promising hope for desalinating waters with a low salt concentration, which include many large inland pools of brackish water.

FRESH WATER RESOURCES

The hydrologic cycle provides fresh water through the flow of rivers, streams, and springs, the filling of lakes and playas, and the saturation of aquifers.

The total amount of precipitation falling on the earth each year is about 380 billion acre-feet,[13] over 79 percent of

[11] The average price for municipal water obtained from conventional sources is 30 cents per 1,000 gallons; from the same sources, irrigation water is delivered at the farmer's gate for 8 to 12 cents per 1,000 gallons.

[12] One megawatt is equal to one million kilowatt hours.

[13] An acre-foot, the amount of water required to cover a level acre of land to a depth of one foot,

which falls on the ocean; the remaining 21 percent (80 billion acre-feet) falls on the land. The volume of water carried to the sea by glaciers, rivers, and coastal springs is approximately 27 billion acre-feet per year with a drainage area of 25 billion acres. Another one billion acre-feet drains into inland seas, lakes, or playas, involving roughly 8 billion acres that drain mostly deserts and well-watered areas. In all, more than one-half of the water that falls on the land evaporates from it each year.

Most river waters run off to the sea virtually unused by man. The United States, a heavy water-user (about 1,700 gallons for all purposes per day per capita), withdraws, by diverting from streams and pumping from the ground, only slightly more than 7 percent of its total rain and snow fall. At the world level, about one billion acre-feet per year, less than 4 percent of the total runoff (27 billion acre-feet), is used by artificial irrigation works, which are the principal consumers of the world's water. This runoff irrigates 310 million acres of land, or less than 1 percent of the land area of the earth.

Over the conterminous United States, this is an average of approximately 30 inches of precipitation each year, the equivalent of over 4 billion acre-feet of water. Only about 30 percent of this total, more than one billion acre-feet per year, or about 1,100 billion gallons per day, is the gross potentially available water supply the 48 states use to meet their water demands. Approximately 350 billion gallons of fresh water are used daily; 171.5 billion gallons are withdrawn for industrial purposes, such as steam generating, electric power production, cooling, separating cellulose for paper, or refining petroleum; 154 billion gallons

for irrigating crops; and the remaining 24.5 billion gallons for domestic and public use. This, of course, does not include the huge volumes of fresh water involved with carrying off wastes, supporting inland navigation, pleasure boating and swimming, turning the generators of hydroelectric plants, and esthetic uses of water.

SUPPLY CHARACTERISTICS OF WATER

In assessing a society's water supply, it is important to understand that there is no recognizable market for water nationally because of the high cost of transporting water over long distances, compared to its value. Thus, the mobility of water as a commodity input is localized.

Another difficulty in assessing national water supply stems from the incompatibility of drainage systems and national boundaries. Here, one is concerned with the proper allocation between societies. The division of runoff water also presents spatial, economic, political, and other problems that must be evaluated not only in terms of their short-run, but also their long-run, affects before an estimate of the national supply of water is made.

Not all nations experience these problems. Some nations' supplies of water can be measured by the quantity of flow in the nations' watersheds. This approach relates supply to demand in a practical fashion. However, where the watershed is spread over two or more nations, there is always an allocation problem. The watershed-basin approach undoubtedly appears to be a more logical solution.

Theoretically, the total fresh water supply of a nation is its average annual runoff, including that which drains into inland seas, lakes, and playas; the effective supply is the quantity that can be made available for various demands. The

is 325,872 gallons. Other measures commonly used for water measurement are gallons per day and cubic-feet per second (cu sec).

average annual runoff is a function of the amount of precipitation, size of the drainage area, annual mean temperature, topography, and soil conditions. These factors explain the average runoff variation among regions, although in any area there are wide variations from year to year. These variations are of three kinds:

1. Regular seasonal variation within a year caused by the seasonal precipitation and melting of snow

2. Irregular variations from year to year

3. Random variations caused by individual storms[14]

Table 3–8 is a compilation of the best estimates of length, area, and discharge of the earth's 38 major rivers. These rivers carry slightly less than half of the total runoff to the oceans. The use of river water depends on the effective supply, which is partially determined by the demand for water. The volume of water used from a river is determined by:

1. Structure and size of the demand for water and the distance of the demand market from the river

2. Technology, including indirect practices, such as efficiency of water use; conservation and mulching methods; development of suitable crops and manufacturing processes; better lining for canals; better irrigation practices; and attempts to modify and improve precipitation patterns by controlling weather and climate to provide the desired amount of precipitation at the desired time and location

[14] The volume of all the runoffs when added together provides the total supply of fresh water. Runoff may be measured by the volume of water discharged, a theoretical measure of which is:

$$D = L + A_c V_m$$

where,

D = the volume discharged,

A_c = cross sectional area of a stream or river,

V_m = mean velocity of a stream or river,

L = volume of water in the lakes and playas.

3. Financial ability

4. Water quality

Because these factors operate in economically advanced countries, these nations can develop large, multipurpose water systems that are economically feasible. For instance, the Ob-Yenisey project in western Siberia calls for a huge dam on the Ob, creating an inland sea connecting the Ob River and the Yenisey River to divert the unused flow from the Arctic to the central Soviet steppes. The Colorado and Snake project is another example of feasibility, with many political ramifications. Plans await leadership and agreements of all concerned for greater, more efficient utilization of international rivers, such as the Rhine, Danube, Rio Grande, St. Lawrence, and Columbia.

In most developing nations, the problem of water use is extremely complicated. This is especially true in arid or semi-arid nations where waterlogging and salt accumulation in the soil occur in vast, almost flat plains due to poor drainage.

Another aspect is the willingness or reluctance to use the water efficiently and to solve the problem of land tenure. In the desert Rajasthan state of India, water from the Bakhra–Nangal dam was offered to the farmers through hundreds of miles of canals. Extension agents reported that many farmers, when told of the way in which water would be made available to them and how many kilowatts of electricity had been generated out of water, refused to use it. The farmers reasoned that the extraction of electricity left the water "dead" and hence not usable for their crops.

Many farmers are sharecropping tenants who have little incentive to use irrigation as a means to increase production. In regions with a savanna climate, characterized by an annual cycle of heavy rainfall during one season followed by

TABLE 3–8 Length, Area, and Discharge of Major Rivers

REGION OR CONTINENT	RIVER	LENGTH (in miles)	DRAINAGE AREA (sq. mi.)	AVERAGE DISCHARGE (cu.-ft. per sec.)
Africa	Zaire (Congo)	2,900	1,425,000	2,000,000
	Niger	2,590	584,000	
	Nile	4,132	1,293,000	420,000
	Orange	1,155	400,000	
	Zambezi	1,650	513,000	
	Total	12,429	4,215,000	
Asia, including eastern USSR	Amur	2,802	787,000	
	Brahmaputra	1,800	361,000	500,000
	Euphrates	1,675	430,000	
	Ganges	1,550	432,000	270,000
	Hwang Ho (Yellow)	2,903	400,000	1,116,000
	Indus	1,980	372,000	300,000
	Irrawaddy	1,425	158,000	
	Jaxartes	1,700	320,000	
	Lena	2,653	1,169,000	325,000
	Mekong	2,600	350,000	600,000
	Ob–Irtysh	3,461	1,131,273	
	Oxus	1,500	115,000	
	Salween	1,730	62,700	
	Yangtze Kiang	3,430	750,000	770,000
	Yenisey	2,566	1,000,000	
	Total	33,775	7,837,973	
Australia	Murray–Darling	3,350	414,000	13,000
	Total	3,350	414,000	
Europe, including western USSR	Danube	1,770	347,000	315,000
	Dnepr (Dnieper)	1,420	202,000	
	Rhine	820	86,000	
	Volga	2,293	592,000	
	Total	6,303	1,227,000	
North America	Churchill	1,000	140,000	
	Colorado	1,450	244,000	23,300
	Columbia	1,214	259,000	280,000
	Mackenzie–Peace	2,525	682,000	450,000
	Mississippi–Missouri	3,860	1,243,000	513,000
	Nelson–Saskatchewan	2,805	360,000	
	Rio Grande	1,885	232,000	5,180
	St. Lawrence	1,900	565,000	400,000
	Yukon	1,800	330,000	
	Total	18,439	4,055,000	
South America	Amazon	3,900	2,772,000	7,200,000
	La Plata–Paraná	2,450	1,198,000	2,800,000
	Orinoco	1,800	570,000	
	São Francisco	1,800	252,000	
	Total	9,950	4,792,000	

drought the remainder of the year and by warm weather at all seasons, many millions of what are now barren acres could be brought under irrigated cultivation. The Nile project is already in progress. The basins of the Niger and the Rufiji rivers lend themselves to water utilization. Similarly, in the area extending from India east through Burma, Thailand, and Vietnam to the northern Philippines, year-round crop-raising is possible.

To capture the supply of water is not an end but a means. Proper use of water for enterprises that provide higher marginal value for water is extremely important. It calls for the evaluation, analysis, and improvement of social and institutional arrangements that surround water use. Supplying adequate water to mankind, whose population is doubling about every 40 years, promises to be one of the major problems facing most societies.

POLLUTION

All pollution problems stem from natural laws, which usually work in a most benign fashion. These laws essentially decree that matter is never really consumed except, as Einstein noted, by transformation into energy. Thus, through all the operations of economic activities, matter is used, altered, and modified, but it still remains matter. Some residual matter is dispersed into the environment through streams and rivers and by conversion into land enrichment or fill. The remainder escapes into the atmosphere in the form of gases, smoke, or vapors. Theoretically speaking, residual matter is what remains after resources have been used; some scholars call residuals "resources out of place."

Historically, man's thinking has been geared to producing and distributing goods for consumption, with little or no concern for what happens after the goods are used. As the earth becomes more crowded, one person's trash is discarded in another's living space; downstream and downwind, other communities are expecting fresh air and potable water. Often they must bear higher social costs for the use of resources by establishing sewage treatment plants, air pollution controls, and water purification systems.

POLLUTION OF RESOURCES

There is a serious lag between the upsurge in population and the disposal of the more rapidly increasing waste accumulations. The impact of resource use upon the quality of a resource has become a major concern for many affluent societies engaged in mass production and consumption. The quality of resources is affected by the disposal of wastes on the land, in the water, and in the air.

Air pollution in the form of smoke, dust, gases, vapors, fumes, and mists greatly affects the health and life of plants, humans, and other animals occupying the land. Polluted air contains minute particles that finally come to rest on the land or in water. If wastes are deposited in rivers, lakes, and bays, not only is the water supply contaminated, but adjoining land becomes less desirable for human habitation. Likewise, wastes deposited on land pollute water through seepage and washing and cause atmospheric contamination by producing foul odors and gases. Incinerator waste pollutes air, and garbage grinders may turn waste into a water treatment problem. Air and water treatment plants often leave solid or liquid wastes that give off fumes into the atmosphere.

There is a noticeable trend, however, toward recycling "out of place" resources. In the United States, more than half of the nation's steel, 56 percent of its copper, 12 percent of its rubber, and 21 percent of its paper are presently derived from scrap or reprocessed materials. Recycling involves sorting out, collecting, and transporting wastes for reprocessing, all of which are laborious and relatively costly. But experts look to the time when trains, trucks, ships, and cargo planes, that now move out empty after supplying the needs of our cities, will carry containers filled with discarded materials. This would be economically feasible if householders were required to sort their trash, perhaps into coded baskets, for collection via conveyor systems built under some cities. Every new product designed for production or manufacture could be accompanied by a plan for disassembly and permanently labeled with its material content.

From the ecological point of view, pollution is the introduction of elements that stop, control, or redirect biological activity. These elements can set in motion a chain of adaptation that may not be revealed for many generations. Such adaptation suggests a variability in the level of tolerance of pollution elements not only over time, but also over areas. The degree of environmental purity depends on the relative tolerance as a result of adaptation and on the required standards. Air surrounding the manufacture of some electronic parts, for instance, must be considerably more pristine than that which seems quite fresh in a living room. And the water used in many industrial processes, including steam generators, in many respects must be more stringently controlled than that which comes, safe and tasty, from a kitchen tap.

No community's water supply is completely independent of the actions of the others in that watershed. Air, too, moves across political boundaries in an airshed analogous to a watershed. Hence the problems of pollution, having complicated structural and areal interrelatedness, lend themselves to the relatively new technique of systems analysis. This technique has been applied to various pollution studies in California.

ECONOMIC EFFECTS OF POLLUTION

From the point of view of economics, pollution is an "external effect," distorting cost curves and resulting in a misallocation of resources in an economy. An upstream plant that dumps a noxious effluent into a river has lower costs if effluent treatment is not required, and therefore finds it profitable to produce more effluent than would otherwise be the case. The downstream plant must pretreat its water, has higher costs, and does not find it profitable to produce as much. Likewise, the householder who decides to incinerate his garbage in the back yard rather than pay for collection, or who chooses to skip a tune-up on his car or leaves a leaky muffler unrepaired, reduces his immediate expenses but increases the burden on society. When used for agricultural purposes, pesticides provide better yields to farmers, but at the possible expense of the consumer's health and at the social expense of disposing of the residues of pesticides.

There are numerous other external costs associated with pollution; for example, in the United States property damage from air pollution alone is estimated at $12 billion a year.

SOURCES OF POLLUTION

Pollution is caused by a multiplicity of increasingly sophisticated substances generated by a wide variety of sources. The following classification of refuse material by kind, consumption, source, and disposal or corrective methods, suggested by the American Public Works Association, has been modified and expanded here to include sources of water and air pollution:

1. Garbage: waste from food preparation and the handling of produce
2. Rubbish: combustibles, such as

57

paper cartons, wood, branches, yard trim-mings, wood furniture; noncombustibles, such as metals, tin cans, glass, crockery

3. Smokes and ashes: ordinary ashes and residues from incinerating plants, smoke

4. Street refuse: sweepings, leaves, and contents of receptacles

5. Dead animals

6. Combustion-engine vehicles: abandoned autos; moving vehicles giving off exhaust, such as cars, planes, locomotives, ships

7. Industrial wastes: solid, gaseous, liquid

8. Demolition wastes: from wrecking buildings

9. Construction waste

10. Special waste: such as, hazardous solids and liquids, radioactive and patho-logical materials

11. Sewerage: sludge and effluent from septic tanks and sewer treatment plants

12. Agricultural pollutants: washed or blown pesticides, herbicides, dung and urine, and the residue left in consumption items

These sources of pollution need not nec-essarily be determining factors for the relative degree of pollution in a location. Spatial variation in pollution, in general, is a function of:

1. The total population

2. The percent of population living in urban areas

3. The number, size, model, and use frequency of combustion engine vehicles

4. Type and level of economic activities

5. Type and level of human con-sumption

6. Human awareness, education, and sense of responsibility for pollution control

7. Topographical and meteorological factors—temperature inversion[15] and wind movements

[15] A temperature inversion is a layer of air that shows an increase in temperature with an increase in altitude. It is called a temperature inversion because air temperature normally decreases with an increase in altitude. The effect of such a layer

8. Climatic factors permitting the level of biochemical oxygen demand (BOD) in waste-carrying waters

The effluent from the pulp and paper industry is much more than that which comes from an auto assembly plant of comparable size. The emission of con-taminating substances from areas of heavy population with their attendant economic activities is larger than those areas that are sparsely populated and have relatively no industry. The nearly permanent temperature inversion in the atmosphere over the California coast is a unique phenomenon associated with the relatively stationary high pressure area over the North Pacific Ocean. Thus, as a mass of air moves down the California coast, the upper part sinks and is heated by compression. At this time, the air next to the ocean surface is cooled from below. This process gives rise to two layers of air: above, a layer of warm, dry, descending air; and below, a layer of cold, moist, ocean-cooled air. Where these two layers meet and intermix a temperature inversion and pollution is the result. These inversions, which man so far has been unable to alter, are now found to be quite common not only in California, but also in major SMSAs[16] in varying degrees during peak morning and evening traffic (*see* Figure 3–4). Fig-ure 3–5 shows the extent of water pollu-tion.

Analysis of pollution has not yet ad-vanced to a stage permitting accurate analysis of the national picture or of the

is to trap the air beneath it and to stop upward movement. This creates a predisposition to air pollution that is especially pronounced when there is little wind or when topographical features restrict lateral air movements.

[16] Standard Metropolitan Statistical Areas. An SMSA is an urban region involving one or more contiguous counties and containing a city of 50,000 or more inhabitants. A region is rela-tively homogeneous in terms of social and eco-nomic characteristics.

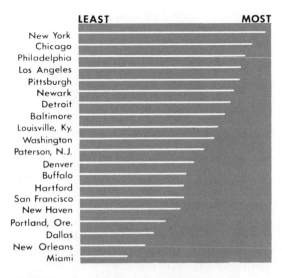

LEAST	MOST
New York	
Chicago	
Philadelphia	
Los Angeles	
Pittsburgh	
Newark	
Detroit	
Baltimore	
Louisville, Ky.	
Washington	
Paterson, N.J.	
Denver	
Buffalo	
Hartford	
San Francisco	
New Haven	
Portland, Ore.	
Dallas	
New Orleans	
Miami	

FIGURE 3–4 *Air Pollution in U.S. Cities*

global phenomenon. Nevertheless, the determining factors can be used to areally differentiate the pollution problem. For example, the primary sources of atmospheric pollution in the United States, which account for approximately 125 million tons of pollutants each year, can be analyzed areally to provide regional pollution estimates for the regional air quality commissions established under the Air Quality Act of 1967. The primary sources of atmospheric pollution are shown in Table 3–9.

Policy recommendations can be improved if they are based on the regional distribution of the pollution content. The major contents of air pollution during 1970 in the United States are shown in Table 3–10.

POLLUTION CONTROL

Pollution relates to society's leftovers, its economically unuseful outputs, which are discharged into air, water, or land, reusing them in one or more activities. In Figure 3–6, a simplified diagram of the process of producing paper products, some of the outputs are directly recovered and reused in the modification process; for example, chemicals from the pulping process and fiber from the paper machine. In the absence of environmental quality control, the waste, which may or may not be residual, would be reused depending upon the costs of the alternative inputs. Figure 3–6 shows waste as material—liquid, gaseous, and solid—and in the form of energy—heat and noise.

Bower emphasizes the importance of the interrelationships among the three forms of material residuals. One form of material residuals can be transformed into another, and additional material and energy residuals are often produced by modifying a particular residual. Further-

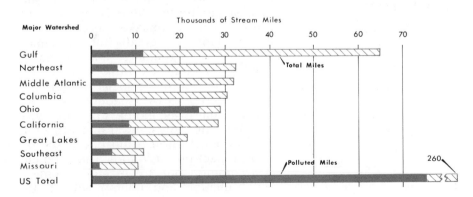

FIGURE 3–5 *Extent of Water Pollution in U.S.*

TABLE 3–9 Primary Sources of Atmospheric Pollution in the U.S., 1970

SOURCE	MILLION TONS PER YEAR	PERCENT
Transportation	143.9	54.5
Stationary Fuel Combustion	44.6	16.9
Industrial Processes	34.8	13.2
Miscellaneous	29.6	11.2
Solid Waste Disposal	11.1	4.2
Total	264.0	100.0

Source: The Conference Board, Road Maps of Industry: Pollution, Dimension, Abatement, No. 1700, Oct. 15, 1972.

more, material residuals can be traded off for energy residuals.

These interrelationships can be simply illustrated by considering a power plant using coal as the fuel for electric energy generation. The particulates formed by combustion can be discharged into the atmosphere in a gas stream as a gaseous residual. If, however, there are constraints on such discharge, a wet scrubber could be installed to wash the particulates out of the gas stream, thereby

TABLE 3–10 Major Air Pollutants in the U.S., 1970

	MILLION TONS PER YEAR	PERCENT
Carbon monoxide	147.3	55.8
Hydrocarbons	34.6	13.1
Oxides of sulphur	33.8	12.8
Particulate matter	25.3	9.6
Oxides of nitrogen	22.7	8.6
Other	.3	.1
Total	264.0	100.0

Source: The Conference Board, Road Maps of Industry: Pollution, Dimension, Abatement, No. 1700, Oct. 15, 1972.

transforming the gaseous residual into a liquid residual of suspended solids that could then be discharged into an adjacent river. Such discharge might adversely affect water quality and damage fish life. To prevent such an impact, a settling basin could be installed to settle out the suspended solids in the liquid residual, thereby yielding a solid residual for "ultimate" disposal.

Similar possible transformations exist for energy residuals. In the case of the power plant, approximately 2 kilowatt hours (kwh) of residual heat are generated for every kwh of desired energy (the "product") produced. This residual heat —waste heat, by traditional terminology —must be dissipated in some manner.

Perhaps we cannot rely on market forces to lead us to the amount of recycling most desirable for society. A major difficulty relates to changes in social values. For example, our present efforts at species preservation or wilderness preservation are more valuable to us if we believe that the next generation will increase our efforts at preservation. Diversity of species is an asset whose value continues over many generations. Our efforts at species preservation are not just for our generation or the next, but for many generations. Our valuations of our efforts of preservation depend on our hopes for the future. Since all the "traders," present and future, cannot bargain in a single room, there is no way for present markets to take these concerns into account. Even greatly improved markets give us no guarantee that the planet will be inhabitable a century from now.

If some form of social immortality is considered to overshadow the more narrow goal of economic efficiency, the goal becomes the survival of the planet. Present policy choices must be based on their impact on the future. The problem is a common one for macroeconomics. With inflation and unemployment, for example, economists decide that a 6 per-

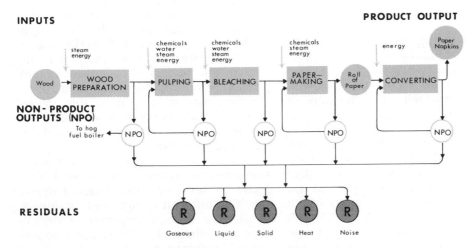

INPUTS

PRODUCT OUTPUT

steam
energy

chemicals
water
steam
energy

chemicals
water
steam
energy

chemicals
steam
energy

energy

Paper
Napkins

Wood

WOOD
PREPARATION

PULPING

BLEACHING

PAPER—
MAKING

Roll
of
Paper

CONVERTING

**NON - PRODUCT
OUTPUTS (NPO)**

To hog
fuel boiler

NPO

NPO

NPO

NPO

NPO

RESIDUALS

R R R R R

Gaseous   Liquid   Solid   Heat   Noise

FIGURE 3–6   *Definition of Residuals*

cent inflation rate is "unacceptable," but a 3 percent rate is "acceptable." The goal seeming right and feasible, the money supply is then manipulated to achieve it.

One obvious policy instrument to move the economy toward a steady state of social immortality is the severance tax. Long-run population policies are perhaps even more crucial than material-flow policies. The two policy areas are similar in that, for both, very gentle incentives can have enormous effect over a 200- to 300-year period. A severance tax leads us toward spaceship earth in several ways. It raises the price of primary materials relative to secondary materials, and thereby encourages recycling. More important, in the longer run it stimulates technology to develop production processes that further take advantage of the relatively cheaper recycled materials. In the long run, severance taxes favor product durability and service commodities over material ones. Severance taxes are like import tariffs in that they are collected at a small number of entry "ports"

in the production and distribution process. They are far easier to collect than disposal taxes levied upon the final owner of a material.

States with anti-litter laws have found out that it is impossible to prevent surreptitious dumping. Schemes to collect disposal taxes from the final manufacturer have to provide for recycled content. And then definition and certification of "recycled" becomes a difficult problem, while the problem of surreptitious dumping remains with processors, not with the final manufacturer. Administrative costs of collecting a disposal tax are much higher for the final consumer than for the first processor. The best point at which to collect a disposal tax is at the processor, when it becomes a severance tax. To resolve the question, one must weigh the reduction in administrative cost against the efficiency lost in collecting the disposal tax "too early."

Severance taxes are understandably unpleasant to mining companies and

61

something of a pipedream to recycling companies. How can severance taxes be approved if depletion allowances, which are negative severance taxes, are so well entrenched?

It is misleading to talk about specific resources as immutably nonrenewable with dates upon which each will "run out." But the entire planet can be viewed as a single asset which, when managed in one way is renewable and, when managed in another way, is nonrenewable. Economic theory tells us that even greatly improved markets will provide us with "too little" of the renewable asset. The earth is an asset whose type can be changed; we have a choice as to which type of asset we want it to become. A hundred years from now the choice may no longer exist. We may have irrevocably transformed spaceship earth into a progressively more hazardous and time-limited spaceship Apollo.

With the emerging patterns of metropolitan areas and suburbia, the once "no man's land" around these centers is now "somebody's" living space. This means there has to be a joint effort by parties concerned with pollution control. Three groups can build and operate pollution-control facilities and can pay for them in the same or different proportions: those who require pure resources, those whose activities create pollution, and the community as a whole. Each of the three groups pays some of the bills. A recent survey of 3,000 American corporations by the National Industrial Conference Board revealed that these corporations now have a capital investment of approximately $1 billion in facilities to reduce or to control water pollution, with yearly operating expenses of $100 million. Consolidated Edison Company has recently announced that it is switching to less-polluting fuel for its power plants; the Tennessee Valley Authority has also announced plans to cut smoke at its electric generating plants.

The question of which units should undertake pollution control is one of technical feasibility, economic efficiency, and the maximization of welfare to the whole community's watershed, region, or airshed. To propose and design alleviating measures, detailed analyses of the sources and factors of pollution content, possibilities of recycling, salvaging, or reclaiming wastes, improving the present methods and channels of disposal, and the development of new methods of disposal are important.

A major campaign to combat pollution presently is underway in the United States. A series of laws enacted during the 90th and 91st Congresses sharply expanded or initiated important programs in water, air, and solid waste management; President Nixon's declaration of "War on Pollution" in the 1970s is further testimony to the seriousness of the problem. The attack on water pollution, first a subject of federal research a century ago and which received broadening support in 1948, 1956, and 1961, was significantly amplified by several measures passed in 1965 and 1966. Under the 1965 Water Resources Planning Act, a cooperative program for long-range planning for water resources in all U.S. river basins was established. States were warned to set up satisfactory standards for pollution control by July 1967, or the federal government would step in.

Federal air-pollution control has also accelerated considerably since the first legislation was passed in 1955. With the Clean Air Act of 1963, as amended in 1965, related research and regulation have been established. Regulatory vehicle emission standards have been applied to all cars built since 1968. Likewise, the Solid Waste Disposal Act of 1965, initiating federal support in this area, authorized $92 million over four years for demonstration projects and planning for state and local programs of research and training. Stimulated by federal activity,

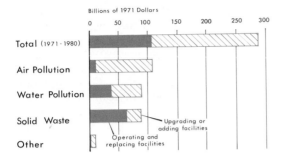

Billions of 1971 Dollars

FIGURE 3–7 *Pollution Control Expenditures*

other levels of government have stepped up their programs. Some states like New York and California have gone beyond federal requirements for water pollution control.

The battle to combat pollution is an expensive one. United States industry and government are now spending over $10 billion a year to combat pollution by factories, garbage incinerators, car fumes, sewage, etc. Figure 3–7 shows pollution control expenditures programmed for 1970 to 1980. A whole new occupation to invent, build, test, install, and repair anti-pollution equipment is developing rapidly. This rapidity is, however, likely to be redefined in the wake of the deepening recession and pressures from industry and powerful interest groups.

references

1. Armstead, Christopher H. *Geothermal Energy and Development*. Paris: UNESCO, 1973.

2. Barlow, Raleigh. *Land Resource Economics: The Political Economy of Rural & Urban Land Resource Use*. Englewood Cliffs, N.J.: Prentice-Hall, 1958.

3. Brewer, Michael, F. "Natural Resources Problems of the Next Decade." In *Departmental Personnel Conference Proceedings*. Washington, D.C.: U.S. Department of the Interior, 1967.

4. Brinkworth, Brian J. *Solar Energy for Man*. New York: John Wiley & Sons, 1972.

5. Brooks, D. B. *Supply & Competition in Minor Metals*. Baltimore: The Johns Hopkins Press, 1966.

6. Clark, R. H. "Energy From Fundy Tides." *Canadian Geographical Journal* 85 (November 1972): 150–163.

7. Clawson, M. E. *Natural Resources and International Development*. Washington, D.C.: Resources for the Future, Inc., 1964.

8. Davis, Kingsley. "Rise and Growth of Cities." In *Readings in Urban Geography*, ed. by Harold M. Mayer and Clyde F. Kohn, Chicago: University of Chicago Press, 1959.

9. English, T. Saunders, ed. *Ocean Resource and Public Policy*. Seattle: University of Washington Press, 1973.

10. Fisher, Joseph L. "Limits on the Exploitation of Natural Resources." *Technological Review* 70 (1968).

11. Feiss, Julian. "Minerals." *Scientific Monthly* 209 (September 1963): 128–147.

12. Frey, Krause, and Dickason. "Major Uses of Land & Water in the United States with Special Reference to Agriculture." *U.S. Department of Agriculture*, Agricultural Report No. 49 (1960).

13. Guyol, Nathaniel B. *Energy in the Perspective in Geography*. Englewood Cliffs, N.J.: Prentice-Hall, 1971.

14. Hammond, Allen L.; Metz, William D.; and Maugh, Thomas II. *Energy and the Future*. Washington, D.C.: American Association for the Advancement of Science, 1973.

15. Healy, Timothy J. *Energy, Electric Power, and Man*. San Francisco: Boyd & Fraser Publishing Co., 1974.

16. Kauger, Paul, and Otte, Carel. *Geothermal Energy: Resources, Production, Stimulation*. Stanford, Calif.: Stanford University Press, 1973.

17. Landsberg, Hans H.; Fischman, L. L.; and Fisher, J. L. *Resources in America's Future*. Baltimore: The Johns Hopkins Press, 1963.

18. Mosley, Leonard. *Power Play: Oil in the Middle East*. New York: Random House, 1973.

19. Odell, Peter R. *Oil and World*

Power: A Geographical Interpretation. New York: Taplinger Publishing Co., 1971.

20. Peach, W. N., and Constantin, James A. *Zimmerman's World Resources and Industries.* 3rd ed. New York: Harper & Row, 1972.

21. Searl, F. Milton. *Production of Energy: U.S. Atomic Energy Commission.* Washington, D.C.: U.S. Government Printing Office, 1962.

22. Thomas, Trevor M. "World Energy Resources: Survey and Review." *Geographical Review* 63 (April 1973): 246–258.

23. Warren, Kenneth. *Mineral Resources.* New York: John Wiley & Sons, 1973.

24. White, Gilbert F. "The Mekong River Plan." *Scientific American* (April 1962).

economic
framework

4

4

The major identifiable parts of the economic framework of any market-oriented society are generally recognized as: demand, supply, market, substitution, cost, price, and the interrelationships among these parts as a function of their spatial location. In this chapter, each of these concepts or parts of the economic framework will be differentiated, analyzed, and reassembled to reflect a unified economic framework.

DEMAND

Prices of commodities, i.e., goods or services, reflect their relative desirability and availability. Prices are variously determined according to the market system involved, which can range from a perfectly competitive market to an absolute monopoly operated by the state or private interests. Under competitive conditions, price is the result of the Law of Supply and Demand.[1] Price, representing the relative value of a good or service, influences the demand and supply of a good or service.

In any society, forces of demand and supply basically perform four functions:

1. Determination of commodities and the relative quantities that are produced

2. Rationing or distribution of commodities among individuals and/or groups at various locations

3. Partial determination of the location and relative scale of output of the economic activities

4. Indicating sites of possible relocation of economic activities and the change in scale or output over time

Demand is the relation between the various amounts of a commodity that might be bought and the determinants of those amounts. The determinants reflect all human motives, desires, and aspirations for commodities. The demand can be looked at: (1) as an individual consumer's preference for one or several commodities, and (2) as a business firm's preference, reflecting the number of customers, where they are located, and the volume of commodities they will purchase. The former is called an *individual demand* and the latter a *market demand*. The sum of market demands of firms represents the *industry demand*. A firm, while having a market demand for its commodities, also has a business demand for its inputs, generally referred to as *derived demand*, i.e., derived from market demand and therefore immediately or ultimately dependent on it.

Overall, demand for goods and services depends on many factors, principally:

1. Price of the commodity concerned

2. Prices of other commodities, especially of substitutes and complements[2]

3. Income of the buyer

4. Tastes and preferences

5. The buyer's existing stock of similar commodities

6. Future expectations of income, prices, and new commodities

7. Degree of information about the commodity

8. Spatial relationship of buyers or consumers

---

[1] Alfred Marshall, *Principles of Economics*, 9th ed. (New York: The Macmillan Company, 1961). Marshall's analysis assumes that the rationale behind the demand for a given commodity is its utility, which decreases as more of the commodity is acquired or consumed. Modern treatment of demand also recognizes many other factors.

[2] The concept of *substitution* refers to a buyer's option to do without a given good or service because he can buy a similar article that will fulfill a similar function, or because he does not need the product at all. *Complementary* refers to products that are bought and used together. For in-

The relative effect of any factor varies, depending upon the commodity involved, size of the area to be served, and the time (day, month, year, etc.).

The larger the area, the greater the significance of the spatial distribution of customers. The trend toward growing specialization and concentration of market demand into a few oligopolistic corporations[3] or firms illustrates the importance of the location of customers in determining the demand for any commodity. This is particularly so in considering the demand for spatially fixed commodities that cannot be transported to other areas. A few examples of such commodities are outdoor recreation services and facilities (fishing, hunting, boating, park and zoo visitation, seeing fairs and festivals, watching games), education for residency degree or diploma, and hospital services.

For the sake of simplicity, the demand for a commodity has conventionally been demonstrated in terms of a *demand schedule* (Table 4–1) and *demand curve* (*see* Figure 4–1). A demand schedule states the relations between price and quantity. A demand curve is the transformation of demand schedule into a curve, even when it happens to be

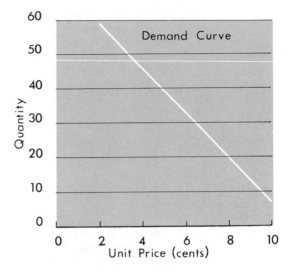

FIGURE 4–1 *Demand Curve*

a straight line, using a two-dimensional graph.[4]

A demand schedule does not necessarily indicate price but does indicate what amounts of a commodity will be bought at different possible prices, given the market area, the time, and the commodity. Generally, the lower the price, the larger the quantity purchased. Likewise, the higher the price, the smaller the quantity purchased. *The inverse relationship between price and quantity is often called the Law of Demand.* The law stands confirmed by many empirical investigations.

A demand schedule may include quantities that would be bought by customers at different distances. The distance, however, may not represent the actual arrangements of transport facilities, time, and conveniences. Transportation

TABLE 4–1   A Demand Schedule

PER UNIT PRICE	QUANTITY
$.10	6
.08	19
.06	32
.04	45
.02	58

---

stance, an increase in the sale of automobiles would increase the demand for gasoline; the same holds true with phonographs and records, spareribs and sauerkraut.

[3] Oligopoly, as defined in Table 4–2, pertains to an industry with only a few firms.

[4] These are charts of a general character and do not represent any one commodity but can be used to represent the relations of price and quantity of any commodity. The demand schedule is in tabular form; the same data in the demand schedule is represented on the demand curve in graphic form.

cost is often suggested as a replacement for distance. But this too, although superior to a distance factor, falls short of reflecting proper spatial relationships. For example, Seattle, in terms of time, might be much closer to Chicago than a town in the Shawnee Hills of southern Illinois.

For actual estimation of the demand curve, distance complexities can be partly alleviated by introducing appropriate additional variables into the model.[5] For example, the size of population of areas would partially explain the spatial distribution of the demand, because the growth of transportation facilities and the size of the population correlate positively.

Analysis of demand can also be helpful to explain the location pattern of an economic activity and its growth and to select an optimum location by:

1. Identifying the spatial distribution of the total market demand and its relation to the industry demand

2. Estimating individual market demand as related to respective areas or clusters

3. Indicating the elasticities of demand estimates

In economics, *elasticity* means a ratio of the relative change (generally measured as a percent of change) in two quantities or variables. The relative change is used in order to recognize the dissimilarities of the units of measurement and the scale of the two variables. The two variables may be commodity price and quantity, distance and quantity, income and quantity, price of a substitute or complementary commodity and quantity (known as cross-elasticity), transportation cost and quantity, and the like.

[5] A model is a complete system of mathematical equation(s) expressing a relationship between given variables. The system may be as broad or as narrow as the problem requires, or as the researcher using the model wishes.

The data in Table 4–1 illustrate the meaning of *price elasticity*. Let E stand for elasticity, which, when expressed in numerical form is called *coefficient of elasticity:*

$$E = \frac{\text{percent change in quantity bought}}{\text{percent change in price}}$$

In the above relationship, two observations must be known for each of the two variables; thus, an estimate of E represents only that part or arc of the demand curve between those observation points. The E at the midpoint of the arc is considered to be the best estimate. This is called an *arc elasticity*, often simply referred to as an elasticity. The usual formula for arc elasticity is:

$$\frac{(q_1 - q_2)/(q_1 + q_2)}{(p_1 - p_2)/(p_1 + p_2)}$$

where q stands for quantity and p for price. Using the above formula, the elasticity (E) between the prices of 10 cents and 8 cents is approximately −4.68, and between 6 cents and 4 cents, −1.78. E always bears a negative sign because of the inverse relation between the two variables of the demand schedule; however, it is customary to disregard the minus sign and use only the absolute value of E. When the value of the coefficient is greater than 1, the demand is elastic; when equal to 1, demand per unit is elastic; when less than 1 but greater than 0, demand is inelastic; and when the coefficient is zero, the demand is perfectly inelastic.

An elastic demand means that the quantity purchased responds to price change; i.e., the percent change in the quantity is larger than the percent change in price. Therefore, other things being equal, it is more profitable to lower the price and sell larger quantities. An inelastic demand indicates that the percent change in quantity is smaller than the percent change in price, so lowering the price is not advisable. Unit elasticity reflects an equal percent change in both the quantity and the price. The relative size of *E* determines how much change would occur in the volume or quantity purchased in response to certain price changes.

The elasticity equation is an application of the concept of elasticity related to price and quantity. The same can be readily applied to demand functions involving distance, transportation cost, time, income, and the like.

SUPPLY

Supply represents the total quantity of a commodity that is offered for sale within a given space and time. Assuming that other determinants are constant, the *supply schedule* refers to pairs of possible prices and quantities offered for sale. The *supply curve,* a graphic version of the supply schedule, also can be a straight line and still be called a curve. In general, a supply curve exhibits a positive relation between prices and quantities: the higher the prices, the greater the quantities producers are willing to supply.

However, this may not always be true. There can be supply schedules where larger quantities are sold at lower prices, as the American farmer has experienced. Farmers tend to compensate for lower prices by producing more in order to maximize their net returns. Net return is equal to the price of a commodity multiplied by its quantity, minus the total cost of production and transportation (if applicable).

The analysis of supply is similar to that of demand. The industry supply function is a horizontal summation of the individual supply functions of the firms. However, unlike the demand function, the industry supply function and the market supply function are identical for a given space.

Elasticity of supply is just as important as elasticity of demand and has the same meaning. In general, since both quantity and price go up and down together, the elasticity of supply has a positive sign. Both time and space are more important for the elasticity of supply than they are for the elasticity of demand. The larger the supply area and the longer the period of adjustment, the more elastic the supply is likely to be. A relatively longer period may permit firms to adjust their costs of production, and hence their productive capacity. A larger area permits greater mobility for products of a firm in response to changes in the relevant determinants.

The nature and scope of the determinants of the supply function vary by commodity and location. Hence, it is difficult to offer a generalized statement about the determinants of supply. However, the following variables or determinants are considered to be the common denominators for most supply functions:

1. Price of the commodity
2. Prices of the closely related commodities and the length of time period
3. Size of supply areas
4. Technology of production
5. Future expectations and aspirations for the commodity
6. Cost of production
7. Random disturbances, such as those related to weather, strikes, etc.

While helping to explain the supply of a given commodity, these determinants also suggest solutions as to why a given location produces a certain amount and how its level of production varies from that of other locations.

For example, in the United States iron ore is extracted from over 300 mines of various kinds and sizes. The ages of these mines range from newly excavated to some that are remarkably ancient.

Some are deep and difficult to work, others are shallow and convenient. Costs of operation vary. The result is that whatever the price of iron ore of a given grade, there will be some mines and parts of mines that can be operated profitably and some that cannot be. The industry supply curve can indicate which mines or locations are on the break-even point (where total costs are equal to total revenue), above, or below the break-even point.[6] At certain prices it will pay to operate mines capable of producing quantities that correspond to the price on the supply curve. As the price changes, so will the areal distribution of iron mining.

For a given industry, the spatial supply functions can be utilized to make effective policy. For example, United States federal farm programs and policies can assist in achieving desired objectives more effectively when modified in view of the spatial supply functions and their elasticities.

Supply should not be confused with *production function*. The latter is the functional relationship between inputs, or resources, and output, or the product. The conventional use of the production function is to predict the total output curve. Marginal products for individual resource inputs then can be predicted by computing the derivative of the product in respect to the particular resource. These derivatives then can be equated (1) to the resource/product price ratio to determine the optimum quantity to use of a particular resource; and/or (2) to the resource/resource price ratio to determine the optimum combination of resources for a particular output. Through

[6] The course of the supply curve of a firm or industry is guided largely by the marginal cost. Marginal cost at any level of output is the increase in total cost required to increase output by one unit from that level. The most profitable level of output on the supply curve is the one at which marginal cost is equal to market price.

this process optimum efficiency in resource use or management may be achieved. But, given other variables of production function, the existence in varying degrees of *externalities, indivisibilities,* and *factor immobilities* in resource use produce spatial variation in the production functions of various areas. Therefore, areas vary in productive capacities as well as in actual supply of the commodity demanded.

Externalities refer to the external economies and diseconomies—changes in the long-run cost function of a firm caused by the growth of the industry—over which the firm has no control. Firms and areas enjoying external economies have a lower per-unit cost of production; firms experiencing external diseconomies have a higher per-unit cost of production. Educational facilities, resource pollution, ownership of resources, longevity of a firm, public facilities, and access to transportation all influence external economies or diseconomies of a firm. Established firms have numerous advantages over their newer competitors in terms of easy access to the capital market with favorable terms, experienced personnel, and the elimination of inappropriate policies.

The effects of resource pollution are examples of external diseconomies. The costs of a firm located downstream on a polluted river may be higher because of the additional cost involved in pretreating their water. Externalities may also appear in the consumption sector with the same effects.

The *indivisibility characteristic* of resources or plant equipment refers to units of inputs comprising a single complex of resources or equipment that must be employed as a whole in order to produce even one small range of output. An indivisible resource is exemplified by a river basin or an oil field whose development or exploitation is economically justified only by multipurpose project structures. Blast furnaces, refineries, and distilleries are other examples of plant equipment that can be employed for only one purpose. In contrast, a divisible plant consists of several complexes of more or less identical equipment. Here, output can be increased by putting another machine into operation, adding another shift, or accelerating the operation. Examples are textile mills and hydroelectric plants with several units of turbines and generators.

Areas vary in their adaptability and suitability for exploitation of resources. Given two areas with an identical natural resource base, different demand structures may invoke indivisibility conditions in one area, limiting its comparative development. Changes in capacity of a firm or area do not occur continuously, but through abrupt steps conditioned by the magnitude of indivisibilities.

Immobility of factors of production —land, labor, capital, management, and technology—may exist between occupations, firms, industries, or between geographic locations. Under optimum conditions of efficiency of resource use, the marginal productivity of a particular resource must be the same in all occupations and locations. This proposition requires that the factors of production be mobile in all respects. Consequently, the resultant distribution of economic activities exhibits a maximum degree of specialization, lending itself to the trade patterns led purely by the law of comparative advantage.

This immobility is more pronounced between nations. Natural resources and land are immobile geographically. The social overhead capital is relatively immobile; other factors, too, have some degree of immobility. Impediments to free mobility materially affect the production function and, hence, the supply potential of an area.

The overriding determinant for demand and supply is price, which changes as do the forces of demand and supply. Demand follows wants, and changes in wants can occur rather quickly in response to relevant determinants. However, supply changes usually require production changes, or moving production and/or output, which are more time-consuming adjustments. Thus, demand changes are faster and usually force the supply to adjust accordingly. How demand and supply balance each other and how prices are determined under spatial markets are discussed in the following section.

MARKET

The word *market* has diverse connotations: a place of business transactions, the process of trading a given commodity, the total area occupied by consumers, and the character of salability. Here, market is defined as:

> A communicative process or mechanism within which the forces of demand and supply determine the terms of transactions for a given commodity in a given area.

Communication is an essential element of a market. The contacts may be face to face at a particular site, or by mail, telephone, or cable. The same person(s) may be in different markets for different commodities, at the same or at different times. The area of the market may range from a small settlement to the entire inhabited earth. Local markets may produce commodities that are too perishable and expensive to be shipped very far without canning, freezing, drying, or being processed in some other way, such as fresh milk and certain fruits and vegetables. Worldwide markets may involve wheat, sugar, tobacco, cotton, hardware, and other easily transportable items.

What differentiates one market from

71

TABLE 4–2   Market Types and Their Characteristics

MARKET TYPE	GENERAL CHARACTERISTICS
Pure Competition	Many sellers and buyers; no one "big" enough to influence the market price and the decisions of competitors; factor mobility unrestricted; all firms in a given industry produce identical or nondifferentiated products; both sellers and buyers possess equal knowledge of the forces of demand and supply for a product; the same price faced by sellers and buyers
Imperfect Competition Monopolistic Competition	Many sellers, as in a pure competition market; each firm in a given industry produces a different product, which can be substituted for by another firm; some restrictions on factor mobility invoked by product differentiation; some control over prices
Oligopoly	A few large sellers, each with a significant share of customers in the industry; factor mobility generally difficult; price controls often possible; advertising channels frequently used to increase one's share of the market's product differentiation and improvement, an effective means of market and price control
Monopoly	One seller; no close product substitutes; factor mobility extremely difficult; almost total control of price; less responsive to change; sometimes practices price discrimination[1]

[1] Price discrimination refers to different prices that exist in separate markets for the same product. The markets are separated by the relative degree of demand elasticity, which means that different prices are charged based on the earning power of the buyers, age, sex, military status, location of buyers, status, use of the product, labels, and the like.

another for a given product is determined by the criteria employed. Here we focus on competition as influenced by the number of firms in the industry; the degree of product homogeneity and factor mobility also distinguishes markets. Table 4–2 is a conventional classification of markets and their associated characteristics.

Table 4–2 presents markets primarily from the seller's point of view. The same characteristics apply when they are viewed from the buyer's side. For example, a monopoly can identify a market situation where there is one buyer. Likewise, an oligopoly can refer to a market involving a few large buyers.

Any of the market types in Table 4–2 can exist in a given market area. How is the market area determined? The simplest criterion for market area delineation is price uniformity, commonly called the Law of One Price. This law states that under competitive conditions of demand and supply, the price of a given commodity tends to be equal throughout the whole market area.[7] (In a perfectly or purely competitive market, the price equality is very clear.) Thus, if prices of the product differ between areas by more than the cost of transporting the product from one area to the other, two market areas are involved instead of one.

Improved means of transportation and related facilities continually widen market areas. As market areas expand,

[7] Wholesale prices of a product tend to maintain equality more closely than retail prices in a given market. At the wholesale level, price competition virtually does not exist. At the retail level, individual dealers may deviate from the market price by offering additional customer services and conveniences, but even then the tendency to one price is at work, setting limits beyond which price deviations cannot go.

trade areas based on commuting patterns for shopping within the market area emerge. The establishment of trade areas reflects a situation where buyers have accepted, perhaps unaware, the transportation cost. This often provides a partial basis for the location of economic activity. The continuous agglomeration of industry in large metropolitan areas illustrates this point.

Determination of price under the varying market types is generally a function of the forces of demand and supply. The behavior of these forces varies with the market type. Different prices are determined in different markets. A generalized mechanism of price determination, employing the schedules of demand and supply, will be offered here since analyses of individual market types are beyond the scope of this text.

The hypothetical demand and supply schedule in Table 4–3 shows the amounts sellers would sell at different prices; similarly, the demand schedule in the same table shows the amounts buyers would purchase at different prices. At any given time, only the price at which the amount offered and demanded are exactly equal will affect the transaction. This is the market price. In Table 4–3, at the per unit price of 6 cents, 32 units are demanded and the same number of units supplied; hence the market is *cleared* (see Figure 4–2). A *cleared market* has no surplus and no shortage. Six cents is then the equilibrium price, which can change as the forces of demand and supply change. Demand and supply are viewed as in constant motion, producing new equilibrium prices with every related change. Areas with more stable and steadily rising demand attract economic activities at the expense of those with a greater degree of fluctuation in demand. With a predictable demand, it is convenient for suppliers to adjust their production.

Traditional market classifications do

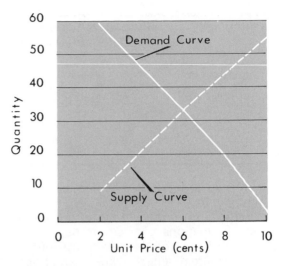

FIGURE 4–2 *Supply and Demand*

not consider spatial relations between buyers and buyers, sellers and sellers, and sellers and buyers, except relations reflected by transportation cost and rent.[8] Theoretically speaking, these spatial relations can exist in infinite numbers. Nevertheless, spatial relations for any given market can be classified under four general groupings:

1. Clustered buyers (consumers) and scattered sellers (producers)
2. Clustered sellers and scattered buyers
3. Buyers and sellers both scattered
4. Buyers and sellers both clustered

The groupings are illustrated in Figure 4–3 with no reference to any particular market type. The spatial size and shape of the market vary, depending on the definition of the market, the commodity

[8] Rent represents income accrued to owners of factors of production that are limited (less than perfectly elastic in supply). This may involve land, capital, and, in some cases, labor. The level of rent accrued is closely related to location and special characteristics of the factors attributed to spatial considerations.

73

TABLE 4–3 **Hypothetical Demand and Supply Schedules for Price Determination**

NUMBER OF UNITS DEMANDED	PER UNIT PRICE	NUMBER OF UNITS SUPPLIED
58	$.02	9
45	.04	21
32	.06	32
19	.08	43
2	.10	54

involved, and the communication chan-nels. Within the general group, any modification produces a different set of spatial relations. For example, under Group 3 there could be even distribution of buyers and sellers in the market area or some other modification. Any one of the market types mentioned in Table 4–2

GROUP I — Clustered buyers & scattered sellers

GROUP II — Clustered sellers & scattered buyers

GROUP III — Both buyers & sellers scattered

GROUP IV — Both buyers & sellers clustered

Market area boundary

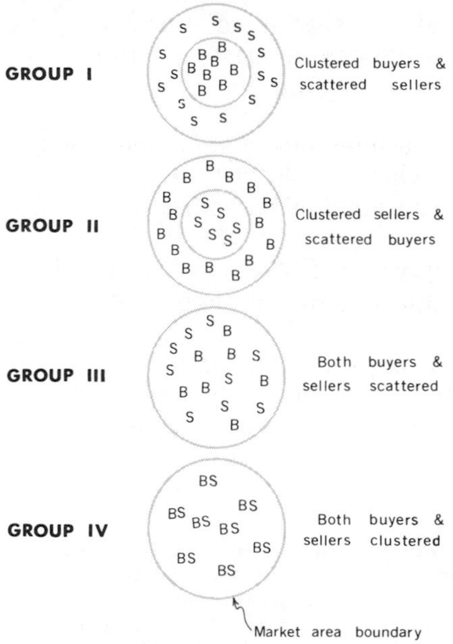

FIGURE 4–3 *Market in Four General Spatial Groupings*

may be assumed for each of the four spatial-relation groupings. The adapta-bility of various market types to the grouping or to a subgroup thereof pro-vides an inference to predict the spatial arrangements of economic activities.

In Group 1 in Figure 4–3, the con-ception of a spatial market where the buyers are clustered or point-located and the sellers are scattered around the buyers bears some resemblance to the Von Thünen model. Assuming an isolated area with a village type of settlement and uniform soil fertility, climate, topography, and transportation facilities throughout the market area, Von Thünen discovered that differences in land use were due to variations in transportation cost. Von Thünen defined transportation cost as a composite representation of distance in-volved, weight, volume, perishability of the commodity, and ease of transporta-tion.

Under this model, the sellers will maximize net profit by a concentrated effort to minimize (1) transportation cost for the supplies of materials, labor, and other inputs, and the delivery of the products, and (2) cost of resource inputs, especially rental cost, which is partly affected by distance from the buyers. The higher transportation cost may be offset by lower cost of materials. Since the areal location of buyers is clustered and cannot be extended, the product price would tend to be the same for all consumers, irrespective of the quantity sold to any

74

given consumer. (4) All market types are possible; however, pure competition is more likely to occur at the initial stage of development of the market, with eventual blending into monopolistic competition as the rates of substitution between transportation cost and rent become equal.

The market pertaining to Group 2 in Figure 4–3 reflects a situation where buyers are scattered around the production center at varying distances from sellers. In this case, sellers are maximizing profit by minimizing rental cost and/or by maximizing productivity. From the point of view of spatial strategy, this may involve agreements or cartels, extensions of the sales radius, achieving economies of scale, and minimizing transportation cost of inputs within the production center. (The strategy of *industry-mix*, where each industry is integrated with another by using each others' intermediary products, is an example of minimizing the transportation cost of inputs by means of underground conveyors, pipes, and other methods of fast and efficient delivery.)

Transportation of products is not a variable from the seller's point of view, except when the seller absorbs part or all of the transportation cost. All firms with a similar rental cost would lean toward expanding their areal market. This can be accomplished through product differentiation and/or lowering the price, assuming the buyer is paying the transportation cost of the product. If firms behave as this model suggests, then the purely competitive market does not seem to prevail under the spatial conditions of Group 2. When sellers are located at one point, with their customers scattered at varying distances from them, there most likely will be a strong tendency toward the development of oligopolistic and monopolistic markets.

Group 3 shows buyers and sellers located in a random pattern. The particular spacing between buyers and sellers is influenced by the spatial distribution of resources and population. Under conditions of homogeneity, the distribution of buyers and sellers would be even, and all of the market area would be covered. The trade pattern of each buyer and seller would tend to overlap, resulting in a tendency by each firm or seller to square off his boundaries, forming a hexagonal trade area pattern within the general market area. This is a suitable structure for pure competition, as Losch (11) demonstrated, and it would eventually push profits to zero, a situation sellers do not relish.[9] To increase their profit, sellers most likely would cut their transportation cost, which would result in some form of interdependence between buyers and buyers and between sellers and sellers. This would be the result only if the resources and population were heterogeneously distributed.

Since the basic spatial facts indicate heterogeneity and sometimes indivisibility of resources, the hexagonal pattern of trade areas cannot be realistically defended. In fact, as Losch points out in his empirical work, the spatial discontinuities in economic activity would produce "hills" and "valleys" in the location of economic activities, as well as of buyers and sellers. The hills represent locations and concentrations where the resources, consumers, and market type, in general, make the best combination to achieve the minimum cost of rent and transportation. These conditions point to the oligopolistic type of market, which, in fact, is the pattern of U.S. space economy.

In Figure 4–3, Group 4 is a market in which the distance factor is less important. All buyers and sellers are located adjacently to each other. All types of market are possible, but pure competi-

[9] In Loschian terminology, this would be referred to as *supernormal profit*.

tion and monopolistic competition are most likely to prevail.

SUBSTITUTION

In the section on minerals in chapter 3, substitution was considered as a dynamic force alleviating depletion problems. Subsequent discussion referred to substitution as a determinant of demand function. In this chapter, a detailed analysis of the substitution concept is developed.

Substitution refers to the process by which (1) alternative locations are evaluated in terms of substitution between various transportation routes or means, between diverse inputs, costs and revenues, outlays in various time periods, and between a combination of these substitutions; and (2) a consumer best satisfies his wants by substitutions among various commodities and various time periods. All of these substitutions, in essence, reflect a course of rational behavior resulting in a unique combination of various inputs or outputs—a situation where no alternative move could result in a further favorable substitution, i.e., in reduction of total production and delivery cost or in the increment of use for consumers.

Production of dissimilar commodities frequently requires different ratios of inputs. Likewise, different consumers consume different proportions of various commodities, even if the total use derived by each consumer is identical. Such differences are more pronounced on the regional basis, as a result of relative prices, incomes, tastes, and beliefs.

For certain items there are no substitutes. Man must have water and salt to survive. Similarly, to raise agricultural crops a certain amount of space is a necessary input, no matter how much labor or capital have been substituted for it. Inputs and outputs may be substituted for each other only within certain limits. Substitution may take place at various rates. A constant rate of substitution, i.e., one-for-one or a fixed proportion replacement is a rare phenomenon. However, many substitution decisions involve a diminishing rate of substitution, sometimes referred to as *imperfect substitution*. What this imperfect substitution means and how an *ideal* substitution is achieved are illustrated by the hypothetical data in Table 4–4.

Imperfect substitution of inputs means that as more and more of a particular input is substituted for another input in a given production process, the substituted input becomes increasingly *less* effective. In other words, the marginal rate of substitution (MRS) of any input *diminishes as the proportion of that input to other inputs increases.*[10] Marginal substitution refers to the amount of an input for which an extra unit of another input can be substituted without affecting the output.

In Table 4–4, column 2, the MRS of capital (K) for labor (L) is denoted by the ratio $\Delta L/\Delta K$, where Δ refers to "change"; it is the amount of labor for which an extra unit of K can be substituted while maintaining the same output of 100 units. Any of the four combinations of K and L in Table 4–4 can yield 100 units of output. Starting with the second combination, a second unit of K substitutes four units of L; the addition of a third unit of K substitutes two units of L; and finally as a fourth unit of K is added, only one unit of L can be withdrawn. The MRS of K for L in Table 4–4 is diminishing with subsequent substitutions of K for L. Similarly, the MRS of L for K (column 3), when Table 4–4 is read from the bottom up, shows a diminishing substitution.

[10] This is a consequence of the Law of Diminishing Returns or the Principle of Variable Proportions, which says that given the state of technology and fixed quantities of all other inputs, the addition of units of a variable input will eventually lead to ever smaller increases in output. The law stands empirically proven.

TABLE 4–4 Combinations of Capital (K) and Labor Units (L) to Produce 100 Units of Product, Rates of Substitution, and Cost Outlays Illustrating Cost Minimization

QUANTITIES OF INPUTS		MARGINAL RATE OF K FOR L ($\Delta L/\Delta K$)	SUBSTITU- TION OF L FOR K ($\Delta K/\Delta L$)	UNIT INPUT COST (C) K = \$8 C_K/C_L	RATIOS L = \$4 C_L/C_K	TOTAL COST (100 UNITS)
K	L					
1	10			2	0.50	\$48
		4.0	0.25			
2	6			2	0.50	40
		2.0	0.50			
3	4			2	0.50	40
		1.0	1.00			
4	3			2	0.50	44

The question of which substitution is ideal from the cost minimization point of view is answered by the relative per-unit costs of the inputs. As a general principle, the point where the MRS is inversely equal to the ratio of per-unit costs of the inputs represents the ideal combination. For example, Table 4–4 shows that three units of K and four units of L is the ideal combination, beyond which mutual substitution between K and L is not favorable. This is further seen by the following relationships, using data from Table 4–4:

$$\frac{1}{\Delta L/\Delta K} = 2 = \frac{C_K}{C_L}$$ corresponds to the combination of 3*K* and 4*L*,

$$\frac{1}{\Delta K/\Delta L} = 0.5 = \frac{C_L}{C_K}$$ also corresponds to the same combination of 3*K* and 4*L*.

In this combination, the \$40 total cost is minimum.[11]

[11] The total cost is also \$40 for the combination 2K and 6L because the average MRS has been used in Table 4–4. If the exact, rather than average, MRS is used, the combination of 3K and 4L would be a unique one. The exact MRS can be derived by calculus, computed as a derivative with K/L or L/K expressed as dK/dL or dL/dK, where the change in K and L becomes infinitely

The concept of substitution can be applied to a multitude of problems involving competition or substitution between existing and potential variables.

COMPARATIVE ADVANTAGE OF LOCATION

The concept of *comparative advantage* and its analysis is useful to explain why certain areas or spaces specialize in specific types of economic activity, even though they may be suitable for other activities.

The continuous process of seeking and using locations offering the greatest promise for the most efficient and profitable operation of an economic activity results in areal differentiation or specialization. Thus, specialization tends to become more pronounced with increasing degrees of industrialization and the broadening of knowledge of inputs.

Four general types of specialization —business, task, occupational, and spatial—are all interrelated. A specialized occupation may result in a specialized task, which in turn reflects specialization of business; specialized business gives

small and approaches zero. To accomplish this, the production function must be estimated.

rise to specialized location since it is established at a specific location or set of locations.

Specialization, an excellent method of using scarce resources that provide the greatest output, in a real sense measures the economic ability of an area to compete with other areas in the production of the same or similar commodities. Thus, each area bears a comparative advantage (or disadvantage) in producing the given commodity.[12]

Comparative advantage is linked not only with fixed resources—favorable climate, soils, and topography—but also with favorable combinations and considerations of other inputs and social frameworks that enter into the production process. Inadequate facilities for transporting inputs to and commodities from their points of production often outweigh any fixed resource advantage associated with an area. Quarantine restrictions, protective tariffs, public subsidies, special tax concessions, regional price supports, and many other institutional arrangements may enhance the comparative advantage of one area at the expense of other competing areas. An abundant supply of skilled labor or management, investment and operating capital available at favorable terms, industry-mix facilities, efficient allocation and management of the factors of production, and the ingenuity and skill in marketing outputs and procuring inputs all may combine to provide an area with comparative advantage.

[12] Theoretically, each area can attain self-sufficiency for its residents by employing modern technology and capital. But this would be expensive and wasteful, and ever-increasing human wants would push towards specialization, should those wants be realized. This particularly applies to situations where the productive ability of an area is definitely limited to the demand (e.g., deserts, mountain passes, proven mining locations, water power and reservoir areas, and other resource sites).

Almost all considerations affecting comparative advantage are manifested in terms of costs of (1) assembling the necessary materials, processing, and marketing the output, and (2) depreciation and maintenance of capital. The costs are relative, as are the prices. Not only are costs for a particular operation affected by the cost of other activities, they are also affected by the price of the commodity involved. Therefore, the structure of costs and prices must be examined to fully understand the concept of comparative advantage.

COSTS

For valid comparison of the comparative advantages of various locations, standard cost criteria is important. The term *cost* generally refers to the outlay of funds, direct or indirect, needed for production of commodities. There are a number of concepts related to what constitutes cost. One fundamental concept is *opportunity cost* or *alternative cost,* which means that the cost of anything is the value of the alternative, or the opportunity, that is sacrificed. The alternative cost of producing fuel oil is the value of the gasoline that could have been produced from the same crude oil.

The cost of lending or using capital is the interest it could earn in another use of equal risk. The rent earned by land growing wheat becomes the cost of growing oats when using the land to grow oats is contemplated. Similarly, the alternative cost of a commodity represents the alternative use to which the same resources and location may be put. The foregone alternative constitutes a cost under any economic system. Thus, the concept of alternative cost is used to compare past and future benefits. This concept also offers a rationale for the compensation of funds invested in a firm and services of an entrepreneur.

Another concept is *money cost,* or business cost, which includes all payments and contractual obligations measured by the producing unit. Full costs may be divided into *variable costs* and *fixed costs.* Variable costs vary with output and represent payments for materials, labor, taxes, fuel, power, etc. Fixed costs normally do not vary with output, except when the firm's capacity is enlarged or when other administrative changes occur with respect to tenure and long-term contracts. Fixed costs, or the overhead costs, include certain taxes (e.g., for real estate), some salaries, allowances for depreciation,[13] opportunity cost of the firm, normal profits, rent, and certain insurance payments.

The level of the cost of production for a location is influenced by:

1. Length of the time period for cost calculation and the method of prorating the cost associated with the selected time period

2. The method of allocating cost among commodities when one firm is producing more than two commodities during the same time period

3. Method of allocating cost among plants located at different points but under the same management

4. Method of determining output level or the size of the firm

5. Size of the profit considered "minimum"

6. Technical and economic combination of inputs

7. Types of inputs employed in the production process

The spatial cost variation is not only a function of input price differentials but also of these seven variables.

---

[13] Depreciation may be computed by a variety of methods. Bad (unrecoverable) debts may be estimated as a certain percentage of all sales, of charged sales alone, or of accounts receivable. Each method gives a different answer. It is important that standard criteria be applied for comparative cost analysis.

PRICES

Prices are discussed here in terms of prices of commodities, although a similar analogy extends to input prices. The price of commodity at various market locations may vary because of different demand–supply relationships, demand elasticity, and market type; it can also be the same at all locations. In the former case, costs are clearly relative to the commodity price; a higher price can justify a corresponding higher cost and vice versa. The latter case may be a result of spatial oligopoly with scattered buyers and sellers.

The conditions of the oligopolistic market type in general tend to establish a relatively stable price, which limits competition among sellers to sales volume, securing optimum location, and minimizing cost.

Under these conditions of competition, two pricing systems have been operational in the United States: 1) F.o.b. ("Free on Board") pricing and 2) basing point pricing. F.o.b. pricing uses the seller's price quotation of the mill or factory price. Freight costs are absorbed by the buyer; closer, more conveniently located buyers pay a delivered price (mill price plus freight) that is lower than that of buyers at distant and remote points. In other words, production costs do not include freight charges for outbound shipments; the buyer's delivered price is composed of a mill price constant for all sellers, plus freight charges, which are a function of distance, means of transportation, and regional freight rates. Under f.o.b. pricing arrangements, new entrants would seek a "phantom" freight advantage over established sellers by selecting a location near the periphery of buyers or one where the difference between the per-unit delivery price and the per-unit total cost of production is greater than, if not equal to, that of the established competition.

79

Basing point pricing (12) refers to a system where all producers agree to quote delivery prices based upon prices assigned to some basing point or points, plus freight. Basing points usually represent important production or distribution centers. The simplest form of basing point pricing involves the single basing point system and the quoted delivery price, consisting of the agreed mill price of the seller (irrespective of the seller's location), plus the transportation charges from the basing point. For example, if a buyer orders from a seller so situated that the actual freight rates are lower than from the basing point, he still pays the seller a delivery price that includes phantom freight, i.e., an amount equivalent to the rate from the basing point. Similarly, if the purchase is made from a seller located where freight cost is higher than the cost from the basing point, delivery price is still based on the lower cost from the basing point.

The steel industry used a single basing-point-pricing system called the Pittsburgh-Plus system. Under this system, steel prices in Birmingham, Alabama, and Gary, Indiana, represented the Pittsburgh price plus freight from Pittsburgh. The single basing-point-pricing system was ruled unlawful by the United States Supreme Court in 1948 under the provisions of antitrust acts. Since then various modifications for this system have been suggested. Several industries, including cement, gasoline, steel, and lumber, have used a multiple basing-point-pricing system in which several regional basing points were established throughout the country, instead of one single basing point.

The delivery price quoted to the buyer consists of the general mill price, plus the freight cost equivalent from the nearest basing point to the buyer's location. This multiple basing-point system tends to equalize or neutralize the freight advantage or disadvantage; thus it forces sellers to compete in terms of cost (devoid of outbound freight) minimization, which means greater efficiency. But the freight rate contained in the delivery price may have little relationship to the actual transportation costs charged by the hauling carriers. Furthermore, the multiple basing-point system may inhibit competition by limiting the number of new entrants and the advantages of phantom freight.

Finally, other variations of the basing-point system may be found. The "postage stamp" pricing system, for example, has a positive freight absorption: the greater the shipping distance, the greater the freight absorption by sellers. The f.o.b. mill price absorbs the freight charge. The absorption of freight charges by more and more sellers at greater shipping distances tends to result in uniform delivery prices to all points.

TRANSPORTATION

Transportation, or the means of directly or indirectly connecting spatially dispersed people and their diverse activities, is indispensable in understanding social similarities, economic interdependence and development, and levels and types of economic activities in a particular area. Transportation analysis lends insight to the location and distribution of economic activities. Development of railroads, waterways, freeways and turnpikes, air transportation networks, and large pipelines all reflect the significant role of transportation. The economic importance of transportation is evident in the production and distribution process, the relationship that exists between transportation cost and delivery price, the price stabilizing effect of transportation;[14] the relation between the trans-

[14] Periodic studies by the Interstate Commerce Commission show that a certain relationship exists

portation bill and gross national product, and in the general contribution of transportation toward regional economic development.

Since the distribution of economic activity partly influences freight rates, or transportation costs, freight rates and the location of economic activity are interrelated. Once the location establishes freight rates, any deviation is resisted by firms whose cost–price relations are adversely affected.

The forces that establish transportation rates also initiate any change in rates. These forces may be classified as related to:

1. Carriers
2. Producers and producing areas
3. Consumers and consuming areas
4. Commodity characteristics

Transportation also helps to bring price stability to a commodity and encourages specialization. In general, the price rise in any market in time of local shortage is equal to the transportation cost of shipping the commodity from the surplus areas. The surplus area, reflecting a higher degree of specialization, may even have a lower production cost, so the delivery price in the shortage area may remain the same, or rise only slightly above what it was before the shortage.

Carrier-related forces involve competitive relations that are intramodal (between the same type of carrier firms); intermodal (between different types of

---

between the transportation cost portion of the delivery price and the type of commodity transported. For example, sand and gravel transportation cost makes up over half the delivery price for those commodities; for business machines and the like, the ratio is less than one percent. Such a wide range of between less than 1 percent and over 50 percent indicates the variability of the relative degree of transportation cost as a part of the delivery price, which influences the scope of the market and the distribution of a particular economic activity.

carriers), or both; government control and/or subsidies; and the special privileges afforded to some carriers, routes, or areas. Carrier competition, besides affecting the level and structure of freight rates, may also include services such as greater speed, pick-up and delivery, less damage to a product, and other services.

Public assistance granted to some carriers and routes serving certain points in the social interest may benefit certain economic activities and areas with subsidies and special privileges. These forces, individually or collectively, bring to some areas lower rates than otherwise would have been the case. The same forces may be unfavorable to other carriers and areas, forcing other carriers to increase their rates in order to offset revenue losses. Thus, the larger the ratio of freight rate to delivery price, the greater the effect of freight rate on the location of the economic activity concerned. Consequently, the relative development of the area is also affected.

Producer-related transportation forces may mean survival for some producers (or the areas where these producers are located), at the expense of lower rates for the carriers hauling their shipments. At locations[15] where competitively squeezed producers are able to convince their carriers that closing down production means the carrier's loss of a client, the carriers are likely to accept lower freight rates. Previously, carrier investment was often based on the competitively favorable position of the producers. Carriers affected in such circumstances may seek public assistance and subsidies.

Consumer-related transportation forces affect the location and further growth of economic activities through the relative demand elasticities of differ-

---

[15] The point beyond which nontransportation costs cannot be lowered if a firm is to stay in business.

ent consuming areas. For example, two competitive carriers hauling from a given point to different consuming centers may encourage new entrants to that production center or the growth of those already existing there, by lowering freight rates. Lower rates would cause lower delivery price and greater demand.

The volume of increased demand depends on demand elasticity: the more elastic the demand, the greater the increase in the volume of sales and vice versa. Consuming areas with relatively greater elastic demand are likely to be more influential in causing growth in output. The carriers linking these consuming areas not only move the production centers toward specialization, but also increase their traffic volume and revenues. This may put other producing areas not linked to the preferred consuming centers in a disadvantaged position; hence their locational value is downgraded for new entrants or expansion by existing competitors.

The commodities, or inputs and outputs, involved in transportation also may affect the comparative advantage of location. If the movement of commodities between areas is such that the carrier's service is fully used in two-way traffic, producers located at those points may enjoy lower freight rates and consequently be able to sell their products at lower delivered prices. These points, therefore, have cost advantage over other locations that do not have comparable return commodity flows.

Finally, assuming that inputs are mobile and can be transported to any location at a cost, the spatial cost differentials can be reduced logically to transportation cost differentials. In a sense, locations or sites are mobile; i.e., they are available anywhere but at a different cost or rent. The rent is a function of accessibility of the site to markets, inputs, aesthetic facilities, cultural attractions, educational facilities, and the time and convenience involved in reaching the site. A location most accessible to the desired use involves a lower transportation cost to reach it and thus commands higher rent. Conversely, less accessible locations require a higher transportation cost resulting in lower rent value. Thus, transportation costs are important in helping to explain why economic activity locates itself in certain areas.

INTERNATIONAL TRADE

Earlier, locational comparative advantage (or disadvantage) as a basis for regional trade was discussed in terms of its physical characteristics, costs, prices, and transportation forces. There are numerous other considerations that influence the comparative advantage of an area.

Although the following discussion concerns the basis, significance, and effects of international trade, the same analysis lends itself to international trade flows. It must be recognized, however, that while the fundamental analysis of all trade is essentially the same, there are some limitations upon international trade largely because of policies of the nations involved. Limitations may involve a certain level of output beyond which the comparative advantage becomes ineffective. Tariffs, quotas, the problems of foreign exchange, and credit restrictions on certain international carriers and routes tend to discourage international specialization and trade.

International financial institutions, such as the International Monetary Fund (IMF), International Bank for Reconstruction and Development (IBRD), United Nations International Financial Corporation (UNIFC), Special United Nations Fund for Economic Development (SUNFED), and the United States Agency for International Development (AID), have facilitated international trade and economic development and assure sufficient credit in coming years to finance the noncommunist world's continued economic growth.

In 1967, the noncommunist world revised the provisions of the General Agreement on Tariffs and Trade (GATT) signed in 1947, completing the greatest tariff cuts in history and laying the foundation for a vast expansion of international trade.

A plan to create new Special Drawing Rights (SDRs) was drafted by the finance ministers of the "Group of Ten" (The United States, Great Britain, France, West Germany, Japan, Italy, Sweden, Belgium, The Netherlands, and Canada), submitted to the IMF in 1967, and approved by IMF members in 1970. Under the plan, a specified amount of SDRs would be issued each year to member nations in accordance with each nation's demand for SDRs and the quota in the IMF. The SDRs, another name for international currency, perhaps will never be seen or used by most citizens. Only government central banks will use them to settle international payments, along with their reserves of gold and other hard currencies.

Since different commodities require different relative amounts of inputs for their production, and countries are variously endowed with these inputs, the relative supplies of the inputs are reflected in their relative prices; and the relative costs of producing different commodities reflect relative efficiency. Therefore, the variation in relative costs forms the fundamental basis of trade. Other factors that may influence foreign trade are the satisfactions associated with the novelty of possessing or consuming foreign goals, altruistic motives toward other countries, and the demand for foreign materials, fruits, and other food items which a country cannot procure at home.

The relation of cost of commodities in one country to the cost of the same commodity in another country determines whether a country has an equal, absolute, or comparative advantage as a basis for engaging in trade. The comparison of cost can be made either on the basis of price, which normally covers cost, or with some index representing the standard transformation of physical inputs. Price comparison measures the social or market value of the commodity expressed in terms of the country's currency. An index measures the amount of physical inputs used to produce a given amount of the commodity. Both approaches have their advantages and disadvantages.

The price method is convenient because it is a common denominator for various inputs, but it requires the establishment of a conversion factor, commonly called the *exchange rate*, i.e., the value of one currency expressed in terms of another currency. Not only do different currencies have different units of measurement, but their purchasing power also differs. The input method, however, divorces the institutional effects (union strength, public subsidies, the degree of industry competitiveness, etc.) from the price and represents the actual amount of physical inputs used. Differences in the quality of inputs present a difficult problem.

For illustrative purposes, however, the price method will be employed. For covenience, let us suppose that the world contains only two countries, the United States and West Germany, and only two commodities, chemicals and steel. Let us further suppose that each country has its own monetary unit, the dollar ($) and the mark (M.). Given the prices for some specified units of chemicals and steel in both the countries, and the exchange rate between the two currencies, the nature of advantage for both countries can be determined.

83

TABLE 4–5   Prices of Steel and Chemicals Showing a Relation of Equal Advantage

	U.S. (prices in dollars)	WEST GERMANY (prices in marks)
Steel (*S*)	6	9
Chemicals (*C*)	2	4
	$1\,S_{U.S.} = 3\,C_{U.S.}$ $1\,C_{U.S.} = 1/3\,S_{U.S.}$	$1\,S_G = 3\,C_G$ $1\,C_G = 1/3\,S_G$

EQUAL ADVANTAGE

The hypothetical data and related equations in Table 4–5 show that the price ratios between steel and chemicals in both countries are identical. If the initial exchange rate is one mark for 25 cents, then $6.00 is the equivalent of 24M. and steel would be cheaper in Germany by 15M. (24 minus 9); similarly, chemicals would be cheaper by five marks (8 minus 3). At this exchange rate of marks for dollars, Germany could profitably export steel and chemicals to the United States.

But one-way trade is possible only for a relatively short time. German financial institutions dealing with foreign exchange will accumulate demand deposits in U.S. banks or deplete U.S. deposits in German banks. As the German banks continue to pile up their inventory of dollars, they will be willing to accept more dollars but only at a lower price. At the exchange rate of 1M. = $0.25, the German banks paid four marks to get one

dollar; the lower price means that to buy one dollar they will pay less than four marks. The exchange rate of marks for dollars will continue to fall until it reaches 1.50M. = $1.

At this rate, steel and chemicals are equally priced in both countries, which means that there is no basis for trade, not even for one-way trade. Therefore, it may be concluded that in the absence of trade barriers, any two nations whose domestic price ratios are equal in the manner shown in Table 4–5 possess equal advantage, and hence make no net gain from engaging in mutual trade.

COMPARATIVE ADVANTAGE

Now, suppose the data in Table 4–6 represent domestic prices of steel and chemicals, which may also be referred to as costs because prices in general have a close association with costs. Note that the price or cost of *S* is three times the price or cost of *C* in the United States, while

TABLE 4–6   Prices of Steel and Chemicals Showing a Relation of Comparative Advantage

	U.S. (prices in dollars)	WEST GERMANY (prices in marks)
Steel (*S*)	6	9
Chemicals (*C*)	2	4
	$1\,S_{U.S.} = 3\,C_{U.S.}$ $1\,C_{U.S.} = 1/3\,S_{U.S.}$	$1\,S_G = 9/4\,C_G$ $1\,C_G = 4/9\,S_G$

it is only two and a quarter times as great as chemicals in Germany. Comparatively speaking, this means that steel is more costly to produce in the U.S. than in Germany; similarly chemicals are more costly to produce in Germany than in the United States. Indeed, the the relative costs of the two commodities are reciprocals of each other; this can be verified from the equations at the bottom of Table 4–6. The equations show that while steel is relatively cheaper in Germany than in the United States, chemicals are relatively cheaper in the United States than in Germany.

Based on this information, the United States would be expected to import steel from Germany, and Germany would be expected to import chemicals from the United States in order for both countries to benefit from mutual trade. Both countries will benefit from trade if the commodities are exchanged at a ratio of terms that falls between their internal cost ratios. The United States gains no advantage when it trades three units of chemicals to obtain one unit of steel; similarly, Germany has no advantage when it trades a whole unit of steel for 2¼ units of chemicals. The United States enjoys the greatest benefit when it can receive one unit of steel by trading as few as 2¼ units of chemicals. Germany benefits most when it receives three units of chemicals in exchange for one unit of steel. Therefore, one unit of steel must be exchanged for between 2¼ and 3 units of chemicals.

Now, let us suppose that the terms of trade are agreed upon as 1S = 2½ C. The United States gains one dollar[16] on every unit of steel imported. It costs $6 to produce one unit of steel at home and $2 to produce a unit of chemicals, but by importing one unit of steel at the expense

of exporting 2½ units of chemicals, one dollar per unit is saved [$6−($2 × 2½)]. In other words, the cost of the United States of an imported unit of steel is 2½ units of chemicals, which, without trade, is 3 units of chemicals. Likewise, Germany gains one mark [(4M. × 2½) −9M.] for every 2½ units of chemicals imported; that is, the cost to Germany of an imported unit of chemicals is ⅖ units of steel, instead of 4/9.

Examining from the view of exchange rate: if the exchange rate is ⅔ M. = $1, neither country can underprice the other in steel; if the exchange rate is 2M. = $1, neither country can underprice the other in steel; if the exchange rate is 2M. = $1, neither can underprice the other in chemicals. An effective exchange has to be within these limits: the mark price of one dollar being less than 2M. and greater than ⅔ M. Suppose the rate is 1.75M. = $1.00.

Stating the prices in Table 4–6 in either of the two currencies, it can easily be verified that steel is cheaper in Germany and chemicals are cheaper in the United States. At the exchange rate of 1.75M. =$1.00, the net gains of the United States and Germany are approximately $.86 and 1.29M., respectively.[17] This exchange rate is slightly unfavorable to Germany, since 1.25M. is about $0.71. But, as American banks continue to pile up their inventory of marks, as a result of the favorable exchange rate, they will be willing to accept more marks only at a lower price until an equilibrium is reached. At that point, the benefits of trade are identical to both nations. (The lowering of the price of the mark may be accomplished either through the exchange-rate mechanism, the terms of trade, or both.)

[16] The gain would be affected when the relative transportation cost and other barriers to trade are taken into consideration.

[17] The net gains are computed based on the trade of 1 unit of steel with equivalent units (18/7) of chemicals.

ABSOLUTE ADVANTAGE

Absolute advantage is a special position a country may enjoy. When the United States, having created a variety of efficient factors of production, is able to produce most commodities more efficiently (i.e., maintain a higher output per unit of some specified input, e.g., labor) than other countries, it enjoys a position of absolute advantage. The general productive superiority of a country may seem to disqualify it from engaging in trade. Although a country might have absolute advantage, it can best use its resources by specializing in producing commodities where its comparative advantages are greatest. For example, a physician would not be expected to use his time nursing, although he may do a good job nursing. A lawyer might be a good typist as well as a competent lawyer, giving him an absolute advantage in both fields. But the opportunity cost of his time when he is typing is much higher than what he may save (say $4,000 a year) by not hiring a professional typist. A similar analogy may be extended to a nation possessing an absolute advantage. The United States, for example, can still benefit by selling commodities to other nations where its comparative advantage is the greatest, and buying commodities from nations for which their comparative disadvantage is the least.

Absolute advantage is a special case of comparative advantage. The analysis of comparative advantage also applies here. To recapitulate, the Law of Comparative Advantage states that, with no trade barriers, a nation tends to import goods and services the relative cost of which are less abroad than at home, and exports items the relative cost of which are greater abroad than at home.

The bilateral, two-commodity trade example of Germany and the U.S., although a simplified explanation of the process of international trade, provides a basic rationale for the process. The multiplicity of commodities in multilateral trade, coupled with the various levels and kinds of trade barriers, foreign aid, and institutional problems of settling the balance of payments all complicate determination of the terms of trade and exchange rates.

The student of geography is not concerned with the detailed process of determining exchange rates and settling problems of balance of payments; his or her contribution lies in analyses of the trade patterns and trends that result and in the evaluation of associated institutions that affect commodity flows. These flows provide a variable to explain why a region has certain economic phenomena, the volume of economic activity, and the degree of specialization. Generally speaking, both measurements should reflect a positive correlation. Exceptions would be countries like the United States and the Soviet Union where domestic markets are sufficiently large to permit specialization without significant exportation.

EFFECTS

During the 1960s, world trade of goods and services averaged about 10 percent of world income. This proportion doubles when data for the United States and the Soviet Union are excluded. According to the Standard International Trade Classification (SITC), adopted by the United Nations Economic and Social Council, there are 150 categories involving 570 different kinds of goods and services that are traded internationally.

During 1965, the value of exports was $165 billion currency equivalents, excluding the People's Republic of China, the USSR and its satellites, and United States military exports. The rate of growth in international trade has averaged about 6 percent since 1950 and about 9 percent since 1962. These statistics, impressive as they are, have multiple repercussions for real income and general economic welfare, the allocation pattern of resources among various activities and locations, relative costs and prices, and the scale of production.

It is invalid to conclude that if a nation's exports or imports were 5 percent of its national income, its national income would be affected only by 5 percent if foreign trade were cut off. The United States perhaps might be able to maintain its present standard of living by drawing from its vast territory and wide variety of resources and by making numerous substitutions. But when one considers consumer sovereignty and preferences, types of goods and services being traded, and cost-and-benefit aspects of the standard of living, the effects of cutting off foreign trade become obvious. Consider the effect on the standard of living if Americans had to forego items such as coffee, tea, cocoa, bananas, crude rubber, tin, jute, and spices, the domestic supply of which is now totally imported. The United States has only two metallic minerals, magnesium and molybdenum, in sufficient quantities to meet domestic needs without importation. Substitutes could be developed, but the costs of readjustment are great, even without taking into account benefits lost as a result of cutting off international trade.

DYNAMICS

In international trade, *dynamism* pertains to changes in domestic cost ratios, technology, artificial barriers, state of international relations, transportation costs, and institutional arrangements and facilities. This makes the network of world trade one of perpetual motion of composition, volume, direction, and speed. Classical theory about the basis of international trade, which says that comparative cost differences are due to different production functions, stands up to em-

pirical investigations under the short-term phenomena of trade. In the long run, production functions tend to be the same for all countries. Thus, a dynamic theory[18] of international trade for both short- and long-term considerations involves three variables: 1) production function, 2) resource prices, and 3) product prices. Based on the interdependent results of these variables, a country tends to export commodities that use large amounts of resources that are in relatively scarce supply at home. Thus, relative resource price differentials at national levels may be attributed to relative differences in the uses of national resources. Differentials of relative demands influence relative costs for all situations where industry is operating either at an increasing or at a decreasing cost.

Although other considerations previously mentioned quite frequently influence the trade pattern, differences in relative factor endowments, relative demands, and relative production functions remain the basic and dynamic forces underlying foreign trade.

SPATIAL DISPERSION AND EFFICIENCY

Spatial dispersion of economic activities is a function of the distribution of resources and consumers, the type of market, the nature of institutions, and social goals and directions. Efficiency refers to the ratio of output and input associated with the dispersion pattern. There are numerous considerations in the measurement of efficiency. Suffice it to say that each dispersion pattern has a degree of

[18] The dynamic, sometimes called the modern theory of international trade, has come to be known as the Hackerscher–Ohlin theory of trade. Bertil Ohlin, benefitting from the work by Eli Hackscher, presented the theory in his *Interregional and International Trade* (Cambridge, Mass.: Harvard University Press, 1933).

87

efficiency which may or may not be a society's goal.

Given the type of market, theoretical spatial relations between buyers and sellers can be portrayed (*see* Figure 4–3). The situation of clustered buyers suggests that sellers tend to seek locations that promise cost minimization regardless of rivals. If buyers are scattered, however, sellers seek locations that not only minimize cost but also secure a larger buyers' market. This means that sellers are faced not only with the need to determine relative elasticities of demand fairly accurately, but also to determine marginal cost functions, freight rates, degree and importance of amenity factors, and other institutional and custom considerations at alternative locations.

references

1. Balassa, B. "An Empirical Demonstration of Classical Comparative Cost Theory." *The Review of Economic and Statistics* 45 (August 1963): 231–38.

2. Brehm, Carl. *Introduction to Economics*. New York: Random House, 1970.

3. Chisholm, Michael. *Geography and Economics*. New York: Frederick A. Praeger, 1966.

4. Eagly, Robert V. *The Structure of Classical Economic Theory*. New York: Oxford University Press, 1974.

5. Finkelstein, Joseph, and Thimm, Alfred L. *Economists and Society: The Development of Economic Thought from Aquinas to Keynes*. New York: Harper & Row, 1973.

6. Greenhut, Melvin L. *Microeconomics and the Space Economy*. Glenview, Ill.: Scott, Foresman and Co., 1963.

7. Hansen, N. M. "Development of Dole Theory in a Regional Context." *Kyklos* 32 (1965): 176–190.

8. Heilbroner, Robert L. *The Economic Problem*. 2nd ed. Englewood Cliffs, N.J.: Prentice-Hall, 1970.

9. Hoover, Edgar M. *The Location of Economic Activity*. New York: McGraw-Hill Book Co., 1948.

10. Isard, Walter; Schooler, E. W.; and Vietosisy, T. *Industrial Complex Analysis and Regional Development*. New York: John Wiley & Sons, 1959.

11. Losch, August. *The Economics of Location*. New Haven: Yale University Press, 1954.

12. Machlup, Fritz. *The Basing Point System*. Philadelphia: The Blakiston Co., 1949.

13. Marshall, Alfred. *Principles of Economics*. 9th ed. New York: The Macmillan Co., 1961.

14. Moore, Basil J. *An Introduction to Modern Economic Theory*. New York: Free Press, 1973.

15. Nourse, Hugh O. *Regional Economics*. New York: McGraw-Hill Book Co., 1968.

16. Spann, Othmar. *The History of Economics*. New York: Arno Press, 1972.

17. Suits, Daniel B. *Principles of Economics*. New York: Harper & Row, 1970.

18. Suranyi–Unger, Theo. *Economic Philosophy of the Twentieth Century*. De Kalb, Ill.: Northern Illinois University Press, 1972.

19. Ward, Benjamin. *What's Wrong with Economics*. New York: Basic Books, 1972.

20. Weber, Alfred. *Theory of the Location of Industries*. Chicago: University of Chicago, Press, 1928.

sociopolitical
framework

5

5

The analysis of economic activity traditionally has depended on physical, economic, and, occasionally, social aspects. However, the changing and spatially varying emphases and roles of various political concepts and the emergence of new states have challenged the ability of existing analyses to explain and reflect the spatial variation of economic phenomena. Society, which is influenced to some degree by communication between cultural regions, has a direct impact on the level and type of economic activities. The impacts are relative, however, and in continuous flux due to changing technology. Thus, culture and material resources have a dynamic relationship.

This chapter will identify some of the major sociopolitical factors and explore how they may influence the type of level of economic activities. This relationship has been investigated by many scholars who have reached the general conclusion that social and political factors significantly influence economic growth. But there are interesting philosophical and empirical differences in the interpretation of the character and degree of these influences. Everett E. Hagen (14) concludes that social and political factors are decisive and serve as the basic vehicle for economic growth.[1] In any case, the relevance of social and political factors is well recognized, although the complexity of their manifestation has not permitted or attracted penetrating empirical study.

[1] The purposes of this text do not warrant a detailed discussion of this controversy. Generally, very little empirical evidence exists on this topic; most of the work related to it has philosophical or theoretical implications.

POLITICAL FACTORS

The goals of governments, whether international, national, or regional are manifest in the type, level, and location of their economic activity.[2] Countries placing high priorities on economic development tend to allocate their resources primarily toward productive capital goods. Economically advanced countries promote greater levels of research and development to find new products and processes in order to maintain and increase a high level of consumption. Regions with declining levels of economic activity have often been stimulated by government-initiated programs and activities. Government actions may also adversely affect areas.

The effects of political factors may be direct or indirect. Government owned and operated activities are examples of direct effects. Social values associated with property, contracts, individual opportunity and rights, modern money,[3] trade, fiscal policy, monetary policy, and institutions affecting the size of economic units and the activity of labor unions are almost invariably instituted through a political framework, directly or indirectly. The structure and degree of political influences is determined by the relative political doctrines and modern concepts of the nation-state.

[2] Regions once labeled as monocultures have and are introducing diversification, partly as a result of government-directed movements for a higher degree of self-sufficiency and national security. These diversifications have been justified even at the expense of established profitable markets and benefits associated with trade based on relative comparative advantage.

[3] Money, in the modern sense, is anything that serves as a medium of exchange, standard of value, store of value, and a standard of deferred payments; it is produced and controlled by government, which also establishes the legal mechanism for its acceptability. Ideal money is durable, portable, divisible, uniform within its denomination, recognizable, difficult to counterfeit, and relatively inexpensive to produce.

NATION-STATE

A *nation* traditionally refers to a group of people with a common language and, sometimes, a common religion. A *state* is a territorial boundary over which a government exercises sovereignty. A nation can be stateless but a state cannot be nationless. For example, Israel has existed as a nation for a long time. It was only in 1948 that she attained her statehood by acquiring Palestine.

The classical European nation–state, with a relatively homogeneous cultural base, effective sovereignty, and loyalty and adherence to the law, is no longer realized as it was during the nineteenth century. Although some European nations still closely conform to the classical nation–state, the two World Wars, the end of colonialism, the cold war, limited warfare, and domestic instability and disharmony have produced numerous loosely structured societies, which, for the sake of socioeconomic progress and survival, are progressing toward the so-called modern nation–state.[4]

The modern nation–state is not a cohesive, homogeneously structured unit; it is a society structured primarily by a political framework. The great number of government activities are designed to stimulate and diffuse economic and social progress and cohesiveness and to promote unity of purpose in the political realm. Fisher illustrates the impact of government rhetoric in the U.S.:

> Associated with the names of most Presidents in this century have been certain watchwords. Theodore Roosevelt proclaimed his Square Deal; Wilson the New Freedom; Harding preferred Back to Normalcy; Franklin Roosevelt the New Deal; Truman the Fair Deal; Kennedy

the New Frontier. Although he had no one pet phrase, Eisenhower emphasized partnership. President Johnson has proclaimed his goal for America as achieving the Great Society.

> Running through these bold proclamations are several themes: a better deal for those groups suffering disadvantages; a higher level of social justice in the distribution of wealth and income among all people; the harnessing of science to economic and social development; an emphasis on freedom and range of choices in national policy; a regard for efficiency and the holding down of costs. The Great Society, it would seem, draws from all of these, but in the main, it is a restatement of American democracy in political, economic, and social terms suitable for the last third of the twentieth century. Its grandiloquent ring causes some persons to wince and others to smile; all the same, it does seem to find positive response from a much larger number of citizens who sense that to the earlier goals of individual freedom and a better deal for certain groups must now be added an all-embracing design for improvement of the whole American society.[5]

Government activity is a never-ending process in contemporary nation–states. Here, we will discuss the conceptualization and the effects of political factors as they influence economic activity. Our analysis will not attempt to theorize the process of political evolution or policymaking.

POLITICAL SYSTEMS AND DIVISIONS

Governments vary in how they are constituted and maintained, their relation to the governed, and the type and level of economic role they play. The spatial

---

[4] For further study of the concept of nation–state, see Alfred Cobban, *National Self-Determinism* (Chicago: University of Chicago Press, 1944), and K. H. Silvert, *Expectant Peoples: Nationalism and Development* (New York: Random House, 1964).

[5] Joseph L. Fisher, *Resource Development in the Public Interest* (Washington, D.C.: Resources for the Future, 1965), p. 1.

variation in political behavior roles is manifest in the different decision-making processes of producers and consumers, resulting in spatial variation of economic phenomena. Conceptually speaking, there are as many forms of political behavior roles as there are political entities. But some functional groups can be made and analyzed. The behavior roles within these groupings may be either constitutionally defined, professionally attained, or both.

For example, it has been suggested that democratic governments act rationally within the constraints of a democratic political structure, an electorate of rational voters, and the varying degrees of uncertainty. The government, i.e., the individuals in government, rationally designs efficient strategies to accomplish selected political and economic goals of the individuals in government. The constitutional and economic role of the government may be minimal, but government rationality alone is a sufficient condition to invoke spatial variability.

In totalitarian economies, the condition of rationality to produce variability is stronger. However, in these economies, variability may be a result of one-directional rationality (a single party or an organization) as compared to the two-directional interplay of the electorate and the government found in democratic societies.

Politicoeconomic systems are characterized in many ways: by their organization, structure, development, conduct, control, and direction.

From the viewpoint of *organization*, three systems—capitalism, socialism, and communism—are basic in the world today. There are no universally accepted definitions of these systems; for our purposes, we shall discuss the characteristics they embody (*see* Figure 5–1).

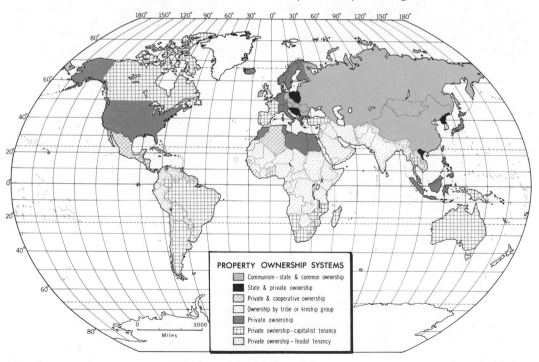

PROPERTY OWNERSHIP SYSTEMS
- Communism – state & common ownership
- State & private ownership
- Private & cooperative ownership
- Ownership by tribe or kinship group
- Private ownership
- Private ownership – capitalist tenancy
- Private ownership – feudal tenancy

FIGURE 5–1

92

CAPITALISM

Pure capitalism involves the following institutions and assumptions:

1. Private property
2. Freedom of enterprise and choice
3. Individualism
4. Competition
5. Consumer sovereignty
6. A limited role for government
7. Market-directed allocation of resources and distribution of wealth

Under a capitalistic system, property, or the means of production (material resources, buildings, plant, and equipment used in the production process) is owned by private individuals or corporate bodies. The institution of property is maintained by a legal mechanism, and individuals or corporations holding the property may negotiate contracts and control, employ, buy, and sell their property to any market they wish. Laborers are free to sell their services wherever and to whomever they choose. There is no visible government control on the individual's choice. However, the individual is guided by the market forces, and market conditions and coordinates individual decisions.

The consumer exercises his sovereignty by paying ("casting his vote") for the things he wants. The desirability of products is indicated by the amount bought; lower prices are bid for less desired commodities. Price is a basic organizing force through which the activities of both buyers and sellers are synchronized. The businessman, in response to consumer sovereignty, seeks to secure and organize his enterprise in such a way that it will provide profit. The allocation of resources and the distribution of wealth are impersonally determined, primarily by market demand and the individual's contribution. Those who pay heed to the market are rewarded and

those who do not are "punished." The inequality of income distribution is justified on the basis that each person's income represents the relative value of his contribution to production.

These are the major characteristics of capitalism in its *pure* form. With growing realizations of capitalism's shortcomings, many variations have occurred, principally in five areas:

1. Consumer sovereignty has been affected to the degree that the consumer has the choice to buy only goods and services producers make available and persuade consumers to buy through advertising.

2. Decline of producer competition has tended to increase the gap between prices and costs, affecting the distribution of income that would have existed under pure capitalism.

3. The tendency to monopolize resources has limited resource mobility.

4. Incomes are also being earned from sources other than those directly contributing to the production process, e.g., monopoly profits, capital gains, and inheritance wealth.

5. Capitalism does not adequately provide for the production of social goods, or equitable allocation of social costs and social benefits.

Remedial actions have occurred and are occurring to alleviate these shortcomings through numerous laws and direct interventions by government. The salient feature of the capitalistic system is that the allocation of resources and the distribution of wealth is brought about largely through the interplay of market forces.

COMMUNISM

Communism, in practice, primarily involves:

1. Complete or nearly complete public ownership and control of the productive and distributive processes, and the property resources used therein
2. Central planning
3. Command-directed economy

4. Circumscribed freedom
5. Prescribed prices

Public ownership extends to the property, means, and instruments of production and distribution: material resources, capital, transportation and communication, most retail and wholesale enterprises, banking systems, and most urban housing. Supreme authority is likened to a dictatorship interested in enhancing its own power, privilege, and prestige. Economic planning may or may not reflect consumer interests. Central planning determines what and how much is to be produced, where enterprises are to be located, and how the output will be distributed among production units and consumers.

Consumer sovereignty is limited solely to the consumer's freedom to spend his income as he sees fit, and on those services and goods for which the central plan provides. The kinds of goods and services produced according to the plan establish the number and kinds of jobs available. Resource prices, set by the planning committee, vary between occupations and localities in a fashion and to a degree that provide for the needed number and types of workers in various occupations. The labor force, save occasional compulsory job assignments, is relatively free to choose or change jobs in response to spatial and occupational wage differentials. Product prices are used merely as a rationing tool. The planning committee or its related agency sets the consumer goods prices at levels that will leave no shortages or surplus.

SOCIALISM

Socialism basically involves:

1. Public ownership and management of all producers' goods that are strategically important to the society[6]

[6] The producers' goods are given priorities that command a relative degree of eligibility for so-

2. Large-scale production in all economic sectors requires relatively large numbers of employees and great economic power
3. Equality of income distribution
4. Economic growth and elimination of business cycles
5. Partial reliance on market mechanism
6. Economic planning
7. Social democracy
8. "Meaningful" freedom

Not all property and enterprises are publicly owned and managed in socialist systems. Public ownership and management are limited to only enterprises and property that are crucial to output, employment, resource use, pricing, technological development, and the location of economic activity. Control of these economic factors translates into political power, which may be exercised toward more abundant satisfaction of luxury desires and more political and social dominance. This may produce an inequality of income and freedom (under the assumption that economic, social, and political liberty are inseparable—it is impossible to have one without the others), and imbalance (in favor of public goods) between social and private goods. A situation of "public opulence and private squalor" may result in continued intensification of the inequality of income distribution and, consequently, further inequality in the society.

In theory, the public role of socialism would replenish the "starved public sector," resulting in more stable economic growth, improved income distribution, and greater equality of opportunity and freedom to choose an occupation, location, and goods and services. Because in theory the government is elected democratically, an individual's significance in

cialization. First priorities would be banking and public utilities; second, communications; third, energy, steel, chemicals, transportation, and construction, and on down the line.

effecting change is enhanced. Under socialism, he gains more "meaningful" freedom, otherwise circumvented by the elite of wealth in pure capitalist systems.

Each politicoeconomic system, capitalism, socialism, and communism, provides a different organizational framework for viewing and resolving questions of resource ownership and allocation, location of enterprises, and distribution of output. The spatial arrangement of economic activities tends to be different in each of these frameworks, and modification of them occur country by country. In communism, the activities tend to be resource-oriented; in capitalism, market-oriented; and in socialism, some mixture of resource- and market-oriented.

The *structural* aspect of a policy is closely associated with its organizational pattern. For example, the capitalistic system with market and price mechanisms as the basic forces of resource allocation and output distribution employs a market structure that may fall anywhere on the continuum between pure competition and monopoly. The spatial patterns of economic activity likely to be yielded by pure competition, monopoly, monopolistic competition, and oligopoly were discussed in chapter 4. The economic structures of communist and socialist political economies are dependent on the type and the degree of command, which may range from a high degree of centralization to complete decentralization. Each economic structure produces a different spatial pattern of economic activities. The control and direction of a highly centralized structure tend to develop large complexes of activities with a high degree of specialization. Decentralized control of the economy may foster specialization, but not on as large a scale as is possible under a centralized system.

A political framework may envelop economies at different points in the stage and rate of economic development. Five such stages have been identified (26):

1. Tradition
2. Preconditions for take-off
3. Take-off
4. Drive to maturity
5. High mass consumption

Traditional societies are predominantly agricultural, with a primitive technology; low productivity; limited entrepreneurial endeavors; a high rate of illiteracy; high birth and death rates; limited social and economic mobility; local and provincialized political orientation, and limited trade.

The second stage is transitional; traditional ways of thinking, attitudes toward work and life, and methods of government change. In this transition, political and social attitudes and economic institutions conducive to development are constructed. A spirit of nationalism emerges and many nations within the state are united in a single nation–state.

Societies in the take-off stage lower resistances to economic growth, increase new and productive investments, and use new technology. Manufacturing is generally of increasing importance.

The fourth stage reflects mass industrialization, a high level of literacy, increased mobility of labor, lower birth and death rates, higher productivity, and a high degree of economic interdependence.

In the last stage, a society experiences an increase in income to a level where durable consumer goods beyond the needs for food, shelter, and clothing can be afforded. The society's resources are basically oriented toward consumer satisfaction and enjoyment. A polity may experience all five stages simultaneously within its boundaries because of spatial variations in the components of its society.

Polities may also be differentiated by their rates of economic growth, commonly measured by the average percent increases of the real gross product from year to year. The rate of growth basically depends on the proportion of the net national product invested.[7] And, the rate of investment is a function of many factors: availability and accessibility of raw materials; availability and adoption of technology; entrepreneurship; educational, social, political, and economic institutions; national solidarity and cohesion; and the general willingness of the populace to advance economically.

To recapitulate, the politicoeconomic systems of the contemporary world are numerous and diverse. Classification of these systems can be accomplished wherever possible with respect to selected criteria. The list of criteria or characteristics discussed earlier are by no means exhaustive. Other criteria, such as freedom, justice, personal security, and social equality could also be employed, although they are difficult to measure. Functional political systems can be adequately defined by the criteria used here; a structural as well as functional understanding of these systems provide a reference for the explanation of economic activity.

POLITICAL INSTITUTIONS

Basic to all political or government institutions is the individual member of society, with his or her expectations, aspirations, attitudes, participation, and vigilance—qualities known to political scientists as "raw materials." With these raw materials, the political individual moves to establish and direct the institutions conducive to favorable processing of his raw materials. When organized with the rest of the political individuals

[7] The rate of growth contributes toward gains in social welfare only when it exceeds the rate of population increase.

in the society, these raw materials may show a wide range of goals.

How are these raw materials acquired? They are related to psychological, economic, and social variables of the individual (9, 20). A personality that exhibits fear, suspicion, and insecurity, and shudders at uncertainty, complexity, and change, tends to seek and accept authority and leadership from others. The social experiences related to education, work, interest groups, clubs, political parties, political views of the family, religious affiliation, age, and sex influence the raw material. Katz and Lazarsfeld (18) observe a strong relationship between the character of primary groups and the political behavior of an individual. Dye (12) and Reagan (24) show that economic status and aspirations also influence the political behavior of an individual.

The political system, which partially influences and molds the political raw material, influences the effect of micropolitics on macropolitics and related institutions. For instance, capitalism under democratic institutions not only establishes and maintains supportive institutions, but it also contains the mechanism by which the local political units have dynamic control over the structure and direction of these institutions. Under a communist system, the degree of influence of local political units on institutions is perhaps minimal.

LAW AND THE LEGAL SYSTEM

The law is the body of rules and regulations of conduct established and enforced by authority, legislation, or custom and tradition. The law involves the *legal order system* and *sociological norms*, both of which condition economic phenomena. The legal order system is manifest in the guarantees, protection, licensing, controls, indemnities, subsidies, prohibition, and coercion or punishment. These constitute the "rules of the game" in the emergence and performance of economic phenomena in which the players, or the producers and consumers, engage for the attainment of certain goals. Sociological norms are an induced expression of approval or disapproval about economic activity, produced without any outward coercive force, physical or legal. The inducement may be a composite force of custom, religious ethics, expectation and acceptance of novelty, public opinion, etc. The location and survival of many economic phenomena are influenced by the social-based law.[8] As economic activities are affected by political systems, legal order systems are the direct result of particular political orientations.

POLITICAL VARIABLES

The variation in national political systems provides a reference for nation–state regions. However, as in the United States and other democratic countries, despite the universality of constitutional frameworks, political frameworks of internal regions or states differ significantly. This differentiation is caused by the relative strength and competition of political parties, political participation, voting district apportionment, interest-group activity and strength, and factors related to the personality, role, and status of political figures at the national level.

Our interest does not lie in political differentiation as such, but rather in its effect on the economic phenomena. For such purposes, the identification of political variables is imperative. Adelman and Morris (2) have identified twelve political variables that affect the level and type of economic activity of an area:

[8] A stimulating text for those interested in a philosophical treatment of social-based law is Max Rheinstein (ed.), *Max Weber On Law in Economy and Society*, trans. by Edward Shils and Max Rheinstein (New York: Simon and Schuster, 1967).

1. Degree of national integration and sense of national unity
2. Degree of centralization of political power
3. Strength of democratic institutions
4. Degree of freedom of political opposition and press
5. Degree of competitiveness of political parties
6. Predominant basis of the political party system
7. Strength of the labor movement
8. Political strength of the traditional elite
9. Degree of administrative efficiency
10. Extent of leadership commitment to economic development
11. Extent of political stability
12. Political strength and role of the military

These variables demonstrate the significant interrelationship between political patterns and economic phenomena.

Other variables with roots in the political system include property rights, tenancy and leasing, acquisition and transfer of ownership rights, bequeathing of property, protection and guarantees, taxation, subsidies, and the employment of fiscal and monetary policies for influencing the economic performance of the region. Our interest here is to identify the relevant variables in order to provide a perspective for the student of economic geography and to open avenues of study about the precise nature and level of the interrelationships of these variables and the dependent variable of economic activity.

SOCIAL FACTORS

The relevance of social factors that can be identified and interpreted depends on the validity with which these factors can be measured. There have long been efforts to enumerate social aspects: Mary and Joseph going to Bethlehem for enumeration, and provisions for decennial census and the State of the Union message[9] of the U.S. Constitution are examples. The High Moore Fund of New York (a population policy panel), the Social Science Research Council, the American Statistical Association, the Bureau of the Budget, and UNESCO (United Nations Educational, Scientific and Cultural Organization) all have made strides toward the definition and measurement of social indicators or factors. The U.S. Department of Health, Education, and Welfare in 1961 initiated monthly and annual indicators, which may provide a parallel service to economic indicator series published by the departments of Labor and Commerce and to the Economic Report of the President. Progress to date on this series has involved measurement of:

1. The spatial distribution of the population by age, race, skill and training, marital status, and head of the household

2. Estimates of propensities to move and actual spatial mobility

3. Estimates of present population and projections of the future, the basic variables of which are birth rates, death rates, fertility rates, and population migration

These kinds of data, although useful for many purposes, do not reveal the overall character of a society. Many significant measures associated with value systems, beliefs, social stimuli, goals, perceptive mechanisms, dexterity, attitudes toward life, change, etc., are lacking.

[9] Historically, the presidential State of the Union messages have been dominated by so-called "economic philistinism," i.e., economic statistics and issues, leaving the condition of the social fabric relatively minimized, if not ignored. Contemporary State of the Union messages are dominated by the Budget (required by the Budget and Accounting Act of 1921), the Economic Report (under the Employment Act of 1946), and the Manpower Development and Training Act of 1962).

The Committee on Space of the American Academy of Arts and Sciences has prepared for the National Aeronautics and Space Administration an innovative and provocative volume (3) in which the authors deal primarily with the social ramifications of space programs. The substance of this volume yields valuable insight into the means by which a society's character, as well as that of a state, can be evaluated or anticipated. This volume also attempts to define the type and value of social statistical series necessary for policy decisions.

There are numerous difficulties involved in compiling social data because: (1) Attempts to obtain unbiased data, especially in societies where individual freedom is highly valued and guaranteed, elicit the charge that any attempt to measure the "real" character of the society is an act of "dehumanization." And (2) Presently we are unable to measure human values and "personal" affairs. Aside from technical difficulties, other factors of concern include invalidity, inaccuracy, conflicting indicators, lack of data, incompatible models, and value consensus.

Invalidity refers to situations where an indicator reflects only a limited validity, where the meaning of the events that generate the data does not exactly correspond to the meaning attached to the indicator. There may be differences in the meaning of a concept at different periods. For example, a certain number of people with a particular religious affiliation does not necessarily mean that all affiliates of that particular sect represent a homogeneous affinity with its "articles of faith." Hence, a social series on religious affiliations may involve invalidities. There are similar invalidities related to data on educational achievement, poverty, etc.

Inaccuracy is associated with sampling and enumeration errors and biases. *Conflicting indicators* are ones that show contradictory implications when applied or used for the same judgment or conclusion. The strengthening of the family unit in the United States holds a respectable value as a basic building block toward strengthening the democratic process. Yet some contend that Social Security and welfare programs tend to weaken the family bond and thus have an adverse effect on the national goal of a strong democracy. *Lack of data* may occur simply because of discontinuity in the series, or because of the difficulty of defining and measuring certain social aspects. *Incompatibility* of models is related to the manner in which the indicators are statistically treated or analyzed. The difficulty of determining a *value consensus* stems from individual differences in preferences, standards, and relative values.

Man's behavior is a composite representation of his biological structure and physiocultural environment. No attempt is made here to analyze spatial variations in the biological structure and motivational forces of man and their effects on economic phenomena. The focus here is on the social factors as they develop and manifest themselves in diverse ways at different times and places; therefore, they are conceptualized as causes of spatial variation in economic phenomena.

POPULATION

Population has many aspects: size, density, spatial distribution, age and sex, fertility rate, birth and death rate, life expectancy, migration, and rate and trend of population growth. The implications of these aspects tend to produce regional differentials in the spatial distribution of economic activities and their growth patterns.

The world population is now approaching 4 billion, which, according to the geometric progression of Malthus, may be looked upon as the result of two dozen individuals increasing at the rate of 0.02 percent per year over a period of approximately 100,000 years. Philip Hauser (17), using the estimates of Harrison Brown, reports that projection of the average post-World War II rate of increase of the population existing then would give a population of 50 billion by 2160 AD. At this rate of increase, by the mid-twenty-eighth century, if all the land on earth were divided equally, each person would receive only one square foot.

Can any set of economic activities support this population? Brown thinks so, assuming that technological achievements in the capturing of solar and nuclear energy will enable energy to be produced at such a low cost that the conventional energy-producing resources will become available for other uses, including food, and the change in food habits will be such that food raised from algae farms and yeast factories will satisfy the need.

These speculations and voluminous figures may be fantasies, but they do indeed reflect a crisis. Table 5–1 shows that the rate of the world's population growth has been increasing rapidly, and future projections indicate an even faster rate of increase.

Man can avert the population crisis in the same way he is creating it: with enormous preventive and remedial technology. Medical technology has reduced mortality rates and increased life expectancy; birth rates may also be checked by modern medical technology. However, modification of the value systems that promote fertility and unchecked reproduction must occur; this complex problem is compounded in societies whose religious practices do not allow birth control.

According to the United Nations, few, if any, countries are willing to commit themselves to halting population growth, even if technically possible, because they fear that the "numbers game"

TABLE 5–1 Size and Increases in Populations by Continental Regions

	POPULATION (in millions)					AVERAGE ANNUAL INCREASE				
	1900	1925	1950	1975*	2000*	1650–1750	1900–1925	1925–1950	1950–1975*	1975–2000*
Africa	120	147	199	303	517	—%	0.9%	1.4%	2.1%	2.8%
Asia	857	1020	1380	2210	3870	—	0.8	1.4	2.4	3.0
Europe (including USSR)	423	505	574	751	947	—	0.8	0.6	1.2	1.0
North America	81	126	168	240	312	—	2.2	1.3	1.7	1.2
South America	63	99	163	303	592	—	2.3	2.6	3.4	3.8
Oceania	6	10	13	21	29	—	2.3	1.4	2.4	1.6
World	1550	1907	2497	3828	6267	0.3%	0.9%	1.2%	2.1%	2.6%

* These are medium-level UN projections.

Source: Philip M. Hauser, "Demographic Dimensions of World Politics," in T. Morgan, G. W. Betz, and N. K. Choudry (eds.), *Readings in Economic Development* (Belmont, Calif.: Wadsworth Publishing Co., 1963), p. 62. By permission of the publisher.

TABLE 5–2 Determinants of Population Growth

NATURAL INCREASE IN A REGIONAL POPULATION IS AFFECTED BY:		
BIRTH RATES INFLUENCED BY:	**DEATH RATES INFLUENCED BY:**	**MIGRATION INFLUENCED BY:**
Fertility rate	Mortality rates	Employment opportunities
Age, sex, and income distribution	Climate	Amenity factors
Religion and cultural values	Health measures and facilities	Barriers to in-and-out migration
Technology of birth control	Education	
Working hours patterns	Environmental pollution	
Privacy	Population intensity	
Education	Caloric consumption	
Marriage rate	Type of economic activities	
Composition of food		

Source: Philip M. Hauser, "Demographic Dimensions of World Politics," *Science* 131 (June 1960): 1641–1647, Tables 2 and 3. Copyright © 1960 by the American Association for the Advancement of Science. Reprinted with permission.

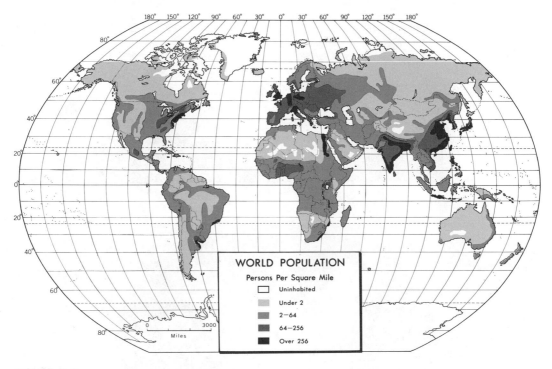

Persons Per Square Mile

☐	Uninhabited
	Under 2
	2–64
	64–256
	Over 256

WORLD POPULATION

0 3000
Miles

FIGURE 5–2

may shortchange them in world politics. Thus, solutions to the problem are of international concern and scope. The problems are further compounded by barriers to international migration.

Table 5–1 and Figure 5–2 demonstrate that the growth in population is occurring unevenly among the various regions, and the prospective rates of population growth even more so. Population growth rates are a function of birth rates, death rates, and migrations, as shown in Table 5–2. Based on the correlations among these variables and the per capita income for a selected number of countries, international differences in standard of living are phenomena caused partly by these variables. For example, death rates and birth rates are negatively correlated to the per capita level of national income; there are varying reasons for this relationship. In some countries,

such as Ireland and Japan, the scarcity of local material resources has provided the impetus for family limitation (lower birth rates), which has been partly responsible for more efficient units of economic enterprise, resulting in higher per capita incomes. In many societies, the desire for a higher standard of living has provided the impetus for family limitation.

Other aspects of population growth, such as the structure of societies with a smaller share of the economically productive world population, may mean lower total production of output. In many developing countries, there is a relatively high child-dependency ratio, and a much smaller proportion of the population survives to working age. Assuming that the economically productive population of a nation is between the ages of 15 and 64, poor countries average something like 55 percent of their popu-

101

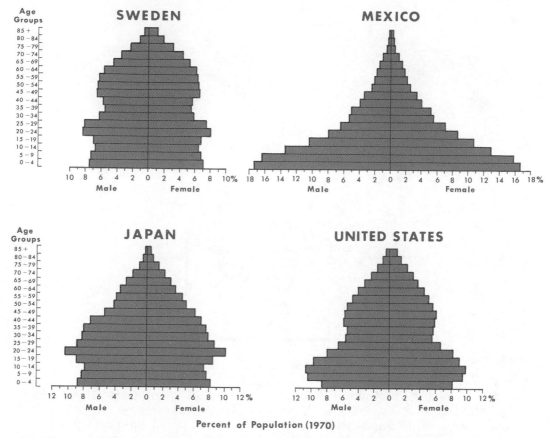

FIGURE 5–3 *Population Pyramids*

lation in this category, compared to 65 percent for developed countries (*see* Figure 5–3).

The size of population may or may not be a deterrent to the improvement of living standards. To a point, the increase in total population encourages exploitation of resources that would otherwise not be used or perhaps be used less efficiently. In general, the present consensus falls into the "Malthusian population trap." The consensus says that at very low per capita income levels, health and nutritional levels decline to the point where the mortality rate exceeds the birth rate. But higher per capita income levels bring about an increase in population under the pressure of a falling mortality rate; the increase may well be faster than the rate of per capita income change until a 3 percent maximum limit of population increase is reached. At that point, various forces would promote efforts to limit or decrease population and aggressive economic development in order to increase the per capita income at a faster rate. India, for example, has reached the outer limit of this "trap" after having experienced reasonable rates of economic growth as a result of her five-year plans. In summary, whether or not a society will be caught in the Malthusian trap depends basically on the levels of absolute and relative change in the rates of population and income.

Finally, the spatial variability in population density patterns directs economic activities into labor-intensive economic activities; low density areas are oriented toward capital-intensive activities.

RELIGION

Religion is a system of beliefs and faith in divine or supernatural powers to be revered, worshiped, and obeyed as creators, rulers, and regulators of the universe. The expression of beliefs is manifested in the manner of worship and in associated institutions, buildings and valuables, rituals, practices, ethical codes, and expressions of conduct. Our interest lies in the way religious aspects affect

and influence resource recognition and exploitation and economic activities (*see* Figure 5–4). Occasional inadvertent effects of religion are recognized but not treated as an exogenous force on economic activity.

The influences of religious factors on economic phenomena may be examined in the following ways:

1. Economic activities owned or operated by religious institutions and the claim to income of the region

2. The regional density, structure, and coherence within and between religion(s)

3. The relation between religion and the state and associated concessions and restrictions

4. The effect of religion on resource use and economic activities

Property owned by religious bodies, in terms of its monetary value, location, and

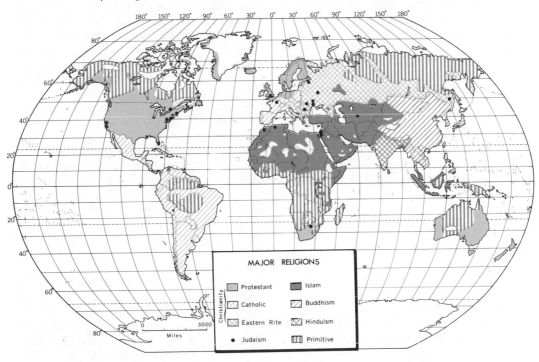

FIGURE 5–4

103

tax exemptions, not only restricts and conditions land use, but also helps to explain the development of commercial and population centers where religious interests were or are foci around which these centers develop. Claims on income affect economic activity in the ways this income is spent on certain types of goods and services.

The extent of property ownership and claims to income of religious bodies varies over time and place. In the United States, the value of church-owned real estate was estimated at $80 billion in 1967. Estimates of the annual income flowing into religious treasuries from business profits, rentals, and dividends runs into billions. The importance of religious properties and income, which are mostly exempted from taxation, is likely to increase as more and more religious bodies hold titles to various forms of economic activities.

Frequently one finds churches and their agencies holding title to farms, ranches, office buildings, apartment houses, parking lots, bonds, stocks, securities, etc. For example, a garbage dump in Chicago and the ground under Yankee Stadium in New York are owned by religious groups. With the existing tax shelters and with prudent management of properties and incomes, which result in lower costs, church owned and operated businesses may control greater and greater shares of the market and influence economic activities.

Voluntary contributions also provide a sizable income for religious bodies. And, the amount of income left unclaimed by religious bodies may also affect economic phenomena.

The greater the degree of density, homogeneity, and coherence within a religion, the greater the growth and stability of economic activities yielding goods and services desired by that religion. Israel is a prime example. Some regions

with many religious denominations or beliefs have suffered from lagging economic growth because they lack a healthy social atmosphere for new business investments. The higher average rate of economic growth in West Pakistan during the last two decades, compared to that of India, which is religiously more homogeneous, demonstrates this effect.

The relationships between religion and state have some bearing on the level of economic activity in a region. The economies of religious states differ significantly from secular states. Often secular states may grant concessions to religious institutions, such as tax exemptions. Or secular restrictions may penalize or discourage certain actions and manifestations of religious faith influencing the location and type of economic activities (e.g., the Soviet Union).

Economic activity is affected by religious beliefs, taboos, and value systems that relate to respect for authority; the status of the future; man's dominion over minerals, plants, and animals; transmigration; work and leisure; stewardship; the relation of planets to God, seasons, and holidays; worship practices; festivals, customs, and the like.

Numerous illustrations can be cited to substantiate the influence of religion on economic activities. Taboos against eating particular foods and working on certain days of the week have greatly affected economic phenomena. For over a thousand years, the Roman Catholic Church required its members to abstain from eating meat on Friday in the spirit of penance. Acting on recommendations from Catholic bishops throughout the world that renunciation of meat is not always the most effective means of practicing penance, Pope Paul VI relaxed the rules on fasting and abstinence in 1966. Catholics no longer need to abstain from eating meat on Fridays, except during Lent. With this authority, bishops of many

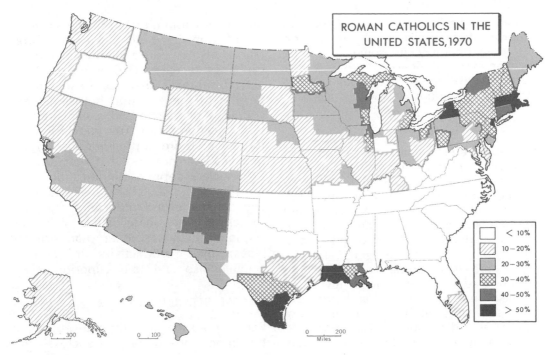

ROMAN CATHOLICS IN THE
UNITED STATES, 1970

	< 10%
	10 – 20%
	20 – 30%
	30 – 40%
	40 – 50%
	> 50%

FIGURE 5–5

countries, including the United States, in 1966 terminated meatless Fridays except during Lent (*see* Figure 5–5).

The problems of fishing industries in Catholic countries have since been compounded by a decline in landings and sagging revenues, while the principal competitors of fish, meat and poultry, have been gaining. One study (4) revealed that landed prices of New England fish, on the average, were 12.5 percent lower than normal (extrapolated from the past ten-year pattern) as a result of decreased demand for fish. This short-run decline in the demand for New England fish (excluding lobsters, clams, oysters, and miscellaneous marine products) caused approximately $3 million in revenue losses to the industry over a seven-month period in 1966–1967.

The economic loss is distributed among many localities in Massachusetts, Maine, Rhode Island, and Connecticut. The greatest absolute and percentage loss of revenue occurred at New Bedford where fish most sensitive to a lower demand are landed.

The Hindu belief in the transmigration of souls has resulted in keeping alive large numbers of monkeys, rats, and cattle (which are regarded as sacred), causing both losses in crop production and the nation's agricultural capacity. Without this element of belief to which approximately 66 percent of India's population adheres, the type and spatial structure of economic landscape in India would perhaps be different.

Mining explorations in Tibet were discouraged for many years by religious objections. The efforts to harness solar energy in India have partially been dwarfed by Hindu belief in the Sun god. In Moslem cultures, the development of

105

a pork-raising industry does not seem to be promising because of religious values.

Religion may in some cases be weakened, but the habits, traditions, and customs developed by religious cultures still affect economic activity.

EDUCATION

Education refers to knowledge of physical and social sciences, humanities, the arts, self-awareness, and physical, social, economic, and political environments, and attainment of skills—all of which are learned and acquired. There is marked spatial variation both in quantity and quality of education (see Figure 5–6).

There is a strong correlation between a region's educational level and its economic productivity and progress. Harbison (15), employing an index of educational development that measured enrollment in secondary schools and universities, found that in seventy-five selected countries the coefficient of correlation between educational level and per capita gross national product (GNP) is .89. This means that approximately 90 percent of the variation between these countries' per capita GNP is explained by the education factor. This conclusion, although it requires further verification and qualification, indicates that the progress of a society depends significantly upon the educational level. Societies with relatively higher levels of education are likely to earn a larger share of the GNP from economic activities other than primary types; their productivity in primary activities also tends to be superior.

RACIAL STRUCTURES

Race, and especially the perception of the importance of race, are closely re-

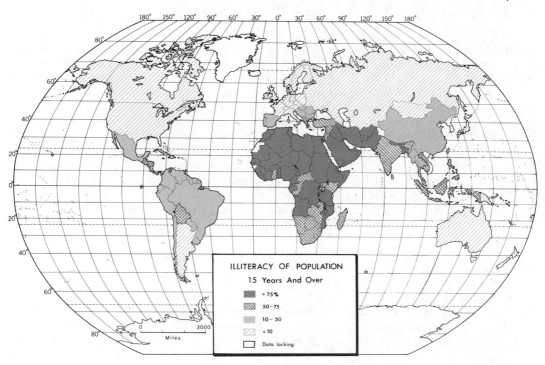

ILLITERACY OF POPULATION
15 Years And Over
> 75%
50 – 75
10 – 50
< 10
Data lacking

FIGURE 5–6

lated to the geography of religion. Our interest here does not lie in the physiological differences of races,[10] but rather in regional racial structure, its quantitative measurement, its perception by a society, and the impact of these aspects on economic phenomena. Kindelberger (19) states that a positive correlation exists between the percentage of white people in a nation and the per-capita income. He says that racial behavior is actually cultural behavior, which conditions the attitudes of a people toward occupation and income. These attitudes reflect a group's desire to progress. There does not, however, exist a positive relationship between race and type of economic activity. Dravidians consume more spices than Americans and hence engage in related economic activities; this reflects a cultural difference, rather than a racial one.

Attempts to measure racial factors in a region may face problems of:

1. Lack of data, especially in regions where racial enumeration and discrimination are illegal

2. The definition of racial stratifications

3. Difficulty of distinguishing between racial and social (class or caste) stratification

4. Construction of an index of statistical skills

The concept of race carries many ethical and political implications. These implications bear a relation to economic geography. When one considers the results of racial tensions, the loss of energy and capacity, and economic disruptions and

dislocations due to racial discrimination, its impact becomes evident.

FAMILY STRUCTURE

The meaning assigned to the family as a social unit or institution varies from society to society. An extended family with three or more generations living under the same roof differs in its economic impacts from a nuclear family involving one generation. Economic impacts of family structure are reflected through the social communication circle. Extended family structure may restrict migration, trade, flow of ideas, breaking of revered roles for the aged, and aspirations, and national patriotism. This type of social structure inhibits spatial communication and economic growth, and also generates ubiquitous congeries of economic units comprising basically primary types of economic activities.

Nuclear family structures, by virtue of the need for broader social life, tend to create a more plastic and mobile society. They encourage social changes that increase communication, literacy, globalism, rationality, and specificity in the relations of man to his environment. Also, the confidence and monetization of trade developed by the broader social circle brings specialization, which promotes easier transformation of agricultural societies into industrial and mass consumption societies.

These generalizations, supported by many anthropologists and sociologists including Robert Redfield (25), although providing a basic framework for the role of family as a social unit, need further verification and modification, taking into account mass communication systems, cultural heritage, number of households, and efforts to develop one national language.[11]

---

[10] Modern anthropological studies refute the centuries-old notion of physiological differences between races which also refutes the argument that occupational patterns are strictly related to climatic regions. The argument that blacks are better able to withstand the heat involved in cultivating cotton, sugar, and coffee is actually a cultural rather than physiological phenomenon.

[11] Over three-fourths of the world's states are multilingual.

PERSONALITY STRUCTURE

In addition to social indicators, there are other factors, grouped here under the term "personality structure," that affect man's economic behavior. These factors include an individual's attitudes, goals, aspirations, expectations, motivations, ethics, spirit of cooperation and competition, and the values he attaches to security, achievement, change, progress, and the like. Many of these bear the imprints of family structure, religion, education, and the perception of race within an area. Regardless of how these traits are classified or produced, their impact on the economic structure is frequently observed.

A paramount difficulty, however, exists in quantifying these personality aspects. Complicating the analysis is the fact that the standards by which people judge or evaluate their personality aspects are relative to their experience and level of economic development. For geographic analysis involving spatial series data, data comparability is highly important. Although this concern is applicable to all spatial data, the data on personality aspects are more susceptible to this problem.

Based on the responses of 20,000 people from thirteen representative nations (U.S., West Germany, Yugoslavia, Poland, Brazil, India, Nigeria, Israel, Egypt, Cuba, the Dominican Republic, Panama, and the Philippines), including 600 members of legislative bodies of some of the countries studied, Hadley Cantril (7) has presented interesting and informative data on personal values and character, personal economic situation, job situation, health, family, and political and social values. He concludes that the "concerns of people are patterned largely according to the phases of development they are in both culturally and ontologically within their society."

McClelland has attempted to measure human "achievement motivation" and its relation to the level of economic activity:

The "achievement motive" is ordinarily measured by performing a "content analysis" on imaginative thought. The scoring criteria for the "content analysis" were derived by comparing the thought processes of people under the influence of achievement motivation with the thought processes of people not under its influence. "Thought processes" were sampled by asking subjects to write imaginative stories to pictures. It was found that they introduced more ideas of a certain kind into their stories when their motivation to achieve—to do well—was aroused than when it was not aroused. An objective coding definition has been worked out for detecting these "ideas" with high agreement among different observers. Nearly all of the "ideas" can be classified under the heading of "desiring to do well" or "competing with a standard of excellence." This then became the scoring definition for a variable which was named technically *n*-achievement score for an individual is simply a sum of the number of instances of achievement "ideas" or images and their subtypes, and the score for a group of individuals is some measure of central tendency (the average, the mode) of the score of individuals who make up the group. In this way, it can be determined, for example, that the average *n*-achievement of a group of teen-age German boys is slightly but significantly lower than the average *n*-achievement of a carefully matched group of American boys, or that American boys from lower class background have lower average *n*-achievement than boys from middle class backgrounds.[12]

[12] D. C. McClelland, "Community Development and the Nature of Human Motivation: Some Implications of Recent Research," paper presented to the 1957 Conference on Community Development and National Change, Center for International Studies, M.I.T.

McClelland found a positive correlation between *n*-achievement and economic growth and claims that by using the *n*-achievement measure for various regions the level of economic activity can be explained or predicted.

The analysis presented in this chapter is not of empirical rigor, but is a conceptualization of social frameworks, which play a part in explaining the spatial variability of economic activities in terms of type and level.

references

1. Abler, R.; Adams, J. S.; and Gould, P. *Spatial Organization: The Geographer's View of the World*. Englewood Cliffs, N.J.: Prentice-Hall, 1971.

2. Adelman, Irma, and Morris, Cynthia T. *Society, Politics, and Economic Development: A Quantitative Approach*. Baltimore: The Johns Hopkins Press, 1967.

3. Bauer, R. A., ed. *Social Indicators*. Cambridge: Massachusetts Institute of Technology, 1966.

4. Bell, Frederick W. "Economic Impact of the Abolition of Meatless ·Fridays." *New England Business Review* (December 1967).

5. Brown, Lawrence A., and Longbrake, David B. "Migration Flows in Intraurban Space: Place Utility Considerations." *Annals of the Association of American Geographers* 60 (June 1970): 368–384.

6. Bensen, P. H. *Religion in Contemporary Culture: A Study of Religion Through Social Science*. New York: Harper & Row, 1960.

7. Cantril, Hadley. *Patterns of Human Concerns*. New Brunswick, N.J.: Rutgers University Press, 1965.

8. Caruso, Douglas, and Palm, Risa. "Social Space and Social Place." *The Professional Geographer* 25 (August 1973): 221–225.

9. Dahl, Robert. *Who Governs?* New Haven: Yale University Press, 1961.

10. Dikshit, Ramesh D. "Geography and Federalism." *Annals of the Association of American Geographers* 61 (March 1971): 97–115.

11. Dodo, Robert, J. "The Use of Speculative Social Thought in Geographic Research." *The Professional Geographer* 23 (October 1971): 295–297.

12. Dye, Thomas R. *Politics, Economics, and the Public: Policy Outcomes in the American States*. Chicago: Rand McNally, 1966.

13. Fisher, J. L. *Resource Development in the Public Interest*. Washington, D.C.: Resources for the Future, 1965.

14. Hagen, Everett E. *On the Theory of Social Change: How Economic Growth Begins*. Homewood, Ill.: Dorsey Press, 1962.

15. Harbison, Frederick. "Education for Development." *Scientific American* 209 (September 1963): 140–147.

16. Hartshorn, Truman A. "The Spatial Structure of Socioeconomic Development in the Southeast: 1950–1960." *Geographical Review* 61 (April 1971): 265–283.

17. Hauser, Philip M. "Demographic Dimensions of World Politics." In T. Morgan and G. W. Betz, eds. *Economic Development: Readings in Theory and Practice*. Belmont, Calif.: Wadsworth Publishing Co., 1969.

18. Katz, Elihu, and Lazarsfeld, Paul F. *Personal Influence*. Part 1. New York: The Free Press, 1964.

19. Kindleberger, C. P. *Economic Development*. 2nd ed. New York: McGraw-Hill Book Co., 1965.

20. Lipset, Seymour M. *Political Man: The Social Bases of Politics*. New York: Doubleday & Co., 1959.

21. Lowry, Mark. "Race and Socioeconomic Well-Being: A Geographical Analysis of the Mississippi Case." *Geographical Review* 60 (October 1970): 511–528.

22. McClelland, D. C. "Community Development and the Nature of Human Motivation: Some Implications of Recent Research." Paper presented to the Conference on Community Development and National Change, Center for International Studies, M.I.T., 1957. Mimeographed.

23. Oxtoby, F. E. "The Role of Political Factors in the Virgin Islands Watch Industry." *Geographical Review* 60 (October 1970): 463–474.

24. Reagan, M. D. *Politics, Economics, and the General Welfare.* Glenview, Ill.: Scott, Foresman Co., 1965.

25. Redfield, Robert. *The Primitive World and Its Transformation.* Ithaca, N.Y.: Cornell University Press, 1953.

26. Rostow, W. W. *The Stages of Economic Growth: A Non-Communist Manifesto.* Cambridge University Press, 1960.

27. Schultz, T. W. "Investment in Human Capital." *American Economic Review* (March 1961). Reprinted in Teodore Morgan, George Betz, and N. K. Choudry, eds. *Readings in Economic Development.* Belmont, Calif.: Wadsworth Publishing Co., 1963.

28. Soja, Edward W. "The Political Organization of Space." *Association of American Geographers.* Commission on College Geography, Resource Paper No. 8, Washington, D.C., 1971.

29. Sommers, Lawrence M., and Gade, Ole. "The Social Impact of Government Decisions on Postwar Economic Change in North Norway." *Annals of The Association of American Geographers* 61 (September 1971).

30. Stanley, William R. "Transport Expansion in Liberia." *Geographical Review* 60 (October 1970): 529–547.

31. Tawney, R. H. *Religion and the Rise of Capitalism.* New York: Harcourt, Brace and World, 1952.

technological
framework

6

6

The sum total of the knowledge, skills, tools, and techniques developed to satisfy human wants shall be used as a generalized definition of *technology* here. Human wants may be divided into three parts: those related to utility, those related to "know-how," and the final consumer items. While the outer limits of technological feasibility are determined by knowledge of nature, the selection and design of technology is controlled by social, political, and largely economic criteria. Societies choose from an array of available or conceivable technological options to suit specific social and cultural requirements. Any change in these criteria will change the technology and its related knowledge.

KNOWLEDGE

Knowledge is developed, learned, and acquired through mental processes, particularly through the ability to store, retrieve, and transmit information. Knowledge is a consequence of man's desire to attain goals; man learns through experience, and experience is a result of mental processes.

Human experience in cumulative form is enormous and complex. Only when it is sorted, organized, and related to the environment does it become useful knowledge. *Knowledge is the set of human experiences that is properly sorted, organized, and related to the environment*. In this context, knowledge is only an instrument applied to social activities to achieve social goals.[1]

Social goals are dynamic and culture-oriented. A society's desire for knowledge is a consequence of its desire to understand, satisfy curiosity, explain, intervene, modify, control, predict, and improve its environment. Culture affects spatial and time variations related to resources, and thus affects knowledge in the same way.

Learned experience or stored information is the building block for constructing knowledge. The methods of gaining knowledge are numerous, ranging from "trial and error" to scientific methods.[2] A particular methodology is a function of not only the type of experience and cost restraints, but also of the already existing state of knowledge. However, the scientific method is the most commonly and widely used by almost all branches of learning. The scientific method is generally recognized to include the following steps:

1. A lucid statement or definition of the problem
2. A review and evaluation of related knowledge or literature
3. Selection of appropriate analytical tools
4. Construction of testable or reputable hypotheses, which yields provisional solutions of the problem
5. Procurement of data
6. Data synthesis and analysis
7. Testing of hypotheses
8. Derivation of conclusions
9. Recommendations
10. Distribution of results

Not all research endeavors necessarily follow every step listed. The particular

---

[1] This definition of knowledge accords with the "instrumentalist" school of thought, which holds that knowledge is only an instrument or means to an end, the end being human evaluation and purposes. "Nominalism" is another related theory, which says the meaning of words, which signifies knowledge, lies in the conventions that define their use.

[2] Other methods include generalization from experience, logic, magic, reliance on authority, and deductive and inductive reasoning. These methods are not exclusive of each other; for example, the scientific method partially employs mechanisms of inductive and deductive reasoning and logic.

steps and sequence followed depend upon the character and scope of the research project.

SKILLS

Knowledge precedes mastery of skills. Skills refer to the capabilities of an individual laborer that can be used to perform a productive task in the economy. Some skills are acquired by short periods of observation, while others require considerable training and specificity. A conventional classification of skills includes: unskilled, semi-skilled, skilled, administrative, organizational, clerical, and professional. The composition and relative level of skills found in a labor force are functions of the amount of applied knowledge, social processes of diffusing knowledge, social objectives, and economic demands for those skills. It is possible that poverty of skills may occur with an abundance of knowledge. In that case, the society lacks an adequate educational process and perhaps has not clarified its objectives and demands.

The United States has developed vast amounts of new knowledge and, more important, readily translated that knowledge into skills. Today the average American farmer produces enough food to adequately feed himself and approximately forty other people. Since World War II, the productivity of American agriculture has increased at twice the rate of industrial productivity. Scientists and extension agents based at land-grant colleges and universities in the United States have helped to realize this technological marvel. The amounts spent on research and development (R & D) by industry and the federal government have improved many skills. In 1972, approximately $28 billion was spent in the U.S. for R & D, of which the government accounted for over 70 percent.

Patent law tends to limit the dissemination of technology, although several government agencies and departments, as well as private organizations, diffuse technical information. For example, the National Aeronautics and Space Administration (NASA) has fashioned an elaborate computerized system to facilitate information transfer, to use either to develop physical capital (tools) or to improve the labor force. The following are a few examples of spinoffs (3):

1. An electromagnetic hammer was developed that removes dents from sheet metal in microseconds without structural weakening. It is proving useful in metal fabrication and repair (automobile repair shops, for example).

2. Using principles of the Lunar-Walker, the means of locomotion of the moon's first earth visitors, a walking chair has been devised that allows paraplegics to go up and down curbs and even climb stairs.

3. Spray-on electrodes were developed to monitor the heart action of test pilots and astronauts. They are now being used for children's heart examinations and for electrocardiograms because they do not slip and provide good electrical contact. Their potential use is impressive; for instance, coupled with a tiny transmitter they can keep a constant check on heart patients and alert a nurse if any trouble occurs.

4. A paint for the outside of space crafts, which is unusually resistant to heat and scratching, was developed. It has obvious commercial possibilities.

Not too long ago, the whole thrust of government-supported research was to win a war; if peacetime uses could be found after victory, they amounted to windfall benefits. Now, however, any knowledge gained for military use, space exploration, and problem solving is systematically gathered, evaluated, and disseminated.

The beneficiaries of this technological spinoff include business interests, hospitals, state and local governments, and, most important, educational and vocational institutions. In short, the entire society benefits.

The degree of effectiveness and substitution of skills has great bearing on the spatial differentiation of technology and, consequently, on economic activity. The effectiveness of substitution depends on the suitability of skills for employment opportunities, the level of specialization, and the availability of relevant equipment and tools and their spatial mobility. Regions with incongruent skills may produce sets of economic activities quite different from those that otherwise might be expected.

TOOLS

Tools, technically referred to as physical capital, are labor-saving or labor-aiding objects used in human activities, which may or may not be directly operated by man. They are an extension of man's efforts and include hand tools, automated tools, machines and equipment, and buildings.

The determination of level and composition and how tools are acquired has long baffled social scientists, and a thorough treatment of it requires a textbook itself. Only salient features are pointed out here.

The development of tools is a function of social objectives, knowledge, material resources, the relative size of the labor force and its entrepreneurial and organizational skills, and the arrangements of international trade and aid. Social objectives provide the basic initiative and direction to attain tools.

Analysis of alternatives of material resources may suggest various choices. The relative quality of labor points to substitutional and complemental support for the achievement of objectives. For example, the U.S. depends on foreign nations for a major share of domestic needs for copper, lead, tin, cobalt, alumi-

num, columbium, tantalite, nickel, tungsten, and uranium, all of which are important to the implementation of objectives. Cobalt is used in high-speed tools, jet turbines, and atomic power; columbium and tantalite are used in guided missiles, rockets, and apollos; uranium is an important fuel for generating nuclear energy.

TECHNIQUE

Technique refers to the operational or innovative aspect of technology. It is a set of instructions or steps: a computer program, convocation exercises, cookbook recipe, registration procedure, mechanical steps in operating a machine, etc. Techniques appear as choices at various levels of economic activities. At initial stages, the choices may be few, but they multiply at succeeding levels.

Energy may be generated by thermal, hydro, solar, and nuclear techniques. The choice of a technique of power generation also depends on other factors:

1.   *Locations* need to be evaluated in terms of spatial distribution of demand for the power, transportation cost of inputs and outputs, relative economic efficiency, and long-run considerations of the supply of raw materials to the plant.

2.   *Size* affects the economies of scale and total transportation cost. The diseconomies of scale may be outweighed by the economies realized through lower transportation cost associated with smaller units (if possible) located in proximity to demand centers.

3.   *Rate of change* of the substitution between tools and labor, which may capitalize savings during peak and slump periods, is a factor.

4.   *Continuity*, i.e., a plant may be run on one or multiple shifts to achieve a better substitution between labor and physical capital; when the interest rates are high resulting in higher cost of the physical

capital, multiple shifts offer an economical choice in substituting labor for capital.

5. *Plant life and maintenance* reflects the overhead and operating costs.

6. *Input mix,* or the choice between various proportions of different inputs, is made with a view to increasing economic efficiency.

7. *Product mix* is concerned with economic efficiency.

These choices can be further expanded, depending on the type and level of economic activity. Each power source envelops a relatively different set of technological choices.

That technique can often be partially formulated from accumulative and diverse knowledge gives it a distinctive meaning. For example, building and use of a dolly to transport heavy objects is a technique. A person may be able to figure out how to build and use the dolly based on knowledge of the weight of the objects, physics of inclined planes, strength of material to be used, the distance of hauling, texture of the floor, etc.

THE PROCESS OF TECHNOLOGICAL CHANGE

It is widely recognized that technological progress is the major factor that accounts for the difference between medieval and modern standards of living, or between economically developed and less economically developed societies. Why does a certain period or place excel over another in technological progress?

Technological progress occurs over a spectrum of changing "knowledge-accumulating" and "knowledge-utilizing" activities. Conventionally speaking, the former refers to discovery and the latter to innovation. However, these conventional terms do not adequately reflect the total process of technological progress. Contrary to popular thought that

technical or scientific discovery occurs in an unplanned and unpredicted fashion, the process encompasses integrated and interdependent involvement of three broadly identifiable activities: basic research, applied research, and dissemination commonly summed up under the label research and development.

TECHNOLOGICAL DEVELOPMENT

In theory, technology is international in its occurrence, scope, and imitation. However, the sociopolitical facts, attitudes, and values remain stubbornly national, reflecting a spatial and time variability in technology. This variability is a function of many factors, particularly social objectives, relative scarcity of resources, planning, and economic systems.

Objectives are a product of a multitude of forces, often spearheaded by a political process. Certain objectives, such as an improved standard of living or economic progress, are assumed to be nearly universal and only vary in intensity and scope. Other objectives are quite distinctive, such as military power, dominance, and prestige.

The seventeenth-, eighteenth-, and nineteenth-century European drive to conquer the great centers of wealth, the "gorgeous East" and the South American El Dorado, encouraged technological progress in defense, transportation, and production. The struggle for power and empire was reflected by the invention of new methods of transportation, resources, production, and innovations in money and marketing. The goals of conquering outer space and being "first on the moon" have not only produced a highly specialized technology, but have also induced a broad spectrum of research and development in numerous economic activities and resulted in a variety of new consumer goods.

The relative scarcity of resources

115

strongly influences technological progress. A basic economic principle states that demand for a relatively small supply of a resource results in increased price and vice versa.[3] An increased price gives man two choices: (1) to substitute the relatively scarce resource with something cheaper; or (2) to increase the resource, which would require increasing the productive efficiency through different input proportions or through affecting the quantity or quality of the resource. For either of these choices, man must resort to technology.

Automation, for example, is the result of an effort to substitute machines for the higher cost of labor. Also, a more skilled labor force may be realized by equipping the labor resource with additional tools and skills. These conditions are quite common in the modern Western world.

It is not surprising that after reading Malthus' "An Essay on the Principle of Population as It Affects the Future Improvements of Society" (1798), Thomas Carlyle called economics "the dismal science," and William Godwin remarked that Malthus and David Ricardo had converted enthusiasm and progress appeal, churned by the stunning inventions and innovations of the 18th century, into gloom and despair. Both Ricardo and Malthus argued that material resources are fixed, while the population increases in a geometric progression, resulting in eventual starvation. They apparently did not consider that material resources can be increased, improved, or substituted by application of technology. Karl Marx won the praise of many intellectuals by articulately demonstrating how technological advances could increase material resources, resulting in highly unequal distribution of wealth and in class conflicts.

Rewards, in terms of related technological advances, are often conferred on a society that recognizes the value of technology. The establishment of patent rights,[4] copyrights, and merit or incentive systems are examples of social recognition and reward. It has been argued that patent and merit policies may have adverse effects. The patent laws were originally conceived within the context of nineteenth-century laissez-faire philosophy to encourage the independent inventor working in his woodshed or small shop. Now, however, about 60 percent of all patents in the United States are issued directly to corporations. This diminishes innovative competition, and competition tends to promote technological change and advancement.

Insecurity on the part of individuals, which is caused by internal or external forces, at times tends to promote technological progress. Many societies, in efforts to avoid unpleasant feelings of insecurity, tend to work harder, seek greater efficiency, and to invent newer techniques and tools.

Planning is a more recent factor, which provides for technological change through systematic programming. In the Soviet Union and some other totalitarian societies, the planning factor of technology is common. Also, among the member governments of the Organization for Economic Cooperation and Development (OECD),[5] the concept of planning for "science policy" is fast replacing an older idea that technological

---

[3] An increase in price may occur because of an improved bargaining position for labor or for corporate monopolies. Under these circumstances, technological progress may not be as great (*see* chapter 4).

[4] In the U.S., a patent is a grant of a seventeen-year monopoly to an inventor, giving him the right to exclude all others from duplicating his discovery for use or sale.

[5] The OECD is a twenty-member international organization designed to foster permanent cooperation between member countries in order to harmonize national policies. Member countries include the U.S., U.K., France, W. Germany, Canada, Japan, Greece, Norway, and others.

116

innovation is a purely random activity. For example, to promote the systematic programming of technological progress in Italy, Spain, Turkey, and Ireland, OECD suggests the following planning process:

1. Making a complete inventory of all scientific and technical resources, including scientists and engineers
2. Making an economic analysis to determine research priorities
3. Formulating programs for allocating inventoried resources among selected priorities
4. Construction of a detailed plan for the development of all aspects and phases of pure research, applied research, and blueprinting

A meaningful coordination among all institutions is also suggested by OECD.

By virtue of its operation, an economic system may affect technological progress. A competitive economic system tends to force progress and economic change. Competitors force each other to change, resulting in variety and improved quality of goods and services as alternative choices to cutting prices. To produce variety and quality, technology must be favorably affected.

RESEARCH PROCESS

The previously discussed factors are important to the level of technology in respect to the knowledge-accumulating and knowledge-utilizing processes of basic research, applied research, and innovation.

Basic knowledge-accumulation involves a search for the basic fact or relationship, which may itself serve as a source for applied research and innovation. The process often involves highly trained scientists. Although the results of their engagement may potentially benefit all societies, political frameworks may confine the results of their activity to only certain places. Basic researchers also

benefit from the problems associated with practical applications of and reactions to basic knowledge. Since basic research often has no immediate application, its effect on economic activity is of little significance unless applied research and blueprinting processes evolve from it. This depends on how effectively basic research findings are spun-off to potential users. The spinning-off process involves an array of activities: cataloging, classifying, printing, and disseminating.

Applied research infuses basic knowledge with practical considerations. Thus, the motivational force behind applied research, contrasted to basic research that appears only in intangible forms, is the "tangible" return. Such returns may be physical products, tools, solutions to problems, or explanation. The activity of applied research is usually greater than basic research. If basic research is an international commodity and flows freely between societies, poorer regions then tend to concentrate primarily on applied research to solve local problems. The results of applied research also serve as feedback to basic research.

Innovation or *blueprinting* focuses on the detailed application of basic and applied research outputs. This process adapts basic and applied knowledge into techniques, plans, and consumer and investment products. The motives of direct application and diffusion are the distinguishing features of innovation. With tools of basic and applied knowledge, county agents quite often are engaged in innovation endeavors while adapting and diffusing knowledge to a particular situation, factory, farm, or home. Entrepreneurs, too, with the assistance of their technostructure, practice blueprinting. The practical planning profession is another instance where various bits of knowledge are brought together into an integrated whole, resulting in a technique or plan to effectively achieve the goals of the planning area.

117

To summarize, all three of the processes involve inputs and outputs. The processes are differentiated by the particular motivation of research and the character of the inputs and outputs. The fixity and certainty seen in actual production processes, however, are not present in the same degree. There is always an uncertainty whether knowledge will emerge, and, if it does, there is doubt about its character and usefulness in achieving a society's goals.

Assuming technological development is measured by the dollar amount spent on R & D, the varying allocation among basic, applied, and innovative research would produce variability over space and time, even though over all of these places and during all of the time period the same dollar amount is spent. The varying allocation between these research activities will be reflected in the relative productivity and efficiency of the economic activities. However, the actual application of technology would produce regional differentiation in productivity. For example, productivity in the U.S. economy, whether measured as output-per-man-hour or by the more comprehensive output-per-unit of total input, has been advancing at half the rate of the previous two decades. The slowdown has been sharper and lasted longer than that usually associated with final stages of an economic boom and a recession in economic activity. Figure 6–1 shows the smallest improvement in output-per-man-hour occurred in the U.S. This is largely due to the slower and fewer applications of technology to production processes.

TECHNOLOGY AND ECONOMIC ACTIVITY

Technology is commonly thought to result from specific efforts or routine roles

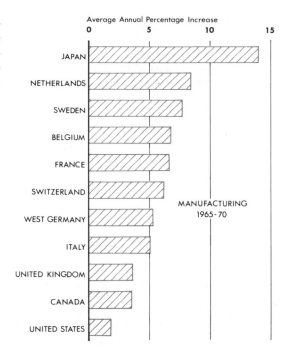

FIGURE 6–1 *Output-Per-Man-Hour*

of specific segments of a society. Technological activities are not confined to one segment of society, although one may produce more than another. More important, the knowledge-accumulation process depends, directly or indirectly, on all facets of social activities; therefore, technology affects the level and spatial dispersion of economic activities. The impact of technology upon economic institutions and activities is so significant and complex that it requires comprehensive studies of the overall relationships. Only the basic relationships are highlighted here.

CHANGE

All technology reflects change, but all change may not yield newer technology. Technological change may be an initiating force that alters not only the level and structure of economic activity, but also socioeconomic institutions. Techno-

118

logical change, as opposed to social change, is more readily accepted by society and thus acts as a potent and practical force for causing eventual social change. Social change is often resisted because it directly affects the established patterns of social interaction and behavior.

For example, besides affecting the production techniques of many economic sectors and consequently affecting regional differentiation, the technology of outer space has acted as a social diverter of various human activities. President John F. Kennedy's innovative idea of the Peace Corps has been labeled a "safety valve" for helping to reduce restlessness among youth; it offers an opportunity for the constructive use of energies of students who want to help others. The substitution of iron and coal for stone and wood, respectively, were powerful initiators of change for the entire spectrum of economic, social, and political activities. James Watt's steam engine of the eighteenth century produced diverse applications and caused modifications and transformation of economic and social aspects of society. Thus, it is logical to conclude that technology, as an entering wedge of economic change, has nourished the evolution of capitalism. Many contend that technological change is the basic source of economic progress in any society.

Technological change is interdependent, cumulative, and irreversible. The invention of the steam engine, for example, promoted new developments in textile, iron, and other types of economic activities that employed mechanical power. And, without the boring machine invented by John Wilkinson, the ultimate success of Watt's engine would perhaps have never become a reality.

Being cumulative in its effects, technology acts as a multiplier of economic activity, producing a conglomerative complex. Nearly every technological

change, irrespective of where it occurs, provides a springboard from which greater leaps may be made in other economic activities.

The irreversibility of technological change yields promise of continued economic progress. A given technological change necessitates other changes; the process is never reversed. The irreversible character of technology serves as a strong force for sustained economic growth of a society.

ECONOMIC PROGRESS

Each society and its respective technology exhibits a distinctive spatial pattern of economic phenomena.[6] With technology, material resources can be increased through new techniques of procuring resources, through finding feasible substitutes, or through changing proportions of resource-mix or product-mix. The reorganization or allocation of resources may result in efficiency, yielding larger output-per-unit of input. Labor often becomes more productive with additional education, training, and apprenticeship experiences. However, a proper balance between liberal and vocational education must be struck to achieve the best use of technology and skills. Change in techniques of production, marketing, and distribution may result in greater demand, which is realized through lower delivery prices, which may further lower the production cost as a consequence of economies of scale.

[6] Lewis Mumford in his *Technics and Civilization* (New York: Harcourt, Brace and World, 1963) identified three broad, overlapping, and penetrating phases, each with a distinctive technological complex. The *eotechnic* is typified by a wood, wind, and water power complex. The *paleotechnic* is associated with a coal, steam, and iron complex. And the *neotechnic* is identified with elements such as electricity, internal combustion engines, alloys, and chemicals. Each phase is thought to embody a distinct social and economic arrangement of human activities.

119

references

1. Barbour, Ian G. *Western Man and Environmental Ethics: Attitudes Toward Nature and Technology.* Reading, Mass.: Addison-Wesley, 1973.

2. Basiuk, Victor. *Technology and World Power.* New York: Foreign Policy Association, 1970.

3. Bernard, H. Russell, and Pelto, Pertti J. *Technology and Social Change.* New York: Macmillan, 1972.

4. Briggs, Asa. "Technology and Economic Development." *Scientific American* 209 (September 1963): 52–61.

5. Bronwell, Arthur B. *Science and Technology in the World of the Future.* New York: John Wiley & Sons, 1970.

6. Brozen, Y. "Invention, Innovation, and Imitation." *American Economic Review* (May 1951): 239–59.

7. Calder, Nigel. *Technopolis: Social Control of the Uses of Science.* New York: Simon and Schuster, 1970.

8. Capron, William M., ed. *Technological Change in Regulated Industries.* Washington, D.C.: The Brookings Institution, 1971.

9. Cardwell, Donald S. C. *Turning Points In Western Technology: A Study of Technology, Science, and History.* New York: Science History Publications, 1972.

10. Carter, Anne P. *Structural Change in the American Economy.* Cambridge, Mass.: Harvard University Press, 1970.

11. Chase Manhattan Bank. "Space Research Comes Down to Earth." *Business in Brief* (December 1966).

12. Clarke, Arthur C. *Profiles of the Future: An Inquiry Into the Limits of the Possible.* New York: Harper & Row, 1973.

13. Dewhurst, J. F. *America's Needs and Resources: A New Survey.* New York: Twentieth Century Fund, 1955.

14. Fellner, William. "Measures of Technological Progress in the Light of Recent Growth Models." *American Economic Review* 57 (December 1967).

15. Gabor, Dennis. *Innovations: Scientific, Technological and Social.* London: Oxford University Press, 1970.

16. Higbee, Edward C. *A Question of Priorities: New Strategies For Our Urbanized World.* New York: William Morrow, 1970.

17. Kaufman, Richard H. *The Technology Gap: U.S. and Europe.* New York: Frederick A. Praeger, 1970.

18. Kuhns, William. *The Post-Industrial Prophets: Interpretations of Technology.* New York: Weybright and Talley, 1971.

19. Leiss, William. *The Domination of Nature.* New York: George Braziller, 1972.

20. Mesthene, Emmanuel G. *Technological Change: Its Impact on Man and Society.* Cambridge, Mass.: Harvard University Press, 1970.

21. Nelson, Richard R.; Peck, Merton J.; and Kacheck, Edward D. *Technology, Economic Growth and Public Policy.* Washington, D.C.: The Brookings Institution, 1967.

22. Nikolaieff, George A., ed. *Computers and Society.* New York: H. W. Wilson Co., 1970.

23. Piel, Gerard. *The Acceleration of History.* New York: Alfred A. Knopf, 1972.

24. Schwartz, Eugene S. *Overkill: The Decline of Technology in Modern Civilization.* Chicago: Quadrangle Books, 1971.

25. Spencer, Daniel L. *Technology Gap in Perspective: Strategy of International Technology Transfer.* New York: Spartan Books, 1970.

26. Teich, Albert H. *Technology and Man's Future.* New York: St. Martin's Press, 1972.

27. Thring, Meredith W. *Man, Machines, and Tomorrow.* London: Routledge and Kegan Paul, 1973.

28. Tilton, John E. *International Diffusion of Technology: The Case of Semi-Conductors.* Washington, D.C.: The Brookings Institution, 1971.

29. Vacca, Roberto. *The Coming Dark Age.* New York: Doubleday, 1973.

30. Willia, C. S., ed. *Toward Century 21: Technology, Society, and Human Values.* New York: Basic Books, 1970.

III

PRIMARY
ECONOMIC
ACTIVITY

CHAPTERS

7 Location Theory of Primary
  Activities
8 World Agricultural Systems
9 Fishing
10 Forests and Forest Products
11 Mining

introduction

In Part II, we enlarged upon the conceptual model of man as the dynamic agent of change within the global system. Specifically, we explored how various frameworks within this model, which are common to all societies, are contrived in order to promote and achieve social goals.

In Part III, we relate the frameworks to the phenomena of primary production. Primary activity location theory, an integrative statement of the relevant variables identified under the frameworks, is the subject of chapter 7. Chapters 8 through 11 apply the theoretical material by describing and analyzing a selected set of primary economic activities.

Primary economic activities embrace all activities associated with producing or extracting from nature and with the rearing and reproducing of animal life. Agriculture, animal husbandry, forestry, hunting and fishing, and mining are examples of primary economic activities.

location theory
of primary activities

7

7

Numerous theories and hypotheses attempt to explain the location patterns and characteristics of economic activities. This chapter mainly concerns activities commonly referred to as primary economic activities, with an emphasis on agriculture. The specific model developed here is associated with Johann Heinrich Von Thünen's theory, initially developed in the early 19th century from his observations of agricultural landscapes and marketing practices in Germany.

Von Thünen, like every theorist, sought to explain general patterns, rather than specific, more heterogeneous observations. By concentrating on the general, Von Thünen, among others, has allowed us to acquire a more substantial understanding of a global pattern, while including significant principles that bear on local and regional patterns. This attention to general processes and patterns, however, is accompanied by a diminution of some factors which, in some parts of the world, may be the more important factors.

Like any thesis of reality, Von Thünen's theory of the location of agricultural activities is based on a set of ideal conditions—conditions which make the theory more operable but also which result in a highly abstract model. Our concern initially is to analyze Von Thünen's general theory and model and then to illustrate how several modifications render it applicable as an explanatory tool.

THE VON THÜNEN THEORY

Von Thünen suggested that "if a laboratory could be constructed according to

several specific conditions, then agricultural endeavors would tend to locate in a specific, determinable, and predictable pattern." The conditions Von Thünen imposed to construct his model are discussed in the following paragraphs.

ELEMENTS OF VON THÜNEN'S MODEL

Isolated Area. The existence of an isolated area consisting of one city and its agricultural hinterland. This condition is imposed initially to reduce the number of variables. The agricultural hinterland affords opportunities for city residents to acquire food, fiber, and building materials. The city is the market for products from the agricultural hinterland; it receives products from no other area, and vice versa. The price received by farmers is the market price, which is set by the local market (see chapter 4).

These conditions do not allow the "isolated city" to trade with any other hinterland or city, any farmer to trade with any other farmer, or farmers to trade with any other city. Thus, the residents of the agricultural hinterland and the city are forced into an exchange economy whereby agricultural products must come from the adjacent hinterland and urban residents must buy them. If we move to the "real" world equivalent, it is obvious that generally the residents of a city may acquire their food and fiber from any agricultural hinterland, even if it is not the most adjacent one.

Homogeneous Physical Environment. The hinterland has a homogeneous physical environment within which there is no variation in slope, soil, climate, drainage, and so on. By imposing this condition, Von Thünen avoids the necessity of contending with minor or major variations in the physical environment and so is better able to contend with the elements that are most applicable to an isolated economy.

Rational Producers. The hinterland is occupied by rational farmers who desire to maximize their profits per unit area and who are capable of adjusting their agricultural practices to the demands of the local market. For any one commodity, the production techniques are sufficiently similar so that production costs do not vary. "Maximization" of profit objective does not allow for the occurrence of farmers who would "just get along" or would be satisfied with a minimal profit. Obviously, there are differences in the attitudes of farmers from place to place; we analyze these attitudes in chapter 8.

Agricultural practices must be adjusted to the demands of the market because if farmers did not produce what the market desired, they would soon be operating at a loss and hence would quickly be put out of business. In order to continue a viable agricultural practice, farmers must occasionally change the type of plants or animals grown or the methods used to produce them.

One Mode of Transportation. The hinterland is traversed by only one means of land transportation and is equally accessible to all farmers; all products are carried by man, hauled by horses or oxen, or transported under their own power.

There are two prime variables in this set of conditions: 1) location of agricultural production units, or farms, and 2) variability of transport costs. Both variables are tied directly to a specific location in the area, the city or the market. From this summary, we may isolate four major concepts:

1. *Production costs* (PC), which vary from commodity to commodity but are the same for all farmers who grow the same commodity. These include expenditures for taxes, labor, seed, tools, maintenance, etc., which occur in association with production activities on the farm, including payment to

the entrepreneur for his own labor. Like all other costs, they are computed on a unit-area basis.

2. *Transportation costs* (TC), which vary from commodity to commodity, are computed on a unit-area basis and are proportional to the distance that commodities have to be moved from the farm to the market.

3. *Market price* (P), the price received by the farmer at the market after he has transported his crop there; this price is set by the market and must be adhered to by the farmer.

4. *Total revenue* (TR), the revenue computed by multiplying the quantity sold and the market price.

5. *Economic rent* (R), the total revenue per unit area of farmland which the farmer is left with after having paid production and transport costs. This is the value which all farmers seek to maximize.

The principal economic relationship between these four concepts is defined by the formula:

$$R = [TR - (PC + TC)].$$

ZONES OF LAND USE

Von Thünen's model is concerned primarily with the role that TC's play in allocating land resources between different agricultural uses at varying distances from market. Having recognized that TC's involve not only the transfer of produce to market but also the time, effort, and inconvenience associated with moving workers and supplies to and from various production sites, Von Thünen indicated that the first zone around his central city would be used to produce crops and livestock products that are highly perishable, heavy, or bulky to transport. Because of the tendency for wagon transportation costs to increase with distance, the lands located farther away would suffer an economic handicap which would dictate their use for enterprises involving lower transportation costs. Thus, as Figure 7–1A shows, the

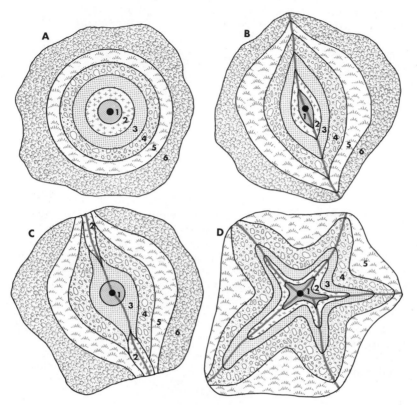

FIGURE 7–1 *Von Thünen's Model of Land Use at Varying Distances and Its Generalized Modifications*

first concentric zone around the city would be used mostly for gardens, truck crops, and some facilities needed for stall-fed milk cows and laying hens; all of these activities reflect intensive use, care, and high transportation costs.

The second zone would be used for forest products. Forest products once provided fuel and were the primary source of building materials. Since these products are both bulky and heavy to haul, it seemed reasonable to produce them near the city.

The second zone grades into the third, which in Von Thünen's model would be used for bulky and heavy crops, such as potatoes, root crops, and hay, and for grain or pasture grown in rotation with these crops. The third zone merges into the fourth zone where the primary crops are cereal grains, rotated with fallow or pasture. Zone five would be used primarily for grazing purposes and sheep and cattle produced or fed in this area would be driven to market. Lastly, the surrounding wilderness area would be used for possible hunting and trapping.

MODIFICATIONS OF THE VON THÜNEN MODEL

Modifications in Von Thünen's model may be made by adjusting various assumptions. For example, if one assumes that a navigable stream flows through the "isolated state," the water transportation facility will cause changes in land use. A series of adjustments may cause an *elongated* pattern to emerge, as suggested in Figure 7–1B. This change would be most pronounced for the forestry zone and lead to a situation where forest production is shifted farther away from the city along the navigable stream (see Figure 7–1C).

The introduction of additional improved transportation routes and carriers are likely to cause a *star-shaped* land-use pattern. Although the speed and variety of transportation processes have reduced transport costs and made it economical to use many areas for production, this would not have been practical in the past. However, Von Thünen's conclusion about the importance of TC's as a factor affecting land-use patterns still stands firm. Regardless of the type and sophistication of a transportation facility, there will always be a cost of overcoming *friction, gravitation,* and *loss of time* in moving goods and people.

Two conclusions involving economic rent can be drawn from Von Thünen's work: 1) R and TC are inversely related; the higher the R, the lower the TC, and vice versa. 2) The level of rent defines definite agricultural regions around the city; no crop will be grown beyond the radius where TC's completely consume rent costs.

Figure 7–2 illustrates economic rent as it relates to distance. The vertical line represents the monetary value of economic rent. The horizontal line represents distance from the isolated market (M) and has four arbitrarily chosen points: a, b, c, and d. The broken lines rising from a and b and intersecting the diagonal line show the relative economic rent to be derived by farmers operating at those points. At point c, the economic rent is zero; this is the break-even level

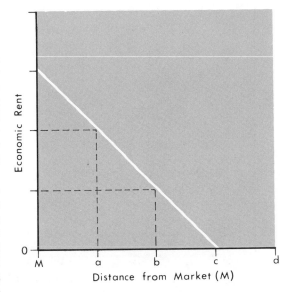

FIGURE 7–2 *Economic Rent Diagram: One Crop*

of production for a commodity with this economic rent–distance relationship.

Considering Figure 7–2, farmers wishing to maximize economic rent obviously would attempt to get as close to the market as possible. In a highly competitive situation where farmers are mobile and possess sufficient capital over a period of time, the more efficient individuals compete for locations closer to the market and the least efficient are located at distances farther from the market. Thus, in the ideal situation, farmers in the bc zone are less successful than those in other zones closer to the market.

This process, extended to several crops with different economic rents, is illustrated in Figure 7–3. The gradient of each of the three diagonal lines, E, F, and G, is different. E, with the steepest rent gradient incurs the highest transportation costs and reaches its break-even point before the other two crops. G, with a lesser economic rent near the market but with a lower rent gradient, extends over a greater distance. In the maximiza-

127

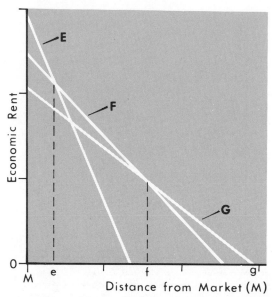

FIGURE 7–3 *Economic Rent–Distance Relationships: Three Crops*

tion of economic rent, each of the three crops is allocated to specific zones along the distance line Mg.

Since the economic rent process extends outward from the market in all

directions, we can make a simple rotation of Figure 7–3 at point M to transform the graphic rent process to geographic space. This is shown in Figure 7–4. The very high transport costs of E confine it to a zone very close to the market. The slightly lower transport cost of commodity F results in its production on the outer margins of zone E, but within the lower rent gradient of crop G.

Figure 7–5A shows a more complete image of the original Von Thünen model of agricultural location resulting in other modifications as illustrated earlier in Figure 7–1A–D. The general pattern from the market to the outer limits is one of decreasing economic rent. An acre devoted to market gardening or dairying will yield a higher rent than an acre devoted to grain farming, livestock grazing, or potentially useable forests. Market gardening and dairying, which involve high inputs of labor, capital, fertilizer, and yield highly perishable crops with a high demand, can command a high market price. In a competitive situation, they

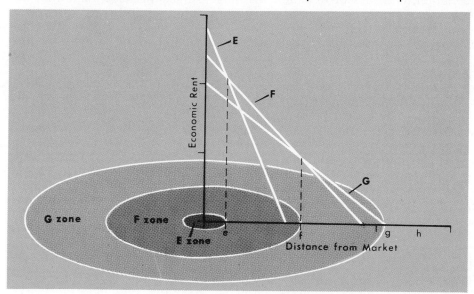

FIGURE 7–4 *Transformation of Economic Processes to Geographic Space*

128

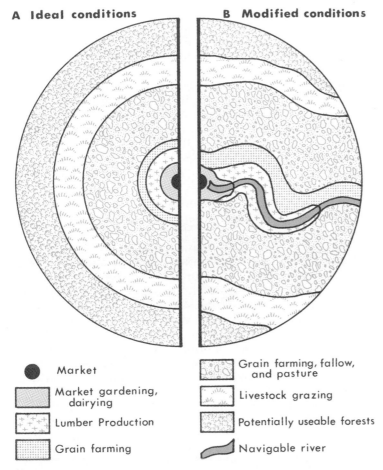

A **Ideal conditions**
B **Modified conditions**

● Market	Grain farming, fallow, and pasture
Market gardening, dairying	Livestock grazing
Lumber Production	Potentially useable forests
Grain farming	Navigable river

FIGURE 7–5 *Von Thünen Model: Ideal and Modified Conditions*

occupy the most favorable (closest to the market) locations. The transport costs for these commodities are relatively high. Thus, the economic rent gradient for both is steep and we may expect them to be located adjacent to markets. Later we will discuss the influence of more rapid transportation systems, mobile-refrigeration units, and suburbanization on market locations.

The second ring in Von Thünen's model, as noted earlier, is devoted to forest products, including lumber and firewood. In an earlier urban setting with

a low production cost, high transport cost, but high market value, it is logical to assume that wood products would be located near the market. However, in almost all instances this zone is now non-existent because lumbering practices have exhausted the supply in this zone.

Farmers in the next two zones are associated with grain production; in the nearer zone without fallow, and in the farther, with fallow. On the next to the outer ring is commercial livestock grazing, which generally has a low-per-acre yield, low transport cost, but good

129

market value. (Prior to rail and truck transport transit cattle were driven to market on hoof.) Since the amount of space necessary to adequately produce one steer may be as much as 3 to 15 acres, this extensive form of agriculture could not produce sufficient revenue to compete with higher economic rent activities nearer the market.

The most obvious limitation of Von Thünen's model is that the agriculturalists of a country, state or the world do not consciously arrange their operations so that precise concentric circles appear around markets.[1] This does not mean that the model is without value, but it must undergo other modifications for greater applicability to the real world.

The model assumes that all agriculturalists are completely economically rational and do indeed operate at a maximum economic rent. The theory does not allow for the existence of markets that compete for the produce of spatially scattered farms, nor does it allow for different forms of transport systems, government subsidies, acreage allotments, tariffs, or variable physical environments. The model's constraints are not defects because no theory can accommodate all the conditions of the real world. Von Thünen himself was aware of these limitations and sought to introduce other variables by modifying or deleting his original conditions.

Von Thünen's condition of only one means of land transportation available to producers can be modified to allow for land and water transportation. By

bringing the transportation factor closer to reality, the model in Figure 7–5B is created. Water transportation, which provides for cheaper costs and greater volume, though at a slower speed, tends to extend the economic rent gradient, thereby permitting affected commodities to expand their area of production. In Figure 7–5B, the navigable stream tends to *elongate* the zones of production of the several commodities.

Another relevant modification is associated with the choice of variables. In the ideal model, all producers maximize economic rent, but this is hardly the situation in the real world. We can assume that this condition is modified to allow any farmer at any point along line Mh (*see* Figure 7–3) to produce any commodity he chooses among the three possible crops. (We could also create a scattergraph with 200 different economic rent gradients and then allow freedom of choice among possible crops, but the resulting diagram and discussion would be extremely cluttered and complicated.) In zone Me, all three crops are possible, but there is a difference in their rent-yielding capacities; the rank order of economic rent is E, F, G. In zone EF, the rank order changes so that on the market side the order of decreasing rent is F, E, G, but opposite the market side, the order is G, F, E. Prior to point F, option E completely disappears and hence is not possible.

As one moves from M to G, the number of profitable options decreases, as does the absolute profit. Within these economic rent gradients, if any producer engages in an activity to the right of the point where the rent gradient intersects the horizontal axis, he is operating at a loss. Continued operation obviously results in bankruptcy, and another farmer (or real estate developer) purchases the land and brings it into economically compatible production.

We may also modify the original

[1] Two examples of real concentric zones of agricultural practice may be suggested: The Zande of Central Africa arrange their household gardens in concentric zones of decreasing fertility away from their houses. One also often observes household or botanical gardens with some degree of concentricity. These essentially similar patterns, however, are not to be explained by the same process considered here. The green ring effect in the North China Plain also illustrates this phenomenon.

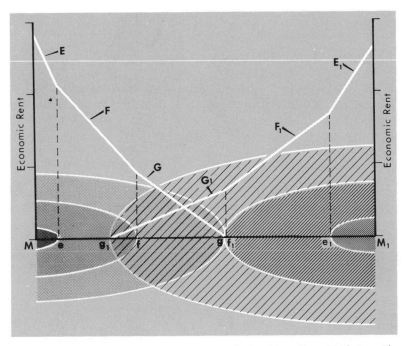

FIGURE 7–6 *Economic Rent–Distance Relationships: Two Markets with 3 Crops Each*

model by the addition of another market (M_1) that competes for products going to M. The result is illustrated in Figure 7–6. The addition of the new market, three more crops, new transport and production costs, and economic rents in turn influences the zones of production of the other market. The zone of greatest competition is the one shown by the overlaps in the figure. Here, the two markets may compete with each other for the produce of the farmers. Markets compete not only for the raw materials and supplies secured from their hinterland, but also for the goods produced there. The nature and extent of this competition are defined by the market structure (*see* chapter 4) and several economic variables like the cost of production, transfer cost, and economies of scale. When producers residing in different areas quote standard F.O.B. prices to their customers, their actions often have an automatic effect in dividing and allocating market areas. Such delineation is much easier under uniform transportation costs. Complications, however, arise when some producers enjoy more favorable transportation rates than others, absorb their freight charges, or adhere to a "leasing point sytem" (*see* chapter 4).

A further modification is illustrated by Figure 7–7. Here all conditions except the fifth (rational farmers) have been modified. From this perspective, it is irrelevant how many market or crop options we add to the model because the result will be decreasing economic rent away from the individual markets until the influence of the next market becomes operative and begins to bid the economic rent higher.

A change in the economic rent gradient over time may be prompted by any one or several factors, such as decreasing transport costs, improved technology

131

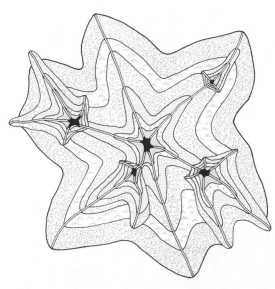

FIGURE 7–7 *Modified Von Thünen Model with Four Markets*

with increased crop yields, or increasing market demands with higher market prices. Figure 7–8 illustrates the economic rent–distance relationship as it changes over time.

Figure 7–8A shows an increased economic rent for all producers, usually associated with an increase in market productivity or price or both. In Figure 7–8B, all producers benefit by some absolute increase, but with great variations in the relative increase; the rent at point a increased by about 30 percent, at point c by about 50 percent. The economic rent at point c jumped from zero to almost the level of b at T_1. Farmers in the vicinity of point d, who at T_1 were excluded from the exchange economy, are now able to participate at a break-even profit.

Decreasing transport costs at longer distances with no increase in market demand and price might also result in a changed rent gradient (see Figure 7–8B). Although absolute and relative increases in rent are greater in Figure 7–8B

at increasing distance from the market, the producers nearer the market still retain the larger economic rent. Such a change, however, may easily and quickly result in the situation shown in Figure 7–8B where decreased transportation costs and increased productivity for zone cd cause the economic rent to fall as represented at point a, reflecting TC and PC per-unit advantages to distant producers. Producers nearer the market might then adjust their agricultural practices by switching to another crop or combination of crops.

Figure 7–8D illustrates an increase in market demand and price unaccompanied by decreased transport costs. In this situation, the area of production is not expanded beyond c, but the increased market price increases economic rent. Over a period of time, producers beyond c may be able to participate in the economy by virtue of a shift to the gradients represented by T_2 in Figure 7–8D.

SPATIAL DYNAMICS OF AGRICULTURAL LOCATION

What occurs when the forest zone is exhausted and demand for wood and lumber to build houses, bridges, and schools and to heat and cook continues? Generally, there are two alternatives: (1) substitution of resources, and (2) expansion of the exchange economy to bring new areas into production. In reality, both of these have and do occur. In industrializing, urbanizing Western Europe, the rapid consumption of forest products was associated with a shift to mortar, brick, stone, steel, iron, petroleum, and electricity as substitutes for diminished wood supplies. The areas previously occupied by large forests have given way to expanding cities, suburbs, and agricultural and recreational uses. As early as the 17th century, forest-destitute Eng-

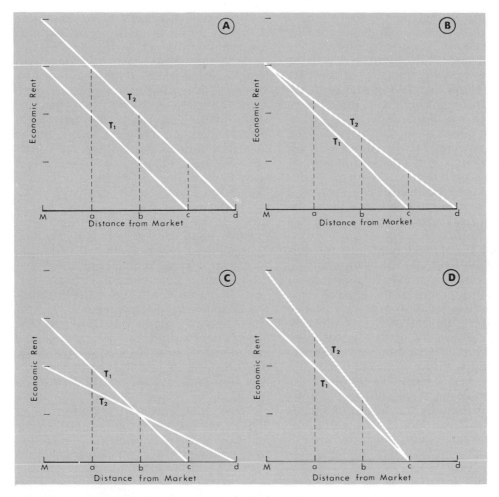

FIGURE 7–8 *Economic Rent–Distance Relationships: Changes over Time and Space*

land was acquiring oak for hulls and keels and pine for masts from the forests of its New World colonies. Changes in transportation, including the modification of the sailing ship, demand, and market price were all involved in this spatial shift of wood sources in England's economy.

What might be the result if people unrelated to market activity were resident in the potentially usable forests shown in figures 7–5 and 7–7? We will

assume that within these forests reside societies that practice subsistence economic activities and are not functionally related to the exchange economy. From the changes briefly discussed with respect to European woodland use we may readily foresee the process by which these subsistence societies may be brought into the exchange economy. Here, in a brief historical economic geography, we will attempt to do just that.

Modifying our concept of an "isolated state" to include the early urbanizing, industrializing Northeast of the United States (Boston, Philadelphia, New York, and later Pittsburgh), we will explore the general process of primary location. Numerous factors will be omitted in order to highlight those most relevant to the basic model.

From about 1650, the forests of the Northeast were heavily lumbered for wood products and cleared for agricultural land. Within these forests, Amerindians engaged in essentially subsistence economies. Brought into contact with the expanding exchange economy, they had several alternatives: (1) forceful resistance to the encroachment into the forests by the commercial economy; (2) join the commercial exchange economy; or (3) abandonment of the present location for a new location at some distance farther from the influence of the expanding commercial economy. All three options were exercised by various Amerindian groups. Those who continued their traditional near subsistence economic activities, however, were subsequently removed, voluntarily or involuntarily, as the frontier expanded.

By the late 1800s, the major area of forest production had shifted to the Appalachian Mountains, an area of extensive and still near subsistence agricultural use. By the 19th century, forest production was concentrated in the Upper and Western Great Lakes region of Minnesota and Michigan. By this time, the dominant "potentially usable area of forests" being brought into the national exchange economy was in the Northwest in Washington and Oregon.

As the forest economy relocated, the market side, which was now nearer the Northeast, experienced other spatial changes in livestock production, especially grazing and ranching, and grain production (wheat and corn), which also moved successfully outward from the market. Fueling this spatial expansion of

the exchange economy were increasing demands by an urbanizing, industrializing population which itself was increasing by birth and immigration, by innovations in agricultural production, including new types of crops and techniques, government policies, all linked together by stagecoach, pony express, railroads, highways, and other transport forms. In the interim, major markets other than those agglomerated in the Northeast arose, such as the Chicago–Detroit and the San Diego–San Francisco areas.

Indeed, one may now argue that in order to observe the more significant positive relationships between the Von Thünen theory and reality, one has to survey large areas, whole continents, and often a large portion of the Earth's surface, to isolate one or several commodities or major market centers.

Applying these principles to the global distribution of several selected commodities will also tend to verify some aspects of our explanatory models and principles.[2] Figure 7–9 shows the distribution of major world population clusters; the Northeast of the United States, Northwest Europe, India, China and Southeast Asia and, to a lesser extent, southeastern Australia, and southeastern South America.

Assuming these major nodes as global markets for agricultural products, we may then analyze their distribution relative to dairy-farming commodities. The distribution of major dairy-farming zones conforms to the major markets in only two instances: Northwest Europe and Northeast United States (see Figure 8–3). It fails almost completely in the other market areas. The numerous rea-

[2] The major limitation in the following discussion and figures is that the latter do not show economic rent of commodities, but the general world distribution of commodities. However, we do know generally that dairying, wheat production, livestock ranching, and subsistence gathering have lesser unit-area productivity, respectively.

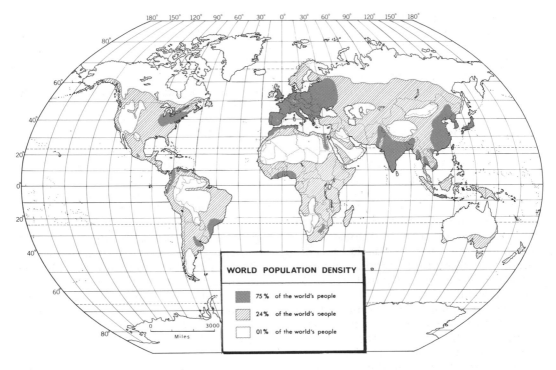

WORLD POPULATION DENSITY

75% of the world's people

24% of the world's people

01% of the world's people

FIGURE 7–9

sons for this lack of conformity are beyond the scope of the present discussion
but generally include some of the principles outlined in the initial chapters of the
text that are associated with culture, society, and economy.[3] One explanation for
this lack of dairying is the relatively high
cost of operation, transport, and maintenance in developing economies, prevent-
ing its extensive establishment. (In the
United States the average investment in
a commercial dairy farm is approximately
$100,000.) The lack of dairying adjacent

to these markets, however, does not
mean that the land does not have a relatively high economic rent. Indeed, it
does, and one of the more common features of the agricultural landscape of
these markets is the intensively tilled and
highly productive market gardens.

The distributions of Figures 7–9 and
7–11 also reveal some degree of conformity to decreasing land-use intensity
with increasing distance from the global
market zones (see Figures 8–6 and 8–7).
The general location of wheat production
for each major market tends to be at a
distance greater than that of dairying and
less than that of livestock ranching. The
major exceptions in these two isolated
examples are associated with the ranching economy. In the United States from
colonial times, from the late 19th century
in Australia, and from the 1930s in the

[3] Arguments for the lack of demand by Asians for
dairy products rest on sets of facts. There is evidence to suggest that the domestication process
of the bovine was diffused from Southwest Asia
to East Asia but before the process of milking was
introduced. While the milking process was being
developed and diffused in Western culture, Ori-
entals who used the bovine for other reasons did
not generally see a need for its milk products.

135

USSR, livestock grazing has been allotted peripheral or marginal space, in deference to more productive grain or grain *and* meat zones. This continued competition and movement away from the higher-economic-rent zones have combined to result in a similar pattern around several major markets.

These illustrations also do not show the large-scale movement of commodities from zones of production to consumption. For example, a great portion of the beef production of Argentina and Australia–New Zealand is exported to either the United States or Europe, and wheat production from both these countries and from the United States is exported to numerous other countries, including those of Western Europe, Japan, and South Asia.

The general economic rent–distance relationships between the selected commodities on the world maps is graphically shown in Figure 7–10. Among the three commodities, dairying, which returns the highest economic rent, is close to the market, followed in proximity by

zones of wheat production and livestock ranching. Beyond the outer limits of functionally related and integrated space, are zones not directly related to the exchange economy. These zones do not possess an attractiveness or sufficiently high economic rent in terms of contemporary technology to warrant expansion of the exchange economy. Many of these zones are characterized by environmental limitations and political or technological limitations. Some are uninhabited and others are occupied by the world's few remaining residents who see no profit in joining a large-scale exchange economy. Figure 7–11, showing the distribution of the major areas of subsistence gatherers, indicates global zones with relatively low economic rent, from the perspective of urban–industrial societies. This distribution should be closely compared with distributions in figures 7–5, 7–7, and 7–9 through 7–11.

WORLD AGRICULTURAL REGIONS

The locational factors and intrinsic characteristics of world agricultural activities are much too complex and vast to be adequately described and explained by one or even several theories or models. However, since its inception and modifications, the theory and model offered by Von Thünen appears tentatively as the most satisfactory. Even with modifications, there are numerous regional variations that must still be relegated to the category of anomaly or irregularity, and whose explanation is more acceptable when examined individually. Although the basic tenets of Von Thünen have been supported by numerous scholars, including Chisholm, Dunn, Marble, and Garrison, there are traditions and innovations bearing on the spatial organization of agriculture that must be examined in other ways. The following chapter

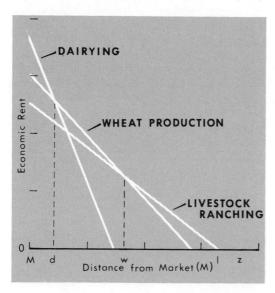

FIGURE 7–10 *Economic Rent–Distance Relationships: Dairy, Wheat, and Livestock*

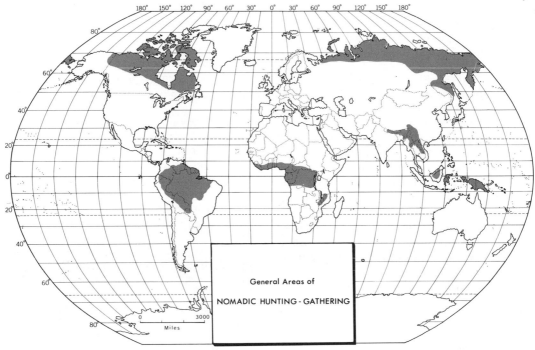

Miles

General Areas of
NOMADIC HUNTING - GATHERING

FIGURE 7–11

does this by first observing world agricultural regions and then analyzing them individually.

references

1.   Brown, Lester R., and Finsterbusch, Gail W. *Man and His Environment: Food.* New York: Harper & Row, 1972.

2.   Casetti, Emilio. "Spatial Equilibrium Distribution of Agricultural Production and Land Values." *Economic Geography* 48 (April 1972): 193–98.

3.   Chrisholm, M. "The Relevance of Von Thünen." *Annals of the American Geographers* 59 (June 1969): 401.

4.   Griffin, Ernst. "Testing the Von Thünen Theory in Uruguay." *Geographical Review* 63 (October 1973): 500–16.

5.   Grigg, David B. *The Harsh Lands: A Study in Agricultural Development.* New York: Macmillan and Co., 1970.

6.   Hall, P., ed. *Von Thünen's Isolated State: An English Edition of "Der Isolierte Staat."* By Johann Heinrich Von Thünen. Translated by C. M. Wartenberg. New York: Pergamon Press, 1966.

7.   Heiser, Charles Bixler. *Seed to Civilization: The Story of Man's Food.* San Francisco: W. H. Freeman Co., 1973.

8.   Hutchinson, Sir Joseph Burtt. *Farming and Food Supply.* Cambridge: Cambridge University Press, 1972.

9.   Isaac, Erich. *Geography of Domestication.* Englewood Cliffs, N.J.: Prentice-Hall, 1970.

10.   Jacoby, Erich H., and Jacoby, Charlotte. *Man and Land: The Essential Revolution.* New York: Alfred A. Knopf, 1971.

11.   Johnson, David G. *World Agriculture in Disarray.* London: Macmillan and Co., 1973.

12.   Lloyd, Peter E., and Dicken, Peter. *Location in Space: A Theoretical Approach to Economic Geography.* New York: Harper & Row, 1972.

137

13. Mabogrinji, Akin L. "Manufacturing and the Geography of Development in Tropical Africa." *Economic Geography* 49 (January 1973): 1–20.

14. McLaughlin, Peter F. *African Food Production Systems: Cases and Theory.* Baltimore: Johns Hopkins Press, 1970.

15. Morrill, R. L. *The Spatial Organization of Society.* Belmont, Calif.: Wadsworth Publishing Co., 1970.

16. Muller, Peter O., and Diaz, Gregory J. "Von Thünen and Population Density." *The Professional Geographer* 25 (August 1973): 239–41.

17. Muller, Peter O. "Trend Surfaces of American Agricultural Patterns: A Macro-Thünian Analysis." *Economic Geography* 49 (July 1973).

18. Owens, Denis F. *Man in Tropical Africa.* New York: Oxford University Press, 1973.

19. ———. *Man in Tropical Africa: The Environmental Predicament.* New York: Oxford University Press, 1973.

20. Parr, John B., and Denike, Kenneth G. "Theoretical Problems in Central Place Analysis." *Economic Geography* 46 (October 1970): 568–86.

21. Peet, J. R. "The Spatial Expansion of Commercial Agriculture in the Nineteenth Century: A Von Thünen Interpretation." *Economic Geography* 45 (October 1969): 283–301.

22. Preston, Richard E. "The Structure of Central Place Systems." *Economic Geography* 47 (April 1971): 136–55.

23. Ruthenberg, Hans. *Farming Systems in the Tropics.* Oxford: Clarendon Press, 1971.

24. Struever, Stuart. *Prehistoric Agriculture.* Garden City, N.Y.: Natural History Press, 1971.

25. Webber, M. J., and Symanski, Richard. "Periodic Markets: An Economic Location Analysis." *Economic Geography* 49 (July 1973).

26. Weitz, Raanan. *From Peasant to Farmer: A Revolutionary Strategy for Development.* New York: Columbia University Press, 1971.

27. ——— ed. *Rural Development in a Changing World.* Cambridge, Mass.: M.I.T. Press, 1971.

world agricultural
systems

8

8

The regional application of the Von Thünen model requires relaxing all his assumptions and considering additional realities of government policies and transportation innovations that have occurred since he proposed his model. These considerations become much more relevant when engaging in global analysis. For example, some countries relatively separated by navigable seas may enjoy lower transportation costs, and thus they create disturbances in the Thünenian formulation of land use. Tax subsidies and production scales would affect a location pattern even if homogeneous physical conditions were assumed. National cultural variations seriously influence the rational and entrepreneurial traits assumed in the Von Thünen model.

The pattern of world agriculture is conditioned by culture, technology, resources, climate, socioeconomic variables, and government policies. These patterns generally can be identified in terms of broad activity groupings, such as *agricultural systems*. Agricultural production has been organized in several different ways over space and time. These various forms of organization have had significant effects upon the rates of change and growth of agricultural productivity and, in some cases, upon the entire society in which they exist. In most respects, different types of organization of agricultural production are not distinct and clear cut. Any form of organization is, in part, a function of society. Units on subsistence farms that would be classified as low-production farms in the United States might be classified as medium- or large-scale farms in other agricultural economies.

Garrison and Marble recognize the need for a more vigorous treatment of the spatial structure of agriculture, but they observe that "nowhere does there appear any explicit proof of one of the basic theorems, namely: 'that for every spatial location there is some jointly optimum intensity of land use, type of land use, and group of markets, the selection of which by the agricultural entrepreneur leads to spatially ordered patterns of land use.' " (6)

There are several ways of comparing an agricultural system of one region with that of another. It can be done in terms of crop distribution, relative productivity, or effect on the rural landscape. For purposes of classification, it is useful to consider four elements: (1) the quantity of resources (land, labor, and capital) involved in the production unit; (2) the proportions of those resources involved in a typical production unit; (3) who decides how the resources of the production unit are used; and (4) the extent to which economic factors, such as product and resource prices, determine the way in which the resources of the production unit are used. Before proceeding with an analysis of agricultural systems, however, a brief discussion of the origin and dispersion of agriculture is in order.

Agriculture, the art of cultivating the soil to raise grain and other crops for man and domestic animals, is the oldest of occupations and the basis of all other arts. The two most epochal steps in the civilization of man were the invention of the wheel and the birth of agriculture. The former initiated technology, and the latter marked the beginning of man's attempts to shape the environment to his own ends.

ORIGIN AND DISPERSION

When and where did agriculture begin? For many years, scholarly attention has focused on the Middle East, where archaeological remains seem to indicate

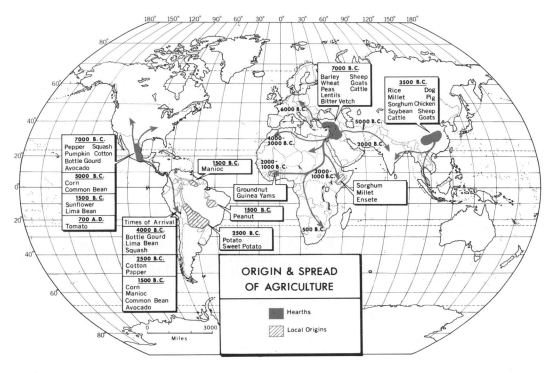

FIGURE 8–1

that that area was the cradle of modern man's culture. But information on the early domestication of plants is scarce and scattered. Recent discoveries about the birth of agriculture, based largely on carbon–14 datings,[1] are summarized in Figure 8–1, which shows the spread of agriculture. The most remarkable discovery is the almost simultaneous appearance of agriculture on opposite sides of the world, in the Middle East and in Mexico, around 7,000 BC.

This discovery implies that the in-

vention of agriculture, vital to the progress of the human species from the aboriginal to the technological stage, did not occur merely by chance. According to Sauer (16), the origin of agriculture had to be linked with:

1. A sedentary society because planted land, especially that of primitive cultivators, must be watched over continuously against plant predators

2. The production of surplus and leisure because hungry people lack the opportunity and incentive for the slow and continuing selection of domesticated forms

3. Woodlands, which permit abandonment of planting after a time to the resprouting and reseeding of wild, woody growth and provide a form of crop rotation where the soil is replenished by nutrients carried up from deep-rooted trees and shrubs

[1] Carbon–14 is a radioactive form of carbon that decays slowly into nitrogen–14. Half of a given amount of carbon–14 decays in this manner in roughly 5,600 years. Carbon–14 is produced at a constant rate by the action of cosmic rays in the high atmosphere. Since carbon likewise decays at a constant rate, there is a uniform, equalized level of carbon–14 in the air at all times.

SYSTEMS OF AGRICULTURAL PRODUCTION

The environment is an important factor in determining the type of agricultural production that develops in an area. Within the environment, climate marks the broad outline. Soils largely controlled in the broad agricultural belts by climate are locally modified by topography and by parent materials, the basic materials that formed the soils in a locale. Vegetation soils show on the broad basis a correlation with climate and locally a close correlation with topographic and soil differences; soils are in turn affected by plant cover.

Man directly or indirectly uses naturally or artificially produced plant cover. In modern agriculture, except for forage, timber, and wildlife production, plants and soils are modified to increase production, and domestic animals and plants have largely replaced native forms.

Natural plant cover is adjusted to conditions of soil and climate. If properly interpreted, the natural cover indicates not only climatic and soil conditions but also the effect of fire and the biological impingements that have determined the appearance and composition of natural covers. The natural cover is a summary of the conditions that control plant growth and is therefore the best guide to the potential for crop production in an area.

Climate is also one of the major factors influencing the selection of specific crops by man to satisfy his needs. Types of farming are linked closely with climate; this introduces a whole field of agricultural geography. In most cases, it is possible to draw geographical limits for the cultivation of a crop. Near the marginal areas, crops may fail in one out of two or three seasons. But nature is perverse and often rewards the adventurous who farm near the margin with crops of exceptional quality and quantity in favored years. Moreover, it is the constant aim of agricultural science to extend the limits of cultivation by developing strains resistant to cold, drought, or excessive moisture. Where economic forces or incentives are sufficiently strong, adverse climatic conditions may be overcome by irrigation, pest control, and other means.

The most widely accepted classification of systems of agriculture was made by Derwent Whittlesey in the 1930s. (23) Whittlesey recognized two main forces in his classification: (1) "the combination of environment conditions which sets the limits of range for any crop or domestic animal and provides, within those limits, optimum habitats" and (2) "the combination of human circumstances which applies the habitat possibilities of plants and animals to human needs." The interaction of the pertinent elements of the natural environment (climate, soil, and slope) and the "chief elements of the cultural circumstances—density of population, stage of technology, and inherited position—produces the "functioning forms which appear to dominate every type of agriculture." Whittlesey lists these forms as:

1. Crop and livestock association
2. Methods used to grow crops and produce stock
3. Intensity of application to the land of labor, capital, and organization, and the product that results
4. Disposal of the products for consumption, i.e., whether used for subsistence on the farm or sold off for cash or other goods
5. Ensemble of structures used to house and facilitate farming operations

There are areas of the world where the land is totally unsuitable at present for agricultural use. These environments, termed restrictive by Whittlesey, pose such serious obstacles to any notable increase in population that by and large man only occupies outposts in such places. These areas include: high mountains with rugged surfaces, shallow stony soils, restricted flat land, and inhospitable climates; deserts where water for irrigation is nonexistent; icecaps in Antarctica and most of Greenland; and tundras with permafrost and poor drainage.

Figure 8–2, based on Whittlesey's classification, recognizes thirteen types of agricultural occupancy. A description of these agricultural systems follows.

COMMERCIAL DAIRY FARMING

Commercial dairy farming represents the agricultural activity that is profitable only where the products can be sold to an urban market. Von Thünen (see chapter 7) recognized this in his land-use model where competition for land, reflected by the desire to maximize economic returns, tends to distribute various types of land use in such a way that each tract is occupied by the use that can earn the highest economic rent there. Commercial dairy farms producing fresh milk for daily consumption of necessity must be located near densely populated industrial areas.

Fresh milk cannot be shipped distances farther than twelve hours away; cream can go twice as far without perishing, and refrigerated butter can cross a continent on rails and from the antipodes in ships. Cheese will keep for up to three or four years, depending on the kind. These facts explain the worldwide distribution of Danish and New Zealand butter, the special trademark value of

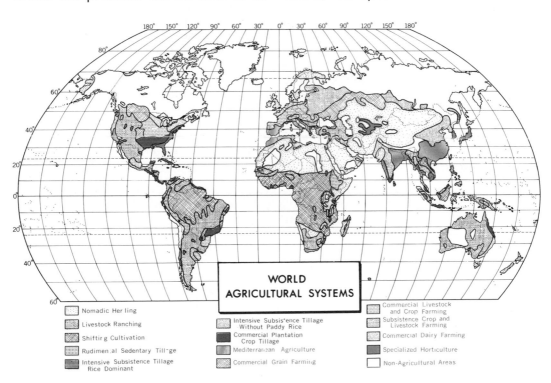

WORLD AGRICULTURAL SYSTEMS

Nomadic Herding
Livestock Ranching
Shifting Cultivation
Rudimental Sedentary Tillage
Intensive Subsistence Tillage Rice Dominant

Intensive Subsistence Tillage Without Paddy Rice
Commercial Plantation Crop Tillage
Mediterranean Agriculture
Commercial Grain Farming

Commercial Livestock and Crop Farming
Subsistence Crop and Livestock Farming
Commercial Dairy Farming
Specialized Horticulture
Non-Agricultural Areas

FIGURE 8–2

many cheeses, chiefly of European origin, and the abundant supplies of milk and cream in cities adjacent to major dairying regions.

Dairying is an intensive form of agriculture. It is elaborately mechanized and the capital investment in buildings and equipment on high-grade dairy farms exceeds that in any other type of agriculture. In only a very few other agricultural activities is the amount of labor needed greater than in dairying, and then, not in terms of the total number of people, but in man-hours per value of product (the relationship between the number of man-hours to produce a product and the price the product will bring in the marketplace).

Every step in feeding, milking, and processing is critical. Dairy cattle must be milked twice a day to produce their maximum capacity. Milking must be done every day of the year. In addition to milking, a farmer usually has hogs and chickens to feed. According to the season, other tasks are cutting and storing hay, harvesting corn and oats, preparing seedbeds for the next planting, cultivating newly planted crops, selling animals and fluid milk, and repairing equipment and machines. The percentage of tenantry is low. Apparently the personal stake that keeps the farm owner on the job is a cornerstone of prosperity in commercial dairy farming.

Table 8–1 shows raw milk production in the world and in selected leading countries. Of these, the USSR leads. Although the United States is second in production, it is the only major producer that had a drop in output in the last decade. Diet and cholesterol-conscious Americans are cutting down on milk consumption.

The chief dairy regions of the world are in Europe, North America, and Oceania (see Figure 8–3). The major producers of dairy products in Europe are France, the Federal Republic of Germany, Poland, the United Kingdom, Italy, The Netherlands, the Democratic Republic of Germany, Czechoslovakia, Denmark, and the Soviet Union. In North America, the Northcentral United States and adjacent parts of Canada contribute about 95 percent of the total world output. Production in Oceania is about equally divided between Australia and New Zealand. The latter specializes in the production of manufactured dairy products—dried and condensed milk, butter, and cheese—marketed chiefly in Europe. In contrast, the large urban industrial populations of northwestern Europe and the American Midwest provide a ready market for dairy products from nearby dairy farms.

TABLE 8–1 Total Raw Milk Production in the World and Selected Leading Countries (in thousand metric tons)

	1963	1972	PERCENT CHANGE
USSR	61,248	83,200	+35.84%
U.S.	56,791	54,557	− 3.93
France	23,737	30,347	+27.85
India	20,241	23,750	+17.34
W. Germany	20,857	21,343	+ 2.33
Poland	12,644	15,769	+24.72
United Kingdom	11,904	14,200	+19.29
Pakistan	8,028	11,212	+39.66
World	350,554	414,303	+18.19%

Source: Based on the *U.N. Statistical Yearbook, 1973* (New York: United Nations, 1974), pp. 118–122.

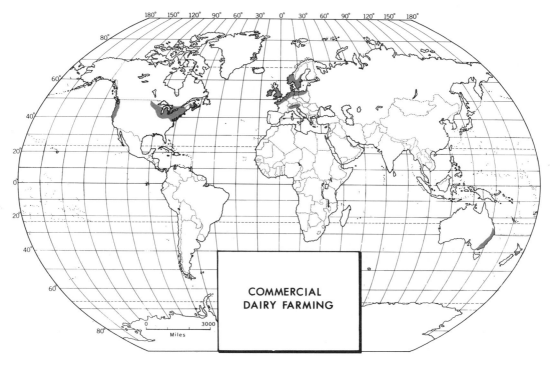

COMMERCIAL
DAIRY FARMING

0   3000
Miles

FIGURE 8–3

SPECIALIZED HORTICULTURE

Like dairy farming, growing fruits and vegetables is linked to large urban populations and rapid transportation to market. Horticultural distribution (*see* Figure 8–4) correlates with the Von Thünen model because the first ring of land use around the market center is occupied by economic activities that yield higher income because of higher rent.

Market gardening was the earliest type of commercial fruit and vegetable production. It developed coincidentally with the growth of cities to meet the demand for perishable vegetables from nearby sources. Until about 1900, market gardening was mainly restricted to an area lying within 10 to 15 miles of a city, but since then production has been extended to distances of a 100 miles or more from the market. The increased use of trucks and the development of improved roads have been important factors in this expansion.

Market gardening is a very intensive form of cultivation. The land adjacent to cities is relatively high-priced, large labor forces are used, and heavy applications of fertilizer are made. Production close to the market benefits from lower expenses for transportation and packing compared with production at a distance. Crops from market gardens, however, come on the market mainly at the peak of production, rather than at the peak of prices, so that prices are comparatively low. The market gardener can supply only in-season vegetables, and the small amount of out-of-season vegetables produced near the market are grown in hot-houses at great expense.

A second, and the most recent, type of vegetable production is *truck farming*,

145

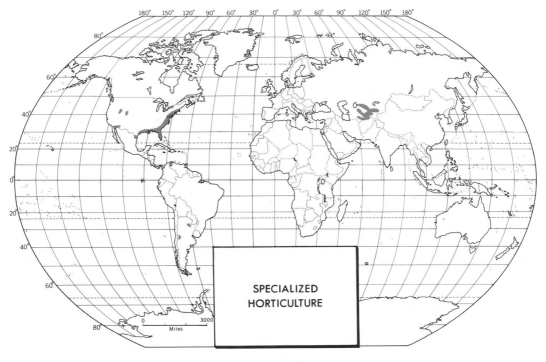

FIGURE 8–4

where the producer, unlike the market gardener who grows a variety of crops, specializes usually only in one crop and uses less intensive methods. Truck farming is carried on at a distance from the markets. Each truck farmer concentrates on a crop particularly adapted to the soil conditions and seasonal climate of his region. In each trucking region, crops are grown at a time of the year when there is little competition with crops grown in other sections. For instance, vegetables from Mexico and the West Indies reach the eastern cities of the U.S. first, and then crops are successively received from Florida, Georgia, South and North Carolina, and other sections as far north as Canada. This progression occurs over about a six-month period, and each locality can count on about two to three weeks' advance in maturity over a region

immediately to the north. During this period of a few weeks, the district must market its crop if it is to obtain favorable price and market conditions. Any delay in the maturity of a crop as the result of unfavorable weather conditions may seriously affect the returns for the season's work.

The location of market gardens and truck farms depends chiefly on climate and soil conditions and proximity to market. The location of truck farms depends mostly on soil and climate that favor a particular crop, and market gardens depend chiefly on proximity to market.

All cities, large and small, have outlying areas devoted to market gardens. In some cases, a market-gardening area may be bounded by a river, a swamp, or another urban area, or it may be confined to small, favorable soil areas. Long Island and northern New Jersey are important market-gardening areas for the New York City region. In England, London receives a large portion of its vegetables from the nearby counties of Middlesex and Bedfordshire and from the Isle of Ely; East and West Ridings of Yorkshire are important sources of vegetables for the northern counties. In the Netherlands vegetables are grown over so wide an area it would be difficult to define those supplying each city.

The more important trucking sections of the United States are the Atlantic Coastal Plain from southern New Jersey to Florida; the Gulf Coastal Plain from Alabama to Texas; California; and certain north central states. Important trucking areas are also found in Algeria, Tunisia, Egypt, and the French Riviera.

Commercial fruit orchards are found in many truck-farming regions. All but hardy fruits, such as apples, cherries, and pears, are confined to climates milder than the urban regions of either Europe or North America. Irrigation has evolved the large and handsome fruits common in the western United States. Small pockets of intensive fruit cultivation also occur near: (1) large water bodies which retard the early blossoming of fruit trees until the danger of frost is past, and (2) in hill country which permits air drainage (the flowing of colder air downslope to low spots below the fruit trees), which minimizes frost hazards. Examples are the apple district of southwestern Germany and the fruit zones of Nova Scotia, the lower Great Lakes, the middle Appalachians, and the Ozarks. The wine districts of North Europe also belong in this category.

In dry regions where irrigation must be practiced, cotton may dominate the business of small districts. Cotton grows well on the irrigated lands of Central Asia, south Kazakhstan and the Transcaucasus (USSR), the coastal oases of Peru, parts of the lower Colorado Basin, and the Argentine Chaco. Sugar beets in the Platte River and Salt Lake oases of the western United States and sugar cane in coastal Peru and northern Argentina are also benefitted by irrigation.

COMMERCIAL LIVESTOCK AND CROP FARMING

This mode of agriculture, also called mixed farming, is an extensive form, based on a combination of crop cultivation and animal husbandry. It occupies the humid middle latitudes in all continents. The monetary return generally is less than that of commercial dairy farming or specialized agriculture. Periodic rather than daily shipment to market is the rule. Farm population density is high, and large urban centers are interspersed within the mixed farming belts. Smaller cities, towns, and villages dot the landscape, providing market outlets and services.

Table 8–2 reveals that the USSR and Brazil lead the world in total number of livestock. However, the United States still dominates in the production of grain-fattened livestock because in the United States most grain is converted to meat through the medium of livestock. In most areas outside of the United States, grain is grown primarily as human food.

The two largest commercial livestock and crop-farming regions are in the United States and Eurasia. In the United States, this activity prevails in the Midwest (Ohio, Indiana, Illinois, Iowa Nebraska), the South (Virginia, Tennessee, Georgia), and the Southwest (Oklahoma and much of Texas). In Eurasia, it encompasses much of northern Portugal and Spain, the Po River plain of Italy, a large portion of the Danube Basin countries of Hungary, Yugoslavia, and western Ro-

147

TABLE 8–2   Total Livestock in the World and Selected Leading Countries (in thousands)

	1968	1972	PERCENT CHANGE
China	366,520	382,530	+4.37%
USSR	295,228	321,647	+8.95
India	225,480	226,460	+0.43
U.S.	197,079	207,079	+5.07
Brazil	193,380	206,510	+6.79
Australia	188,634	193,964	+2.83
Argentina	104,932	100,640	−4.09
World	2,883,692	3,120,647	+8.22%

Source: Based on the *United Nations Statistical Yearbook, 1973* (New York: United Nations, 1974), pp. 107–115.

mania, and the Amur Valley in the USSR (see Figure 8–5).

Minor regions are found in Argentina, southeastern Brazil, south central Chile, and South Africa. Elsewhere, occasional patches of this type of activity occur near the larger occidental cities.

The commercial livestock–crop-farming system concentrates on breeding and plant selection and a well-established crop rotation in which legumes and hay play a part in proper soil management. Grains are produced for sale as a cash crop and as feed for livestock. Some farmers specialize only in growing wheat, corn, or soybeans for sale; others produce only corn to feed to animals which they sell as meat for human consumption.

Farm animals use roughage, which may be produced in any system of mixed livestock–crop farming. On a typical midwestern farm with a rotation of corn, oats, and clover, approximately 1.75 tons of roughage are produced for every ton of grain. Animals convert these by-products of grain production, which are of little value in themselves, into products of much greater market value.

In Eurasia, root crops planted in rotation with grain crops in order to maintain soil fertility are fed to farm animals. Hay is a substitute for corn in most of Eurasia; corn is an important feed crop only in the Danube Valley. Elsewhere potatoes, turnips, sugar beets, and oats are the major feed crops.

Farms in Eurasia are smaller and less mechanized than their U.S. counterparts, with higher production per acre but lower production per worker. Average livestock–grain operations in the U.S. occupy approximately 150 acres (ranging from 120 to 200 acres); in South America and South Africa, they are about the same size; in Eurasia, about half as large.

The close interdependence between this farm system and centers of trade and manufacturing is disclosed by its weak development in eastern Europe and in the southern continents, even where the natural environment is satisfactory, and by its absence in eastern Asia where intensive hand tillage held sway long before Europe outgrew the medieval three-field system of farming.

Livestock and crop production are complementary activities on general farms. They make possible a more even seasonal distribution of labor, the heavy labor demands coming at a time when labor is released from caring for the crops. For these reasons, cattle raising plays an important role in the intensive agriculture of northwestern Europe and the American Midwest.

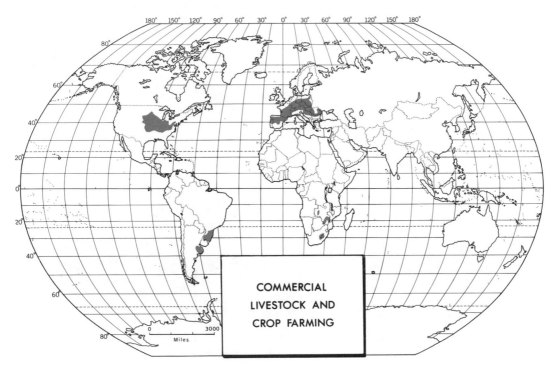

COMMERCIAL
LIVESTOCK AND
CROP FARMING

FIGURE 8–5

Nearly everywhere in North America the farmer lives on the acres he works; this is also true of many regions in Europe and the southern continents. Since farms are of medium size, this does not impose severe socioeconomic isolation. Marketing towns are numerous, because in a cash system there is much trade. The standard of living varies, but in every country it is relatively high, except in rugged or infertile districts where it is hard to produce enough from the niggardly ground to pile up a surplus for sale.

COMMERCIAL GRAIN FARMING

Commercial grain farms lie on the border between humid and semiarid climates, where summers are short and winters are cold. Most of these regions are deep in the interior of continental land masses. Land values per unit are low, population density is sparse, varying from 2 to 25 people per square mile. Wheat has often been called a frontier crop, not only because of its distribution (see Figure 8–6), but because it is adapted to frontier conditions of scarce labor and extensive cultivation on vast tracts of land at a distance from markets. These factors explain the importance of wheat in Canada, Argentina, and Australia, where wheat is grown because there are few alternatives and because land is cheap.

The crop and stock association is simple and standardized. Wheat is the cash crop, with flax or barley substituting at times in places. Oats and hay feed draft animals, unless tractors have supplanted them. Other animals are kept for local supplies. No other association has been found that will provide a livelihood,

149

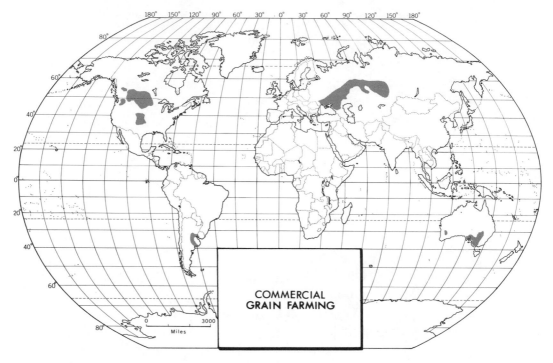

COMMERCIAL
GRAIN FARMING

0   3000
Miles

FIGURE 8–6

except where standards of living are so low and population is so dense that oriental agriculture can be adopted.

Technological improvements are vital factors that determine the regions where wheat will be grown, as well as the type of wheat grown and the amount produced in each region. Three technological improvements are of particular significance:

1. Well-drilling machinery for artesian wells made water available for domestic use in semiarid regions.

2. Railroads made transportation facilities adequate for handling the wheat.

3. Despite a scarcity of labor, new types of agricultural machinery made it possible to cultivate large tracts of land in the short seasons available for seeding and harvesting.

Without these three developments, it would have been impossible to cultivate

the vast middle-latitude grasslands that have become the world's chief wheat-growing regions.

Tractor power, self-propelled combines, and other large-scale machinery enlarged the acreage that one man could handle. Now one man can handle about 300 acres on the eastern border of the Great Plains in the United States and about 800 to 1,200 acres in the western United States, and even more on a farm with an especially good manager with adequate equipment. The hours of work for each acre of wheat have been reduced from 6.1 hours in 1902 to less than 2 hours in 1973; this includes time spent in the field and in repairing and maintaining machinery.

The major world regions of commercial grain farming are concentrated in the middle latitudes of the Northern and Southern hemispheres between 30°

and 55°. The percentage of land used for commercial grain farming, less than 5 percent of the earth's surface, is relatively small compared to that used for other agricultural activities.

Table 8–3 shows the importance of wheat production in the USSR, the world's leading producer of the commodity. Canada's wheat production declined drastically from 1963 to 1972, while India showed the greatest percentage gain. China stressed wheat production during that period, also. China leads all other countries in rice production, but Indonesia had the greatest percentage increase in the last decade. The

United States still produces the most corn; this commodity is mainly used as animal feed and as such is the key to the importance of corn in the United States' agricultural system.

In North America, there are several major areas of commercial wheat production. The largest lies in the northern Great Plains and includes the Canadian prairie provinces (Alberta, Saskatchewan, and Manitoba) and the Dakotas in the United States. A second area centering in Kansas continues south to include the panhandles of Texas and Oklahoma. Smaller areas occur in eastern Oregon and Washington, southern Idaho, eastern

TABLE 8–3 Total Production of Wheat, Rice, and Corn in the World and Selected Leading Countries (in thousand metric tons)

	1963	1972	PERCENT CHANGE
Wheat			
USSR	49,688	85,950	+ 72.98%
U.S.	31,212	42,043	+ 34.70
China	21,800	34,500	+ 58.26
India	10,776	26,410	+145.08
France	14,760	18,123	+ 22.78
Canada	19,691	14,514	− 26.29
World	239,595	347,740	+ 45.14
Rice			
China	81,000	101,000	+ 24.69
India	55,497	57,950	+ 4.42
Indonesia	11,595	18,031	+ 55.51
Japan	16,649	15,281	− 8.22
Bangladesh	15,935	14,387	− 9.71
Thailand	12,171	11,669	− 4.12
World	254,045	292,936	+ 15.31
Corn			
U.S.	102,093	141,053	+ 38.16
China	22,800	23,500	+ 3.07
Brazil	10,418	14,892	+ 42.94
USSR	11,143	9,830	− 11.78
Romania	6,023	9,817	+ 62.99
S. Africa	6,100	9,630	+ 57.87
World	221,308	302,232	+ 36.57

Source: Based on the *United Nations Statistical Yearbook, 1973* (New York: United Nations, 1974), pp. 133–34; 27–28, 116–17.

Montana, eastern Illinois, and northern Iowa.

The Pampa of Argentina is the major commercial grain area in South America. Australia devotes considerable acreage in the southeastern and southwestern parts of the continent to grain farming. Eurasia's commercial grain area stretches from west to east for some 2,000 miles and north to south for 700 miles. It includes all of the Ukraine except its extreme southeast corner, Crimea, much of the northern Caucasus and the irrigated regions of Central Asia and Transcaucasia, the middle and lower Volga Basin, the south Ural Mountains, western Siberia, and Kazakhstan.

The acreage available for wheat production is reduced by competition from other crops for the land. Corn and cotton have much narrower geographical limits than wheat, so their farm values per acre have been greater. Cotton has even narrower limits than corn, so cotton has first choice of the land that is available for these crops, and corn has second place.

LIVESTOCK RANCHING

In general, livestock ranching occupies the wetter margins of steppe lands in the middle latitudes and the savanna areas of the tropics. This type of economic activity is characterized by:

1. Relatively large land areas, as opposed to smaller areas for field agriculture and livestock farming

2. Upgrading of natural vegetation

3. Erection of permanent buildings, roads, fences, etc.

4. Extensive use of the land, as opposed to intensive use, more commonly associated with livestock farming

5. Awareness of and dependence upon economic factors that primarily determine the success or failure of the venture, such as: government policies, world-market prices, financial management, application of scientific principles of animal husbandry, production for sale, and great distances from markets (a reflection of the need for low land values)

Livestock ranching, then, tends to occupy the outer fringe of the Von Thünen model because land values are cheap and distances to market are too far to permit anything but low rent. The dominant factor in this endeavor is distance. Population is sparse, with many areas having less than 2 people per square mile. The range or "spread" of the ranch is usually measured in square miles called sections. Towns are small and far apart, and there are no big cities. In no other agricultural activity do schools, libraries, public health units, road maintenance divisions, and other social and economic agencies suffer so much from lack of an adequate population base. Either these services do not exist at all or they are very costly. The settlement pattern is either dispersed, as is the case with individual ranch homes and associated buildings, or agglomerated. The latter type comprises the service centers found only in commercial economies. Surplus production from the surrounding ranches, such as wool, skins, and so on, are collected at the service centers for shipment to major markets, and ranchers secure their needed supplies here.

Cattle, sheep, and goats are the major domesticated animals tended by man. The development of animal husbandry, a significant step in man's history, is primarily the result of man's ability to add to the naturally occurring resource base by improvising on its carrying capacity.

Table 8–4 shows the United States as the principal producer of beef in the world, followed by the USSR. The tremendous percentage increase in beef production in Australia and Brazil from 1968 to 1972 should be noted.

TABLE 8–4   Total Production of Beef and Veal in the World and Selected Leading Countries (in thousand metric tons)

	1968	1972	PERCENT CHANGE
U.S.	9,789	10,360	+ 5.83%
USSR	5,513	5,800	+ 5.21
Argentina	2,561	2,198	−14.17
Brazil	1,694	2,088	+23.26
China	1,909	1,949	+ 2.10
Australia	935	1,434	+53.36
France	1,624	1,395	−14.10
World	38,849	41,112	+ 5.83%

Source: Based on the *United Nations Statistical Yearbook, 1973* (New York: United Nations, 1974), pp. 211–17.

Location. In North America, livestock ranching is an important activity in the more arid parts of the Great Plains, stretching from Texas through the prairie provinces of Canada and throughout the intermontane basins and plateaus between the Rocky Mountains and the Sierra Nevada–Cascades from Canada to central Mexico.

South America has two zones. The first begins at the southern tip of the continent at Tierra del Fuego and continues for some 4,000 miles through Argentina, Uruguay, and Brazil on the east. The northern zone, much smaller in size, occupies the llanos of Colombia and Venezuela.

Large cattle and sheep ranches dominate much of the interior of Africa south of Angola and Rhodesia. The greater parts of Australia and New Zealand are used for livestock ranching; in no other area does this economic activity occupy so much space. Except for the Kazakhstan–Turkmenistan region northeast of the Caspian Sea, formerly the habitat of nomads, livestock ranching is largely absent from the Eurasian realm (*see* Figure 8–7).

Carrying capacity, a term used to describe the number of animals an amount of land can support, varies considerably. In deserts, 100 acres or more are required for forage to support one steer. Steppes and mountain meadows vary from 25 to 75 acres, depending on the availability of moisture. In the subhumid part of the Great Plains, the carrying capacity improves, averaging 10 to 15 acres. Because carrying capacity is often low, large acreages are required for an economic unit. In western Texas many ranches have 20,000 acres; one ranch in southern Texas covers over 1,000 square miles. In Arizona and New Mexico many ranches have 30,000 to 40,000 acres. The world's largest ranches are found in Australia, where several encompass 5,000 or more square miles, and one even spreads over 12,000 square miles.

In the stock and crop association the ratio of browsing animals—cattle, sheep, goats—to total area is very low, and the ratio of cropland—mostly hay—to the total area is even lower. The land is used extensively because several acres are required to feed an animal. This means huge holdings and a small and scattered farm population. Isolation urges absentee ownership, and some holdings are organized as stock companies.

Livestock ranching is likely to be the mode of occupying an expanding frontier. Near the margin of settlement, the number of people and animals may be negligible. This is notably the case in the southern part of the Amazon Basin, and scarcely less so in interior Australia.

153

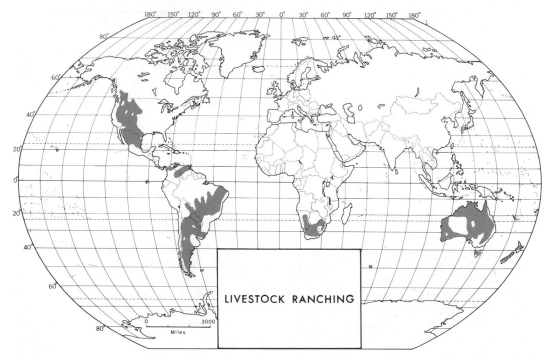

FIGURE 8–7

MEDITERRANEAN AGRICULTURE

Mediterranean agriculture refers to a diverse crop–livestock economic system that evolved from the Roman and Greek civilizations as a major land-use pattern. Four other non-Mediterranean areas have similar climatic patterns: southern California, Central Chile, the region about Capetown in South Africa, and southwestern Australia and its lands around Spencer Gulf. This type of climate occurs on all western coasts of countries in the subtropics (latitude 30° to 40°), but it is usually called Mediterranean because it occurs most extensively around the Mediterranean Sea (see Figure 8–8).

From a geographic standpoint, Mediterranean agriculture is the most satisfactory of all types, probably because it represents an ancient and stable collabo-

ration between man and the land. So vital has this proved that it stoutly maintains its character in the region of its origin, despite the worldwide shift from isolated to interdependent economies. The environment of Mediterranean lands encourages a distinctive, interrelated stock and crop association:

1. Winter grains, such as wheat and barley, grown without irrigation
2. All-year crops, such as olives, grapes, and carob, grown without irrigation
3. All-year or summer crops grown with irrigation, such as oranges, lemons, pomelos, deciduous fruits, corn, rice, and vegetables
4. Livestock, mainly small animals, grazed on highlands in winter and on lowlands in summer

Citrus and vine crops have long been important in world trade. Table 8–5

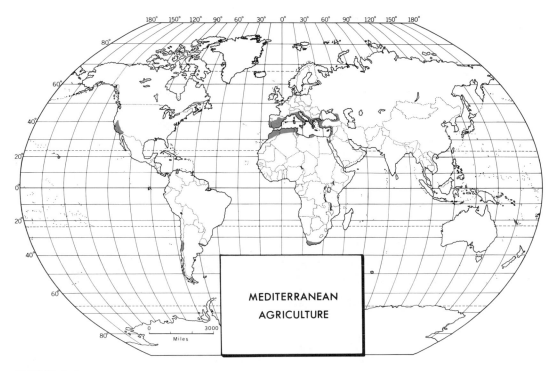

MEDITERRANEAN
AGRICULTURE

0   3000
Miles

FIGURE 8–8

shows the leading producers of these Mediterranean crops. Not all grapes are produced in Mediterranean countries; Argentina's interior steppe where irrigation is practiced produces enough grapes to qualify as a major producer.

Because animals are a major feature in the Mediterranean agricultural economy, some observers give the name *bioculture* to this type of agriculture. In no other major agricultural economy do both plants and animals occupy such an important position.

Both subsistence and cash crops are important in the economy of every region of Mediterranean agriculture, although not on every farm. The relative emphasis on the several products varies with the amount of rainfall. Thus, North Africa produces more barley and goat skins, and South Europe more wheat and sheepskins. Tradition, market, and government favor may sway attention to a particular crop, but the elements remain constant. Southern France, Italy, California, and Chile are important wine producers; California and Spain stress oranges. More wheat is grown in Italy, where it is supported by tradition and tariff, than in California, which must compete with commercial wheat raising in the interior United States. California markets fresh citrus and deciduous fruits and has an active canning industry for perishable, deciduous fruits. South Africa makes jams and preserves for the English market.

Despite the importance of agriculture, only about one-fifth of the land in the Mediterranean climatic regions is intensively cultivated. The remainder is too steep, too dry, or too rocky. Due to this limitation, a definite pattern of land use has evolved over the centuries. Small fruits and vegetables occupy the low-

155

TABLE 8–5 Total Production of Grapes, Oranges, and Lemons and Limes in the World and Selected Leading Countries (in thousand metric tons)

	1970	1972	PERCENT CHANGE
Grapes			
Italy	10,724	9,369	−12.64%
France	11,445	8,938	−21.90
USSR	4,011	4,500	+12.19
Spain	4,140	4,250	+ 2.66
Turkey	3,850	3,396	−11.79
Argentina	2,462	2,600	+ 5.61
U.S.	2,830	2,329	−17.70
World	55,532	51,435	− 7.38
Oranges			
U.S.	7,491	7,952	+ 6.15
Brazil	3,099	3,200	+ 3.26
Spain	1,950	2,493	+27.85
Mexico	1,555	1,650	+ 6.11
Italy	1,325	1,490	+12.45
Israel	938	1,080	+15.13
World	25,623	27,512	+ 7.37
Lemons and Limes			
Italy	798	726	− 9.02
U.S.	526	615	+ 9.43
India	450	450	0.00
Mexico	199	210	+ 5.53
Argentina	202	182	− 9.99
Spain	97	165	+70.10
World	3,480	3,557	+ 2.21

Source: Based on the *FAO Production Yearbook 1972* (Rome: FAO, 1973), pp. 147, 156–57.

lands where temperature and soil favor such cultivation near urban markets. Wheat and barley are grown in the more arid portions of the lower slopes. Tree and vine crops dominate the upper slopes, reducing erosion and yielding desirable food crops. Frequently, interculture is practiced to make the most of the usable land.

Livestock grazing is based primarily on natural vegetation. The marginal nature of so much of the land use in the Mediterranean, and the extent of open woodland and scrub, has stressed the importance of pastoralism. Generally, cattle tend to predominate in the wetter areas, sheep over vast areas of the arid zone, and goats in the driest, more rocky areas. Pastoralism has been divorced from agriculture, and this, together with the abrupt physical contrasts of relief and climate, has encouraged *transhumance*, the seasonal movement from lowland to highland. It is traceable to remote antiquity and is a climatic response. During the wet winter season, the lush green lowlands with mild temperatures are ideal for grazing livestock. In summer, when the lowland pastures are dry and dormant, the cool grassy upper slopes are ideally suited to pastoral activities.

Over much of the Mediterranean, sheep far outnumber all other domestic animals. The natural grassland is too scanty for large-scale grazing of cattle. In southern California, sheep ranches at one time dominated the land, and they are still numerous. In central Chile and southwest Africa, sheep ranching is very important. The breeding and raising of sheep for wool is the most important of the agricultural and pastoral activities in Australia.

Livestock farming in Mediterranean agriculture is based on irrigated meadows planted in alfalfa, hay, clover, sown grasses, or other forage crops. The animals are stall fed. Meat, milk, and cheese are produced both for local consumption and export in northern Algeria, northern Italy, southern France, and southern and eastern Spain. Dairying is especially important near the larger cities. Italian cheeses (Parmesan, Gorgonzola, and Stracchino) are highly esteemed in Western Europe and the United States. In other areas of the Mediterranean Basin, such as southern Italy, central Spain, northern Greece, Yugoslavia, Turkey, and Syria, subsistence livestock farming largely prevails.

Large-scale commercial livestock farming is important in California. Irrigated pastures and imported grain support huge dairies and meat-packing plants near Los Angeles and San Francisco. The San Joaquin Valley is a large milk-producing center, serving the urban population.

COMMERCIAL PLANTATION– CROP TILLAGE

Plantation agriculture is usually a corporate enterprise that organizes the production of valuable commercial crops, such as cotton, rubber, rice, sugar cane, sugar beets, pineapple, bananas, coconut, tea, cacao, cloves, nutmeg, allspice, and citrus fruits. This is accomplished through factory production methods, with headquarters, a marketing organization, transport facilities, housing for workers, and welfare facilities. Its *corporate organization* distinguishes it from other forms of large-scale intensive agriculture.

This system is not characterized by a predominant crop, but rather by the manner in which crops are produced and the land is managed. Neither is it strictly a phenomenon of the tropics or subtropics; the system is employed in a wide range of extratropical regions. The type of plantation ranges from those producing bananas or rubber in the wet tropics to state and collective enterprises in the USSR, the People's Republic of China, and Cuba. Plantations may cultivate potatoes and sugar beets in California or grow varieties of fruits, vegetables, cotton, or tobacco in the southern U.S.

Monoculture no longer prevails as it once did. Even the tropical plantation system has tended toward crop diversification. For example, rubber and bananas are commonly paired, as in Haiti; citrus fruits and bananas are produced in tandem on plantations in British Honduras; cacao and oil palms in other parts of Central America; sugar cane, citrus fruits, and cattle in Florida.

Table 8–6 shows the three most important commercial tropical plantation crops—bananas, sugar cane, and rubber—and their principal producers. Brazil leads the world in production of bananas, but Ecuador, with a much smaller population, is the major exporter. While India is the largest producer of sugar cane, the bulk of it is consumed domestically. Cuba, once the major producer of sugar cane, has reduced its acreage because of economic pressures and loss of the U.S. market. Malaysia continues to dominate in the production of natural rubber.

Many crops usually identified with

157

TABLE 8–6 Total Production of Bananas, Sugarcane, and Natural Rubber in the World and Selected Leading Countries (in thousand metric tons)

	1970	1972	PERCENT CHANGE
Bananas			
Brazil	6,408	7,000	+ 9.24%
Ecuador	2,700	3,100	+14.81
India	3,234	3,100	− 4.14
Burundi	1,400	1,500	+ 7.14
Costa Rica	1,146	1,400	+22.16
Honduras	1,200	1,366	+13.83
World	30,753	32,964	+ 7.19
Sugarcane			
India	135,024	115,378	−14.15
Brazil	79,753	84,000	+ 5.33
Cuba	80,981	45,000	−44.43
China	35,746	38,600	+ 7.98
Mexico	33,550	34,000	+ 1.34
U.S.	21,769	26,756	+22.91
World	621,036	580,894	− 6.46
Natural Rubber			
Malaysia	1,269	1,325	+ 4.41
Indonesia	809	845	+ 4.45
Thailand	289	337	+16.61
Sri Lanka	159	140	−11.45
India	90	109	+21.11
Liberia	83	64	−22.89
World	2,940	3,060	+ 4.08

Source: Based on the *FAO Production Yearbook 1972* (Rome: FAO, 1973), pp. 161–62; 149–50; 179–80.

tropical plantations also are grown by nonplantation methods. Cacao and peanuts in Nigeria, rubber in Amazonia and Malaysia, bananas in Central America, and tea in Ceylon are produced by individual farmers and even gathered without cultivation and sold to the plantations for export.

Although not the general rule, diversification also is present in a plantation system. Many tropical plantation enterprises operate in several countries to minimize crop failures, destruction by hurricanes, attacks by pests or fungi, and other such destructive forces. Although the tropical plantation system of agricul-

ture varies widely in operation, the following generalizations can be made:

1. Cultivated land is more than one geographical region, often with separate tracts.
2. Large land areas are cleared.
3. Large capital investments are made.
4. Scientific techniques relating to meteorology, soil, feed, and fertilizer are applied.
5. Managerial arrangements are highly structured.
6. Production is for commercial purposes.
7. Transportation and communication facilities are highly integrated.

The tropical plantation system was evolved to meet the world demand for certain staple crops. As part of the imperialist era, it rested on European acquisition of areas of suitable land sufficient to make economically attractive units, where managers and assistants were established to provide commercial organization and technical direction. Manual labor had to be cheap, so that the product could be sold at a price that would ensure a large and growing volume of demand. However, these conditions no longer are as valid as they were in the 18th and 19th centuries, when Europeans established colonial systems after their commercial ventures in the tropical and subtropical regions of the Americas and Southeast Asia (*see* Figure 8–9).

INTENSIVE SUBSISTENCE TILLAGE WITH RICE DOMINANT

In south and east Asia, the dominant subsistence, sedentary, agricultural techniques are more complex than any in the world. Its agricultural characteristics do not fit the Von Thünen model. This is a land of real tropical farmers. Asia's dry and cool monsoon season gives man more energy than in the wet tropics, and the task of clearing and maintaining a farm is relatively easy. The young trees and dry grass are burned near the close of the dry season, the ground is then hoed, and crops are planted at the beginning of the rainy season.

Soils, generally alluvial in nature, occur in major drainage basins, such as the Irrawaddy, Salween, Menam, Me-

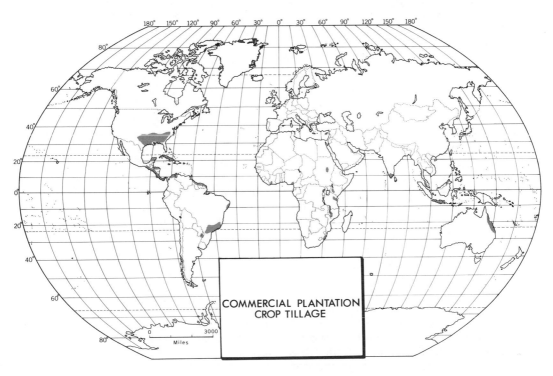

COMMERCIAL PLANTATION CROP TILLAGE

FIGURE 8–9

159

kong, Red, Yangtze, and Si river basins. These soils are naturally fertile, but owing to intensive tillage they require large amounts of fertilizer from animals and human sources. The latter is by far the most widely used in Southeast Asia because the population is so dense that animals are relatively few.

Fields are rather small, often averaging less than 2 acres per farm. In order to feed, clothe, and house a family of up to ten people, yields must be high and methods intensive. Labor is mainly manual, although a few highly skilled groups use animal power, such as in parts of South Vietnam. Due to the high labor requirements of rice cultivation, the dominant food crop, 90 percent or more of the agricultural population often is employed in planting, cultivating, and harvesting this important grain.

Before the monsoon rains begin, the fields are tilled by hand or with draft animal power and flooded with water. The rice is then planted and the fields remain flooded until a few days before harvest. Almost every member of the family, young and old, in some manner helps to produce the rice crop. Terraces are built and mended. To prevent soil erosion, soil, washed from the fields, is carried on the backs of men to the upper fields. The water inundating the paddy field is planted with fish, which serve not only as food but also supply fertilizer for the rice.

Rice forms the staple food of well over half the world's people. It is so prevalent in the peasant economy that an agricultural system based on intensive tillage, night soil, multiple cropping, and hand labor has been developed around this dominant crop. The Southeast Asian farmer's methods of agriculture would no doubt remain the same whether the crop were rice or soybeans or manioc (see Figure 8–10).

Rice cultivation covers much of Ceylon, southern India, Bangladesh, the delta of mainland Southeast Asia, Java, Sumatra, the Philippines, and southern China and Japan. The total area under "wet" rice cultivation—as distinct from "dry" rice grown by shifting or rudimentary cultivation—exceeds 200 million acres.

Because rice exists in so many varieties, it can be grown under widely varying conditions, from brackish or even saline soils to deeply flooded deltas like those of Thailand and South Vietnam. In many places, given enough water, rice can supply two crops from the same land each year. It can give worthwhile yields on the same land year after year for generations without fertilizing, although yields may be greatly increased by the judicious use of manure. Dry crops under similar conditions in the tropics tend to give declining yields that often stabilize at an uneconomic level.

Among the populations supported by plow cultivation of rice there are, not surprisingly, many variations in agricultural economy and technology. Some rice cultivators have highly developed techniques of terracing hillsides and of controlling water in the terraces (e.g., in the hills of Ceylon, in Java, and in the interior of Luzon); others tackle land that is almost flat (e.g., in southern Thailand and in the Malay Peninsula). Again, some rice cultivators, as in China, employ almost incredible ingenuity to see that every scrap of waste organic matter finds its way back to the soil. Indeed, their technology tends to be intensive gardening rather than plow culture. Other rice cultivators that until recently felt little population pressure, used no manure at all until pressure was exerted by a cash economy and by government agencies (e.g., in lowland Ceylon).

Regardless of where rice is grown as a subsistence crop in Southeast Asia, rice cultivation generally involves the following:

1. Back-breaking labor
2. Intensive tillage
3. High moisture requirements—38 to 40 inches of annual precipitation or its equivalent through irrigation
4. Relatively heavy clay soils, with relatively impervious subsoils
5. Green manuring and/or night soil
6. Use of hand tools
7. Great population density

INTENSIVE SUBSISTENCE TILLAGE WITHOUT PADDY RICE

Although still cultivated intensively, much of interior India, dry inland portions of Southeast Asia, and China north of the Yangtze differ in nature and methods of crop production. Where rice is dominant, water is supplied either through man-made irrigation systems or by natural rainfall and flooding. Where the natural rainfall is insufficient or undependable and man is unable to afford costly irrigation systems, grains other than rice become the staples of diet. India and China are classic examples of intensively cultivated, densely populated lands with the bulk of their labor force engaged in subsistence agriculture. As such, they merit further attention (*see* Figure 8–11).

India. Agriculture is the mainstay of India's economic life, as well as its greatest economic problem. India has too many people on too little land. Productivity is among the lowest in the world because of primitive techniques, poor

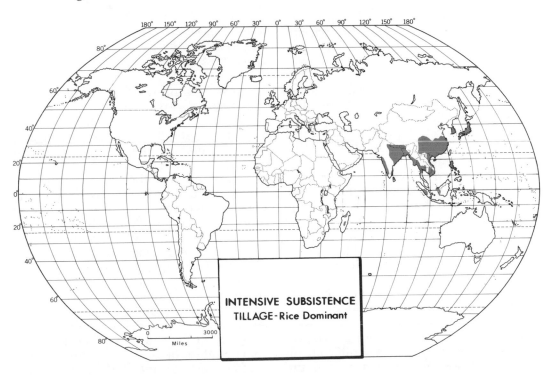

INTENSIVE SUBSISTENCE TILLAGE-Rice Dominant

FIGURE 8–10

161

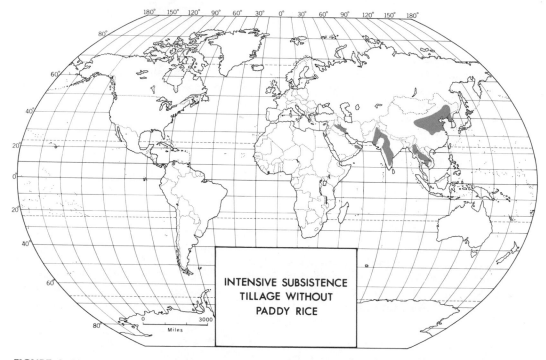

INTENSIVE SUBSISTENCE
TILLAGE WITHOUT
PADDY RICE

FIGURE 8–11

seed, a highly seasonal distribution of rainfall, and land-tenure systems that have provided little incentive to the cultivator. In the last decade, land reform, agricultural extension services, better seed, and a rapidly expanding use of fertilizer have put the increase in food production slightly ahead of the increase in population. However, there are an estimated 45 million landless agricultural laborers in India, and population pressure on the land remains. India will continue to have a food deficit for many years.

To a very great extent, the cultivator in India labors not for profit or a net return but for subsistence. The overcrowded population, lack of alternative means of securing a living, difficulty of finding any avenue of escape, and the early age at which man is burdened with dependents combine to force the farmer

to grow food on whatever terms he can. Illiteracy, conservatism, superstition, and fatalism, which are common among Indian farmers, play a large part in preserving India's ancient agricultural methods. These cultural deterrents reflect the real problems of the Indian economy.

Crop failures in various parts of the country have been a recurrent feature of India's agriculture. Approximately four-fifths of the cultivatable area in India is dependent on the rainy seasons or monsoons. Of the major subsistence grains cultivated in the drier parts of India, sorghum, millet, and wheat occupy the greatest acreage of inefficiently worked land. Sorghum is widely distributed over the Deccan Plateau, but is most heavily concentrated on the black soils in the central part of the Indian peninsula. Millet is the major grain in the extreme northwest and Rajasthan portions of

India bordering Pakistan. Wheat is grown mainly in northwestern and central India.

Other secondary crops include gram or chickpea, which extends from the Punjab plains eastward up to the delta region; peanuts, which are highly concentrated in the southern half of the peninsula; and cotton, produced mostly in the northwestern and central parts of the Deccan Plateau.

People's Republic of China. China, like the United States, can be divided into fairly well-defined regions. The most clear-cut separation is between north and south, and the dividing line follows generally along the Yangtze Valley. South of the Yangtze River, the green of South China is the green of the rice fields. Rice is the universally cultivated crop in this region because rainfall is plentiful, and the air is moist and warm almost year round.

North of the Yangtze, the green countryside dies away quite suddenly into brown, except for a momentary revival where the Yellow River forges its treacherous way to the sea. North China is a region of fertile and barren plains, and of bare mountains. Like the south, there is much rich soil, but the richness is less stable because of infrequent and uncertain rainfall. Prolonged droughts may parch the soil and burn the crops out before harvest, or, sudden outbursts of rain produce devastating floods.

Despite this climate, north China is a highly productive region. The area near the coast, the famous north China (Yellow River) Plain, is one of the most densely populated and most intensively cultivated parts of the country. Better known as the winter wheat–kaoliang region, it comprises most of Hopei, Shantung, and Honan provinces. Because of its high percentage of cultivable land (60 percent or more under cultivation), the winter wheat–kaoliang section produces a wide variety of crops without irrigation. Fortunately, the maximum rainfall of 24 inches annually occurs during the hot summer. Winter wheat is the principal crop and occupies about 45 percent of the cultivated land. No other winter crop is planted to any extent, although barley and peas are grown in a few districts.

Kaoliang, a kind of sorghum, is the chief summer crop. It is well adapted to the climate and produces large amounts of grain and stalks for human food and fuel. Soybeans, cotton, corn, and sweet potatoes also cover a considerable area in the summer. Delicious persimmons and hard pears are important fruits. Peanuts are cultivated in many districts, especially in Shantung and Honan, and flue-cured tobacco is grown in a few localities. No other agricultural area in China has so much diversification.

To the west of the winter wheat–kaoliang region are the Loess Highlands, an area of wind-blown silt deposits 300 or more feet thick in places, with fertile soils, steep slopes, and marginal rainfall. More than one-third of the cropland is terraced to check erosion of the steep hillsides. The best agricultural districts are along the Yellow River in southern Shansi and northern Honan, extending west into Shensi. Winter wheat, the major crop, is confined to the plains and valleys; other winter crops, of only minor importance but extensively planted in some localities, are rapeseed, peas, and barley. Millet is the most widely grown summer crop, followed by corn, soybeans, sesame, and buckwheat; cotton is important in some of the more productive agricultural districts.

The spring wheat region forms a fringe along the Mongolian frontier, lying on either side of the Great Wall. The percentage of cultivatable land is small, owing to the colder climate and very limited rainfall. Spring wheat is the principal crop, with millet, oats, peas, flax, and buckwheat following.

SUBSISTENCE CROP AND LIVESTOCK FARMING

This form of agriculture land occupancy is mostly outside the money economy. The farmer produces for his own sustenance and sells little or nothing. Having no cash income, he cannot buy expensive machinery, save the best seed from his fields, or buy breeding stock. His return is correspondingly low, and he cannot market his rare surpluses in competition with the high-grade and reliable output of commercial regions. Lacking the stimulus of a competitive market, methods are crude.

Subsistence crop and livestock farming occupies large tracts of semidesert, hilly, or mountainous lands in the Anatolian and Iranian plateaus in southwest Asia, portions of Soviet Siberia bordering the Mongolian People's Republic, and small segments in Soviet Europe north of the 55th parallel. The Carpathian and Rhodope mountain areas of east-central and southeastern Europe also have small tracts of land that are still classified as subsistence crop and livestock farming areas. The only area of significance outside the Eurasian realm is the Mexican plateau.

Few people are engaged in this type of agriculture. In the past, most of them followed a nomadic way of life, but inroads are constantly being made on the lands they occupy through government intervention, improvement in agricultural techniques, and resettlement programs. For the most part, agriculture and animal husbandry tend to become separate occupations. The mixed type of farming characteristic of many parts of the world is practiced only on a small scale, and many villages maintain one or more

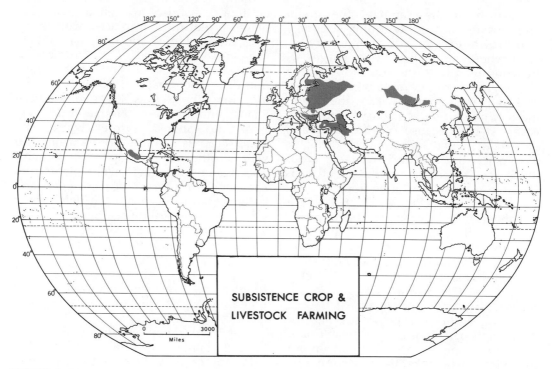

SUBSISTENCE CROP & LIVESTOCK FARMING

FIGURE 8–12

164

shepherds to look after all animals in common, while the great majority of owners devote themselves entirely to cultivation.

Herding tends to be restricted to less favorable regions. People who still persist in this endeavor have become seminomadic villagers who move their flocks in summer to hillsides or alpine mountain slopes where the animals graze until cold weather threatens. This transhumance system of vertical seasonal movement of flocks and herds is an ancient practice in Eurasia.

Because of population pressure, all lands capable of cultivation are given over to cereal growing, which produces a greater quantity of foodstuff per unit of area than land under pasture. Wherever possible, vegetables and fruits are cultivated. The Kurds of eastern Turkey and Armenia, the Buryats of southeastern

Siberia, and the Yakuts north and west of Lake Baikal, USSR, are former nomadic herders who have become sedentary agriculturists. They are still somewhat dependent on livestock farming, although it is carried on as a semivillage function.

RUDIMENTARY AND SEDENTARY TILLAGE

Throughout areas inhabited by hunter–gatherers practicing shifting cultivation, many groups have changed their economic systems generally in a more progressive direction. In general, many of the more primitive forms have gradually evolved into rudimentary and sedentary tillage systems of agriculture (see Figure 8–13).

People will change their entire pattern of living only when there is considerable pressure from some source to

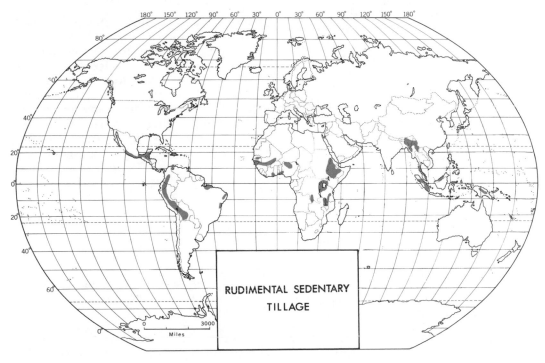

FIGURE 8–13

cause such a radical shift. For example, population pressure results in:

1.   A lower standard of living and a switch to other forms of resources
2.   Migration to other areas
3.   A change in the socioeconomic activities that will maintain the essentials of the existing patterns while transforming those of lesser necessity or tradition

Production of foodstuffs and other plants solely for local use takes many forms in terms of the products grown (rice, tubers, fruits), the techniques used (hand tools, irrigation, use of work animals), intensity (settled agriculture, minor gardening), organization (ownership of land, financing, work methods), and other variables. Native communities often supplement their subsistence cropping to some extent with marketable products. Growing rubber or pepper or making copra from coconuts, for example, provides communities with money to help fill minimum needs for imported goods.

Much of the sedentary subsistence farming in Latin America is still characterized by extensive employment of human labor, little use of machinery, forest destruction, and soil waste and erosion. The pattern of farming in Latin America usually followed consists of:

1.   Felling with axes all but the largest trees, which are girdled
2.   Burning of forest and ground vegetation
3.   Planting with hoe or stick crops such as corn, beans, rice, manioc, and even cotton
4.   Chopping weeds with a machete
5.   Harvesting few crops, usually not more than three or four
6.   Planting grasses to be grazed until scrubby trees choke them out, or simply abandoning the land for a newly cleared plot

Traditionally, Congolese agriculture has been little more than subsistence agriculture. Small, family-owned farms grow cassava and plantain bananas, along with sweet potatoes, yams, rice, and sugarcane for home consumption.

The hoe is the most important tool in African sedentary subsistence farming. Other important agricultural implements are the axe and the bush knife, used to cut threes and shrubs when new clearings are made. The cultivated crops of the wet-dry savanna lands are mainly shrubs, such as the cotton bush, small plants, such as tobacco and peanut, or domesticated grasses, such as maize and millet. Corn, wheat, barley, rice, sorghum, sweet potatoes, and various types of beans are staple items of the diet. Secondary crops commonly grown in the savanna lands are manioc, sesame, artichokes, peppers, tomatoes, pumpkins, henna, and indigo.

SHIFTING CULTIVATION

In most cases, shifting cultivators dwell in greatest numbers in the tropical wet and tropical wet-dry climates. Generally, the location of these economic activities not only coincides with the above climates but also is adjacent to the hunting-gathering societies. In many instances, the shifting cultivators are located in these relatively isolated areas for the same reasons as the hunting-gathering systems are (see Figure 8–14). These include:

1.   A forcible exile into remote areas by advanced cultures occupying the more desirable lands
2.   Self-exile to preserve cultural characteristics
3.   A socioeconomic organization that can be manifested better in these climates than elsewhere

Subtypes.   Three major subtypes of shifting cultivators may be recognized. The

166

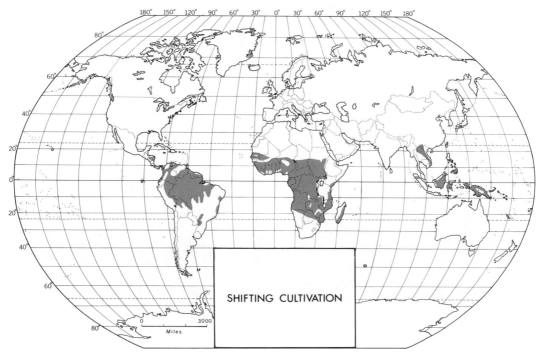

SHIFTING CULTIVATION

FIGURE 8–14

first, or least advanced, usually consists of a hunting-gathering tribe that supplements its activities with very primitive agricultural techniques. Quite often no tools are employed, not even sticks. The ground is not plowed in any way. Wherever there is a natural clearing in the forest, seeds are placed in holes dug by hand or stick. This subtype of shifting cultivators does not till or care for the crops. As the crops grow, they practice an economic system almost identical to the simple hunting-gathering economy. When the crops mature, however, the shifting cultivators return to harvest them. Due to insects, fungi, and other such pests, crop yields are low. In this socioeconomic system, the hunting-gathering economy is the major source of livelihood, and the very limited agriculture

that is practiced is only supplementary.

The next type of shifting cultivation consists of semipermanent dwellings made of materials easily gathered from the immediate area. These dwellings usually are occupied for about three to four years, and the agricultural activities occur in the adjacent area.

The third and most common subtype of migratory agriculture is that in which the tribe is relatively well settled in the same area for periods of up to twenty to thirty years. Here the forest is cleared in patches, one clearing will be used for several years, then an adjacent one. After several clearings are made and their soil resources depleted, migration occurs. The dwellings and fields are abandoned, and a new area is sought. Table 8–7 shows the general distribution

167

TABLE 8–7   Distribution of Migratory Agriculturalists

Central America	250,000
South America	1,100,000
Africa	30,000,000
Madagascar	1,000,000
India	5,000,000
Southeast Asia	5,500,000
Philippines	200,000
New Guinea	500,000
Indonesia	10,000,000
Total	53,550,000

and number of people classified as migratory agriculturists.

Agricultural Techniques.   Migration cultivation, or the annual production of food or fiber crops in temporary clearings in the forest, is widespread. The practice is called *milpa* in the Amazon Valley, *fang* in the Congo Basin, and *ladang* in Southeast Asia. Trees are girdled or felled with stone or iron axes. After the trees have been dried by high temperatures, they are piled and burned. Later the ashes are spread over the ground to restore fertility. The temporarily enriched soil is stirred with a digging stick by the more primitive groups or with a hoe among more advanced peoples, after which the crops are planted.

Crops.   Usually only one or two vegetable crops are planted per family in the wet tropics, although a wide variety of tree crops (coconuts, breadfruit, oil palm, mangoes, avocados, bananas, plantains, cacao, guava) and vegetable crops (yams, sweet potatoes, pumpkins, beans, and peanuts) are cultivated throughout the area. A little rice and corn are grown in a few places where outside forces have introduced them. Sugar cane and millet are also grown here and there.

Within a year or two, however, weeds and other pests become serious or the fertility declines. Then the land is abandoned to forest and a new clearing is made.

Bread is made from cassava or manioc, which is a staple in the diet of the more sedentary cultivators. Bananas, yams, and sweet potatoes provide abundant starch; coconuts and oil palms supply the needed fats. But there is a dearth of protein in the diet, and these people consume too much starch, which results in protruding abdomens, even among little children.

Production and Soil Nutrients.   It would appear that tropical humid areas are rich in soil nutrients because they support a dense vegetation. In some cases, this is true. However, the nutrients, climatic conditions, and vegetable growth is such that almost all nutrients are used or stored in the vegetation or are leached from the soil by the constant rains.

As the plants absorb and use minerals from the soil, they are not returned to the soil until the leaves fall or until the tree matures, dies, falls, and decays. Since the growing season is all year in the wet tropics and at least six months in the wet-dry tropics, the density of fallen, decaying trees and ground vegetation is rather slight at any one time. Also, the constantly high temperatures produce a high density of organic decaying bacteria. Therefore, almost all nutrients present are not available for man to use. Portions of the forest must be cleared and burned to make soil nutrients available. When the vegetation is burned, the cycle of nature is broken, and for a time the soil is relatively rich. Unfortunately, the bulk of these nutrients are valuable only to starchy plant foods.

The period of soil enrichment is rather short. Usually the first crop yield is good, but the second is only a fraction of the first, and the third and fourth harvests fall off appreciably. Since these people do not possess the technology, tools, and techniques to cope with soil depletion, they are forced to move on.

NOMADIC HERDING

Animal husbandry is not the same, nor is it directly associated with, the hunting-gathering system. The Kalahari Bushmen, the Semang, and most of the Amerindians, among others, were not engaged in animal husbandry. Animal husbandry is associated only with activities in which animals are domesticated. The Eskimo, for example, generally is not engaged in animal husbandry, since he is a hunter and not a herdsman; in some cases, however, with the introduction of domesticated reindeer or caribou, the Eskimo has taken up reindeer herding instead of hunting.

Knowledge of the original domestication of animals is lost in the dark period of prehistory. The methods of domestication can only be surmised from indirect evidence, such as the attitudes and habits of primitive peoples about the animals around them. Presumably the initial steps were taken largely through the widespread practice of making pets of captured young or crippled wild animals.

People in a Paleolithic culture generally had no truly domestic animal, except perhaps the dog. Cattle and sheep were domesticated as early as 7000 BC in Asia Minor. Horses first appeared as domesticated animals about 3000 BC, and mounted invaders from the north brought them into the Tigris–Euphrates Valley as early as 2000 BC. Chickens were domesticated in southeastern Asia perhaps by 2500 BC. Only the llama, alpaca, guinea pig, and turkey were domesticated in Latin America. American Indians north of Mexico had no domesticated animals except dogs.

Whatever and wherever the first domesticated animals were, it is quite certain that many animals in many places were domesticated for a multitude of uses. For example, in the great original division of agriculture—between vegetable planting and seed planting—animals, such as cats, chickens, and ducks were considered household animals. With the seed planters go the herd animals, such as camels, goats, sheep, yak, horses, *Bos indicus*, and *Bos taurus*.

Animals commonly associated with nomadism were not domesticated by nomads but by sedentary agriculturists. Nomadism originally developed *after* sedentary agriculture and *after* the domestication of sheep, cattle, goats, and camels. The origins of nomadism are not in deserts now traveled by nomads, but in areas of original domestication and cultivation. The vegetation that now is the food supply for many grazing animals developed from the cultivation of seed or grain.

It is quite a tribute to early man that no major species of plants or animals have been domesticated since about 2000 BC. All of the so-called modern plants and modern animals are not newly domesticated species, but only crossbreeds of species domesticated thousands of years ago.

Nomadism as an Economic Activity. Nomadism occupies more of the earth than any other single economic activity (*see* Figure 8–15). It is characterized by:

1. Location in semiarid or arid regions
2. Migratory habits
3. Grazing of animals on native or wild plants
4. Almost complete dependence of man on the animal population for his transportation, food, shelter, tools, clothing, and fuel
5. A level of technology often too low to apply any principles of crossbreeding or

169

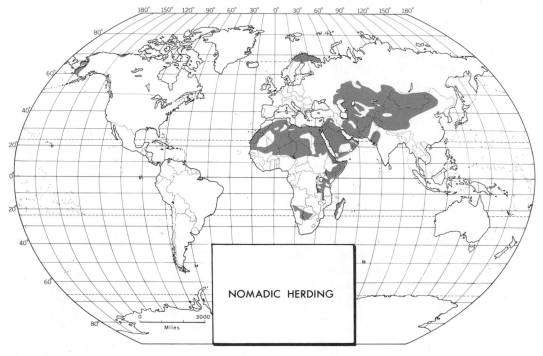

NOMADIC HERDING

FIGURE 8–15

hybridization to animals to improve their quality

6. Near-subsistence production

In many areas, nomadism is a product of cultural associations that may be as dominant a factor in the activity as the physical landscape, which has a greatly limited resource base. Many Moslem Arabs prefer nomadism to a sedentary way of life because of long tradition and history. In other areas without the benefits of modern technology and capital investment, nomadism is the only economic system that can survive.

Perhaps one wonders why, instead of migrating from one seasonal pasture to another, the nomads do not head straight for the perennial green pastures and settle there. In many cases this has been done, for example, by the Israelites

who settled in Canaan. When a nomadic society attempts to inhabit an already settled area of perennial grass, warfare invariably is the result. Often the warfare may not be limited to the local area. For example, the Huns, a nomadic people from the Asiatic steppe, ravaged northwestern China for centuries. In 375 AD the first wave of Huns appeared in Eastern Europe, in the steppe lands north of the Caspian and Black seas. By the end of the 5th century they almost reached the Atlantic. The Moors, a Moslem, Arabic-speaking race of mixed descent, overran Spain around 700 AD and pushed northward into France. They were repulsed by Charles Martel at the Battle of Tours in 732, after which they were restrained to Spain south of the Ebro. In 1241 Mongol nomads invaded the West as far as Poland. Turkish nomads laid

170

siege to the city of Vienna in 1529, and during the 16th and 17th centuries the Manchus invaded China.

Often these invasions were triggered by a series of unusually dry years in the steppe areas occupied by nomadic tribes. With no grass to eat, the herds die, famine results, and the desert clans raid the oases of other clans. If the drought is prolonged, vast migrations take place. The law of survival of the fittest tends to operate to some degree.

Often nomads are assimilated into the existing population. The Huns, for example, never returned to eastern Asia. Instead, they were gradually absorbed into the European milieu. The Manchus, Tatars, and other nomadic tribes of northern and eastern Asia were fused into the population of China. Almost invariably, when a nomadic tribe inhabits an area of sedentary agriculture over a sustained period, nomadic activity disappears. It blends in with the livestock-crop associations and ceases as a way of life.

There has been a conscious effort on the part of some governments to make nomads sedentary. Egypt has attempted this with moderate success. Iran and Iraq have taken measures to permanently settle more than 3 million nomads. Somali, Israel, Tanzania, and the Soviet Union also have experimented with settling nomads.

The principal regions of pastoral nomadism are in the arid lands of the Old World, extending from North Africa through Saudi Arabia to inner Asia. This type of highly specialized livelihood involves frequent movement of livestock in response to the need for grazing lands and water. Settlement is generally characterized by small clusters of homesteads temporarily established near a common watering point and pasture. Subsistence is maintained almost entirely by domestic stock, such as cattle, camels, goats, and sheep (see Figure 8–11).

Today agriculture is practiced throughout the world—in some areas by methods not far removed from the conditions of several thousands of years ago, in others with the aid of science and mechanization, as a highly commercial endeavor. Regardless of the particular system employed, several important generalizations about agriculture may be made:

1. Agriculture is the major sustainer of life.

2. Agricultural activity covers a greater portion of land surface than any other economic activity.

3. Every society of significance is dependent either directly or indirectly on agriculture.

4. More people are engaged in agriculture than in any other economic activity.

5. The total value of agricultural products exceeds the value of all other forms of economic activity, and the value of animal products exceeds the value of all minerals mined.

6. Without agriculture, the type of culture with which most of the world's inhabitants are familiar could not exist.

7. No other economic activity yet devised or proposed can supplant agriculture.

A HUNGRY WORLD: THE CHALLENGE TO AGRICULTURE

Few, if any, problems confronting modern man are more complex than that of assuring an adequate food supply to the peoples of the world in the decades to come. With near-famine conditions in some parts of the world pushing the problems to the forefront, specialists in the analysis of interacting global issues have begun to apply their expertise and their computers to search for possible solutions.

They emphasize that success will depend on identifying key factors that will control the outcome and, not unexpectedly, they have found that curbing population growth is by far the most vital element.

Some suggest that if food sources are not found soon where food supplies are already short, mass starvation by the end of this century is inevitable.

This conclusion has emerged from an international effort of computer analysis of all factors believed to bear on food and population growth over the next half century. The analysis indicates that unless births are brought down to the death-rate level within a few decades, half a billion children will die between 1980 and 2055.

In a keynote address at the opening session of the World Food Conference in Rome in 1974, Secretary of State Henry Kissinger emphasized the global nature of the world food crisis and proposed "a comprehensive program of urgent, cooperative worldwide action" to prevent catastrophe. (12)

Food has become a central element of the international economy. A world of energy shortages, rampant inflation, and a weakening trade and monetary system will be a world of food shortages as well. And food shortages, in turn, sabotage growth and accelerate inflation.

The food problem has two levels: first, coping with emergency supplies of food, and second, assuring long-term supplies and an adequate standard of nutrition for the growing populations of the world.

During the 1950s and 1960s global food production grew with great consistency. Per capita output expanded even in the food-deficit nations, and the world's total output increased by more than half. But at the precise moment when growing populations and rising expectations made a continuation of this trend essential, a dramatic change occurred. During the past three years, world cereal production has fallen, and reserves have dropped to the point where sig-

nificant crop failure can spell a major disaster.

The long-term picture is starker still. Even today hundreds of millions of people do not eat enough for decent and productive lives. Since increases in production are not evenly distributed, the absolute number of malnourished people are in fact probably greater today than ever before. In many parts of the world, 30 to 50 percent of the population die before the age of five, millions from malnutrition. Many survive only with permanent damage to their intellectual and physical capacities.

World population is projected to double by the end of the century. It is clear that we must meet the food needs of this potential population. But it is equally clear that population cannot continue to double every generation indefinitely. At some point, we will inevitably exceed the earth's capacity to sustain human life.

In short, the world faces a challenge new in severity, pervasiveness and global dimension. The minimum objective of the next quarter century must be to more than double world food production and to improve its quality.

One hope for increased food supply is better use of the world's oceans. The nations of the world appear to be more and more interested in the seas as a major source of food and other needs. Fisheries and their importance to man are discussed in the next chapter.

references

1. Barrett, Ward. "The Meat Supply of Colonial Cuernavaca." *Annals of the Association of American Geographers* 64 (December 1974): 525–40.

2. Borchert, John R. "The Dust Bowl in the 1970's." *Annals of the Association of*

American Geographers 61 (March 1971): 1–22.

3. Chakravarti, A. K. "Green Revolution in India." *Annals of the Association of American Geographers* 63 (September 1973): 319–30.

4. Chisholm, Michael. *Rural Settlement and Land Use*. London: G. Bell, 1966.

5. Dickinson, J. C. "Alternatives to Monoculture in the Humid Tropics of Latin America." *The Professional Geographer* 24 (August 1973): 217–22.

6. Garrison, William L., and Duane F. Marble. "The Spatial Structure of Agricultural Activities." *Annals of the Association of American Geographers* 47 (June 1957): 137.

7. Glassner, Martin Ira. "The Bedouin of Southern Sinai under Israeli Administration." *Geographical Review* 64 (January 1974): 31–60.

8. Hart, Fraser. "The Middle West." *Annals of the Association of American Geographers* 62 (June 1972): 258–82.

9. Igbozurike, Matthias U. "Ecological Balance in Tropical Agriculture." *Geographical Review* 61 (October 1971): 519–29.

10. Jumper, Sidney R. "Wholesale Marketing of Fresh Vegetables." *Annals of the Association of American Geographers* 64 (September 1974): 387–96.

11. Kiefer, Wayne E. "An Agricultural Settlement Complex in Indiana." *Annals of the Association of American Geographers* 62 (September 1972): 487–506.

12. Kissinger, Henry. "No Child Will Go to Bed Hungry." *War on Hunger: A Report from the Agency for International Development*, vol. 8, p. 1.

13. Mather, E. Colton. "The American Great Plains." *Annals of the Association of American Geographers* 62 (June 1972): 237–57.

14. Mausel, P. W., and Johannsen, C. J. "An Application of Remotely Sensed Data to Agricultural Land Use Distribution Analysis."

The Professional Geographer 25 (August 1973): 242–48.

15. Prunty, Merle C., and Charles S. Aiken. "The Demise of the Piedmont Cotton Region." *Annals of the Association of American Geographers* 62 (June 1972): 283–306.

16. Sauer, Carl O. "The Agency of Man on Earth." In William L. Thomas, Jr., ed., *Man's Role in Changing the Face of the Earth*. Chicago: University of Chicago Press, 1956, p. 56.

17. Seavoy, Ronald E. "The Transition to Continuous Rice Cultivation in Kalimantan." *Annals of the Association of American Geographers* 63 (June 1973): 218–26.

18. Shortridge, James R. "Prairie Hay in Woodson County, Kansas: A Crop Anomaly." *Geographical Review* 63 (October 1973): 533–52.

19. Simoons, Frederick J. "The Antiquity in Dairying in Asia and Africa." *Geographical Review* 61 (July 1971): 431–39.

20. Spencer, J. E., and Norman R. Stewart. "The Nature of Agricultural Systems." *Annals of the Association of American Geographers* 63 (December 1973): 529–44.

21. Stanislawski, Dan. "Dark Age Contributions to the Mediterranean Way of Life." *Annals of the Association of American Geographers* 63 (December 1973): 397–410.

22. Trueman, H. L. "The Hungry Seventies." *Canadian Geographical Journal* 83 (April 1971): 114–29.

23. Whittlesey, Derwent. "Major Agricultural Regions of the Earth." *Annals of the Association of American Geographers* 26 (December 1936): 199–240.

24. Wilken, Gene C. "Microclimate Management by Traditional Farmers." *Geographical Review* 62 (October 1972): 544–60.

25. Wood, Harold A. "Spontaneous Agricultural Colonization in Ecuador." *Annals of the Association of American Geographers* 52 (December 1972): 599–617.

fishing

9

9

Fishing is considered an extractive industry because it involves the removal of resources that have been stored in the environment by natural processes. Fishing activity must be carried on where the raw material occurs in nature. Power, labor, capital, and transport facilities must be brought to the raw materials, and the product is conveyed to market from the resource site.

Since fishing activity must be conducted principally at the resource site, the economic, technological, and cultural frameworks of the primary activities model determine the level and location of the activity. Fishing resources are frequently located far away from markets, involving substantial transportation and capital costs. However, these costs are mitigated by a rental subsidy, i.e., the "free" use resources that are publicly or internationally owned. The analysis of fisheries in this chapter reflects resource orientation.

From earliest times, fisheries have played a vital part in the life of people living near the oceans. Fishing was one of the earliest methods of food gathering. Our forefathers were hunters or fishermen before they were tillers of the soil. It was probably to seek good fishing grounds that man first built crude boats and risked the dangers of the unknown ocean. Fisheries played an important part in the early development of all the leading maritime powers of the world. Today fisheries make valuable contributions to the world's food supply, although the total annual value of the products of fisheries is less than that of the American crop of wheat, cotton, or corn.

The organisms of the sea are born, live, breathe, feed, excrete, move, grow, mate, reproduce, and die within an interconnected medium. Interactions of marine organisms and interactions of organisms with the chemical and physical processes of the sea range across the entire spectrum from simple, adamant constraints to complex effects of many subtle interactions.

The first creatures with backbones that inhabited the waters of the earth probably were fishes. Fossilized fragments of heavily armored, apparently cumbersome beasts that were the evolutionary precursors of fish have been found in deposits 450 million years old. During the next 40-million-year portion of the earth's existence the first true fishes appeared, and probably between 300 and 350 million years ago, the ancestors of the bony fishes we know today evolved.

Various fishery experts estimate there are about 40,000 kinds of fishes in the world today. Of these, approximately 25,000 are marine varieties; and the remainder inhabit freshwaters. Marine fishes are at the end of a vast food chain which has its beginning in microscopic plant and animal material called plankton.

As the sun's rays shine down into the upper layers of the ocean, oxygen and carbon dioxide are dissolved in the ocean from the atmosphere. Various mineral salts, principally phosphates, nitrates, and iron compounds, along with minute amounts of essential vitamin-like substances are continually poured into the sea by land erosion. These processes produce ideal conditions for the growth of billions of microscopic plants called phytoplankton, or plant plankton. Feeding upon these minute floating plants are crustacea and other little animals ranging in size from a pin's head to somewhat larger than a grain of rice (zooplankton). All these plant and animal creatures, which drift more or less passively in the water, are referred generally by the term plankton. A great many fish, such as herring, pilchard, and mackerel, feed directly upon these minute plankton animals in the upper layers of the ocean. Other zooplankton, sinking to greater depths and to the sea floor, form food material for starfish, worms, sea urchins, and a host of voracious, crawling animals who in turn form the food of bottom-dwelling fish, such as cod, haddock, and sole, which must eat 10 pounds of plankton to grow one pound. Demersal, or bottom-feeding, fish and pelagic, or surface, feeders are in turn heavily preyed upon by many species of large, voracious fish during all stages of their lives.

It is easy to see the all-important role plankton play in the food web. All sea life depends on the sunlit "pastures" of floating microscopic plants for their basic food supply. In essence, man too depends on it for his sea food. This interdependent plant and animal chain of life is known as the biotic pyramid.

DISTRIBUTION AND CONSUMPTION

Although distribution of fish is worldwide, distribution of desired species is not. Differences in fertilty of the sea can vary as much as those of the land, ranging from virtual deserts in mid-ocean to fantastic abundance off the Peruvian coast. In general, shallow waters yield the greatest quantities of fish currently in demand, but even there differences are widespread. Fish are more abundant, as far as number of species is concerned, in tropical waters; however, large numbers of one species tend to be concentrated in colder waters of the mid-latitudes and

subpolar seas. A number of natural settings that contribute to the development of an area as an important source for fish have been recognized.

SHALLOW WATER

Sunlight, required by all plants for photosynthesis, diminishes rapidly below 600 feet. Coastal waters and the water over continental shelves or elevated areas in the seas are richer in plankton materials. Here, too, plant nutrients tend to drift downward and accumulate on the sea floor where they may be affected by sunlight and regenerate nutrient material.

Some of the world's great fishing grounds are associated with coastal shallows and banks (see Figure 9–1). Northwestern Europe has several hundred thousand square miles of coastal or offshore shallows, with famous cod, herring, and flounder fishing grounds, such as the Dogger Banks, the waters around the Faeroe Islands, Iceland, and the coast of Norway.

TURBULENCE

In sea water, plant and animal remains sink toward the bottom and decompose mostly at depths where photosynthesis cannot occur. Without turnover of surface and bottom water, the upper layers of the ocean would become sterile except near river mouths where nutrient salts erode from the land. However, several forces tend to provide replenishment of the upper zones: current mix, wind and upwellings, and winter cooling.

Current Mix. When warm and cool currents meet, a mix occurs. Generally, the warm currents glide over the cooler ones, forcing the latter downward and producing a churning effect on the lower water levels. Plant and animal plankton from both currents are intermixed and provide

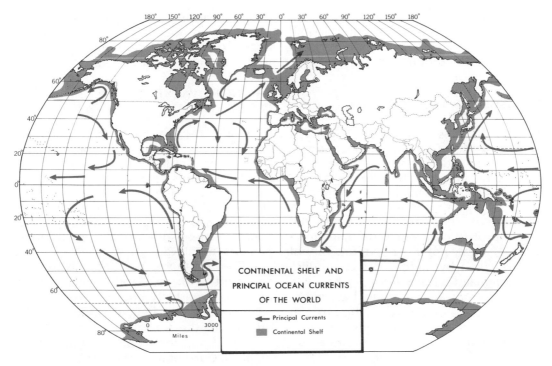

CONTINENTAL SHELF AND
PRINCIPAL OCEAN CURRENTS
OF THE WORLD

← Principal Currents

■ Continental Shelf

0   3000
Miles

FIGURE 9–1

rich food material for fish. Most of the world's great fishing areas are identified with a conflict of currents. For example, the Grand Banks off Newfoundland are located between the cold Labrador Current flowing out of Baffin Bay and the warm Gulf Stream (North Atlantic Drift) flowing from the American tropics.

Wind and Upwelling. The force of wind is generally sufficient to mix waters up to several hundred feet in depth. When wind movement forces surface water away from coasts, deep-water upwelling from great depths replaces it, bringing upward rich plant nutrients that support large populations of plants and fish. The extensive fish concentrations off the coast between Iquique, Chile, and Salinas, Ecuador, are a result of such wind action and resultant upwelling. Similar upwellings occur off the coasts of California,

Morocco, and the west coast of South Africa.

Winter Cooling. Surface water in the higher latitudes becomes colder, and thus denser and heavier, with the advent of cold weather. Surface water tends to sink and be replaced by relatively warmer water from the depths, which contains rich plant nutrients. The weather cycle thus develops a turbulence or mixing cycle that fosters renewed plant growth and the food web.

COOL WATER

Tropical and subtropical waters are not as productive of commercially valuable fish species as are cool waters. Fish from warm water regions tend to have a higher oil content, which often makes them less desirable as food. Cool water fish also

177

tend to congregate in schools of one species, making it economically feasible to fish for and market one species with less unit cost of production.

THE OCEAN'S PRODUCTIVITY

Although oceans cover over 70 percent of the surface of the earth, they supply little of man's food needs. In some cases, this is a function of distribution, but more often it is a case of economics, marketing practices, or transportation. Often, it is a function of consumer preference; the severe protein deficiencies in many low-income, highly populated nations cannot be overcome by increased fish production if demand is not present.

Five areas of the world have high-volume fisheries. All possess the physical characteristics previously referred to as instrumental in fishery development. Four of these are in the Northern Hemisphere and oriented to fish as food; one is a recent development specializing in fish meal and fertilizer.

Table 9–1 shows the productivity of the leading fish-catching nations of the world. Peru, the USSR, and China showed a remarkable percentage increase from 1963 to 1972. Peru, once leading the

world in tonnage caught, had significantly less productivity. Thailand, not a large producer, had more than a 300 percent increase.

THE NORTHWEST PACIFIC OCEAN

Currently, the foremost fishing area in the world is in the northwest Pacific Ocean, encompassing seas from the Aleutian Islands to Indonesia. Although the principal catch is from waters in the Northern Hemisphere, an important segment of this fishing area exists in the Southern Hemisphere between Borneo, Sumatra, and Java.

The northern part of this realm, abundant with fish food, possesses a number of partially enclosed seas and a wide continental shelf; it is the meeting ground for the warm Kuroshio or Japan Current from the south and the cold Okhotsk Current from the north.

In the north, large numbers of salmon, herring, and cod are prevalent. Salmon leads in terms of both value and weight of catch. The five species of salmon found along the Pacific coast of North America are present here, and, in addition, a sixth species, the masu. Masu salmon occur in commercial quantities,

TABLE 9–1 Total Fish Catches in the World and Selected Leading Countries (in thousand metric tons)

	1963	1972	PERCENT CHANGE 1963–72
Japan	6,716	10,248	+ 52.59%
USSR	3,977	7,757	+ 95.05
China	4,336	7,574	+ 74.68
Peru	7,091	4,768	− 32.76
Norway	1,388	3,163	+127.88
U.S.	2,777	2,650	− 4.57
Thailand	419	1,679	+300.71
Spain	1,125	1,617	+ 43.73
World	48,400	65,600	35.54

Source: Based on the *United Nations Statistical Yearbook, 1973* (New York: United Nations, 1974), pp. 139–40.

but because of their small size, they are much less valuable than any of the other five species.

To the south, the warmer seas around China and Japan are intensively fished, and tuna, mackerel, sardines and allied varieties, as well as great tonnage of shellfish, are annually taken. Although large amounts are eaten immediately by the Japanese, who consider fish an integral part of every meal, an increasing amount is being canned for export. The People's Republic of China, which like Japan annually ranks in the "big three" of world fishing nations and consumes most of its catch immediately, has not yet adopted the long-range trawl ships used so extensively by Japan. Most of China's fishing vessels are small and fish only coastal waters.

The Japanese and Russians are increasingly using inedible or "trash fish"

for fertilizer. Their far-flung search for these items, off the Pacific coast of North America, for example, has prompted considerable criticism from American fishermen.

In Southeast Asia, fish constitute a major protein source and an essential part of the daily diet. Almost all islands and coastal communities have local fishing fleets, but catches generally are small and for local, immediate consumption (*see* Figure 9–2).

SEAS OFF WESTERN NORTH AMERICA

A major fishing region occurs along the Pacific coast of North America from Alaska to California. In the north, salmon dominate the catch, both in value and numbers. North Pacific waters are the true home of salmon because many cold,

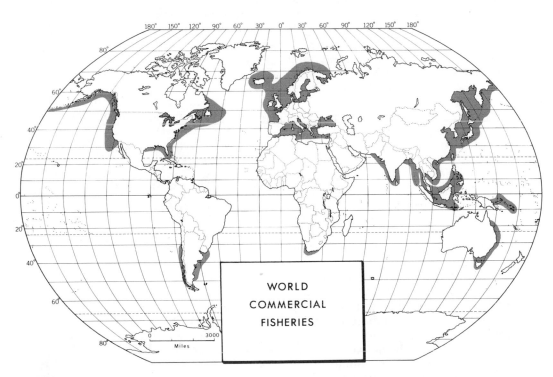

WORLD COMMERCIAL FISHERIES

FIGURE 9–2

fresh-water streams along the shores invite spawning and protect the abundant eggs and fry. The North Pacific, into which the fingerling salmon later disappear, is an ideal rearing ground because of its cooling Arctic currents and rich food supply of smaller marine organisms.

Five species of salmon inhabit the waters of the Pacific coast of North America: the pink (humpback) salmon, chinook (king) salmon, sockeye (red) salmon, coho (silver) salmon, and chum (dog) salmon. All species of Pacific salmon are anadromous, i.e., the adults migrate from the ocean into freshwater streams to spawn, usually in the summer and autumn and in the same streams where they began life. How they manage to return to their "home stream" after their sojourn to the sea is still a mystery. The female salmon deposits her eggs in a nest, which she digs by fanning her tail in the gravel of the stream or shallow lake shores. Digging is alternated with egg laying, followed by fertilization by the male salmon. In this process, the fertilized ova are covered with successive layers of gravel to a depth of several inches.

There is considerable variation in the life cycle of salmon, depending upon the species and character of the freshwater habitat. Incubation time, usually about three months, also depends on water temperature. Newly hatched fish live in the protective gravel of the nest, gradually absorbing food in the abdominal yolk sac. At the end of this time, they wriggle up through the gravel and begin the search for food.

The length of time the young stay in freshwater varies. For some species, such as pink salmon, the young begin their migration to the sea immediately. Others stay in freshwater for as long as three years. Once they reach the rich feeding grounds of the ocean, they remain there from one to four years, growing rapidly.

On approaching sexual maturity, they return to freshwaters to spawn and thereby complete the cycle.

California, Oregon, and Washington coastal waters principally support fishing for chinook, silver, and sockeye salmon. Fishing for chinook and silver salmon is carried on by small boats dragging skillfully fashioned hooked lures. Because of their fine flavor, size, attractive appearance, and the individual care they receive in catching, chinooks command a premium price on the fresh-fish market or for a salting process known as mild curing. Only a small proportion are taken by nets and canned. Chinook salmon are voracious feeders, averaging over twenty pounds; specimens of fifty pounds are not uncommon, and the record size is 125 pounds.

The Alaskan fishery deals mainly in sockeye, pink, and chum salmon, in that order. Along the Alaskan coast, halibut, a bottom fish, supports a large spring and summer fishery of unusual stability. Taken on long lines of baited hooks strung out along the bottom, halibut are marketed almost exclusively fresh or frozen.

A specialty fishery of some renown is the king crab operation located in the Gulf of Alaska. The crabs are taken in deep water with trawls or pots and are very large, ranging up to eighteen pounds and five feet long. In the southern part of the Pacific coast region, albacore tuna, pilchards, and mackerel are taken in limited quantities.

NORTHWEST ATLANTIC REGION

European fishermen began exploiting the vast resources of the western Atlantic during the 15th century. Documentary evidence recently found in England and in Spain suggests that this fishery was established even before Cabot "discovered" Canada in 1497. The Portuguese,

180

Basque, and Bristol fishermen may all have been in this area by 1490, and certainly before 1500. Nearly 500 years later, the "Spanish sailors with bearded lips" seen by Longfellow in Boston made their appearance in this region, along with Portuguese and other Europeans. Now, Russian and Japanese fishermen swell the ranks of visiting ships.

Fishing in this region is of two types: inshore and offshore. The fisheries along Canada's Atlantic seaboard cover some 12,000 miles of bays, coves, inlets, protruding headlands, and offshore islands. The coast is dotted with fishing hamlets issuing myriad fleets of dories, motorboats, and other vessels to reap the wealth of cod, herring, mackerel, haddock, pollack, and hake, along with shellfish.

Offshore fishing occurs on the Grand Banks east of Newfoundland. The Grand Banks consist of a submarine plateau rising abruptly from deep ocean to general depths of less than 300 feet below the water surface. The central plateau is quite level, but a number of isolated shoals exist between the center of the bank and the ocean deep, some as shallow as twelve feet. The Grand Banks extend as far as 230 miles eastward of Cape Lace, Newfoundland; their maximum width extends in an east–west direction for about 400 miles. The St. Pierre Bank and the Green Bank are associated with the Grand Banks.

On these banks the warm, indigo Gulf Stream and the cold, olive-green Labrador Current converge. A water temperature range of 54° to 32° F. might take place in less than a ship's length. Along the convergence, water from the Labrador Current recurves eastward to flow parallel to the northern edge of the Gulf Stream, gradually losing its identity through mixing processes. As the cold waters of the Labrador Current chill the warm, moist southwesterly winds from the Gulf Stream, dense sea fogs are cre-

ated throughout May, June, and July. Icebergs, drifting with the Labrador Current, persist until July. The uneven ground of the shoals and banks, coupled with the strong, flowing currents, produce rough seas in bad weather or even with strong breezes.

Braving these dangers are veteran blue-water fishermen from all over the world. Even with 200,000 square miles of deep-sea grounds, the fisherman population has been compared to the crowds in Times Square on New Year's Eve. Otter trawlers of many varieties are assembled here, dragging their otter trawls across the bottom. The great ocean-going schooner fleet of Portuguese dory fishermen and the giant factory ships of the United Kingdom and the USSR also fish heavily in this area.

Since its discovery, cod has been the principal species caught in the Northwest Atlantic. In recent years, haddock, halibut, hake, pollack, redfish, varieties of flatfish, swordfish, scallops, and seals have also gained importance.

Great changes have taken place in the vessels and gear used to take the marine harvest. Faster vessels with powerful engines and the use of otter trawls instead of lines with hooks now provide larger catches and allow quicker trips to and from fishing banks. The catch is no longer salted at sea, but is chilled on ice and delivered fresh to the markets. Increased efficiency in catching and handling the fish at sea and ashore has resulted in expanded fishing efforts and wider markets for species previously discarded. Technological improvements have industrialized the Northwest Atlantic fisheries, resulting in greater variety and improved quality of fish products.

NORTHWESTERN EUROPE

The seas of northwestern Europe constitute the greatest of the world's historic fishing regions. This extensive area of fishing opérations covers the Norwegian Sea, the North Sea, including the famous Dogger Banks, the Barents Sea, the fjords of Norway, the gulfs of Bothnia and Finland, the Irish and English channels, and the waters surrounding Iceland.

Although most of these waters are in very high latitudes, sea surface temperatures are mild. The North Atlantic Drift, an extension of the Gulf Stream, is mainly responsible for the extremely favorable climate and hydrography that produce an abundance of aquatic resources. This drift results in comparatively moderate water temperatures that are suitable for the herring and bottomfishes that approach the coast on spawning or feeding migrations. As is characteristic of high-latitude waters, the number of species is not large, but the fish are concentrated in vast schools.

The physiography of much of the adjacent coastline, particularly that of Norway, also lends itself to extensive coastal fisheries. Fjords and archipelagoes of large and small islands, islets, and rocks provide many sheltered parts and fishing grounds.

The major fish taken are herring, cod, saithe (dogfish), and similar species. Deep-water shrimp and European lobster are also secured; mackerel, flounder, halibut, and shark are taken in quantity. Some lesser operations are concerned with small whales and seals.

The fishermen of northwestern Europe are usually full-time fishermen, with the exception of Norwegians who traditionally operate as farmer–fishermen who fish the fjords. Declining catches of coastal herring and cod have led fishermen to build larger craft and intensify distant-water fisheries. Since large craft with high operating costs and upkeep must be kept fishing at all times, the fisherman population has been steadily declining. However, over 15,000 part-time fishermen are found in Norway alone. These individuals fish on a sea-

sonal basis; small-scale farming and work in fish processing or other industries are their off-season employment.

The catch from the waters of northwestern Europe goes to many countries, with the United Kingdom, West Germany, France, and Sweden the principal consumers. Fresh and frozen fish, canned fish, fish meal, and marine animal oils and fats are marketed. Some African nations, such as Nigeria, take large quantities of dried fish. Dry-salted fish are also shipped to Portugal and some Latin American nations.

WESTERN COAST OF SOUTH AMERICA

Since World War II, attention has been focused on the rapidly developing fishery along the west coast of the South American continent. Here the emphasis has not been on fish for food but fish for fish meal. Principally in Peruvian waters, but also in Chile, the anchovy fish meal sector of the fishing industry is paramount.

Fishermen here have ready access to a rich variety of marine resources. High productivity is accounted for mainly by the movements of oceanic water masses and by associated changes due to prevailing winds. In the southeastern Pacific, there is a net eastward movement of water known as the West Wind Drift. This surface current, rich in plankton, approaches the Chilean coast around latitude 50 degrees south, where it divides. One branch flows southeastward around Cape Horn; the other, known as the Humboldt, or Peruvian Coastal Current, flows northward along the Chilean and Peruvian coasts.

At various places along these coasts, southerly and southeasterly winds carry surface waters away from the coasts and colder waters are drawn from moderate depths toward the surface, causing upwelling. The colder waters, rich in nutrient salts, further enhance the growth of the plant plankton that is the basis for the variety and abundance of aquatic resources in these waters.

The most abundant species off this coast is the anchovy, which feeds on the enormous growths of plant plankton associated with the upwelled waters of the Humboldt Current. Other pelagic surface-swimming species, such as the bonito, sardine, and jack mackerel, are found in these waters. Tuna, especially yellowfin tuna, inhabit the warmer waters to the west of the colder Humboldt Current. These tuna generally stay offshore, except at certain times and in certain localities when the warmer waters extend inshore and cover the colder upwelled waters. Bottomfish and shellfish are negligible resources except in the northern area because of the narrowness of the Continental Shelf.

A warm ocean current threatens economic disaster for Peru. Flowing down the South Pacific coast, the warm waters of "El Nino," as the current is known, have sent millions of anchovies and other marine species scurrying in search of cooler waters. The anchovy has all but disappeared from Peruvian fishing waters, and this in turn has virtually shut down Peru's fishing industry.

Because Peru earns 40 percent of its foreign exchange from fishing, the situation is one of mounting concern for Peruvians. Peru's situation also could have major international repercussions, perhaps altering the world fish market which in recent years has come to accept Peru as the largest producer of fish products in the world.

"El Nino" is not an unusual phenomenon. In the past the current has come every five or six years, around Christmas time. Born off the coast of Ecuador, the current moves south to confront and override the strong, cold Humboldt Current that sweeps up the west coast of South America from Antarctic regions. Ordinarily "El Nino" diminishes and conditions return to normal in two or three months. But in 1972 "El Nino" lingered off the coast idling the fishing industry; not only did it destroy the year's fish harvest, it also seriously, and perhaps permanently, damaged the entire fishing industry.

Peruvians are beginning to wonder if their hard-won struggle to become the world's largest fish producer may have been destroyed as a result of an ecological phenomenon.

A larger variety of fish and shellfish is taken wherever the Continental Shelf has rich hake grounds. Other bottomfishes are also plentiful, and among the pelagic species, jack mackerel and sardine predominate. Moreover, the fishing grounds are closer to the densely populated consumer markets, so a variety of food fishes, such as snake mackerel, cusk eel, and croaker are also taken in this region. Shrimp, plated lobster, clams, and sea snails are among the many shellfish available in the central region.

Whales, especially sperm whales, are abundant in waters up to 200 miles from the coast. They inhabit the rich feeding grounds of the Humboldt Current, migrating north from the Antarctic during the Southern Hemisphere's fall and winter; in spring and early summer, they migrate southward to the tropics. Sperm whales yield a waxy oil for industrial use. Five species of baleen whales are also taken, the principal species being the fin and blue whale. Baleen oil is the well-known whale oil of international trade and is used mainly in the manufacture of margarine.

Export trends for fishery products have closely followed developments in the producing segments of the industry. A substantial trade in exports of fish meal and oil has been fostered with government support and marketed in the United States, Belgium, Venezuela, West Germany, the Netherlands, and Spain, among other nations.

183

In a 1954 compact, Chile, Ecuador, and Peru claimed jurisdiction for conservation purposes over waters extending 200 miles from their coasts. This extensive territorial claim is in conflict with the three to twelve-mile limits recognized by most coastal countries. These three nations have adopted regulations that govern fishing and whaling in the 200-mile zone off their coast. Foreign fishing vessels planning to operate in these waters must apply to the respective governments for permits to fish and must pay duties on their catches. Special conferences sponsored by the United Nations have studied the problem of territorial waters and fishery zones, but international accord on their extent has not been reached.

OTHER MARINE SOURCES

Several species of sea mammals make a significant contribution to either the economy of the major fishing nations or to a local economic base. Whales and seals in particular fall in this category. Whaling today is principally located in the South Pacific off Antarctica. Norway, Japan, the United Kingdom, the USSR, and the Netherlands are the major nations engaged in whaling. Modern explosive harpoons and specialized equipment, notwithstanding world conservation agreements, are rapidly depleting the fishery.

The Pribilof Islands in the Bering Sea are the chief center of the seal fur industry. Strict U.S. regulation here has managed to support quite a flourishing industry.

Specialized fisheries, such as operations for sponges, pearls, lobsters, crabs, oysters, and other crustacea, also contribute to the worldwide fishing economy. Sponges are obtained mainly from the waters off the West Indies, the coast of Florida, and the Red and Mediterranean seas. Although many sponges are still

caught by hooking them with a pole in shallow water, most are now obtained by divers operating at depths less than fifty feet. The diver gathers the sponges to place in a net and hauls the net to the surface when it is full. Increasing competition from synthetic and rubber articles contributes to the economic pressure facing this industry.

The major pearl fisheries are in the tropical waters of Australia, Southeast Asia, Ceylon, the Persian Gulf, and northern South America. The pearl, an accretion formed from irritation, occurs in a number of oysters and mussels. Divers gather oysters and mussels and extract the much valued item for decorative use. Pearl shell, used to make buttons, knife handles, and other items, is actually of equal or greater value. In certain countries, notably China and Japan, scientific pearl culture is carried on. In recent years, the industry has faced considerable competition with artificial pearls.

Oysters, a large variety of mollusk, are a very valuable shellfish. The major source regions occur along the east coast of North America from Maine to Florida, in the Gulf of Mexico, along Chinese and Japanese coasts, and in Western Europe from northern Spain to the Netherlands. Chesapeake Bay, of long historic importance in the U.S. fishery, has had a lengthy period of decline due to pollution and overfishing. The bays of the Gulf Coast are heavy producers, however, and an oyster industry is developing on the coast of the state of Washington. Dredges gather most of the U.S. oyster catch.

Lobsters are found worldwide. Caught in traps or pots and with baited lines at a depth of about forty feet, this seafood commands a high price. Most of the North American catch comes from Atlantic waters from New York to Labrador. Northwest Pacific waters lead in the world catch, lobsters occurring principally around Japan northward to Sak-

184

halin. The Atlantic coast of Europe is also a large producer, and the waters off southwestern Africa and Chile are developing extensive lobster fisheries.

Crab and shrimp fishing supports a large industry, particularly in several regions. San Francisco is a notable crab center, as is the Pacific Northwest coast, including Alaska and its lucrative king crab fisheries. The dungeness crab is the major species caught in the eastern Pacific. The shrimp, a small crustacean, is gathered extensively in the Gulf of Mexico and Mexico's Sea of Cortez, as well as worldwide for local use.

INLAND FISHING

Commercial fishing in inland waters is practiced extensively throughout the world, accounting for about 6 percent of the total catch. Several areas are prominent, particularly Southeast Asia where densely populated areas with limited meat sources demand a cheap protein food that is supplied by fish. "Fish farming" is widely practiced with carp and other fish. Almost all freshwater fish are marketed fresh.

The USSR also has an important freshwater fishery in large rivers, such as the Volga, Don, Dnieper, and others. Sturgeon, salmon, beam, carp, pike, and perch are representative species of the USSR. The fisheries are particularly important in the delta areas of the rivers and in the inland seas.

Africa ranks high in her freshwater fishery operation, particularly in Central Africa and Egypt. Fish are an important dietary item to combat the over-rich starch diet. Almost all fish are consumed fresh, due to high temperatures and lack of refrigeration.

Freshwater fishing in Anglo-America is insignificant in the total world picture, but important locally. The Great Lakes and the Mississippi system constitute the major source regions of species such as perch, carp, catfish, smelt, and white bass.

Since 1945, untreated or inadequately treated sewage discharged into tributary streams and directly into lakes has destroyed great numbers of fish. The United States and Canadian governments have passed laws to stop pollution, but it will take many years to restore these waters as major fishing grounds.

A LOOK AHEAD

Never before has man had so many effective tools for finding and catching fish. Boats can roam far afield, locating rich schools in new waters, tracking the mid-ocean depths, as well as the traditional surface and bottom fish sources. And instruments standard on the most modern boats are coming more and more within the reach of fishermen who yesterday could not have dreamed of owning them.

Midwater trawling, long thought impractical, is today a reality. Underwater lights lure fish to the fishermen. Fleets that roam the world, complete with mother and factory ships and spotter boats, allow tens of thousands of fish to be caught, frozen, and canned miles away from home ports.

The use of electrical fields to stun fish and suction pumps to gather them is no longer only experimental. Even primitive fishing has felt the force of this technological wave. In Sri Lanka, for example, catamaran fishermen who used to land, at best, fifteen to twenty pounds a day often make catches five times as large. Their rafts have been equipped with outboard motors, increasing their range and fishing time, and they have modern synthetic fiber nets which resist rot and hold fish as securely as steel mesh.

However, the efficiency of modern fishing methods has intensified proportionately the more pressing problem of how many fish are there in the sea? And how many of each species may be caught without depleting, perhaps irreparably, natural stocks? Whale stocks have already been reduced to crisis levels by ruthless commercial competition and exploitation. Other stocks are now also endangered.

A proper assessment must be made of the populations of commercially important species and the rate at which they can be fished without overwhelming their regenerative capacity. If it is discovered that we are taking too much from the sea of any particular species, the fishery nations must establish yearly catch quotas. The problem of controlling the activities of thousands of ships from scores of nations operating on the high seas may appear almost insurmountable. But the alternative could be a sharp fall in catches of some species presently being fished close to the limit.

With the exploitation of new fishing grounds, fish species unknown to the consumer will be landed, creating new markets. New fish products acceptable to the consumers will be developed. Such product development may also lead to greater human consumption of species now taken in very large quantities for conversion to stock feed. We must therefore offer the developing nations more technical assistance to build their own fishery industries.

Fish culture has been practiced with great success in Asia for thousands of years. In India, about one-third of the national catch comes from rivers, lakes, or ponds. Asian farmers who might otherwise never receive enough protein to maintain their own and their families' health raise fish in their own small ponds for food and profit.

The so-called limitless abundance of the sea has been exposed as a myth in the past decade, as the catch of species after species has declined in the older fishing grounds.

DECLINING STOCKS

The beneficial effect of two world wars on North Sea fishing is frequently cited to support establishment of fishing quotas. This oldest of European fishing waters was badly depleted of fish, flat fish in particular, when World War I broke out. Hostilities prevented large-scale fishing for four years and, when peace brought fishing fleets back into the area, stocks had replenished themselves remarkably. Fish size as well as quantity was up dramatically. The same situation recurred when trawlers ventured out after almost six years of war in late 1945. When extensively depleted, fish stocks appear to have a remarkable capacity for replenishing themselves.

Since World War II, various international commissions have sprung up to devise common policies governing fishing in an area or for a species. Eight commissions currently monitor fishing in the greater part of the world's oceans. At present, these commissions represent a

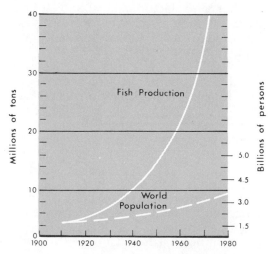

FIGURE 9–3 *Growth in World Fisheries Compared to World Population Increases*

patchwork of national, binational, and multinational agreements, supported only by a vague international accord.

For example, the International Commission for North Atlantic Fisheries (ICNAF) is an area commission dealing with all fishing in the vast northwest Atlantic. Sixteen member nations regularly trawl the area, including the once rich George's and Brown's Banks off the northeast coast of North-America. For several years now, ICNAF has imposed catch quotas on most Atlantic fish. The results have been marginal, slowing up the decline rather than improving fish stocks. Too little too late has been a frequent criticism of their approach.

Incidental catches upset the effectiveness of quota rulings. For example, a ship trawling for mackerel inevitably pulls in other species at the same time. If the number of trawlers fishing the region is considered, the total "additional" catch can reach impressive proportions. Biologists point out that these incidental catches frequently push the volume of landed fish well beyond the quotas set for the year.

STOCK REPLENISHMENT

The major problem is obtaining international agreement on what steps should be taken to conserve fish stocks. Biologists from all countries tend to arrive at similar conclusions; however, political acceptance of their recommendations does not always follow. A call for a cutback in fishing is not readily accepted by a nation already troubled by unemployment in its fishing industry.

As far back as 1961, biologists warned that a rapid decline of haddock lay ahead unless stingent rationing of the catch was introduced. The warning was ignored. Now the annual haul is a mere 10 million pounds, compared with 85 million when the warning was issued.

Many marine biologists are pressing for limitations on the total catch. This attitude emerged strongly at a recent U.N. Food and Agriculture fishery management conference in Vancouver. Under such a scheme, specie quotas would be set, plus an overall catch limit for an area, such as George's Bank. When that limit is reached, all fishing would be banned.

NATIONAL MANAGEMENT

There is growing support for coastal nations to manage fishing adjacent to their own territorial waters. Coupled with this is a call for national quotas whereby each country may take only a predetermined quantity of fish from a given area. ICNAF has recently begun this form of rationing for some species, such as herring and haddock. Those proposing extended local control do so in the belief that a coastal nation will be more concerned with conserving stocks in its own backyard than in those of distant nations.

Iceland contends this is the motivation behind its recent claim to a fifty-mile territorial limit. Ecuador, Chile, Peru, and more recently Brazil have unilaterally extended their fishing boundaries 200 miles out to sea. They use the term "patrimonial waters," as opposed to "territorial waters," where full sovereignty is exercised. Under this system, the coastal nation would set all quotas but could not exclude foreign fleets from the area. When the host nation saw fit, for conservation purposes, to cut back on the fishing effort, it would be obliged to restrict its own activities, too. A major advantage of the system is that nations without modern fleets would be guaranteed an equitable share of the harvest, although less sophisticated equipment means spending many more hours at sea.

According to Sir John Boyd, formerly head of the U.N. Food and Agricultural Organization, "A lifetime of malnutrition and actual hunger is the lot of at least two-thirds of mankind." Clearly, the

187

world's demands upon its seas will increase in years to come. How will these demands be met?

Research and technology suggest some possibilities: A concentrate of fish protein intrigues nutritionists; at present, this powdered fish flour has only been tested as a dietary supplement in a few of the world's famine areas. And experts contend that if produced in volume, it could supply the hungry of the world with their basic protein needs for less than half a cent a day per person. Furthermore, it would give fishermen an enormous market for fish that they now ignore or throw away.

references

1. Alford, John J. "The Role of Management in Chesapeake Oyster Production." *Geographical Review* 63 (January 1973): 44–54.

2. Bardach, John. *Harvest of the Sea.* New York: Harper & Row, 1968.

3. Borgstrom, George, ed. *The Hungry Planet: The Modern World at the Edge of Famine.* New York: Macmillan Co., 1965.

4. Browning, Robert J. *Fisheries of the North Pacific: History, Species, Gear and Processes.* Anchorage, Alaska: Alaska Northwest Publishing Co., 1974.

4. Coull, James R. "Faroese Fish for Properity." *The Geographical Magazine* 47 (January 1975): 124–227.

6. ———. *The Fisheries of Europe: An Economic Geography.* London: Bell, 1972.

7. Craig, Alan K. "Patrimony of the Sea and Fisheries Development in Latin America." *The Professional Geographer* 26 (November 1974): 421–24.

8. Eydal, A. "Fisheries." *Proceedings of the Association of American Geographers* 2 (1970): 56–68.

9. Gillespie, C. J. "The Atlantic Salmon." *Canadian Geographical Journal* 76 (June 1968): 186–99.

10. Holt, S. J. "The Food Resources of the Ocean." *Scientific American* 221 (September 1969): 178–94.

11. Hunter, J. G. "Fisheries Research Board Studies in Canada's Arctic." *Canadian Geographical Journal* 82 (March 1971): 100–07.

12. Idyll, Clarence P. *The Sea Against Hunger.* New York: Thomas Y. Crowell, 1970.

13. Isenberg, Irwin. *Japan: Asian Power.* New York: Wilson Publishing Co., 1971.

14. Manzer, J. I. "The Sea Life of Canada's Pacific Salmon." *Canadian Geographical Journal* 72 (January 1966): 2–15.

15. Padgett, Herbert R. "Some Physical and Biological Relationships to the Fisheries of the Louisiana Coast." *Annals of the Association of American Geographers* 56 (September 1966): 423–39.

16. Rothschild, Brian J. *World Fisheries Policy: Multidisciplinary Views.* Seattle: University of Washington Press, 1972.

17. Royce, William F. *Introduction to the Fishery Sciences.* New York: Academic Press, 1972.

18. Tarraka, Kakuei. *Building A New Japan: A Plan for Remodeling the Japanese Archipelago.* Tokyo: Simul Press, 1973.

19. Weatherley, A. *Growth and Ecology of Fish Populations.* New York: Academic Press, 1974.

20. Wimpenny, R. S. *The Plankton of the Sea.* New York: American Elsevier Publishing Co., 1966.

forests and
forest products

10

10

In Von Thünen's land-use model, forestry occupies the second ring, after horticulture and dairying, providing the basic raw material for construction and fuel. Historically, the demand for forest products resulted in higher prices and greater income nearer the market than any other economic activity, except horticulture and dairying. Although forest products still command high prices, they no longer dominate the economy. Competition from alternative land-use activities, i.e., from manufacturing, suburban development, and recreation has pushed forest industries to great distances from densely populated centers.

Forest industries generally tend to locate near the source of the raw material. The sawing of lumber tends to be done as close to the forest as possible because the removal of slab, the loss in sawdust, the culling of knotty, splintered, decayed, or otherwise undesirable portions, usually accomplishes a reduction in weight of 25 to 40 percent, which reduces freight costs. In addition, there is a marked compression in volume. Only a few logs can be carried on a flat car or truck because of the large interstices between logs, but sawed lumber can be packed more compactly into box cars or trucks. Furthermore, lumber can be loaded and unloaded more cheaply, whereas large logs require expensive equipment for manipulation.

FORESTS

Forests are one of the chief forms of natural vegetation cover and have always been of great significance in the lives of the people living in or near them. The presence of forests in the tropics, subtropics, and temperate lands has challenged man for millenia. His struggle against the forest has left its mark everywhere, sometimes in his now fruitful fields, sometimes in man-made deserts, and sometimes in tiny agricultural clearings, as in the equatorial rain forest. Since man's attack began thousands of years ago, and particularly since 1900 when world population began to increase rapidly, the forests increasingly have been felled to give way to cities, shopping centers, railroad rights-of-way, highways, airports, industrial complexes, and farm fields and pastures. Agriculture demands the removal of natural vegetation. Consequently, the world's forests of the 1970s are to be found for the most part on the poorer lands, which are unsuited to farming because of unfavorable climate, infertile soils, or remoteness of location.

THE NATURAL ENVIRONMENT OF FORESTS

There are scientific reasons for the distribution of the world's forests, although on a world map the distribution seems strikingly haphazard (see Figure 10-1). Although trees grow under a wide range of climatic conditions, they are in general limited to areas where midsummer temperatures average 50° F or above. Along the equatorial margins of the high latitudes, approximately 15 inches of rainfall are required for forest growth; in the mid-latitudes, more than 30 inches with more than half falling during the warm months; and in the tropics, roughly 45 to 90 inches for deciduous and 90 to 150 inches for rain forest. Forests shun the low deserts, the true polar lands, and the highest parts of mountains and plateaus above timberline.

Climate is not the only factor affecting the growth and distribution of forests. Other influential factors include:

1. Presence of porous soils and bedrock

2. Fire, a destructive agent that destroys millions of acres of forest land annually

3. Logging off of forested areas without replenishing them

4. Grazing of animals, particularly sheep and goats, which kills young tree seedlings

5. Removal of forests for development

6. Clearing of forest land for cultivation

7. Cultural preferences, i.e., societies that prefer to use forest land for highway construction, golf courses, etc.

Forests once covered about half the land area of the earth. They were absent or rare only in ice-capped polar regions, barren mountains, deserts, and dry grasslands. Over the centuries, man has cleared forests for farming and has overcut, overgrazed, and burned forests, so that today only about one-third of the earth's land is classified as forest land.

Of the 11 billion acres of forest land that remain in the world, one-third is unlikely to be commercially valuable because of adverse climate or soil conditions. Another one-third is commercially valuable and in use, and the remaining third has commercial potential but presently is not used or is inaccessible.

LOCATION

The world's forests are fairly well distributed regionally. Although Europe, except the European part of the Soviet Union, has less forest than other larger regions, it is 28.4 percent forested, which is more than Africa (21.8 percent) and Oceania (9.5 percent). The world's two most densely populated areas, Asia (except the Asiatic Soviet Union) and Europe, have a

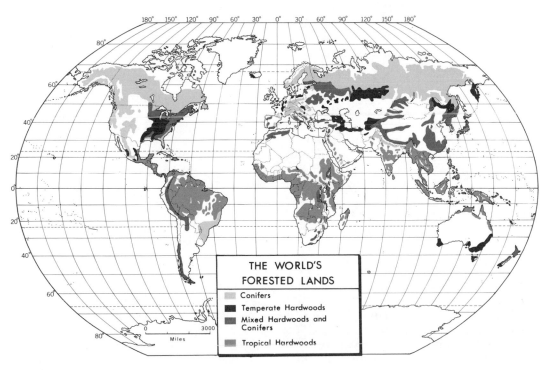

THE WORLD'S FORESTED LANDS

Conifers
Temperate Hardwoods
Mixed Hardwoods and Conifers
Tropical Hardwoods

Miles

FIGURE 10–1

per capita forest area of only 0.8 acre, compared with 17 acres in South America and 13.6 acres in the Soviet Union (*see* Table 3–1).

ACCESSIBILITY

Slightly more than half of the world's forested area is accessible by waterways, roads, railways, or other transportation. Nearly all forests in Europe are accessible and in use, but other regions have large tracts of inaccessible forest, particularly the Amazon Basin, the northern parts of the Soviet Union, and North America north of Mexico.

The accessible forests not in use are not necessarily a ready reserve from which rising timber requirements will be met in the future. Generally, these forests are not in use because they grow on poorer sites, are understocked, or are stocked with species less desirable than those in use. Often they are noncommercial. Stands of scrubby alpine birch in Norway and the sparsely wooded savannas in Tanzania and the Republic of Sudan, for example, produce little but fuelwood.

Much of the inaccessible forest in the middle and high latitudes is also noncommercial, especially where climate limits growth (such as in northern Canada and the Soviet Union), in high mountains, and in dry areas. Inaccessible areas in the tropics are likely to contain good timber stands, such as in the Amazon Basin, and the Andes, middle Africa, and Southeast Asia.

OWNERSHIP

Most forests, especially inaccessible and less commercially desirable forests, are publicly owned. More than three-fourths of the accessible forests are owned by the state or public entities. Private ownership of accessible forests is most marked in Europe (55 percent), in South America (45 percent), and in North America (43 percent). Nearly all forests are publicly owned in communist countries, and there is a tendency toward public ownership of forest land in less developed regions.

CLASSIFICATION OF FORESTS

Native species of trees are divided into two classes: hardwoods, which have broad leaves, and softwoods, which have scalelike leaves (cedars) or needlelike leaves (pines). Hardwoods, except in the warmest regions, are deciduous and shed their leaves at the end of each growing season. Native softwoods, except cypress, tamarack, and larch, are evergreen. Softwoods also are known as conifers because all native species of softwood bear cones of one kind or another.

The terms "hardwood" and "softwood" have no direct application to the actual hardness or the softness of the wood. In fact, hardwood trees, such as cottonwood and aspen have softer wood than white pines and true firs, and certain softwoods, such as longleaf pine and Douglas fir, produce wood as hard as that of basswood and yellow poplar.

CONIFEROUS FORESTS

Conifers occupy slightly more than one-third of the world's forest area, and broadleaf species, slightly less than two-thirds. Conifers occur mostly north of the Tropic of Cancer. On an area basis, 98 percent of the coniferous forests, composed mainly of pine, spruce, fir, and larch, are in the Northern Hemisphere. Conifers in the Southern Hemisphere generally are mixed with broadleaf species and are not abundant. An exception is the Paraná pine, which occurs in fairly pure stands in southern Brazil where it has been greatly exploited.

Plantings of the useful conifers have been made in the Southern Hemisphere.

192

Conifers have been the mainstay of large-scale wood industries for generations because they are adaptable for many purposes, notably construction, packaging, and pulp and paper. Oddly enough, the most widely planted conifer, Monterey pine, is an import from the United States, where it occurs in a restricted area along the coast of central California and is not used extensively. Monterey pine has been planted in New Zealand, Australia, Chile, and South Africa.

BROADLEAF FORESTS

Vast tracts of tropical broadleaf forests in Central and Latin America, Asia, and Africa are not in use because of inaccessibility and the bewildering number of species. Unlike temperate forests, tropical forests are generally a mixture of a great many species, with low volume per acre of any one species. In the mahogany-bearing part of the Amazon rainforest, the number of marketable mahogany trees probably is less than one tree per acre.

Indonesia has at least 4,000 species of native trees that reach saw log size. Indonesian foresters estimate that about 400 of these will become commercially important because of useful wood properties or abundance. Only a few are not known in foreign markets and not many more are used domestically because the properties and proper use of most of these timbers are unknown or because steady supplies cannot be guaranteed.

VOLUME

The volume of growing stock in forests in use is estimated at 5.5 trillion cubic feet, two-thirds of which are coniferous and one-third of which are broadleaf. This proportion is just the opposite of the actual existing world supply of conifers and broadleafs. Volumes of growing

stock in North America, Europe, and the Soviet Union have been estimated at 4.1 trillion cubic feet. The total volume in all forests is probably twice that of forests in use. Because a large part of the forests not in use is in the tropics, the proportion of volume in broadleaf species is large compared to coniferous stands.

Gross annual growth is estimated at 1.8 percent of the growing stock, which is equal to about 100 billion cubic feet. Since 1960, the drain on forests in use from removals, waste, and losses from fire, insects, disease, shifting cultivation, and transportation has probably been less than the growth during the same period.

DISTRIBUTION

There appears to be no wood shortage for the world at present consumption rates, but the uneven distribution of forests, lack of conifers in local areas, current quality and species requirements, high transportation costs, and waste in the woods and at processing plants produce timber shortages in certain areas.

The Soviet Union, Europe, and North America, with less than one-third of the world's population, have two-thirds of all forests, nine-tenths of the coniferous forests in use, and account for two-thirds of all removals. This roundwood volume includes more than 90 percent of the world's output of industrial wood. (Roundwood refers to peeled logs, in contrast to sawed timber.)

PRODUCTION

Table 10–1 shows that the volume of timber removed from the world's forests in 1972 totaled about 2,447 million cubic meters of solid volume of roundwood without bark. Wood for fuel accounted for nearly three-fourths of all trees lum-

TABLE 10–1   Total Production, Solid Volume of Roundwood Without Bark, in the World, Continents, and Selected Countries, 1972 (in million cubic meters)

	CONIFEROUS	BROADLEAF	TOTAL
Country			
USSR[1]	321	64	385
U.S.	272	83	355
China	79	95	174
Brazil	26	138	**164**
Canada[1]	109	11	120
Sweden	52	7	59
Japan[1]	26	20	46
Finland[1]	31	12	43
Continent			
Asia (except USSR)	136	513	649
North America	395	120	**515**
Europe (except USSR)	202	120	322
Africa	11	296	307
South America	32	206	238
Oceania	11	18	29
World	1,107	1,340	2,447

[1] 1971 figures

Source: Based on the *U.N. Yearbook 1973* (New York: United Nations, 1974), pp. 136–37.

bered in the less developed regions of Africa, Latin America, and Oceania, but less than one-fourth in North America, Europe, and the Soviet Union. Although a little less than half of all removals is coniferous, three-fourths of the industrial wood is coniferous, and four-fifths of the fuelwood is broadleaf.

Coniferous Forests.   These generally are used more completely and efficiently than broadleaf forests. Because of the prevalence of pure stands and the economic utility of small trees and logs, greater usable volumes per acre in coniferous forests favor mechanization in logging and utilization of smaller trees in this dense forest.

Broadleaf Forests.   In these forests, particularly in the tropics, the mixture of

species with widely varying wood properties, utilities, and marketability favor low-investment animal logging and waste. Logging in broadleaf stands in Latin America and Asia is primitive and expensive in many places, and only choice logs of desirable species may be brought out. Other logs are left to rot in the woods. Sometimes the best logs, such as butt logs, are also left because they are too big to handle manually.

COMMERCIAL PRODUCTS OF FORESTS

The major processed forest products are lumber, plywood, fiberboard, and particle board (panels made from scrap wood). The order cited corresponds to the order in which these industries developed; it also corresponds to the present order of importance, measured by roundwood consumed, value of output, and direct employment afforded.

SAWMILLING

Sawmilling employs two-thirds of the labor force of the forest industry, uses about two-thirds of the industrial round-wood, and furnishes nearly half of the gross output value of all forest industries. The pulp and paper industry, employing one-fourth of the industrial roundwood, furnishes more than two-fifths of the gross output value.

Capital investment by the pulp and paper industry is three to four times that of the sawmilling industry. Plants tend to be larger and more mechanized, and they yield a much higher gross value per unit of raw material used. Compared with the pulp and paper industry, the wood-based panel industries—plywood, fiberboard, and particle board—are of comparatively minor importance.

LUMBER

About four-fifths of the world's lumber output, estimated at 2,447 million cubic meters in 1972 (see Table 10–1), is derived from coniferous forests. Because the wood of conifers can be readily sawed and planed and is strong in relation to its weight, it is preferred for many purposes. The Soviet Union, Europe, and North America produce most of the coniferous lumber and two-thirds of the broadleaf lumber. Temperate broadleaf species, such as oak, maple, and black walnut, are used mainly in furniture, flooring, and a great variety of highly valued wood products.

The sawing of heavy logs into rough lumber is carried on near the forest because boards are easier to ship than logs. The only exceptions are woods of high quality, such as mahogany and walnut. The principal products of the sawmills are rough lumber, shingles, lath, railway ties, cooperage, and veneer stock. The lumber is usually dried and seasoned by passage through a kiln or by exposure to the air before it is sent to the planing mills. There seems to be a definite tendency to manufacture rough lumber products near the forests and to locate processing mills nearer the markets.

From the planing mills, the lumber is shipped to wholesalers, retailers, and industrial users, to be used in the production of an infinite number of different products.

PRODUCTS OF TROPICAL WOODS

The trees of the equatorial rain forest are all hardwoods, and most of them are evergreen because there is no dormant season. Over half of these hardwoods are located in South America, and a little less than 40 percent are in Asia and Africa. The annual cut from the equatorial forests is relatively small, even though they represent almost half of the total world timber stand.

Several factors account for this: In contrast with the coniferous forests, these forests seldom contain pure stands. A great variety of trees are found in a small area, and trees of any particular species are likely to grow singly. Some woods are very hard, and often the trees are of poor quality. The equatorial climate is very enervating, and in places the dense undergrowth and soft swampland make transportation to shipping points difficult and expensive. The shipping points are often at a great distance from the markets, which are mostly in the mid-latitudes in the Northern Hemisphere.

All of these factors tend to limit commercial lumbering for tropical hardwoods. Only species that excel in

195

hardness, grain, color, or fragrance are lumbered despite the high costs of cutting and marketing. Because of the extreme hardness of the native woods, many equatorial regions import softwoods for construction.

Tropical woods vary greatly in physical properties. Balsa, mainly from Ecuador, is lighter and softer than cork, while species of ironwood in Burma are extremely heavy and so hard that they bend nails. U.S. imports of lumber or logs of tropical broadleaf species are mainly specialty woods. They include fine woods, whose ornamental grain and desirable physical properties make them suitable for furniture and cabinet work, such as true mahogany from Latin America, African mahogany, and some Philippine mahogany.

The United States also imports woods with unusual properties. *Lignumvitae,* from Central America, is one of the hardest and heaviest of woods and has the unique property of being self-lubricating. It is especially good for bearings under water and is widely used for bearing or brushing blocks that line the stern tubes of propeller shafts for ships. *Lignumvitae* wears better than metal and needs no lubrication in such cases. Teak from Southeast Asia is one of the outstanding woods of the world. Its strength, durability, and dimensional stability under varying moisture conditions make it ideal for many uses, particularly in shipbuilding.

WOOD PULP

North America and Europe account for more than four-fifths of the production of wood pulp. Somewhat less than one-third of the pulp is mechanically produced wood pulp, used mainly for newsprint and fiberboard. Nearly two-thirds is chemically and semichemically prepared wood pulp, used chiefly in papers other than newsprint and for paperboard and synthetic materials, such as rayon, plastics, and films. About 6 percent of the pulp comes from non-wood sources—straw, bamboo, bagasse, and grasses, such as esparto in Spain and northern Africa and sabai in India.

About 90 percent of the wood pulp is made from the long-fibered conifers, but the use of broadleaf pulp, usually mixed with coniferous pulp, has been increasing.

Paper. Paper production is distributed in these proportions: 19 percent, newsprint; 18 percent, printing and writing paper; 30 percent, other paper, including tissues, wrapping paper, and wallpaper; and 33 percent paperboard, largely for corrugated containers, cardboard boxes, and food containers.

Plywood. More than half the world's plywood is produced in North America, largely from the coniferous Douglas fir. Oregon produces almost 57 percent of all U.S. plywood. The South began producing plywood in 1963, and today it accounts for 30 percent of total U.S. plywood production. Most of the plywood produced in the rest of the world is broadleaf and used for furniture, cabinetwork, or paneling. Broadleaf plywood in Europe and the United States is faced with a veneer of choice domestic species, such as black walnut and birch, or ornamental woods from tropical Latin America and Africa, such as mahogany and okoume. Japan, a major producer and exporter of broadleaf plywood, operates largely on lauan veneer logs imported from the Philippines.

Plywood can be made into other products, such as blockboard, battenboard, and cellular wood panels. Blockboard and battenboard consist of a thick core composed of blocks, laths, or battens glued together and surfaced with veneer. In cellular wood panels, the core consists of battens or laths spaced one from the other in parallel or lattice form.

NONWOOD FOREST PRODUCTS

Nonwood forest products include a multitude of items collected for industrial and home use, medicine, and food. Some products are important only locally, but many enter international trade. The United States normally imports crude or slightly processed nonwood forest products valued at more than $100 million annually.

Bamboos, essential to existence in parts of Southeast Asia, are giant perennial grasses, some species of which grow more than 100 feet high and up to a foot in diameter. Like other grasses, the stems, or culms, attain total height and diameter in one growing season. Uses of bamboo include fencing weapons, furniture, clothes, paper pulp, farm implements, fuel, and food. With some exceptions, notably in Ecuador, bamboos have not been extensively used in the Western Hemisphere.

Cork, the dead outer bark of the cork oak native to the Mediterranean region, was used extensively by the ancient Greeks. Cork is periodically stripped from trunks, and if the operation is carefully done with no injury to the live inner bark, the trees are not harmed and continue to produce. Because of its lightness and resistance to moisture and penetration by sound, the product is valuable for flooring, life preservers, bottle stoppers, and insulation.

GUMS, RESINS, AND LATEXES

Many gums, resins, and latexes are obtained by tapping or wounding the live inner bark or the live sapwood. *Gums,* most common in trees of drier regions, are used in adhesives, paints, candies, and medicines, and in printing and finishing textiles and sizing paper. Gum arabic, gum tragacanth, and karaya gum are the most important and better known gums.

Resins include many substances, such as copal, dammar, lacquer, turpentine, balsam, and elemis, that have many uses, particularly in the paint and varnish industry. The turpentine industry in the southern pine region of the United States is the world's largest producer of turpentine and resin. The flow of pine resin is often increased by spraying the chip or wound with sulfuric acid.

Guttapercha and chicle are best known among the many *latexes* tapped from wilderness trees. One of the important uses of guttapercha is in the construction of submarine cables, and no suitable substitute has been found. Guttapercha is a poor conductor of electricity, resistant to salt water and pliable, but with the right amount of rigidity. Chicle is the basis of the chewing gum industry.

Tannin extracts are prepared from the whole bark of many species, especially wattles and mangroves, and from the wood of quebracho trees in Argentina and Paraguay. Tannin also comes from the fruits of myrobalan trees in Southeast Asia, divi-divi and tara trees in tropical America, and the acorn cups of the valonia oak of Asia Minor. It is used to tan perishable hides and skins to make them durable and flexible.

Quinine, valuable in the treatment of malaria, originally was extracted from the bark of cinchona trees, native to the Andes of northern South America. Most quinine now comes from large cinchona plantations in the Far East, particularly Java.

NATURAL RUBBER

Man's best source of natural rubber, the tree *Hevea brasiliensis,* is a native of the

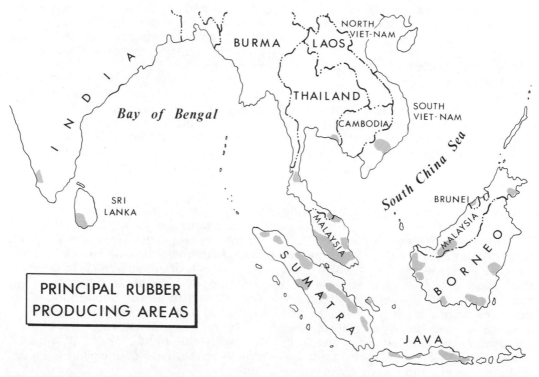

FIGURE 10–2

Amazon Basin. Nearly all the world's supply of natural rubber comes from this source (*see* Figure 10–2). Until 1876, this area was synonymous with rubber. However, in 1876 an Englishman, Henry A. Wickham, collected 70,000 seeds of the tree from the valley of the Rio Tapajos. He smuggled the seeds to England where they were planted in London's Kew Gardens. The 2,800 that germinated and survived were later sent to Ceylon and to Malaya, where they were planted. Those that lived formed the bases for the 9 million acres of plantations and small native holdings there today.

Wild Rubber vs. *Plantation Rubber.* In 1972 more than 95 percent of the world's natural rubber came from plantations in Southeast Asia, another 2 percent from plantations in Africa, and only 2 or 3 percent from the forests of Amazonia (*see* Table 8–6). Costs of production in Southeast Asia are but a fraction of those in Amazonia, and the yield per tree is much higher—10 to 17 pounds, compared with 3 pounds. Moreover, one Asiatic worker attends up to 500 trees, whereas his South American counterpart handles 175 to 200.

In the Amazon there is no supervision of tapping methods and no tree cultivation, whereas in Southeast Asia trees receive extensive care from scientists. At the Rubber Research Institute's headquarters in Kuala Lumpur, Federation of Malaysia, efforts are made to discover and promote ever better methods of growing and processing rubber. The institute's field workers help hundreds of thousands of small holders to improve their rubber production. In the Amazon forest, workers are exposed to all the dangers and hardships of a remote, wild, and sparsely settled region. Moreover, they receive a very small return for their effort. Most are forced to supplement their small income from rubber by hunting and fishing and by engaging in subsistence shifting agriculture (*milpa*). In Southeast Asia, plantation rubber workers are carefully housed, receive medical care, and are supplied with a well-regulated diet. In Southeast Asia, labor is abundant, skilled, used to routine tasks, and cheap; in Amazonia, labor is scarce, unskilled, by comparison, and not so low in cost. Although Southeast Asia produced only 9 percent of the world's rubber in 1910, the percentage had leaped to 60 by 1914, to 93 by 1924, and to 95 by 1972.

World Trade in Natural Rubber. Besides being only a forest or plantation product, natural rubber is a very important item in world trade. Its properties of elasticity, impermeability, softness, and electrical nonconductivity have made it an essential industrial material. It enters into the manufacture of tires, industrial rubber goods, sponge products, footwear, wire and cable insulation, and a host of other products.

World trade in rubber is largely from Southeast Asia and Central Africa to the United States and Western Europe; much rubber is also imported by the Soviet Union, China, and Japan. Although synthetic rubber effectively competes with natural rubber, natural rubber is growing in world importance. The United States alone consumed 3.3 million tons of natural and synthetic rubber in 1972, more than double the quantity used in 1958 and more than four times the amount consumed in 1941. Two conditions encourage continued use of natural rubber in the U.S.: (1) Many products made from it are superior to those made from synthetic rubber. (2) The economic

and political stability of Malaysia and Indonesia are so dependent upon rubber that a closing of the American market could mean their national ruin.

OTHER NONWOOD PRODUCTS

Curare, the arrow poison of some South American Indians, is extracted from the barks, roots, and woody stems of certain lianas. Various alkaloids found in curare are used in medicine. The demand for fragrant *sandalwood* and sandalwood oil, an essential oil, has been so great that sandalwood has been almost exhausted in many parts of the East.

Palms furnish fibers for brushes, cordage, hats, baskets, and mats. Fatty oils are pressed from palm nuts and important waxes are scraped from the leaves. Carnauba wax, chiefly from northeastern Brazil, is valuable because it is hard and has a high melting point. It is used in polishes (for floors, furniture, and shoes), coatings for paper (carbon paper), phonograph records, and in pharmaceutical and cosmetic preparations.

Rattans, stems of climbing palms that may attain a length of 200 feet or more, are used for furniture, ship fenders, canes, and in planting or coarse weaving of many articles. Rattans occur in many tropical rainforests, but the most pliable and best quality whole and split rattan comes from Southeast Asia.

INTERNATIONAL TRADE

International trade in wood and wood products is extensive, mainly because forests in use are unevenly distributed in relation to population density; forest industries are concentrated in North America and Europe. Densely populated Europe is a major importer of roundwood, processed wood, and wood pulp,

199

but it is also a major exporter of paper and paper products. Although the Soviet Union and North America are net exporters of wood, their different degrees of industrialization are reflected in the kind of products they export: The Soviet Union exports mainly lumber and round-wood; North America, a net importer of roundwood, exports wood pulp, paper, and processed wood. The less developed regions tend to export roundwood and import maufactured wood products, particularly paper. Because of the need for a variety of wood products and because the flow of raw materials into Europe and North America for processing and out of these areas for marketing, these two highly industrialized areas account for about four-fifths of international trade in wood.

Per capita consumption of wood is highest in North America. The world's industrialized areas—North America, Europe, and the Soviet Union—use much more industrial roundwood per person than fuelwood, but the reverse is true in the less developed regions of Latin America, Africa, and Oceania.

Consumption of industrial wood products varies tremendously from country to country, depending primarily on the degree of industrialization. In some less developed countries, almost all the wood used is fuelwood. For example, per capita consumption of industrial wood in the United States is more than 300 times that of Ethiopia. But fuelwood consumption in Ethiopia is six times that of the United States.

Some forest-rich countries, such as Finland, the Soviet Union, Sweden, and Norway use lumber as lavishly as the U.S. and Canada, but none come close to North America in the use of plywood and paper. North American per capita consumption of paper is three times that of Europe, twelve times that of the Soviet Union, and fifty times that of Africa.

TRENDS

World production trends indicate that outputs of all wood products except fuel-wood will probably increase in the next decade. The output of lumber has not kept pace with the rise in general industrial output or with the increase in population. As a result, per capita consumption has been decreasing.

Unlike the sawmilling industry, the pulp, paper, fiberboard, and particle-board industries are able to use small-size timber and frequently less valuable species. To an ever-increasing extent, they employ wood residues from saw-mills and veneer and plywood plants and even residues from forest operations. The percentage increase in output of these products has been double or more that of lumber.

The particle-board and plywood industries have grown rapidly in the last decade because they use the less processed material. Although large, good logs are needed for face veneer, plywood has several advantages over lumber: it does not split, warps little, and can be made in large, easily used panels. Lumber is being displaced by wood panel products, by masonry, metals, and plastics for construction, furniture, and other products, and by paperboard for packaging.

In the near future, deforestation for agricultural purposes will tend to be balanced by reforestation of denuded land near population centers in order to avoid the expense of opening up inaccessible areas. Tropical forests contain huge supplies of wood, but use of these areas will be slow to develop because of problems of accessibility, use, and marketing. The increasing demand for wood products probably will quicken the current trend of better and more intensive management of forests now in use and greater utilization of what was formerly considered unavoidable waste in the woods and at processing plants.

Man is becoming more conscious of the multiple uses of forests—for wood, water, forage, recreation, wildlife, and protection from floods and soil erosion. As this understanding grows, forests, which are renewable resources, will be more wisely managed for the benefit of all people.

references

1. Barr, Brenton M., and Fairbairn, Kenneth J. "Some Observations on the Environment of the Firm: Locational Behavior of Kraft Pulp Mills in the Interior of British Columbia." *The Professional Geographer* 26 (February 1974): 19–26.

2. Barr, Brenton M. "Regional Variation in Soviet Pulp and Paper Production." *Annals of the Association of American Geographers* 61 (March 1971): 45–63.

3. Bone, Robert M. "The Soviet Forest Resource." *The Canadian Geographer* 1 (1966): 94–116.

4. Critchfield, William B., and Little, Elbert L. J. *Geographic Distribution of the Pines of the World.* U.S. Department of Agriculture, Forest Service Miscellaneous Publication 991. Washington, D.C.: U.S. Government Printing Office, 1966.

5. Denevan, William M. "Development and the Imminent Demise of the Amazon Rain Forest." *The Professional Geographer* 25 (May 1973): 130–35.

6. Dinsdale, Evelyn M. "Spatial Patterns of Technological Change: The Lumber Industry of Northern New York." *Economic Geography* 41 (July 1965): 252–74.

7. Frome, Michael. *The Forest Service.* New York: Frederick A. Praeger, 1971.

8. Gorovili, N. S. "The Timber Industry of Northern European Russia." *Soviet Geography* 2 (April 1961): 53–59.

9. Hare, F. Kenneth, and Ritchie, J. C. "The Boreal Bioclimates." *Geographical Review* 62 (July 1972): 333–65.

10. Harman, Jay R. "Forest and Climatic Gradients Along the Southeast Shoreline of Lake Michigan." *Annals of the Association of American Geographers* 60 (September 1970): 456–65.

11. Harrington, Lyn. "Timber in Western Australia." *Canadian Geographical Journal* 78 (January 1969): 24–25.

12. Harrington, Robert F. "Prince George: Western White Spruce Capital of the World." *Canadian Geographical Journal* 77 (September 1968): 72–83.

13. Ketchum, Richard M. *The Secret Life of the Forest.* New York: American Heritage Press, 1970.

14. Kromm, David E. "Sequences of Forest Utilization in Northern Michigan." *The Canadian Geographer* 12 (1968): 144–157.

15. Kummerly, Walter, ed. *The Forest.* Washington: R. B. Luce Co., 1973.

16. Miller, Jesse W., Jr. "Forest Fighting on the Eastern Front in World War II." *Geographical Review* 62 (April 1972): 186–202.

17. McDougall, Harry. "Water Bombers Protect Canadian Forests." *Canadian Geographical Journal* 77 (August 1968): 38–45.

18. Roberge, Earl. *Timber Country.* Caldwell, Idaho: Caxton Printers, 1973.

19. Silverberg, Robert. *The World of the Rain Forest.* New York: Meredith Press, 1967.

20. Spurr, Stephen H., and Barnes, Burton V. *Forest Ecology.* New York: Ronald Press Co., 1973.

21. Strahler, Alan H. "Forests of the Fairfax Line." *Annals of the Association of American Geographers* 62 (December 1972): 664–84.

22. Thomas, Dana L. "Money Does Grow on Trees." In Howard G. Roepke, ed. *Readings in Economic Geography.* New York: John Wiley and Sons, 1967, pp. 81–90.

23. Tseplyaev, V. P. *The Forests of the U.S.S.R.* Translated from the Russian by A. Gourevitch. Jerusalem: Israel Program for Scientific Translations, 1965.

24. United States Forest Service. *Timber Trends in the United States.* Forest Resource Report No. 17. Washington, D.C.: U.S. Government Printing Office, 1965.

mining

11

11

Extractive industries are economic activities that involve removal of resources that have been stored in the natural environment by natural processes. Although enormous amounts of minerals exist, they can be used only when brought into recoverable concentrations by the combined forces of technology and economics. Minerals become recoverable resources only after they are culturally recognized and economically justified (see chapter 2).

Because of the nature of the industrial process in almost all extractive industries, it must be carried on at the point where the resource occurs. Power, labor, capital, and transport facilities must be brought to the resources, and the recovered product conveyed from that point to the market. In other words, these industries are resource-oriented in their localization.

However, many extractive activities, such as mining and quarrying, are carried out closer to the market before sites are exploited that are farther away and of poorer quality. Many regions presently supporting extractive industries will eventually cease to do so as their supplies become exhausted. The central value of the mining sites is positively related to the distance from the market, given the constant quality of the sites. However, this relationship is frequently distorted by the random dispersion of the quality of ore.

Chapter 3 discussed the structure, relevance, grade, reserves, and quality of minerals and presented a general overview of U.S. production and consumption of minerals. This chapter deals with the more important producers of industrial minerals, which include iron ore, ferroalloys, nonferrous metals, and fossil fuels. The distribution of these materials and their utilization in major manufacturing nations are discussed in detail.

IRON ORE

Iron is the most useful material of civilization; it has made possible tools, machinery, and many of the products of the Industrial Revolution. It is used principally when alloyed with other elements, notably carbon. A moderate amount of iron ore produces steel, and an excess produces cast iron. The availability of adequate supplies of iron ore is important to industrial nations.

Sixty-one countries of the world produce iron ore, and more than 150 million tons of iron ore are sold outside the country of origin each year. Seven countries account for the bulk of the iron ore mined. Of these, the USSR leads all others, followed by the United States, Australia, Brazil, People's Republic of China, Canada, Liberia, Sweden, India, and France, in the order named (see Figure 11–1).

Table 11–1 shows that, next to France, the United States experienced the smallest growth in iron-ore production from 1963 to 1972; France's output dropped by 12.7 percent during this period. All major producers substantially increased their output of iron ore from 1963 to 1972.

MINING METHODS

Open-pit and underground mining are the principal methods used to recover iron-ore deposits. The method used depends on the position of the ore body in the earth. Deposits that occur relatively near the surface are excavated by first removing the overburden with power shovels, draglines, or scrapers. Ore is then transported from the pits by rail, truck, ship, conveyor belt, or combinations thereof; with few exceptions,

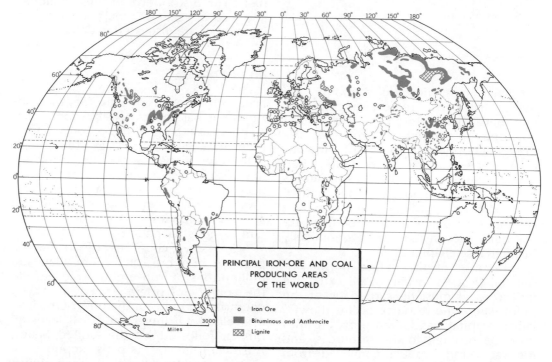

PRINCIPAL IRON-ORE AND COAL
PRODUCING AREAS
OF THE WORLD

o   Iron Ore

▪   Bituminous and Anthracite

▨   Lignite

FIGURE 11–1

the choice of transport is ruled by the grade of haul and the size of the operation.

Underground mining methods are employed where ore deposits lie deep within the earth. Large underground mines have been mechanized to the same extent as open-pit mines, and wherever possible loaders, conveyors, and hoists have been fully automated.

MAJOR PRODUCING REGIONS

USSR. Iron ore reserves are officially estimated at 95 to 100 billion tons, including 50 billion tons in the commercial category. About half the reserves are located in the eastern regions of the USSR. The largest ore deposits are situated in the so-called Kursk magnetic anomaly in the central European region,

in the Krivoy Rog basin in the Ukraine, the Kustanay basin in Kazakhstan, and in eastern Siberia. Substantial deposits are also located at Kachkanar in the central Urals, on the Kola Peninsula in the Northwest, at Kerch in the Crimea, and at several other sites throughout the country.

United States. Most of the iron ore produced in the U.S. comes from the Lake Superior iron-mining district in Minnesota and Michigan. There are relatively small but significant mines producing iron ore for domestic consumption in New York, Pennsylvania, Alabama, Missouri, Texas, Wyoming, Utah, and California.

The United States produced essentially all of its iron ore needs prior to the end of World War II, when depletion

TABLE 11–1   Total Production of Iron ore in the World and Selected Leading Countries (in thousand metric tons)

	1963	1972	PERCENT CHANGE 1963–1972
USSR	71,206	113,467	+ 59.35%
U.S.	41,542	45,798	+ 10.25
Australia	3,615	39,254	+985.86
Brazil	7,629	28,628	+275.25
China	19,250	25,300	+ 31.43
Canada	16,150	24,387	+ 51.00
Liberia	8,843	22,543	+154.92
Sweden	14,436	21,317	+ 47.67
India	12,567	22,126	+ 76.06
France	18,815	16,525	− 12.17
World	266,600	433,800	+ 62.72

Source: Based on the *United Nations Statistical Yearbook 1973* (New York: United Nations, 1974), pp. 175–76.

of domestic high-grade ore and development of even higher grade foreign ores resulted in an increasing dependence on imported ore. This dependence diminished about 1955 when taconite began to be processed competitively with foreign ores. Foreign supplies constitute approximately 40 percent of primary domestic iron needs.

Canada normally supplies about one-half of U.S. imported ore; essentially, the remainder comes from Venezuela, Liberia, Brazil, Chile, and Peru.

Australia.   Discovery of vast iron-ore deposits in western Australia brought a mining boom to desolate areas in the northwest in 1965. Today, Australia is the world's largest producer of iron ore, after the USSR and the United States (*see* Table 11–1).

The main iron-ore reserves presently being worked are the Iron Prince and Iron Monarch ore bodies in the Middleback Ranges near Whyalla, South Australia, the Cockatoo and Koolan Island deposits at Yampi Sound, and the newly developed deposits at Koolanooka Hills, Koolyanobbing, Mount Tom Price, and Mount Goldsworthy in western Australia.

Other deposits are being developed in the Pilbara and Ashburton regions of western Australia, where reserves estimated at some 15 billion tons have dramatically changed Australia's resources position. Deposits in the Savage River area of northwest Tasmania, estimated at more than 1 billion tons, are also being developed.

People's Republic of China.   China's supply of ferrous and ferroalloy minerals is sufficient to support a major iron and steel industry. Iron-ore deposits, mostly low-grade and requiring beneficiation, are fairly widespread, although nearly all of the major mining areas are located north of the Yangtze River. Mines now being worked are near Anshan in Liaoning, northwest of Peking, in the Pai-Yun-o-po area north of Paot'ou, and near Ta-yeh and Ma-an-shan in the Yangtze Valley. The high-grade ores mined on Hai-nan Tao Island are mostly exported. Numerous other iron-ore deposits exist, and the output from ore bodies in Kansu, Kueichou, and Kuangtung is potentially great (see Figure 11–1).

205

OUTLOOK

Within the last decade, iron ore has become a major item of trade around the world. European countries import iron ore from Canada, Brazil, Morocco, Mauritania, Guinea, Sierra Leone, Angola, the Republic of South Africa, and India. The southwestern European countries receive ore from Sweden and Norway and relatively small quantities from the USSR. Japan imports iron ore from more than twenty exporters.

The iron-ore industry will be a vital part of the expanding industrialization brought about by worldwide rise in living standards and growth in population. New mines will be opened to share in the markets created by the iron and steel industries now being planned by the recently independent, less developed nations. Others will be opened to satisfy demands foreseen for already industrialized areas. Mines producing high-grade, low-silica pellets or their equivalent will tend to capture world markets.

Technology will continue to exert a strong influence on the development of the iron-ore industry. Except in unusual circumstances, iron ore will be mined in open pits from large, low-grade, and easily beneficiated deposits. The trend toward larger equipment and automation of transportation and crushing plants will continue. Drilling and blasting practices in the taconite mines will improve but not at the fast rate of the last decade.

FERROALLOYS

When added to iron, ferroalloy minerals contain elements that impart some desirable quality to the iron. Chromium, nickel, manganese, tungsten, vanadium, molybdenum, silica, and magnesite are commonly used ferroalloys. Depending upon the materials and amount added, steel can be made stronger, tougher, more heat resistant, and more resistant to corrosion.

DISTRIBUTION

Though widely distributed, ferroalloys do not exist in large reserves, so it is fortunate that they are used in small quantities. Moreover, they are not equitably distributed throughout the world. For the most part, they are located in remote and thinly populated areas; few of them are found in countries that lead in the manufacture of iron and steel. No modern industrial nation is an important producer of all or even most of the ferroalloys, and some of the world's leading steel-producing nations possess almost none (see Figure 11–2). Although the United States is prominent in steel-making, it is forced to depend on foreign countries for the bulk of its ferroalloys. The U.S., which produces only 1.6 percent of the world total of ferroalloys, is the greatest market for them, consuming about 35 percent of the total world output.

OUTLOOK

Growth of the ferroalloy industry roughly parallels that of the steel industry. Demand for individual ferroalloys fluctuates due to the substitutability of many ferroalloys, but the majority of the output will continue to be alloys of manganese and silicon. Overproduction is a worldwide problem, resulting in keen competition for markets. The emergence of relatively less-developed ore-producing countries as producers of ferroalloys has aggravated the problem. Low profit margins result from lower prices desired by domestic producers to meet competition for restricted markets from foreign imports, in addition to domestic competition. These low profit margins limit funds for research and engineering development to spur the growth of the industry.

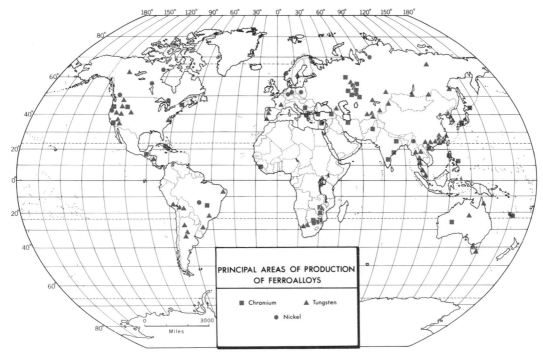

**PRINCIPAL AREAS OF PRODUCTION
OF FERROALLOYS**

■ Chromium   ▲ Tungsten

● Nickel

0   3000

Miles

FIGURE 11–2

NONFERROUS METALS

While iron and steel are the largest single metallic bases for industry, in the aggregate, nonferrous metals are only slightly less significant. Some of them, such as tin and zinc, find their main uses in connection with iron and steel as protective coatings. Others, such as copper and lead, owe their major consumption to the electrification of the industrial world, which has done much to increase man's productivity and comfort. Again, copper and aluminum, aside from their own uses, are alloyed with steel to give it special qualities (see Figure 11–3).

COPPER

The use of copper has increased rapidly in the last fifty years because, next to silver, it is the best known conductor of electricity and also because many types of electrical equipment are made of brass, a composite of copper and zinc.

The United States leads the world in trade of copper. Crude materials used to produce copper, such as ores, concentrates, matte, and blister, as well as refined copper, are imported. Refined copper and fabricated copper, fabricated copper products, and manufactured goods containing copper are exported.

Table 11–2 presents the leading copper-producing countries: the U.S., USSR, Chile, Zambia, Canada, Peru, and the Philippines. All of these countries expanded their output of copper ore from 1963 to 1972.

The USSR has moderate reserves of copper ore, estimated to be sufficient for several decades at present rates of production. In the past, the USSR has regularly imported part of its copper

207

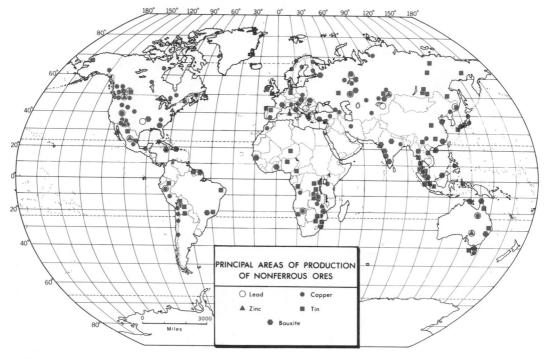

PRINCIPAL AREAS OF PRODUCTION
OF NONFERROUS ORES

○ Lead   ● Copper
▲ Zinc   ■ Tin
◉ Bauxite

FIGURE 11–3

requirements, but in 1964 when production was started at a third major center,
Almalyk, the country achieved self-sufficiency and had a net export. West Germany and the United Kingdom regularly
import most of their copper. Japan and
South Africa both produce and consume
moderate amounts of copper. Japan imports copper ore, mostly from Canada
and the Philippines.

**TABLE 11–2   Total Copper-Ore Production in the World and Selected
Leading Countries (in thousand metric tons)**

	1963	1972	PERCENT CHANGE
U.S.	1,101	1,510	+ 37.15%
USSR	600	1,050	+ 75.00
Chile	602	724	+ 20.27
Zambia	588	718	+ 22.11
Canada	411	709	+ 72.51
Peru	180	217	+ 20.56
Philippines	64	214	+234.37
Australia	115	172	+ 49.57
World	4,620	6,780	+ 46.75

Source: Based on the *United Nations Statistical Yearbook 1973* (New York: United Nations, 1974), p. 180.

BAUXITE

A rock consisting chiefly of aluminum hydrate or hydroxide minerals, bauxite is the principal raw material used by the world's immense aluminum industry. The aluminum industry consumes about 90 percent of the bauxite mined. The remaining 10 percent is used to make refractories, catalysts for petroleum refining, cements, abrasives, chemicals, and for other purposes.

The largest bauxite deposits are in Australia, which has 2 billion tons of reserves and about 1 billion tons of potential resources and in Guinea, which has 1.2 billion tons of reserves and about 2.4 billion tons of potential resources. Cameroon and China each have at least 1 billion tons of potential bauxite resources that are unfavorably situated or otherwise unsuitable for mining. Table 11–3 indicates that Australia and Jamaica are now the leading bauxite producers. They both mine over 40 percent of the world's bauxite. Surinam occupies third place in bauxite output and is the major supplier of bauxite to the United States.

Bauxite is concentrated into commercially pure aluminum oxide, or *alumina* as near as possible to where it is mined. In the United States, the chief concentration plants are in East St. Louis, Illinois, and Mobile, Alabama. The alumina is shipped to points that have low cost power and is there converted by the use of electricity into the metal, aluminum.

FOSSIL FUELS

The fossil fuels—petroleum, natural gas, and coal—are becoming increasingly important as more and more nations change their economic status from underdeveloped to developing. Energy resources were analyzed in chapter 3 in terms of their regional structure, production, consumption, and adequacy. Energy resources are so crucial to the functioning of a national economy that attempts of oil-rich nations to exert political leverage have caused intense international friction.

PETROLEUM

Origin of Petroleum. Scientists are not certain how petroleum was formed. Most geologists believe it is derived from the remains of plants and animals that lived in the sea or were washed into the sea by rivers and streams about 500 million

TABLE 11–3 Total Bauxite Production in the World and Selected Leading Countries (in thousand metric tons)

	1963	1972	PERCENT CHANGE
Australia	360	13,697	+3,704.72%
Jamaica	7,078	12,989	+ 83.51
Surinam	3,508	6,777	+ 93.19
USSR	4,300	4,700	+ 9.30
Guyana	2,861	3,707	+ 29.57
France	2,029	3,258	+ 60.57
Guinea	1,664	2,650	+ 59.25
Hungary	1,363	2,358	+ 73.00
U.S.	1,860	2,235	+ 20.16
World	31,700	65,800	+ 107.57

Source: Based on the *United Nations Statistical Yearbook 1973* (New York: United Nations, 1974), p. 178.

years ago. If they are right, oil and natural gas are being formed today in still backwaters where decaying marine life and vegetation lie undisturbed and in tropical reefs teeming with fish. Over millions of years, layers of mud and organic matter gradually change into rock and petroleum.

From its source beds, oil and gas seep toward the surface, perhaps into layers of porous rock. When upward migration is blocked by nonporous rocks, the petroleum collects in reservoirs or traps. The job of the geologist is to find these traps. Exploration is risky, expensive, and time consuming. Oil companies must estimate how much oil or natural gas the reservoir is likely to contain, acquire the right drill, and bring in expensive drilling equipment. The cost of a simple exploratory well, known as a "wildcat," may range from about

$100,000 to more than $5,000,000, depending on where it is drilled and how deep it must go.

World Reserves. The maximum petroleum reserves of the earth can only be conjectured. The term "proved reserves" is invariably employed when figures are given; it refers to the *known* stores of underground oil that can be produced under present engineering methods and price conditions. When the initial well in a new field is brought in, engineers are able to assign the pool a figure of probable production, a figure that is constantly revised as more wells are drilled and the limits of the field are determined.

Estimates of the total world oil reserves proved in million metric tons are shown in Table 11–4 and Figure 11–4 which clearly show that the major proved oil reserves are in the Middle East.

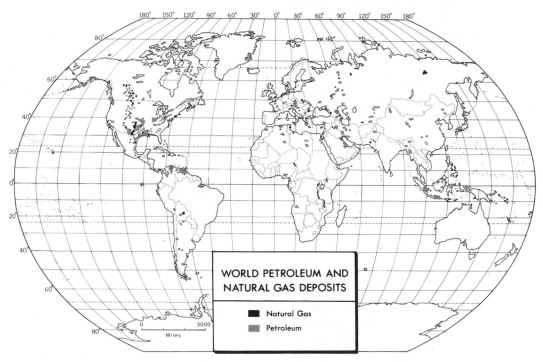

FIGURE 11–4

TABLE 11–4 **1972 Total Reserves and Production of Crude Petroleum in the World and Selected Leading Countries (in metric tons)**

	RESERVES	PRODUCTION
U.S.	4,899,000	466,956
USSR	5,716,000	400,440
Saudi Arabia	18,658,000	285,583
Iran	8,515,000	248,498
Venezuela	1,978,000	168,066
Kuwait	10,197,000	151,097
Libya	3,184,000	106,394
Nigeria	1,729,000	90,914
Canada	1,080,000	72,997
Iraq	4,433,000	71,125
United Arab Emirates	2,654,000	58,140
Indonesia	1,466,000	54,080
Algeria	1,235,000	50,477
China	1,709,000	29,600
Neutral Zone	1,861,000	28,610
Qatar	776,000	23,493
World	76,800,000	2,527,400

Source: Based on the *United Nations Statistical Yearbook, 1973* (New York: United Nations, 1974), pp. 170–71.

World Production. Since 1859 the United States has led in petroleum production, for decades contributing more than 60 percent of the world output. Although it is still the leading producer, the U.S. now contributes only about 20 percent. For many years, Venezuela ranked second and the Soviet Union third, but in 1959 the Soviet Union moved into second place. In 1972 the U.S., Soviet Union, Saudi Arabia, Iran, Venezuela, Kuwait, Libya, and Nigeria, respectively, were the major producers. As table 11–4 shows, these eight countries produced over 75 percent of the world's output of crude petroleum. The extensive network of Saudi Arabian refineries, oilfields, and pipelines is shown in Figure 11–5.

United States. The U.S. leads the world in production of petroleum and natural gas. Not only is it the largest producer, but it is also the leading consumer. The leading petroleum provinces are Appalachia, southeast Illinois–southwestern Indiana, the midcontinent (Texas, Oklahoma, Arkansas, and Louisiana), the Gulf Coast, the Rocky Mountains, southern California, and the northern Great Plains. Thirty-four states are oil and gas producers; the highest production comes from Texas, Louisiana, California, Oklahoma, Kansas and Wyoming, respectively. Some of the best areas, based on present knowledge, are off the coasts of California and Louisiana. Their development is a matter of economics because operation costs run two to ten times the cost of drilling oil on land.

In 1968, what may prove to be the largest petroleum deposit in the United States and one of the largest in the world was discovered on the north slope of Alaska near Prudhoe Bay, 150 miles southeast of Point Barrow. Reported reserves of 10 billion barrels are confirmed, and others have estimated 20 billion. But oil and gas from the north slope will not be available to consumers until the Alaska pipeline is in operation. Lengthy delays were largely caused by concerns of environmentalists who feared that the pipeline would destroy the ecology of the areas through which it passed. They have also discouraged further searches for oil in Alaska.

Importance. Crude oil provides more than 5,000 products, ranging from medicine to synthetic fur. In addition, it is the only primary energy source used by all of the energy markets—transportation, industrial, commercial, residential, and electric power generation. It is the basis of the petrochemical industry that today contributes synthetic rubber, clothing, utensils, plastic, and chemical fertilizers and pesticides. Petroleum is also vital to national defense.

Demand. With only one-seventeenth of the world's population, the United States uses more than one-third of the world's energy. At the end of 1972, one-fourth of the nation's oil supply was imported. By 1985, the U.S. may be spending more than $30 billion yearly to import foreign oil and gas, mostly from the Middle East.

A decade from now a gallon of gas may cost twice as much as it does today. Heating and lighting the home may cost 100 percent more. The same percentage added onto the fuel bills of the nation's factories will increase the price of consumer goods over the entire manufacturing range.

Beyond this, most Americans only dimly realize what the developing energy shortage may mean to the security, independence, and economic well being of their country. As imports rise, the United States will become increasingly dependent on the political and economic policies of a small number of distant countries. Saudi Arabia, Kuwait, Libya, and a few small nations may feel they have the power to shape U.S. foreign policy by threatening to withhold vitally needed oil.

USSR. The USSR ranks second to the U.S. in oil production, being responsible for a little more than one-sixth of the world's oil output and possessing almost 8 percent of the world's oil reserves. Commercial production in the Soviet Union began in 1873 when the Baku oil field, the major source of petroleum for decades, was discovered. Great expansion in the search for new oil fields and the transition to the use of petroleum as a major source of energy did not occur until the Seven Year Plan (1959–1965), when particular attention was given to the development of petroleum and natural gas reserves.

The most important deposits being exploited in the early 1970s are situated between the Volga River and the Ural Mountains, north of the Caspian Sea. This region, often referred to as the second Baku, has far surpassed the old Baku fields and the northern Caucasus in reserves and in output, although new reserves are being found in these older areas through deeper drilling and offshore sites. Other exploited deposits in the European USSR are fields in the western Ukraine, Belorussia, and the Komi autonomous republic where rich additional sources of oil along the western slope of the Urals were found in 1968. In the same year, commercial oil strikes were reported to have been made in Lithuania and the Kaliningrad province on the Baltic Sea.

Present plans call for output from the western Siberian fields of 75 million tons by 1975, out of a total planned production of 460 million tons. Surplus Siberian production will then be transported westward to European Russia by existing pipelines, reversing the present eastward

212

pipeline flow to Siberia from the Volga–Ural fields.

The bulk of the USSR's exported petroleum and natural gas products moves through the pipeline terminal of Ventspils, Latvian SSR. From there it is pumped into tankers and shipped to many Western European nations. Discovery of new oil reserves also has been made at a great depth in the older producing area of Grozny in the Caucasus, where shallower deposits were depleted by the late 1950s. Deep drilling during the 1960s yielded new reserves whose exploitation is advantageous because of the existence of an established extraction and refining industry around Grozny. Baku, the principal producer until World War II, is still holding its own with annual production of about 20 million tons, although it has long been surpassed by the Volga–Ural fields.

Offshore oil production has been expanded with the start of new operations in the Caspian Sea. Oil had begun to flow in 1972 from wells on the Zdanov Bank, a section of shallow water off the Cheleken Peninsula of the Central Asian republic of Turkmenia.

The Soviet Union's petroleum needs are such that it could become a net importer in the 1970s. The problem is not entirely one of quantity; the USSR is being forced to develop its new oil fields in remote areas, away from its industrial centers and farther and farther away from its partners in Europe. Faced with mounting demand from its allies and enormous transportation problems, the Soviets have urged their Eastern-bloc partners to look beyond the USSR for their increased petroleum needs.

Middle East. The world's largest petroleum reserves lie in a sedimentary basin bounded by the Taurus Mountains of Turkey in the north, the mountains of Lebanon and Syria and the highlands of Saudi Arabia on the west, and the mountain ranges of Iran and Oman on the east. The valley of the Tigris–Euphrates rivers and the Arabian Gulf is in this basin. The area's geology has a structural and a topographic basin, particularly well suited to the generation and accumulation of petroleum (see Figure 11–5).

The Middle East accounts for 40 percent of the noncommunist world's production and for 68 percent of its oil reserves.

Production costs in the Middle East are the lowest in the world. Average daily production of a Middle East oil well is about 4,500 barrels, compared to an average of less than 300 barrels for Venezuelan wells and only 15 for wells in the United States. Most Middle East wells also are free flowing; oil must be pumped out of U.S. wells and in a high percentage of wells of other major producing areas, such as the Soviet Union and Venezuela. Additionally, much of Middle Eastern oil is produced at fields close to the Persian Gulf's marine shipping points. These savings more than offset the high costs of plant and equipment and other operation expenses.

The huge reserves and low productions costs inevitably have attracted more and more oil companies to seek concessions in the Persian Gulf area. Middle Eastern governments, too, have sought a wider role in the development of their oil resources. For most of these nations, petroleum accounts for a large part of their income and foreign exchange earnings.

The governments of the Arab oil-producing countries profit most from U.S. oil company operations. Arab government oil revenues average about 65 percent of the profits and in some cases as high as 80 percent. This great new wealth has been created principally in the last two decades and most notably since the establishment of Organization of Petroleum Exporting Countries (OPEC) and has catapulted some of the Middle

213

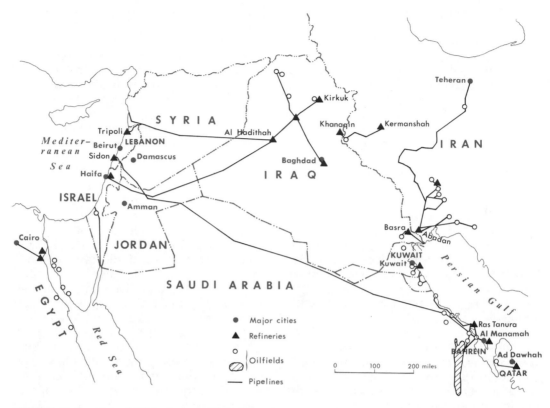

FIGURE 11–5 *Major Middle Eastern Oil Fields and Pipelines*

East countries from feudalism into the last half of the twentieth century.

Other Producing Regions. Next to the Soviet Union, Romania has been Europe's leading producer of petroleum. Several fields on the plains east of the Carpathian Mountains, most famous of which is the Ploesti area, supply almost all the country's oil. Production amounts to 13,770,000 metric tons, ranking Romania twentieth among the oil-producing nations of the world.

Indonesia is the largest oil producer in the Far East, ranking thirteenth in world production. Although the principal oil fields are in Sumatra, there is some production too in Kalimantan (formerly Borneo), in Java, and in Sarawak, Malaysia. Sumatra's principal producing fields lie across the Strait of Malacca opposite Singapore. Virtually the entire output is consumed in the Far East.

By world standards, the People's Republic of China is neither a major producer nor a major consumer of petroleum. China's total production of 18 million metric tons amounts to about fourteen days' output in the U.S., placing China at approximately the same level of production as Mexico or much smaller Middle Eastern producers, such as Oman and Qatar.

Of the several oil fields discovered in the 1950s, the Karamui field in Sinkiang and the fields in the western portion of the Tsaidam Basin are most productive. By 1960 these new fields, along with the older Yii-men field in western Kansu, provided the bulk of China's crude oil. In recent years oilfields have been developed in northeastern and northern China. The famed Ta-Ch'ing oilfield in Heilungkiang, where development began in 1960, now accounts for more than half of China's production of crude oil. A more recent discovery, the Sheng-li oilfield, is believed to be approaching large-scale production and could contribute significantly to future output.

NATURAL GAS

The United States, Canada, and Mexico produce about 90 percent of the world's output of natural gas, and the U.S. alone accounts for about ⅔ of the total (*see* Figure 11–4).

United States. The gaseous hydrocarbons (mainly methane), or natural gas, are closely allied to and often associated with petroleum. Because of its sootless and essentially odorless qualities, low cost, ease of transport, and high heat value (100 cubic feet equals 8 to 12 pounds of coal), natural gas is the most rapidly growing energy source in the United States.

With less than one-fifth of the reserves, the U.S. produces more than 60 percent of the world's natural gas. A system of pipelines of more than 165,000 miles distributes natural gas to all parts of the country, supplying 32 percent of the total energy fuel needs of the nation. Two states, Texas and Louisiana, have roughly 72 percent of the proved reserves and account for about 73 percent of the nation's natural gas production. Other large producers are Oklahoma, New Mexico, Kansas, and California. Esti-

mated proved reserves total 275 trillion cubic feet.

Natural gas is the second largest source of energy in the United States. Prices have been controlled by the U.S. government at an artificially low level, accelerating demand but not providing adequate incentives to explore intensively enough to find the additional supplies required. As a result, reserves of natural gas are dwindling; not even substantial new volumes from Alaska and Canada are expected to reverse this trend. The contribution of natural gas to the total U.S. energy supply is expected to decline from about 32 percent today to about 21 percent in 1985.

Canada. Proved marketable reserves of Canadian natural gas are placed at 47,666 billion cubic feet, with average withdrawals totaling 4.45 billion cubic feet per day. Alberta continues to be the leading producer, supplying more than 60 percent of Canada's natural gas. Saskatchewan accounts for about 25 percent and British Columbia 4 percent. Manitoba, Ontario, the Northwest Territories, and New Brunswick produce the small remainder. Although natural gas is by far the cheapest source of energy in Canada, it currently supplies only about 17 percent of Canada's energy requirements. More than one-third of the natural gas produced in Canada is marketed in the United States and transmitted by pipeline as far as California.

USSR. The bulk of the Soviet output, which is about a third that of the U.S., has been produced in the European areas, which provide roughly 70 percent of the USSR's total output. New discoveries of deposits in western Siberia and Central Asia, however, are scheduled to reduce the share of European fields to about 41 percent in the next few years.

The potential reserves, including the least certain ones, are rather widely distributed over forty locations. These reserves were roughly estimated at 67.3 trillion cubic meters. The largest reserve, amounting to about 72 percent of total reserves, is in eastern and western Siberia and in central Asia, including Kazakhstan. Some of the most important industrial and population centers, however, have almost no reserves. These areas include central and northwestern USSR, the Baltic republics, and Belorussia.

Developed and commercially exploitable fields are officially estimated to contain about 2 trillion cubic meters of gas. Seventy-five percent of these reserves are located in the northern Caucasus, the Ukraine, and Uzbekistan. These three regions account for the bulk of the output.

Western Europe. Over many decades, deposits of natural gas had been found in West Germany, France, Italy, and elsewhere, but before the early 1960s, production and market was limited. In 1959 the Groningen field in the northern Netherlands was discovered. The Netherlands is now the country in Western Europe richest in supplies of natural gas, with about half the entire area's known reserves of 141 trillion cubic feet.

In the mid-1960s, natural gas was discovered 34 miles from shore in the British sector of the North Sea. Several gas fields have since been found and developed there, and Great Britain ranks second now in natural gas reserves, with about one-third of the supply of the Netherlands. Other discoveries have increased the level of reserves to 11 trillion cubic feet in West Germany, 7 trillion in France, and five trillion in Italy.

Latin America. Mexico is the largest producer of natural gas in Latin America. Gas is piped from the Poza Rica field to Mexico City and from Ciudad Pemex, close to the Guatemalan border, via a natural-gas pipeline that is more than 500 miles long and crosses marsh, plain, and mountain. A gas pipeline about 155 miles long serves the manufacturing city of Monterrey. Mexico's gas is used for industrial purposes.

COAL

Coal is by far the most abundant of the fossil fuels. However, it produces more sulfur compounds than any other fuel source. Sulphur compounds, when mixed with moisture in the atmosphere, erode steel and marble and contribute to an increased incidence of respiratory disease.

Moreover, extracting coal from the ground without major damage to the environment has become a serious problem, notably with the advent of ruthless strip mining. Progress has been made in removing excess sulfur from coal burning, and conversion of coal into gas is technically possible. Desulfurization and gasification of coal, however, are expensive processes which will continue to reduce the desirability of coal as an energy source. Of course, to the extent that the shortage of natural gas and petroleum leads to higher prices, coal could become more attractive as an energy source.

TYPES OF COAL

The three main types of coal are anthracite, bituminous, and lignite; all types contain some bituminous matter and are further distinguished by the degree of hardness or softness and the limits of fixed carbon or BTUs. Anthracite is the hardest coal; it burns slowly with a pale blue flame and requires a minimum of attention. Lignite is the softest; it disintegrates rapidly in air and is liable to spontaneous combustion. Bituminous coal is the most abundant and most widely used variety, varying from medium to high grade. Medium- to low-grade volatile bitumious coals may have a coking quality; coking, or caking, is a property of coal that softens, swells, and runs together when heated almost to its burning temperature. When further heated in a closed oven, without oxygen or with very little, the volatile matter is driven off in the form of gas, water vapor, light oil, and tar. The gray porous residue consists largely of fixed carbon and is called coke, which is used extensively in blast furnaces for smelting iron ore.

PRODUCING AREAS

The bulk of the world's coal is mined in the middle latitudes of the Northern Hemisphere. Table 11–5 shows that Anglo-America, Europe, the USSR, and China are the largest producers, accounting for about 93 percent of the world's mined output. South of the equator, only the Republic of South Africa and Australia mine coal in appreciable amounts.

United States. Coal is the most abundant conventional energy resource in the U.S. Currently the nation is consuming roughly 535 million tons of coal per year, which contributes to about one-fifth of the total energy used (*see* Table 3–6). Oil companies have started to acquire coal lands and coal-mining companies, the natural gas industry has started an advertising campaign praising coal as the energy of the future, and several government agencies have been promoting development of new coal technologies.

In spite of the high-polluting nature of many coal deposits and massive transportation needs to get it to market, coal has two distinct advantages over the other fossil fuels, oil and gas: It is abundant, accounting for 88 percent of the nation's proven reserves, and it can be converted to clean-burning oil and gas

TABLE 11–5 Total Reserves and Production of Coal in the World and Selected Leading Countries, 1972 (in metric tons)

	RESERVES	PRODUCTION
U.S.	1,100,000,000[1]	535,242
USSR	4,121,603,000[2]	451,119
China	1,011,000,000[3]	400,000
Poland	45,741,000[4]	150,697
W.Germany	70,000,000[4]	102,707
India	106,260,000[1]	74,771
Australia	16,000,000[4]	49,056
France	2,800,000[1]	29,763
Japan	19,248,000[5]	28,098
World	6,641,200,000	2,144,800

[1] 1966 figure
[2] 1960 figure
[3] No current figure available; this is a 1913 figure.
[4] 1967 figure
[5] 1961 figure

Source: Based on the *United Nations Statistical Yearbook, 1973* (New York: United Nations, 1974), pp. 166–67.

through new developmental technologies.

DISTRIBUTION OF COAL

Coal deposits are widely distributed within thirty-seven states (*see* Figure 11–6). The northern Appalachian basin was the first to be developed because of its proximity to population and industrial centers. Pennsylvania, long the leading coal producer, has been superseded by West Virginia and Kentucky. These three states, along with fourth-ranking Illinois, currently produce two-thirds of the industry's output.

From the standpoint of reserves, the richest region is the northern Rocky Mountain basin, which embraces parts of Montana, Wyoming, Idaho, and the Dakotas. Most of the deposits in the Dakotas and some in Montana are lignite, the lowest-rank coal in energy per ton, al-

though useful for some purposes. Substantial coal deposits are also found in the southern Rocky Mountain basin, which includes parts of Colorado, Utah, Arizona, and New Mexico. The northern and southern Rocky Mountain basins are estimated to have the largest portion of the country's coal reserves.

Over 75 percent of the country's economically strippable coal lies in thirteen states west of the Mississippi River. Many of these deposits are also unusually thick; one bed of coal in Wyoming, for example, is almost 90 feet thick. Western coal seams are said to be an average of about twelve times thicker than those in the East.

Another quality of western coal, which is mostly bituminous, is its low-sulfur content. With growing awareness of air pollution, states and municipalities are imposing stricter limits on the sulfur content of coal used by electric utilities.

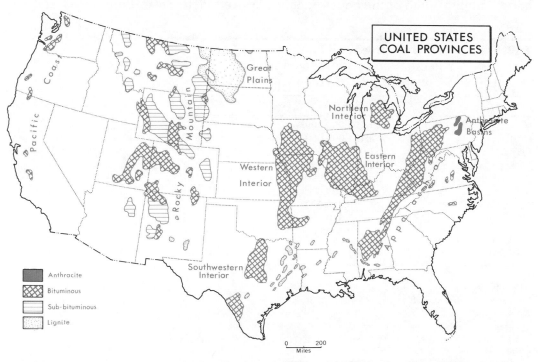

UNITED STATES COAL PROVINCES

Anthracite
Bituminous
Sub-bituminous
Lignite

FIGURE 11–6

Wyoming, Montana, New Mexico, and North Dakota have the most low-sulfur, strippable coal and lignite. Coal-burning electric utilities have been operating for a long time in the West, and new plants are going up in Texas, New Mexico, and Washington. Moreover, western coal is coming east. Chicago utilities have brought low-sulfur coal from Montana and Wyoming and are considering purchasing low-sulfur coal from Colorado, Utah, and New Mexico.

TRANSPORTING COAL TO MARKET

Most mines are far away from markets, and coal is too heavy and costly to haul. Railroads are still the primary transport means for coal. Pennsylvania Power and Light Company uses five fleet trains of specially built coal cars that shuttle between coal mines in western Pennsylvania and the company's power plants in the eastern part of the state. Ten thousand tons can be loaded and unloaded rapidly, and the savings are worth the investment in rolling stock.

The quest for lower-cost transport has also led to use of pipelines. Coal, finely ground and mixed with water to form a slurry, can be pumped through a pipeline. In eastern Ohio, coal was pipelined to Cleveland until railroad freight rates made this venture unprofitable. A plan to pump coal from West Virginia and Pennsylvania to the Atlantic Seaboard never materialized, more because of legislative and right-of-way obstacles than technical difficulties.

Instead of railroading bulky coal from the mine to a distant power plant, why not build the power plant atop the mine and send the kilowatts to market by wire? That is now being done, thanks to improvements in long-distance power transmission. Most Philadelphia–Baltimore–Washington consumers receive electricity from a trio of huge mine-mouth plants atop Chestnut Ridge, an immense coal-bearing mountain in western Pennsylvania. Three plants devour 1,700 tons of coal an hour around the clock. At one plant, a pile of coal over a million tons high is collected to assure uninterrupted service, and it is estimated that the underground mine has enough coal to feed the plant for thirty years. Four vase-shaped cooling towers, 325 feet high, curb any thermal pollution of the little stream that supplies the water. Towering above the landscape are two 800-foot high smokestacks that disperse whatever combustion by-products that may escape the electrostatic precipitators into the upper atmosphere.

COAL RESERVES

USSR. The Soviet Union ranks first in the world coal reserves (62.1 percent) and second (21.3 percent) to the United States (24.96 percent) in world production (*see* Table 11–5). The great bulk of the large and easily worked deposits is situated in remote, sparsely populated regions of the country. Deposits in the principal settled areas are of poor quality, requiring expensive cleaning operations, or are difficult to mine and therefore too costly.

The major suppliers of coal are the Donetsk, Moscow, and Pechora basins in the European USSR; the Kuznetsk basin in western Siberia, the Urals; and the Karaganda basin in Kazakhstan (*see* Figure 11–7). The Donets Basin (the Donbas) is the largest single producer of coal and the most important source of coking coal for metallurgy; it accounts for about one-third of the coal output and more than half the output of coking coal. The coal seams in the Donbas, however, are thin and steep, and they lie at relatively great depths, which makes extraction costly.

The Kuznetsk Basin (the Kuzbas) contains what is said to be one of the richest deposits of coal in the world, one-

219

FIGURE 11–7   *Distribution of Coal in the Soviet Union*

third of which is of coking grade. Its output is consumed primarily by the iron and steel mills in the Urals and western Siberia and by nonferrous metallurgy plants in eastern Kazakhstan. Although the cost of mining in the Kuzbas is relatively low, owing to the thickness of the seams and the possibility of open-pit mining, the great distance of this basin from industrial consumers (1,375 miles from Magnitogorsk in the Urals) reduces its importance and limits its potential development.

The Karaganda Basin, also rich in coking coal, supplies primarily the southern Urals and Kazakhstan. Its distance from the Urals is only half that of the Kuzbas. The Pechora Basin provides for the needs of the European north and northwest USSR and supplies coking coal to the Cherepovets steel mill. The Moscow brown-coal basin, exploited for about 100 years, is gradually losing importance because of the high cost of its

low-grade output and the growing use of oil and gas in the central industrial region.

The huge deposits in eastern Siberia, representing over three-fourths of the country's total, are located between rich sources in western Siberia and the Far East. The cost of mining in the Kansk–Achinsk Basin of the Krasnoyarsk Region is only one-sixth of the national average because economical use of its coal for purposes other than local fuel is precluded by the coal's high moisture and low-heat content. Long-range plans envision the conversion of this coal into electric power for transmission to the Urals and the European USSR.

People's Republic of China. Coal accounts for about 90 percent of all the primary energy available in the People's Republic of China. Possessing 15.22 percent of the proved resources and producing 18.65 percent of the world's coal,

220

China is third after the USSR and the United States (*see* Table 11–5). Most of the coal reserves are located in Shensi and Szechwan, although deposits of various sizes are claimed to have been discovered in every province. Chinese coals range from lignite to anthracite, with bituminous types predominating. Most deposits are poor to fair in quality and must be upgraded by preparation and cleaning before use. There are ample reserves of good coking coal, but in some areas they are far removed from the widely dispersed coke plants.

Over half of China's coal is produced in the north and northeast. In northern China, mines are located in an arc extending from near T'ang-shan to Chengchou in Shantung, and in the southern portion of the North China Plain. In northeastern China, several mining complexes located in Liaoning, including the famous open-pit mine at Fu-shun, serve the heavy industry base of southern Man-churia. Large and important mining complexes are located near the Soviet border in Heilungkiang, away from the major industrial areas. Efforts have been made to increase production in coal-deficient areas of the south, but local self-sufficiency has not yet been attained. Current policy emphasizes working small local mines, using labor-intensive methods of coal extraction. A similar policy during the Great Leap Forward created havoc in the industry, but it appears that operations are now being more carefully planned and implemented.

Western and Central Europe. In Europe the most important coal deposits extend in a broken belt from Great Britain through northern France into southern Russia (*see* Figure 11–8). Within it are the six major British coal fields; the important French–Belgian–Dutch fields; Germany's famous Ruhr and Saar basins and her intensively mined lignite fields near

FIGURE 11–8   *Coal Fields of Western and Central Europe*

Cologne; Czechoslovakia's Bohemian fields; and the important Upper Silesian–Moravian field of southern Poland and Czechoslovakia. Few areas of equivalent size anywhere on earth possess greater power potential than this 300-by-1,200-mile belt.

Great Britain has long been regarded as a country rich in coal deposits and outstanding in coal production; it is the world's fourth largest coal producer, and for decades during the 19th century it was first.

The nation has been particularly fortunate in having coal fields near tidewater areas, in the interior, and near deposits of iron ore. Moreover, British coal is semianthracite and bituminous, which are of high quality and excellent for all purposes.

Belgian coal fields lie in the north and south of the country. In both areas, the high cost of mining, owing to the thin and deep coal seams and irregular occurrence, has caused production levels to fall.

West Germany possesses bituminous and lignite coal, the best coal being located largely in the Ruhr and Saar basins. The Ruhr, which ranks as one of the world's outstanding coal areas, possesses three-fourths of the total German output. The coal is of excellent quality, and the Ruhr has the highest percentage of coking coal among the several fields of Europe. Besides the deposits of coal in the Ruhr, there are several large reserves with important production in the Saar and the Aachen areas. The Saar was one of Germany's largest coal-producing areas prior to World War II. Actually this field is relatively small; also, the coal is highly volatile and does not alone make high-grade metallurgical coke.

In addition to the bituminous coal deposits and mines in the Ruhr and Saar basins, enormous reserves of lignite are present in the Rhineland west of Cologne. The principal deposits extend from near Bonn and Cologne to Aachen in the west and to the Dutch border on the north. More and more brown coal is being mined and used in Germany because it is a cheap source of energy when used at the mine. Lignite in Germany is mostly converted into electrical energy; most electrical power stations use coal.

Poland ranks among Europe's coal-producing leaders in reserves and production (see Table 11–5). The principal fields, the Dombrawa and the Krakow in eastern Upper Silesia, possess reserves ranking with those of the Ruhr Basin in Germany. Coal seams 3 feet thick are numerous, and some reach 30 feet; sporadically, two or more seams combine to form beds 50 to 60 feet thick. The mines are at depths of 1,300 to 2,600 feet, which obviously involve mining difficulties.

Other Coal Reserve Areas. Only a few areas outside those previously discussed are conspicuous on the coal map of the world. Japan's coal reserves are moderate; its recoverable coal is estimated at about 3 billion tons, a very small amount compared to the U.S. or the USSR. The major coal fields are located at opposite ends of the country, in Kyushu and Hokkaido. Japanese coal is mostly low-grade bituminous, with low heating value, and its coal seams are thin, tilted, and badly broken.

India has rich deposits of coal in Bengal, Bihar, and Orissa. Fortunately, the deposits are close enough to large iron-ore deposits, which gives India the potential to be one of the world's cheapest producers of iron and steel. In the south, there are deposits of low-grade brown coal, which has not been easily used by industry in the past; with the development of new processing and burning techniques, this lignite coal will become a suitable source for thermal power.

Australia's coal discoveries in Queensland in 1960 have more than doubled the country's estimated reserves. Although current published reserves are not large by world standards, there is evidence that considerable veins of coal still await discovery.

Coal underlies vast areas of the Transvaal and of the Orange Free State in the Republic of South Africa. However, with the exception of 300 million tons in Natal, all of this coal is noncoking and present production is relatively small.

TYPES OF COAL MINING

Coal mining depends upon several factors, the most important of which are:

1. The area where coal is available

2. The thickness and inclination of the seam and overlying strata

3. The value of surface land and other economic factors

The major coal-mining methods are underground or deep mining, where coal is extracted from the seam without removing overlying strata; strip or overcast mining, in which the strata overlying the coal seam (the overburden) are removed and coal is extracted from the exposed seam; and auger mining, in which coal is recovered by means of larger-diameter augers boring horizontally into the outcropping system (*see* Figure 11–9).

NUCLEAR FUELS

Uranium is the primary nuclear fuel, which, with thorium, forms the only new energy source developed during this century. Reserves and resources are sufficient to supply the world's long-range energy demand for many generations as gas, oil, and coal sources become depleted.

Uranium is a fairly rare element, comprising about 0.0002 percent of the earth's crust. It never occurs free in na-

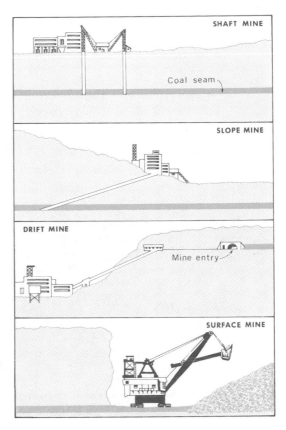

FIGURE 11–9 *Methods of Mining Coal*

ture. More than 150 uranium-containing minerals have been identified, but the chief ones are pitchblende and coffinite. The major sources are the western United States, the Elliot Lake and Beaverlodge areas in Canada, the Republic of South Africa, France, Australia, and several areas in communist countries.

references

1. Aschmann, Homer. "The Natural History of a Mine." *Economic Geography* 46 (April 1970): 172–189.

2. Bronitsky, Leonard, and Wallace, William R. "The Economic Impact of Urban-

ization on the Mineral Aggregate Industry." *Economic Geography* 50 (April 1974): 130–39.

3. Cicchetti, Charles J. *Alaskan Oil: Alternative Routes and Markets.* Baltimore: The Johns Hopkins University Press, 1972.

4. Cuff, David J. "Mineral Distributions." *The Journal of Geography* 69 (September 1970): 367–74.

5. Doherty, William T. *Minerals.* New York: Chelsea House Publishers, 1971.

6. Dugas, Jean. "Mineral Development in Quebec." *Canadian Geographical Journal* 84 (February 1972): 36–49.

7. Durrenberger, Robert. "The Colorado Plateau." *Annals of the Association of American Geographers* 62 (June 1972): 211–36.

8. Federal Power Commission. *Natural Gas Supply and Demand: 1971–1990.* Staff Report No. 2. Washington, D.C.: Bureau of Natural Gas, 1972.

9. King, L.; Casetti, E.; Odland, J.; and Semple, K. "Optional Transportation Patterns of Coal in the Great Lakes Region." *Economic Geography* 47 (July 1971): 401–13.

10. Finnie, Richard S. "North American Arctic Petroleum Development." *Canadian Geographical Journal* 83 (November 1971): 146–61.

11. Gilmor, Desmond A. "Irish Mineral Development and Canadian Participation." *Canadian Geographical Journal* 22 (May 1971): 172–81.

12. Haynes, James B. "North Slope Oil: Physical and Political Problems." *The Professional Geographer* 24 (February 1972): 17–22.

13. Manners, Gerald. *The Changing World Market For Iron Ore: 1950–1980.* Baltimore: The Johns Hopkins University Press, 1971.

14. Melamid, Alexander. "Satellization in Iranian Crude-Oil Production." *Geographical Review* 63 (January 1973): 27–43.

15. Prieto, Carlos. *Mining in the New World.* New York: McGraw-Hill Book Co., 1973.

16. Riddell, W. A. "Potash: New Wealth for Saskatchewan." *Canadian Geographical Journal* 89 (September 1974): 16–23.

17. Stewart, Keith J. "Minerals and Canada's Prairie Provinces." *Canadian Geographical Journal* 84 (April 1972): 104–15.

18. Valeton, Ida. *Bauxites.* Amsterdam, N.Y.: Elsevier Press, 1972.

19. Warren, Kenneth. *Mineral Resources.* New York: John Wiley and Sons, 1973.

IV

SECONDARY ECONOMIC ACTIVITY

CHAPTERS

12 Location Theory of Secondary
    Economic Activities

13 Manufacturing Systems

14 Manufacturing: Iron and Steel
    and Lesser Industrial Metals

15 Metal-Fabricating Industries

16 Textile and Garment Industries

17 The Chemical Industries

18 Electrical Machinery and
    Equipment

introduction

Secondary economic activities involve converting material resources into intermediary or finished goods through the application of labor, capital, and technology. Intermediary goods characterize secondary activities as possessing a hierarchical and spatially differentiated structure. The differentiation evolves through the combined influence of the frameworks discussed in parts I and II. Although there are as many secondary activities as there are different processes and products, selection of secondary activities for discussion is arbitrarily limited to a few topics here.

Part IV begins with a chapter on the location theory of secondary activity, followed by chapter 13 which discusses world manufacturing whose distribution patterns shed light on chapters 14 through 18, illustrating secondary economic activities.

location theory
of secondary
economic activities

12

12

Secondary activities encompass all activities that transform materials procured by primary activities into semi-finished or finished goods. Because inputs and outputs are variable for secondary activities, these activities follow highly uneven patterns of location. Their location patterns are not static, but are responsive to the changing conditions of input and output markets (*see* Figure 12–1).

Industry is constantly on the move, especially in economically developed societies. It does not locate randomly; the decision of where to locate an industrial plant is a crucial management problem. As industry has gained international markets, population shifts have occurred, transportation structure and costs have changed, and the need for new labor reserves has grown. The magnitude of the problem is indicated by the billions of dollars spent annually for the process of locating new plants in the United States alone.

FACTORS OF INDUSTRY LOCATION

A paramount problem facing executives of any large corporation is where to locate a plant or plants. Obtaining the best location requires consideration of a great array of interdependent factors. In general, industries often are oriented to one or a combination of criteria—raw materials, transportation, and markets—and sometimes others. For example, industries whose raw materials lose much weight in the manufacturing process (pulp mills, packing plants, or saw mills), tend to locate close to their raw material source; these industries are generally classified as *resource based*. Conversely, if the product gains in bulk or weight (soft-drink bottling, for example), the plant tends to orient itself near the market; such industries are often classed as *market based*. Industries that produce bulky or heavy material often feel compelled to locate near transportation facilities where lower transport costs assure them of competitive economic advantage. Industries that do not have specific orientation may be called "foot-loose" industries.

RAW MATERIALS

Although technological and transportation developments continually tend to reduce the significance of the location of raw materials, their procurement as a necessary condition for production is still a factor in deciding where to locate an industry. The location decision involves consideration of the following dimensions of raw materials: perishability, number of materials used, materials-mix, material substitution, freight-rate structure, and weight-loss ratio. Industries using highly perishable materials tend to be resource based. As the number of materials used increases, the significance of raw materials to the location decision proportionately reduces.

The increasing feasibility of substituting one material for another due to technological and environmental developments may substantially affect the location decision. For example, scrap metal is fast becoming an effective substitute for pig iron. Freight-rate structures, such as lower rates for water transportation, may influence management to locate away from the source of raw materials. However, transport costs proportionately add less to the cost of a material of higher value than to one of lower value, although there might be freight-rate advantages.

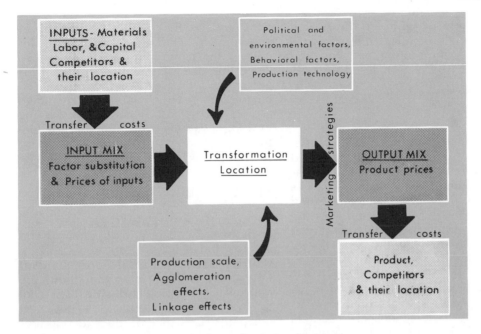

FIGURE 12–1 *Basic Flow of Production and Location Decisions*

MARKETS

The term market has various meanings. In this context, it refers to the location or concentration of households and firms that use or consume outputs. The size and capacity of a market, its purchasing power, the value and perishability of the industry's products, transportation cost, and available labor pool are all factors bearing on where to locate an industry. The size of the market can be varied and diverse—local, regional, national, or international. Localized markets encourage market-based industries.

For larger and extended market sizes, the location decision involves weighing the transportation cost against cost reduction achieved by greater plant capacity that permits economies in large-scale production. Because larger, scattered markets have information and communication facilities, availability of a trained labor pool, and higher income levels that mean greater purchasing power, plants generally locate near concentrations of people and other industries. Firms producing perishable and bulky products tend to locate near their market. Sand and gravel plants, which produce a bulky good with a low initial cost, would not survive away from the markets.

LABOR SUPPLY

Employee wages average about two-thirds of the total cost of U.S. firms. Regional differentials in wage rates, degree of skill and numbers in the labor force, the extent and strength of union activity, and attitudes toward work and commuting facilities are of crucial concern in location decisions. Labor-intensive industries, such as clothing, textiles, leather, electronics, jewelry, optical, and gun-making industries, are attracted to sites with a skilled and

229

plentiful supply of labor. A site near a labor pool would be affected by the consideration of commuting patterns and facilities, which reflect on absentee rates and lateness for work.

CAPITAL

From an economic point of view, capital represents all manmade things that aid in production. Economists list tools, machines, buildings, equipment, etc., as capital. However, the meaning assigned by the general public to capital is the money that may be used to buy capital goods and related inputs to produce outputs.

Capital in this sense is the most mobile factor of production, which reflects a negligible spatial variation in its supply. Nevertheless, financial centers like New York, Chicago, Los Angeles, Boston and other headquarters of the U.S. Federal Reserve Banks tend to agglomerate and perpetuate for reasons of security, communication, and cost reduction associated with face-to-face transactions.

TRANSFER COST

Transportation cost has traditionally been viewed as a direct cost of moving inputs and outputs. However, with increasing specialization and realization of the value of consumer time used to acquire products, the concept of transfer cost now includes freight charges. The cost to the consumer of acquiring a product, although it does not enter the accounting ledgers, influences the location decision particularly in situations where there is active competition between producers. The transfer cost is primarily dependent on freight rates and their structure, which, in turn, is affected by the direction, distance, volume, form of shipment, mode of transport, competition between car-

riers, and by the regulatory statutes of government. Common to all transfer costs is the packaging and loading cost. Since this part of the transfer cost progressively decreases with increasing distance, firms may consider this advantage against other cost items if considering locating away from the market. For further discussion, students may wish to refer back to chapter 4.

STRUCTURAL FACTORS

Structural factors relate to plant size and economies of scale and to internal and external linkages between plants and industries. Such links result in agglomeration affects because cost reductions are realized by locating industries adjacent to each other. Certain locations may permit plant sizes that produce economies of scale because the per-unit cost of production decreases with increasing output. A larger plant size may result from convenient and closer links with other firms and industries. As one firm's output becomes input for another, both firms tend to achieve stability and growth. Numerous firms and industries agglomerate at one location to take advantage of a situation that permits them to share certain cost items, such as research and development, volume transportation, or the elimination of transportation cost through vertical linkage,[1] and the publication of market and business conditions and opportunities. The impetus for per-

---

[1] Vertical linkage refers to a situation in which several firms are interrelated, each normally forming one stage in a series of operations. For example, mining, beneficiating, smelting, etc., are separate firms functionally linked together. Horizontal linkage, on the other hand, refers to a relationship between firms producing similar products that all may serve as input to another firm. An example would be automobile-component manufacturers and their converging linkage to Detroit from a radius of 200 miles.

petuation and mutual growth leading to the possibilities of mergers is provided.

TECHNOLOGICAL FACTORS

Although technological considerations are relevant to all factors bearing on location, their impact is specifically evident through transport technologies that are continually lessening the frictions of distance and through organizational and production technologies which provide economies of scale and agglomeration. Areas with many research and development activities attract other industries seeking to take advantage of the spin-off. Although technology is highly mobile over longer distances, it is generally adopted intensely in the immediate surrounding areas.

BEHAVIORAL FACTORS

Behavior patterns related to varying motivations often reflect diverse decisions about business goals and consequently about the location. The profit motive may be subordinated to sociological and psychological motives where habit, individualism, identity with certain institutions, community, friends and relatives, power and prestige, and such other considerations play a significant role in location decisions.

SOCIAL FACTORS

Social factors are listed separately but their separate listing is purposely done to emphasize that the social involvement of the entrepreneurs—membership in local clubs, churches, governments, and school boards and considerations of the goals and interest of the family members—may exert considerable influence on a firm to select a specific location. Proximity to a favorite golf course, church, circle of

friends and relatives may merit consideration.

CLIMATE

For some time, of course, climate has related to site selection. Industries involved in flight testing have often selected locations as devoid as possible of bad weather conditions that prevent flight observation and analysis. The rapid amalgamation of aircraft companies in southern California is testimony to this effect. In addition, lower construction and maintenance costs can be secured in favorable climatic regions. The advent of technical and aerospace research added a further dimension to the role of climate. Launching of multimillion or even billion dollar space capsules demands excellent weather conditions over extended periods of time. Restricted geographic regions met such conditions, and as such influenced industrial site selection of plants or complexes serving such functions.

SITE CONDITIONS

Site conditions have become a more prominent factor, particularly for industries that emit smoke, noise, or waste products. The increasing urbanization of the world adds a further dimension to the purchase of plant sites adjacent to markets, raw materials, or transportation. Some industries, such as those involving rocket testing, are forced to acquire large tracts in isolated areas to satisfy public health and safety standards and conservational criticism.

The site problem has undoubtedly led to the popularity of the industrial park, a term denoting all types of privately owned industrial areas that have full-time personnel devoted to attracting industries. In addition to acquiring pros-

231

pect leads from other agencies, industrial parks develop their own prospects via direct contacts, direct-mail solicitation, and advertising. Large-scale industrial parks advertise in national business periodicals. They provide detailed factual data about their sites, as well as area economic data.

Industrial parks have experienced problems that were not envisioned when the concept first developed. Deterioration in standards has occurred when original covenants were not strictly enforced and when managers or tenants were succeeded by others less concerned with maintaining the intended quality of the environment. Another problem, closely related to the first, is the addition of tenants needed for expansion programs that the park management is not able to meet. These are three partial remedies for this:

1. Persuade the original tenant to acquire more land than he thinks he needs
2. Hold adjoining land for a tenant's future expansion
3. Make larger sites available outside the industrial park to provide for future needs

Private land owners and developers of industrial property may operate on a local, regional, national, or international scale. In many cases, they use the services of industrial realtors for promotion and marketing of their properties. Sometimes they operate jointly with railroads, universities, or municipalities, and sometimes they set up complete merchandising programs of their own.

POLITICAL INFLUENCES: SPENDING AND REGULATIONS

Defense considerations have also become factors of location practice. Since World War II, the U.S. Department of Defense has awarded contracts based on regional dispersion. In several cases, plant construction of critical industries (e.g., electronics) was directly influenced by such national policy decisions. This is also true for other types of government spending; research and development spending in a region provides a significant stimulus or inducement for other industries to locate in that area. Spatial dispersion of industries in totalitarian nations from the point of view of national security has long been an important factor in site selection. U.S. economic policy has also tended to encourage spatial dispersion of industry to minimize the loss from a surprise attack.

Taxes are an increasingly important factor in the location of industrial plants. States and private municipalities, faced with rising costs for services and increased citizen apathy toward personal taxes, have instigated tax concessions, special deductions, and other tax incentives to attract industry in order to provide more jobs, more income, and consequently greater tax revenues. For example, Puerto Rico has created a climate of good will toward industry, which along with tax concessions and favorable loan policy has lured a number of international firms. Concessions offered by various political subdivisions usually include:

1. Exemption from local or state property taxes for from two to ten years, frequently with the understanding that the exemption will be extended
2. Guarantee that a new firm's property tax will not be increased for a specified number of years
3. Exemption from state income and excise taxes. Some states accomplish this by allowing a new firm to accelerate the depreciation of certain of its investments
4. Exemption from property taxes on goods and materials stored for interstate shipment, a practice known as the "free-port" exemption (25)

In most cases, tax concessions are confined to some form of relief from property taxes, which generally means that local governments bear the entire burden of the exemption. This is one of the major disadvantages of the practice; it leads to an additional tax burden on long-established firms, as well as limiting the tax base of the community.

Increasing the tax base and expanding existing industries are important objectives of a community, presenting a great dilemma for the leaders of every community. Obviously, new firms seeking locations are going to shy away from any city or location with a group of unhappy industrialists. The "happy" industrialists in the area may accelerate more economic growth by being "better advertised" than the tax incentives.

Tax concessions and special arrangements are often offered by local governments as inducements to industry. Some of these arrangements are legal, some are extralegal, and some may be illegal. Generally, the inducements are of two types: 1) sub rosa tax concessions and 2) arrangements for free or low-cost extensions of access roads, sidewalks, utility mains, power connections, or parking lots. Some local governments provide training schools for prospective employees of a new plant. These inducements may be accompanied by assistance from community leaders in zoning hearings, in waivers of building code requirements or fire regulations, and in modification of planning commission rulings on land–building ratios or esthetic architectural requirements. In some states, individual cities or state agencies assist industry with market research studies, special raw material or labor market studies, and other technical services, which if not obtained free would have to be purchased by the incoming firm.

Sub rosa arrangements, because of their secrecy, are not assigned a dollar value, but they are believed to be rather common occurrences. Problems of such arrangements, however, are obvious:

1. Lack of accountability means that objective and accurate estimates of comparative costs cannot be determined

2. The duration of the arrangements is uncertain because exposure and publicity may bring their cancellation

3. To the extent that arrangements are illegal or extralegal, considerable risk of exposure, litigation, and possible imposition of penalties and fines is borne by the parties that solicit, accept, or assent to such arrangements

SITE AMENITY FACTORS

The "good life" is rarely discussed in texts dealing with manufacturing geography, but its importance is apparent, if rarely calculated. Senior executives invariably stress casual living as a decisive factor in site location. Although this may pose problems for those who heavily rely on detailed cost-benefit ratios for industrial site location, its persistence as a factor of geographic location is indisputable. What is meant by casual living? It could mean living in an area where ice and snow are minimal, if not totally absent. It could mean that the sun shines from a blue cloudless sky. It could suggest homes built around a patio or garden, where many meals, particularly evening meals, are barbecued and eaten outdoors. It might suggest engineers and executives wearing cool, open-throat, short-sleeved sport shirts. Or it might suggest proximity to ski slopes, scenic paths, lakes, and trout streams. Whatever it connotes, it is a factor that has definite accountability in site selection by industry.

In a sense, cultural atmosphere is more definitive. Engineers, scientists, and skilled workers who comprise a significant segment of the labor force are largely an exceptionally well-educated group who desire the best cultural advantages for themselves and their children. Among these advantages are attractive homes on large lots, superior schools and libraries, efficient community government, outstanding medical and hospital facilities, active little-theatre movements, and often universities and research facilities.

The interaction between industrial firms, particularly research-based industrial complexes, and educational institutions and activities are many and diverse. First, research and research-based manufacturing establishments have a demand for skills at various levels. Second, their employees, if not the firms themselves, often demand a better general education and training in work-related, specialized areas. Third, science-oriented firms need faculty consultants, research from colleges and universities, and other specialized services of educational institutions.

Many science-based firms also contribute directly to vocational training by conducting their own in-house training programs. This reduces the need for outside facilities and adds to the supply of local skills available to other firms. Better opportunities and better working conditions will effect levels of occupational and educational aspiration, occupational mobility, and educational achievement.

WATER

Always an important consideration, water has taken on increasing significance in recent years as a location factor, partly because new industrial technology has greatly intensified the demand for water. The quantity and quality of water available for industrial purposes is becoming more scarce as a result of rapid urbanization.

Of equal importance to many firms is water temperature and impurity. Hard water must be treated or otherwise it would cause corrosion in pipes and circulating systems that would elevate repair and replacement costs. Since cold water is necessary in a number of industries, such as steel, water temperature at the source becomes important. In certain regions, for example, southern California, cooling towers are required to cool water before it is used in the manufacturing process.

WASTE DISPOSAL

Waste disposal is also a location factor of no small import, both in terms of disposal of fluids and of gases. Most states now have stringent requirements for disposal waste material, and many cities, Los Angeles, for example, have even stricter regulations to reduce pollutants into the atmosphere. Dye plants and woolen mills discharge unusually heavy amounts of fluid waste material in the form of grease and suspended solids; these industries, as well as chemical industries, are usually extensively regulated by law. Consideration of the means of waste disposal, the costs of disposal, and related legal restrictions (which all vary from one place to another) occupy a prime place in the process of deciding where to locate an industry.

PERSONAL REASONS

Personal reasons are not given the credit they deserve as an industrial location factor. The classic question, "Why did the Boeing Aircraft Company decide on Seattle for its plant location?" and the answer, "Because Bill Boeing, the president, liked his home town," leads to the supposition that a key to the formation of new enterprises in particular places is the entrepreneur himself. From a location standpoint, he may appear anywhere. This is the reason that every area is presumed to have a potential for the development of "homegrown" industry. Some

evidence seems to indicate that entrepreneurs are more numerous in the
highly technological and high-growth
industries than in others. However, the
entrepreneur tends to start his business
where he lives. He may fail if it is a poor
place to start such a business, but initially
this will probably not inhibit him. More
businesses are started in urban areas because more entrepreneurs live there, not
because of any conscious relocation of
entrepreneurs to what is a better seed-
bed for new firms.

COMMUNITY ATTITUDES

Often the local warmth of the populace
becomes a dynamic factor of industrial
location, even if tax advantages are not
apparent. The rise of local industrial development corporations in small towns
and the aggressive work of chambers of
commerce and local bankers often swing
industries, particular small- and medium-
sized firms, to locate where they are
wanted.

Citizens of small towns and rural
areas often do not want industry, or
rather, do not want the accompanying
changes that it brings. Firms are often
highly sensitive to local feeling, and more
than one community has lost a large industrial plant after town-hall meetings
with vigorous, outspoken opposition.
Industry must be wanted by the community; otherwise, many problems may
evolve: harassment of legitimate zoning
requests, resurrection of antique city
ordinances that restrict operation, and
measures that might make it more difficult for the firm to recruit a work force.

Firms seeking new locations are very
conscious of how they will be received
in a community. They often take personal
surveys of potential locations; for example, a representative of a potential
industry in an area, walking along the
main street of various towns stopped
local people to ask, "How would you like

to work for company X?" In some towns,
he received the nearly unanimous reply,
"I'd like to work for company X, especially if that fine company were located
in my town." In other towns, he also
received an almost unanimous reply, "I'd
like to work for company X, but I wish
they would locate in a nearby town."
There is no doubt which community the
site selector chose.

Community attitude-formation is the
beginning of any conscientious program
of industrial development. It may require
organized effort to mount a campaign
through all media, including personal
appearances at clubs and gatherings, to
spread the message about the benefits,
as well as the problems and effects, of
industrial growth.

CURRENT TRENDS IN MAJOR LOCATION FACTORS

In the United States, various changes in
the importance of the major industrial
location factors of market, labor, transportation, and material resources may be
cited. Early industrialization patterns in
the U.S. reflected a matching of the
dominant locational factors of certain
industries with the areas that were most
favored by that factor. Thus, market-
oriented industries were highly concentrated in the Northeast, on the Atlantic
seaboard, and around Chicago. Raw ma-
terial-oriented industries were located at
the best source of those raw materials,
which in many cases was the West. Many
labor-intensive industries sought location
in the South, where labor was abundant,
cheap, and not affected by union activity.

The relationships between location
factors and area of the nation have been
changing. Slowly at first, but accelerating
after World War II, these changes are
shifting comparative advantages (see
chapter 4) that certain regions have traditionally enjoyed. Nevertheless, there

are still important regional differences that correspond more favorably to certain location factors, and these are likely to persist.

It is important to differentiate between consumer markets, which are generally a function of population and income patterns, and industrial markets, which are a function of manufacturing concentrations. There are important differences in the geographical distribution of consumer and industrial markets, although these differences are not as great as they once were. Markets, in this context, shall refer to regional markets, rather than district or local markets.

Consumer markets are still highly concentrated. As Harris (9) points out, half of the retail sales in the United States are in the Northeast. Some states in this area have a market density several hundred times higher than some western states. Consumer market densities in most of the mountain and plains states are also very low.

This situation is slowly changing because of the higher population growth rates of western and southern states. However, much of this growth, up to now, has been concentrated in oasis-like areas in the West and in the South, such as southern California, Phoenix, Arizona, and parts of Texas. In the mountain states, there are vast areas of very sparse consumer markets, which affect the market pull of these growth areas. Although there is a general trend toward developing significant markets in regions other than the Northeast, the differences in regional market densities remain sizable.

Industrial markets are even more highly concentrated. About two-thirds of all manufacturing employment is still in the Northeast. According to industry, these markets have traditionally been concentrated in certain regions or cities. For instance, the automobile industry market has been concentrated in Detroit, the rubber industry market in Akron,

Ohio, and the steel industry market in Pittsburgh and the areas around Chicago.

Another factor that varies significantly among regions is wages. Wage differences as high as 25 percent between developed urban areas are not uncommon; differences between urban and rural areas are even more striking. There are forces, however, that are narrowing these differences: union organization and collective bargaining, particularly at the national level, federal minimum wage laws, and the migration of industry itself. When industry moves into an area of low wages, it increases employment. If other plants later locate close by, demand may put an upward pressure on wages and tend to reduce the differential that previously existed.

Four additional, related trends may be noted in the contemporary industry location process. Two of these are spatial in nature, reflecting shifts in the concentrations of industrial activities:

Regional decentralization from the Northeast to the South and West
Local decentralization from large central cities

The other two trends are functional in nature, resulting from a variety of socioeconomic changes that have caused shifts in the relative importance of the kinds of industry locating new plants. These shifts are due to differential growth rates, which in turn reflect changes, such as the rise in personal income levels, the growth of the service sector of employment, and the increasing role of research and technology. These trends are:

Increasing market orientation of industry
Growth of highly technological industries

Manufacturing industry in the United States has traditionally been concentrated in the Northeast. This area, often referred to as the "manufacturing belt," includes the New England states, Middle Atlantic states, and Great Lakes regions. In 1870 this area accounted for 83 percent of the industrial employment of the nation.

During the past century, the growth of the western and southern regions of the U.S. has generally been faster than that of the Northeast, accelerating particularly rapidly in the last two decades. From 1940 to 1960, while the Northeast increased its manufacturing employment 70 percent, the Southwest enjoyed an increase of 160 percent and the Far West an increase of 200 percent.

As impressive as these growth rates are, they are large percentage increases derived from relatively low base figures. Thus, despite differences in growth, the Northeast still predominates in manufacturing. As Perloff (19) points out:

> Looked at in terms of each region's share of the nation's manufacturing development, however, the enduring strength of the urban-industrial Northeast is evident. After ninety years of continuing industrial transformation, nearly two-thirds of the nation's manufacturing labor force was still located in the Northeastern industrial belt in 1960. (p. 50)

A continuation of the trend toward regional decentralization in favor of the South and West is to be expected. Inherent in this shift, which accelerates in periods of economic expansion, are opportunities for areas and communities that lack an industrial base.

A second trend of industrial location is toward changes in the type of area or community selected. Traditionally, manufacturing plants were located in large cities in order to draw on a large labor force and to secure the materials and services necessary to their operation. For the past thirty years or more, however, there has been a tendency for industry to move out of the central city, in many cases to a nearby suburban community or to some other point on the periphery of the urban concentration. In other cases, however, smaller industrialized areas or even rural towns were the favored locations.

The third trend in industrial location is toward market orientation, based on the declining pull of other location factors, particularly the raw materials factor. Proximity to raw materials is no longer as important to the production process of the average plant as it once was.

Another aspect of the increasing market orientation of industry is the relatively greater growth of market-oriented industries. As Perloff pointed out, resource-oriented activities of the economy have been declining in relative importance since 1870. In the past two decades, manufacturing industries, and particularly those producing consumer goods, have proliferated and expanded rapidly. Companies that have been building and serving these markets tend to be market-oriented by nature. As personal incomes grow and equalize across the nation, markets for new consumer products expand. The producing companies follow these markets, giving rise to the "filling in" process described by Perloff. As quickly as a regional market passes the threshold of size that permits economical operation, company after company puts branch plants into the market. Even when the economic advantages are small, when one company in an industry branches, competitors tend to follow suit.

A final trend concerns the growth of what might be called the highly technological industries. This term, admittedly vague, includes some of the so-called "footloose" industries, which are generally not footloose at all. In considering this aspect of recent economic growth, the term industry must be broadened from its customary meaning which is synonymous with manufacturing. While

237

many companies in this field do manufacture a product, or "hardware" as it is often called, many others produce "software," which is really a service. However, highly technological industries will be considered together with manufacturing industries in defining this trend because they are almost always "export industries" in the regional sense and thus provide the same economic stimulation that the more traditional manufacturing activities do. Furthermore, they are among the fastest growing segments of the economy, and they are attractive in terms of wages and a high propensity to generate new business enterprises.

A well-recognized principle in location theory is the tendency of companies using new technologies and pioneering new fields to locate in urban environments. However, this tendency provides only part of the explanation for the pattern of concentration that has emerged in the "intellect-oriented" industries. These industries are concentrated in five geographical areas: southern California, San Francisco Bay area, New York–northern New Jersey, Boston, and Washington, D.C. This type of industry also needs technological resources, such as those provided by universities and research organizations, and also requires many kinds of specialized services, components, and supplies. In addition, there is often a need for high-risk capital financing and above all for a large pool of professional people from a variety of disciplines.

In light of this combination of location requirements for business enterprise, as well as for the people whose satisfactions are the substance of its success, the pattern of urban concentration is not surprising. In each case, the reasons for the development of the complex are probably different, but the presence of entrepreneurship and the availability of risk capital are common and significant factors.

THEORIES OF LOCATION OF SECONDARY ACTIVITIES

WEIGHT LOSS AND TRANSFER COSTS

The principle that illustrates the relationship between weight loss ratio and transfer cost is important to the understanding of secondary location theories. The weight loss ratio is the ratio between the product weight and the weight of raw material processed.

Assuming that a firm transforms raw materials (I) from a single site (I_R) into a single product (O) for sale at a single market (M) located away from the site of raw materials and that the transfer cost (T) is higher per ton for O than I, the pull toward locating at the market site increases with the increasing weight loss ratio. This principle is illustrated in Table 12–1, where the weight loss ratio varies inversely with the percentage of weight lost during processing. For example, a weight loss ratio of .10 means that 90 percent of the weight of the raw materials was lost during processing.

The firm's location would be determined by the minimization of the transfer costs, given the prices of O and I. In Table 12–1, the location is indeterminate when the weight loss ratio is .70. Such situations call for location decisions influenced more by other factors and by the intermediate location opportunities.

The question of intermediate locations between market and raw materials involves consideration of freight-rate structures. The freight charges normally increase at a declining rate with distance. As freight rates tend to taper off with distance, intermediate locations are at a competitive disadvantage with sites of raw materials or markets. The intermediate locations may become attractive when there are deviations from the tapering rate structure. Such deviations are possible when transshipment trans-

TABLE 12–1 Hypothetical Relationship Between Weight Loss and Transfer Costs

TRANSFER COSTS ASSOCIATED WITH THE PROCESSING
OF 100 TONS OF RAW MATERIALS

WEIGHT LOSS RATIO (0/I)	MARKET LOCATION (@ $7.00 per ton transfer costs)	LOCATION AT THE SITE OF RAW MATERIALS (@ $10.00 per ton transfer costs)
.10	$700	$ 100
.20	700	200
.30	700	300
.40	700	400
.50	700	500
.60	700	600
.70	700	700
.80	700	800
.90	700	900
1.00	700	1000

fers are involved or when carriers grant special rates because of complementary and return shipments permitting the carriers to fully use their capacity in each direction.

THE WEBER THEORY

Alfred Weber, a German economist, published his famous *Theory of the Location of Industries* in 1900. His theory was designed to apply to all types of economic activity and to a homogeneous political and economic system. Like Von Thünen, he based his theory on simplified assumptions and premises: (1) a uniform transportation system where transportation costs vary directly with the length of the haul and the weight of the shipment; (2) homogeneous culture under a simple sovereignty; (3) nonmobility of labor and (4) a sporadic and fixed distribution of material resources. Given these conditions, Weber theorized that secondary economic activities would locate in response to the dynamic forces of relative transfer costs, labor costs, and agglomeration factors. (An agglomeration

factor is a force that tends to attract industry at certain points within a region because of various economies, such as transportation economies, internal and external economies, and the scale of the firm.)

While Von Thünen concentrated primarily on the role that transfer costs play in allocating land resources at varying distances from a market between agricultural uses, Weber attempts to explain the location of secondary activities with additional variables.

Weber's simplest formulation involved one input (or one material resource) and one market. In his model, location is affected by the distribution of only one input, the amount of weight loss of the input in manufacturing, and the ratio of transportation charges to weight and distance. The ubiquity of an input would suggest location close to or at the market, because at that point transfer cost would be the lowest. If the input is sporadically distributed and there is no weight loss, the location will be either at the source of the input or at the market. If the input is sporadically

239

distributed and there is weight loss in manufacturing, then location would tend to occur at the source of the input because of the advantage in transfer cost. (Weber assumed that transfer costs were directly proportional to the weight of the shipment, whether it was a raw material or a finished product.)

However, if the analysis is extended to two inputs (i.e., material resources) and one market, the choices of location increase. Of course, ubiquitous distribution of both inputs would suggest the location for the market. If one of the two inputs is sporadic in distribution, and there is no weight loss of either input, the advantage of transfer cost would suggest locating at the market. If both inputs are sporadically distributed and involve no weight loss, the plant will locate at the market, except when one of the inputs is on the route of the other input being shipped to the market. In the latter case, the transient point of input incidence would be equally attractive to location.

The location problem becomes more complex when both inputs are sporadically distributed and a weight loss is incurred for both. Figure 12–2 assumes that the two raw materials (I_1 and I_2) and the market (M) are equidistant, 25 miles from each other. To process 100 tons of I_1 and I_2 at M would involve 5,000 ton miles (100 tons of I_1 × 25 from I_1 site to M and 100 tons of I_2 from I_2 site to M). The location at I_1 would involve 5,000 ton miles, shown below:

100 tons of I_2 × 25 miles from I_2 to I_1	= 2,500
100 tons of O × 25 miles (with weight loss ratio) from I_1 to M	= 2,500
(Total in ton miles)	5,000

Similarly, the location at I_2 would also involve 5,000 ton miles. However, the location at point N in Figure 12–2 would add ton miles, computed below:

100 tons of I_1 × 12.5 miles from I_1 to N	= 1,250
100 tons of I_2 × 12.5 miles from I_2 to N	= 1,250
100 tons of O × 21.6^2 miles from N to M	= 2,160
(Total in ton miles)	4,660

The distance between N and M in Figure 12–2 can be computed using the following relationship:

$$\sqrt{(\overline{I_1N})^2 + (\overline{NM})^2} = \overline{I_1M}$$

Obviously location N has a better competitive advantage over sites M, I_1, and I_2, assuming the freight rates are uniformly applied to all directions of the triangle. Other points of location may similarly be determined with the objective of minimizing the transfer costs when weight loss and relative amounts of inputs are varied. However, minimizing transfer costs does not necessarily mean minimum cost location.

Weber illustrated the rationale for locating at several intermediate points by the use of isotims and an isodapane. Isotims are concentric circles representing transfer costs of raw materials and products. An isodapane is the line connecting the locus of points of equal cost. In Figure 12–3, isotims around M show transfer costs from all points to M; simi-

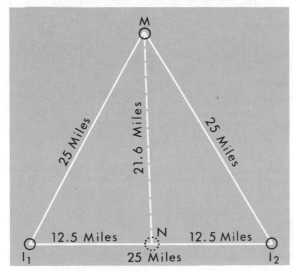

FIGURE 12–2 *Weber Triangular Model of Industrial Location*

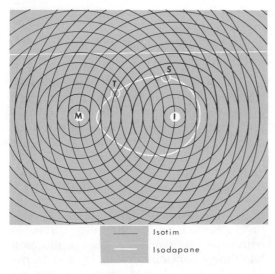

Isotim
Isodapane

FIGURE 12–3 *Weber's Location of Industry with the Aid of Isotims and Isodapane*

larly, isotims around I reflect transfer charges to all points from I. Figure 12–3 reflects assumptions that transfer costs are the same per ton-mile for raw materials and products and that the two sets of isotims are spaced to represent one unit of transfer cost per ton. With the further assumption of a weight loss ratio of .50, the location at I would involve 9 units (9 isotims equidistant between I and M) of transfer cost as the product is shipped from I to M.

Similarly, if the firm were located at M, the transportation cost would be 18 units, since two tons of material would have to move the 9 distance units from I to M for every ton of product made at M location (based on the weight-loss ratio of .50 and the 10 equidistant isotims between I and M).

The intermediary locations would be determined by relative levels of the transfer cost. When connected, the locus of points showing equal transfer cost forms an isodapane in Figure 12–3. For example, at points S and T the transfer costs are identical. At point S, the aggregate

transport cost would involve eight units of new material (4 isotims multiplied by 2 tons of raw material), plus nine units on product (9 isotims multiplied by 1 ton), totaling 17 units. At point T, the transfer cost is also 17 units (approximately 12 and 5 units for raw material and product, respectively). The heavy solid line in Figure 12–3 is an isodapane connecting points at which the transfer cost would total only 17 units. (Students may wish to verify this observation and the other locations on the isodapane from the data of Figure 12–3.) The isodapane identifies locations with their relative transfer costs which need to be compared and weighed with other costs, such as labor, and agglomeration effects on costs.

Weber emphasized that the first step is to determine the point where manufacturing is possible with a minimum inbound and outbound transfer cost. The location from the site with the least transfer cost may deviate because of lower labor costs. If the saving in labor costs exceeds the additional transfer costs resulting from the shift, the location will move to the point offering a saving in labor costs. This also holds for the saving in cost or attraction offered by the agglomeration force.

Thus, by using these analytical tools based on assumptions about the distribution of materials and weight-loss ratios, Weber was able to predict the location behavior of groups of industries with knowledge of three variables: transfer costs, labor costs, and the sum total of agglomeration effects.

Weber offers a schematic process for choosing a location that overall offers the least cost, given the distribution of materials, labor, the transportation network (rates affected only by weight of cargo and distance of haul), the location of market, and the relative prices. Weber's analysis lacked consideration of: (1) the nature and distribution of markets as

241

demand centers, and (2) the significance of a route network of junctions, long-haul economies, and group, class, commodity, and transient rates, which affect the transport cost—the most important variable in Weber's analysis.

THE LÖSCHIAN THEORY OF LOCATION

Contrary to Weber, whose location theory was primarily concerned with minimum cost location, in 1954 August Lösch offered a theory that assumed cost functions as given and sought optimum locations in terms of maximizing sales revenue. Like Von Thünen, Weber was concerned with optimum location around market centers. Lösch, however, treats the market as spatially dispersed and views firms as seeking locations that maximize sales revenue from sales over wider market areas.

Lösch establishes that for each product there exists a hexagonal system of market areas. Under this system, market boundaries and all spatial areas are served. In Figure 12–4, the circular market boundary system (which also may be perceived in the Thünenian scheme) shows that some areas are unserved; they

do not contribute toward the goal of maximizing the revenue.

Lösch postulated that even if the resources were homogeneously spread over an area, economic differentiation would occur because of economies of scale and no transport cost all production in the given region would be one, or a few, optimum-sized plants located at random. On the other hand, with the absence of any economies of scale and given the transport costs a ubiquity pattern of economic activity would prevail. With economies of scale and transport costs, the result is intermediate: several production sites at definite distances comprise between mass production (yielding economies of scale) and transfer costs. This phenomenon is more pronounced for secondary activities than for primary activities, where space is an input.

The pattern of secondary location could be conditioned by demand and level of competition. A firm would maximize revenue by expanding the demand; graphically, a demand cone is produced by rotating the demand curve around the vertical axis (discussed in chapter 4). Larger sales area would make it possible to achieve economies of scale to cause the profit to increase.

As long as firms realize profit, new entry would take place, which would intensify competition (see chapter 4). Competition squeezes together the round sales areas into equal regular hexagons (see Figure 12–4), leading to a situation where profits and transport costs are minimized. The size of hexagons would depend on the size of the market for each firm and for each product. If the hexagons of various products and firms are arranged in an overlay chart, a complex network of market landscape would appear.

Given the state of technology, cost functions, and economies of scale that the firm possesses, the optimum location

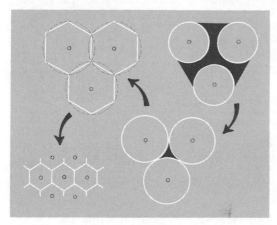

FIGURE 12–4 *Löschian Market Area Boundaries*

responds to the consumer distribution to arrive at an isorevenue point. Since it is very likely that several separate products may have the same pattern and so produce the same size of hexagons, a firm would then choose a location point from the various isorevenue points which serves as a central point to the maximum number of hexagonal networks of market areas. Thus, over time such locations would produce a large metropolis with all the advantages of agglomeration effects. The locations selected with this rationale would not only reduce the transfer costs, but would also realize the agglomeration effects (possible under Löschian schema) and promote industrial concentration. The changes in the hexagonal pattern around the center, caused by the changing consumer and industry demand and by the number and variety of the hexagonal market areas, may result in a composite market network which looks like a honeycomb.

Walter Isard has modified the Löschian model to make it more realistic. Isard recognized that the price of products is determined by many factors, such as tastes and preferences, incomes, future price and income expectations, status, and prices of substitutes. His view of the market landscape is shown in Figure 12–5.

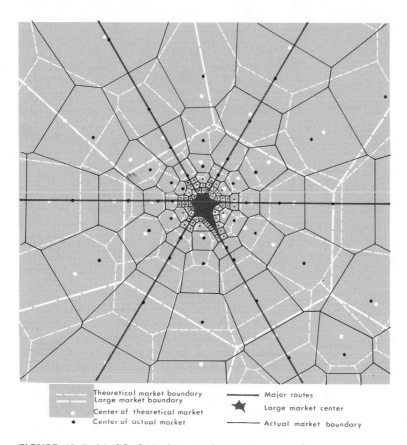

Theoretical market boundary
Large market boundary
Center of theoretical market
Center of actual market
Major routes
Large market center
Actual market boundary

FIGURE 12–5 *Modified Löschian Market Landscape*

From a purely economic viewpoint, the location at which economic profit is maximized will be the optimum one, given the scale of production and time period. On one hand, this means cost will be minimized in assembling the necessary inputs; processing or transformation; and marketing the output. On the other hand, revenue will be maximized by proper product-mix; proper price and delivery schedule; and a better knowledge of the structure and characteristics of demand. In terms of maximum economic profits, the problem of optimum location offers a challenge and opportunity to scholars from the various academic disciplines. The proper understanding of the location process not only benefits a firm's success and survival, it also benefits social welfare through proper and wise use of resources.

references

1. Alexander, J. W. *Economic Geography.* Englewood Cliffs, N.J.: Prentice-Hall, 1963.

2. Berry, B. J. L., and Garrison, W. L. "The Functional Bases of the Central Place Hierachy." *Economic Geography* 34 (1958): 150.

3. Boyce, Ronald R. *The Bases of Economic Geography: An Essay on the Spatial Characteristics of Marr's Economic Activities.* New York: Holt, Rhinehart and Winston, 1974.

4. Christaller, Walter. *"Die Zentralen Orte in Suddeuschland."* Jena: Gustave Fischer Verlag, 1933.

5. Dunn, Edgar S. *The Location of Agricultural Production.* Gainesville: University of Florida Press, 1954.

6. Fetter, F. A. "The Economic Law of Market Areas." *Quarterly Journal of Economics* 39 (1924): 520–29.

7. Garrison, W. L., and Marble, Duane F. "The Spatial Structure of Agricultural Activities." *Annals of the Association of American Geographers* 47 (June 1957): 137–44.

8. Greenhut, M. *Plant Location in Theory and Practice: The Economics of Space.* Chapel Hill, N.C.: University of North Carolina Press, 1956.

9. Harris, C. D. "The Market as a Factor in the Location of Industry in the United States." *Annals of the Association of American Geographers* 44 (December 1954).

10. Hoover, Edgar M. *Location Theory and the Shoe and Leather Industry.* Cambridge: Harvard University Press, 1937.

11. ———. *The Location of Economic Activity.* New York: McGraw-Hill Book Co., 1948.

12. Isard, Walter. *Location and Space Economy.* New York: John Wiley and Sons, 1956.

13. ———. *Regional Input–Output Study: Recollections, Reflections, and Diverse Notes on the Philadelphia Experience.* Cambridge, Mass.: M.I.T. Press, 1971.

14. ———, and Isard, P. *General Social, Political and Economic Equilibrium for a System of Regions.* Occasion Papers, Series No. 2. Philadelphia: Regional Science Research Institute, 1965.

15. Lösch, August. *The Economics of Location.* First published in Germany in 1939. Translated by William H. Woglam and W. F. Stopler. New Haven: Yale University Press, 1954.

16. Lloyd, Peter E., and Dicken, Peter. *Location in Space: A Theoretical Approach to Economic Geography.* New York: Harper & Row, 1972.

17. Morrill, Richard L. *The Spatial Organization of Society.* 2nd ed. North Scituate, Mass.: Duxbury Press, 1974.

18. Palander, Rord. "Beitrage Zur Standortstheorie." *Amgvist Och Wiksells Boktryckeri-a-b,* 1935.

19. Perloff, Harvey S., and Dodds, Vera W. *How a Region Grows.* New York: Committee for Economic Development, 1963.

20. Reilly, W. J. *The Law of Retail Gravitation.* New York: The Knickerbocker Press, 1931.

21.   Riley, Raymond C. *Industrial Geography.* London: Chatto and Windus, 1973.

22.   Smith, David M. *Industrial Location: An economic Geographical Analysis.* New York: John Wiley and Sons, 1971.

23.   Webber, Michael J. *Impact of Uncertainty on Location.* Cambridge, Mass.: M.I.T. Press, 1972.

24.   Weber, Alfred. "Weber Den Standort der Insustrien." In *Reine Theorie des Standorts,* part I. Tubingen, 1900. Translated by C. J. Freindrich as *Alfred Weber's Theory of the Location of Industries.* Chicago: University of Chicago Press, 1928.

25.   Weiss, Stephen J. "Tax Structure, Tax Competition, and Tax Burden on Industry: Comparisons Across State Lines," part I. *New England Business Review* (January 1968).

26.   Von Thünen, Johann Heinrich. *Der Isoliterte Staat in Beiziehung auf Land-wirthschaft und Nationalokonomie.* 3 vols.

manufacturing
systems

13

13

The theories of the location of secondary economic activities did not attempt to integrate all of the location factors outlined in the first part of chapter 12, but rather attempted to identify important common denominators and to simplify and construct modifiable and predictive models. All of these models held that transfer costs are theoretically the most fundamental element determining the location of secondary activities.

The location theories are generalized relative to the size of the geographic space being analyzed. At first glance, one has the impression that these theories are functional only at the local level because they are easily applicable and modifiable at local levels. At larger levels of spatial units, such as the world, their application is complicated by substantially different markets, political conditions, diversity of transport modes, and frequent discontinuities of data.

The application of these theories may not be as apparent in this chapter as in the following chapters in Part II because here the primary objective is to discuss manufacturing, or secondary, activities: first, as an evolutionary process and second as a broad classification at a given point in time.

Manufacturing is the processing or combining of materials to make a desired product. It is a continuous process, carried out on a substantial scale, transforming commodities for sale to buyers over a wide area. Manufacturing, in the sense of transformation of raw materials, historically developed in the form of work to provide the requirements of a house community. In this connection, it was an auxiliary occupation; it first became of interest when production was carried beyond household needs.

Looking back over the last thousand years, one can divide the development of the machine and machine civilization into three successive but overlapping phases, so termed by Mumford in 1934 as: eotechnic, paleotechnic, and neotechnic. (11)

EOTECHNIC PHASE

The eotechnic phase refers to the socio-economic organization characterized by craft guilds and household, or cottage, industries and the simplest type of transformation of local raw materials into finished products, primarily at the site of consumption. Cottage industries are not confined to the historical past but are found widely scattered throughout the less developed nations of the world today. Necessary items, such as clothing, furniture, pottery, brick, tools, ornaments, and utensils are produced on a small scale with limited capital and crude equipment. Enterprises are necessarily small and scattered. Mumford refers to this phase as the "water and wood complex," where energy and raw material were abundant almost anywhere, and man could harness the wind or water for power to transform local clays, sands, hides and skins, wool and wood into products for domestic consumption. The eotechnic phase called for high labor inputs by skilled craftsmen who serviced widely dispersed populations. Differences in regional outputs encouraged intraregional trade at a time when transport was slow, difficult, and very costly.

RISE OF CRAFT GUILDS

The second reason for transforming raw materials for needs other than household, is production for sale, which originated with craft guilds, which flourished in Western Europe between 1150 and 1350 AD.

The craft guild was an association for

the promotion of its particular industry in a town. Its economic functions were:

1. Regulating wages
2. Fixing prices and conditions of sale
3. Determining working hours and working conditions of labor
4. Inspection of workmanship and quality of materials

In order to perform these functions, each craft had to obtain a local monopoly of its particular product. In general, the craft guild protected its members against competition at all levels—from production to consumption of their product. In addition, it served its members in time of need, provided them with opportunities for common religious and social activities, and furnished their children with schools.

DISINTEGRATION OF CRAFT GUILDS

The disintegration of the craft guilds, which took place after the close of the Middle Ages, proceeded along several lines. Certain craftsmen within the guilds rose to positions of merchant and capitalist, i.e., became employers of home workers. Masters with considerable invested capital purchased the raw materials and turned over the work to their fellow guildsmen, who carried on the process of production for them and sold the finished product. The guilds were thus transformed into guilds of dealers in which the full members were those who produced for the market, while those who had sunk to the level of wage workers and home workers for others lost their vote in the guild and hence their share in its control.

DEVELOPMENT OF THE DOMESTIC SYSTEM

During the late Middle Ages, distinctions arose between the craft guilds. In the chief cities in England and on the Continent, there were a handful of industries whose guilds (or livery companies, as they were later called) had come to dominate not only the other crafts but the town government as well. The democracy of the guild system was attacked and weakened.

The disappearance of quality within and among the craft guilds paved the way for the domestic, or "putting out," system of industry inaugurated by the Commercial Revolution, when the capitalist organization of business began to develop in Western Europe during the 16th century.

The textile industry, whose beginnings go back to the early Middle Ages, became the main industry of the domestic system. From the 11th century onward, there was a struggle between linen and wool industries, and in the 17th and 18th centuries between wool and cotton industries; wool and cotton won in each case. Charlemagne wore nothing but linen, but later, with increasing demilitarization in France, the demand for wool increased; at the same time, forests were cleared, the fur industry disappeared, and furs became more expensive. In the Middle Ages, woolen goods were the principal commodity in the markets of France, England, and Italy. Wool became the foundation of the economic prosperity of the medieval city. Here again one finds early traces of the putting-out system. In general, the system first appeared in Flanders, and later in England where the Flanders woolen industry called forth mass production of wool.

THE FACTORY AND ITS FORERUNNERS

Shop production, which implies separation between household and place of work, has appeared in varied forms in the course of history:

1. *Isolated small shops* are formed everywhere, for example, in the bazaar system, with its grouping together of a number of workshops to facilitate working together.

2. The *ergasterion* also is universal; its medieval designation was *fabrica*, an ambiguous term which may designate a cellar den leased by a group of workers and used as a shop or a manorial institution for wage work.

3. *Unfree shop industry* on a large scale seems to have occurred during late Egyptian civilization. It undoubtedly originated from the gigantic estate of the pharaoh, out of which developed separate shops with wage labor.

In the West, the industry of the craft guilds was carried on without fixed capital and hence required no large initial cost. But even in the Middle Ages, there were branches of production that required capital investment; industries were organized either through provision of capital by the guild communally, by the town, or feudally by an overlord. Among establishments of the workshop type that existed alongside craft work organized in guilds were various kinds of mills, breweries, iron foundries, and hammer mills.

PALEOTECHNIC PHASE

The paleotechnic phase, dominated by coal and iron and so called the "coal and iron complex" by Mumford, began with the breakdown of medieval European society and carried the process of disruption to a finish. There was a sharp shift in interest from spiritual values to pecuniary values which previously had been latent and restricted in great measure to the merchant and leisure classes that now pervaded every walk of life.

This phase was an outgrowth of the Industrial Revolution, the roots of which run far back into the history of mankind, at least as far back as the first time man tied a stone to a club in order to make an axe to help him in his work. The most primitive man of whom we have any record used tools in his work. But tools are passive objects, manipulated by human hands, dependent on a craftsman's skills, and powered by human energy. Throughout most of his history, man was compelled to use his own energy to supply himself with goods and services. Later he brought into his service domesticated work animals, although he was still dependent upon animate, living creatures for power and energy. If he or his livestock were to work, both had to be supplied with food, and part of the work was therefore lost in order to make work possible. Man and beasts had to labor in order to be fed and had to be fed in order to labor. They were caught in a cycle of food-energy-work-food and never seemed able to push far beyond subsistence.

The turning point in man's effort to be productive came about with the invention of machines and the use of inanimate energy to supply power to the machines. These two developments broke the cycle. A machine is a device that does much the same work as the human hand. It performs a task, more or less complicated, which prior to the invention of the machine either could not be done or could be done only with the human hand. Whatever the method of capturing and exploiting power, the result is always the same: men and domesticated animals are displaced by machines driven by sources of energy other than their own. The final outcome is a great increase in productivity.

THE NATURE OF MACHINERY

Though ancient and medieval people possessed machines, such as the potter's wheel and the water mill for grinding corn, their industry rested primarily on manual labor and hand tools. Furthermore, the so-called "machines" of the ancient and medieval periods did not possess all the characteristics of the true machine, which are:

1. Complexity
2. Regulation by controls that are part of the machine
3. Limitations and regularity in action
4. Relative independence of the machine operator; fully developed, the machine is automatic

The machine as a basic element of industrial activity was a product of the Industrial Revolution, and as new industries expanded, machines played an even greater role.

GROWTH OF THE FACTORY SYSTEM

Several basic technological inventions made possible the growth of modern industry. Among the most important were Kay's flying shuttle, Hargreave's spinning jenny, Arkwright's water frame, Crompton's spinning mule, Cartwright's power loom, Whitney's cotton gin, Howe's sewing machine, Dudley and Darby's use of coke in smelting, Smeston's air-blast, Onion and Cort's puddling process, Cort's rolling mill, Bessemer's converter, and Watt's steam engine.

These inventions became effective in industry largely through the development of the factory system. Successor to the putting-out system, the factory system became the characteristic form of modern industrial organization. By successfully organizing the means of production, it was fully as important as machinery and the steam engine in producing the remarkable transformation of the industrial process that brought into existence a new type of society in the West.

The factory system organizes labor and management in machine-equipped plants operated by artificial power. Centralization of control and the division of labor are carried to extreme limits, and the dissociation of labor from capital is almost complete. Labor is thoroughly disciplined by the pattern of the production process and by the compulsion of the plant owners. The factory system facilitates the production of goods in large quantities for sale in world markets.

EFFECTS OF THE INDUSTRIAL REVOLUTION'S DIFFUSION

In general, the European continent began to experience the characteristic industrial changes about a hundred years after England did. The industrial changes on the Continent brought about:

1. The overthrow of the guild system where it still functioned
2. Widespread introduction of machinery and steam power
3. Rise of the factory system
4. Reduction in the relative importance of agriculture compared with industry and commerce

By introducing a new economic basis for social organization and by intensifying the rate of social change, the Industrial Revolution transformed the nature of Western society. One of its primary social results was the gradual transformation of Western civilization from a rural to an urban basis—perhaps the chief social transformation in history.

The age of the Industrial Revolution was also characterized by great population movements. Until 1865, most immigrants in the U.S. were from Western Europe. After 1865, many people emigrated from Central, Southern, and Eastern Europe to the U.S. In general, the course of European migration was to the United States and South America, where industry and cheap lands offered apparently unlimited possibilities to ambitious men. Curiously enough, the exodus from Europe did not cause population to decline there because the losses were made up by a rapid increase of the birth rate. The countries to which the immigrants came benefited by the creation of a large labor supply and the transplantation of cultural forms.

Population changes in the Old World and the New World were accompanied by the rapid rise of the middle class. Equally important was the appearance of a new social class during the Industrial Revolution, the industrial proletariat. By concentrating workers in the cities, the factories made it possible for the working class to achieve conscious and effective organization.

During the paleotechnic phase, efficient low-cost transportation was the key to the movement of bulky raw materials to manufacturing centers. Coal fields became the focus for large-scale industrialization, especially where water transport made possible the low-cost movement of iron ore and associated raw materials to coal centers for the manufacture of iron and steel. New technology and growing urban markets in the 19th century, however, began to free industry from raw material sites, resulting in greater mobility.

NEOTECHNIC PHASE

In the past century, Mumford's electricity and alloy complex, or his neotechnic phase, has been a period of even greater industrial shifts. The neotechnic phase began in 1832 with the perfection of the water turbine by Fourneyron. By 1850 a good part of the fundamental scientific discoveries and inventions of the new phase had been made: the electric cell, the storage cell, the motor, the electric lamp, and the spectroscope.

With the neotechnic phase came the scientific method, which advanced knowledge of mathematics and the physical sciences. In short, the concepts of science, previously associated largely with the cosmic, the inorganic, and the mechanical were now applied to every phase of human experience and every manifestation of life.

MASS PRODUCTION

Modern manufacture and assembly in the neotechnic phase require making and then putting together myriad bits and pieces that are interconnected, standardized, and produced according to a time schedule. Modern mass-production systems depend upon science and technology to produce new materials, new products, and new production techniques. Automation has emerged from three centuries of industrial evolution that has provided metallurgies, mechanical equipment, and power sources.

Modern industrial systems differ from traditional artisan industries in several important ways. In mass-production systems, every step and phase is conceived and perfected to minimize unit costs and to standardize output. An artisan craft entails great heterogeneity in product design and little emphasis is given to time and cost control.

This basic difference often leads to difficulties in adopting artisan skills to factory labor. For example, a U.S. diesel-engine manufacturer experienced considerable difficulties with his plant in Shotts, Scotland. Labor was recruited from among local craftsmen who were simply unwilling to yield individual skills developed over long years to the precision and standardization built into "mindless machines." This example points to the substantial gap between traditional artisan societies and the human requirements of modern industrial systems.

An important contribution to the automation process has been the development of modern high-speed electronic computer and data-processing machines. Such machines have certain capacities that are almost human, such as remembering, learning from past experience, and quickly sorting a multiplicity of facts and instructions.

They also have superhuman qualities, for example, the ability to perform a million acts of addition or subtraction in *one second*. Such a machine renders obsolete the old process of bookkeeping, auditing, account-keeping, inventory control, payroll handling, and many other business and fiscal operations. It also makes a major contribution to the automatic industrial process. And it makes possible a host of scientific, engineering, and technical calculations never before feasible.

GENERAL PATTERNS OF MANUFACTURING ACTIVITIES

Since manufacturing activities depend upon movable rather than fixed raw materials, localization is a matter of considerable complexity. Every manufacturing activity, in addition to securing raw materials, must have at least five component elements: capital, transportation, market, power, and labor, as indicated in chapter 12. Where the raw materials become mobile, each of the five elements is free to exert a localizing influence.

INDUSTRIES ORIENTED TOWARD RAW MATERIALS

Every raw material exploited for use in a manufacturing activity must eventually be transported from its point of origin to its market. At some point, it will undergo the application of labor and management and capital and power in a process called manufacturing or fabrication. Fabrication may be at the site of exploitation, at the market site, or somewhere in between.

The exact fabrication point will be determined by either single or multiple factors, depending on the nature of the raw material, its weight, value, demand, and other such criteria (*see* Figure 13–1). Precisely how this process operates can be seen only after an analysis of each element.

Although raw materials exert a decreasing pull on modern industrial plants due to increased transportation efficiency of bulk cargo, especially by water, about 20 percent of all world manufacturing is still largely tied to the source of raw materials. For example, where perishable raw materials are converted into nonperishable, or at least less perishable, products must be processed near their sources. For example, sugar beets and sugarcane, vegetables, fruit, milk, and seafood are made into marketable products at the site where they are found. Sweet corn is canned near the cornfield; butter and cheese are made near the dairies which contribute the milk; fish canneries are located as near to the fishing grounds as possible.

Some raw materials and all fuels lose weight in the process of manufacturing, but some materials do not (*see* chapter 12). With materials that lose weight in processing, there is usually a distinct saving if the industry is located at the source of the raw materials or fuel supply because the total weight that must

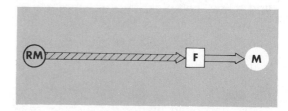

FIGURE 13–1 *Every exploited raw material moves from its point of origin (RM) to its market (M). At some point F, it will undergo fabrication.*

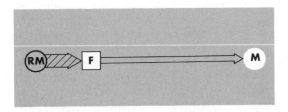

FIGURE 13–2 *If bulky raw materials are markedly reduced during the manufacturing process, the point of fabrication is located as near to the source of the raw material as possible. RM = raw material, M = market, and F = factory.*

be shipped is reduced, and the costs of transportation are thereby lessened (*see* Figure 13–2).

The tanning industry, long dependent upon the bark of oak and hemlock trees for tannin, illustrates another influence of raw materials on location. The industry migrates from one region to another as the supply of bark becomes exhausted. The industry was first freed from this dependence to location when the process of leaching the tannin from the bark was developed and only the tannin extract needed to be shipped. The leaching process, which is a weight-losing process, is carried on close to the source of raw materials, and the bark itself is not shipped. Tannin from quebracho is extracted from the bark near forests in South America, and then shipped to the tannin centers.

Many ores are smelted near their point of origin or concentrated there and shipped to distant points for further refining. Bulk copper mined at Butte, Montana, is smelted at Anaconda, 20 miles away; the smelted copper is then shipped to Great Falls, Montana, for refining.

Fuels, an important item in manufacturing costs, are outstanding examples of weight-losing materials. The location of coal mines exerts a strong influence upon the location of modern iron and

steel production centers, although recent developments have somewhat lessened this influence. When beehive coke ovens were used, good coking coal was essential to steel production, and so the steel industry in the U.S. developed in the Connellsville district of Pennsylvania. The invention of the by-product method of coking made it possible to use a much wider range of coals and resulted in the use of coal from sections other than Connellsville. Another result of the use of by-product ovens is that the gas and other by-products of the coking process provide fuel for the blast furnaces.

However, the shift to the basic oxygen process in steel making has greatly reduced the steel industry's dependence on coal fields. At the same time, the use of ore of less iron content and the beneficiation process of ore have increased the amount of ore necessary to produce a ton of steel. The significance of coal in determining the location of steel-making plants has thus been decreased, and the significance of iron ore increased.

Slaughterhouses are located near the source of their raw materials, the livestock-producing centers. They, in turn, provide the raw materials for a host of by-product industries, such as soap making, glue making, and the manufacture of bone products. In this way, materials that would otherwise be wasted are turned into marketable products.

The partial control exerted over industrial location by raw materials, then, is exerted for all manufacturing industries that use perishable or highly condensable raw materials, i.e., where fabrication involves a preserving or bulk-reducing process (*see* Figure 13–3).

Iron smelting is another illustration of the effect of raw materials on where industry tends to locate. At Birmingham, Alabama, where ore, coking coal, and limestone resources occur juxtaposed within a small radius, a naturally determined locus of fabrication occurs. (In

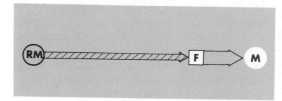

FIGURE 13–3 *If an industry uses two major raw materials, the more remote of the two moves to the one nearer the market, where fabrication takes place. RM = raw material, M = market, and F = factory.*

most instances the three are not closely associated in nature.) The proper location of a smelter is not a simple matter, however, because the two major raw materials, iron ore and coke, do not usually coincide. Consequently, one of them usually must be transported to the other before fabrication can be effected. Ore moves to coal only if the coal lies on the road to market (see Figure 13–4). Where ore lies closer to the ultimate market, coal will move to ore. In the Gary–Chicago area, coal and ore are moved toward one another in the direction of this market and point of movement of raw materials.

INDUSTRIES ORIENTED TOWARD POWER SOURCES

In all industries where the amount of mechanical energy required in processing is very large and where the cost of that energy is the principal cost item, proximity to the source of power becomes the primary consideration in the decision to locate.

Power is necessary to all manufacturing, but there is great variation in the amount required by individual industries. The Industrial Revolution in the 18th and 19th centuries was based on the use of energy. Most early industrial regions were oriented to natural power resources. At first, waterfall sites were chosen for industries. New England early became the seat of manufacturing with textile mills, shoe factories, grist mills, and sawmills that utilized that region's numerous rapids and falls for power to drive the machinery in the mills. Industry was confined to the water-power site and heavy concentrations of similar industries developed.

With the advent of coal as the primary source of industrial power, a large number of industries were geographically liberated, at least with respect to power. For most industries, an adequate power supply could be obtained at any point that might be reached by railway cars, river boats, or canal barges. This liquidity of power was further enhanced by the development of electrical transmission, which made coal power and water power readily transportable up to a radius of about 350 miles. The result of this development has been to almost entirely destroy the locative influence of power for most industries. In spite of this, electric power cannot be transported without some cost, and, if the distance is great, the line loss together with transforming loss may be considerable.

Consequently, in industries where

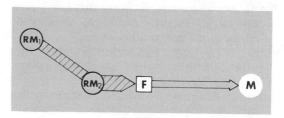

FIGURE 13–4 *If bulk perishability or the likelihood of obsolescence is increased by the manufacturing process, the point of fabrication locates as close to the market as possible. RM = raw material, M = market, and F = factory.*

huge amounts of power are consumed and where power input costs are large in comparison to raw material, labor, or transportation costs, nearness to the source of power is essential. Wherever power costs constitute the major percentage of the total cost of the finished product, the manufacturing plant is forced to locate as close to the locus of power generation as possible. Examples of industries requiring large amounts of power are: aluminum smelting, electrolytic refining, electroplating, electric-furnace iron smelting, manufacture of firebrick and crucibles, and synthetic nitrogen manufacture, among others (see Figure 13–5).

INDUSTRIES ORIENTED TOWARD LABOR

Certain industries require large numbers of unskilled workers; others require large numbers of skilled workers; still others require varying amounts of both. All industries require the service of entrepreneurs: enterprisers, promoters, managers, or operators. These three types of workers may be classified under the term "labor." It is quite commonly believed that labor plays a locative role in many fabricative industries. In one sense, this

is true, but it is often much less significant than is supposed.

In the past, manufacturing was extremely localized and very slow to develop. In many instances, local craftsmen became highly skilled in producing a quality product that was relatively safe from imitation or competition. As a result, geographical place names often became an integral part of the name of the product, e.g., Swiss watches, Dresden china, Pilsen beer, Toledo blades, Brussels carpets, or Gouda cheese. Rooting of an industry in local labor persists, even in the present, although it has ceased to have much significance.

Large numbers of relatively unskilled laborers are employed in industry. Large reservoirs of unskilled labor exist primarily in metropolitan areas or urban centers. Many factories and mills were established at points which were as near as possible to reservoirs of unskilled and semiskilled labor.

The same may be said of entrepreneurs, or management. In earlier days the promoter, enterpriser, or manager arose only in localities where certain skills and attitudes had developed. Thus capitalist adventurers, foremen, or managers in weaving arose only in areas where weavers lived and plied their craft. Owing to provincial ties and lack of geographic knowledge, the enterpreneurial class was usually reluctant to remove themselves to new areas.

Certain relaxations of labor immobility, however, have been taking place during the past half century, particularly in the United States. Improved communication and increased facilities for travel have affected the managerial class. The mobility of the managerial classes, largely a product of education, is becoming so marked that their labor can no longer be regarded as a locative factor for industry. To a large extent, the same was once said of unskilled labor.

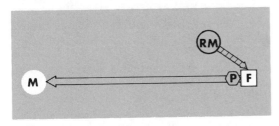

FIGURE 13–5 *In any industry where excessive mechanical energy is required, the point of fabrication is as close to the source of power as possible. RM = raw material, M = market, F = factory, and P = power source.*

255

Skilled labor, however, seems to behave in quite a different manner. It was developed over a long period of time through the craft guilds. Men served long periods as apprentices and journeymen before being accepted as master craftsmen. Their skill was the foundation upon which the fabricative industries were built. They jealously guarded their talents. The immobility of unskilled labor is an established fact. The textile workers of the Merrimack and Blackstone valleys, the shoemakers of Boston, Lynn, Brockton, and Haverhill, the jewelry makers of Attleboro, or the cloak and suit workers of Greater New York are difficult if not almost impossible to move to new locations.

Concentrations of skilled labor are definitely locative for certain types of fabricative enterprises (see Figure 13–6). For example, diamonds from various parts of the world go to Amsterdam and Antwerp to be cut into gems; bits of gold, silver, brass, and steel go to Switzerland to be made into watches. The Naugatuck Valley of Connecticut makes half of the brass products of the nation, and yet New England produces neither copper nor zinc, the two raw materials of which brass is composed.

Not all industries employing large

numbers of skilled laborers are located in this manner. Only if labor costs constitute a preponderant percentage of manufacturing costs can an industry go to the reservoir of skilled labor. If the expense of transporting the finished goods to market would make up a very large proportion of the total cost of production, such an arrangement would be economically unwarranted.

Unskilled labor is largely mobile, and so labor is ordinarily nonlocative except during the industrial infancy of a country. But in industries that employ large numbers of skilled artisans (i.e., where wages of skilled workers are a large item in the total cost), then labor may be the locative factor.

INDUSTRIES ORIENTED TOWARD TRANSPORTATION

All fabricative enterprises require adequate transportation in order to have access to raw materials and markets. Established main lines of transport would appear to be powerful magnets that draw a great number and variety of industrial plants. Upon further examination, this attraction does not necessarily prove to be the case.

The history of industrial development in the United States suggests that transport facilities follow rather than precede the establishment of industries. Railways, for example, were built wherever there were promises of large and profitable traffic. A mill located near raw materials or a factory erected at a power or fuel site was almost invariably supplied with transportation facilities if it created sufficient cargo.

The general outlines of the American transport system today are the result of building roads and railways from one industrial location to another. In many recorded instances, the presence of transport facilities did not constitute the

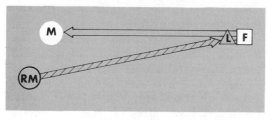

FIGURE 13–6 *If an industry employs large numbers of skilled workers, it tends to locate as near as possible to some concentration of laborers possessing the requisite skills. RM = raw material, M = market, F = factory, and L = labor.*

reason for an industry's coming to a site.

A classic example of an industrial complex developed along an access route is the New York–Mohawk Valley region of central New York. With the Great Lakes at one end and the Atlantic Ocean and New York City at the other, this gateway early attracted settlement. Industries developed for a variety of reasons. After the completion of the Erie Canal, a string of population centers arose, and industries grew to process the raw materials flowing through the region to serve not only local markets but also a national market. A wide array of industrial products are produced in this region: cameras and microscopes at Rochester, New York, electrical equipment, washing machines, and typewriters, and chemicals at Syracuse, New York, and textiles, copper, electrical machinery and fabricated metals in the Mohawk Valley cities of Rome, Utica, Amsterdam, and Johnstown; and electrical equipment, apparel, and textiles in the Schenectady–Albany–Troy district.

Certain heavy industries are exacting in their transport requirements and may need waterside facilities as well as rail connections. These industries are generally most suitably situated at port sites. Such industries include petroleum refining, iron and steel, oilseed crushing, heavy chemicals, sugar refining, paper manufacturing, and marine engineering. Their coastal locations also enable them to use imported raw materials, thus making them among the most permanently rooted of all industries.

INDUSTRIES ORIENTED TOWARD MARKETS

Many industries find that the best place to locate is as close to the market as possible. In general, industries of this kind fall into three groups: 1) industries whose process of fabrication results in a product bulkier than the raw materials used. In this class belongs the fabrication of bulky hardware and machinery and cheap furniture and pianos. Even the assembling of cheaper automobiles tend to fall into this class. It is cheaper to ship auto parts and to assemble them near the market than to ship the finished car. The manufacture of boxes, barrels, and crates is a close parallel. The staves, heads, bungs, and spigots for a barrel are made near the forest, but barrel manufacturing is done far away from the forest near a brewery, glass factory, or other concern that ships its products in barrels because barrel parts can be shipped compactly, reducing small freight charges per unit. Barrels consist mostly of empty space, although only a few of them fill a freight car. Hence empty barrels would be considerably more expensive to ship to market than their unassembled parts (see Figure 13–3). The same principle is illustrated by all industries whose manufactured products have very little value per unit of weight, that is, by all whose raw materials are fairly widespread in occurrence, such as brick and tile factories, cement and ice plants, breweries, bottling works, and others.

The second group of industries that tend to locate as close as possible to their markets includes those that produce perishable or breakable finished goods. For many of these, location near their consumer markets is an absolute necessity. Bakeries, ice cream plants, wood veneer factories, and glassworks illustrate this relationship of market to industrial site.

The third group of industries for which location close to market is desirable are manufacturing undertakings whose products are constantly changing in style, material design, or technical improvement. Principal examples are women's dresses and hats, men's clothing, newspaper publishing, and the writing of plays, radio and television scripts, movie scenarios, and popular music. Further examples are the manufacture of factory machinery, machine appliances, and machine tools.

Proximity to market tends to be a prime requisite for all fabricative enterprises where (1) the original materials are markedly increased in bulk or weight during their conversion into finished products; (2) the processing creates a fragile or perishable product; or (3) the product is subject to rapid change in style design, technological character, or popular interest.

FACTORS MODIFYING THE OPERATION OF ECONOMIC FORCES

Thus far we have discussed physical and economic factors that affect the distribution of fabricative industries and have developed several working principles that summarize the operation of these factors. The discussion has proceeded on the assumption that in response to these factors, adjustments in the distribution of production take place smoothly and without artificial restrictions. Actually, an analysis of individual manufacturing activities will soon show that certain special situations exist that may interfere in a greater or lesser degree with smooth and rapid adjustments to the economic factors we have explored.

Inertia. An adjustment of location is often delayed or entirely prevented by the failure of producers to respond to changing conditions. Sometimes this inertia is due to a lack of complete information as to the need for a change, and at times it is largely a matter of the conservatism of the producer. In the case of laborers, the number of men in any particular trade changes slowly in response to altered opportunities in the trade. It takes time for workers to learn a trade, and it also takes time for workers already in a trade to acquire new skills if they decide to shift to some other occupation.

ADVANTAGES BROUGHT BY INDUSTRY TO A LOCATION

When an industry is established in a location, the location soon acquires additional advantages that were not originally factors determining the choice of the location, but do play an important role in holding the industry there. In fact, these derivative advantages may be sufficient to hold an industry in a region long after the favorable factors that determined the original choice have disappeared. Because the work has been carried on by one generation after another, skilled labor force is built up. This creates a tendency for new companies interested in the same industry to locate where this supply of skilled labor is available. People who have been employed by the older concerns and who are able to start new concerns with savings will most likely prefer to start business in the same locality.

Moreover, once an industry becomes important in any one section, other complementary industries grow up—industries that supply necessary materials for the major industry and industries that utilize some of the waste products of the major industry. These other industries make various economies possible and increase the attractiveness of the location for the leading industry. Regions that have become known for a certain product have many advantages which accompany an established reputation.

The advantages of a well-established industry make it difficult for a new concern in a region to compete successfully. To offset these advantages that are common to older industrialized nations proposals are often made for tariffs to protect infant industries in regions becoming industrialized.

MANUFACTURING REGIONS OF THE WORLD

Almost 250 million workers in the world are engaged in manufacturing and handicraft industries. According to censuses, the proportion of the world's labor force engaged in manufacturing and handicrafts ranges from less than 10 percent in primarily agricultural countries, such as Colombia, Bolivia, Iran, Egypt, Thailand, and most African countries, to over 30 percent in highly industrialized countries, such as the U.S., Belgium, Luxembourg, West Germany, and the United Kingdom.

With about 30 percent of the world's population, four major areas produce about 85 percent of its industrial output: (1) Anglo-America from the Mississippi

River eastward to the Atlantic Ocean, including the Lower Great Lakes states and the adjoining parts of southern Canada, the Middle Atlantic States, and southern New England; (2) Western Europe, especially the United Kingdom, West Germany, Belgium, and France; (3) the USSR, extending eastward to the Kuznetsk Basin of central Siberia; and (4) Japan. The close relationship between high wages and high productivity is shown in Figure 13–7.

Other significant industrial centers occur along the Carolina Piedmont, the Gulf States, and the Pacific Coast of the United States, and in southeastern Australia. Other important manufacturing areas are developing in the People's Republic of China, India, the Republic of South Africa, Brazil, Argentina, and Chile (*see* Figure 13–8).

The breadth and scope of these industries are so varied that only a few are selected for discussion in chapters 14

Average Hourly Earnings of Wage Workers in Manufacturing, 1970

US $

Italy	$ .96
Japan	$ .96
France	$1.01
United Kingdom	$1.25
Netherlands	$ 1.27
Belgium	$ 1.32
West Germany	$ 1.62
Sweden	$ 2.33
Canada	$ 2.98
United States	$ 3.36

FIGURE 13–7

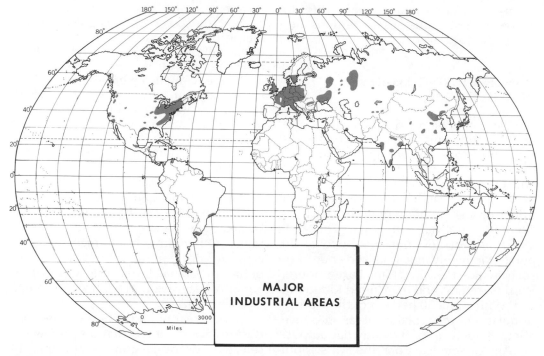

MAJOR
INDUSTRIAL AREAS

0   3000
Miles

FIGURE 13–8

through 18: iron and steel and lesser industrial metals, metal fabricating, textile
and garment industries, chemicals, and
electrical machinery and equipment.

references

1. Bahl, Roy W.; Firestine, Robert; and
Phares, Donald. "Industrial Diversity in Urban
Areas: Alternative Measures and Intermetro-
politan Comparison." *Economic Geography*
47 (July 1971): 414–25.

2. Berman, Mildred. "The Location of
the Diamond-Cutting Industry." *Annals of
the Association of American Geographers* 61
(June 1971): 316–28.

3. Best, Alan C. G. "South Africa's
Border Industries: The Tswane Example."
*Annals of the Association of American Geog-
raphers* 61 (June 1971): 329–43.

4. Dienes, Leslie. "Investment Priorities in Soviet Regions." *Annals of the Association of American Geographers* 62
(September 1972): 437–54.

5. ———. "The Budapest Agglomeration and Hungarian Industry: A Spatial Dilemma." *Geographical Review* 63 (July 1973):
356–77.

6. Grotewold, Andreas. "The Growth
of Industrial Core Areas and Patterns of
World Trade." *Annals of the Association
of American Geographers* 61 (June 1971):
361–70.

7. Haddad, Paulo Roberto, and
Schuartzman, Jacques C. "A Space Cost Curve
of Industrial Location." *Economic Geography*
50 (April 1974): 141–43.

8. Hay, Alan M. "Imports Versus Local
Production: A Case Study From the Nigerian
Cement Industry." *Economic Geography* 47
(July 1971): 384–88.

9. Lonsdale, Richard E., and Browning, Clyde. "Rural-Urban Locational Preferences of Southern Manufacturers." *Annals of*

the Association of American Geographers 61 (June 1971): 255–68.

10. Miller, E. Willard. *A Geography of Industrial Location.* Dubuque, Iowa: William C. Brown Co., 1970.

11. Mumford, Lewis. *Technics and Civilization.* New York: Harcourt, Brace, and Jovanovich, 1963.

12. Okunrotifa, P. O. "Manufacturing Industries in Lagos, Nigeria." *The Professional Geographer* 22 (March 1970): 62–66.

13. Ray, D. Michael. "The Location of United States Manufacturing Subsidiaries in Canada." *Economic Geography* 47 (July 1971): 389–99.

14. Rogers, Allan. "The Location Dynamics of Soviet Industry." *Annals of the Association of American Geographers* 64 (June 1974): 226–40.

15. Steed, Guy P. F. "Plant Adaptation, Firm Environments and Location Analysis." *The Professional Geographer* 23 (October 1971): 324–27.

16. Steed, Guy P. F., and Thomas, Morgan D. "Regional Industrial Change; Northern Ireland." *Annals of the Association of American Geographers* 61 (June 1971): 344–60.

17. Struyk, Ramond J. "Spatial Concentration of Manufacturing Employment in Metropolitan Areas: Some Empirical Evidence." *Economic Geography* 48 (April 1972): 189–92.

18. Sweet, David C. "An Industrial Development Screening Matrix." *The Professional Geographer* 22 (May 1970): 124–27.

19. Turnock, David. "The Pattern of Industrialization in Romania." *Annals of the Association of American Geographers* 60 (September 1970): 540–59.

manufacturing:
iron and steel
and lesser
industrial metals

14

14

The history of iron-ore smelting is an excellent illustration of the locative effect of raw materials. When the industry was dependent upon charcoal for fuel and on water or human energy for power, it was conducted on a small scale in scattered plants, with local iron deposits supplying a sufficient quantity of ore. The industry today is concentrated and highly integrated, and the mass production methods require large supplies of ore and coal, large amounts of capital, a large market, and considerable organizing ability and technical skill. The pattern of this industry's development illustrates Weber's agglomeration theory.

In studying the location of steel plants, we will first consider materials that play a relatively minor role in the location of the industry. Limestone is an essential raw material, but it is used in smaller quantities than either iron ore or coal, and it is also more generally distributed. Very large quantities of water are required, which affects the specific location of the plant, but not the general location of the industry. Fairly widely distributed raw materials are not important location factors. Alloy metals, such as manganese, nickel, molybdenum, chromium, and tungsten, are commercially available in only a few places; they are used, however, in very small quantities and can be shipped to steel centers at small transportation cost. A large plant requires many acres for buildings and storage facilities, and so a site would not be chosen in a rugged region with little level land, or in a large city with high land values. Most regions, however, have available land suitable for steel mills.

Large investments are necessary to yield economies of scale, and a large steel center cannot be developed unless

this scale is available. This would seem to limit the industry to regions with capital; however, any region possessing all the other necessary elements would be financed by other regions.

Labor is not of major importance as a locational factor in metal industries. There are two reasons for this. In the first place, the industry is highly mechanized, reducing labor requirements. In the second place, locations determined by the factors discussed below are also regions which have an abundant supply of labor.

LOCATIONAL FACTORS

Three factors play a major role in determining the location of the iron and steel industry: iron ore, coal, and markets. The ratio between coal and ore and between coal and steel varies, depending on the characteristics of the original ore and the nature of the final products. It is estimated that between 1 and 1.5 tons of coal are necessary to convert one ton of ore into steel products in the United States. Low-grade ore loses more weight than high-grade ore. Therefore, the higher the grade of ore, the greater the attractive pull of coal; on the other hand, all technological improvements in the direction of great fuel economies reduce the attractive power of coal.

Coal fields also afford the most favorable location for the steel industry because of the nature of the market for steel products, a large part of which is furnished by the machine-making and machine-using industries. Since these industries need power and since coal is an important power source, they tend to be located near the coal fields. The coal fields, therefore, exert their attractive pull on the steel industry not only directly but also indirectly through their pull on the industries that furnish the market for steel.

The location of the steel plant obviously must be one with excellent facilities to transport bulky raw materials and finished products cheaply. The early development of Pittsburgh, Pennsylvania, as a steel center was favored by its situation at the point where the Allegheny and Monongahela rivers join to form the Ohio River, which was connected by canals with Lake Erie, and later with the Hudson River via the Erie Canal. Today, Pittsburgh has excellent railroad connections with all industrial sections of the Northeast.

IRON AND STEEL INDUSTRY

The iron and steel industries include the smelting and refining of iron ore to convert it into iron and steel and the shaping of iron and steel into products that serve as raw materials for a wide range of other industries. Companies engaged in steel production generally enter related fields; they carry on mining operation and transportation and manufacture finished products, such as ships and automobiles, as well as a variety of by-products, including coal-tar products, gas, and Portland cement.

About 2.5 tons of coke, iron ore, limestone, scrap, and other materials are required to make a ton of ingot steel. This estimate does not include the substantial tonnage of coal and iron ore that must be washed and beneficiated to obtain the high-quality materials required for efficient iron production (*see* Figure 14–1).

STEELMAKING

Steelmaking is a highly technical art, which assumes many forms, depending on what element is added or taken away. Steel is made into numerous physical forms, comprising a virtually limitless range of products that vary according to metallurgical content, shape, width, thickness, length, surface finish, and many other characteristics. The result can

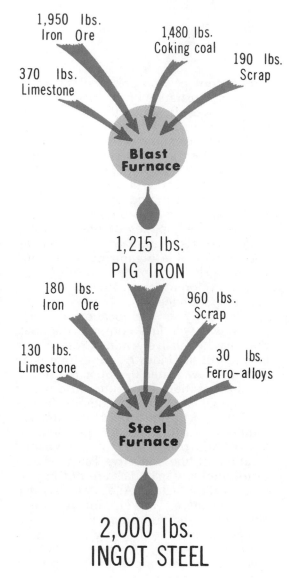

FIGURE 14–1 *Elements Required to Make a Ton of Steel*

be any of the many types of steel used by metal-working industries, which include carbon steels, the original "workhorse" steels that account for over 90 percent of the output; alloy steels; high-strength, low-alloy steels; stainless and heat resisting steels; and tool steels of carbon or an alloy.

All these types of steel have the same beginnings. They are a result of a chain of production starting with the combination of coke produced from coal, iron ore (pelletized or sintered), and limestone, which is prepared by crushing and screening to produce pig iron.

Broadly speaking, the steelmaking processes consist of refining blast-furnace iron to remove excess carbon and impurities. At the same time, the steelmaker controls the quantity of the elements other than iron that are an essential part of steel by changing or reducing elements already in the metal and adding others.

Steel is stronger and more pliable than cast iron and can be rolled, forged, or drawn into useful shapes. Blast-furnace iron, or pig iron, must be cast into shape.

Steel is made by three types of processes: open hearth, basic oxygen, and electric.

Open Hearth Method. Open hearth furnaces produce about one-third of the steel in the United States. The furnace is called "open hearth" because its hearth, or bottom, where the metal is held, is open to the sweep of flames that melt the steel. The hearth is shaped like a large, oval dish and is lined with heat-resistant materials. The front side of the furnace contains doors through which the raw materials are inserted. The refined steel is drawn off or "tapped" from the rear (see Figure 14–2).

Gas, oil, coal, or tar may be used as fuel. To aid combustion, the fuel is mixed with hot air in burners located at each end of the furnace; these burners operate alternately as the flames sweep down and across the open hearth, directly

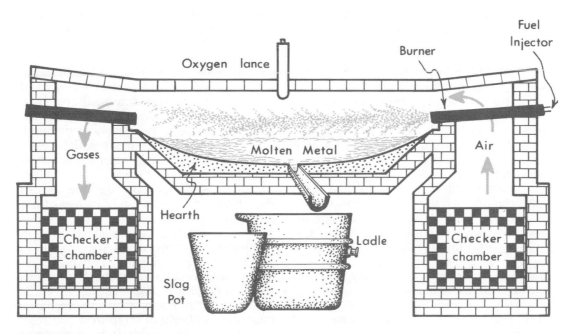

FIGURE 14–2 *Open Hearth Furnace*

above the metal bath, and exit at the opposite end. The furnace is built to operate at about 3,000° F.

Limestone and scrap are then put in the furnace. After a period of melting, molten pig iron (hot metal) is poured into the furnace from a large ladle. Steel can be made in an open hearth from scrap or pig iron, but it usually is a combination of both; a frequent ratio is 48 percent scrap and 52 percent pig iron.

Basic Oxygen Process. Dating from the mid-1950s, the basic oxygen process now accounts for about one-half of the total steel output in the United States. This process produces steel very quickly compared with the other major methods. For example, a basic oxygen furnace may produce up to 300 ton batches in 45 minutes compared to 5 to 8 hours for the same amount in the older open-hearth process. Most grades of steel can be produced in the refractory-lined, pear-shaped furnaces.

The principal ingredient used to manufacture steel by the basic oxygen process is molten iron, so most basic oxygen facilities are built near blast furnaces. Some scrap steel is used in the process. Oxygen-producing facilities are usually built at the same plant.

The first step in heating steel in a BOF is to tilt the furnace and charge it with scrap steel. The furnaces are mounted on trunnions and can be swung through a wide arc. Molten pig iron is used for between 65 and 80 percent of the charge and is poured from a ladle into the top of the tilted furnace. The furnace is then returned to an upright position. A water-cooled oxygen lance is lowered into the furnace and highly pure oxygen is blown onto the top of the metal at supersonic speed. Oxygen combines with carbon and other unwanted elements, eliminating these impurities from the molten charge and converting it to steel.

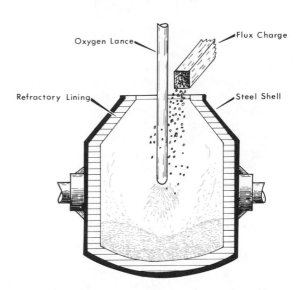

FIGURE 14–3 *Basic Oxygen Furnace*

During the oxygen blow, lime is added as a flux to help carry off the oxidized impurities as a floating layer of slag. Lime is consumed at a rate of about 150 pounds per ton of raw steel produced. After steel has been refined, the furnace is tilted and molten steel pours into a ladle. Alloy additions are made into the ladle (*see* Figure 14–3).

Electric Furnace Method. The electric furnace process of steelmaking is used for the most exacting compositions, such as stainless steels, where melting and refining must be very closely controlled. The electric furnaces most widely used are steel shells, lined with heat-resistant brick. Large sticks of carbon, called electrodes, extend down through the roof of the furnace to within a few inches of the metal in the furnace. When the current is turned on, electric arcs similar to those in arc lights used for street lighting or in sun lamps are struck between the electrodes and the charge of metal provides the heat (Figure 14–4).

Electric furnaces may use a charge consisting entirely of scrap iron and steel as raw material, although sometimes

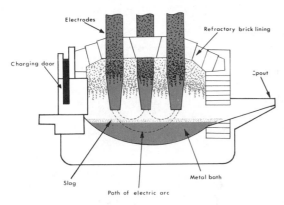

Electrodes

Refractory brick lining

Charging door

Spout

Slag

Metal bath

Path of electric arc

FIGURE 14–4 *Electric Furnace*

molten open-hearth or bessemer steel is further refined in the electric furnace. When alloy steels are made, alloys such as nickel, chromium, and tungsten, are added as pure metals or as ferroalloys. When heating is completed, the furnace is tilted to release the steel into the ladle. About 12 percent of the steel made in the U.S. today is made in electric furnaces.

Steel Products. After the molten steel has been poured into ingots and allowed to cool, the subsequent processes de-

pend upon the nature of the desired finished product. It is impossible to follow through all of these subsequent processes, so only one important section of the steel industry will be described.

In the production of steel sheets, the ingots are handled mechanically. They are first taken to the soaking pit, where they soak up heat until they are of a uniform temperature throughout. They are then taken to the "blooming" mill where they are passed back and forth between rollers, which shape them into thick slabs. In the rolling mill, they are rolled into sheets of desired sizes and shapes. Other steps, such as removing the "scale," also are necessary.

Many varieties of finished steel products are manufactured: sheets, plates, structural steel, pipes, rails, wire, and specialty steel, such as that used for cutlery. Table 14–1 shows the percentage distribution of steel consumption by category of use.

MAJOR STEEL-PRODUCING NATIONS

Figure 14–5 shows the iron and steel production centers of the world. These cen-

TABLE 14–1   Percentage Distribution of U.S. Steel Consumption with Projections for 1980

CATEGORY OF USE	1940	1960	1980
Construction (excluding railroad)	25%	31%	32%
Automotive	16	18	17
Rail Transportation	10	4	6
Water and Air Transportation (including military aircraft)	2	1	1
Producer Durables	9	12	18
Consumer Durables	6	6	4
Containers	8	10	7.98
Ordnance	—	—	0.2
Ferrous Castings	24	18	14
Total	100%	100%	100%

Source: American Iron and Steel Institute, "Distribution of Steel Consumption," *Steelways*, 24 (March–April 1968): 13.

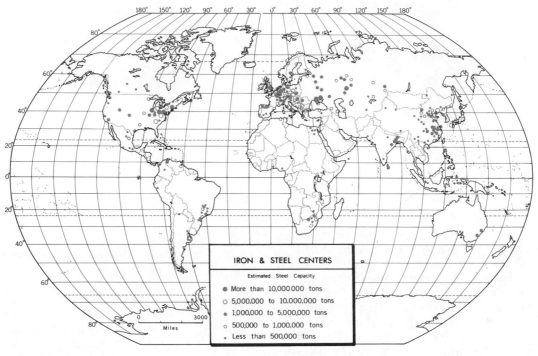

IRON & STEEL CENTERS

Estimated Steel Capacity

- ● More than 10,000,000 tons
- ○ 5,000,000 to 10,000,000 tons
- • 1,000,000 to 5,000,000 tons
- ∘ 500,000 to 1,000,000 tons
- · Less than 500,000 tons

FIGURE 14–5

ters correlate positively with the level of industrial maturity. A similar conclusion is evident from Table 14–2.

The U.S. Steel Industry. The United States produces about 20 percent of the steel in the world. Plant capacity in the U.S. is 150 million tons, but present demand is still not sufficient to engage plants to this capacity.

There are more than 200 individual companies with plants located in 300 communities in 37 states engaged in the production and finishing of iron and steel. About one-third of these companies make the raw steel required to produce their finished products. The remainder are engaged in further finishing or in semifinishing of steel produced by others (*see* Figure 14–6).

Nine-tenths of the steel made in the U.S. is produced in the main manufactur-

ing belt, which enjoys low-cost water transport for its raw materials of coal from Appalachia, iron ore from the Lake Superior district and Labrador, local limestone, and imported ferroalloys. The Chicago area, including Chicago, Gary, Calumet, and East Chicago, leads all others in output. The Pittsburgh district, with many plants on the Ohio, Monongahela, and Allegheny rivers, is second in importance. The Lake Erie district, which extends from North Tonowanda to Detroit, has nearly a dozen centers with integrated iron and steel plants and nearly three times as many centers with rolling mills. Other less important U.S. steel districts are:

1. The southern New England, east-central New York, and New Jersey district, which operates plants that are not fully integrated establishments, but which convert

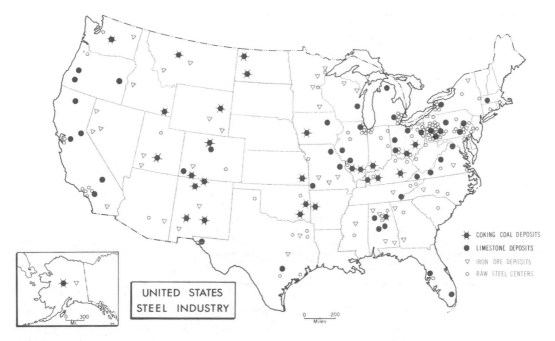

UNITED STATES
STEEL INDUSTRY

COKING COAL DEPOSITS
LIMESTONE DEPOSITS
IRON ORE DEPOSITS
RAW STEEL CENTERS

FIGURE 14–6

pig iron, steel scrap, and alloy metals into special steels.

2. The fully integrated mills in eastern Pennsylvania (Morrisville) and Maryland (Sparrows Point), which are based on local coal and imported high-grade iron ore from Chile and Venezuela.

3. The Birmingham, Alabama, district, which has most of the necessary raw materials for making steel within a 20-mile radius.

4. The Houston and Daingerfield integrated plants of northeastern Texas.

5. The western iron and steel districts at Pueblo, Colorado; Provo, Utah; Fontana, South San Francisco, Pittsburg, and Torrance, California; Seattle, Washington; and Portland, Oregon.

Of the far western mills, only three—at Provo, Fontana, and Portland—are fully integrated.

USSR. The Soviet Union is the world's largest steel producer (*see* Table 14–2).

However, her raw materials are far less well located than those in the United States and cross-haulage is the rule, not the exception.

There are four major iron- and steel-producing districts and many minor ones. The four major centers are the Southern Ukraine, the Central and Southern Urals, the Moscow Basin, and the Kuznetsk Basin (*see* Figure 14–7). The Southern Ukraine is the oldest of the important iron and steel centers; it possesses the necessary raw materials, transportation, labor, and markets. It is also the part of the Soviet Union that was first influenced by the modern manufacturing practices of Western Europe. Donets coal to the east and Krivoy Rog iron ore to the west and south at Kerch, have contributed to an iron- and steel-producing area similar to the Great Lakes, based on its Mesabi Range iron-ore deposits and Pennsylvania coal. Once rail links between coal field and ore field were established in the

269

**TABLE 14–2   Total Crude Steel Production in the World
and Selected Leading Countries
(in thousand metric tons)**

	1963	1972	PERCENT CHANGE
USSR	80,231	125,589	+ 56.53%
U.S.	99,120	120,875	+ 21.94
Japan	31,501	96,901	+207.61
W.Germany	31,597	43,706	+ 38.32
France	17,557	24,054	+ 37.01
China	12,000	23,000	+ 91.67
Italy	10,156	19,815	+ 95.11
Belgium	7,529	14,477	+ 92.28
Poland	8,004	13,476	+ 68.36
Canada	7,436	11,859	+ 59.48
World	386,500	626,300	+ 62.20%

Source: Based on the *U.N. Statistical Yearbook, 1973* (New York: United Nations, 1974), p. 297.

late 19th century, an interchange of coking coal and iron ore occurred. This not only stimulated iron and steel production in the Donets Basin, it also resulted in the establishment of larger facilities on the Dneiper River at Dnepropetrovsk, Dneprodzerzhinsk, and Zaporozh'ye. Though on smaller scale, a similar interchange between the Donets and the Kerch ore fields in the Crimea led to iron and steel production at Kerch and at transshipment ports on the Sea of Azov, notably at Zhdanov.

Large scale metallurgy began on the east slope of the Urals in 1934 with the building of Magnitogorsk, near a mountain of magnetite ore. A giant new blast furnace, the tenth to be erected, began working at Magnitogorsk in 1966.

The Urals now turn out nearly 40 percent of Soviet steel. Although new methods of coke production make it possible for coal from the Urals to be used in iron-smelting to a greater extent than in the past, the dependence on outside sources of coal remains heavy. The region produces only 2 million tons of coking coal annually but more than 13 million tons of steel. There are several important iron- and steel-producing centers in the Urals; the biggest are at Magnitogorsk, Nizhniy Tagil, Chelyabinsk, and Sverdlovsk.

The Moscow Basin, an old industrial area, until recently obtained some iron ore from deposits near Tula and Lipetsk, where there are blast furnaces. The steel works near Moscow depend heavily on scrap from local engineering industries to attain their annual output of 3.5 million tons. In 1973, the Soviets opened their largest blast furnace in the iron and steel center at Lipetsk, 230 miles southeast of Moscow. It reflects both a continuing trend toward larger iron-smelting furnaces in the Russian steel industry and an effort to build up productive capacity near the metal markets of central Russia, where most of the population and industrial capacity are concentrated. The new furnace, which is the fifth at the Lipetsk mill, raises the plant's pig-iron output from about 4.5 million tons to close to 7 million. Under the current expansion program, iron and steel output at Lipetsk is planned to reach 15 million tons by the early 1980s.

The Ukraine, the Urals, and the

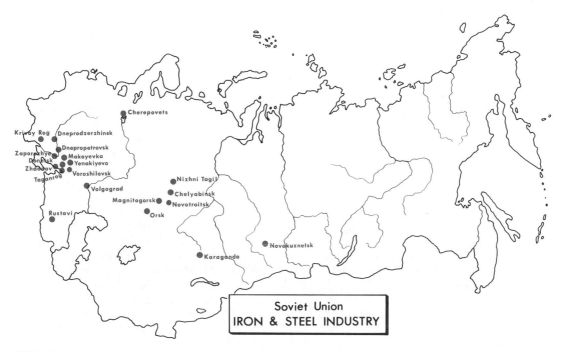

Cherepovets

Krivoy Rog · Dneprodzerzhinsk

Zaporozhye · Dnepropetrovsk

Donetsk · Makeyevka

Zhdanov · Yenakiyevo

Taganrog · Voroshilovsk

Nizhni Tagil

Volgograd

Chelyabinsk

Magnitogorsk · Novotroitsk

Orsk

Rustavi

Novokuznetsk

Karaganda

Soviet Union
IRON & STEEL INDUSTRY

FIGURE 14–7

Moscow Basin combined produce at least 85 percent of the Soviet pig iron and more than 75 percent of the steel. Compared with these three regions, the steel production of the remaining districts is relatively minor, though steadily increasing. The most important of these is the Kuznets Basin which, with its works at Novokuznetsk (formerly Stalinsk) and Gur'yevsk, produces about 8 percent of Soviet steel. A second blast furnace, with a 2-million-ton capacity, was opened at Novokuznetsk in 1971. The two plants use locally mined coking coal as well as iron ore from a mine at Zheleznogorsk, 700 miles to the east in the Irkutsk Region.

Japan. Despite its relative deficiency of raw materials, Japan ranks as the world's third largest iron and steel producer (*see* Table 14–2); its rank as a world steel producer is not likely to diminish, either.

After World War II, the industry made large investments to increase capacity and improve productivity with the most modern techniques, such as large-capacity blast furnaces and converters using oxygen and heavy oil instead of the older open-hearth method for producing crude steel. Because of highly modernized production systems, and despite the necessity of importing a high percentage of raw materials, iron and steel are produced at a relatively low unit cost, which enhances the country's ability to compete in the world market of steel and steel products.

The iron and steel industry in Japan is controlled by a few very large firms made up of numerous subsidiaries specializing in some phase of the process. Firms are integrated from ownership of raw materials through production of special-purpose steels and steel forms. Since the merger of Japan's two largest

271

steel concerns into one giant, the Nippon Steel Corporation, Nippon's output of raw tonnage is slightly higher than that of the United States Steel Corporation, long the world leader. Other Japanese steel producers of note are Sumitoma Metal Industries, Kobe Steel, and Kawasaki Steel. With Nippon, these firms produce about two-thirds of Japan's total steel output.

Of the ten largest blast furnaces in the world, eight are in Japan and two are in the Soviet Union; these blast furnaces substantially reduce the cost of pig iron.

Size alone is not the only explanation for Japan's success in steel making. Japanese mills use advanced technology to improve efficiency. Japan has several built-in competitive advantages in steel making: (1) labor costs are lower; (2) steel mills enjoy lower transportation costs because almost all are built at seaports accessible to cheap coastal or direct export shipping; and (3) Japanese steel companies have evolved a comfortable system of "grouping" to buy raw materials and scrap at lower prices and are able to shop throughout the world for the best ore prices.

Japan's steel mills are not subsidized, although the government does provide tax breaks on steel purchased for the manufacture of exports and allows capital accumulation for reinvestment in plant and equipment.

Federal Republic of Germany. Iron and steel manufacture form the backbone of German industry: rolling and drawing mills, structural steel fabrication, transportation, and machine and precision-tool industries. West Germany produces every type of steel. The nation ranks fourth in world steel production and first among the steel-producing nations of Western Europe (see Table 14–2).

The Lower Rhine Valley in the Westphalia industrial region mines most of the bituminous and brown coal produced in West Germany. About one-third of the country's industrial plants are located here. The center of this heavy industrial concentration is the Ruhr Valley, a triangle only 35 miles wide and 60 miles long, extending from Wesel to Dusseldorf to Hamm. The Ruhr industrial region is today a vast conurbation of nearly 5 million people, almost 30 percent of the Federal Republic of Germany. It is served by a labyrinth of railroads, canals, and navigable rivers, and freight moves cheaply in any direction.

A second important steel-producing region is the Saar Valley which abuts the French border. The industries of the Saar Valley are primarily associated with coal mines and iron and steel works. Its peripheral location formerly tended to restrict industrial growth, but it is now central to the European community and has a brighter future.

France. French iron and steel production has also risen rapidly. Steel mills have been expanded to supply new rolling mills, such as Uninor at Denain and Montataire, and Sollac at Seremange as well as new tube-producing mills. Steel output rose from 6.2 million tons in 1938 to 24.1 million tons in 1972 (see Table 14–2). The main steel-producing area is Lorraine, followed by northern France, south-central France, Normandy, and Brittany.

Italy. Italy is very poor in most minerals, particularly in those that enter into the manufacture of iron and steel. Yet, because of the importance of her secondary enterprises that depend on steel, Italy uses much primary steel.

Italy is unique in having a relatively small iron industry but a rather impressive steel industry, operating primarily with imported raw materials. Of necessity, her steel mills use hydroelectric power. Many rivers in the north, whose sources are in glaciers and snow fields, provide abundant hydroelectric power, at least during the summer months. Italy fabricates mostly high-quality electric steel.

The industry, located in the north at Bagnoli, Corniguiano, Piombina, and Terni, produced more than four times as much steel in 1972 as in 1947 (*see* Table 14–2). Nearly all the mills are new.

People's Republic of China. According to Western standards, the manufacture of iron and steel in China until the late 1950s was unimpressive. Except for Manchura, where, during the Japanese occupation, a large integrated plant had been built at Anshan, there were only two blast furnaces: one at Hanyang near Hankow and the other at Yang Chuan in Shansi. Their combined capacity was only 120 tons of pig iron per day.

In little more than two decades, China's production has soared from 120 tons to 24 million. Large-capacity steel mills with giant furnaces, rolling mills, and associated heavy industry have developed at Anshan in southern Manchuria, Wuhan on the Yangtze River, Paotow on the middle Hwang where it wends south from Inner Mongolia, and at Shanghai, despite lack of local raw materials there. Each of these mills has an annual capacity of several million tons. A dozen other steel mills are rated at over one-half million tons each, notably those at Peking, Tientsin, Tsingtao, Taiyuan, Chung-king, and Penki, Manchuria (*see* Figure 14–8).

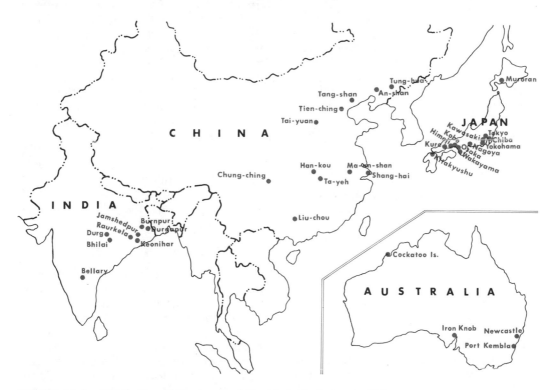

FIGURE 14–8 *Distribution of the Iron and Steel Industry in Japan, China, India, and Australia*

WORLD TRENDS IN STEEL CAPACITY AND CONSUMPTION

Expansion in world steel-producing capacity since 1947 has been marked by three stages of development.

1.   During the early postwar period, growth in world steel output and consumption kept pace with the expansion of steel capacity, and there was only a small margin of unused capacity. In contrast, during the late 1950s world steel capacity expanded considerably faster than world steel consumption, and utilization rates of world steel eased, although they were still high.

2.   The doubling of world steel-producing capacity during the 1950s was accompanied by major shifts in the pattern of world steel production. The proportion of U.S. steel capacity in relation to world capacity diminished, and the relative proportions accounted for by Japan and the European Coal and Steel Community (ECSC) countries rose. The most significant expansion in capacity occurred in the USSR, where capacity more than doubled.

3.   Although the USSR continued to increase her relative proportion of world steel-producing capacity in the 1960s, the most dramatic change took place in Japan, where capacity nearly tripled and the Japanese proportion of steel-producing capacity in relation to world capacity rose from 6.4 percent in 1960 to 15.5 percent in 1972. Great expansion also occurred in Canada, Latin America, and India. Although still not adequate to meet total domestic steel needs, increased steel production in those areas lessened the dependence of those countries on imported steel.

LESSER INDUSTRIAL METALS

Since 1900, there has been an unprecedented revolution in man's use of light metals, such as aluminum, magnesium, titanium, and others. This revolution is creating new industries in which the advanced nations of the world have been investing heavily. Not only have their companies built up complex corporate relationships, but they have gone far afield to ensure adequate supplies of raw materials, principally bauxite, the major sources of which are to be found in the underdeveloped countries.

MANUFACTURE OF ALUMINA

Alumina plants are generally located: (1) relatively near bauxite mines or (2) on navigable waterways close to or far away from the mines. They are situated at either of these two types of location to save on otherwise costly transportation, since about 2 tons of bauxite are required to make 1 ton of alumina. After washing and drying (a process designed to decrease weight), bauxite from Guyana and Surinam is sent to Mobile, Alabama; to Burnside, Baton Rouge, and Gramercy, Louisiana; and to La Quinta and Point Comfort, Texas. Ore from Guyana destined for Canada is treated at Arvida, Quebec, whereas that mined in Jamaica but destined for reduction at Kitimat, British Columbia, is first converted into alumina in Jamaica. Bauxite from Arkansas moves by rail to Bauxite and Hurricane Creek, Arkansas.

Most bauxite is mined by the big aluminum companies for their own use, so when the mineral moves to alumina plants in developed countries, it is not only moving toward the ultimate market but to manufacturing plants.

MANUFACTURE OF ALUMINUM

The conversion of alumina into aluminum requires a great deal of power: 17,000 kilowatt hours of electric energy, or 6.8 tons of coal, are required to make 1 ton of aluminum metal. No other electrometallurgical operation consumes so much power. In the past the aluminum industry sought locations for its plants where large amounts of hydroelectric energy were available 24 hours a day,

274

365 days a year, at low cost. Often such locations were available only in remote areas where there was little competition for power. Even when the plants received cheap power, the cost of reducing aluminum averaged 16 percent in contrast to 2.8 percent for most industries.

In the United States, as the demand for hydropower soared during World War II and particularly during the Korean War, new aluminum works could no longer depend on adequate, dependable sources of hydropower at low cost. Many new plants were located in southern states, such as Alabama, Louisiana, and Texas, where natural gas and lignite are abundant and cheap. As the demand for aluminum in the U.S. continued to soar, new plants sprang up in the Ohio Valley, where coal could be delivered economically via barge. By 1972 approximately 48 percent of the total primary aluminum output of the United States was derived from plants utilizing coal-based power.

Aluminum manufacturing, then, is a prime example of an industry in which the source of power is the primary locative consideration. Industries in which huge amounts of power are consumed and in which power costs are large in comparison with raw materials, labor, or transportation costs, proximity to the source of power is essential. Wherever power costs constitute the major percentage of the total cost of the finished product, the manufacturing plant is driven as close to the locus of power generation as possible (*see* Figure 14–9).

WORLD PRODUCTION OF ALUMINUM

The huge power requirements of the aluminum industry have made it imperative that the industry be located where power is developed, which is primarily in the industrialized countries of the United States, the Soviet Union, Japan, Canada, Norway, the Federal Republic of Germany, France, and Australia (*see* Table 14–3).

The U.S. produces about one-third of the world's aluminum. Seventy-five percent of the U.S. output is from three regions: the Gulf Coast (29 percent), the Pacific Northwest (28 percent), and the Ohio River Valley (18 percent).

U.S. Aluminum Production. The Pacific Northwest's industry along the Columbia River was developed to supply the needs

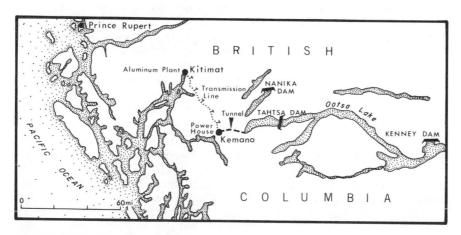

FIGURE 14–9 *The Kitimat Complex*

TABLE 14–3 Total Primary Aluminum Production in the World and Selected Leading Countries (in thousand metric tons)

	1963	1972	PERCENT CHANGE
U.S.	2,098	3,740	+ 78.27%
USSR	760	1,250	+ 64.47
Japan	224	1,015	+353.12
Canada	653	907	+ 38.90
Norway	225	548	+143.56
W.Germany	209	445	+112.92
France	298	392	+ 31.54
Australia	42	213	+407.14
World	5,280	10,760	+103.78%

Source: Based on the *United Nations Statistical Yearbook, 1973* (New York: United Nations, 1974), p. 298.

of the booming aircraft industry, which was war-nurtured and rose to prominence suddenly. Although no primary aluminum was produced until 1940, by 1944 the area was making 40 percent of the national output.

The Pacific Northwest has the largest hydroelectric potential in the United States. The area boasts the lowest firm power costs in the nation—2.1 mills per kilowatt hour, contrasted with 4 mills in Tennessee and the Gulf states and 3.1 to 4.5 in the Ohio Valley. Initially, its low-cost power sources compensated for long rail hauls of alumina from the Gulf Coast and of aluminum to markets in the Midwest and East. It was the availability of cheap power that attracted the industry to the Northwest, permitting the Columbia River drainage basin to produce more than half of the nation's primary aluminum in 1949.

Alumina, the raw material for these plants, is transported about 2,500 miles via boxcar from the Gulf Coast. Alumina is transported via rail, rather than via water, because railroads provide low rates in order to get the business.

The Pacific Coast market presently is of minor importance. Half or more of the aluminum manufactured in the Northwest is shipped some 2,500 miles to the American Manufacturing Region for fabrication. Despite the distance of these plants from their sources of alumina and from their markets, they have been able to operate successfully. Since the Korean War, however, competition within the industry has been so keen and the logistics problems so complicated that the most recently constructed plants tend to locate in the Midwest, closer to their market and power source, and to receive their alumina by barge via the Mississippi and Ohio rivers.

The South has grown in stature in the manufacture of aluminum since World War II, the result primarily of hydroelectric power shortages in the Pacific Northwest. The South's nine plants account for almost 60 percent of the nation's primary aluminum output. This situation has resulted from a combination of circumstances: (1) the ease of receiving bauxite or alumina, since almost all bauxite and much alumina come from the Caribbean area; (2) the presence of substantial waterpower, natural gas, and lignite; (3) the proximity to needed raw materials, such as lime and sodium carbonate; (4) the growing industrialization in the South; and (5) greater proximity than the Pacific Northwest to the American Manufacturing Belt, the major market for primary aluminum.

In the past only hydroelectric power was considered cheap enough for smelting of alumina. Now, however, a number of plants in Texas, Arkansas, and Louisiana use low-cost natural gas as fuel. A plant at Rockdale, Texas, uses lignite.

It is axiomatic that production is simplified and made more efficient and economical if plants of multiprocess industries can be located near one another. This is no problem in the South.

The aluminum industry's last major move was to the Ohio Valley. A fundamental reason for this move is that some traditional economic and geographic assumptions have been discarded. The sole justification for locating alumina-reducing plants in remote regions was the availability of ample power at reasonable cost, which was believed to offset the larger transportation costs of raw materials in and of manufactured products out. Recent developments make clear, however, that several other factors must be considered.

After considering one hundred sites, the Kaiser Aluminum and Chemical Corporation selected a 2,500-acre site on the Ohio River at Ravenswood, West Virginia, because it was near the center of the midwestern and eastern markets, especially for sheet and foil; furthermore, there were great advantages in quick delivery by truck: one day to Cleveland and Cincinnati and two days to Detroit and New York. The company, previously located in Washington, was thus able to reduce its transportation costs to eastern and midwestern markets by about 70 percent. Other Ohio Valley plants are located at Evansville, Indiana (Aluminum Company of America) and Clarington, Ohio (Ormet Corporation).

All the Ohio River reduction works utilize coal. And because of more efficient coal mining and steam-plant design,

power costs are constantly being reduced, although these costs are not as low as those of hydropower.

Soviet Union. Although its industry dates only from 1932, the Soviet Union ranks second in aluminum output in the world (*see* Table 14–3).

The Russian industry is located at widely dispersed points west of Lake Baikal: in the Kola Peninsula, near Leningrad, on the Dnieper River, north and east of the Black Sea, southeast of the Aral Sea, in the Northern and Southern Urals, and in the Kuznetsk Basin. Very large plants were recently constructed at Pavlodar on the Irtysh River in eastern Kazakhstan and near Shelekhovo on the Irkut River. Both these plants rank among the largest in the world. All of these plants reflect obvious consideration of the proximity of fuel supply.

The most authoritative sources state that between 50 and 60 percent of the Soviet output comes from the two plants at Krasnoturinsk and Kamensk-Uralsky. Both draw bauxite from nearby sources and both use electricity from steam plants.

Canada. Availability of low-cost power was the main factor in the establishment of Canada's aluminum industry, which uses only imported bauxite and alumina. Aluminum Limited, a conglomerate, operates forty-nine fully owned or affiliated companies in twenty-eight countries and ranks among the most powerful aluminum corporations in the world. Canada as a nation ranks fourth in world output of aluminum (*see* Table 14–3), an interesting and impressive achievement considering that the country imports a substantial part of its raw material.

Rivers draining Quebec's Canadian Shield furnish power for smelting ores from Guyana and Guinea. Quebec Province accounts for 65 percent of Canada's aluminum pig.

The reduction works are located at Shawinigan Falls, La Tuque, and Beauharnois on the St. Maurice River and at Arvida and Isle Maligne on the Saguenay River. All plants in Canada capitalize on the enormous potential for hydropower; Canada now has more hydropower capacity than any other nation.

Arvida, which boasts the world's largest aluminum smelter, started in 1926; an alumina works was added in 1928. Arvida thus enjoys the distinction of being the first integrated plant in North America. The Arvida area was able to benefit from three basic needs of the aluminum industry: (1) large amounts of uninterrupted, low-cost power; (2) cheap transportation for handling inbound raw materials and outbound fabricated products; and (3) satisfactory labor supply. Actually, Arvida is not on navigable water; the river terminal facilities are at Port Alfred, 20 miles distant, with which Arvida is connected by railway.

Huge amounts of electricity are generated within the 30-mile stretch between Lake St. John and tidewater where the raging Saguenay River drops 330 feet. The Shipshaw Power Development, with a dam only a few miles distant from Arvida, has a developed 1.5 million horsepower and a total capacity of 2 million horsepower in the valley.

In Canada's far west, at Kitimat in northern British Columbia, is probably the greatest challenge to engineering science in setting up a fully integrated plant. Its location shows how strong the pull of abundant low-cost hydropower is.

Here, as in all the other Canadian aluminum projects, low-cost hydropower was the principal location factor. The water for power is procured by damming the Nechako River, which made a reservoir or storage basin 150 miles long. A 10-mile tunnel was made to penetrate the Coast Mountains so that the water from the lakes can fall 2,600 feet to the hydroelectric plant located at Kemano in a cavern at sea level. Power lines then deliver the electricity over high-tension lines some 50 miles to Kitimat, at the head of a deepwater fjord, where there is enough flat land for the smelter and a town. The plant began operating in 1954. It draws alumina 5,600 miles from Jamaica and then ships the finished aluminum ingots 2,500 to 3,000 miles to manufacturers in eastern Canada and the United States.

France. France ranks seventh in aluminum production in the world and second in Europe (see Table 14–3). Fortunately, she has her own supply of bauxite. In France, all reduction works are oriented to sources of hydropower in the Alps and Pyrenees, which means that the industry is centered largely in the south, east and west of the Rhone River. Especially prominent is the Alpine department of Savoy which has four plants. Most French plants, like most European plants, are small. The largest, at St. Jean de Maurienne in Savoy is an exception because it reduces 37 percent of France's aluminum.

West Germany. Although it mines almost no bauxite, West Germany ranks sixth among world producers of aluminum, fourth in Europe, and third in Western Europe. The industry is located in Bavaria, Westphalia, and the Rhineland. Three factors are responsible for West Germany's present high rank: (1) low-cost coal and lignite; (2) relative proximity to sources of European bauxite in France, Greece, and Yugoslavia and to imports from Indonesia and West Africa; and (3) proximity to the important market for primary aluminum.

Norway. Like Canada and West Germany, Norway has an impressive aluminum industry. Although it mines no bauxite and does not have a large do-

278

mestic market for aluminum, Norway ranks fifth in world production and is the largest producer in Western Europe.

The Norwegian industry exemplifies well the strong locational pull of low-cost waterpower. Their power is abundant and their output is reasonably constant— a factor of considerable importance in the aluminum industry. Finally, this power is available at tidewater, at excellent ports which, despite quite high latitude, are ice-free throughout the year. On a per capita basis, Norway leads all nations in production of electricity and in low-cost per kilowatt hours.

The aluminum-reduction works are located along the coast at Stangfjord, north of Bergen; at Höyanger, on the Sognefjiord; and at Haugvik in the north. The Norwegian industry manufactures aluminum from alumina imported principally from Canada and France. In addition, bauxite is imported, chiefly from France and Greece.

Japan. Japan is the leading aluminum producer in Asia, and it ranks third among world producers. Japan's aluminum industry is based on cheap hydroelectric power. The lack of suitable domestic ores and the consequent total reliance upon imports are the major problems facing the industry. Two-thirds of the bauxite is imported from Bintan Island, Indonesia, which is the only large proved reserve of high-grade bauxite ore in the entire Far East.

Aluminum reduction works are scattered widely over the island of Honshu, at seaboard sites and at interior points, principally at Niigata, Kitakta, Oomachi, and Kambara, and at Niihama on the Inland Sea coast of Shikoku.

MAGNESIUM

Lightness is the striking quality of magnesium, whose weight is two-thirds that of aluminum, less than one-fourth that of iron, and only a fifth that of copper or nickel. In short, magnesium is the lightest of all structural metals and also possesses strength and machineability. It can be cast, rolled, drawn, spun, forged, blanked, and coined. Its alloys are also resistant to corrosion.

Half of the magnesium consumed is commercially used: 33 percent by the aircraft industry, 20 percent by the aluminum industry, 10 percent for machinery, and 37 percent for miscellaneous uses. The automotive industry would use from 25,000 to 50,000 tons of magnesium per annum, if the price were reduced. American automobiles contain less than 1 pound of magnesium on the average.

Magnesium is the third most abundant of the engineering metals. It can be extracted from underground salt brines and seawater or from ores containing magnesium—chiefly brucite, dolomite, and magnesite.

The processing of sea water is by far the most important method of magnesium reduction. Immense mills employ this process at Freeport and Velasco, Texas. At Painesville, Ohio, underground brine is used. Silico-thermal plants are located at Canaan, Connecticut; Wingdale, New York; Manteca, California; and Spokane, Washington.

World Production. Currently only twelve countries produce magnesium in the world. However, only five of these are important and only two, the Soviet Union and the United States, account for the bulk.

TITANIUM

Titanium, a light metal, has been known as a common element for well over 150 years, but the employment of metallic titanium as a useful metal dates only from 1948. Titanium has one very great advantage over aluminum and magnesium, both of which are lighter in weight: it holds its strength at temperatures as high as 800° F. Titanium has other valuable qualities: it performs better than stainless steel, but is only half as heavy; it is six times stronger than aluminum and almost as rust-resistant as platinum; and it is extremely resistant to corrosion by saltwater.

Titanium, however, owes its rise solely to the Cold War and to the aircraft industry's precise specifications. Its ability to hold its strength without much expansion at temperatures between 300° F and 800° F obviously gives it priority for use in the fabrication of air frames, rockets, turbojets, and ram-jet engines, where lightness is especially crucial and where temperatures to be withstood are so high as to discourage the use of alloys made with aluminum and magnesium. It is expected also that titanium alloys will be used commercially for high-speed fly-shuttles, for textile machinery in cotton mills, for high-speed cutting tools, and for pipes and tanks in food-processing plants.

Titanium is abundant, being found as *ilmenite* (iron and titanium oxide combined) and *rutile* (a high-grade titanium oxide). Large deposits of ilmenite and rutile have been found in Norway, Sweden, and Finland; in the Transvaal of South Africa; in the Ilmen Mountains (an extension of the Urals) in the Soviet Union; in New York, North Carolina, and Virginia; in the Allard Lake region 400 miles northeast of Quebec City, Canada; in Oaxaca in southwestern Mexico; and in Brazil. And extensive beach-sand concentrations exist in Australia, extending 50 miles on either side of the Queensland–New South Wales border; in Travancore, India, and elsewhere. The United States, India, Canada, and Norway currently account for more than 90 percent of the world output. There is no foreseeable world shortage of titanium minerals.

ECONOMIC OUTLOOK FOR LESSER INDUSTRIAL METALS

Primary aluminum has become an international commodity whose raw material, bauxite, exists in areas all over the world that cross many international boundaries. This circumstance makes clear two conclusions: (1) the aluminum industry does not lend itself to restrictive regional practices; and (2) in order to prosper, the industry requires world peace.

The other light metals are no less vital than aluminum, but their present production is on a comparatively small scale. They are employed mostly for military uses as alloying agents. If they are to be produced in greater quantity and to be used commercially, they must be much reduced in price, and price reduction can only occur with cheaper methods of extraction.

Only aluminum appears to be assured of large output now and in the near future. It alone has adequate raw materials and sufficiently low production costs to guarantee worldwide use.

references

1. Brody, David. *Steelworkers in America: The Non-Union Era*. New York: Russell & Russell, 1970.

2. Burtenshaw, D. "Regional Renovation in the Saarland." *Geographical Review* 62 (January 1972): 1–12.

3. Cannon, James S. *Environmental Steel: Pollution in the Iron and Steel Industry*. New York: Frederick A. Praeger, 1974.

4. Chang, Kuei-Sheng. "Nuclei Formation of Communist China's Iron and Steel Industry." *Annals of the Association of American Geographers* 60 (June 1970): 257–85.

5. Clark, M. Gardner. *Development of China's Steel Industry and Soviet Technical Aid*. New York: New York School of Industrial and Labor Relations, Cornell University, 1973.

6. Dury, G. H. *The British Isles*. 5th ed. London: Heinemann Education Books, 1973.

7. Friden, Lennart. *Instability in the International Steel Market: A Study of Import and Export Fluctuations*. Translated by R. Tanner. Sweden: Vallingby, 1972.

8. Hunker, Henry L. *Industrial Development*. Lexington, Mass.: D.C. Heath and Co., 1974.

9. Isenberg, Irwin. *Japan: Asian Power*. New York: Wilson Publishing Co., 1971.

10. Kawahito, Kiyoshi. *The Japanese Steel Industry with an Analysis of the U.S. Steel Import Problem*. New York: Frederick A. Praeger, 1972.

11. Lydolph, Paul E. *Geography of the U.S.S.R.* 2nd ed. New York: John Wiley & Sons, 1971.

12. McCarthy, Harold M, and Black, William R. *A Locationally Oriented Classification of American Industries*. Bloomington: Indiana University Department of Geography Monograph Series, 1973.

13. McDivitt, James F., and Manners, Gerald. *Minerals and Men*. Baltimore: Johns Hopkins University Press, 1974.

14. Miller, E. Willard. *A Geography of Industrial Location*. Dubuque, Iowa: Wm C. Brown Co., 1970.

15. Starkey, Otis P.; Robinson, J. Lewis; and Miller, Crane S. 2nd ed. *Anglo-American Realm*. New York: McGraw-Hill Book Co., 1975.

16. Steinhart, Carol E., and Steinhart, John S. *Blowout*. North Scituate, Mass.: Duxbury Press, 1972.

17. Stone, Joseph K. "Oxygen in Steelmaking." *Scientific American* 218 (April 1968): 24–31.

18. Spelt, Jacob. "The Ruhr and Its Coal Industry in the Middle 60's." *Canadian Geographer* 13 (Spring 1969): 3–9.

19. Warren, Kenneth. *The British Iron and Steel Industry Since 1840: An Economic Geography*. London: Bell, 1970.

20. ———. "The Changing Steel Industry of the European Common Market." *Economic Geography* 43 (October 1967): 314–32.

21. White, C. Langdon; Foscue, Edwin J.; and McKnight, Tom L. *Regional Geography of Anglo-America*. 4th ed. Englewood Cliffs, N.J.: Prentice-Hall, 1974.

metal-fabricating
industries

15

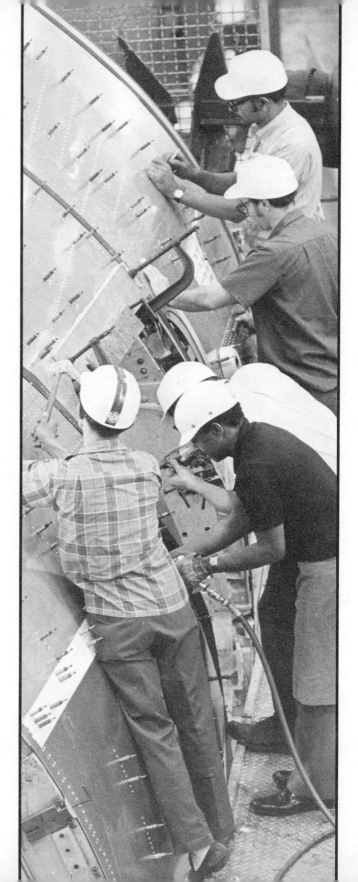

15

MACHINE TOOLS

The process by which iron, steel, copper, aluminum, and other metals are converted into usable products is known as metal fabrication. The first step, shaping raw materials as they come from refining furnaces, is done by rolling, casting, and hammering. But these processes give only crudely shaped castings or forgings or rolled stock, such as sheets, plates, rods, and bars. For most purposes, metal parts must be accurately and precisely shaped, and this requires machine tools to drill, bore, plane, grind, turn, mill, and shear or press.

There are more than two hundred major types of machine tools. The industry is unique because it makes not only the machine tools used in all the metal-fabricating industries, but also the machine tools that make the machines. It consists of some five hundred manufacturers in the U.S., heavily concentrated in Ohio, Michigan, Illinois, and southern New England. The lower Great Lakes area dominates, with about 60 percent of the national output. Many of the firms are small; companies with less than 1,000 workers account for almost 75 percent of the total U.S. machine-tool output.

A well-developed iron and steel industry is a prerequisite for the establishment of large machine-producing industries. Large amounts of capital, a labor force with technical skill, and inventive genius are also essential. Skilled labor is necessary for the production of complicated machinery, which requires great accuracy of workmanship. Even more important is the availability of men with technical education, skill, and inventiveness who can improve old machines and develop new ones.

The foundation of the machine-tool industry in the United States was laid in 1798 when Eli Whitney invented the system of interchangeable parts, the basic principle of mass production. In the 1790s, Samuel Slater contributed to mass production techniques by setting up a system of manufacture in which the successive steps of the skilled artisan were broken down into such simple components that a group of children could outproduce the finest craftsman. Combined with Whitney's system of interchangeable parts, New England's manufacturing economy was launched and, it soon became the most highly industrialized region of the Western Hemisphere. They also set the two basic patterns of industry that still predominate in New England: metal-working and textile manufacturing.

With these basic devices for precision metalworking, New England quickly became the machine shop of the new nation. In addition to turning out machine tools, New England manufacturers developed, for their own use and for sale, a great variety of specialized machinery for making textiles, guns, shoes, ships, sewing machines, farm and household equipment, hardware, and many of the necessities and luxuries demanded by a rapidly expanding nation.

By 1900 the basic geographic pattern of the machine-tool industry was well established. Lower New England, the Middle Atlantic, and lower Great Lakes states had essentially equal distributions of the industry; Ohio, Pennsylvania, Connecticut, and Massachusetts led in production.

The automobile industry, the largest consumer of machine tools and the prime example of mass production, is the basis for the machine-tool industry in the lower Great Lakes region, which accounts for roughly 60 percent of the national machine-tool output; Ohio alone has

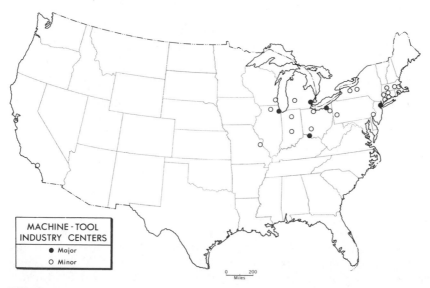

FIGURE 15–1

approximately one-third of the machine-tool industry. Production in the Middle Atlantic states has declined to about 10 percent of the nation's production. New England has experienced a gradual decline, but it is still an important center, especially in the electrical and textile machinery fields and in light-metal manufacturing (*see* Figure 15–1).

Metalworking industries remain competitive by reducing costs through investment in machine tools that are modern and more productive. In 1972, for the first time in decades, the U.S. was not the leading producer or consumer of machine tools; it fell to third place in production, behind West Germany and the Soviet Union, and to fourth place in consumption, behind the Soviet Union, West Germany, and Japan.

METAL FABRICATING

The geographical distribution of steel consumption by manufacturers closely follows the distribution of steel-making facilities. Tonnages of steel shapes consumed by metal-fabricating industries are largely concentrated in a belt about 350 miles wide, running from the Mississippi River to the East Coast. The top of the belt runs just above Milwaukee and Buffalo; the bottom extends from St. Louis to Baltimore.

Located inside this 350-mile band are over two-thirds of the nation's metal-fabricating plants, consuming more than three-fourths of the steel shapes used by manufacturing industries. Within the heavily industrialized belt, metal-fabricating plants are even more concentrated. Over one-third of the steel-mill shapes are consumed by plants in seven metropolitan areas: Detroit, Chicago, Pittsburgh, Cleveland, Philadelphia, northeastern New Jersey, and Milwaukee.

Almost another third of steel production is consumed by metal fabricators in thirty-two specific state economic areas inside the heavily industrialized belt. Manufacturers' use of steel-mill shapes and forms in these thirty-two areas range from 200,000 to 1 million

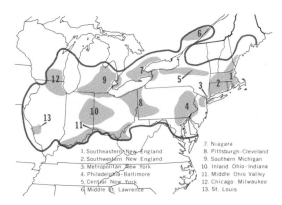

1. Southeastern New England
2. Southwestern New England
3. Metropolitan New York
4. Philadelphia-Baltimore
5. Central New York
6. Middle St. Lawrence
7. Niagara
8. Pittsburgh-Cleveland
9. Southern Michigan
10. Inland Ohio-Indiana
11. Middle Ohio Valley
12. Chicago-Milwaukee
13. St. Louis

FIGURE 15–2 *The   American   ·Manufacturing Region*

tons. Only eight other areas in the rest of the country have steel consumption that falls within this range.

Most of the nation's machine making, metalworking, automotive, and transportation-equipment industries are located in this 350-mile belt. This concentration of steel-making and steel-fabricating industries is based upon the natural advantages of plentiful supplies of iron ore and coal. Coupled with the Great Lakes transportation system, this combination of location factors may continue to attract a large number of the new steel-producing and steel-consuming plants to be built in years to come (see Figure 15–2).

METAL-CUTTING TOOLS

Metal-cutting tools are the replaceable cutting units that are inserted into power-driven, metal-cutting machine tools that do the actual cutting or removing of metal, in the form of chips, when the machine tool is operating.

Two of the principal consumers of metal-cutting tools are the automotive and aircraft industries. Despite their increasing demand for metal-cutting tools, the domestic industry faces increased competition at home and abroad. U.S.

imports of metal-cutting tools amount to about $15 million per year, as West Germany, Sweden, Great Britain, and Japan become more successful in their efforts to penetrate the U.S. market.

USSR.   The Soviet Union leads the world in machine-tool manufacture with an annual output of 160,000 machines. This eminence has been gained recently; as late as 1955, the USSR was reported to have only 56 percent as many machine tools as the United States.

In prerevolutionary Russia the share of metal fabrication and machine-building production amounted to roughly 6 percent of world production. In value, this industry was approximately four times less than Soviet textiles and six times less than that of the Soviet food industry. The technical level of machine-building factories was low, and the range of items produced very limited; mainly uncomplicated types of equipment were produced within the country.

During the pre-World War II Five-Year plans in the USSR, several large-scale enterprises were constructed: the Moscow, Gorky, and Yaroslavl automobile plants; the Kramatorsk and Ural'sk heavy machine-building plants; the Chelyabinsk, Kharkov, and Stalingrad (Volgorgrad) tractor plants; the Rostov and Tashkent agricultural machinery plants; the Ordzhonikidze machine-tool plant in Moscow; the Gorky milling machine plant; the Kiev automatic machine plant; and the Moscow ball-bearing plant.

West Germany.   Germany long has held an important place in the world as a producer of high-quality machine tools and other fabricated metal products. German skilled labor operates at a high degree of efficiency and turns out a wide array of desired metal goods for sale on the world market for about one-third the cost of comparable U.S. products.

285

The machine industry is the key to the high level of German postwar industrial development, accounting for 7.5 percent of all industrial production and over one-fourth of all exports. Machinery exports are about 15 percent of the world total. About 25,000 varieties of machines are produced, of which the most important are machine tools.

The industry suffered relatively little from war damage and the postwar policy of the Allies, but the loss of one-fourth of the prewar German machine-production capacity through partition of the country created serious problems during the early postwar period. Most of the prewar production of machine tools was concentrated in what became East Germany.

The enormous demand for consumer goods after 1948 sparked the rapid recovery of the machine industry. A number of enterprises employing skilled workers, technicians, and managers moved from East Germany to West Germany after the war and reestablished themselves with the help of the government and foreign aid. By 1950 the machine industry was producing at a rate 16 percent higher than the 1936 level. Production in 1972 was 280 percent of the 1936 level.

The lower Rhineland associated with the Ruhr is a major production center; it includes the industrial cities of Dortmund, Cologne, Remscheid, Solingen, Düsseldorf, Duisburg, Rheydt, and München Gladbach. The Neckar, a second center, contains important industrial cities, such as Stuttgart, Reutlingen, Göppingen, Heilbron, and Karlsrue.

United Kingdom. Britain was the birthplace of the modern machine-tool industry. By the early 1830s, it had developed the boring machine and screw-cutting lathe, as well as other machine tools, to an advanced stage. Today there are some 350 firms making machine tools, although the greater part of the industry's output comes from about 150 firms. The high degree of specialization makes it possible for the small firms to flourish.

Despite its prestige as a pioneer, by 1900 Britain had lost its leadership. Largely because of its failure to modernize its plants, it now lags behind the Soviet Union, West Germany, and the United States in the manufacture of machine tools.

The British machine-tool industry is centered mainly in the Midlands, Yorkshire, and Lancashire, and to a lesser extent near London and Glasgow. The Machine Tool Trades Association of Great Britain is the representative body of most of the machine tool manufacturers and importers and is responsible for the International Machine Tool Exhibition, held in Britain every four years.

Japan. Japan, the only highly industrialized nation in Asia, has become one of the world's leading manufacturing powers since World War II and the world's fifth largest exporter of material goods. Of these, metal-fabricating products rank high. Government tariffs support this industry by allowing only noncompetitive machine tools to enter the country.

Today Japan produces machine tools comparable to those made in the United States and Western Europe. Production is centered in the Tokyo–Yokohama, the Kobe–Osaka, and the Nagoya, Karatsu, and Niigata areas.

In the postwar period a large and increasing part of resources has been poured into private investment in plant and equipment in Japan. The ratio of productive investment to gross national product has risen to nearly 20 percent in recent years. Coupled with technological innovation, this large investment has swiftly modernized Japan's industries and raised the productivity of workers. Consequently, wage costs per unit of output in manufacturing have not increased, in spite of the substantial rise in wages. This has contributed to the improved competitiveness of Japanese commodities on world markets.

AGRICULTURAL IMPLEMENTS AND FARM MACHINERY

Since 1831, when Cyrus McCormick invented the reaper, inventions and improvements in farm implements and farm machinery have led to almost complete mechanization of agricultural activity. Machines now enable the United States with fewer farmers to produce more food and fiber than at any time in its history. With these labor-saving machines, the American farmer produces four hundred times more food than he eats.

Conditions in the United States were just right for the development of the farm-implement industry: (1) huge areas of flat to undulating land with fertile soils; (2) cheap land, some of which was available for as little as $2½ per acre; (3) relatively small farm population with a costly labor force; and (4) growing mar-

kets in northwestern Europe and eastern United States. Table 15–1 indicates that nearly 70 percent of the world's farm implements are invented, manufactured, and used in the developed, highly industrialized countries, such as the United States, France, Great Britain, West Germany, Australia, and the Soviet Union.

United States. The American farm implement industry had its inception along the eastern seaboard, but with the opening up of the Midwest the industry began to migrate westward via New York, Pennsylvania, and Ohio. Illinois ultimately became the leading producer, contributing today about half the national output. Three-fourths of all American farm implements are made in the "Implement Belt" (see Figure 15–3). For implements to be used in the Midwest there could be no better locations than Chicago, Detroit, Louisville, Milwaukee, Peoria, Racine, South Bend, and Indianapolis.

California has had to specialize in manufacturing farm implements because many of its agricultural problems differ from those of the East or the Midwest. The principal California center is

TABLE 15–1 Total Number of Tractors and Combined Harvester–Threshers in the World and Selected Countries

	1963	1972	PERCENT CHANGE
U.S.	4,755	4,387	− 7.74%
USSR	1,442	2,112	+ 14.65
W.Germany	1,053	1,430	+ 35.80
France	868	1,400	+ 61.13
Italy	339	698	+105.90
Canada	568	645	+ 13.56
U.K.	475	450	− 5.26
Australia	284	335	+ 17.96
Spain	114	305	+167.54
World	12,487	16,066	+ 28.66%

Source: Based on the *United Nations Statistical Yearbook, 1973* (New York: United Nations, 1974), pp. 97–99.

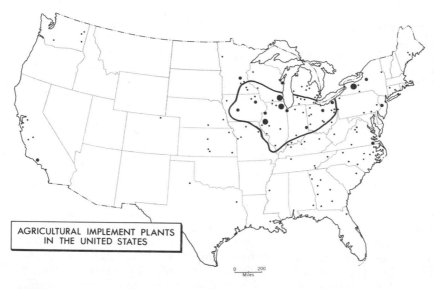

AGRICULTURAL IMPLEMENT PLANTS
IN THE UNITED STATES

0   200
Miles

FIGURE 15–3

Stockton, in the middle of the Central Valley; Fresno, Bakersfield, and Sacramento, other valley cities, as are Los Angeles, San Diego, San Francisco and San Jose.

Canada. With vast expanses of attractive farmland, a small agricultural population, and an enormous farm output, Canada logically has an outstanding agricultural-implement industry. Moreover, Canada desires to manufacture as many as possible of her own goods, including agricultural implements. Her companies, particularly the larger ones, function precisely as do the larger ones in the United States. The Massey-Ferguson Company, with branches in the United States, Europe, and elsewhere, is one of the oldest and largest in the world. At Coventry, U.K., it operates the largest tractor plant in Europe.

Most of Canada's factories are concentrated in the Ontario peninsula and in the St. Lawrence lowland in Toronto, Brantford, and Woodstock. Ontario accounts for about 95 percent of the total Canadian output. Plants are located near the farmlands of Ontario and close to the primary iron and steel and machine-tool industries.

Great Britain. The farm-implement industry was established early in Britain, where many early machines were invented and manufactured. Britain's advantages are its early start, availability of well-distributed iron and steel and machine-tool industries, and a pool of highly skilled workers. In the past the industry was based on an export market because agriculture was largely neglected until World War II. Now, however, Britain produces 70 to 80 percent of her own food. The equipment used to grow food crops is supplied mostly by British companies or Canadian and American companies operating in Great Britain.

The farm-implement industry is distributed throughout the south and east of England, the leading centers being Greater London, particularly Dagenham, but also Gainsborough, Grantham, Hounslow, and Southampton, Coventry,

288

Doncaster, Kilmarnock, Leeds, and Newark.

Soviet Union. Among the many claims being made by the Soviet Union is the assertion that its agriculture is today the world's most highly mechanized and that the USSR correspondingly has the largest agricultural-implement production. Farm operations in areas of extensive production are indeed highly mechanized but the bulk of Russian farm work still is performed by human labor rather than by machinery. The level of farm mechanization in the USSR is at a level where the U.S. was more than 25 years ago.

The manufacture of agricultural implements is one of the most important industrial enterprises in the Soviet Union, output having increased more than fortyfold since the Revolution. The leading centers are at Zaporozhe in the Ukraine; Rostov in the North Caucasus, one of the largest and best equipped in the country; Saratov in the Volga region; and Lyubertsy near Moscow. A more recent center is Irkutsk, 2,600 miles distant from Moscow.

INDUSTRIAL MACHINERY

TEXTILE MACHINERY

The manufacturing of textile machinery developed very early and located near the textile industry itself. The old American textile-manufacturing regions of New England and the Middle Atlantic states still produce most of the country's textile machinery.

There is considerable specialization in this industry. Some companies make only looms for weaving; others make machines for dyeing, washing, carding, and spinning; some make machines for humidifying operations; and still others specialize in air-conditioning equipment.

The principal location factors in all of the specialized industries in the textile-machinery field have been the momentum of an early start, availability of highly skilled labor and technical skills, availability of laboratory facilities for testing machines, and proximity to markets for finished products.

In Great Britain, the textile-machinery industry is located on both sides of the Pennine Mountains, thereby representing an adjustment to the cotton and woolen textile industries. In addition to nearness to market and momentum from an early start, this area originally had a large supply of hardwood timber, which was an important raw material in the early stages of development of the industry. Furthermore, the area was near iron and steel mills. The towns in Lancashire specialize in making cotton-textile machinery; those in Yorkshire are important in the manufacture of woolen- and worsted-textile machinery. And there are several towns in the area where all types of textile machinery are manufactured.

Textile machinery is also made in Belgium, France, Germany, Italy, and Switzerland, and more recently, in the USSR, India, and Japan. Prior to the Second World War, some Japanese cotton machines that were superior to those of Britain and the U.S. were reputedly developed.

ENGINES AND MOTORS

In highly industrialized countries, engines and motors are widely used in all industries. Generally, the engine and motor industry developed in areas consuming much electrical power that also possessed, or were near to, adequate supplies of raw materials, fuel, and labor. The availability of secondary steel industries, especially machine-making ones, and technical knowledge and skill were also important. The engine and motor

289

industry is important in the U.S., Great Britain, Belgium, Holland, France, Germany, Sweden, Switzerland, Italy, and the USSR. The locative reasons for manufacturing engines and motors resemble fairly closely those for the machine-tool industry.

In Britain, the cities of Birmingham, Manchester, and London are the leading centers of production.

Some of the heaviest engines made in the United States are fabricated in Milwaukee, which, because of its position on the Great Lakes, can distribute engine motors cheaply by ship to other cities on the lakes and by rail to the Northwest, West, and South. Pittsburgh, a major center of the world's iron and steel industry, is a great center for the manufacture of engines and electrical equipment (see Figure 15–4). Philadelphia, New York City, and southern New England have important engine-manufacturing industries. One of the most im-

portant electrical manufacturing plants in the world is located at Schenectady, New York, 15 miles northwest of Albany, on the main railway line between New York and Boston on the east and Chicago on the west.

Germany's poverty in petroleum has stimulated her to manufacture economical power generators. The Diesel engine, which burns low-grade fuel oil, is a German invention. The machine and automotive equipment industry had the sixth largest labor force in the nation prior to the Second World War. In the 1930s, Germany ranked among the three leading countries in this branch of manufacturing. Standards of quality are high, and the industry is greatly concentrated. Seven plants have been responsible for 90 percent of the nation's output of generators and electric motors, and four large plants have accounted for almost the entire transformer production. The principal centers are Berlin and its en-

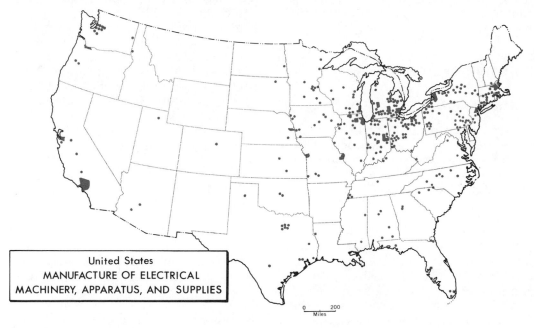

United States
MANUFACTURE OF ELECTRICAL
MACHINERY, APPARATUS, AND SUPPLIES

0   200
Miles

FIGURE 15–4

virons, but there are clusters of plants in the Ruhr Valley, in the Province of Saxony, in Bavaria, and elsewhere.

According to official Soviet statements, there is now no branch of machinery production that does not exist in the Soviet Union and no machine that Russia does not manufacture. According to the Russian aim of distributing industry widely, a considerable number of cities now make machinery; especially notable are Leningrad, Kharkov, Tula, and Izhevsk.

In Asia, only Japan is a significant producer of engines and motors. As Japan became a great industrial and commercial nation, she developed an important industry in the manufacture of transportation equipment and in the production of equipment for the generation and transmission of power, light, and heat. A few firms dominated the industry and made a wide range of products. Single companies and individual plants made a greater variety of products than those in America and Britain. Among the leading manufacturing centers are Kobe, Osaka, and Tokyo.

MINING MACHINERY AND EQUIPMENT

The mining machinery industry, with annual shipments more than double those of a decade ago, has used progressive management, research and development, improved technology, and efforts of an active association to bring it rapidly toward the billion-dollar mark. About 190 firms own or control some 200 manufacturing establishments, which produce the machines and equipment that extract and beneficiate most of the nation's mineral output (see Figure 15–5). The largest producing states in terms of value of shipments are Colorado, Ohio, Pennsylvania, and Wisconsin.

The primary reason for the industry's

CONSTRUCTION & MINING MACHINERY CENTERS
● Major
○ Minor

0   200
Miles

FIGURE 15–5

growth is the increase in mineral production in the United States, which is growing at the rate of approximately $1 billion a year. Every ton of metallic and nonmetallic ore and every ton of solid fuel has to be extracted from the earth and beneficiated in some way before it is ready for industrial use which requires a great variety of mining machinery and equipment. In the same way, the kind and quality of the ore and the characteristics of the coal dictate the particular type of machinery required for proper beneficiation.

SHIPBUILDING

Shipbuilding is custom construction; every ship is different and must be tailored to customer specifications. Mass-production methods have been tried but have not as yet proved successful. To make ships, a country or area must have technological knowledge, skilled and relatively low-cost labor, a long history of shipbuilding, an iron and steel industry of impressive dimensions, and numerous subsidiary industries to install the many machines, instruments, and fittings that go into a ship. A shipyard may be regarded as an assembly plant, to which various lines of manufacturing contribute: steam engines, turbines, furniture, pumps, etc. All these are brought to the shipyard to fabricate into a ship.

Production of merchant ships reflects a nation's concern for maritime trade. Any country or area that builds ships must benefit from a combination of favorable circumstances:

1. It must have a large, experienced, and low-cost labor supply. Labor accounts for about 35 percent of the cost of a ship. A shipyard employs thousands of workers, draftsmen, craftsmen, and engineers. Labor costs vary widely.

2. It must have at hand important iron and steel mills or have easy access to them. Materials comprise about 65 percent of the total cost of ships, and among these steel makes up about 20 percent for the hull and superstructure alone. Steel also is the principal ingredient in the main engines, auxiliary engines, and deck machinery.

3. It must have a climate and harbor facilities that permit outdoor work for many days in the year.

WORLD PRODUCTION

As shown in Table 15–2, Japan is responsible for 48 percent of new merchant ship construction. Sweden, Germany, and the United Kingdom follow; the United States occupies thirteenth place, with less than 2 percent of new construction (see Figure 15–6).

The leading shipbuilding nations are mostly in Europe (see Figure 15–7). The only large producers outside Europe are Japan (see Figure 15–8) and the United States (see Figure 15–9), though some other countries do build ships.

Japan. Japan has long been important in this industry, but only since World War II has she moved into first place. In 1972 Japan set a peacetime construction record, accounting for 48 percent of the total world output. Japan also led the world in oil-tanker construction, with over 50 percent. The Japanese are a hardworking and realistic people and are determined to adapt their economy to the changing times. Shipbuilding has been a major factor in restoring prosperity to Japan.

Japan's advantages for shipbuilding are: (1) the world's biggest yards, important since the trend is definitely toward larger vessels, particularly oil tankers; (2) low cost of production, about 20 percent below the European costs; (3) exceptionally attractive credit terms; (4) early deliveries; (5) high level of industrialization; (6) favorable exchange rates;

TABLE 15–2   Total Tonnage of Merchant Vessels Launched in the World and Selected Leading Nations (in thousand gross registered tons)

	1963	1972	PERCENT CHANGE
Japan	2,367	12,866	+443.55%
Sweden	888	1,814	+104.27
W.Germany	971	1,606	+ 65.39
U.K.	928	1,233	+ 32.86
Spain	175	1,142	+552.57
France	447	1,129	+152.57
Norway	341	975	+185.92
Italy	492	948	+ 92.68
Denmark	323	905	+180.19
U.S.	294	611	+107.82
World	8,539	26,714	+212.84%

Source: Based on the *United Nations Statistical Yearbook, 1973* (New York: United Nations, 1974), p. 308.

(7) much skilled labor procurable at low wages; (8) ships built for delivery at fixed prices, whereas European yards make contracts with escalator clauses; (9) occasional government subsidization of ships for export; (10) a very large home market for ships as a result of the outstanding fishing and trading activities; (11) a relatively mild climate; and (12) numerous good harbors and ports.

Japan's most spectacular shipbuilding achievement is the construction of giant ships in the 200,000-ton category. Earlier giants, the 17,000-ton tanker of two decades ago, for example, were later outmoded by 100,000-ton giants. The development of new construction techniques and larger shipbuilding docks has increased the potential size of ships. Four Japanese yards now contain docks with 200,000-ton ship capacity, and an even larger dock is now underway.

These giant tankers are an entirely new phenomenon, resulting from the spectacular increase in world petroleum demand and the spectacular economies available in moving oil in bulk from Persian Gulf fields to Western markets. The mammoth ships are, of course, re-stricted to special-purpose runs and to specially built ports. In fact, one major firm plans to supply the European market from a million-ton tank farm on the Atlantic Coast of Ireland, since it considers the North Sea and the English Channel to be too shallow for Japanese supertankers to enter.

The industry is concentrated in a number of centers: Kure, Kobe, Nagasaki, Tokyo, Maizuru, Taman, Aioi, Yokohama, mostly on the big island of Honshu (see Figure 15–8). Today it has 34 yards capable of building ships of 10,000 tons or more, and it increases its yard facilities by 20 percent annually. Two-thirds of Japanese shipyard production is exported, representing $700 million in overseas sales. This accounts for one-tenth of the nation's total exports, a far cry from the occupation period when Japan was completely prohibited from replacing its destroyed merchant fleet.

United Kingdom. Until 1956, when Japan moved into first place, Britain led the world in shipbuilding, in keels laid, tonnage launched, and tonnage completed. Leadership stemmed from the

FIGURE 15–6

availability of iron and steel produced at centers on tidewater, skilled labor at reasonable wages, which were cheaper than in continental Europe and the United States; an early start in the machine-tool industry; mild climate; adequate capital for financing; a tradition of shipbuilding; government aid and stimulation; and a large domestic market for ships as well as prestige in foreign markets. However, Britain has slumped into fourth place during the past several years.

The British shipbuilding industry is located in several different areas, but well over three-fourths of the tonnage of ships built in Britain comes from four areas: the River Clyde in Scotland; the northeast coast of England, along the lower reaches of the Tyne, Wear, and Tees, and at West Hartlepool and Blyth; the northwest coast of England, on the

River Mersey and at Barrow-in-Furness; and Belfast, Ireland.

West Germany. Possessing one of the world's outstanding primary iron and steel industries, skilled labor, technological leadership, and deepwater bays, and being relatively poor in natural resources, Germany logically should have a great shipbuilding industry.

During the last fifty years, astonishing progress has been made in shipbuilding. Begun in order to construct warships with which to challenge Britain's mastery of the sea, the movement naturally spread to the creation of a merchant navy that would provide the experience and familiarity with the sea so necessary for a nation of landsmen to take to the ocean. Today there are large shipyards at Hamburg and its outport of Elmshorn,

FIGURE 15–7 *Principal Shipbuilding Centers of Europe*

at Kiel, Lubeck, Bremerhaven, and Emden. The total tonnage of shipping launched has exceeded that of Great Britain since 1958.

Scandinavia. The three great seafaring nations, Norway, Sweden, and Denmark, rank high in shipbuilding, despite their

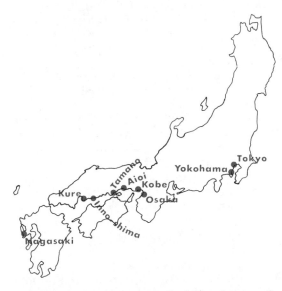

FIGURE 15–8 *Principal Shipbuilding Centers of Japan*

unimportance in iron and steel industries. Sweden is most important in Scandinavia and ranks fourth in world tonnage output. With construction costs lower than the United Kingdom, Sweden is a strong competitor. Chief centers are Göteborg, Uddevalla, and Malmö.

Sweden, like Japan, has been a pioneer in developing shipbuilding techniques. As evidence of this, the U.S. recently negotiated for license rights on a number of Swedish patents after the U.S. Secretary of the Navy investigated the mechanized yards at Ardenal, Sweden. The Ardenal yard can produce a 70,000-ton tanker with only 40 percent of the man-hours required by the same firm's conventional shipyard. The new yard emphasizes prefabrication, although this is now a standard technique. What is unique is the use of a small work force with very advanced equipment, operating under cover along a straight production line.

Shipbuilding is in many respects Denmark's most important industry. She ranks tenth in world output and exports more than half the ships she constructs. Largest yards are at Copenhagen, but ships are constructed also at Nakskov, Odense, Elsinore, Aalborg, and Frederikshavn.

Norway, one of the world's great maritime nations, builds ships at Bergen, Oslo, and Stavanger, and ranks ninth in world tonnage output.

France. The French shipbuilding industry is concentrated and dispersed. The industry is concentrated at the shipyards of the lower Loire River, which possess 60 percent of the country's shipbuilding capacity. The remaining 40 percent is distributed among many other ports.

The most widely dispersed shipbuilding centers include Dunkerque, Cherbourg, Brest, Lorient, La Pallice, and

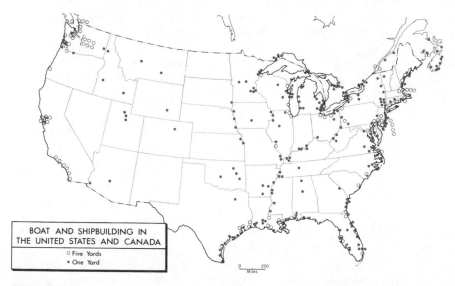

BOAT AND SHIPBUILDING IN
THE UNITED STATES AND CANADA
○ Five Yards
• One Yard

FIGURE 15–9

Queyries. Brest and Lorient have naval bases and share some of the naval construction work with Toulon and La Seyne.

Altogether, there are fourteen yards that are capable of building vessels of 3,000 tons or more. France has a total capacity of some 700,000 tons, but average yearly output is only about 450,000 tons. As in Britain, the industry has had to struggle with foreign competition, especially Japanese.

Italy. Italy has long ranked among the ten top shipbuilding nations and now ranks eighth. She builds passenger freighters and whaling vessels and tankers, and some of her craft rank among the world's finest. The industry is stimulated by a state subsidy amounting to 27 percent of the cost of every ton of new shipping. Some of the shipyards are among the world's best, and many of the techniques (e.g., electric welding and the manufacture of aluminum-alloy bodies) are unsurpassed. Principal yards are in the Genoa area; but Monfalcone, La Spezia, Palermo, and Trieste are also important.

United States. The United States does not rank high in shipbuilding (*see* Table 15–2). It costs twice as much to produce a dead-weight ton in American shipyards as it does in Japan. In the United States approximately 80 percent of the cost of building a large ship consists of wages for labor. Moreover, construction standards in American shipbuilding are very high, adding more to the cost.

The chief shipbuilding areas in the U.S. are the Atlantic Coast, the Gulf Coast, the Great Lakes, and the Pacific Coast. The chief points are on New York Harbor, Delaware River and Delaware Bay, and Chesapeake Bay (*see* Figure 15–9). The principal yards in the New York area are Staten Island, Brooklyn, and Kearney. The Delaware River is sometimes referred to as the "American Clyde"; its most important yards are in Philadelphia, Camden, Chester, and Wilmington.

Sparrows Point and Newport News are the two most important shipbuilding centers in the Chesapeake Bay–Hampton Roads area. They enjoy the advantages of proximity to steel factories, availability of skilled labor, proximity to supporting industries, and excellent harbors.

Gulf Coast yards have risen in importance in the past several years. West Coast yards, at Los Angeles, San Diego, San Francisco, Portland, and Seattle, are hampered by higher wage costs and costlier steel, machinery, and equipment; they cannot compete well with East Coast or the Gulf Coast yards on cost. The Great Lakes shipyards at Manitowoc, River Rouge, and Toledo specialize largely in lake carriers, except in time of war.

Soviet Union. In the past shipbuilding in Russia was never important. But since World War II, it has expanded greatly as a result of enlarged merchant, fishing, and naval marines. However, compared with the United States, the United Kingdom, Norway, Liberia, and Japan and West Germany, the Soviet Union still operates a relatively small fleet of ships of 1,000 gross tons and over.

Shipbuilding is widely distributed from the Baltic Sea to the Pacific and from the Arctic to the Black Sea. Seagoing vessels are constructed at Leningrad, Nicolayev, Riga, Sevastopol, Vladivostok, Komsomolsk, Kaliningrad, Odessa, and in a few other places. The industry is also important on many rivers, for example, at Predivinsk on the Yenisey; in the vicinity of Chkalovsk on the shore of the Gorki Reservoir on the Volga; and at Rostov on the Don. These centers construct river boats and barges.

THE AUTOMOTIVE INDUSTRY

In about three-quarters of a century the motor vehicle has completely changed the way of life and altered the distribution of population in many portions of the earth. The manufacture of motor vehicles uses mass production techniques of assembly, involving standardized and

TABLE 15–3 **1972 Total Motor Vehicle Production in the World and Selected Leading Countries**

	PAS-SENGER CARS	COM-MERCIAL VEHICLES
U.S.	8,824	2,447
Japan	4,022	2,277
W.Germany	3,514	303
France	2,993	345
U.K.	1,921	408
Italy	1,732	107
Canada	1,155	320
USSR	730	651
World	27,630	7,850

Source: Based on the *United Nations Statistical Yearbook, 1973* (New York: United Nations, 1974), pp. 209–10.

interchangeable parts. The assembly line turns out a finished car every minute. Eight countries account for over 90 percent of the entire passenger car production: the United States (31 percent); Japan (15 percent); West Germany (13 percent); France (11 percent); the United Kingdom (7 percent); Italy (6 percent); Canada (4 percent); and the Soviet Union (3 percent) (see Table 15–3). The remaining 10 percent is produced in some fourteen other countries, including Australia, Brazil, and Spain. These countries mainly have branch plants that assemble auto or truck units for U.S., West German, and Japanese firms. Favorable tariffs and labor-saving costs are factors that have encouraged the establishment of assembly units in these countries (see Figure 15–10).

United States. The U.S. leads the world in the production and consumption of automobiles. Highway travel accounts for 98 percent of all private transportation, 85 percent of which uses cars. Eight out of 10 people travel to work by car, and

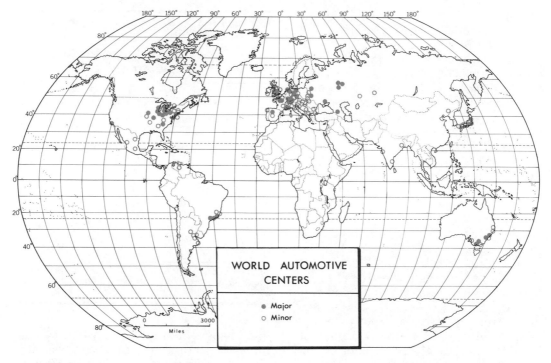

FIGURE 15–10

almost 9 out of 10 go by car when they travel between cities. More than 90 million cars and trucks are registered and more than 111 million people are licensed drivers.

The huge market of the auto industry in the U.S. is made possible because of the high per capita annual income in the U.S.; the incomparable highway system of over 3 million miles, two-thirds of which is surfaced; the large population in the suburbs, which the automobile made possible; and the desire, largely created by advertising, to possess one or more cars (see Figure 15–11).

The industry is concentrated primarily in the Lower Lake area, where the following combination of conditions is highly favorable:

1. An early start by imaginative "pioneers" of the industry, such as Henry Ford and Ransom Olds

2. Cheap water transportation for all raw materials needed to make iron and steel

3. The Great Lakes and the St. Lawrence Seaway for shipping parts and assembled cars

4. Excellent railway and highway networks for assembling raw materials and distributing assembled cars

5. Ample flat land for the huge, sprawling plants

6. Proximity to makers of parts

7. A large pool of skilled, semiskilled, and unskilled labor

8. A large market at hand

Detroit is the automotive-manufacturing center of the world. During the early years of automobile manufacturing, however, operations were widely scattered: in eastern Massachusetts, northern New Jersey, the Hudson–Mohawk Valley, the Connecticut Valley, southeastern Pennsylvania, Cleveland, and Chicago.

United States
AUTOMOTIVE INDUSTRY

● MAJOR CENTER
○ SECONDARY CENTER

0   200
Miles

FIGURE 15–11

In 1909 the center of activity shifted to the Midwest. Detroit's supremacy was ensured in 1914 when the moving assembly line was perfected by the Ford Motor Company.

Actually, Detroit had no economic-geographic advantages over Chicago, Milwaukee, Cleveland, or Buffalo as a center for automobile manufacturing. It became the automotive center largely because it was the hub of a circle within which were many of the pioneers of the business, notably Henry Ford. However, the choice of Detroit proved to be advantageous. In the first place, it is conveniently located for shipment of parts to assembly plants anywhere in the nation. The automotive industry had to be located centrally with respect to steel; Detroit is an important and growing iron and steel center itself. And, during the seven or eight months of the navigation season, it is accessible by water from the great steel-making centers at South Chicago, Gary, Cleveland, Loraine, and Buffalo. Outstanding automotive-making centers besides Detroit are Flint, Lansing, Pontiac, Kenosha, and Toledo.

Actually the automotive industry is decentralizing toward both sea coasts and even overseas to assembly plants located close to foreign markets. The equivalent in parts of ten automobiles can be transported in a single boxcar that can hold only four assembled cars. There are at present more than 100 plants engaged in some phase of automobile assembly to better serve local markets. This does not mean, however, that Michigan and Detroit are withering on the production vine; nearly all the qualifications that made this area the center of the industry in the beginning are still functioning.

Decentralization and the rise of the assembly plant result also from high labor costs in Detroit. The industry there is particularly vulnerable to strikes and

299

work stoppages because of the heavy concentration of the industry, the strength of the unions, and the high cost of living in the Detroit area. Finally, the automotive industry appears to be assuming a traditional industrial pattern: in the early stages, there is much concentration, followed later by decentralization and dispersion.

Canada. Canada, in seventh place, has an impressive automotive industry. On a per-capita basis, its output roughly equals that of the United States. There is one major center, Windsor, which is the largest automotive center in the British Commonwealth, but there are dozens of "automobile cities." As in the United States, the companies purchase most of their parts from sources in Chatham, Galt, Hamilton, Ingersoll, Kitchener, Merritton, Niagara Falls, Sarnia, St. Catharines, Stratford, and Wallaceburg. Windsor, across the river from Detroit, shares all the advantages of Detroit, except its large market. It also has branches of big American companies. Since Canada's volume is comparatively low in this mass-production enterprise, the Canadian automotive industry is protected by a high tariff of 17½ percent. It was this protection, plus British Commonwealth preferential tariffs, that caused U.S. companies to establish manufacturing plants in Canada.

West Germany, France, the United Kingdom, and Italy, respectively, are the leading automobile producers in Europe. The industry has become an increasingly important sector of European economy through its share in total output, employment, and exports and through the growing number of dependent subsidiary industries and services (see Figure 15–12).

West Germany. In a country of nearly 60 million inhabitants, motorization is gradually approaching American proportions, with cars functioning for transportation and as symbols of prestige. More

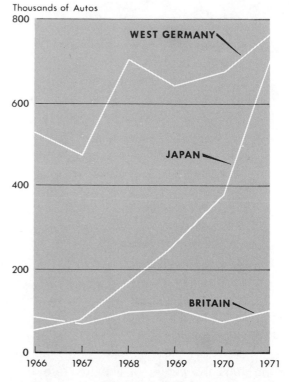

Thousands of Autos

FIGURE 15–12 *Auto Imports: Landings in the U.S.*

than 10 million automobiles clog West German streets and *Autobahnen*—one for every six people—and pleasure is rapidly replacing business as the main buying motivation. Output and exports to all destinations are still expanding, and the flow of orders suggests that prospects for the future are good.

However, a substantial shift from export sales to domestic sales has occurred, with the result that delivery times for home sales have been shortened. As incomes rise, new classes of buyers are entering the car market. For the same reason, demand for large cars is growing strong, while sales of some domestically produced small and midget cars have decreased, creating difficulties for some branches of the industry.

300

Five companies—Volkswagen, Mercedes, Opel, Borgward, and Ford—have experienced the greatest increases. German automobiles are still popular in the United States although other foreign imports have cut into German sales. The Mercedes competes in the luxury class and is rated as one of the best in its field.

France. Four companies produce passenger cars in France—Renault, Citroen, Simca, and Peugeot. The first three have their main factories in Paris. Despite attempts since World War II to decentralize the industry, the Paris market absorbs a quarter of the cars sold in France and, like Detroit, is the center of the industry, which evolved from coach-building and other craft enterprises involving skill in the use of metals, wood, and fabrics.

Unlike the others, Peugeot makes its cars in the provinces, with the main plant located at Sochaux on the edge of the Jura Mountains. Like other firms, Peugeot also built new factories since the war at Dyon, Vesaul, and Mulhouse, with subsidiaries at Lille and St. Etienne.

United Kingdom. The British automotive industry is located mainly in the Midlands and the London area. It consists of a relatively small number of assembly firms, headed by the "Big Five" (British Motor Corporation, Ford, Rootes, Standard, and Vauxhall) and backed by a large number of specialist body and component manufacturers. The "Big Five" are responsible for about 90 percent of the output of vehicles of all kinds. The balance of the industry's motor production, other than tractors, consists of heavy commercial vehicles, sport, and other specialty cars.

There are roughly twenty specialty car producers. Of these, the best known are Rolls-Royce, Daimler, Armstrong Siddley, Jaguar, and Rover. They cater either to the luxury class, such as Rolls-Royce, or to sport-car enthusiasts.

The largest foreign market for Brit-

ish-made cars is the United States, which accounts for more than one-third of total exports, followed by Canada, Australia, and South Africa. The largest European market is Sweden.

Automotive research is carried out at Lindley, Warwickshire, by the Motor Research Industry Association, an autonomous body founded in 1946 and partly financed by the Department of Scientific and Industrial Research, but mainly by the industry itself. Individual firms also have their own research and development facilities.

Italy. No country has embraced the automobile revolution with greater enthusiasm than Italy, which ranks a strong fourth in Europe. As in many other fields of engineering, production is dominated by the vast integrated concern of Fiat at Turin, where Lancia's main factory is also located. Fiat employs about 80,000 persons in the area, and makes 80 percent of the Italian motor vehicles as well as many other forms of transport. Other centers of the industry are Milan and Naples, where the Alfa Romeo is assembled; Madena, home of the Ferrari plant; and Bolzano, where the Lancia is made. Fiat has several factories overseas, notably in South America, as well as designers and technical connections in Spain, Poland, and the USSR. Italy is second to Japan in the production and export of motorcycles, producing approximately 600,000 per year. Export trade for Italian cycles is largely with other European nations.

USSR. Although the Soviet Union is slowly expanding car production, an automobile revolution has yet to take place in this land of 240 million people. For the foreigner, a striking feature of Soviet towns is the relative absence of automobile traffic. Moscow is perhaps the only capital in the world where one can drive to the finest theater, the

Bolshoi, and park his car right in front on the evening of a soldout performance.

In car production, the Soviet Union stands today about where the United States was a half century ago. The USSR produced 1,381,000 motor vehicles in 1972, more than one-half of which were cars. However, the majority went to state agencies or were exported; private Soviet customers bought only 217,000.

If the objectives of the current five-year plan are realized, 4.1 million new cars will roll off assembly lines by the end of 1975, and 2.5 million will be sold to private citizens. The rest will be shipped abroad or sold to public agencies. Although the Russians intend to expand private auto use rapidly, they are quick to disavow any intent to overtake the United States. They regard American output and the overall fleet of American cars as excessive, a burden rather than a blessing.

Only four makes of cars are currently available to private buyers in the USSR: the Zaporozhets, the Moskvich, the Zhiguli, and the Volga. There are only a few station wagons, and no sport cars or convertibles are offered.

The little Zhiguli, named for a mountain range near the factory where it is made, is making the Soviet auto revolution. The Zhiguli, modified for rugged Soviet road and weather conditions, is a country cousin to the Fiat-124, and it will soon be joined by a version of the Fiat-125. The first Zhigulis came off the assembly line in 1970, but they already account for 75 percent of the new cars sold in Moscow.

The proportion is likely to rise slightly as the Italian-designed $1-billion factory moves into full swing on three assembly lines. The factory is situated 500 miles west of Moscow at Togliatti, a Soviet town renamed for the great Italian Communist. Last year, 170,000 Zhigulis rolled off one line and this year two lines

will produce 320,000. For 1975, the target is 660,000.

Japan. The growth of the motor industry in Japan has been spectacular. While other industries have been cutting production, motor manufacturers have maintained a 10 percent growth rate, emphasizing the dominant position they have achieved in the economy. The million mark was reached in 1963, and production has since continued to soar beyond two million. Japan now is second in world automobile production, surpassed only by the United States.

The heavier motor vehicles made in Japan have long been highly regarded, and now the new passenger cars rival the best that the United States and Europe can offer. Toyota and Nissan are the two leading manufacturers; others include Isuzu, Hino, Mitsubishi, Prince, Fuji, Toyo Kogyo, Daihatsu, Honda, and Suzuki. Japan leads the world in the manufacture and export of motorcycles, producing about 2,600,000 annually; Honda accounts for about 65 percent of this total. The bulk of foreign sales are made to the United States and Great Britain.

The U.S. is Japan's biggest export market. Because of the U.S. dollar devaluation, it is also the market in which Japan is having the most trouble. The Japanese say they are being forced to raise prices 10 to 12 percent on most cars exported to the U.S. because of the yen's rise in value against the dollar. Such increases in price would put Ford's subcompact Pinto about $100 below the cheapest Toyota and Datsun and would put General Motor's Chevrolet Vega about equal in price to the Japanese compact cars.

Although the Japanese were disturbed that exports to the U.S. sputtered in 1972, they were pleased that shipments to Europe jumped 71 percent in 1972. However, that large rise may have badly hurt Japanese efforts to increase sales in Europe during the rest of this decade. Japan still has less than 5 percent of the European market, but the size of the 1972 increase has alarmed some Europeans. Among those concerned are many in the United Kingdom, where Japan shipped 86,478 vehicles in 1972, or four times more than in 1971. There is already some talk among British businessmen that Britain should emulate Italy, which allows only 1,000 Japanese cars a year to be imported.

AEROSPACE INDUSTRY

The combined aerospace industry is one of the largest employers in the United States. The bulk of missile and space employment is carried on as a separate operation from aircraft plants, although many aircraft plants have shifted some of their operations to the missile and space field as they have procured government contracts. Missile components are produced by about twenty different industries, but between 70 and 80 percent of the total is produced by three industries: aircraft and aircraft parts, ordnance, and electrical machinery.

AIRCRAFT INDUSTRY

The American aircraft industry, regarded as the world's outstanding, was a relatively insignificant enterprise prior to World War II. In two years it jumped from twentieth to fourth place in the world. Aircraft manufacture is carried on only in the large, highly advanced, and wealthy countries of the world, particularly in those that have strong military forces. Recently, almost 90 percent of the total sales of U.S. companies were made to the Air Force and the Navy. However, military production is highly uncertain. With the unpredictability of

international relations, the aircraft industry will probably persist, though it is developing more and more into a producer of missiles and spacecraft.

Commercial production consists of four separate and distinct parts of an aircraft: *engines, air frames, propellers,* and *instruments.* Only the engine and airframe parts are treated in this chapter.

Engines. During World War I, the eastern United States dominated airplane production, although a large part of the engines were manufactured in Detroit. Today most airplane-engine factories are located in the East, principal centers being Wood-Ridge, New Jersey; East Hartford; Farmingdale, Long Island; Trenton; Cincinnati; Indianapolis; and Muskegon, Michigan.

Among the most important location factors are local pride, skilled labor supply, access to markets, and industrial inertia (after the industry is established). None of these factors, however, has exerted sufficient influence to cause the concentration experienced by the automotive industry.

There is little similarity between the manufacture of airplane engines and airframes. Engines are made largely by machine, airframes largely by hand. The production of engines requires hundreds of separate and specialized skills and five years, on the average, to bring an engine to quantity production from the time design and engineering begin.

About half the dollar volume of an engine producer's prime contracts goes to subcontractors and suppliers. Thus, although the number of engine manufacturers is limited, the number of suppliers is legion. The Aircraft Industries Association estimates that some 50,000 different firms feed it.

Airframes. Automation and mass production are not important in the manufacture of airframes, primarily because of the restricted number of any one type and model sold and their early obsolescence. Moreover, although a modified mass-production technique is followed, it appears that mass production will be delayed as long as designs change so rapidly.

LOCATION FACTORS

Only a few countries in the world can afford the luxury of an aircraft industry. The two leaders obviously are the United States and the Soviet Union. In the United States, there is a complete lack of geographical centralization in this industry, allegedly because the leading companies to whom scientific location might presumably be important have not been dependent upon location for profit. The government has been the largest source of business for the aircraft industry, ensuring against financial loss in any business and normally guaranteeing a profit.

The four most important location factors are climate, suitable terrain in large tracts, skilled labor (automation has not been able as yet to displace experienced men and women), and proximity to market. However, location factors are not the same for all countries. For example, in the Soviet Union resources, transportation, and established industrial metallurgy are the dominant location factors; because of the type of government, technicians and workers in large numbers could be forced to go to determined sites anywhere. Vent and Monier well state the situation:

> Location of aircraft production facilities in both the United States and the USSR has assumed definite locational patterns, each with its peculiar criteria for location. In the United States, it is dictated by climate, skilled labor pools, and basic economic conditions. In the Soviet

Union, resources, transportation, and political considerations are more significant. (17)

Suitable Climate. Climate is the most important location factor affecting the industry, and it is more important than in most industries. A mild climate is advantageous in four ways: (1) good flying weather permits year-round flight testing of planes; (2) warm and relatively dry climate allows storage of parts and equipment out of doors; (3) mild temperatures reduce heating needs and consequently construction costs, important where hangars cover millions of square feet; (4) work may be carried on out-of-doors throughout the year, especially important because the final assembly process requires a great amount of space owing to the huge wing span of modern planes. All operations should, if possible, be carried on out of doors. Accordingly, much of the airframe industry is in California, Texas, Georgia, and Arizona.

Labor Supply. The availability of a large pool of skilled labor is another major location factor. Such skills take a long time to develop. Skilled aircraft workers seem to be more mobile than workers in other industries. (11)

Level and Inexpensive Land in Large Tracts. Few industries demand so much room. The buildings are enormous, and there must be landing fields, hangars, storage space, parking areas for the automobiles of workers, and room for future expansion. For example, one company has a mile-long, 200-foot-wide assembly line. The land should be level and free from obstructions for take off and landing.

The Strategic Factor. In a world where destruction of industrial capacity by an enemy is possible in a matter of minutes, there is danger in locating as vital an industry as aircraft in certain locations, the Northeast and Pacific Coast areas.

At the beginning of World War II, more than 80 percent of the floor space devoted to airframe production was concentrated on the Pacific and Atlantic coasts, two-thirds of it in southern California alone. The same proportion of engine-production facilities was located in the Northeast, as were all the propeller producers and most of the instrument producers. The government urged dispersal of aircraft-fabricating facilities, and by 1944 much new integrated capacity had been constructed in the Midwest and the Southwest. This is the major reason for the rapid growth of aircraft manufacture in Texas and Kansas. Currently, airframe, engine, propeller, and instrument aircraft factories are not concentrated in any one area. Components must

be gathered from widely scattered sources throughout the nation for final assembly.

WORLD PRODUCTION OF AIR FRAMES

Principal producing countries are the United States, the Soviet Union, Great Britain, Canada, and France.

United States. The United States airframe industry is located mostly west of the Mississippi River (*see* Figure 15–13). The principal centers for airframe construction are Los Angeles and San Diego, Dallas and Fort Worth, Seattle, Baltimore, Buffalo, Wichita, and Atlanta. In San Diego and Wichita, 70 to 75 percent of workers employed by manufacturers are in the aircraft industry or its suppliers. Los Angeles and San Diego together account for about one-fourth of all

United States
AIRCRAFT INDUSTRY

FIGURE 15–13

employment in the American aircraft industry. Aircraft and now missile manufacturing, along with ancillary industries, such as electronics and scientific instruments, comprise an industrial core.

The number of companies is few, but they operate on a gigantic scale. Douglas Aircraft, the largest employer in southern California, has four plants and employs about 60,000 persons; the Lockheed plant at Burbank has 32,500 employees.

Today Texas ranks second only to California. The industry, centered in the Fort Worth–Dallas area, employs 15 percent of all workers engaged in it. The Texas plants are not raw-material or market-oriented. The chief locative factors were strategic location, suitable climate, and ample flatland at reasonable cost.

The Seattle area is the home of the Boeing Aircraft Company, leader in the manufacture of heavy aircraft and long-range guided missiles. Founded in 1916, the company is the largest employer in the Pacific Northwest; its payroll constitutes about a fourth of the total industrial payroll of the state—five times that of the aluminum industry and four times that of the pulp and paper industries. Although it undoubtedly plays too vital a role for the economic health of the state of Washington, the industry does complement the resource-based industries.

Boeing has remained in Seattle largely because of industrial inertia and because national dispersal of the aircraft and missile industry has been regarded as essential. However, it is not as good a location as southern California because it lacks a warm, sunny, dry climate and large tracts of flatland.

Soviet Union. Since the Soviet Union encompasses one-seventh of the land surface of the globe and since its surface transport is as yet but modestly developed, its airways are extremely well developed. To move people into all parts of the country and to become ever more powerful militarily, the Soviet Union has had to build up an impressive aircraft industry. Major emphasis is on military planes. Moreover, the aircraft industry is government owned and operated.

The Soviet industry is located in four areas, making for effective economic-geographic distribution: (1) Moscow–Gorki; (2) Volga–Urals (Kazan, Votkinsk, Perm, Chelyabinsk); (3) the Southwest (Kiev, Rostov, Osipenko, Tambov); and (4) the Far East (Komsomolsk, Khabarovsk). All these areas have important types of manufactures other than aircraft. Moreover, all were established centers of considerable importance industrially, the opposite experience of the airframe industry in the United States. During World War II, there was considerable dispersal of the industry to the interior, to the Urals and to the Far East. Much industry, however, remains in European Russia.

Great Britain. Britain has long been and still is a leader in the manufacture of aircraft. However, because of the financial strain of producing costly items that quickly become obsolete, the country in 1957 withdrew from military-aircraft production and began concentrating upon missiles.

Although Britain lacks weather conditions comparable to those of southern California or Texas, weather has been taken into consideration in locating the plants. The majority of them are in the south, principally in the Greater London area, at Hayes, Kingston, Luton, Hatfield, Dagenham, and Weybridge. A second area of importance lies to the south at Portsmouth and East Cove, and a third is in the Midlands at Coventry and Wolverhampton.

AIRCRAFT INDUSTRY COMPETITION

In 1971, 76 percent of all transport aircraft operated by noncommunist countries were made in the U.S., compared with 83 percent in 1958. Because of increasing foreign competition, the U.S. share of the aviation fleet of the noncommunist world is expected to drop to about 64 percent by 1980. Although the difference in the number of aircraft is still not great, unless the U.S. counters programs of foreign aircraft manufacturers and governments to penetrate world markets, composition of the world's airline fleet will significantly change. For some existing aircraft, for example, the Boeing 747, the Lockheed L-1011, and McDonnell Douglas DC-10, the United States remains the sole supplier. Beginning with the British/French Concorde and standard, wide-body twin jets and advanced medium-range transports, the new technology of other nations is expected to account for an increasing proportion of world aircraft sales.

In addition to the competition from transports developed and produced by other nations, the U.S. faces competition from other governments who are actively seeking military sales to support their domestic industries. Some countries have negotiated agreements providing for rising military sales to Latin America and African countries. European helicopters are increasingly displacing U.S. helicopters in world use. Recent studies indicate that the U.S. share of the world military aircraft market will decline from 60 percent in 1970 to 47 percent in 1980.

World technological leadership earned by the United States aerospace industry during the 1960s is being eroded in the 1970s because of a lack of new programs. In contrast, there are continuing achievements by the European and United Kingdom consortiums and by the Soviet Union. The United States' traditional major share of the world aerospace market in 1980 can be achieved only with leadership and funding required to develop and launch major new programs.

references

1. Adams, Walter, *The Structure of American Industry*. 3rd ed. New York: The Macmillan Co., 1961.

2. Alexandersson, Gunnar. *Geography of Manufacturing*. Englewood Cliffs, N.J.: Prentice-Hall, 1967.

3. Clark, Mills Gardener. *Development of China's Steel Industry and Soviet Technical Aid*. Ithaca, N.Y.: Cornell University Press, 1973.

4. Davies, Wayne K., and Briggs, Ronald. "Automobile Establishments in Liverpool: A Steady State Distribution." *The Professional Geographer* 19 (November 1967): 323–29.

5. Gibson, Jay James. "An Analysis of the Location of Instrument Manufacture in the United States." *Annals of the Association of American Geographers* 60 (June 1970): 352–67.

6. Horvath, Ronald J. "Machine Space." *Geographical Review* 64 (April 1974): 167–188.

7. Hurley, Neil P. "The Automotive Industry: A Study in Industrial Location." In Howard G. Roepke, ed. *Readings in Economic Geography*. New York: John Wiley and Sons, 1967, pp. 416–29.

8. Jerome, John. *The Death of the Automobile: The Fatal Effect of the Golden Era, 1955–1970*. New York: W. W. Norton and Co., 1972.

9. Kawahito, Kiyoshi. *The Japanese Steel Industry: With an Analysis of the U.S. Steel Import Problem*. New York: Frederick A. Praeger, 1972.

10. Lydolph, Paul E. *Geography of the U.S.S.R.* 2nd ed. New York: John Wiley and Sons, 1971.

307

11. McKnight, Tom L. "Aircraft Manufacturing in Texas." Southwestern Social Science Quarterly 38 (June 1957): 44.

12. Mandell, Melvin. "The New World of Machine Tools." In Howard G. Roepke, ed., *Readings in Economic Geography*. New York: John Wiley and Sons, 1967, pp. 481–85.

13. Miller, E. Willard. *A Geography of Industrial Location*. Dubuque, Iowa: William C. Brown Co., 1970.

14. Patterson, J. H. *North America*. 5th ed. New York: Oxford University Press, 1975.

15. Rothschild, Emma. *Paradise Lost: The Decline of the Auto-Industrial Age*. New York: Random House, 1973.

16. Steed, G. P. F. "The Changing Milieu of a Firm: A Study of Manufacturing Geography." *Annals of the Association of American Geographers* 58 (September 1968).

17. Vent, Herbert J., and Monier, Robert B. "The Aircraft Industry in the United States and the USSR." *The Professional Geographer* 10 (May 1958): 7–8.

18. Warren, Kenneth. *The American Steel Industry, 1850–1970: A Geographical Interpretation*. Oxford: Clarendon Press, 1973.

19. ———. *The British Iron and Steel Sheet Industry Since 1840: An Economic Geography*. London: Bell, 1970.

20. White, C. Langdon; Foscue, Edwin J.; and McKnight, Tom L. *Regional Geography of Anglo-America*. 4th ed. Englewood Cliffs, N.J.: Prentice-Hall, 1974.

21. White, Lawrence J. *The Automobile Industry Since 1945*. Cambridge: Harvard University Press, 1971.

textile and garment
industries

16

16

When man domesticated plants and animals, and thus assured a food supply for himself, he was able to cease his interminable roaming and to use his time, his energy, and his ingenuity for technical development; in short, he established the basis for a permanent civilization. The arts of spinning and weaving, the most ancient and universal manufacturing activities, were born at this time in human history.

Most natural fibers utilized for modern textiles are the same ones used in ancient times. As trade developed during the age of exploration, the West became acquainted with the East's great fabrics: Egypt offered linen; Mesopotamia, wool; India, cotton; and China, silk. By the late 1600s, Europe's textile industries were sufficiently advanced to stimulate spinners, weavers, fullers, and dyers to organize powerful craft guilds.

TEXTILES

Today more than forty countries have substantial textile industries, especially the United States, the Soviet Union, India, Japan, Pakistan, France, West Germany, Poland, Italy, and the United Kingdom.

COTTON

The cotton-textile industry is unique in its geography (see Table 16–1). It is a widespread, major industry and usually the first to be developed when nations experience industrial revolutions. The following causes underlie these two basic and closely related factors:

1. The processes of the textile industry are simple and, especially in coarse goods,

similar to the original handicraft operations. Thus, areas lacking skilled industrial labor can develop the industry quite rapidly.

2. A comparatively small amount of capital is needed to set up a plant of economical size, particularly in comparison with the vast initial outlays required for the iron and steel or automotive industries.

3. The market for cotton yarn and cloth is extensive even in nonindustrial societies.

4. The locational pattern of the industry is affected little by the location of materials, although the cost of raw materials comprise the chief elements in the total production cost.

5. The industry tends to expand in areas with low wage scales, since labor costs comprise the second most important element in the cost structure of the industry and show the widest variation both interregionally and internationally.

U.S. Cotton Production. The ascendancy of the United States as the world leader in cotton-textile production parallels the decline of the English cotton-textile industry. The U.S. today accounts for about 25 percent of world production.

The cotton industry in the U.S. offers a valuable study of industrial location. Since 1880, and especially since 1923, the great shift of the cotton mills from New England to the South has been dramatic in its economic, social, political, and technological impacts.

A number of decided advantages, aside from an early start, propelled New England's industry: (1) high humidity that, by reducing the frictional electricity caused by rubbing the fibers during processing, retards tangling during spinning and reduces breakage during weaving; (2) water power; (3) soft, clean water, excellent for bleaching; (4) skilled labor working for low wages, the original labor force being gradually replaced by successive waves of European immigrants, each group poorer than the last; (5) ample capital available for investment, provided initially by merchants and seamen whose business had been cut off by wars and later by the whaling industry;

TABLE 16–1   Cotton Yarn Production in Selected Leading Countries (in metric tons)

	1963	1972	PERCENT CHANGE
U.S.	1,683	1,517	− 9.86%
USSR	1,220	1,504	+23.28
India	893	973	+ 8.96
Japan	473	527	+11.42
Pakistan	175	336	+92.00
France	298	275	− 7.72
West Germany	301	222	−26.26
Poland	160	212	+32.50
Italy	193	155	−19.69
United Kingdom	222	121	45.50

Source: United Nations Statistical Yearbook, 1973 (New York: United Nations, 1974), pp. 238–39.

and (6) location in a major market area close to wholesale centers of the coastal cities of Boston, New York, and Philadelphia.

In every New England state except Vermont the cotton-textile industry is still important, but Rhode Island and Massachusetts have the majority of the mills and workers. Although the textile industry for the past seventy years has been one of the slowest-growing industries in the nation and at various times has suffered substantial losses, New England has been the hardest hit. Why did the industry decline so severely? Low labor productivity; the static nature of management; lack of enterprise; archaic organization; obsolescent plants and equipment; high cost factors, such as labor, power, fuel, and taxes; subsidies in regions soliciting new industries; and poor employee relations, improved only when it was too late to affect most of the industry.

The cotton-manufacturing industry of the South, which has contributed so immeasurably to the economic growth of the region, actually had its beginnings forty years before the much-publicized "Cotton-Mill Campaign" of the early 1880s. In the depression of the 1840s, the Piedmont South, recognizing the advantages of its location and its cheap labor, established several mills, employing mostly women and children and relying on Northerners for the management of the plants. However, several disadvantages, among them inadequate transport facilities, marketing difficulties, and a paucity of operating capital, hampered progress.

In 1880 the cotton-textile industry was well launched in the South. Relative political and economic stability, a railway network into the Piedmont, and a vigorous campaign to recruit northern investment capital, machinery, and managerial talents incited a new surge of activity. With an abundant labor supply as a foundation and the promise of realizing economies of scale, the South exerted an attraction for industry through the large number of advantages it enjoyed over the North:

1. A lower wage scale and longer working hours. A large labor force was at hand, labor laws were far less stringent, labor unions were weak, and high-priced skilled labor became less necessary with advanced technology. The wage differential historically has been cited as the most significant factor in the North-South textile

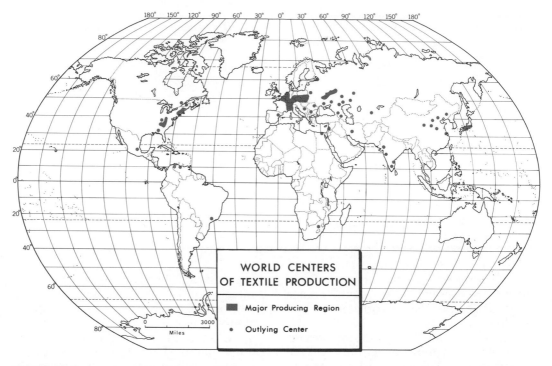

FIGURE 16–1

movement; but following 1940, because of minimum-wage laws and pressures from high-wage industries, wage differences became much less marked.

2. Lower living costs. Most southern mills are located in rural communities or on the outskirts of larger cities. Milder winters mean lower fuel bills. Moreover, longer frost-free seasons enable workers, many of whom are rural residents, to grow some of their own produce.

3. Cheaper power from both coal and hydroelectric sources. Most southern mills are about 400 miles closer to coal deposits than those of New England. In hydroelectric power, the South was and still is definitely favored.

4. Scientific location of mills was emphasized; plants were scattered rather than concentrated as in New England. More modern machinery is used, and many mills open operations with the lastest equipment.

5. Subsidized housing, from the outset a universal characteristic of the southern

industry. Building can be carried on year round, and materials and labor for construction cost less in the Piedmont. Workers were given reduced rents in lieu of higher wages.

6. Lower corporate taxes.

7. Since 1930, a marked increase in mergers. Southern firms have acquired northern plants and some of their machinery, resulting in a greater capacity for diversification and increased facilities to supply, process, and market goods.

The Piedmont, then, had every advantage except two—experience and proximity to market, which was later mitigated by improved transportation. New England neglected her opportunities in both respects. Today the South is the unchallenged center of the nation's cotton-textile industry, and the Piedmont is the throbbing heart of it. Among the outstanding centers are Anderson,

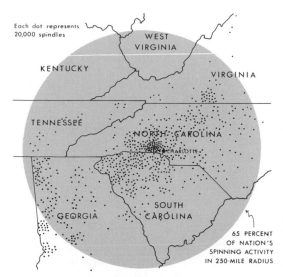

Each dot represents 20,000 spindles

65 PERCENT OF NATION'S SPINNING ACTIVITY IN 250-MILE RADIUS

FIGURE 16–2 *Distribution of the Textile Industry in the Southern Piedmont (by Spindles)*

Atlanta, Augusta, Charlotte, Columbia, Columbus, Danville, Gastonia, Greensboro, Greenville, Macon, and Spartanburg (*see* Figure 16–2).

Both the South and the North have been hard hit by textile slumps recently and by substitution of petroleum-based fabrics. In the last forty years, textiles seem to have earned their way only when wartime shortages created unusual demands. Cotton manufacturers have been seriously concerned about the decrease in per-capita consumption of cotton. The textile decline is in large part a result of foreign imports, which comprise so strong a threat that even the expected gain in the American textile market in the 1960s may be submerged by them. However, this trend may be reversed in the 1970s due to increasing petroleum prices that would affect the price of man-made textiles.

Soviet Union Textile Production. Textiles is the basic industry that directly serves the needs of the Soviet people;

and cotton manufacture is the principal branch of production, employing about half the total number of textile workers. Before the 1917 Revolution, when heavy industry was woefully backward, textile manufacturing was the country's dominant large-scale industry.

Cotton manufacturing developed in the central region of European Russia, at Vladimir, Moscow, Yaroslavl, and Ivanovo, and in Leningrad. Raw-cotton production expanded into Central Asia to serve the industrial center when Russia was cut off from American cotton during the Civil War. Prior to the Revolution, half of the cotton used in Russian mills was imported, largely from the United States; the other half came from Central Asia and Transcaucasia. Today the Soviet Union claims self-sufficiency in raw-cotton production.

After the Russian Revolution, the industry concentrated even more heavily in the industrial center of the Ivanovo Oblast, where it had the advantages of agglomeration effects, i.e., the clustering of the industry in one location facilitating the processing and distributing of manufactured goods. The Ivanovo Oblast became one of the densest textile areas in all Europe, although the Moscow Oblast surpassed it in production. Since the 1920s, the Soviets have built cotton mills closer to their raw-material sources and consuming centers, for example, in Uzbekistan, Turkmenistan, Western Siberia, Azerbaidzhan, Armenia, and the Volga River region.

India. The making of cotton textiles was the first and remains the foremost large-scale manufacturing industry in India. Although most production is consumed at home, India ranks second only to Japan as an exporter of cotton cloth.

In India output of yarn exceeds that of cloth, which is characteristic of lands where raw cotton is plentiful. Most yarn is coarse because short- and coarse-staple

313

cotton is grown in India. Imported cotton from the United States and Egypt accounts for the increasing quantities of better-quality cloth.

Built on ancient foundations, the modern Indian industry was really born with the establishment of a power-driven mill in Bombay in 1854. India's outstanding industrialist, Jamseti Tata, built his first cotton mill in 1869. In 1880, India provided the market for approximately half of Britain's machine-made cotton goods, which destroyed a substantial portion of India's cottage industries. Although the Indian industry developed slowly, with the country's huge market, its availability of raw cotton, and its abundant and cheap supply of labor, the industry grew in stature.

The main divisions of the industry are the mill industry, producing yarn and cloth; the small power-loom enterprises, producing cloth from mill-made yarns; and the widely distributed handloom industry, producing cloth from both mill-made and handspun yarn.

The cotton-mill industry is concentrated in Maharashtra and Gujarat, where 60 percent of all Indian spindles and looms are located. The next most important state in these respects is Tamilnadu, but the mills in the south have always concentrated on spinning, mainly because of the large demand for yarn from the local handloom industry. The industry is also well established in Madhya Pradesh and Uttar Pradesh.

Japan. Japan is today the world's leading exporter of cotton goods and the largest importer of American raw cotton; Japan grows no cotton. Cotton textiles launched Japan's industrial revolution. The first cotton mill was built in 1868, but the industry really gained momentum after the turn of the century. However, at the beginning of World War I, Japan was still importing substantial quantities of cotton cloth. When the war ended, Japan dominated the textile trade with China and, thereafter, textile trade with the Netherlands East Indies, the Indian Ocean countries, and Africa; this comprised the greatest market in the world for cheap, coarse cotton goods.

Japan developed machinery for spinning India's very short-staple cotton, which was in little demand elsewhere. It devised a process for blending Indian raw cotton with Egypt's long-staple cotton. By the 1930s Japan's cotton goods were being traded worldwide, and Japan became the world's foremost exporter of cotton textiles.

Japan's phenomenal progress hinged on the ability of her mills to produce cotton goods at prices that other sellers could not match. Japan was able to do this through almost continuous operation of mills and rapid amortization of equipment. The nation had an abundant source of cheap and committed labor, fostered by a paternalistic system of training and maintaining mill workers. Children, usually girls, were recruited from farm families to labor for a fixed fee paid to their debt-ridden fathers. The Japanese advanced mill technology introduced the Toyoda automatic loom and European textile machinery.

Japan's cotton mills are to be found in the Kansai district of Honshu, with the greatest concentration around the city of Osaka. Twenty miles to the southwest of Osaka Bay is Kobe, the chief port of entry for Japan's raw-cotton imports.

Great Britain. Although Britain still has more cotton spindles than any other nation (almost 20 percent of the world total), she now has only a slight edge over the United States. In production of yarn and of woven cotton fabrics, she has declined markedly from first to tenth place, being superseded by the United States (see Table 16–1 and Figure 16–3).

In addition to being plagued by export problems, especially since World

War II, the British industry has been hamstrung by the obsolescence of many of its mills and much of their equipment, by inefficient organization, and by apathetic management. In early 1959, a third of Lancashire's spindles and a fourth of its looms were idle. Nevertheless, Lancashire's capacity continued to exceed demand. Its chief competitor, Hong Kong, a part of the British Commonwealth, was persuaded to give a three-year breathing space to Lancashire by restricting its quantity of exports. The industry obviously required a complete reorganization in order to survive. In 1959 a scheme was designed to remove surplus capacity, to re-equip and modernize existing machinery, and to encourage installation of modern equipment.

Europe. As cotton spindles and consumption spiraled downward in Britain, a concurrent increase took place on the European mainland, which now considerably surpasses Britain in both categories. Cotton textiles have long figured prominently among the industries of the Continent, particularly in the major manufacturing area, west-central Europe. The industry there was at the outset favored by (1) a large population supplying cheap labor and working long hours and a big domestic market; (2) numerous

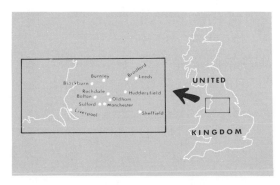

FIGURE 16–3 *Cotton and Wool Manufacturing Centers in the United Kingdom*

foreign markets, especially colonial possessions; (3) ample coal and water power; (4) abundant pure water; (5) an efficient transportation web of rivers, canals, and railways; (6) access to the sea for importing raw cotton; and (7) high tariff walls.

The major cotton-manufacturing area extends from northeastern France, with Lille the leading center, through Belgium, the Netherlands, Germany, Poland, Czechoslovakia, Switzerland, and northern Italy. Raw cotton is imported primarily through Bremen, Dunkirk, Genoa, and Le Havre.

China. Although cotton spinning and weaving was an ancient handicraft in China, the modern cotton-textile industry began only in 1890, when the first mill was built.

In 1918 Shanghai had 80 percent of all Chinese spindles and, before World War II, more than half the nation's spindles and looms. Standing at the mouth of the 750,000-square-mile Yangtze drainage basin and containing roughly one-third of the nation's people, the city had a large and cheap labor supply and a huge market. In addition, after World War I the city offered relative political security, access to imported raw cotton, foreign and domestic capital, and good transportation. During the late 1920s and the 1930s, the industry was decentralized to some extent; in the mid-1930s about half the spindles and looms were in Japanese-owned mills and about 5 percent in British-owned ones.

The People's Republic of China furthered decentralization by dismantling coastal mills and rebuilding them inland, closer to the raw-cotton sources. Mills operating with modern machinery have been built primarily in the important cotton-growing provinces of Hupeh, Honan, Shensi, and Sinkiang. The city of Tsingtao has become an important center, but the Shanghai-Nanking-Hangchow triangle continues to dominate the industry.

WOOL

The transformation of the fleece of sheep into fabric is one of the most ancient and fundamental manufacturing processes. Peoples of high and middle latitudes early recognized the virtues of wool in their cold milieus. Because of its long, barbed fibers, it could be spun easily into thread. It was light, yet durable, and its elasticity and scales produced a cloth that could preserve heat and absorb moisture. Wool was a necessity during the many centuries when cotton was still a luxury. Because of the firmly established traditional methods employed by crafts, as well as the greater complications involved in the manufacture of wool textiles, large-scale mechanization of wool manufacturing developed considerably later than that of cotton.

Although wool-producing areas—notably the belt of nomadic herding from the Mediterranean Basin to Central China, the grazing land of the Andes, and the high plateau and mountain areas of the tropics—are slowly introducing mechanization into wool manufacture, by far the largest portion of woolen cloth in these areas is made by hand in the ancient manner. The wool-manufacturing industry has centered in the advanced industrialized nations of Italy, the USSR, the United Kingdom, Japan, France, the United States, Italy, and West Germany. These nations import raw wool and manufacture about 75 percent of the world's wool yarn. The high value of wool enables it to stand the cost of long hauls to manufacturing centers, and it also can be stored for a long time without deteriorating (see Table 16–2).

The Industrial Revolution had a profound effect on the geography of the wool industry: Yorkshire took the helm and kept it because coal and iron were in close proximity and because this area was better able to adapt to the changed economic conditions created by the introduction of machines. Western England and Scotland continue to turn out high-quality cloth, and Leeds has become the trading, engineering, and clothing-manufacturing focus. The United Kingdom, once the world leader in output of woolen fabrics, is now second after the USSR (see Table 16–2).

Northeastern France, West Germany, northern Italy, Belgium, and the Netherlands today have important wool-manufacturing industries. France is famous for its soft woven fabrics, the product of shorter staple wool, which are utilized chiefly in women's apparel. Pre–World War II Germany developed a substantial

TABLE 16–2 Wool Yarn Production in Selected Leading Countries (in metric tons)

	1963	1972	PERCENT CHANGE
USSR	243	377	+55.14%
United Kingdom	251	233	− 7.17
Japan	122	165	+35.25
France	158	155	− 1.90
U.S.	244	116	−52.46
Italy	92	116	+26.08
West Germany	99	87	−12.12

Source: United Nations Statistical Yearbook, 1973 (New York: United Nations, 1974), p. 238.

woolen industry in Silesia, Saxony, and Westphalia in the coal-field region. Today West Germany's centers are Wuppertal (east of the Rhine) and München-Gladhach (west of the Rhine), which combine coal for power with good transportation facilities. Czechoslovakia, Bulgaria, Austria, and Switzerland produce sizable quantities of woolen goods, too.

Prior to the 1917 Revolution, Russia's woolen industry was outstanding in Moscow and Leningrad, where mills turned out fine cloth, and in the Black Earth Center and Central Volga region, where coarse cloth was produced. In the Soviet period and particularly since World War II, mills have been constructed nearer to the raw-material sources—e.g., Kharkov and Kremenchug in the Ukraine, Kutaisi and Tbilisi in Georgia, and Semipalatinsk in Kazakhstan. The USSR ranks first in the world in output of wool yarn (see Table 16–2).

Japan ranks second in world production of wool yarns and fabrics, although, as with cotton, she must import all her raw material, about 80 percent of her wool coming from Australia. There has been a fairly strong domestic demand for woolen fabrics in response to the desire for Western-style clothes, which feature wool as an important component. But Japan, living on trade as she does, has managed to increasingly export her woolens and worsteds, particularly to the United States. By 1960, Japan's subsidized, staple, mass-produced worsted cloth had so endangered the American industry that stiff tariffs were imposed on such goods.

U.S. Woolen Industry. From the outset the American woolen industry differed from the cotton-textile industry: it began in the home, not in the factory, and it was and still is more widely scattered. Farmers manufactured woolen cloth from their own raw materials. As was true of cotton cloth, Britain used every possible means to stifle woolen manufacture in the colonies—by prohibiting importations of sheep into America and by forbidding exportation of colonial-made cloth; but her efforts were largely in vain.

Two circumstances stimulated native manufacture: the War of 1812, which interrupted trade between Britain and America, and high protective tariffs in 1816 and 1824. New England logically became the production center, by virtue of its textile tradition, humid climate, proximity to markets, adequate waterpower, pure soft water, ample capital, and accessibility to textile machinery.

Wool manufacturing became identified with cities such as Providence and Woonsocket in Rhode Island and Lawrence, Lowell, and Holyoke in Massachusetts. Cities and towns in New York, New Jersey, and Pennsylvania also entered the field. Boston, an excellent central market in the early 19th century, became the capital of the wool trade.

In recent years, the established wool-textile areas of the North have undergone the same frustrating and seemingly relentless decline that has typified the cotton-textile industry, largely because of the migration of mills to the South. The displacement of the wool-textile industry has lagged considerably behind that of cotton, but the trend is accelerating.

Most of the standard wool products are made in very modern plants on the Piedmont. The Piedmont woolen and worsted industry has expanded mainly because northeastern firms have been building branch plants in the South rather than at home, largely for the same economic reasons that apply to cotton manufacturing. Although the development of wool manufacture in the South has been impressive, New England continues to hold on to the major portion of the industry.

LINEN

The ancient cultivation of flax for fiber and the manufacture of linen can be traced as far back as 1200 BC. The Egyptians were the first to cultivate wild flax and to recognize its usefulness. They early gained great proficiency in linen weaving and used exquisite fabric for their sanctuaries and sepulchres.

In Ireland, where the industry was of great antiquity, linen manufacture was fairly well under way in the 13th century. Ultimately, Northern Ireland became the leading linen-manufacturing region of the world. Seventy-five percent of the mills are located within a 30-mile radius of Belfast, which controls the industry today even more decidedly than Manchester does the cotton-textile industry.

Northern Ireland's advantages are several: (1) the early introduction of mechanized equipment; (2) a mild, humid climate, which is not only stimulating but also highly favorable to making quality linen from a rather intractable fiber; (3) absence of a competitive textile industry; (4) a large supply of cheap, efficient labor, derived from wives and daughters of men employed in shipbuilding and other heavy industries; (5) ample sources of pure, soft water; (6) unsurpassed skill in bleaching, dyeing, and finishing processes; and (7) high quality of products. Actually Ireland provides neither the source of the raw material nor the market for the manufactured product. The fiber for the industry is imported from the Low Countries and Eastern Europe; the market for the manufactured product is foreign.

Today northern Europe, from Northern Ireland to eastern European Russia, is the world's foremost flax-growing and linen-manufacturing region. The Flanders lowland of France and Belgium enjoys an enviable reputation for its fine linens, Lille and Ghent being the outstanding centers of production. Other concentrations are Germany's Westphalia and Czechoslovakia's Bohemian Basin. Vyazniki, Kostroma, Smolensk, Vitebsk, and Tallnin are leading linen-milling cities in European Russia, the region that forms the base of the Soviet linen industry.

SILK

Silk, a luxury-apparel fabric for many years, has been severely affected by economic depressions and new, lower-cost, manmade fibers. Its demand, especially of lower-quality silk goods, was considerably curtailed between the two world wars when lower-cost rayon ("artificial silk") underwent so remarkable a development that it replaced silk in most world markets.

In Japan, China, and Korea, where most of the world's raw silk is produced and where silk fabrics are more widely used than anywhere else in the world, the art of reeling and weaving silk is an ancient one. By far the greater portion of silk fabrics, from the cheapest to the most costly, is still woven on hand looms in these lands where an abundant supply of cheap labor is available. Exports of superior-quality silk goods fell off badly in modern times, owing largely to the tariffs levied by importing countries. These countries began to import raw silk, which is of low bulk and high value and therefore can stand the transportation costs, and to do their own manufacturing of silk. Now, more than 75 percent of the machine manufacture of silk takes place far from silk's Oriental homeland.

Japan, which produces about 80 percent of the raw silk in world, most of which is imported by the U.S., manufactures silk fabrics in the central and southern parts of the country. Reeling, formerly a home industry, is performed in factories known as filatures, most of which are located in central Honshu, particularly around Okaya and Nagoya.

Weaving, a separate process, centers on the west coast around Fukui, Kanazawa, and Niigata, in the Kyoto area, and in Gumma and Tochigi west of the Kwanto Plain. In some of these areas, government curtailment of silk production has forced the manufacturers to change over to other textiles, particularly synthetics and woolens, in order to escape bankruptcy.

In China, the homeland of silk manufacture, the industry centers in the traditional sericulture areas—the valley of the Si-Kiang and the lower Yangtze–Kiang. China supplies approximately 5 percent of the world's raw-silk exports.

The USSR is an important silk producer. The major areas of concentration are (1) Transcaucasia, especially at Tbilisi in the Georgian SSR, and Armenia at Malatiya and Sebastiya, which are mainly concerned with the spinning and weaving of silk; and South-central Asia at Chardzhou and Ashkabad in the Turkmen SSR.

The United States, which produces no raw silk, has a silk-manufacturing industry that commands three-fifths of the world supply of raw silk. Americans, with their high standard of living, provide a substantial market for luxury apparel. American silk manufacture initially was a parasitic industry because it tended to locate in surplus-labor areas where women were willing to perform the relatively light work for low wages. Paterson, New Jersey, was the first important center because of (1) a large reservoir of women workers whose husbands and fathers worked in the metal trades; (2) proximity to New York City, the center of women's fashions (roughly half of the world's silk textiles are marketed within a 100-mile radius of the city); and (3) abundant water power from the falls of the Passaic River. Gradually, similar labor advantages prompted the industry to shift to Pennsylvania's anthracite-coal areas of Scranton and Wilkes-Barre and to the cement centers of Allentown and Easton. New England and the southern Piedmont, too, garnered a sizable share of the industry.

JUTE

Hand spinning of jute was practiced in India for centuries prior to the British occupation. In the early 1800s, the British East India Company perfected the cultivation of the "golden fiber" near Calcutta (jute is often called "Calcutta hemp") and introduced the English to its uses as a textile. Under British rule, West Bengal developed the jute-processing industry into almost a world monopoly.

Almost all the world's jute formerly was grown in India in the Ganges-Brahmaputra Delta. With partition, India retained the mills and Pakistan the raw-jute acreage. Each country then attempted to balance the jute economy within their respective nations. Bangladesh, formerly East Pakistan, now has a number of mills, and India today meets four-fifths of its raw-jute requirements. Most of the jute mills, however, still are in India in a 60-mile riparian zone of the Hooghly River in and around Calcutta. Bangladesh's mills are in the nation's river ports.

Most of the jute mills outside Bangladesh are in Europe, primarily in Dundee, Scotland. In India more than 100 jute mills employ some 300,000 workers, and at least 5 million agricultural laborers are dependent on them.

MAN-MADE TEXTILE FIBERS

In only a few decades man-made fibers, the products of man's endless search for newer and better ways to do and make things, have emerged as redoubtable competitors in the textile industry, dominated for so many centuries by natural fibers. Man-made fiber production has increased far more rapidly than have other branches of the industry. It has demonstrated a spectacular ability to invade the textile market, offering seemingly limitless possibilities in apparel, household, and industrial textile materials. In the United States, the synthetic-textile industry has grown so remarkably and steadily that, except for agriculture, it is now the largest single customer for the chemical industry.

With each new man-made fiber created, the natural fibers face a greater competitive threat. At the same time, synthetic fibers can be blended with natural fibers, imparting to natural fibers the qualities for which synthetics have become valued. (*See* discussion on substitution in chapter 4.)

Location of Synthetic-Fiber Plants. All major manufacturers of man-made fibers carefully select sites for their plants to secure the most economical and efficient operation. The location decision involves the respective pull capacities of raw-material areas and of fiber-market areas. Transport cost is apt to be the determining factor; if transport costs of raw materials are substantially less than those of finished products, the plant will locate near the source of the raw materials.

Rayon. Because rayon is a creation of the chemical laboratory, its foremost producers are logically the world's most highly industrialized nations with successful textile industries. Five countries—the United States, Japan, the USSR, West Germany, and the United Kingdom—account for more than half the world's output. The primary locational factor is proximity to an abundant supply of fresh water; from 150 to 200 gallons of water are needed to produce 1 pound of viscose rayon, and 1 pound of acetate requires almost six times that amount.

In the U.S., production takes place predominantly in a crescent-shaped area from southern New Hampshire to Georgia, with a westward extension into Ohio. The rayon industry, like other man-made-fiber enterprises, is an offspring of the chemical and textile industries. It was inevitably drawn to the South where the chemical plants could supply the raw materials, the textile mills could convert the fiber into fabrics, and the parallel growth of these allied enterprises was soundly based on availability of ample supplies of labor, water, raw materials, power, and fuel, complemented by good transport facilities. More than half of the plants have been established in the South, with the greatest concentration in Virginia and Tennessee.

Japan accounts for approximately 20 percent of the world's rayon production. In contrast to her cotton- and wool-textile industries, Japan is able to produce the bulk of the raw materials for rayon manufacture at home.

The USSR ranks third in the world in rayon production after Japan and the United States. The Central Industrial Region, where the textile industry originated in Russia, still maintains leadership in this industry. The rayon mills extend east from Moscow along the Klyaz'ma River at Orekhovo-Zuyevo and Pavlovskiy Posad.

Nylon and Other Synthetic Fibers. Nylon is the most well known and widely produced "miracle fiber," due to its high tensile strength, elasticity, quick-drying properties, light weight, and resistance to wrinkling, moisture, and abrasion. Composed of coal, water, and air, nylon is the result of a complicated manufacturing process involving the conversion of carbon from coal, nitrogen and oxygen from air, and hydrogen from water into a viscous fluid, which undergoes several treatments before filaments can be amassed and wound in a process called melt spinning. Nylon for textile use comes in three main forms: (1) multifilament, for dresses, upholstery, and

TABLE 16–3 **Non-Cellulosic Continuous Filaments Production in the World and the Selected Leading Countries (in thousand metric tons)**

	1963	1972	PERCENT CHANGE
U.S.	323	1,258	+289.47%
Japan	109	503	+361.47
West Germany	58	316	+444.82
United Kingdom	64	196	+206.25
USSR	28	157	+460.71
Italy	46	138	+200.00
World	760	3,330	+338.15%

Source: U.N. Statistical Yearbook, 1973 (New York: United Nations, 1974), p. 249.

tire cord; (2) monofilament, for very sheer hosiery; and (3) staple (a short, wavy strand), for sweaters and socks.

The United States is the world leader in production of noncellulose man-made fibers, which account for approximately 10 percent of the nation's textile fibers. On a worldwide basis, the U.S. produces about 38 percent of the noncellulosic fibers; Japan, 15 percent; West Germany, 9 percent; the United Kingdom, 6 percent; the Soviet Union, 5 percent; and Italy about 4 percent (see Table 16–3).

GARMENT MANUFACTURE

For many centuries garment manufacture was a household industry, and it still is in many parts of the world. In other areas, dressmaking, tailoring, and allied occupations became small-shop enterprises and remained so until the late 1800s. Garment making in industrially advanced countries began its routinized, mechanized life in the factory at this time. By and large, peoples of the industrialized nations are today clothed by the ready-to-wear industry. The mechanization of the industry and the style and quality of its products have been especially notable in the United

States, where good clothes are made at reasonable prices with an amazingly small amount of human labor. The American segment of the industry will be elaborated upon here (see Figure 16–4).

NEW YORK CITY: THE WORLD'S GARMENT CAPITAL

Garment making is New York's most important industry. The city employs approximately 35 percent (or about 300,000 workers) of all workers in the nation's apparel industry, produces 45 percent of its output, and sells 65 percent of all women's and children's garments, although a good amount of the actual production occurs elsewhere. This gigantic industry is encompassed within a remarkably small area; Manhattan's famed garment district is roughly bounded by 34th and 40th Streets and by 6th and 9th Avenues and comprises about 200 acres. In this overpopulated, incredibly congested area, the most concentrated industry in the world is located. Thousands of manufacturers occupy approximately 170 buildings. In their shops an annual $4 billion worth of suits, coats, dresses, undergarments, millinery, furs, and other garments are cut, shaped, pressed, and packed.

321

DISTRIBUTION OF EMPLOYEES
IN THE APPAREL INDUSTRY

- Metropolitan Areas
- Remainder in State

Number of
Employees

5,000
10,000
25,000
50,000
100,000
200,000
400,000

0   200
Miles

FIGURE 16–4

The concentration of apparel firms has led to concentration of ancillary businesses: the design, display, and sale of textiles; cloth shrinking; textile banking; trucking; model agencies; thread and trimming suppliers; belt manufacturers; and machinery-repair shops. These allied activities in and around the garment district contribute substantially to keeping the apparel firms in the city. Of course, the garment district is not the garment making area in New York. Various types of garments are manufactured at many points in the New York metropolitan region, which encompasses twenty-two counties, including nine in New Jersey and one in Connecticut.

The city has an unequaled market outlet because of its metropolitan population of more than 16 million. Moreover, a fourth of the nation's population resides within a 250-mile radius of New York City, and seven of the ten largest

cities in America and the two most populous cities of Canada lie within a two-day drive of the city. Seasonal considerations in the women's apparel industry forces firms to locate in an area with ample reserves of skilled labor available for temporary employment on short notice. Moreover, within New York's nucleus of garment manufacturing, materials in various stages of production can be transferred to different contractors and suppliers with such rapidity that frequent and sudden changes in style can be accommodated.

The influence of fashion is felt throughout the entire industry. It is more conspicuous in women's clothing than in men's, in outer wear than in undergarments, and in the higher-priced lines than in the lower. The more fashion oriented a garment is, the more likely it is to be produced in New York or a smaller fashion center like Dallas or Los

Angeles. Style pirating is commonplace. Normally, the moment a new style makes a "hit" at a high price, manufacturers of lower-priced goods start copying it using less skilled workers and cheaper fabrics. The need for keeping up with the latest in fashion demands that a firm locate its headquarters near other producers of fashion merchandise. New York thus serves as the fashion center of America; buyers from all over the nation converge to compare the output of competing sellers, and they save money by concentrating all their purchasing in one center.

But despite its unique labor pool, its unequaled external economies, agglomeration effects, and its unparalleled mingling and communicating facilities, New York no longer holds the commanding position in women's and children's apparel that it once held, although it remains the greatest source of these garments anywhere in the world. Its decline has been in its share of national production; its fashion leadership and proportion of sales remain stable. Production has undergone more rapid growth outside of Manhattan—in Brooklyn, in outlying counties, in Pennsylvania, New England, the South, and the Far West. The reasons for this shift in production are several:

1. New York suffered a cost disadvantage, primarily in its labor-cost differential in the production of standardized, inexpensive garments. (The supply and cost of labor are the most important factors in determining the industry's location.) Separation of sewing from merchandising enabled the entrepreneurs to establish production wherever costs were lowest. Since New York is a relatively high-cost labor area, production tended to move to lower-cost labor districts, especially those with surplus labor.

2. The decade of the 1950s was marked by a changing pattern of life and a westward movement that brought about a revolution in clothing styles. The spectacular development of suburbs and the growth of cities in the climatically warmer West fostered a more casual way of living. Informal, lightweight sportswear largely replaced dresses, suits, and coats, a trend which strongly affected New York's producers of higher-priced garments.

3. The switch to synthetic and cheaper fabrics adversely affected the New York industry because manufacturers could not easily shift to the less expensive fabrics without lowering the prices of their merchandise in order to compete. Even by entering the lower-priced field, they were unable to match wage costs of other competing areas.

4. Employers searched for lower-cost areas where they would be freer from control of union demands for higher wages and benefits.

5. Along with interregional competition was international low-wage competition, particularly from Japan, Hong Kong, and Puerto Rico, although their exports were chiefly inexpensive goods.

6. A decline in the population of older ethnic groups that had provided the core of the labor reserve necessitated the employment of another labor force willing to work at the lower rungs of the occupational ladder. In the 1930s the blacks and in the 1940s the Puerto Ricans provided the new manpower—or rather, womanpower. These workers, unlike the earlier immigrants, were largely unskilled and therefore worked primarily at the more simple stages in the industry, so that a shortage of skilled operators, especially in sewing, developed.

7. Concomitant with the pull to lower-wage areas, production is being pushed out by scarcity of manufacturing loft space. The growth of section work has made the normal 2,000 to 4,000 square feet per establishment far too cramped a space. Suitable space is not available even at the high rents that prevail in New York; annual rentals are $5,000 more than in New Jersey and almost $7,000 more than in Pennsylvania.

8. Fast transportation by truck now

links the low-wage, low-rent areas with Manhattan. As new highways are constructed and air freight is increasingly used, the distance between the jobbers and the contractors can be feasibly lengthened.

9. Favorable "tax climates" (particularly in Puerto Rico) and inducements such as free buildings and special financial aid (especially in the American South) have also lured production elsewhere.

10. When durable goods are plentiful and per-capita income increases, expenditure for clothing tends to decrease. This decrease has been evident since the early 1950s; in particular there has been a decline in the purchase of formal wear. Clothes as a symbol of status have given way to washers, television sets, cars, and other durable goods.

As early as 1860, Boston ranked second to New York, but it presently is surpassed also by Philadelphia, Chicago, Baltimore, Rochester, Cleveland, and Cincinnati. All these cities specialize in men's clothing, but only Rochester is noted for high-quality men's suits, overcoats, and topcoats.

St. Louis is a center for "junior-miss" clothes and half-size dresses; here the garment industry coordinates its design rooms with the art schools and colleges of the city. Kansas City is noted for its production-line methods, and Milwaukee and Minneapolis have made significant strides in the ready-to-wear field. Dallas and Phoenix have gained prominence as producers of moderately priced sports apparel. Miami specializes in garments that cater to the special markets created by local seasonal patterns that differ from New York's.

New York's greatest competitors are Los Angeles, Hollywood, and, to a lesser extent, San Francisco; they pose a growing threat to New York's dominance, particularly in the sportswear line. Although factory manufacturing dates back to the 1850s, California has enjoyed a meteoric rise in the garment industry only in the past few decades. The emphasis of the California garment industry is a direct response to the California way of life. The products of Los Angeles manufacturers cover nearly the whole field of apparel; sportswear and bathing suits, the dominant lines, are sold throughout the nation and abroad. Hollywood, where some of the leading motion-picture designers operate shops, has become a fashion center of considerable prominence. The magic label "Made in Hollywood," complemented by the mystique of California, has assured the state a permanent place on the apparel map of the world.

EUROPEAN GARMENT CENTERS

Europe's larger cities have thriving clothing industries. However, because of the large supply of cheap and efficient labor, there is far less emphasis on machine-made garments.

Paris has long been, and in most opinions remains, the world's fashion capital; it is a French tradition that "frivolity taken seriously, can be an art." Although Paris still holds the title of fashion's mecca, the city's apparel industry is undergoing a pronounced change. The exclusive shop is slowly giving way. Producers of mass merchandise, who also flock to other European fashion centers, visit the fashion houses to buy outright and to acquire possession of a pattern for a few months, during which time they reproduce it. The fees for this right are a large source of income for the fashion houses. In addition to legitimate, cheap reproduction of expensive patterns, there is style pirating, which is estimated to cost the French fashion industry between $10 and $12 million annually. Mass production, whether legal or illegal, may peril the French industry, which is based on the production of luxurious apparel for the extravagant few. Paris's preeminence is further threatened by the rise of Italian fashion centers.

ECONOMIC OUTLOOK FOR TEXTILE AND GARMENT INDUSTRIES

Paris is said to remain the world's only authoritative source for fashion inspiration, but New York City has unequivocally become the world's fashion distribution center. American designers have demonstrated their own fashion talents and have shown a remarkable ability to adapt Parisian, Italian, or other continental styles to the needs of the huge American market. America's, and particularly New York's, claim to fame is due to its rapid production techniques, which can duplicate thousands of quality units in a season, an operation that cannot be matched anywhere on the globe.

In a world with ever more insistent demands for higher living standards and with a rising population, the garment industry promises to assume an even greater role. At this time, only the American method of production can assure an abundance. With intensified attention directed at the arts of fabric design and garment manufacture, the United States may in time become the unchallenged leader in all phases of the industry.

The location of textile and garment industries has been affected more by technological, political, and agglomeration effects in the long run. In the short run, however, the industry's location has shown marked response to demand, income, and labor factors. Due to a favorable weight-loss ratio, transportation costs do not exert an influence over the location comparable to that of metals and metal fabricating industries. A similar role for transportation cost occurs in chemical and electrical industries, discussed in the following two chapters.

references

1. Alexander, Lewis M. *The Northeastern United States.* Princeton, N.J.: D. Van Nostrand Co., 1967.

2. Alexandersson, Gunnar. *Geography of Manufacturing.* Englewood Cliffs, N.J.: Prentice-Hall, 1967.

3. Dewdney, John C. *A Geography of the Soviet Union.* 2nd ed. Oxford: Pergamon Press, 1971.

4. Dohrs, Fred E., and Sommers, Lawrence M. *Economic Geography: Selected Readings.* New York: Thomas Y. Crowell, 1970.

5. Dury, G. H. *The British Isles.* 5th ed. London: Heinemann Education Books, 1973.

6. Dutt, Ashkok K., ed. *India: Resources, Potentialities, and Planning.* Iowa: Kendall Hunt Publishing Co., 1972.

7. Estall, Robert. *A Modern Geography of the United States.* Chicago: Quadrangle Books, 1972.

8. Hopkins, A. G. *An Economic History of West Africa.* New York: Columbia University Press, 1973.

9. Hunker, Henry L. *Industrial Development.* Lexington, Mass.: D.C. Heath and Co., 1974.

10. Jordan, Terry G. *The European Culture Area: A Systematic Geography.* New York: Harper & Row, 1973.

11. Kish, George. *Economic Atlas of the Soviet Union.* 2nd ed. Ann Arbor: University of Michigan Press, 1971.

12. Malmstrom, Vincent H. *Geography of Europe: A Regional Analysis.* Englewood Cliffs, N.J.: Prentice-Hall, 1971.

13. Miller, E. Willard. *A Geography of Industrial Location.* Dubuque, Iowa: Wm. C. Brown., 1970.

14. Parker, W. H. *The Soviet Union.* Chicago: Aldine Publishing Co., 1970.

15. Paterson, J. H. *Land, Work, and Re-*

325

sources: *An Introduction to Economic Geography.* London: Edward Arnold, 1972.

16. Paterson, J. H. *North America: A Geography of the United States and Canada.* 5th ed. Oxford: University Press, 1975.

17. Shabad, Theodore. *China's Changing Map: National and Regional Development, 1949--1971.* 2nd ed. New York: Frederick A. Praeger, 1972.

18. Sinha, B. H. *Industrial Geography of India.* Calcutta: World Press, 1972.

19. Stanback, Thomas M., and Knight, Richard V., *The Metropolitan Economy: The Process of Employment Expansion.* New York: Columbia University Press, 1970.

20. Wise, M. J.; Rawstron, E. M.; and Buchanan, R. D. *Economic Geography.* London: G. Bell & Sons Ltd., 1973.

21. White, C. L.; Foscue, E. J.; and Knight, T. *Regional Geography of Anglo-America.* 4th ed. Englewood Cliffs, N.J.: Prentice-Hall, 1974.

chemical
industries

17

17

The rapid expansion of the chemical industries during the last half-century represents an economic revolution the effects of which are as great as those of the mechanical revolution of the late 18th and early 19th centuries: The far-reaching nature of these effects is indicated by the fact that it is almost impossible to draw a clear-cut distinction between chemical and nonchemical industries; there are few important industries in which chemical changes do not take place at some stage of production.

Because chemical products affect almost every phase of modern life, they are essential to all industrially advanced nations. The more industrialized the nation, the more important is the role of chemical products. In the United States, for example, the chemical industries rank fourth in the economy, after petroleum refining, primary metal making, and manufacture of transportation equipment.

During the early part of this century, world chemical production grew at a very modest rate, reaching an estimated value of $10,000 million in the late 1930s. Production reached $50,000 million by 1955, and today it exceeds $100,000 million. Eight countries—the United States, the USSR, West Germany, the United Kingdom, France, Italy, Japan, and Canada—account for three-fourths of total world production. In 1950, the U.S. produced about 50 percent of the world's output, but the resurgence of the chemical industry in Europe and Japan has reduced this dominance to slightly less than 40 percent today. Among the major chemical-producing countries, Japan is expected to undergo the greatest growth in the next decade (see Figure 17–1).

LOCATION FACTORS

General considerations for location involve proximity to raw-material sources and markets, the intervening forces of freight costs, agglomeration effects, and the following specific site conditions:

1. Acreage: seldom less than 500 acres for a sizable plant
2. Terrain: the site must not be vulnerable to floods
3. Environmental considerations
4. Proximity to a community: outside corporate limits, but not more than 10 miles from a community
5. Ample water of good quality and low in chlorides
6. Disposal of waste: a major problem for most plants in this industry
7. Access to transportation: on a paved highway and on a main line or a spur of a railway not more than 1 mile from main line
8. Ample electrical-power supply at all times with a constant voltage level and frequency regulation

Energy at reasonable cost, too, is highly advantageous. Additional conditions frequently affect the chemical industry's site selection, such as climate, presence of skilled labor, and amenity factors for plant employees.

Since many of the products of the chemical industries are the raw materials for other industries, nations with a highly developed industrial system offer a powerful attraction in the form of a large market. Industries that are consumers of the chemical industry's products are near at hand in countries such as the United States, the Soviet Union, West Germany, the United Kingdom, France, Italy, and Japan. A large market, therefore, combines with abundant capital and a trained labor force to make these

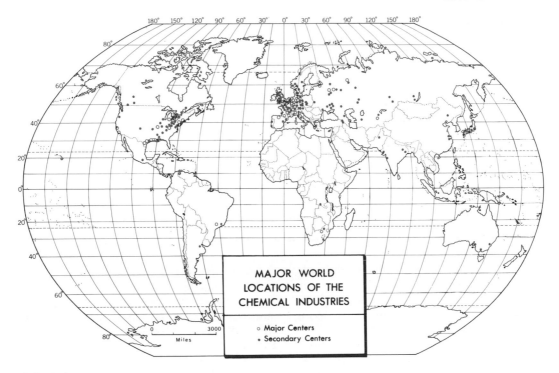

FIGURE 17–1

nations outstanding producers of chemical products.

INDUSTRIAL CHEMICALS

Industrial chemicals, or "heavy chemicals," as they are more commonly called, make up a large and varied list of bulky products that are cheap per unit of weight. They include sulfuric acid, soda ash, caustic soda, chlorine, ammonia, nitric acid, and many others. The value added by manufacture is small, since the processing involves relatively simple procedures, chiefly moving, grinding, mixing, and separating huge amounts of solids, liquids, and gases. In some instances, a loss in weight occurs in manufacture; hence, plants making heavy chemicals tend to locate near the raw materials.

SULFURIC ACID

Sulfuric acid is the most vital of all industrial chemicals. A shortage puts an immediate brake on manufacturing generally, since this acid is used throughout the whole range of modern industry. Included in its long list of users are the drug and dye, leather-processing, oil-refining, paint, rayon, and fertilizer industries; it is even used to pickle steel. About 27 million metric tons of sulfuric acid are produced per annum in the United States, about 14 million in the Soviet Union, and about 7 million in Japan. On a worldwide basis, possibly one-fourth enters the fertilizer industry; one-fifth, petroleum refining; one-fifth, chemical making; and slightly more than one-third, all other industries (see Table 17–1).

329

TABLE 17–1 Sulfuric Acid Production in the World and Selected Leading Countries (in metric tons)

	1963	1972	PERCENT CHANGE
United States	18,993	26,691	+40.53%
USSR	6,885	13,685	+98.76
Japan	4,991	6,714	+34.52
West Germany	3,316	4,735	+42.79
France	2,394	4,114	+71.85
United Kingdom	2,927	3,449	+17.83
Italy	2,711	3,033	+11.88
World	56,730	93,300	+64.46%

Source: Based on the *United Nations Statistical Yearbook, 1973* (New York: United Nations, 1974), pp. 264–65.

The United States.   In the United States, the world's largest producer, most sulfuric acid is made from native sulfur, or brimstone, dissolved from beds along the Gulf Coast. To a lesser extent it is made from pyrites, and it is also obtained as a by-product of zinc and copper smelting. Ducktown, Tennessee, and Anaconda, Montana, are among the largest U.S. sulfur-producing centers.

About one-fourth of the American output normally is used by fertilizer factories; half is consumed in petroleum refining, steel pickling, rubber manufacturing, textile processing, and making explosives; the remaining fourth goes into the manufacture of coal products, pigment and paints, refining of various metals, preparation of chemicals, and making miscellaneous chemical products.

USSR. In Russia the sulfuric-acid industry depends upon flotation residues of copper pyrite and upon sulfurous gases in nonferrous metallurgy. The acid is made chiefly in the Urals.

Japan.   Prior to the Second World War, Japan ranked second to the United States in sulfuric-acid production. The acid was made from iron pyrites and from native volcanic sulfur and also was produced as a by-product of copper smelting. Most sulfuric-acid plants are concentrated in the Tokyo–Yokohama and Osaka districts.

During World War II, much sulfuric acid was diverted into the munitions industries. Normally, however, the bulk of the sulfuric acid is used to manufacture fertilizer, and the lesser amounts are destined for paints, textiles, and minor chemical industries.

SODA ASH

Soda ash is the most important of the alkalies, and it is also the cheapest. It is used in large tonnages to make paper, soaps, and glass; to manufacture other chemicals; and to refine petroleum. Soda ash is almost as important to chemical industries as sulfuric acid.

The two raw materials for soda ash are common salt, which supplies the sodium, and limestone, which supplies the carbonate. Coal and coke provide the fuel to manufacture the soda ash.

The industry tends to locate near deposits of salt and limestone. Outstanding locales in the United States for

TABLE 17–2   Soda Ash Production in the World and Selected Leading Countries (in metric tons)

	1963	1972	PERCENT CHANGE
U.S.	4,205	3,792	− 9.82%
USSR	2,417	3,850	+ 59.29
France	927	1,427	+ 53.93
W.Germany	1,055	1,395	+ 32.23
Japan	641	1,300	+102.80
East Germany	653	721	+ 10.41
Italy	623	664	+ 6.58
Poland	532	709	+ 33.27
Romania	327	665	+103.36
World	12,940	17,470	+ 35.01%

Source: Based on the *United Nations Statistical Yearbook, 1973* (New York: United Nations, 1974), p. 269.

manufacture are Detroit; Syracuse; Ohio's Lake Erie shore, particularly Painesville; Baton Rouge and Lake Charles, Louisiana; Saltville, Virginia; and "Chemical Valley," West Virginia, a 60-mile stretch along the Kanawha Valley from Gauley Bridge on the east to Nitro on the west. Although the United States is by far the largest producer, the Soviet Union, France, West Germany, and Japan also have substantial production (see Table 17–2).

CAUSTIC SODA

Caustic soda (sodium hydroxide) is more commonly known as lye. It is employed in soap and paper making, in oil purification, in treatment of textiles, and in refining petroleum.

The manufacture of caustic soda, commonly associated with the salt industry, tends to be raw-material oriented, but at the same time stresses proximity to its markets as much as possible. Because of keen competition, a plant on navigable water is a distinct location advantage. Plants are widely scattered.

The United States is far and away the world's largest producer, but Japan, the Soviet Union, West Germany, France, Canada, and Italy have impressive outputs (see Table 17–3). Manufacture in the United States is oriented toward raw materials and cheap water transportation. The salt deposits of Louisiana and the Intracoastal Waterway and the Mississippi River satisfy these industry requirements for location.

AMMONIA

Ammonia is one of man's most used chemicals. Like sulfuric acid, it finds a large market in the fertilizer industry. Ammonia is made by combining enormous quantities of atmospheric nitrogen with hydrogen. Much of it is converted into ammonium sulfate, the most widely used nitrogenous fertilizer. Ammonia is also the first ingredient of most military explosives.

Among leading centers in the United States are Hopewell, Virginia; "Chemical Valley," West Virginia; Yazoo City, Mississippi; and Pittsburg, California. In Europe, very large operations are at Oppau and Merseburg in Germany

331

TABLE 17–3 Caustic Soda Production in the World and Selected Leading Countries (in metric tons)

	1963	1972	PERCENT CHANGE
U.S.	5,275	9,311	+ 76.51%
Japan	1,082	2,900	+168.02
USSR	965	1,899	+ 96.78
W.Germany	1,047	1,935	+ 84.81
France	642	1,240	+ 93.14
Canada	440	921	+109.32
Italy	549	1,078	+ 96.35
World	12,280	23,430	+ 90.80%

Source: Based on the *United Nations Statistical Yearbook, 1973* (New York: United Nations, 1974), p. 268.

and at Billingham in England. All industrial nations have large synthetic-ammonia enterprises.

NITRIC ACID

The basic ingredient of nitric acid is the element nitrogen, which constitutes about four-fifths, by volume, of the earth's atmosphere. Its major use is in the manufacture of super-phosphate fertilizer, dyes, drugs, and explosives. It is a vital ingredient for making every type of modern explosive. In some areas—e.g., the United Kingdom, where it is more readily available—it replaces sulfuric acid in converting rock phosphate into phosphate fertilizer.

The United States is the world's largest producer and consumer of nitric acid. Other important producers are West Germany, France, Poland, Italy, and Belgium (see Table 17–4).

CHLORINE

Chlorine gas, a by-product of caustic soda manufacture, is made mainly from

TABLE 17–4 Nitric Acid Production in the World and Selected Leading Countries (in metric tons)

	1963	1972	PERCENT CHANGE
U.S.	3,849	6,370	+ 65.50%
W.Germany	2,281	3,062	+ 34.24
France	1,753	3,019	+ 72.22
Poland	750	1,515	+102.00
Italy	894	1,002	+ 12.08
Belgium	511*	857	67.71
Hungary	191	691	+261.78
Bulgaria	237	672	+183.54
World	11,820	21,880	+ 85.11%

* 1964
Source: Based on the *United Nations Statistical Yearbook, 1973* (New York: United Nations, 1974), p. 267.

electrolysis of salt. Its original use as a raw material was for making bleaching powder, but today it has many applications: as an ingredient in detergent, dye, explosives, and plastics manufacture; as a disinfectant; as a refrigerant; and as a water purifier.

Plants producing chlorine are essentially raw-material oriented, located near deposits of underground salt. Location on navigable water is economically advantageous. One of the world's best locations for the industry is the area of salt deposits in Louisiana where there is raw material, fuel, and access to markets via the Atlantic Intracoastal Waterway, the Mississippi–Ohio–Missouri–Illinois Rivers, and the Panama Canal to the Pacific Coast.

PLASTICS

Plastics, actually invented about a hundred years ago, are regarded as comparatively new chemical products, possibly because their development began to skyrocket in the 1920s, when the infant but fast-growing radio industry provided a market for many new plastic products.

Presently plastics are used in almost all world economies, and they exceed most of the nonferrous and light metals (even aluminum) in annual tonnage.

This widespread use has generated a global trade of substantial volume. Plastics may be substituted for glass, wood, fibers, and even metals. The substitution of plastics for metals ultimately should prove particularly important, since most plastics are made either from very abundant or inexhaustible substances, such as protein from milk, soybeans, and dried blood; phenol compounds; lime; coal; and cellulose.

The United States leads in world production, producing annually about 25 percent, followed by Japan, West Germany, the USSR, Italy, France, the United Kingdom and the Netherlands (see Table 17–5).

In the United States the greater part of the plastics industry is located in the American Manufacturing Region, particularly in the Chicago area, in New England, New York, New Jersey, and eastern Pennsylvania. The South, too, is of growing importance, as are parts of the West, especially southern California,

---

TABLE 17–5 Plastic and Resin Production in the World and Selected Leading Countries (in metric tons)

	1963	1972	PERCENT CHANGE
U.S.	4,068	8,894	+118.63%
Japan	1,069	5,573	+421.33
W.Germany	1,434	5,289	+268.83
USSR	567	2,042	+260.14
Italy	661	1,938	+193.19
France	508	2,100	+313.38
United Kingdom	756	1,608	+112.69
Netherlands	193	1,526	+690.67
World	10,560	34,300	+224.81%

Source: Based on the *United Nations Statistical Yearbook, 1973* (New York: United Nations, 1974), p. 272.

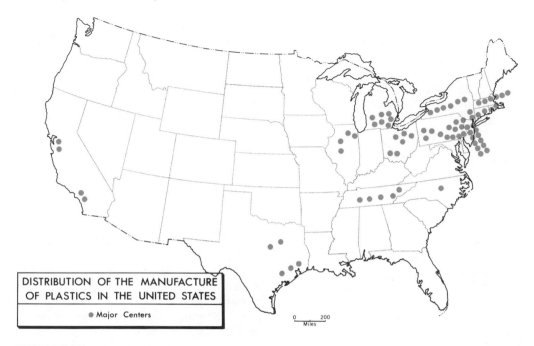

DISTRIBUTION OF THE MANUFACTURE
OF PLASTICS IN THE UNITED STATES

● Major Centers

0   200
Miles

FIGURE 17–2

the San Francisco Bay area, and Seattle. The industry is disseminated into small units everywhere. (Figure 17–2).

ORGANIC DYES

In 1856, W. H. Perkin of London succeeded in producing a purple dye from a coal-tar derivative known as aniline, thereby founding the coal-tar dye industry. Such dyes are used almost exclusively today. Although England made the initial discovery and was the first to make use of the dye industrially, Germany dominated the industry for more than a half a century. Among the leading German centers are Leverkusen, Ludwigshafen, Leuna, and Hannover.

The United States dyestuffs industry, now the world's largest, dates primarily from World War I, when the government seized and held in custody some 4,500 German dye patents. American chemical manufacturers hastily assembled the best chemists available and ultimately succeeded in building an enviable dyestuffs industry. This segment of the chemical industry, located chiefly in response to raw materials, markets, and labor, is found in the east-central portion of the American Manufacturing Region.

England, France, Italy, and Japan today support dye industries that produce more than nine-tenths of their domestic consumption.

EXPLOSIVES

Explosives serve humanity for both war and peace. Most important are the amatols, which are mixtures of ammonium nitrate and trinitrotoluene, or TNT. Many of the world's outstanding feats of civil engineering, such as the Khyber Railway, the Simplon Tunnel, and the St. Lawrence Seaway, would have

334

been impossible without blasting explosives. Mining is greatly simplified by use of blasting explosives.

In the United States the Middle Atlantic seaboard leads in production of explosives, with more than half the annual national output. The Delaware River area, particularly the Wilmington district, is foremost; the Newark Bay area also is outstanding. Here coastal marshes, extensive swamps, pine barrens, and other wastelands are used because the manufacture of explosives is dangerous, and these areas are isolated from populous urban-industrial communities.

AGRICULTURAL CHEMICALS

Agricultural chemicals include a wide array of products that perform many functions, although they are used primarily to enrich the soil and to increase the per-acre yield of crops, and to control insect pests and diseases. Examples of agricultural chemicals are insecticides, fungicides, fumigants, plant-growth regulators, weed killers, and fertilizers.

FERTILIZERS

Few industries are so vital to humanity as those manufacturing agricultural fertilizers. With the world's population doubling every forty years, frantic efforts are being made to maintain and to increase the world's food supply. In Japan, the United States, the Netherlands, West Germany, and several other countries, agricultural output has been skyrocketing as a result of increasing use of chemical fertilizers. Japan is reputed to use more commercial fertilizer than any nation—200 pounds per cultivated acre, contrasted with 1 pound per acre in India. Japan produces a per-acre yield of rice four times that of India.

Nitrogen Fertilizers. World production of nitrogen fertilizer is 38 million tons per year, although this is still not sufficient to meet the world's needs. The United States leads the world in the production of nitrogenous fertilizers, followed by the USSR, Japan, the People's Republic of China, West Germany, the Netherlands, India, and Italy (see Table 17–6).

TABLE 17–6 Nitrogenous Fertilizers Production in Terms of Nitrogen in the World and Selected Leading Countries (in metric tons)

	1965–1966	1972–1973	PERCENT CHANGE
U.S.	5,081	8,472	+ 66.74%
USSR	2,712	6,551	+141.56
Japan	1,615	2,454	+ 51.95
China	827	2,445	+195.64
West Germany	1,419	1,471	+ 3.66
Netherlands	562	1,205	+114.41
Poland	395	1,147	+190.37
India	238	1,051	+341.59
Italy	905	1,046	+ 15.58
World	20,000	38,000	+ 90.00%

Source: Based on the *United Nations Statistical Yearbook, 1973* (New York: United Nations, 1974), pp. 270–71.

Phosphate Fertilizers. Most phosphate fertilizers are obtained from phosphate rock, an exception being the by-product slags of iron and steel mills. Other sources of phosphorus are barnyard manure and guano. Based on tonnage produced, phosphate rock is the dominant mineral-fertilizer product. The reserves of phosphate rock in the world are enormous—about 17 billion tons—but they are restricted to relatively few regions. The United States, North Africa, China, and the Soviet Union are credited with most of the reserves, smaller ones being found in Peru, Egypt, Spain, and the Pacific island of Nauru (*see* Figure 17–3).

The cost of mining phosphate rock is, on the average, low; but cost rises as the distance to the point of use increases.

Potash Fertilizers. Potash fertilizers are obtained from a number of soluble salts in which potassium is present. Since potassium is so highly soluble, soils in humid lands, called *pedalfers,* are usually deficient in potassium.

Until relatively recently, the principal sources of potash were wood ashes and burned kelp. Later, other sources, dust from blast furnaces and cement mills; certain minerals, such as alunite; and the brine of desert lakes, were developed. Major dependence now, however, is on potash deposits, which are known to be present and exploited in only a few countries—chiefly the United States, Canada, East and West Germany, France, Spain, and the Soviet Union (*see* Figure 17–3). Total world proved reserves are placed at 41 billion tons, an amount that

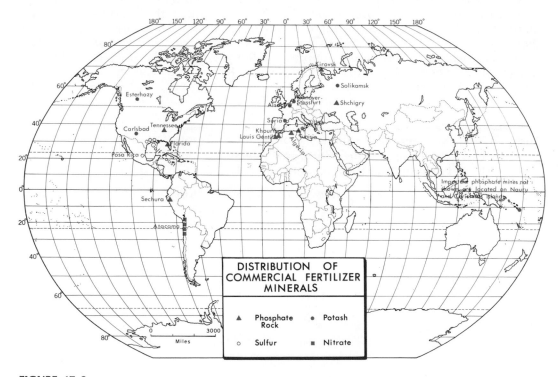

FIGURE 17–3

should last approximately 5,000 years. Three countries—Canada, Germany, and the Soviet Union—possess most of the world's potash resources.

The United States is third among all nations in potash production, but it possesses only about 1 percent of world reserves. Ninety percent of production comes from one area, the Carlsbad region of New Mexico. Recovery is by the room-and-pillar method, from mines about 1,000 feet deep.

The only other important potash-producing area is Searles Lake in southeastern California, which supplies about 7 percent of the domestic output. Here potash salts are extracted from brine in a crystalline salt mass. Unfortunately, both U.S. sources lie far from the principal domestic fertilizer markets, and transportation by rail is expensive.

PETROLEUM-BASED CHEMICALS

As chemical industries have grown over the years, the demand for basic raw materials has exceeded what can be produced readily from coal and coking operations. Accordingly, the industry has turned to petroleum as a source and has attracted petroleum companies into what has been called the petrochemical industry. In all industrial areas of the world, chemical raw materials based on petroleum and natural gas generally have exceeded the growth rate for the chemical industry as a whole.

Recently, the petroleum-based chemical industries have shown a very high growth rate in the world economy. It is a dynamic industry, which supplies intermediate products for a number of other industries and provides substitutes for traditional materials, such as steel, lumber, paper, natural fibers, and soap.

Of the approximately 1,000 petroleum-based chemical plants, more than 50 percent are located in the United States and Canada; over 200 are in Western Europe, about 50 in Japan, and the rest are distributed throughout the world. New plants being planned are spread more evenly among the United States, Western Europe, Japan, and developing areas.

General characteristics relating to industry location include:

1. Product homogenetity and standardization
2. Process continuity and stability
3. High capital intensity
4. High proportion of skilled labor, including technicians and scientists
5. Availability of alternative production processes and raw materials
6. Rapid rate of technological change

United States. About 80 percent of the petrochemical capacity in the United States is in the South, particularly along the Gulf Coast in a 700-mile strip between New Orleans on the east and Brownsville on the southwest and reaching inland for about 100 miles. This represents the most concentrated distribution of this industry in the world. The industry is particularly centered in eight cities of the major region: New Orleans, Baton Rouge, Lake Charles, Port Arthur–Beaumont, Houston, Freeport, Corpus Christi, and Brownsville. Major activity, however, is in the Houston and Port Arthur nodes; the Houston complex alone accounts for 20 to 30 percent of the total capacity.

The Gulf Coast has certain unique advantages for the manufacture of petrochemicals:

1. It possesses 60 to 75 percent of the nation's petroleum reserves and more than 36 percent of its refining capacity.
2. It has a bountiful supply of natural gas, natural-gas liquids, and refinery gases for raw materials and low-cost fuel.

337

3. It has plenty of fresh water for industrial processes.

4. It can call upon a reservoir of trained manpower, including skilled labor, engineers and scientists. (Labor costs comprise a relatively small percentage of the manufacturing costs in this industry, however.)

5. It benefits from a complex system of gas pipelines.

6. It has the advantage of water transport to eastern markets and to export markets.

7. It can dispose of chemical wastes in the Gulf of Mexico beyond a 3-mile limit.

8. It lies close to and enjoys cheap transport costs for many raw materials, such as sulfur, salt, and lime (made from oyster shells).

The Midwest ranks second in petrochemical production, the states of Ohio, Michigan, Indiana, Illinois, and Kentucky accounting for about 16 percent of the operating plants and 8 percent of those under construction.

West Virginia, particularly in "Chemical Valley," is highly favored for petrochemical manufacture and promises to become a particularly formidable competitor to all other areas. It possesses coal, natural gas, petroleum, salt, water, and hydropower. Transport is well developed.

The petrochemical industry on the Pacific Coast, particularly in California, is growing because of an important regional market; however, it currently purchases much crude oil and natural gas from the Southwest, Canada, and abroad. The state is too far distant to compete favorably in eastern markets. The Northeast is important, with about 20 percent of the operating plants. Its big disadvantage is high raw-material costs; its big advantage is proximity to a substantial market.

Europe. Two factors distinguish petrochemical operations in Europe and many other countries from American petro-chemical production. First, in the absence of natural gas, petrochemicals have to be made from imported liquid hydrocarbon fractions. Second, compared with America, many of the European countries are geared to the use of aromatic compounds as by-products from coal processes, and the relative price structure of coal does not make manufacture of aromatics from imported oil attractive.

Late in the 1950s, with the great increase in oil refining in Europe, the petrochemical industry started and has since been one of the fastest growing of all the continent's manufacturing enterprises. The creation of the Common Market (the Six) and the Free Trade Association (the Outer Seven) stimulated production, since these organizations created a continental market, displacing the small regional markets.

Complete economic unification is still in the future, but Western Europe already has up to 472 million consumers —nearly 262 million more than the United States. As a market for chemicals, Europe is worth about $45 billion, only 10 percent less than that of the United States. Its share of world chemical production now is over 30 percent. And at some point in the late 1970s, Europe is expected to surpass the United States in chemical output, which will make Europe the largest chemical production center in the world.

SYNTHETIC RUBBER

Synthetic rubbers are petroleum-based, and their growth has paralleled the growth of basic organic chemicals from petroleum. The synthetic rubber industry began in the 1940s when natural rubber supplies were curtailed as a result of the war. The industry received its greatest impetus in the United States. By 1953, synthetic rubber accounted for nearly three-fourths of total world production of rubber.

Natural rubber was the sole general-purpose elastic material before World War II. General-purpose synthetic rubbers were developed because of the wartime situation, first by Germany and the USSR, and later by the United States. The general-purpose synthetic rubbers were improved over the years and are competitive with natural rubber for many uses. Advantages of the use of synthetic rubbers include custom-tailored materials, better uniformity, technical assistance from producers, and corporate readiness to acquire captive production.

The United States is by far the largest producer and consumer of synthetic rubber, accounting for more than three-fourths of the production in noncommunist countries (see Table 17–7). Since synthetic rubber is based almost exclusively on petroleum, synthetic-rubber plants locate close to petroleum sources. During World War II, the Gulf Coast, with its rich oil resources from Baton Rouge to Houston, was chosen for the location of the major portion of government-financed plants (see Figure 17–4). This area's salient advantages are the presence of: refining gases, which yield butylems and other chemicals; petroleum, from which benzol and ethylene are extracted; natural gas, major source of the carbon black used to reinforce

rubber; sulfur for vulcanizing; and salt, lime, and clays, which have important uses in rubber synthesis.

Butadiene from oil companies and styrene from chemical companies are the major feedstocks of Buna-S rubber. Because it is uneconomical to ship butadiene great distances and because it is employed almost exclusively for making synthetic rubber, the feedstock plants usually form a part of the local industrial complex, consisting of a petroleum refinery, a butadiene plant, and a rubber-producing plant. The flow of materials is usually via pipeline. The styrene, used in smaller quantities than butadiene, is shipped to rubber-producing plants by tank car. The sixteen plants that make synthetic rubber in the Gulf Coast region are on or close to the Gulf and are located with respect to local oil refineries. The only Texas plant not located on water is at Borger in the Panhandle.

Latex rubber must be made close to its market because the high water content, by increasing weight, discourages shipment to distant markets. This product is manufactured close to its local markets in the Midwest, the Northeast, and West Coast. Los Angeles, center of the West Coast synthetic-rubber industry, makes latex and dry rubber, as well as styrene and butadiene.

TABLE 17–7 Synthetic Rubber Production for Selected Leading Countries (in metric tons)

	1963	1972	PERCENT CHANGE
U.S.	1,634	2,455	+ 50.24%
Japan	103	819	+695.15
France	99	368	+271.71
United Kingdom	127	307	+141.73
W.Germany	112	300	+167.86
Italy	96	200	+108.33
Canada	182	196	+ 7.69
Netherlands	85	186	+118.82

Source: Based on the *United Nations Statistical Yearbook, 1973* (New York: United Nations, 1974), p. 258.

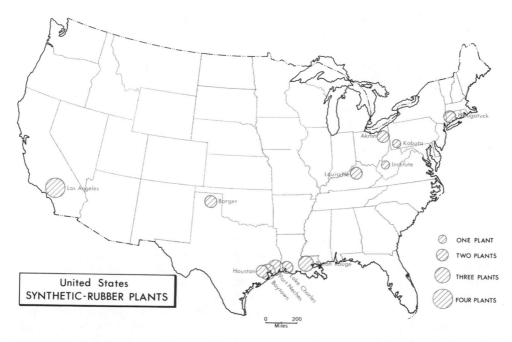

United States
SYNTHETIC-RUBBER PLANTS

ONE PLANT
TWO PLANTS
THREE PLANTS
FOUR PLANTS

FIGURE 17–4

Most synthetic rubber produced in the U.S. is made by divisions or subsidiaries of the major rubber-product manufacturers. The remaining production is divided among oil and chemical companies. As a result, an estimated two-thirds of general-purpose synthetic rubbers is marketed as interplant transfers or as sales to affiliated or constituent companies.

In 1957 Canada ranked second in production of synthetic rubber among all nations but fell to seventh place in 1970. More and more synthetic rubber is being manufactured in Europe, primarily in Great Britain, France, Italy, West Germany. The Soviet Union and Czechoslovakia are greatly increasing their output and consumption. As yet Western Europe manufactures little compared with the U.S., but as a result of the growing role of imported petroleum in the economic life of these nations, the synthetic-rubber industry is growing rapidly.

Appreciable increases in volume were recorded by France, the United Kingdom, and West Germany in the early 1960s; and in Asia, Japan's increase reached 94 percent.

ECONOMIC OUTLOOK FOR CHEMICAL INDUSTRIES

Few industries have the growth potential of the chemical industries, mainly because of the infinite variety of consumer goods to which they contribute. This industry is linked to almost all others and accordingly is sensitive to changes both in its own sphere and in the entire realm of manufacturing.

Two major trends are currently apparent:

1. Many American companies are establishing branches abroad, in developed countries and in less developed ones all over the world. This results largely from the economic revolution now under way, whereby nations as fully qualified as the United States are pitted against one another for the same markets. The quality of their products is often as high as the quality of U.S. products, and their costs are lower.

2. A rising percentage of chemical products sold in the United States bears an import label. In a recent year, United States production of some chemical products declined 14 percent, while imports rose 87 percent.

A democratic economy, with its profit motive, cannot compete with socialist economies, or even with other democratic economies. The United States experiences increasing difficulty competing with the noncommunist nations of Western Europe and in Asia, where wages are considerably lower. Wages, of course, are only one element in the cost of production, but a wide wage differential makes their influence difficult to nullify if all other factors are equal. Until a few years ago, U.S. companies could overcome the low-wage differential with better equipment and production techniques, but this no longer is true. United States exports have not been rising sufficiently fast to offset the rise in imports, creating an imbalance of trade.

The trend in plant sites for many chemicals shows a change from almost exclusive raw-material orientation to a high degree of market orientation, although some plants are still raw-material oriented.

references

1. Alexandersson, Gunnar. *Geography of Manufacturing.* Englewood Cliffs, N.J.: Prentice-Hall, 1967.

2. Bernarde, Melvin A. *Our Precarious Habitat.* New York: W. W. Norton and Co., 1970.

3. Cole, John P., and German, F. C. *A Geography of the U.S.S.R.* 2nd ed. Totowa, N.J.: Rowman & Littlefield, 1971.

4. Dienes, Leslie. *Locational Factors and Locational Development in the Soviet Chemical Industry.* Chicago: The University of Chicago Department of Geography Research, Paper No. 119, 1969.

5. Downs, Ray. *Japan: Yesterday and Today.* New York: Bantam Books, 1970.

6. Elfrod, Jean, and Phelps, Edward. "Oil, Then to Now." *Canadian Geographical Journal* 77 (November 1968): 164–71.

7. Hayden, H. W.; Gibson, R. C.; and Brophy, J. H. "Superplastic Metals." *Scientific American* 220 (March 1969): 28–35.

8. Holdren, John P., and Ehrlich, Paul R., eds. *Global Ecology.* New York: Harcourt, Brace and Jovanovich, 1971.

9. Hunker, Henry L. *Industrial Development.* Lexington, Mass.: D. C. Heath and Co., 1974.

10. Isenberg, Irwin. *Japan: Asian Power.* New York: Wilson Publishing Co., 1971.

11. Jones, Lawrence W. "Liquid Hydrogen as a Fuel for the Future." *Science* 174 (October 1971): 367–78.

12. Lydolph, Paul E. *Geography of the U.S.S.R.* 2nd ed. New York: John Wiley and Sons, 1971.

13. Melamaid, Alexander. "Petroleum Refining and Distribution in Ethiopia." *The Professional Geographer* 20 (November 1968): 388–91.

14. Miller, E. Willard. *A Geography of Industrial Location.* Dubuque, Iowa: William C. Brown Co., 1970.

15. Nicholson, Max. *The Environmental Revolution.* New York: McGraw-Hill Book Co., 1970.

16. Pearse, Charles R. "Athabaska Tar Sands." *Canadian Geographical Journal* 76 (January 1968): 2–9.

17. Roff, William John. *Fibres, Films, Plastics and Rubbers: A Handbook of Common Polymers.* London: Butterworths, 1971.

18. Steed, Guy P. F. "Internal Organization, Firm Integration, and Locational Change: The Northern Ireland Linen Complex, 1954–

1964." *Economic Geography* 47 (July 1971): 371–83.

19. Wagner, Richard H. *Environment and Man*. 2nd ed. New York: W. W. Norton & Co., 1974.

20. Waller, Peter P., and Swain, Harry S. "Changing Patterns of Oil Transportation and Refining in West Germany." *Economic Geography* 43 (April 1967): 143–56.

electrical machinery
and equipment

18

18

The electrical machinery and equipment industry involves a high level of technology, labor skills, and numerous products. The data for this industry's products are not sufficiently standardized at the world level to permit an international comparison. Therefore, this chapter will emphasize aspects and trends of the industry in the United States.

Electrical machinery includes heavy and light electrical machinery and electronic and communications equipment and parts. Heavy electric machinery consists of motors, generators, and circuit apparatus adapted to the special needs of industries, such as electric power, iron and steel, chemical, machine, shipbuilding, and transportation. The most important users of heavy electric machinery are the electric power and iron and steel manufacturers. Light electrical machinery is made up of all types of electrical appliances for homes, such as washing machines; vacuum cleaners; air-conditioning units; small appliances, such as irons; and batteries and electric lamps for home or industrial use. The electronics and communications industry manufactures radio and television sets and parts for home use, electronic computers, and other electronic machines and equipment for telegraph and telephone systems.

The availability of a market is a major factor in the localization of the electrical machinery industry. A manufacturer tends to locate near the largest market because transport costs of raw materials are considerably lower than those of the finished product. Labor costs are high—from 35 to 55 percent of the total cost of producing electrical machinery. Thus a large market is also necessary to provide a reservoir of skilled labor to perform the intricate tasks required by this industry. The advantages of a technologically advanced environment and of the agglomeration effect heavily influence the choice of location.

ELECTRICAL EQUIPMENT

ELECTRIC LOCOMOTIVES

The electrical machinery industry in the United States got its start in New York, Pittsburgh, Boston, and Chicago and expanded to include southern New England, the lower Great Lakes, and southern California.

Heavy electrical machinery for building railway rolling stock in the U.S. is concentrated in Philadelphia, and Pittsburgh, Pennsylvania, and Schenectady, New York, where locomotives are made.

Great Britain, Belgium, and West Germany all rank high in the manufacture of locomotives. Italy, another important manufacturer, has the longest track mileage for electrical railways in Europe.

The USSR ranks first in Europe and second in the world in the number of passenger and freight cars produced. The locomotive plant at Voroshilov and the rail car works at Nizhni Tagil are the largest in the country. The latter, located in the Urals, has attained prominence because of the availability of steel and wood. Among the more important centers in European Russia are Kolomna (south of Moscow), Leningrad, Gorki, Bezhitsa, Bryansk, Sormova, Kharkov, Zhdanov, Poltava, Sverdlorsk, and Tiza. East of the Urals the industry is carried on at Omsk, Tashkent, Barnaul, Chita, Svobodny, Voroshilov, and Ulan Ude. The factories at Ulan Ude are especially important in meeting railway requirements of the Far East.

Japan has attained world stature in the production of railroad rolling stock, including steam, electric, and diesel locomotives, coaches, electric cars, diesel passenger cars, and freight cars. The unit production depends upon domestic and foreign demand and fluctuates from year to year. Tokyo–Yokohama, Osaka, and Kyoto are leading areas producing electrical-machinery.

Switchgear. Major switchgear equipment is customarily installed in major unit substations where transmission lines converge to tie the elements of the grid together and where switching and transformation occur. This equipment is manufactured primarily in the United States and other industrially developed nations.

MOTORS AND GENERATORS

Advances in technology and design of motors and generators have resulted from improved temperature resistance techniques, greater knowledge of thermodynamics, computers that can design motor and generator specifications, and continuing progress in safety. Again, the major producers are the industrialized countries: the U.S., U.K., Japan, Canada, and West Germany.

POWER AND DISTRIBUTION TRANSFORMERS

Demand for transformers of all types is rising at an annual rate of about 8 percent. Demand for specialty transformers, customarily designed for use with signaling apparatus, oil and gas furnaces, fluorescent lights, and other ballast applications, is greatly dependent upon the construction industry.

Although foreign manufacturers maintain a decided advantage over U.S. manufacturers where labor rates are concerned, U.S. economies of large-scale operations, advanced mechanization, and fast delivery have helped American manufacturers to equalize costs.

Canada, Mexico, and Venezuela continue to be the major U.S. customers.

Rather than relying solely on direct export, major United States manufacturers have established foreign subsidiaries in Europe or entered into licensing agreements there. However, attempts of U.S. manufacturers to penetrate Japanese and European utility markets are still unsuccessful. Additionally, in most Third World or developing nations U.S. market penetration is limited. Some foreign suppliers are allegedly selling at 50 to 60 percent below cost, charging only for labor and materials, and subsequently are compensated by some form of government export subsidy or rebate. Only in nations where the U.S. has manufacturing plants or where sales are tied to U.S. funds does the situation improve.

POWER BOILERS AND NUCLEAR REACTORS

Power boilers and nuclear-steam supply systems are used principally by electric-power supply utilities and industries using process steam. The five principal suppliers of nuclear steam systems are mostly also suppliers of fossil-fueled power boilers.

Power boiler and nuclear equipment manufacturers in turn are major customers of the steel forging and fabricated plate industry, rolling and finishing mills, and welding apparatus and accessory suppliers.

The world market for nuclear power plants, equipment, and services is accelerating; nuclear reactors pioneered in the U.S. are now widely accepted as the most economical system for power generation (see Figure 18–1). Of the 19 contracts awarded for nuclear-power reactors outside the U.S. the first half of 1970, 10 were awarded to a U.S. supplier, reflecting the domination of U.S. nuclear reactors in the world market.

Major programs for nuclear projects are in effect or underway in many nations, in developing countries as well as

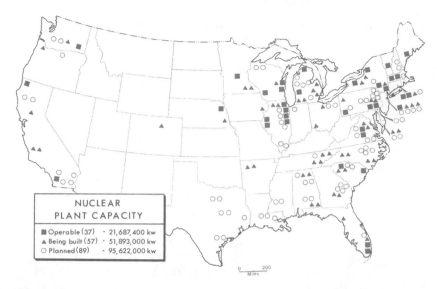

FIGURE 18-1

in industrialized ones. The highly industrialized countries have firm long-range plans that require two to four new nuclear reactors per year up to 10 years. Brazil and Austria acquired their first nuclear plants in 1971. Mexico is bidding for its first, and in 1970 South Korea contracted for its first plant and Taiwan for its second. Argentina recently requested bids for its second nuclear power plant.

France has switched to a U.S. type reactor and the United Kingdom is considering doing the same. Most other industrialized countries started with U.S.-designed nuclear reactors.

West German firms (licensees and former licensees of U.S. nuclear suppliers) are vying strongly for the nuclear equipment market. Japan, Sweden, and other countries are expected to enter the world market as rapidly as possible.

TURBINE GENERATORS

Turbine-generator manufacturing capacity continues to expand rapidly in the United States and abroad. Because of the steadily rising demand for electric energy, manufacturers have invested heavily in recent years in research and development programs to improve mechanical and electrical equipment for power production. The value of overall turbine-generator imports is expected to rise 50 percent by 1980, with imports of gas turbine-generator sets increasing about 12 percent. Manufacturing facilities abroad that are owned by U.S. firms also contribute to rising imports and reduce export markets.

Steam turbine-generator sets come primarily from Switzerland, the United Kingdom, West Germany, and France. Geothermal steam turbine-generators and most hydraulic turbine-generators come from Japan.

AIR CONDITIONING AND COMMERCIAL AND INDUSTRIAL REFRIGERATION

Because a comfortable working area increases productivity and improves workmanship, a high percentage of office building construction now includes air conditioning. Over 75 percent of the

346

dwelling units in the United States are without air conditioning, and in other developed countries of the world, the proportion approaches 95 percent. This low saturation of the potential market and the recent trends in the U.S. (see Figure 18–2) indicate that production shipments in this segment of the industry will continue to rise during the 1970s.

United States commercial and industrial equipment continues to be recognized for its technical superiority. Increasing world requirements, particularly in preservation, processing, and transportation of foods and medicines, will cause shipments of this segment of the industry to continue to rise. The major producers are the United States, Sweden, Japan, Canada, Italy, and West Germany.

More than 50 percent of the ap-proximately 700 establishments in the industry are located in the Middle Atlantic and east north-central states, because of their technological advantages and Weber's agglomeration effects.

ELECTRONICS INDUSTRY

The electronics industry is a relative newcomer to the industrial scene. Although its foundation was laid in 1884 when Thomas A. Edison discovered that a flow of electricity in an electric lamp occurred between the hot luminous filament and a cold electrode, a series of inventions followed that made its success assured. The most important of these were the diode tube, an outgrowth of independent research by the British scientist, John Fleming; and in California in 1906, Lee DeForest invented the "audion," or triode, which put a grid screen between the two primary elements of the diode tube. Other developments soon followed, among them precision magnetic tape recorders, the R-C audio oscillator, and the Klystron tube.

U.S. ELECTRONICS INDUSTRY

This burgeoning industry now ranks fifth in size in the United States with an annual volume of sales of over $20 billion, employing a work force exceeding 2 million people. Because productive capacity continues in excess of current needs and plants are under-utilized, the number of companies producing electronic components continues to decline as mergers and acquisitions take place. Some large companies with diversified production facilities are dropping less profitable component lines. In some cases, companies are leaving the business entirely.

Technological developments now taking place in this industry require ex-

Index 1960 = 100

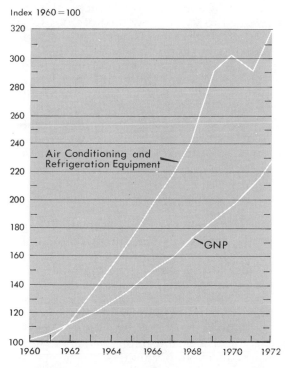

FIGURE 18–2 *Air Conditioning Industry Production, 1960–1972*

tensive research and development. In most cases, it is the larger firms that have this capability. Current research efforts are centered in the solid-state products area, stressing an increasing need for a higher power capability and a continued reduction in size and power requirements. Solid-state microwave power sources utilizing the Gunn effect and the latest developments in the size and color of light-emitting diodes are samples of such technological advances. The search for new products will continue to be the prime mover of this industry.

Imports of electronic components rose more rapidly than anticipated last year, increasing more than 13 percent over 1970 levels. In 1970, 50 percent of all electronic components imported by the United States were entered under Item 807.00 of the Tariff Schedule of the United States. (Item 807.00 allows a U.S. manufacturer to import products assembled from U.S. parts at an offshore plant and to pay duty only on the value of foreign content.)

However, in some individual product areas, this figure was considerably higher. For example, nearly 90 percent of all transistors and 70 percent of all other semiconductors, with a combined value of $72 million, were imported under item 807.00. The U.S. content of these products was $39 million, or 54 percent of the total value. Major sources of components imported under Item 807.00 are Mexico, Hong Kong, and South Korea. These three areas accounted for 31 percent of all such imports in 1970. The electronics industry supplies three general markets: (1) the consumer market that buys radio, television, and high fidelity stereos, which are produced primarily by East Coast manufacturers; (2) the electronics systems and equipment market that purchases radar and myriad control devices for operation of aircraft, missiles, space satellites, artillery, and naval vessels, the

production of which is concentrated in the industrial states of the Northeast and in California and Arizona; and (3) the instrument market that uses business machines, calculators, computers, transistors, and data processors, which are produced largely in the northeastern states, the Greater New York area, and California.

ELECTRONICS EQUIPMENT AND COMPONENTS

The electronics industry is found basically in the U.S., U.K., Japan, West Germany, and other developed nations.

In Taiwan, prospects for new U.S. capital for electronics may be affected by improved U.S.–Peking relations. U.S. electronic producers seeking offshore manufacturing bases will probably be increasingly attracted by other locations, such as Mexico, which has recently been referred to as the new offshore oasis for U.S. electronics firms seeking cost advantages in production and delivery.

Technology and innovations in electronic equipment will continue to show rapid advances. U.S. producers will shift emphasis to all-solid-state circuitry, thus generating a production volume sufficient to bring prices more within the range of present models. (See Table 18–1.)

TELECOMMUNICATIONS

The telecommunications industry is currently undergoing fundamental structural changes. Consumer markets for communication systems are now available to independent equipment suppliers rather than telephone operating companies only. With the advent of new specialized common carriers and regulations regarding the use of the public switched network, many opportunities are available to independent suppliers of PABX systems, intercom systems, multiplexing de-

TABLE 18–1 Value of Shipments of Electronics Equipment and Components (1971–1972) and Projections for 1980 (in millions of dollars)

	1971	PERCENT INCREASE 1970–1971	1972	PERCENT INCREASE 1971–1972	1975	PERCENT INCREASE 1971–1975	1980	PERCENT INCREASE 1971–1980
Consumer products	$ 3,970	7 %	$ 4,100	3%	$ 3,700	−1.7%	$ 3,400	− 1.6%
Phonograph records	505	1	510	1	525	1	600	1.9
Telephone and telegraph equipment	3,528	6	3,740	6	5,000	9.1	8,300	10.
Electronic systems and equipment	8,200	−11	8,600	5	9,600	4	12,000	4.3
Electronic components	6,885	− 4	7,065	3	7,400	1.8	8,500	2.4
Research and development	840	− 8	850	1	900	1.7	955	1.4
Total	$23,930	− 0.4%	$24,865	4%	$30,000	5.8%	$41,500	6.3%

Source: U.S. Department of Commerce, Bureau of Domestic Commerce (Washington, D.C.: U.S. Government Printing Office, 1972), p. 302.

vices, etc. Imports of communications products are increasing, particularly PABX, intercoms, and modems. Domestic producers, particularly the Bell System, are aware of this penetration and are expected to make available in the near future less expensive U.S. equipment, which may eventually supplant these imports.

Telecommunications suppliers may be categorized by major areas of expertise. For example, there are companies that specialize exclusively in either communications hardware or computers. Although there are exceptions, different technologies are required for the two different tasks. For the most part, independent, computer-oriented suppliers of interface devices have not yet made a completely successful transition into the communications area, mainly because of failure to exchange information among communication suppliers, computer suppliers, and users.

MODULAR DESIGN: THE U.S. ANSWER?

U.S. television manufacturers are trying to reduce labor costs in the production and maintenance of television receivers. One large manufacturer's efforts may well mark the beginning of an industry trend to drastically alter the design of TV receivers and many other electronic products. The concept embodies the manufacture of electronic modules which, when combined in the final manufacturing operation, perform the entire function of the product. This may well be the most significant technological innovation in the consumer electronics industry during the 1970s and for an extended period thereafter.

CONSUMER ELECTRONICS

In an electronic device, a controlled and variable flow of electrons must result in a signal containing information. To be classified as electronic, the product must contain vacuum tubes or transistors. Table 18–2 shows television receiver production for selected leading countries. The manufacture of this equipment in the U.S. is concentrated primarily in New York, New Jersey, Indiana, and Illinois. Other important producing states are Pennsylvania, Ohio, Connecticut, Massachusetts, Michigan, Tennessee, and California.

Table 18–3 shows the leading producers of radio receivers. Less than 9 percent of the household radios sold in the

TABLE 18–2 Television-Receiver Production in Selected Leading Countries

	1963	1972	PERCENT CHANGE
Japan	4,916	14,303	+390.94%
U.S.	7,734	10,219	+ 32.13
USSR	2,473	5,980	+141.81
W.Germany	1,920	3,072	+ 60.00
United Kingdom	1,663	3,030	+ 82.20
France	1,152	1,578	+ 36.98
Canada	455	847	+ 86.15
Poland	365	730	+100.00
Spain	315	677	+114.92
Austria	108	363	+236.11

Source: Based on the *United Nations Statistical Yearbook, 1973* (New York: United Nations, 1974), p. 307.

TABLE 18–3   Radio-Receiver Production in Selected Leading Countries

	1963	1972	PERCENT CHANGE
Japan	17,063	26,833	+ 57.26%
U.S.	18,155	14,155	− 22.03
USSR	4,795	8,842	+ 84.40
W.Germany	3,845	5,496	+ 42.94
France	2,838	2,936	+ 3.45
Canada	826	2,314	+180.14
India	418	1,935	+362.91
S.Korea	1,361*	1,858	+ 36.52
United Kingdom	2,782	1,472	− 47.09
East Germany	773	1,041	+ 34.67

* 1968

Source: Based on the *United Nations Statistical Yearbook, 1973* (New York: United Nations, 1974), p. 306.

United States in 1972 were domestically produced, although this proportion is expected to continue to decline. Radio-receiver production in the U.S. dropped from 18.2 million units in 1963 to 14.2 million units in 1972; automobile radios accounted for most of this production.

U.S. imports rose from $1.28 billion in 1970 to $1.7 billion in 1972. Principal suppliers are Japan, Hong Kong, Taiwan, and Mexico. U.S. foreign-based subsidiaries continue to assemble electronics equipment from parts and subassemblies exported from the United States.

Japan continues to be the major U.S. competitor in consumer electronics, with West Germany, the Netherlands, and the United Kingdom providing competition in specialized product areas.

Major new developments expected in the next decade will be associated with color video recording, including color cameras with recording and playback functions from cassette type units. Electronic video recording (EVR) may find its way into the home. However, at the present time, EVR is available only for the educational and business markets because the current cost of equipment and film is too high for the average consumer.

By 1980, cable distribution systems will provide households with two-way communications with educational, banking, retail purchasing, and other service industries. The electronics companies and telephone companies will share in these new developments.

ELECTRONIC SYSTEMS AND EQUIPMENT

Electronic systems include ground, airborne, and marine communications equipment, navigational aids, military electronic equipment, and radio and television broadcasting equipment. This branch of the electronics industry relies heavily on government expenditures that fluctuate greatly with the national defense budget.

During the height of the Vietnam War, there was considerable expansion of this part of the industry, reaching $8.6 billion. Reductions of government subsidies are occurring, however, necessitated by the closing of military bases, laying up of ships, the end of U.S. involvement and the war itself in Vietnam, and further reductions in military weapons-systems procurement.

The National Aeronautics and Space Administration (NASA) is an important customer for electronics and communications products, which they employ in a variety of programs, including an experimental short takeoff and landing aircraft (STOL) for improved short-haul transportation, the Space Shuttle, the Skylab experimental space station, and the unmanned Viking Mars lander.

The Federal Aviation Administration (FAA) also is highly dependent on the electronics industry for electronics equipment, such as navigational aids and communications equipment to support the en route air-traffic control system and the airport improvement program.

One of the most important electronics developments is an aeronautical communications and information-processing system. Implemented by Arinc, Inc., and the airlines, it uses a data link to relay messages between ground and aircraft, to effect channel management, and to select circuits for voice communications. These ground–air messages are electronically switched to a message control center and forwarded via the data link to the aircraft.

Automation will predominate in commercial, industrial, and military electronics systems, with computer techniques being applied to telecommunications operations. The value of industry shipments is expected to expand at 4 percent per year to reach $12 billion in 1980. Use of integrated circuits is constantly increasing, with emphasis on micro-miniaturization. Audiovisual communications will play a major role by 1980 for educational purposes. Satellite communications will be used by ships and aircraft to provide communications channels and navigational data.

Business Machines. Peripheral equipment, which provides a data-processing system with external communications, is the fastest-growing segment of the electronics industry and accounts for almost three-quarters of the cost of a typical electronics data program (EDP). New, specialized input–output devices are appearing on the market that will make possible rapid and accurate capture of data. With automatic tag or symbol readers and credit card readers for credit verification, these units provide direct entry of the transaction into a customer's bank account. Equipment for paperless payroll and accounts payable, bank entries, and securities quotations, with buy-and-sell terminal capabilities, are other examples. Table 18–4 shows U.S. economic projections for business machines to 1980.

Business machines are produced in 575 manufacturing plants in the United States; the Middle Atlantic and north-central states account for 75 percent of total U.S. production. Electronic computers, peripheral equipment, and parts account for more than two-thirds of exports. Major customers are West Germany, Japan, the United Kingdom, France, and Belgium.

Leading imports are calculating machines for which Japan, Italy, West Germany, the Netherlands, and Argentina are the chief suppliers. Japan is the leading supplier of electronic calculators.

MINICOMPUTER TREND

The trend in sales of minicomputers is toward the end-users. This results from a growing sophistication among end-users who want manufacturers to configure and program computer systems for special tasks. The market for the original equipment manufacturer (OEM) will probably diminish as OEM's find it cheaper to buy the components needed to build the minicomputer for their specialized configuration. Most companies sell from 40 to 75 percent of their output

TABLE 18-4 Value of Shipments of Business Machines: Projections 1971–1980 (in millions)

	1971	PERCENT INCREASE 1970–1971	1972	PERCENT INCREASE 1971–1972	1975	PERCENT INCREASE 1971–1975	1980	PERCENT INCREASE 1971–1980
Typewriters	$ 480	2%	$ 494	3%	$ 520	2 %	$ 574	2 %
Electronic Computing Equipment	4,490	5	4,939	10	7,191	12.5	11,025	10.5
Calculating and Accounting Machines	590	5	649	10	864	10	1,392	10
Office Machines	426	5	469	10	624	10	1,000	10

Source: U.S. Department of Commerce, Bureau of Domestic Commerce (Washington, D.C.: U.S. Government Printing Office, 1972), p. 302.

to OEM's, whose profit margins have declined. They view the end-user market as more profitable, although more troublesome, since sales costs will rise as systems analysis, software, maintenance, and customer support increase expenses.

The minicomputer market is growing at the rate of 30 to 35 percent per year in the United States and over 40 percent annually in Europe. Whether this growth rate will continue is open to question. A segment of the industry believes that the larger minicomputer manufacturers will not be able to sustain their volume of sales without entering the general-purpose maxicomputer market. An economic indicator is Digital Equipment Corporation's announcement in 1974 of its five new DEC system-10 models that range in power from that of the IBM 370/135 to the 370/165. DEC, which during the past few years has placed about 200 large systems in the field, sees the need to enlarge its product base. This may be so with all minicomputer companies which, as they approach the $100 million sales base, find that minicomputers alone cannot sustain such volume.

Another sign of this need for a larger product base is evident as peripheral manufacturers enter the main minicomputer market in order to compete with a complete systems approach. This pressure from beneath on minicomputer firms will continue as electronic calculator and semiconductor firms enter the market.

Of about 60 minicomputer firms, 6 control 70 percent of the market. By 1975, industry observers believe that only 20 companies will survive.

OVERSEAS INVESTMENTS

Overseas investments by U.S. electronic-component manufacturers in the past generally were made to accomplish two purposes. The first was to move products and technical services close to the market place to improve a company's foreign competitive position; this has been characteristic of U.S. investments in Europe. The second purpose of companies who invested in overseas production facilities was to take advantage of low-cost labor sources to improve the domestic manufacturer's competitive position in the domestic market. Most of this type of U.S. investment was in the Far East and more recently in Mexico.

However, recent U.S. Customs Court decisions regarding the definition of fabricated parts for transformers and capacitors may adversely affect such investments. With the advancement in production technology and the trend to solid-state electronics, it is extremely difficult to determine exactly what is a fabricated part. This seems to be the focus of recent court decisions. Appeal of these adverse decisions may be necessary to clarify this situation.

Additional problems may arise with Taiwan's recent expulsion from the United Nations, which might affect the flow of U.S. capital to this island in the future.

ECONOMIC OUTLOOK

The outlook for the electronic components industries for the balance of this decade is favorable. Although the annual growth rate is not enormous, estimated product shipments should reach about $6.8 billion in 1980, representing an average annual growth rate of about 2.3 percent.

Continued advancement of the communications-electronics industries is closely coupled with technological achievements in electronic components; in general, these basic building blocks are the foundation for new products. The most crucial electronic component is the transistor, which has opened up the new field of solid-state electronics.

The future of the communications and electronic industries is highly dependent on the level of research and development devoted to electronic components. In the past, military research and development of electronic components has played a most important role in the overall development of the industry. As we move into the 1970s, research and development is expected to center on commercial and industrial products rather than on those exclusively for military application.

Two new products presently promising to influence industry growth are solid-state memory planes and magnetic bubble-switching packs. The latter could be used for telephone switching devices and in computers to replace large magnetic disk files, resulting in extensive reduction in size. Future expansion will also depend on the pace of U.S. economic growth and the demand from international markets.

At present there are no new consumer products exhibiting the potential of color television, which accounted for spectacular industry growth in the mid-1960s. However, two products with a high component content and a potential consumer appeal are home video tape-recorders and quadrasonic stereo systems. At this time, their price is high and they have not yet developed the broad sales appeal of color television.

One of the more promising commercial products is the electronic desk-top calculator. Strong foreign competition already exists in this area from Japan's vigorous promotion of its numerous models. The adaptation of advanced electronics technology to this product has created many improvements such as speed, portability, and the elimination of the mechanical wear factor. Also, some models can be purchased with a lower initial investment than the earlier and more bulky mechanical calculators.

references

1. Boyle, Stanley E. *Industrial Organization: An Empirical Approach*. New York: Holt, Rinehart and Winston, 1972.

2. Boyce, Ronald R. *The Bases of Economic Geography*. New York: Holt, Rinehart and Winston, 1974.

3. Chisholm, Michael, and Manners, Gerald, eds. *Spatial Policy Problems of the British Economy*. New York: Cambridge University Press, 1971.

4. Estall, R. C. "The Electronics Products Industry of New England." *Economic Geography* 39 (July 1963): 189–216.

5. Estall, Robert A. *A Modern Geography of the United States*. Chicago: Quadrangle Books, 1972.

6. de Blij, Harm. *Essentials of Geography: Regions and Concepts*. New York: John Wiley and Sons, 1974.

7. Eyre, John D. "Development Trends in the Japanese Electric Power Industry: 1963–1968." *The Professional Geographer* 22 (January 1970): 26–30.

8. Feuvel, George R. *Poland's Industrialization Policy: A Current Analysis*. Volume 1 of *Industrialization and Planning Under Polish Socialism*. New York: Frederick A. Praeger, 1971.

9. George, Pierre. *France: A Geographical Study*. Translated by J. B. Thompson. New York: Barnes and Noble, 1973.

10. Gerasimov, J. P., et al., eds. *Natural Resources of the Soviet Union: Their Use and Renewal*. San Francisco: W. H. Freeman, 1971.

11. Gottmann, Jean. *A Geography of Europe*. 4th ed. New York: Holt, Rinehart and Winston, 1969.

12. Hull, Oswald. *Geography of Production*. London: Macmillan & Co., Ltd., 1968.

13. Jordan, Terry G. *The European Cultural Area: A Systematic Geography*. New York: Harper & Row, 1973.

14. Kish, George. *Economic Atlas of the Soviet Union*. 2nd ed. Ann Arbor: University of Michigan Press, 1971.

15. Lydolph, Paul E. *Geography of the U.S.S.R.* 2nd ed. New York: John Wiley and Sons, 1971.

16. Malmstrom, Vincent H. *Geography of Europe: A Regional Analysis*. Foundations of the World Regional Geography Series. Englewood Cliffs, N.J.: Prentice-Hall, 1971.

17. Miller, E. Willard. *A Geography of Industrial Location*. Dubuque, Iowa: William C. Brown Co., 1970.

18. Patterson, J. H. *North American*. 5th ed. New York: Oxford University Press, 1975.

19. Starkey, Otis P.; Robinson, J. Lewis; and Miller, Crane S. *Anglo-American Realm*. 2nd ed. New York: McGraw-Hill Book Co., 1975.

20. White, C. Langdon; Foscue, Edwin J.; McKnight, Tom L. *Regional Geography of Anglo-America*. 4th ed. Englewood Cliffs. N.J.: Prentice-Hall, 1974.

V

TERTIARY ECONOMIC ACTIVITY

CHAPTERS

19 Location Theory of Tertiary
Economic Activity

20 Systems of Tertiary Economic
Activities

21 Transportation Services

22 Marketing Services

23 Money, Banking, and Financial
Services

24 Government Services

25 Communication Services

26 Recreation Services

introduction

Goods yielded by primary and secondary types of economic activities are tangible and measurable by conventional weights and indexes of employment. Services are intangible economic activities that are felt or sensed in the process of their consumption; they can be measured by the satisfaction derived from their consumption, which in turn can be translated into monetary units or employment figures. Service industries include government, transportation, utilities, banking, finance, insurance, real estate, recreation, retail and wholesale enterprises, medical and hospital care, etc. Service activities may involve goods in their operation that are produced by primary and secondary types of activities.

Services are measured in terms of the direct satisfaction derived in the process of their consumption; this suggests a closer spatial proximity between consumers and suppliers of services. Buying and consuming of services occur simultaneously, further suggesting that services do not easily lend themselves to transportation.

The spatial distribution of services generally follows the demand of the goods. Besides being related to the number of consumers, demand for services is a function of purchasing power, culture, and productivity levels of the primary and secondary activities, and of the intensity and frequency of transportation of the population.

Part V integrates the variables and frameworks of parts I and II through a theory of location for tertiary economic activities and illustrates by a systems of tertiary and quaternary activities. Quaternary activities, such as recreation, cater to discretionary spending and are considered to be within the general category of services.

location theory
of tertiary
economic activity

19

19

The increasing output per man-hour in primary and secondary activities and the social adherence to the goal of full employment of the labor force have continuously pushed employment of the labor force into nongood producing economic activities.[1] Tertiary and quaternary activities involve employment related not to the production of physical goods, but rather to the distribution and servicing of goods produced in primary and secondary activities. This need not lead the reader to conclude that the only purpose of tertiary activities is to provide opportunities and jobs to earn income which in turn provide claim to the physical goods. Tertiary and quaternary activities perform economic functions by saving time and distance and by providing convenience for the workers engaged in goods-producing activities. If these workers were to pick up their demanded goods from the production locations; to treat illness, to educate, and to serve as a lawyer, etc., by themselves, they indeed would not be as productive in their goods-producing occupations as otherwise. Tertiary and quaternary activities serve to contribute toward the productivity realized in the goods-producing activities. With the increasing degree of specialization and economic wealth, the types of tertiary and quaternary activities is expanding. It is not uncommon for economically developed nations to employ over 50 percent of their labor forces in tertiary and quaternary activities.

Presently, over 65 percent of the U.S. labor force is engaged in tertiary and quaternary activities and all projections indicate that this percentage may climb to as high as 80 percent by the end of this century. This observation suggests that the tertiary and quaternary activities are largely consumer bound, although they indirectly reflect on the productivity of the goods-producing activities. Furthermore, since everyone is a consumer of goods and of some form of services, and everyone is not a direct producer of goods, it is expedient to analyze tertiary and quaternary activities from the point of view of consumers.

Tertiary activities are essentially market-based. Their analysis of location involves considerations of the consumer and the transfer cost. In other words, the location analysis and related theory looks at a service activity in light of consumer behavior and mobility within a general area of consumer density.

Consumer behavior in terms of his wants and needs—what, how much, when, and where—is a complex phenomenon determined by composite forces of income, prices of goods and substitutes, tastes and preferences, prestige and status, etc. (See chapter 4 for a discussion of consumer demand.) All other conditions being equal, the consumer is located at a place that maximizes his satisfaction and also selects the goods and services that provide him with the highest satisfaction. Modes of consumer behavior would be assumed as given in the following analysis of the location of nongoods-producing economic activities.

CENTRAL PLACE THEORY

Von Thünen's central place theory assumed a village to be an area around which economic activities ring themselves into a pattern defined by the distance–rent relationship. Walter Christaller (6), German economist and geographer writing in the early 20th century, sought to restate central place theory by

[1] The labor force is defined as all those that are able, ready, and willing to work. Thus the labor force is a relative concept whose level depends upon the size of the adult population and the social values attached to work.

explaining the size, number, and spatial arrangements of trade centers.

According to Christaller's theory, the town is a nucleus of a region and a mediator of that region's commerce. Christaller's theory was based on two assumptions: (1) uniform topography to enable every site to have equal transportation cost and/or route advantage and (2) uniform productivity characteristics for every site of the region. Christaller postulated that service centers will spring up evenly spaced over the region at a distance equivalent to two hours of nonmechanized travel time. Thus these centers will emerge 7 miles apart because a man could walk 3 miles in an hour. He argued that the boundaries surrounding these centers will emerge in a hexagonal pattern. Figure 19–1 shows that under case 1, involving circular boundaries, it leaves unserved areas and there is overlapping under case 2. Under a hexagonal pattern, as in case 3, there are no areas left unserved, nor is there any duplication.

Christaller further argued that the hexagonal framework would tend to develop into a hierarchy of trade centers. Thus at the first order of this hierarchy would be small hamlets, the most numerous and dispersed 7 miles apart. The second order would be villages, then towns, and finally cities. Each hierarchy offers a respective order of services or functions. For a representation of Christaller's ideas, see Figure 19–2.

Because this theory postulated that service centers tend to be located in the center of the area they serve, it is frequently termed the central place theory. The region, or area served, for which a central place is the center Christaller termed the complementary region—a mutual relationship of town to country and country to town. Complementary regions are also of higher and lower order. They differ for different types of goods, consistently

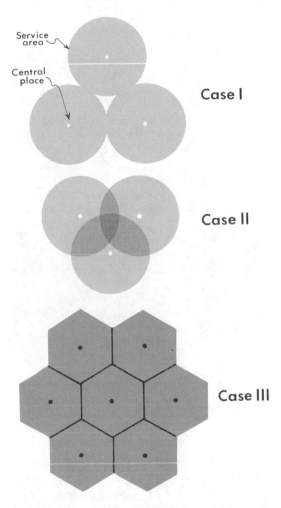

FIGURE 19–1 *Central Place Model*

overlap neighboring complementary regions at the periphery, and undergo periodic and seasonal variations in size and shape.

Recognizing that distance measured by time and cost plays a vital role in any determination of complementary regions and that the size of a central place has an immediate influence on the range of central functions, Christaller reasoned that each type of good (service or function) has its own *threshold* and *market range*.

361

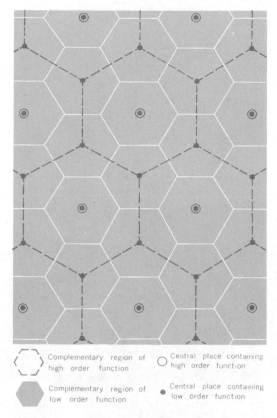

Complementary region of high order function ⬡

Central place containing high order function ○

Complementary region of low order function ⬡

Central place containing low order function ●

FIGURE 19–2   *Christaller Model*

The threshold represents the minimum number of people, and, consequently, the minimum level of demand required to support a technically feasible establishment or firm.[2] *Market range* concerns the distance that the buyers are willing to travel to purchase the good or service at a particular price. An activity will emerge and survive only if there is evidence of a threshold and a market range. The market range, of course, weakens with increasing distance. Buyers farther from the activity location have to pay higher prices (price at the center plus the transfer cost). Buyers closer to

[2] The size of the establishment is determined by the dynamic forces of competitive conditions and the production function.

the activity are able to buy a larger number of units of the good or service than buyers residing farther away. This phenomenon reflects the weakening power of the market range as distance increases.

The emergence of an activity made possible by a threshold and market range would also induce other complementary activities to locate, because most workers associated with the initial activity tend to minimize their commuting effort when their residences are closer to the activity. As they spend their incomes, more services and some manufacturing activities would emerge. Thus, an agglomeration of economic activity locations and worker residences results, which, as it serves the outlying areas, becomes a central place. The market ranges for various activities at the central place may not coincide.

The arrangement of economic activities and residences at the central place is also a locational problem. Usually there is a Central Business District (CBD) conveniently linked to residences and to industrial supply lines.

The market range in practice involves a ring with an upper limit beyond which a service can no longer be obtained from a center, and a lower limit which is determined by the minimum amount of consumption which is necessary before an economic activity will be located. Assuming a uniform plane with equal access in all directions, complementary regions become hexagonal and the lower order centers and their complementary regions nest within those larger centers. In this hierarchical system, several levels of interdependence would emerge. Since it assumes that all areas are able to be served from a minimum of central places, this arrangement has frequently been termed a *marketing principle*.

The marketing principle of the hierarchy would not survive if we relieved the assumptions of uniform topography and economy. Christaller recognized that special traffic or route realities would cause the spatial distribution of central places to be optimum—as many central places as possible lie on the traffic route between larger towns. The administrative or political subdivision may also cause changes in the hierarchy of the marketing system.

Christaller observed that the central place system of southern Germany, dominated respectively by Munchen, Nurenburg, Stuttgart, Strasburg, and Frankfurt, corresponded to his theory with a high degree of exactness.

The revolution in transportation routes and varying productivity of land, either naturally occurring or caused by cultural and technological practices, no doubt, would disrupt Christaller's hypothesis of the hexagonal pattern and of centrality.[3]

This is not to say that Christaller's hypothesis yields no explanation and application. There are areas, such as southwestern Wisconsin, where service centers are dispersed in a pattern similar to Christaller's. Transportation and technological developments may result in distributions that form a linear pattern in which service centers are strung out along transportation routes. Or, a clustered pattern of service centers may emerge and be defined by agglomeration advantages. The clustered pattern may reflect the modern Standard Metropolitan Statistical Area (SMSA).

Modified patterns of distribution do not, however, minimize the concepts of centrality and hierarchy. They modify the hexagonal pattern of distribution.

Fetter (7), using Christaller's assumptions and further assuming that production and transport costs are identical for any two firms located at

[3] Centrality is defined as a state of high accessibility, the quality of being at the center of transport system.

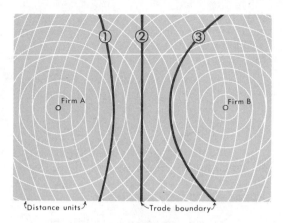

FIGURE 19–3 *Fetter Model*

different central places demonstrated that the boundary between their trade areas will be a straight line perpendicularly bisecting the line connecting the two centers. (see Curve 2 in Figure 19–3). If production costs for the two firms are different, but transport costs are similar, the boundary line is curved and closer to the higher production cost area. The same reasoning applies to a situation where production costs are similar but transport costs are different, resulting in a boundary closer to and curved around the location with the higher transport cost. In Figure 19–3, curves 2 and 3, respectively, show these boundaries.

Reilly (16) attempted to define the boundary between two centers by "retail gravitation," generally referred to as Reilly's Law of Retail Gravitation. He asserted that two cities attract retail trade (T) from any intermediate or intervening city or town (C) in the vicinity; this attraction is in approximately direct proportion to the populations (P) of the two cities (A and B) and in inverse proportion to the squares of the distances (D) from these two cities to the intermediate towns.

The boundary lines may be determined by the contour lines "up to which one city exercises the dominating retail trade influences and beyond which the other city dominates." His law may be expressed as:

$$\frac{T_{(A \leftarrow C)}}{T_{(B \leftarrow C)}} = \frac{P_A}{P_B} \left[\frac{D_{(C \leftrightarrow B)}}{D_{(C \leftrightarrow A)}} \right]^2$$

Actual data are frequently available to calculate the relative retail trade attraction of two cities. Assuming the following hypothetical data:

P_A = population in city A = 70,000
P_B = population in city B = 50,000
D (C↔B) = distance between cities C and B = 150 miles
D (C↔A) = distance between cities C and A = 100 miles
T (A↔C) = trade to city A from city C
T (B↔C) = trade to city B from city C

then, by substitution:

$$\frac{T_{(A \leftarrow C)}}{T_{(B \leftarrow C)}} = \frac{70,000}{50,000} \left(\frac{150}{100} \right)^2 = \frac{7}{5} \cdot \left(\frac{3}{2} \right)^2 = \frac{63}{20}$$

This means that for every $20 of trade that goes to city B from city C, there will be $63 worth of trade to city A from city C.

Additional work has been done by Berry and Garrison (2) to further reinforce the central place theory, expanding it to explain urban agglomeration. The interaction, or "gravitational pull," as Reilly would say, between any two central places may be measured by:

$$i = \frac{P_1 P_2}{d}$$

where i represents interaction, P is population, and d is the distance between cities 1 and 2. This formula suggests that the interaction between cities 1 and 2 will vary positively with the product ($P_1 \times P_2$) of the two populations and inversely with the distance between them.

RECENT MODIFICATIONS OF THE CENTRAL PLACE THEORY

Among the several attempts to modify the central place theory, Berry and Garrison's work is the best known. By relaxing the assumptions of the homogeneity of the spatial distributions of purchasing power and market, they capitalize on the ideas of range and threshold. They demonstrated that with any spatial distribution of income and population, a hierarchical spatial structure of central places will emerge.

In order to survive, each tertiary activity must have a certain minimum threshold. Thus each tertiary activity tends to form a cluster of customers attached to or patronizing it. There might be several firms producing the same service and operating in the threshold; their numbers would tend to cause greater competition among them, increasing the quality of service.

Since each tertiary activity has different thresholds, a hierarchy of thresholds and ranges occurs, as illustrated in Figure 19–4. At the bottom of the hierarchy would be service businesses, such as barber shops, drug stores, or gas stations, which, as "corner store" operations, involve high frequency of use of services.

The highest order recognized by Berry and Garrison is the "Central Business District" (CBD) where activities deal with "shopping-specialty" merchandise. The range of the CBD is the largest in their model. They recognize, however, that other lower-order activities may be carried within the CBD to enhance attraction of customers who may prefer "one-stop" shopping.

364

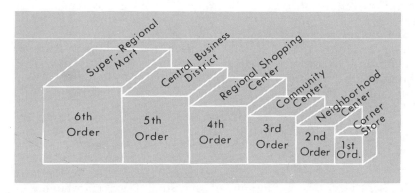

FIGURE 19–4 *Hierarchy of Consumer Shopping Patterns*

With increasing intracity traffic congestion and modern transport facilities, the CBDs have been decaying and the suburban shopping centers of the fourth-order type are fast emerging. It may be that the suburban centers have higher market range, which should make the suburban shopping centers of the fifth order and place the CBD in the fourth order.

The "one-stop" shopping concept has caused further modifications to the central place theory not recognized by Berry and others. This involves the Super Region Marts (SRM), which are frequently centrally located with a maximum of transport access and facilities from several neighboring cities; this is shown as a sixth-order center in Figure 19–4. The location of the SRM's tends to follow the Weber-Lösch model including the consideration of the other location factors mentioned in chapter 12.

In general, modifications of the central place theory have occurred along the following lines:

1. Uniformity of physical plane, economy, and transportation costs is relaxed to permit variation in them which gives rise to a variety of shapes to the declination of market areas; for example, linear patterns, rectilinear patterns (caused by government land survey), clustered patterns, and beaded patterns, etc.

2. The parameters determining threshold, range, and profitability vary with the service, population, purchasing power, prices, and mode and cost of transportation.

3. The places of greater population dominate larger areas than do places with smaller populations, given the same set of goods and services.

4. Customers are not always rational in seeking optimal solutions for transfer costs. Personal considerations may at times become more important than the optimum and efficient location conditions. This uncertainty in consumer behavior would produce irregularity and overlapping of market areas.

5. The agglomeration principle, i.e., grouping of people and activities for mutual benefits, may create "hills and valleys" in the distribution of the service centers.

6. It is possible that trade centers may evolve gradually in response to expanding economic resources and territory.

In summary, the tertiary theories attempt to conceptualize the incidence of activities into a hierarchy of central place areas and to explain the interaction between them. The early theories emphasize the transportation factor, while modern theories place relatively

365

more weight on demand, revenue, and agglomeration considerations. This emphasis stems from the industry promotion and town building activities that produce goods for exporting to other areas or countries; this is made possible through specialization and economies of scale. Processing and manufacturing activities that appear in clusters generate a demand for services—the spatial pattern of which is different from Christaller's hexagonal pattern.

references

1.   Alao, Nurudeen. "An Approach to Intraurban Location Theory." *Economic Geography* 50 (January 1974): 59–68.

2.   Berry, B. J. L., and Garrison, W. L. "The Functional Bases of Central Place Hierarchy." *Economic Geography* 34 (April 1958): 145–54.

3.   Beyers, William B. "On Geographical Properties of Growth Centers' Linkage Systems." *Economic Geography* 50 (July 1974): 203–18.

4.   Brown, Lawrence A., and Cox, Kevin R. "Empirical Regularities in the Diffusion of Innovation." *Annals of the Association of American Geographers* 61 (September 1971): 551–59.

5.   Bucklin, Louis P. "Retail Gravity Models and Consumer Choice: A Theoretical and Empirical Critique." *Economic Geography* 47 (October 1971): 489–97.

6.   Carter, H.; Stafford, H. A.; and Gilbert, M. M. "Functions of Welsh Towns: Implications for Central Place Notions." *Economic Geography* 46 (January 1970): 25–38.

7.   Christaller, Walter. *Central Places in Southern Germany: A Pioneer Work in Theoretical Economic Geography.* C. Baskin, translator. Englewood Cliffs, N.J.: Prentice-Hall, 1966.

8.   Clark, W. A. V., and Rushton, Gerald. "Models of Intra-Urban Consumer Behavior and Their Implications for Central Place Theory." *Economic Geography* 46 (February 1971): 486–97.

9.   Fetter, F. A. "The Economic Law of Market Areas." *Quarterly Journal of Economics* 39 (1924): 520–29.

10.   Garrison, Charles B., and Paulson, Albert S. "An Entropy Measure of the Geographic Concentration of Economic Activity." *Economic Geography* 49 (October 1973): 319–24.

11.   Horton, Frank E., and Hultquist, John F. "Urban Growth and Developmental Models: Transition and Prospect." *The Journal of Geography* 70 (February 1971): 73–83.

12.   Johnson, Lane J. "The Spatial Uniformity of a Central Place Distribution in New England." *Economic Geography* 47 (April 1971): 156–70.

13.   Morrill, Richard L. *The Spatial Organization of Society.* 2nd ed. North Scituate, Mass.: Duxbury Press, 1974.

14.   Odland, J. E., and King, L. J. "Testing Hypotheses of Polarized Growth Within a Central Place Hierarchy." *Economic Geography* 49 (January 1973): 74–79.

15.   Olsson, Gunnar. "Explanation, Prediction, and Meaning Variance: An Assessment of Distance Interaction Models." *Economic Geography* 46 (June 1970): 223–33.

16.   Parr, John B. "Structure and Size in the Urban System of Lösch." *Economic Geography* 49 (July 1973): 185–212.

17.   ———, and Denike, Kenneth G., "Theoretical Problems in Central Place Analysis." *Economic Geography* 46 (October 1970): 568–86.

18.   Reilly, W. J. *The Law of Retail Gravitation.* New York: The Knickerbocker Press, 1931.

19.   Schwartz, George. *Development of Marketing Theory.* Cincinnati: Southwestern Publishing Co., 1963.

20.   Struyk, Raymond J. "Spatial Concentration of Manufacturing Employment in Metropolitan Areas: Some Empirical Evidence." *Economic Geography* 48 (April 1972): 189–92.

21.   Von Böventer, Edwin. "Towards a Unified Theory of Spatial Economic Structure." *Papers of the Regional Science Association* 110 (1962): 163–87.

22.   Webber, M. J., and Symanski, Richard. "Periodic Markets: An Economic Lo-

cation Analysis." *Economic Geography* 49 (July 1973): 213–27.

23. Weber, Alfred. "Weber den Standort der Industrien." In Part I, *Reine Theorie des Standorts, 1909.* Translated by C. J. Friedrich as *Alfred Weber's Theory of the Location of Industries.* Chicago: University of Chicago Press, 1928.

24. White, Roger W. "Sketches of a Dynamic Central Place Theory." *Economic Geography* 50 (July 1974): 219–27.

systems of tertiary
economic activities

20

20

Tertiary systems include a wide variety of occupations and activities. Representative of this diversity are occupations, such as plumber, physician, engineer, educator, athlete, politician, lawyer, garbage collector, salesperson, and secretary. From this diversity we may generalize three tertiary subsystems: services, trades, and finance.

Associated with the tertiary subsystem of services are activities, such as business and repair services (auto repairs, advertising); government services (police, fire); personal services (education, religion); medical services (clinics, hospitals); and recreation, tourism, and leisure time services (hotels, restaurants, theatre, sporting events).

Trading, as a tertiary subsystem, involves retail and wholesale activities. The third tertiary subsystem, finance, includes banking, insurance, and real estate. This chapter deals with generalized patterns or systems of these activities. The term "tertiary" should be construed to include "quaternary activities."

Employees engaged in tertiary systems represent approximately 8 to 12 percent of the world's labor force.[1] Due

to the close correlation between increasing industrialization and the desire of and ability to support increasing numbers of people in tertiary systems, these systems are distributed at least as irregularly over the surface of the earth as are industrial societies. In 1974, 59 percent of the U.S. labor force was employed in tertiary occupations. The United Kingdom's tertiary employment is 48 percent of the labor force, whereas the Soviet Union, Poland, and Niger have 35 percent, 23 percent, and 3 percent, respectively.

Figure 20–1 shows the general correlation of employment between the three general systems of economic activity. Because the industrializing process necessitates that greater numbers of persons be employed in secondary and tertiary systems, there is a general, corresponding decrease in the percent of persons employed in primary systems. In Figure 20–1, countries nearer the bottom of the figure possess a higher percentage of employees in secondary and tertiary systems and fewer employees in primary systems. In other words, there appears to be a positive correlation between the level of percapita income (achieved by industrialization) and the number of people employed in tertiary activities.

TERTIARIZATION OF AN ECONOMIC SYSTEM

The process by which a larger economic system employs an increasing proportion of its labor force in tertiary activities is referred to as *tertiarization*. The commencement of this process is closely related to and may be generally viewed as a fairly direct result of the development of agriculture to a level where surplus production makes possible the feeding and care of populations not

[1] Official definitions and data for tertiary employment and activities vary from one country to another, if such data are gathered at all. In some means of reporting, transportation and related activities are excluded from this set and incorporated into secondary activities. Occupations that are of a transient, seasonal, or part-time nature, especially in less developed countries, are often not considered worthy of tabulation or often escape attention. Additional sources of error occur in the lack of uniformity of categories, definition of labor force, and time or interval of data collection. Often tables or charts with employment data for tertiary activities, especially outside of North America and Western Europe, are based on some

form of statistical interpretation of diverse sources rather than on official surveys.

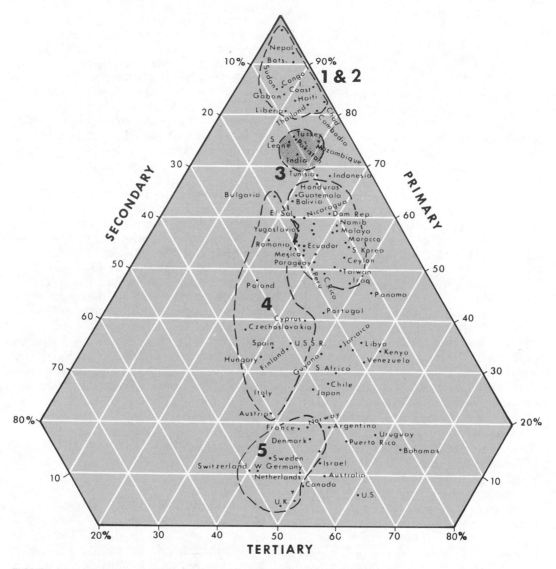

FIGURE 20–1 *Percent of Labor Force in Primary, Secondary, and Tertiary Activities. (After Jan Broek and John W. Webb, A Geography of Mankind, 2nd ed. [New York: McGraw-Hill, 1973]).*

directly concerned with or involved in primary activities. From this level of development in any economic system, we may reckon the initiation of tertiary activities.

The labor force not involved in primary activities is generally associated with specialization in coordinating production, manufacture, transport, consumption, security, and various forms of barter or money exchange. It is difficult to state with certainty which occupations initially developed as tertiary activities; but we can say that they were primarily associated with the beginning of the urban revolution. These initial tertiary occupations appear to have been focussed on sites that allowed for storage, processing, and distribution of agricultural and nonagricultural goods; the security of local people, transients, and their animals; military operations; repair of tools; and the construction of buildings for these functions. Many of these occupations were either directly associated with or controlled by emergent politicians, social workers, and religious leaders.

The overall process of tertiarization —from few people employed in tertiary activities to a majority of the people so employed—may be conceptualized as occurring in stages, such as the following:

Stage 1. Almost total employment in primary activities; majority of the population engaged in some form of subsistence activity; little specialization of occupation; small-scale operations; population density usually low and ratio of goods production to population near a minimum for support of the society; little differentiation between consumer and producer.

Stage 2. Change, via local or diffused invention, leads to increased productivity and commencement of specialization in primary activities; specialization reduces the number of individuals performing similar tasks; spatial separation of economic functions leads to changes and improvements in transportation, storage, and processing, which in turn affords new and different occupations; an increased number of people engaged in activities associated with exchange, growing out of specialization; producer and/or consumer differentiation begins.

Stage 3. Increasing productivity and security results in population increase; more detailed specialization of space, occupation; higher per-capita consumption; increasing rate of exchange internally and with other societies; percent of labor force in primary activities shows significant decline, in asso-

ciation with increasing employment in secondary and tertiary activities.

Stage 4. Secondary activities show increasing specialization and diversity; internal and external exchange linkages become more numerous and complex; development of specialization in money exchange; first major sustained rise in real per-capita incomes and consumption; components of the cultural value system are restructured and directed toward reducing human physical efforts and increasing machine capabilities; percent of total population in the labor force begins to decline although population may continue to increase (the part of the population not involved in the labor force represents non-labor force consumers); employment in primary activities experiences relative and absolute decline; relatively rapid rate of increase in tertiary employment.

Stage 5. Detailed specialization in all tertiary activities and development of new ones; tertiary employment greater than either secondary or primary employment; considerable human effort expended for paper securities, money, machines, and service, rather than for physical labor; specialization in primary and secondary activities continues; flow of goods, services, and people is more intense; increasing interdependency with other economic systems that may be at stages 2, 3, 4, or 5.

This model of tertiarization represents a synthesis of several other models including those by Rostow (18) and Clark (9). Clark, however, emphasizes more general and abstract cultural changes and labels stages as adaptation, domestication, diversification, mechanization, and automation. Our tertiarization system does not represent a rigid ideal through which all societies will or can be transformed. It does, however, afford a broad conceptual network, integrating what otherwise may be extremely diverse and cumbersome parts of reality.

The tertiarization stages presented here may be further illustrated and integrated with previous data arrayed in

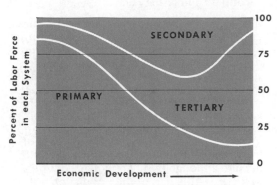

FIGURE 20–2 *Generalized Tertiarization of an Economic System*

Figure 20–1. If we assume that one of the upper points (here representing any hypothetical economic system) is set in motion toward the bottom right of the graph, the conceptual result will be an economic system that is continuously restructured as different alternatives to individual employment appear and disappear. This process may be exemplified more specifically by considering that if a similar graph were prepared around 1820, the United States would appear in the area of the dashed line on Figure 20–1.

Figure 20–2 generalizes tertiarization of an economic system over time. Early in the process the greatest opportunities for employment exist in primary activities. This, however, changes as maximum opportunities appear successively in secondary and then in tertiary activities. As this wave of greater opportunity shifts from primary to secondary to tertiary, the opportunities successively decrease in the lower order activities.

It is instructive to compare this analysis of tertiarization with historical data for the United States and other countries (see Table 20–1 and Table 20–2). Out of the total U.S. population of 211,782,000, only about 90 million were in the labor force during 1974. Table 20–1 shows that about 62 percent of American workers are engaged in tertiary employment and Table 20–2 indicates an increasing trend towards tertiarization.

The tertiary process and stages also may be related to the contemporary data of Figure 20–1 by noting that the countries arrayed on the graph can be loosely associated with one of the five stages. The countries in the upper portion of the graph have employment ratios approximating Stage 1 and/or

TABLE 20–1 Employment Structure in the United States, 1974

ACTIVITY	MILLIONS OF PERSONS	PERCENT
Primary	9.2	10.8%
Agricultural	3.4	4.0
Secondary (manufacturing)	23.3	27.3
Tertiary	52.7	61.9
Transport & Utilities	4.6	5.4
Trade	16.4	19.3
Services	13.3	15.6
Finance & Real Estate	4.1	4.8
Government	14.3	16.8

Source: U.S. Bureau of Census, *Statistical Abstract of the United States, 1974* (Washington, D.C.: U.S. Government Printing Office, 1974), tables 542, 563.

372

TABLE 20–2 Percent Employment in Tertiary Activities in Selected Countries for Selected Years

U.S.		U.K.		FRANCE		JAPAN		MEXICO	
1910	37%	1911	43%	1906	29%	1920	26%	1930	14%
1960	57%	1960	47%	1960	39%	1957	33%	1955	21%
1972	62%	1972	50%	1972	46%	1972	47%	1972	29%

Sources: All data prior to 1961 are from J. Beaujeu-Garnier, *Geography of Population* (New York: St. Martin's Press, 1966), pp. 320–27; 1972 data is computed from the *United Nations Statistical Yearbook* and the *U.S. Statistical Abstract.*

Stage 2. And as one moves to the lower center, the countries are more closely associated with stages 3, 4, and 5, respectively.

REGIONAL TERTIARY SYSTEMS

Tertiarization has significant spatial components. Figure 20–3 shows the general spatial distributions of the countries (or

portions thereof) associated with the various stages previously discussed. Two major characteristics can be immediately observed: 1) most of the earth's surface is not devoted to tertiary activities, and 2) portions of specific countries are undergoing more than one stage.

The first characteristic occurs principally because only 8 to 12 percent of the world's total labor force is involved in tertiary activities and because that

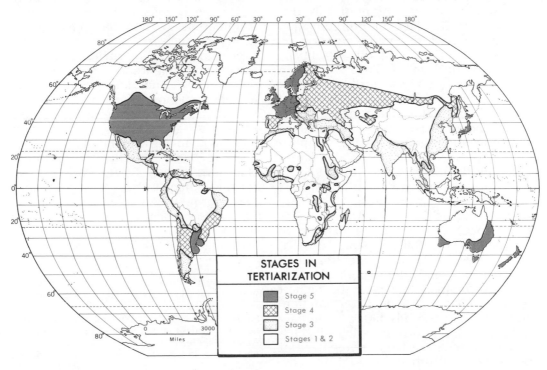

STAGES IN
TERTIARIZATION

Stage 5
Stage 4
Stage 3
Stages 1 & 2

FIGURE 20–3

portion of the population tends to occur in high-density clusters along major transport routes.

The second observation results principally because tertiarization, as a process that transforms socioeconomic systems, does not occur everywhere, or even in the same political space, with the same intensity or at the same time. For example, southern littoral Australia, which contains that country's larger, more productive cities and integrative transport routes, is associated with Stage 5, but the relatively uninhabited and poorly integrated "Outback" has been assigned to Stage 1 or 2. Similarly, the east–west elongation of the tertiary activities of the USSR is chiefly associated with a series of medium- and large-size cities (Gorky, Kirov, Sverdlovsk, Kuybyshev, Chelyabinsk, Omsk, Novosibirsk, Irkutsk, Chita), which lie between Moscow and Vladisvostok.

Another characteristic of this distribution is the lack of differentiation between, but close areal association of, Stages 1 and 2. This is due essentially to the occurrence of Stage 1 only in limited areas among a small number of people. Often in the larger context of Stage 2, primitive hunting-gathering tribes and perhaps more isolated shifting agriculturalists are actually the principal representatives of the conditions that prevail under Stage 1.

The countries with the largest percent of their labor forces in tertiary activities (Stage 5) are the United States and Canada, the cluster of nations on the North Sea, Italy, Japan, Australia, Israel, New Zealand, Argentina, and Uruguay. Generally, these countries represent economies that have the highest per-capita income, energy consumption, and productivity. This block of tertiary states is closely associated with high literacy rates and a larger percentage of population in urban areas. Externally, they represent the highest per-capita

trading partners in the world. The close correlation of these distributions with high employment percentages in tertiary activities is because the demand for tertiary services can exist only in spaces occupied by or connected to other highly specialized and productive primary, secondary, and tertiary systems.

The greater the degree of specialization, the more an individual producer or consumer must rely on other components of his own or other economic systems. This phenomenon is also associated with increased productivity and wealth that is channeled toward other types of services employing other individuals.[2] For example, the quantitative analysis of Denmark's exports in the 1960s showed 71 percent of maximum possible specialization (22). As an example of how specialization and international trade promote tertiary activities and how they in turn service these activities, we may refer to the large number of different occupations involved in facilitating such trade: export managers, foreign bankers, international insurers, brokers and freight forwarders, commercial carriers, and longshoremen and associated labor-union administrators. Primarily to smooth international transactions of goods and services international banking operations, such as Barclay's Bank, The Bank of America, Chase Manhattan Bank, The First National City Bank of New York, and others were formed. All of these maintain numerous branches or affiliates in foreign countries.

In general, then, we may suggest

[2] These components and characteristics of an economic system cannot continue to increase without bounds. As with any system, at some level of input or increase in one variable there will not be a continuation of the behavior of another or several variables. Thus, there is a threshold at which, for example, increasing specialization does not produce increasing productivity. The Law of Diminishing Returns is the general description for this phenomenon.

that high tertiary employment is characteristic of relatively well-developed economic systems that are able to create for the majority of their associated populations a relatively high standard of living. Within the overall operation and measurement of the socioeconomic system, this high standard of living is represented by the ability to purchase and use a wide variety of goods from the primary system, which are manufactured and relocated by the secondary system, and serviced by the tertiary system. This process demands an ultimate consumer population that consumes the services provided by the tertiary system. This brings us to the second and third major features of the tertiary system: the tendency to be consumer oriented, which results in a high-density distribution of tertiary systems.

TERTIARY ACTIVITIES IN CENTRAL PLACES

Due to the tendency of these systems to locate in highly populated areas, a map of the world only generally reveals spaces occupied by tertiary systems. When we change the scale from that of country to components of the tertiary system, the map changes from surfaces to dots that represent central places or foci of urban activity.

This does not imply that central places consist only of tertiary systems. There are towns, usually small, where employment in secondary or primary systems is larger than in tertiary systems; these central places, however, are usually associated with mining, lumbering, or fishing activity. And in Stage 1 and 2 economies, they are associated with agricultural activity and are decidedly less numerous and less significant than central places within which tertiary employment is dominant. Thus, a regional discussion of tertiary occupa-

tions must be essentially associated with urban processes. The central places involved may vary from a small hamlet of 50 people and a general store with gas station to a large metropolitan center with thousands of different tertiary components.

The internal relationships of the city are represented by the actual spatial distributions of various tertiary components (residences of consumers, offices, shops, wholesalers, etc.) and the circulation associated with these components.

CONSUMER–RETAILER LINKAGE

Due to the relative importance of the consumer–retailer linkage in structuring the spatial character of urban areas, this tertiary subsystem will receive the greatest attention here. The consumer–retailer linkage is generally represented by the model in Figure 20–4.

The two principal components of the subsystem begin to interact when the consumer perceives some want and expresses it as a demand on the retailer. In turn, the retailer supplies the item for which a demand has been expressed, for which he receives monetary compensation. This simple process, which can be initiated by the retailer by massaging latent wants via advertising (i.e.,

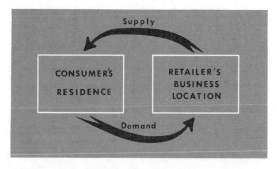

FIGURE 20–4 *Generalized Consumer–Retailer Interaction Model*

expressing that he has a supply which can meet a demand), has a spatial and temporal result in the structure of the urban environment.

The *spatial result* is the actual route taken by the consumer. This will be determined by numerous factors, including perceived alternative retailers who can meet the same demand, relative cost of other opportunities, the distance or travel time involved, other stops that may be integrated into this trip, ethnic background, education level, etc. The proximity of the consumer to the retailer is perhaps the most important.

The *temporal result* is the way in which the consumer makes budgetary decisions concerning the allocation of his income among several different commodities with the same or variable demands. This decision also is influenced by many factors, including income level and periodicity of income receipt.

The businessman also has spatial and temporal responses to the consumer's frequency of shopping and budgetary allocation. These involve delivery of commodity demanded, substitution, promotional advertising, changing inventory, length of time a shop is open, etc. The ultimate objective, as far as the businessman is concerned, is to realize sufficient profit from his services in order to supply his own personal needs from his involvement in this tertiary subsystem. The ultimate concern of the consumer is to achieve his demands in a satisfactory fashion.

From the numerous reasons given for a consumer reaching his decision about where to shop, we may suggest three that appear to be significant: (1) distance, or travel time, from present location to location of retailer; (2) cost of item to be purchased; and (3) frequency with which that item is purchased. Figure 20–5 illustrates the cost–distance relationship which generally prevails in the consumer decision. Es-

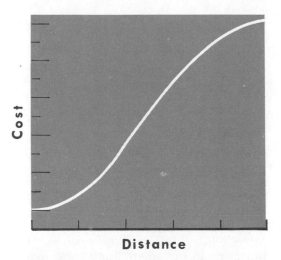

FIGURE 20–5 *Distance–Cost Relationships for Retail Purchases*

sentially, the graph suggests that as the cost of an item increases, the consumer is willing to travel a greater distance; that is, the distance travelled to purchase low-cost items is short, whereas the distance travelled for higher-cost items is farther. The frequency–distance relationship, illustrated in Figure 20–6,

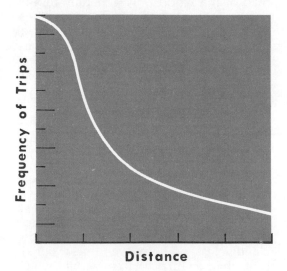

FIGURE 20–6 *Distance–Frequency Relationships for Retail Purchases*

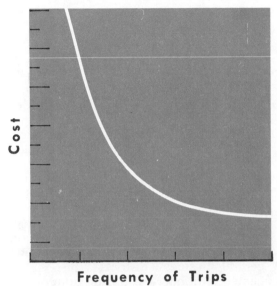

FIGURE 20–7 *Cost–Frequency Relationships for Retail Purchases*

shows that the distance travelled increases with decreasing frequency of trips; thus, generally a consumer perceives that services and goods purchased with a high frequency (such as 2 to 4 times a week) should be closer than goods purchased with lower frequency.

Figure 20–7 illustrates the relationship between cost and frequency and suggests that they are inversely proportional to each other.

THE CENTRAL PLACE RETAIL HIERARCHY

Integrating general consumer-retailer relationships with the previous chapter's theoretical models, we may now direct our attention to the hierarchy of retail establishments.

The *street-corner cluster* of shops is the lowest order and smallest group of retail establishments. It normally consists of one to four or five shops, the more common type of which is the grocery–drug store. The others may in-

clude a gas station, delicatessen, or small cafe. Its hinterland or tributary area is usually small and occupied by consumers who more frequently walk than ride to patronize the establishments. Transactions are usually accomplished casually, the retailer and his customers often being on a first-name basis. These low-order centers appear more frequently in the central place than any higher order cluster of shops.

The *neighborhood center* contains from five to fifteen shops and usually includes a grocery store, beauty salon, barber shop, hardware store, insurance office, small restaurant, local post office, real estate office, clothing store, television and appliance repair shop, and perhaps a dry cleaning establishment. There is a higher density of stores, customers, usually standardized signs, and less contact between consumer and owner or manager. The increased sales of the neighborhood center over the street-corner cluster are associated with more numerous and specialized employees and formal person-to-person contact. This cluster of stores appears less frequently in the urban area than the street corner cluster. The market areas of the neighborhood centers are much larger and farther apart in space from each other and farther from their purchasing consumers than are their smaller kin. Their market areas also commonly overlap at the periphery, but completely overlap the smaller pedestrian-bound market areas of the street-corner clusters.

The *community center* serves several neighborhood areas. Its market area completely overlaps the two smaller tertiary foci. A large parking lot, or multi-level auto-storage facility, indicates that the consumers are generally arriving and departing via automobile. This center contains all of the functions of the street-corner and neighborhood clusters and includes a bank, physicians' offices or medical clinic, legal offices, welfare branch office, food stamp redemption center, supermarket (as opposed to grocery store), department store, and discount store.

The *regional shopping center* provides the central focus for several community-center marketing areas that often involve twenty to forty-five stores. It offers a wider variety of function and greater specialization than the three smaller centers. Large department stores, often a national chain, national chain supermarkets, large parking lots, specialty furniture, clothing, radio-tv-electronics stores, and attractive theatres and restaurants occupy these spaces. The promotional advertising of the stores is often done in cooperation with each other and in competition with other regional shopping centers and the central city. Stores from these centers will advertise full pages in the newspapers and have short commercials, usually locally programmed, on local radio and television stations. The threshold for such a dense concentration of establishments, whether measured in per-capita expenditure per unit of market areas or by population, is much higher than the community center.

One of the major attractions of consumers to these centers is the large variety of alternatives packed closely together and multipurpose shopping at one stop on one trip. Specialization of occupation is relatively extreme here. There are individuals who only sell goods at one counter and not at another; or who only inquire about references when paying with a check; or who only operate a cash register after some other person has made the sale. The highly specialized physician, such as a gynecologist or dermatologist, accepts new consumers only by reference.

The newer regional shopping centers are generally planned centers based on the implementation of the more sophis-ticated consumer and marketing research techniques and theory. Many of the stores or their managers or owners were previously located in the central business district.

The *central business district* is the largest concentration of retail businesses and all components of the tertiary subsystem. It has the largest trade area, encompassing all of the decreasingly smaller portions of the hierarchy: regional shopping center, community shopping center, neighborhood center, and street-corner cluster, and the tributary area external to the city, which may reach for several miles, depending on the spatial distribution of competing central business districts. This is the center of public and private administrative services, highly specialized shops and specialty goods, finest restaurants, theatres, museums, art galleries, and boutiques. The central business district generally, but not always, commands the largest retail sales in the city.

references

1. Bell, Thomas L.; Lieber, Stanley R.; and Rushton, Gerard. "Clustering of Services in Central Places." *Annals of the Association of American Geographers* 64 (June 1974): 214–25.

2. Berry, Brian J. L. "The Impact of Expanding Metropolitan Communities Upon the Central Place Hierarchy." *Annals of the Association of American Geographers* 50 (June 1960): 112–16.

3. ———. *Goals for Urban America.* Englewood Cliffs, N.J.: Prentice-Hall, 1967.

4. ———. *The Geography of Market Centers and Retail Distributions.* Englewood Cliffs, N.J.: Prentice-Hall, 1967.

5. ———. *Growth Centers in the American Urban System.* Cambridge, Mass.: Ballinger Publishing Co., 1973.

6. ———, and Horton, Frank E., eds. *Geographic Perspectives on the Urban Sys-*

tems. Englewood Cliffs, N.J.: Prentice-Hall, 1970.

7. ————; Barnum, H. G.; and Tennant, R. J. "Retail Location and Consumer Behavior." *Papers and Proceedings of the Regional Science Association* 9 (1962): 65–102.

8. Bucklin, L. P. *Shopping Patterns in an Urban Area.* I.B.E.R. Special Publications. Berkeley: University of California Press, 1967.

9. Clark, W. A. V. "Spacing Models in Intra-City Studies." *Geographical Analysis* 1 (1969): 391–98.

10. Claus, R. J.; Rothwell, D. C.; and Bottomley, J. "Measuring the Quality of a Low Order Retail Site." *Economic Geography* 48 (April 1972): 168–78.

11. Eighmy, T. H. "Rural Periodic Markets and the Extension of an Urban System: A Western Nigeria Example." *Economic Geography* 48 (July 1972): 299–314.

12. Gallegde, R. "Conceptualizing the Market Decision Process." *Journal of Regional Science* 7 (1967): 239–58.

13. Good, Charles M. "Periodic Markets: A Problem in Locational Analysis." *Professional Geographer* 24 (August 1972): 210–16.

14. Hurst, M., and Sellers, J. "An Analysis of Spatial Distribution of Customers Around Two Grocery Retailing Operations." *Professional Geographer* 21 (May 1969): 184–190.

15. Perlman, Richard. *Theory of Markets.* Hinsdale, Ill.: Dryden Press, 1972.

16. Pred, Allan R., and Kibel, Barry M. "An Application of Gaming Simulation to a General Model of Economic Locational Processes." *Economic Geography* 46 (April 1970): 136–56.

17. Preston, R. E. "The Structure of Central Place System." *Economic Geography* 47 (April 1971): 136–55.

18. Rostow, W. W. *The Stages of Economic Growth: A Non-Communist Manifesto.* New York: Cambridge University Press, 1960.

19. Semple, R. K., and Galledge, R. G. "An Analysis of Entropy Changes in a Settlement Pattern over Time." *Economic Geography* 45 (April 1970): 157–60.

20. Semple, R. K. "Recent Trends in the Spatial Concentration of Corporate Headquarters." *Economic Geography* 49 (October 1973): 309–18.

21. Symanski, Richard, and Webber, M. J. "Complex Periodic Market Cycles." *Annals of the Association of American Geographers* 64 (June 1974): 203–13.

22. Thoman, R., and Conklin, E. *Geography of International Trade.* Englewood Cliffs, N.J.: Prentice-Hall, 1967, pp. 175–79.

23. Vance, James E., Jr. *The Merchant's World; the Geography of Wholesailing.* Englewood Cliffs, N.J.: Prentice-Hall, 1970.

24. Webber, M. J., and Symanski R. "Periodic Markets: An Economic Location Analysis." *Economic Geography* 49 (July 1973): 213–27.

25. Wheeler, James O. "Trip Purposes and Urban Activity Linkages." *Annals of the Association of American Geographers* 62 (December 1972): 641–54.

379

transportation
services

21

21

The interaction between resources and markets appears to cause certain spatial patterns and systems of location. A location made relevant by its association with economic activities and markets, tends to be linked with other locations by a network of transport routes, which reflect the paths of *circulation* of materials, goods, people, and communication. The frequency and intensity of the circulation depend on the degrees of specialization of production, economic well being, and the spatial distribution of materials, economic activities, and markets.

THEORETICAL CONSIDERATIONS

Traditionally, transportation has been analyzed as a distributive set of activities reflecting socioeconomic interchanges, which are caused by areal differences in the type and level of economic activities. In this analysis, transportation is considered as an index of areal differentiation of economic activities; a higher value index means greater areal differentiation.

Implicit in this association is the recognition that the transportation network is the result of economic phenomena. No commercial activity can survive for very long without adequate and corresponding transport facilities. If a firm is located away from the source of its inputs or if the outputs cannot be moved to the consumer, the survival of the firm is seriously in question.

In specialized and commercial economies, transportation does not merely perpetuate the areal differentiation of economic activities; increasingly, trans-

portation directly effects economic growth.

The empirical evidence strongly supports the thesis that transportation is a prerequisite for the emergence of economic activities and for their growth. The infrastructure of circulation networks tends to lessen the pull toward material resource and market locations and also creates newer patterns of locations with greater areal differentiation. With economic progress, areal differentiation within a nation tends to become more distinct as agglomeration effects and economies of scale cause the means of production to be concentrated in fewer and larger firms. A uniformity in living standards, culture, and ideas tends to make a society more homogenous. These two forces of marked areal differentiation of production units and uniformity of consumer demand are harmonized by the transportation, or circulation, networks.

The modern technology of transportation has brought considerable reduction in the unit costs of movement and consequently has suggested modifications in the classic theories of location. For instance, the transportation components of the Von Thünen and Christaller models treat weight and bulkiness in direct relation to cost over a uniform plane, and this relationship was altered only in special cases where water transportation was possible.

Distance from raw-material sources and from markets affects the spatial distribution of economic phenomena; transportation is a means of overcoming and improving productivity and economic disadvantages that an area might have. The term distance is interpreted in several ways. Geographers frequently refer to it as geodesic, or physical, distance; i.e., the actual measured or mapped index of a physical separation of points on a surface or in space. Economists think of it in terms of economic distance, which is measured by some monetary value or real incurred cost of moving an object between two points. (The cost of transportation is strongly influenced by the structure of freight rates, as discussed in chapter 4). Sociologists view distance as a social phenomenon referring to identity and affinity between various sociocultural groups. A communications specialist may refer to distance as a factor involving communications efficiency.

Distance can also refer to temporal distance, or the time needed to move between two points using a given mode of transportation (see Table 21–1). The factual data in Table 21–1 lead to interesting and ironic conclusions: 1) the surface systems serving the great air terminals are so inadequate that time gained in the air is lost on the ground, moving to and from the airport; and 2) air, mass-transit, and highway systems are separate and unrelated, reflecting disorganization and lack of an efficient system.

Underlying all of the various perceptions of distance is the concept of accessibility, i.e., the permissive link between any two points. The relative degree of accessibility is a function of technology and mode of transportation and demand used to move objects or messages. The demand for the movement of objects and messages between any two locations is dependent upon the conditions of complementarity between them. (The complementarity may be weakened by intervening locations that may qualify as feasible substitutions.) Whenever there exists accessibility between two locations, routes will emerge. The exact path of a route is determined by economic, technological, and physical factors, sometimes collectively called least cost and least effort factors; by connectivity, vehicular capacity, and technical quality of routes; by fineness, i.e., accessibility to local shippers, stress, and density, or route mileage per unit area; and by relative characteristics of the available transport modes.

Spatial interaction through transportation, a circulatory process of overcoming physical distance, produces areal differentiation. Transportation is not

TABLE 21–1   A Comparison of Driving and Flying Time and Cost[1]

DOWNTOWN TO DOWNTOWN	MILES	TOTAL TIME		TOTAL COST	
		DRIVING	FLYING[2]	DRIVING[3]	FLYING[4]
Toledo–Detroit	59	1 hr. 15 min.	2 hr. 50 min.	$ 6.49	$31.75
Milwaukee–Chicago	86	1 hr. 30 min.	2 hr. 25 min.	9.46	25.75
Sacramento–San Francisco	90	1 hr. 30 min.	2 hr. 20 min.	9.90	20.86
Cincinnati–Indianapolis	105	1 hr. 45 min.	2 hr. 46 min.	11.55	26.95
Cleveland–Pittsburgh	131	2 hr. 15 min.	3 hr. 5 min.	14.41	29.95
New Orleans–Mobile	147	2 hr. 45 min.	2 hr. 20 min.	16.71	30.45
Boston–New York	213	4 hr. no min.	3 hr. 5 min.	23.43	31.95
Toronto–Detroit	233	4 hr. 15 min.	3 hr. 35 min.	25.63	36.55
New York–Washington, D.C.	240	4 hr. 15 min.	3 hr. 35 min.	26.40	43.20

[1] This table, when revised, is not likely to yield substantially different interpretation. Proportional upward changes in time and cost do not effect the relationships discussed in the text.

[2] Includes cab to and from downtown, writing and checking time before flight, baggage delay following flight.

[3] At 11 cents per mile.

[4] Includes cab fares and tips. Does not include stack-up times or delays. Add 30 minutes to all flights in bad weather, 2 hours during traffic control slowdown, 8 hours if flight is cancelled.

Source: Caterpillar Tractor Co., "Crisis-Transportation," Form No. AEO 36931, 1971, p. 35. Reprinted by permission.

merely a network of conduits or a matrix of origin or destination; it is a systems framework of interrelationships between physical, social, technological, and economic variables. The circulation system is both a cause and a result of economic activity. The validity of this relationship depends upon the objectives and the stage of economic growth. Our object here is to describe and analyze the circulation network between locations.

Transportation includes services related to railways, waterways, highways, airways, pipelines, and communication pathways. (Communication services are treated separately in chapter 26.) These services are means of circulating various types of items being traded. Thus, an analysis of circulation service activities must not only deal with the means of circulation but also with the associated trade patterns. The interdependence between the means and the related trade patterns, although recognized, has not been widely used in geographic analysis. Such inspection yields helpful information to understand the location patterns of various types of activities.

The underlying motivation for the prevalence of any form of circulation is the need to meet the wants of spatially dispersed producers, consumers, buyers, and sellers through the acts of collecting, rearranging, moving, storing, and selling. On the one hand, circulation flow patterns often serve as a permitting factor in the location or occurrence of an activity at a particular location. On the other hand, a particular activity located at a certain place may give rise to a flow pattern of circulation involving a specific form of transport or communication medium that may influence its level of activity.

Various investigations reveal that the availability of suitable means of circulation are instrumental in the location of economic activities. The location, type, capacity, and development of a particular circulation system or route depends upon existing or potential long-range traffic or use flows, relative benefits and costs, alternatives available to potential users, and political and social considerations. Once again it is difficult to say which is the cause and which is the effect. The question of whether the circulation system is based on the expected traffic flow or vice versa is so complex that studies have attempted to discover the relationship by holding one of the two constant—resulting in findings that both are highly interdependent. However, current research has leaned heavily toward explaining existing circulation patterns and their impact on the location of economic activity.[1]

WATERWAYS

The usefulness and convenience of water as a transport medium evidently occurred to man early in his history. Although the extent of use varies widely among nations, worldwide importance for domestic and international trade remains high. As Figure 21–1 shows, there are basically two types of waterways: ocean and inland.

Oceanways. The routes comprising the oceanways are determined by a multiplicity of factors:

1. *Direction.* In general, the major ocean routes follow east–west directions linking the chief industrial nations and their markets. The north–south routes tend to

[1] Various studies dealing with the analysis of communications systems frequently employ the tools of network geometry and graph theory. With these tools, the circulation system as an integrated whole comprising various means is depicted in terms of a series of links or routes and nodes or vertices (cities or towns), where changes in one part of the system affect all other parts of the network. The links provide information about the efficiency and degree of connectivity of the system.

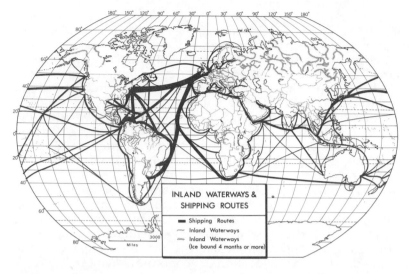

INLAND WATERWAYS &
SHIPPING ROUTES

■ Shipping Routes
— Inland Waterways
〜 Inland Waterways
(Ice bound 4 months or more)

FIGURE 21–1

hug the shoreline, taking advantage of prevailing ocean currents.

2. *Distance.* Quite naturally the routes follow deep waters and the shortest surface distance between two points.

3. *Navigation hazards.* Ocean routes follow deep waters, avoid shoals, rocks, icebergs, and, where possible, fogs and storms.

4. *Harbor facilities.* Natural as well as man-made facilities, especially those with fueling and cargo-handling abilities, play a decisive role in the location of ocean routes.

5. *Volume, perishability, and location of goods destined for international trade.* Recent United Nations statistics indicate that Anglo-America and Western Europe account for approximately two-thirds of the world's trade, most of it via ocean carriers. European nations, including the USSR, account for about one-half of the world total.

6. *Technology.* With the advanced technology of ocean trade, many difficulties imposed by physical factors have been eliminated; for example, the invention and application of the mariner's compass, radar, and loran; larger capacity, length, and draft[2]

of vessels; refrigeration facilities; internal combustion engines; and mechanical loading and unloading facilities are technological factors that influence ocean routes and the kinds of carriers used.

There are three kinds of ocean carriers—the liner, the tramp, and the tanker. Liners are ships in a fleet or line that ply regularly between scheduled ports regardless of the load available. The tramp is the slow dredge of the sea, carrying cumbersome cargoes of great weight or bulk in proportion to value, having no definite sailing schedules, and operating as a single unit of transport. Tankers are carriers of uncartoned or unboxed freights, such as oil, ore, grain, etc.

Figure 21–1 shows the world's major ocean-shipping areas, the most prominent being:

1. North Atlantic

2. Mediterranean–Asiatic

3. European–eastern South America

---

[2] Larger draft vessels cannot visit shallower harbors. The modern super-sized tankers have approximately 50-foot drafts, and there are few harbors deep enough to accommodate them. This necessitates either rerouting the oceanways or deepening the existing harbors.

4. Panama Canal
5. Cape of Good Hope
6. North Pacific

The North Atlantic route links Western Europe and eastern North America. Since 1838, when the first transatlantic steamship line began operations in the North Atlantic Ocean, a well-defined trade pattern has evolved. Today this route is the busiest shipping route, with two major lanes (east to west and west to east) sixty miles apart, mandatorily followed by all carriers under the North Atlantic Track Agreement.

The Mediterranean–Asiatic route, the world's longest single trade route, links Asia and Europe through the Suez Canal.[3] The route is characterized by an unusually large number of integrating branch lines; e.g., the Mediterranean and Black Sea; northwestern Europe and the Mediterranean; Europe and the Far East, South East, and Middle East.

The European–eastern South America route, which links Europe with eastern South American ports, is gaining prominence with expanding trade between Latin American countries and Europe.

The Panama Canal route connects the eastern United States with the west coasts of South America and the United States, as well as Australia with Europe, and the eastern United States with the Far East.

The Cape of Good Hope route links the eastern U.S. and Western Europe with the western, southern, and eastern coasts of Africa and connects Europe with Southeast Asia and Australia. The congestion on this route is affected by the conditions surrounding the traffic flow through the Suez Canal. When the Suez Canal is closed, the traffic that normally goes through it is directed toward the Cape of Good Hope route.

[3] Often closed because of the Arab–Israeli conflict.

The North Pacific route links the west coast of North America with eastern Asia. The increasing importance of eastern economies to the United States has recently intensified traffic on this route.

Inland Waterways. In contrast to oceanways, inland waterways require frequent dredging, widening, and embanking. Their role is keenly competitive with other principal means of transportation, e.g., railways, airways, highways, and pipelines. The incidence of inland waterways is determined by:

1. Depth, length, and width of a channel.
2. Perpetual stream flow.
3. Frequency and height of falls and locks.
4. Speed of water flow. Higher currents fill a stream faster, and also erode banks and alter stream beds, making navigation difficult.
5. Vegetation. Rivers with heavy vegetation make it virtually impossible for boats to pass through.
6. Alternative uses of the streams and rivers. If alternative uses of the flow outbid the navigational use, the waterways may not be economically justifiable.
7. Technology.
8. Religious and cultural values attached to water flows. Some cultures may not permit the use and development of rivers for navigation. The Ganges River, for example, is a sacred river to most Hindus who would regard its use for navigation as sacrilegious.

Waterways are preferred to other means of transport because the cost per ton-mile is considerably less. This is particularly true for oceanways. The inland waterways, however, due to the keen competition offered by alternative means of transportation, specialize in carrying heavy and bulky commodities, such as petroleum products, coal and coke, sand, gravel and stone, iron ore, iron and steel, logs and lumber, chemicals, and grains.

WATERWAYS AND
INTERNATIONAL TRADE

Almost all nations use waterways directly or indirectly in their import–export transactions because the major share of the international trade volume is carried by water transport (*see* Figure 21–1).

World trade has not only increased from $62 billion in 1950 to about $428 billion in 1972, but it has also changed in structure. The U.S. share has fallen slightly—about one percentage point in each of the past two decades—and is now about 15 percent. The growth in the European Economic Community's share of world exports has increased from 15 percent in 1950 to 29 percent in 1972; these figures include trade between EEC members. If other countries that are being taken into the expanding EEC are included, the enlarged EEC will account for over 40 percent of world trade and for 50 percent of world trade in industrial products, or three times the U.S. share. In 1972, West Germany surpassed the U.S. as the leading exporter of manufactures. The story of Japan is similarly told. The share of less developed nations is consistently dropping.

Although since the mid-1960s the overall U.S. aggregate market share entering world trade has increased significantly, it is still a small fraction (13 percent) of our total production compared to 63, 40, 37, 30, and 22 percent in Canada, the United Kingdom, West Germany, Japan, and the European Economic Community (excluding intratrade) countries, respectively. One can understand why a country such as Canada is so concerned about American investment and trade policy when she sees that 63 percent of her production is exported. Likewise, the portion of the United Kingdom's production that is exported is four times that of the U.S. It is therefore important to recognize the perspective of U.S. involvement in foreign trade and to understand the stake foreign economies have in U.S. trade and related negotiations of tariffs and exchange rates.[4]

To the USSR these problems should seem less important, since her ratio of exports to production is far lower than any other nation, being only 8 percent. Her position in world trade, therefore, makes her less vulnerable to outside threats and pressures.

RAILWAYS

Railways as a means of circulation not only play an important role in the initial stages of economic development, but also help to sustain achieved development. Their location is determined by:

1. Collective initiative and action taken either by private enterprise or by government. Collective action is needed because of the relatively large investment involved, which may be provided through private enterprise, if it is large enough, or by government subsidies.

2. Suitability and cost of alternative or competing forms of transportation.

3. Terrain and other natural obstacles, such as areas with high mountains, lakes and streams, and infested areas often discourage the location of railways.

4. Length of haul.

5. Weight of consignment.

6. Related technology.

7. Traffic density. Regions with a relatively higher degree of traffic density on water, air, and land routes tend to intensify rail transportation.

8. Speed and safety.

9. The availability of steel.

---

[4] Interested students wishing to examine the structure and level of imports and exports for a country should consult the *United Nations Statistical Yearbook*. The technical aspects of exchange rates can be found in a standard international economics textbook. Chapter 4 of this text presents a detailed analysis for the basis of international trade.

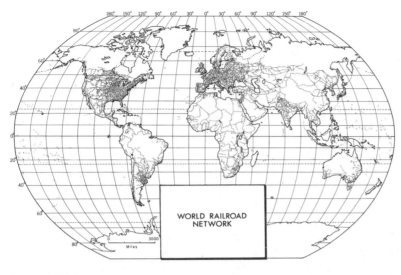

WORLD RAILROAD
NETWORK

FIGURE 21–2

Railways are most heavily concentrated in the industrialized areas of the world, i.e., in Western Europe and the eastern United States. Argentina, India, and eastern Australia also have extensive rail networks (see Figure 21–2).

The gauge or width of the tracks is not universally uniform, varying from three feet in some countries to six feet in others. In 1871 there were twenty-eight different gauges. The standard gauge now used in North America and most of Western Europe is 4 feet 8½ inches. In Spain and Portugal the gauge is 5 feet 6½ inches; 5 feet in the Soviet Union; in most of South America 3 feet 3⅛ inches; in India it is partly 5 feet 6 inches and partly 3 feet 3⅛ inches, as well as other narrow gauges. In Australia rail gauges vary from state to state.

The diversity in gauge sizes is a function of relative topography, source of power, length of railway routes, technology, type of traffic, speed, provincialism, and trade. This diversity makes it very difficult for a network to emerge and operate. Where tracks of different gauges meet, entire trainloads of goods must be transferred through loading operations or through some track-adjusting mechanism.

In comparing the relative cost figures between regional railways, it is particularly important to consider freight-rate territories and group, class, commodity, and in-transit rates. A single group rate applies to all points in a territory; a class rate to small-quantity consignments; and a commodity rate to large consignments. An in-transit rate is a special privilege granted by some authority. The same long-route rate schedule is applied as if there were no intervening stops, although the intervening stops may mean adding to the value of the consignment by further processing.

Table 21–2 presents data on railway passenger kilometers and tonnage kilometers for selected countries, along with population density and per-capita gross domestic product (GDP). The ratio of passenger kilometers traveled and ton kilometers hauled tends to decrease with increasing per capita GDP; however, increasing population density tends to re-

387

TABLE 21-2   Railway Passengers, Tonnage, Population Density, and Per-Capita Gross Domestic Product for Selected Countries, 1972

	PASSENGER KILOMETERS (millions)	NET-TON KILOMETERS (millions)	POPULATION DENSITY	PER-CAPITA GROSS DOMESTIC PRODUCT
Angola	270	4,268	5	$ 200*
Argentina	12,183	12,284	9	1,261****
Austria	6,768	10,000	89	2,758
Australia		25,608	2	3,228****
Brazil	11,489	18,080	12	513
Bulgaria	6,700	15,825	77	NA
Canada	3,288	180,535	2	4,805
Egypt	7,306	2,976	35	216**
France	43,093	68,493	95	3,823
W. Germany	39,638	64,648	248	4,218
India	125,469	133,311	172	94*
Italy	35,394	17,120	180	2,164
Japan	297,888	59,872	287	2,823
Mexico	4,485	23,878	27	781
Poland	38,782	109,777	106	NA
Romania	20,184	53,280	87	NA
Sweden	4,470	16,214	18	5,157
Switzerland	9,502	7,178	156	4,593
United Kingdom	33,902	23,152	226	2,472
U.S.	13,454	1,135,643	22	5,551
USSR	285,792	2,760,823	11	NA

* 1969
** 1970
*** 1971

Source: Based on the *United Nations Statistical Yearbook, 1973* (New York: United Nations, 1974), pp. 411–14.

strain this decrease. With increasing per-capita incomes, more personalized and faster means of travel are preferred, leaving the railways to haul goods. Affluence also permits increasingly market oriented locations to arise through a network of highways. This phenomena tends to promote trucking at the expense of railways because the effectiveness and rate structure of railroads tend to become unfavorable over shorter distances. The history of U.S. railroads illustrates how cost, distance, and rate structure have effected the relative role of railways as a means of transportation.

Railways are characterized as capital intensive, increasing effectiveness with length of distance and haul and complicated rate structures. The analysis of rate structures, briefly discussed in chapter 4, covers a sizable body of literature. In general, it involves several principles: 1) efficiencies in mass and heavy movement warrant lower rates; 2) the consideration of competitive and alternative means of transportation; and 3) the possibility of return traffic or flow warrant lower rates as they would lower the unit cost. For a detailed and classic analysis of the impact of rate structures on the distribution and growth of economic activities, see Alexander, et al. (1).

MOTORWAYS

Highways are a means of transportation to move light loads over short distances involving the least amount of time, although the interstate highway system of the United States and Europe also make long hauls feasible.

The location of highways is determined by factors such as topography, availability of gravel and cement, technology, and competition from alternative means of transportation, intensity of traffic, collective initiative and action, environmental pollution, and alternative uses of land. Like railways, highways vary in width, though to a greater degree. Not only are highways differentiated by the number of lanes, type of pavement, bridges, curves, signs, overpasses, etc., but also by scenery.

Motor transport is an essential part of the total transportation system in North America and Europe. Its importance is so widely recognized that many cultural traits in these regions are related to the automobile and roadways. Today's motorist can drive from New England to the Midwest without encountering a stoplight, saving hours of travel time with a better chance of arriving at his destination safely. The U.S. Interstate Highway System, now almost completed, is responsible for a great deal of the ease and speed of driving in the U.S.

Ideas that had first been used to build city streets were applied to the highways. Versions of center strips, grade separations, and controlled access existed in eastern cities at the turn of the century. New Jersey pioneered the super highway, with traffic circles, grade separations, limited access, and the first cloverleaf and grade separation entrance. The dual-highway concept was not used before 1927, when it cropped up in highway plans in New Jersey and Chicago. During the 1930s, the era of the expressway began. The Pennsylvania Turnpike, a toll road, opened in 1940; it was the first modern, long-distance highway designed for pleasure and commercial traffic.

World War II limited domestic construction, but brought about several notable military roads, particularly the Ledo Road in Burma and the 1,500-mile Alaska Highway. Even more important than the roads were the techniques developed in their construction for using bulldozers, graders, and other modern equipment. The stage was set for the postwar road-building boom that followed the return to peace. In 1944 the

389

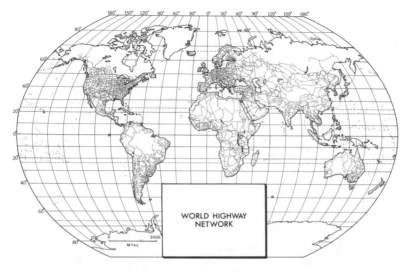

WORLD HIGHWAY
NETWORK

FIGURE 21–3

U.S. Congress, acting on recommendations prepared some years earlier by the Bureau of Roads, passed the basic legislation for the National System of Interstate Highways, the greatest road-building program in the nation's history and one that has given impetus to business and vacation travel, promoted the decentralization of industry, and vastly improved the country's system of distribution.

Figure 21–3 shows the present network of the world's highways. This network positively correlates with the economic well being of corresponding regions. (The regional distribution of motor vehicle production was discussed in chapter 15.) Areas with the highest per capita motor vehicles also reflect the highest level of standard of living. Consistent data for motor passenger and freight traffic is scanty, but it is reasonable to assume their volume corresponds with the number of motor-vehicles.

TABLE 21–3   Toll Road Revenues and Traffic for Selected U.S. Turnpikes and Thruways

Pennsylvania Turnpike		*Ohio Turnpike*	
1951 Revenue	$10,842,586	1956 Revenue	$15,350,966
1972 Revenue	$73,189,300	1972 Revenue	$42,103,507
1951 Traffic	5,494,192	1956 Traffic	9,980,984
1972 Traffic	53,579,861	1972 Traffic	22,719,384
Thomas E. Dewey Thruway		*Chesapeake Bay Bridge and Tunnel*	
1955 Revenue	$ 16,636,222	1965 Revenue	$7,581,296
1972 Revenue	$114,542,582	1972 Revenue	$9,112,025
1955 Traffic	18,300,000	1965 Traffic	1,167,682
1972 Traffic	145,999,293	1972 Traffic	1,402,935

Source: The New York Times, May 27, 1973, p. F15. © 1973 by The New York Times Company. Reprinted by permission.

The production and use of motor vehicles has been phenomenal from 1963 to 1972. In 1963, world motor vehicles in use totaled 154,950,000 units. By 1972 this figure increased to 271,800,000, or 75 percent. The largest increase was shown by Japan and West Germany. Although the U.S. has not shown as significant an increase in the number of motor vehicles in use, it has intensified the use of motor vehicles as shown in Table 21–3. In New York, for example, where the 559-mile Governor Thomas E. Dewey Thruway, the longest toll road in the nation, opened in 1954, gross revenues in 1972 were $114.5 million compared to $16.6 million in 1955, a 590 percent increase over this period. This increase is about 33 percent a year, or more than 11 times the region's annual economic growth rate.

AIRWAYS

Airways are the most versatile and unrivaled means of moving light and highly valued objects and of utilizing advanced technology of containerization, refrigeration, and other devices for quick handling. The air route, vertically and horizontally, is influenced by:

1. Location of population and industrial centers.[5]

2. Location of airports.

[5] Students interested in detailed analysis of air routes use may wish to calculate the ratio between the number of airline passenger departures (or the tonnage shipped) and population of airport cities. The larger the ratio the greater the intensity of air route use and vice versa. The analysis may further be expanded by calculating ratios for various destinations.

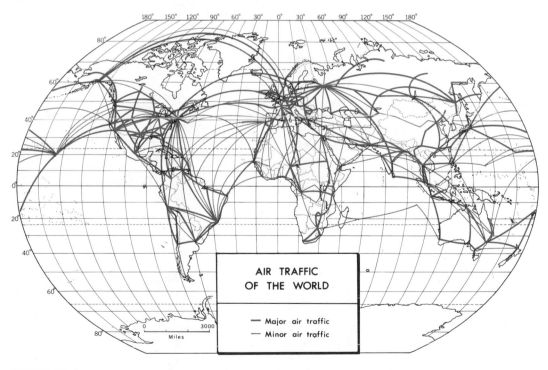

FIGURE 21–4

3. Weather and climate, including the incidence and frequency of fog, heavy clouds, wind, hail, and storms; terrain; navigational technology; size of aircraft; air pollution; government controls.

Figure 21–4 shows the location of major air routes. The concentration of air routes is greatest in the United States and Western Europe. However, in regions where alternative forms of transportation are few and nebulous, air transportation is of great significance.

Air routes and carriers at present are basically engaged in moving people and are only nominally concerned with movement of goods. During most of the 1960s, less than 1 percent of the freight-ton-mileage was handled by the air carriers. However, with increasing size of aircraft, regional specialization, and demand for fresh produce, the trend is toward greater use of airways to move goods.

The manufacturers of airplanes are few: the United States, the United Kingdom, France, and the USSR; India and the People's Republic of China were recently added to this list. Planes are being built that are larger and faster. Aircraft log passenger and cargo kilometers in much greater measure than their production would indicate.

Figure 21–5 shows the changes in airplane capacity and speed. In 1936, the DC–3 had a speed of 185 mph, a passenger capacity of 28, a range of 1,500 miles and a payload of 2½ tons; in 1969, the Boeing 747 had a speed of 624 mph, a passenger capacity of 490, a range of 6,000 miles, and a payload of 62 tons. These changes, coupled with the uncertain prospects of the American Supersonic Transport 1 (SST–1), the British–French Concorde, and the Russian TU 144, will further shrink time and distance by moving an ever greater number and volume of air traffic in ever decreasing time. The SST–1 will carry 100 or so

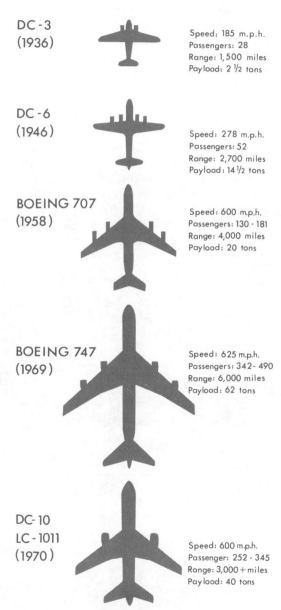

DC-3 (1936)

Speed: 185 m.p.h.
Passengers: 28
Range: 1,500 miles
Payload: 2 ½ tons

DC-6 (1946)

Speed: 278 m.p.h.
Passengers: 52
Range: 2,700 miles
Payload: 14 ½ tons

BOEING 707 (1958)

Speed: 600 m.p.h.
Passengers: 130 - 181
Range: 4,000 miles
Payload: 20 tons

BOEING 747 (1969)

Speed: 625 m.p.h.
Passengers: 342 - 490
Range: 6,000 miles
Payload: 62 tons

DC-10
LC-1011 (1970)

Speed: 600 m.p.h.
Passenger: 252 - 345
Range: 3,000 + miles
Payload: 40 tons

FIGURE 21–5 *Changes in Capacity and Speed of Aircraft: 1936–1970*

passengers from New York to London in less than two hours. Its cruising speed will be Mach 3, or better than 2,000 miles per hour.[6] One SST–1 will replace four 1960-type, 600 mph jet aircraft, or twelve Constellations or DC–7's.

The increasing speed and size of planes have reduced the per-unit cost under conditions of full-capacity use. These phenomena, coupled with the mushrooming demand for air services, have caused growth in civil aviation beyond expectation during the 1950s and 1960s. Table 21–4 shows a very moderate increase (and in some cases a drop) in demand due to large oil-price increases in the 1970s. The large increase in cargo

[6] Mach numbers relate to the speed of sound under various conditions: Mach 1 is rated as 759 mph at sea level, but in thinner air, it is somewhat less than that.

services has implications for strengthening specialized locations since they can reach distant markets by air. An enlarged market frequently results in economies of scale of production, compensating for the increased air transportation cost.

PIPELINES

Pipelines are important means of transporting crude oil, natural gas, refined petroleum products, water, and solids in suspension (such as pulverized coal mixed with water).

The location of pipelines is determined by the location of resources and markets, terrain, the dependability and cost of alternative means of transportation, transit "shrinkage," related

TABLE 21–4   Domestic and International Civil Aviation: Total Scheduled Services in Selected Countries

	MILLION KILOMETERS FLOWN		
	1969	1972	PERCENT CHANGE
United States	3,967	3,823	− 3.63%
Passenger	166	192	+15.66
Cargo ton	5,095	6,285	+23.36
Mail ton	2,000	1,753	−12.35
France	199	228	+14.57%
Passenger	8	11	+37.50
Cargo ton	443	619	+39.73
Mail ton	62	77	+24.19
United Kingdom	298	348	+16.78%
Passenger	15	18	+20.00
Cargo ton	546	715	+30.95
Mail ton	86	104	+20.93
World	6,830	7,210	+ 5.56%
Passenger	298	367	+23.15
Cargo ton	9,970	13,220	+32.59
Mail ton	2,550	2,420	− 5.10

Source: Based on the *United Nations Statistical Yearbook, 1973* (New York: United Nations, 1974), pp. 454–66.

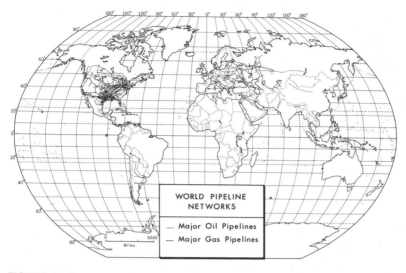

FIGURE 21–6

technology, and the frequency of earthquakes.

As Figure 21–6 shows, most of the world's pipelines are in the United States, Europe, Canada, and the Middle East. The importance of pipelines in the U.S. is evidenced by the fact that in 1972 approximately 24 percent of freight-ton-mileage was via pipeline.

The advantages of pipelines over other forms of land transportation lie in their ability to cross most terrain almost unaffected by weather changes, thereby assuring locations served a continuous flow of materials. In the United States, over three-fourths of crude petroleum consumption is moved through pipelines, about one-fifth by water, and the remainder by truck and rail.

The continuous flow of commodities through pipelines has a significant influence on regions producing petrochemicals and plastics. A region served with pipelines enjoys an economic advantage over regions served by other modes of transportation. Furthermore, the probability of labor strikes is much less in pipeline transport than in other forms of transportation, because the annual operating cost of pipelines is less than 10 percent of the original cost of laying the pipes and of setting up the pumping stations.

Considerable interest has been expressed about the environmental effects of pipelines. For example, the much-debated Alaska pipeline bills, passed by the Congress in 1973, which will transport crude oil from Alaska to the continental states, brought a focus to environmental variables associated with pipelines. The price of this variable might reduce the comparative advantage of pipelines over other competing modes of transportation.

references

1. Alexander, John W.; Brown, S. Earl; and Dahlberg, Richard E. "Freight Rates: Selected Aspects of Uniform Nodal Regions." In H. G. Roepke, ed. *Readings in Economic Geography.* John Wiley and Sons, 1967.

2. Becht, J. Edwin. *A Geography of Transportation and Business Logistics*. Dubuque, Iowa: William C. Brown Co., 1970.

3. Creighton, R. L. *Urban Transportation Planning*. Urbana: University of Illinois Press, 1970.

4. Garrison, W. L. "Fragments of Future Transportation Policy and Programs." *Economic Geography* 49 (April 1973): 95–102.

5. Harvey, David. *Explanation in Geography*. New York: St. Martin's Press, 1970.

6. Hay, Alan M. *Transport for the Space Economy: A Geographical Study*. Seattle: University of Washington Press, 1973.

7. Horton, Frank E.; Louviere, Jordan; and Reynolds, David R. "Mass Transit Utilization: Individual Response Data Inputs." *Economic Geography* 49 (April 1973): 122–33.

8. Hurst, Michael E. "Transportation and the Societal Framework." *Economic Geography* 49 (April 1973): 163–77.

9. ———, ed. *Transportation Geography: Comments and Readings*. New York: McGraw-Hill Book Co., 1973.

10. Mayer, Harold M. "Some Geographic Aspects of Technological Change in Maritime Transportation." *Economic Geography* 49 (April 1973): 145–55.

11. Mertins, Herman. *National Transportation Policy in Transition*. Lexington, Mass.: Lexington Books, D. C. Heath and Co., 1972.

12. Morrill, Richard L. *The Spatial Organization of Society*. 2nd. ed. North Scituate, Mass.: Duxbury Press, 1974, pp. 127–51.

13. New York City Planning Commission. *The Waterfront: Supplement to the Plan for New York City*. New York: New York City Planning Commission, 1971.

14. Robinson, John. *Highways and Our Environment*. New York: McGraw-Hill Book Co., 1971.

15. Stone, Tabor R. *Beyond the Automobile: Reshaping the Transportation Environment*. Englewood Cliffs, N.J.: Prentice-Hall, 1971.

16. Stutz, Frederick P. "Distance and Network Effects on Urban Social Travel Fields." *Economic Geography* 49 (April 1973): 134–43.

17. Sun, Nai-Ching, and Bunamo, Michael C. "Competition For Handling U.S. Foreign Cargoes: The Port of New York's Experience." *Economic Geography* 49 (April 1973): 156–62.

18. Taaffe, Edward J., and Gauthier, Howard L., Jr. *Geography of Transportation*. Englewood Cliffs, N.J.: Prentice-Hall, 1973.

19. Traft, Gerald; Meyer, John R.; and Valette, Jean-Paul. *The Role of Transportation in Regional Economic Development: A Charles River Study*. Lexington, Mass.: Lexington Books, D. C. Heath and Co., 1971.

20. U.S. Department of Transportation. *A Statement on National Transportation*. Washington, D.C.: U.S. Government Printing Office, 1971.

21. Weiner, Paul, and Deak, Edward J. *Environmental Factors in Transportation Planning*. Lexington, Mass.: Lexington Books, D. C. Heath and Co., 1972.

marketing
services

22

22

Once produced, goods must be moved to consumers. This movement involves physical transfer from place to place, pausing now and then for processing and storage. Activities relating to transfer of goods—transportation, preparation for use, storage, pricing and exchange, wholesaling and retailing—may be grouped under two broad categories: transportation and marketing. (Transportation services were discussed in chapter 21.)

Marketing refers to service activities involved in obtaining an exchange of a product between a seller and a buyer. The price at which the exchange takes place is determined by the economic framework of the society, basically either by a tradition, command, or market framework (see chapter 4). A market relies on the judgment of buyers and sellers who interact to determine price, given their objectives, preferences, demands, and the stock of goods.

In practice, none of the price-determining mechanisms operate as strictly as described, but rather with complex behavior. For example, the pricing system in the U.S. is not solely dependent upon a market response; it arises within a market system with numerous modifications of the ideal model (see Heilbroner [6]). Marketing centers on delivering goods in the form, at the time, and to the place that consumers desire. In this process, services of commodity exchanges, brokers, commission houses, wholesalers, and retailers are involved. The location of these services is basically a function of population densities, transportation and communications networks, and the spatial distribution of the goods-producing firms. This suggests that the spatial aspects of marketing activities are more meaningfully analyzed on a local, rather than on a global, basis.

The extent of such services is dependent upon the degree of marketing specialization. James E. Vance, Jr. (14) delineates the distribution process into two systems—open and closed. The *closed distribution system,* which involves direct association of producers with sellers and with customers, assures sufficient interchange between sellers and buyers. It evolves from a self-sufficient unit to Christaller's central place system. The distribution network expands by modification of transportation routes into hexagonal networks over a continuous space.

The *open distribution system* also eventually develops into the central place system's hexagonal pattern, but with discontinuity in continuous space. The trade areas expand into distinct modules of central places with or without spatial links. The most prominent link between producers and consumers in the open distribution system is provided by the agent of trade or marketing services.

FUNCTIONS OF MARKETING

Man constantly strives to produce more per unit of input. In this pursuit he has found it necessary to create a division of labor and to promote specialization. The growth of technology also has depended upon breaking down an overall task into highly specialized jobs, each of them assigned to some individual or group of individuals as the only contribution they make to the productive work of the economy. The degree of specialization is determined not only by the particular skills and activities of an individual but also by the limitations of the firm that employs him and by its current state of technology, research, and development. Whatever the stimulus or forces that cause and promote specialization, the immediate consequence of this phenomenon is economic interdependence that necessitates marketing.

Modern marketing activities have several functions:

1. The marketing systems transfers the ownership title of goods from the seller to the buyer. Ownership includes rights to possess, control, use, and enjoy goods and their benefits and to sell or otherwise dispose of goods according to law. Marketing activities involve the process of transferring a good or service from one possessor to another. In this process, services are performed to create five different kinds of utility values:

a. *Form:* grading, cleaning, minor processing, etc., of a product

b. *Place:* procurement and delivery of goods and services

c. *Time:* storing goods and services to be made available when demanded

d. *Convenience:* closeness to residences to reduce transfer cost

e. *Possession:* provides quick possession at one place (for example, the checkout line) of various kinds of goods and services

2. Marketing accomplishes information exchange between buyers and sellers and between consumers and producers by exposing the consumers to mass displays of what producers offer for sale.

3. Marketing services familiarize the producer with the relative levels of demand at various locations.

4. Although marketing services are induced by the phenomena of specialization, once begun, they tend to perpetuate and enhance economic efficiency in goods-producing sectors.

5. Marketing services spread the risk factor over a larger area of the economy and thus promote stability of the economy. (If spoilage, price, or demand risks are fully born by the producer, his survival is threatened.)

Some view marketing as a passive act and marketing services as merely supplying goods to consumers or buyers. But in a growing, dynamic economy in which competition is the chief coordinator, marketing services try to create new or larger demands for products.

LOCATION OF MARKETING ACTIVITIES

The location patterns of marketing activities are influenced by the theoretical expositions presented in chapters 12 and 19. Only highly relevant concepts are outlined here.

Accessibility. Marketing centers or activities tend to locate at places most accessible to consumers or buyers of services in terms of time, proximity, convenience, means of communication, and transfer cost. Population and the factors governing demand are influential in location.

Population. The location of people has always been pertinent in locating marketing firms. Daytime and nighttime population centers indicate where marketing services may be optimally located.

Transportation Networks. Transportation facilities play an important role in the location of marketing activities. Wholesalers tend to locate close to rail, truck, and water terminals, whereas retailers tend to locate near nighttime population concentrations.

The Locus of Producing Units. The object of locating is to minimize transportation cost from the production to the consumer site; the location of goods-producing units also enters into location decisions of marketing firms.

Agglomeration. Marketing activities tend to concentrate at a single location to permit one-stop shopping; to minimize transfer cost; to meet buyers' desires to compare price and quality, as well as to allow sellers to effectively compete; to reduce overhead cost of buildings, utilities, security, and parking; to minimize risks of robbery and vandalism; and to reduce advertising costs by sharing those costs with other firms.

Space Requirements. Space needed for the performance of service often influences the location of marketing services; for example, furniture stores and automobile dealers would choose locations with relatively lower rent cost.

Homogeneity or Heterogeneity of Products or Services. Services dealing with fairly homogeneous products (groceries, gasoline, laundry and dry cleaning, etc.) tend to follow residential patterns; services dealing with heterogeneous products tend to follow the shopping center pattern to permit convenient and quick comparisons of merchandise.

Spatial Interdependence. The level and structure of marketing activities at one location are directly dependent upon the facilities and attractions at alternative or surrounding locations. The considerations of spatial interdependence partly explain the hierarchical arrangements of wholesalers, retailers, shopping centers, advertising firms, etc. Within this hierarchical system, a metropolis encompasses the city as a service center, the city encompasses the town, and so on, down to neighborhood centers.

Zoning Ordinances. Zoning ordinances are political influences that shape the pattern of activity locations. For example, city or county zoning regulations restrict the type of building and activity that may occur in an area. Firms must choose a location within these defined areas.

PROBLEMS IN MEASURING MARKETING

Fundamentally there are two standards for measuring the amount of marketing: marketing costs and revenues. (Given reasonably accurate measures of these variables, one can compute a ratio to arrive at the "efficiency" of marketing.) Marketing cost can be measured as the sum of dollars spent for marketing by those who buy the product or as a sum of dollars spent in buying labor, materials, etc., by those who distribute the product. Revenue can be measured in dollars received from the sale of goods. The measures of cost and revenue are not direct measures of the contribution made by marketing services, but they are the most frequently used. Volume of sales, number of employees, payroll, etc. are popular measures used by cost-and-revenue approaches.

To calculate the contribution made by marketing, the measure of "value-added" is more appropriate. A value-added measure is basically total sales minus all costs except raw materials. (In marketing, raw materials are the merchandise that is to be sold to the buyers.) Thus the value-added by the marketing process is the dollar value of the utility created by the marketing firms.

Merely changing the terminology of measurement will not make marketing useful and desirable, and "value" and "utility" are ambiguous terms. To an economic geographer, anything has value if it can be exchanged for something else in an open market. Social critics argue that a product has value only if it contributes in some way to social welfare. It is important to measure marketing needs on their merits, not by the play of labels.

In practice, the measure employed is determined by objectives. If the objective is solely to analyze allegations, such as "farmers are shortchanged in the marketing of their products," the *commodity approach* would be appropriate. Under the commodity approach, the analyst looks at classes of goods to determine how they differ in the marketing services they require and the revenues they produce. The *institutional approach* analyzes the behavior of brokers, wholesalers, and retailers. And the *functional approach* examines the activities of marketing—buying, selling, storing, financing, etc.

Ideally, data that provide every statistical detail by firm, trade, geographic area, and time period would be desirable; unfortunately, such data do not exist. There are no standard marketing data published by the United Nations statistical service, and the U.S. and Western European countries publish marketing data that is limited to employees and earnings in wholesaling and retailing only.

WHOLESALING

There are varying definitions of wholesaling in the literature. The following elements are considered important to the nature of wholesaling:

1. The purpose of purchase of the wholesaler is to resell

2. The scale of the sale is frequently relatively large

3. Wholesaling firms selling to retailers act as agents between retailers and producers (and brokers, if involved)

Thus defined, wholesaling is an intermediary activity between producers and retailers. Wholesale firms vary greatly in type and function, although all wholesalers do very little processing and make almost no sales to household consumers. The bulk of their trade consists of buying from producers or other wholesalers and selling to other wholesalers and retailers and industrial users of goods. They conduct business under many different generic names: wholesalers, merchant wholesalers, jobbers, distributors, supply houses, commission merchants, brokers, auctioneers, assemblers, county shippers, converters, etc.

Although wholesaling activity is growing, in some consumer-goods areas independent wholesalers have lost ground to other types of distributors in the last century. For example, department stores, mail-order houses, chain stores, and direct door-to-door sales have taken over large parts of what used to be the business of wholesalers. These concerns often set up their own warehouses to perform wholesaling activities.

Figure 22–1 shows a positive association between population densities and leading wholesale firms. Under Christaller's central place model, wholesale firms would tend to locate at higher order places of centrality, i.e., closer to the central town. The location of firms within standard metropolitan areas is determined by transportation terminals and frequency of retailer demands. For example, grocery and petroleum wholesalers are located closer to retailers, while wholesalers dealing in furniture, dry goods, clothing, etc., locate in central places in fewer numbers.

RETAILING

Retailing involves activities related to selling for final consumption and represents the final link between the producer and the consumer. The nature and size of retailing firms have ben changing. In 1929 there were roughly 1.3 million retailing firms in the U.S. and about 1.8 million in 1958 and 1972. Not all retailing firms have experienced similar trends. Food and drink retailing have experienced substantial reductions in the number of stores. There were about 300,000

LEADING WHOLESALE LINES

M Metals
A Liquor
H Hardware
C Drugs & Chemicals
G Groceries
F Farm products
L Lumber
E Machinery & Equipment
V Motor vehicles
P Petroleum

0   200
Miles

FIGURE 22–1

food retailing stores in 1972, compared to about 461,000 in 1948—a loss of about 35 percent. Most of this loss was in "Ma and Pa" stores that could not compete with the large organizations in retailing.

There has been a general decline in the number of U.S. retailing establishments during the 1960s. The only retail firms showing a substantial increase in the 1960s were gasoline service stations (which now show a decline due to the oil crisis), restaurants and fast-food chains, repair services, radio and television stores, mail-order houses, vending machines and direct-selling organizations.

The most striking recent development in retailing is the conglomeration of large segments of retail trade, particularly evident in food retailing. The success of this approach to retailing has led to experiments with new types of food distribution, ranging from relatively small "superettes" to very large supermarkets. These firms particularly followed the population exodus to suburban areas.

Department stores, in contrast to supermarkets, have traditionally been located in downtown central business districts (CBDs). CBDs have struggled to maintain their position under formidable competition from discount mail-order and discount houses and from specialty stores selling narrow lines of department store goods. The advertising medium best suited to their needs, the newspaper, has strong competition from radio and television. Advertising by manufacturers has tended to make consumers adhere to brand names and to avoid price comparisons at the retailing level.

Discount houses appearing under different names, such as factory stores, "closed-door retailers" (who charge a small membership fee and admit only customers who are members), and "five-and-dime" stores, forced department stores to evolve retailing systems called shopping centers. The locations of shopping centers correspond to suburban neighborhood patterns.

Although vending-machine retailing has resulted in sales of products that gross several hundred million dollars annually, it has not progressed as much as expected, due to difficulties of protecting machines against counterfeit coins and vandalism, of ensuring accuracy and reliability, and the inability of customers to inspect before they buy.

401

Vending machines normally predominate at daytime population centers. Population concentration patterns vary with job and commuting habits.

Other forms of retailing outlets are farmer and consumer cooperatives, government marketing agencies, and periodic markets. Cooperatives are formed to create savings for members who pool their demands to take advantage of bulk buying. Cooperatives do not follow a systematic or predictable pattern of location. The most important marketing operation of government involves government agencies as terminal buyers of defense goods, supplies, and equipment. In times of war and national emergency, government may also perform retailing services by distributing coupons and ration cards. Periodic markets also perform retailing functions, although only on a seasonal basis. The location patterns of periodic markets are largely a function of population and demand densities.

Seasonal retailing is common in large cities of Europe and in the eastern U.S.

Retailing activities involve a bewildering mass of organizations that primarily establish location patterns based on population density. Figure 22–2 shows retail sales of the U.S. by regions. Americans spent about $370 billion for goods and services sold through retailing firms during 1972. Figure 22–3 indicates that food retailers, general merchandisers, and auto dealers received about 60 cents out of every dollar that Americans spent during 1972. Other spending items, all accounting for less than 10 cents of the average consumer's dollar, are also shown in Figure 22–3.

MARKETING AND CONSUMERISM

Marketing activities are associated with and affected by "consumerism." Con-

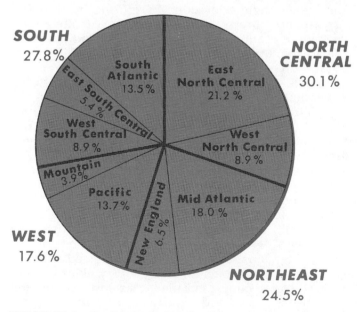

FIGURE 22–2 *Retail Sales by U.S. Regions*

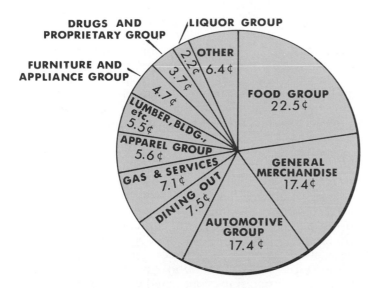

FIGURE 22–3 *How the U.S. Consumer Dollar Was Spent in 1970*

sumerism is basically used to describe the consumer movement of the 1960s and early 1970s, but the meaning of the term varies. Common to definitions of consumerism are efforts by various groups to seek redress or remedy for dissatisfaction experienced in purchasing and using goods. These efforts seek corrective measures for unsafe goods, poor quality goods, polluting goods, broken guarantees, misleading advertising, and fraud in the market place.

Although various consumer movements in early 1900s and in the 1930s have occurred in American history, the current movement has its own set of characteristics and circumstances. Increased discretionary income and leisure time, higher education levels, and greater demand for consumer information, protection, and education characterize the consumer movement of the 1970s.

To protect consumer interest, the government establishes minimum product standards, requires the disclosure of credit and loan costs ("Truth-in-Lend-

ing" act of 1968) and undeceptive packaging and labeling. Consumer protection laws have attracted criticism from business sectors that claim that such laws tend to inhibit initiative and quality improvement and to increase business operating costs. Other critics point out that once a law protecting consumer interest is passed, firms seek to meet only minimum requirements or to discover loopholes. They further argue that additional legislation to close the loopholes would lead to a proliferation of regulations that would ultimately impede effective control.

Some American business interests advocate self-regulation of product quality and protection of consumers. Self-regulation by producing firms would probably be preferable to government regulation in industries where conflict of interest does not preclude setting standards; where standards will not be used to reduce competition in the industry; and where standards are not set at a level such as to reduce product

403

options that many consumers would prefer.

If firms develop standards and quality controls in response to competitive forces, it should not be necessary to enact laws. Often the enactment of laws has prompted firms to regulate themselves. However, because the level of competition is continuing to decline over time as a result of an increased level of market concentration, many believe that self-regulation is unlikely to occur.

Consumer protection achieved by legislation or self-regulation on the part of the producing firm is unlikely to sustain itself without consumer education and information. In 1962 President Kennedy set forth a basic consumer right— the right to be informed—which included possession of the facts needed to make informed choices. Who should provide consumer data and in what form should data be available to consumers? Business firms may provide information too technical, sophisticated, and differentiated to permit meaningful comparisons and choices. President Nixon in 1970 urged that product information be made available to the public by the government "in a manner that is useful to consumers." The limitation of this executive order is that the only products evaluated are the successful bidders for the purchases made by the General Services Administration of the government. Also, the federal specification may not meet average consumer needs, such as color, style, odor, taste, and convenience of installation, safety around children, etc.

The National Bureau of Standards, the Department of Agriculture, the Federal Trade Commission, the Food and Drug Administration, and the Public Health Service, also evaluate and establish standards for products, but they do not distribute information at the right time, or they present evaluations that are too technical for meaningful comparisons.

In 1970 President Nixon created the Office of Consumer Affairs in the Executive Office of the president. This agency is responsible for coordinating all federal activities in the field of consumer protection. The director of the office also engages in regional and state meetings with state officials concerned with consumer issues.

Consumer protection and information have attracted great interest and led to the formation of citizen consumer groups. The crux of the issue is consumer education—an understanding of consumer information and ability to use the information to make day-to-day decisions concerned with job, education, loan, taxes, purchases, etc.

Americans are noted for seeking bigger paychecks but miserably fail in maximizing the utility from what they earn. Partly responsible for this failure are educational systems, the media, and advertising. Until recently, the education industry has ignored offering consumer education in curriculum. As Erich Fromm, a noted psychologist, has indicated, advertising tends to inform the consumer with value-laden ideas about products in such a way that the consumer's choice is decided by the advertiser who does not seek to provide the consumer with relevant data that he needs to compare and choose. Education in decision making helps the consumer to maximize his and his family's satisfaction and to evaluate his own standards—to develop independence and discrimination. In this role of independence and maximizing of material satisfaction, the consumer also forces the producing sector to produce the most highly desired goods and services and to produce them most efficiently.

A substantial number of states and school districts have begun to offer consumer education programs. A viable consumer education program should educate the consumer to function intelligently and effectively in a changing economy and polity. This development bears promise of enhancing the efficiency of the producing sector and of influencing the transportation framework and the location of economic activities.

references

1. Best, Alan C. G. "General Trading in Botswana: 1890–1968." *Economic Geography* 46 (October 1970): 598–611.

2. Dicken, Peter. "Some Aspects of the Decision Making Behavior of Business Organizations." *Economic Geography* 47 (July 1971): 426–35.

3. Epstein, Burt J. "Geography and the Business of Retail Site Evaluation and Selection." *Economic Geography* 47 (April 1971): 192–99.

4. Good, Charles M. "Periodic Markets and Traveling Traders in Uganda." *Geographical Review* 65 (January 1975): 49–72.

5. Good Charles M. "Periodic Markets: A Problem in Locational Analysis." *The Professional Geographer* 24 (August 1973): 210–16.

6. Heilbroner, Robert L. *The Making of Economic Society*. 3rd ed. Englewood Cliffs, N.J.: Prentice-Hall, 1970.

7. Ives, J. D. "Himalayan Highway." *Canadian Geographical Journal* 80 (January 1970): 20–25.

8. McKim, Wayne. "The Periodic Market System in Northeastern Ghana." *Economic Geography* 48 (July 1972): 333–44.

9. Pyle, Jane. "Farmers' Markets in the United States: Functional Anachronisms." *Geographical Review* 61 (April 1971): 167–97.

10. Rawley, Gwyn. "Central Places in Rural Wales." *Annals of the Association of American Geographers* 61 (September 1971): 537–50.

11. Riddell, J. Barry. "Periodic Markets in Sierra Leone." *Annals of the Association of American Geographers* 64 (December 1974): 541–48.

12. Semple, R. Keith. "Recent Trends In the Spatial Concentration of Corporate Headquarters." *Economic Geography* 49 (October 1973): 309–18.

13. Symanski, Richard, and Bromley, R. J. "Market Development and the Ecological Complex." *The Professional Geographer* 26 (November 1974): 382–88.

14. Vance, James E., Jr. *The Merchant's World: The Geography of Wholesaling*. Englewood Cliffs, N.J.: Prentice-Hall, 1970.

15. Walters, C. G., and Paul, G. W. *Consumer Behavior and Integrated Framework*. Homewood, Ill.: Richard D. Irwin, 1970.

16. Yeung, Yue-man. "Periodic Markets: Comments on Spatial-Temporal Relationships." *The Professional Geographer* 26 (May 1974): 147–51.

money,
banking,
and
financial services

23

FEDERAL RESERVE PLAZA

NEW HOME OF THE
FEDERAL RESERVE BANK OF BOSTON

architects
HUGH STUBBINS AND ASSOCIATES INC.
structural engineers
Le MESSURIER ASSOCIATES INC.
mechanical and electrical engineers
JAROS BAUM AND BOLLES

construction consultant
RICHARD J. DONOVAN INC.
heral contractor
PERINI CORPORATION

ng agent
N, ELLIOTT & COMPANY INC.
DERAL STREET
ON

e (617) 357-8220

23

Financial activities involve money creation, exchange, and control, and institutional services related to these functions. People exchange money for goods and services and vice versa, and the frequency and intensity of this exchange depend on the degree of specialization and the level of economic growth. Regional differentiation based on the frequency and intensity of exchange normally coincides with gross regional product and/or employment indices that are derived from the level of economic activity. Therefore, it would be redundant to treat money, banking, and their related institutions as explanatory variables of general economic activity. The importance of finance-related activities is well-established; they facilitate trade and contribute toward the overall development and efficiency of the economy.

Although the location of finance-related activities is primarily correlated with proximity to a market and with degree of economic growth, the exact location of financial activities within an area is influenced by the following considerations:

1. Nearness and accessibility to customers

2. Nearness to other financial institutions, producing agglomeration effects

3. Nearness and accessibility to police protection

Financial activities are frequently situated in close proximity to each other in patterns resembling gas station locations at a crossroads. This pattern exists to realize agglomeration benefits and to claim maximum and continuous protection against theft. Buildings of banks and insurance firms are conspicuous landmarks, partly because maximum public exposure is needed to instill public confidence in the viability and stability of these institutions. Although the incidence of banking activity tends to correspond closely with consumer banking-service locations, the *level* of banking activity, measured by bank debits, reflects the hierarchical order discussed in chapter 19.

The common element of financial activities is money. All financial institutions handle money to create necessary services which in turn aid in the production of other goods and services.

MONEY AND ITS FUNCTIONS

Money is anything that is generally acceptable and serves as a medium of exchange within the boundaries of a defined polity. The physical characteristics of contemporary monies are durability, portability, divisibility, uniformity of denomination, difficulty of counterfeiting, and easy identification.

Historically, many forms of money have been used, ranging from items as common as grains and hides to items as curious or odd as elephant tail bristles and whale teeth. The types or forms of money may be classified as:

1. *Commodity money,* such as grains, cattle, cheese, cocoa, tobacco, spices, leather, beads, metals, and cloth. Obviously, most of these forms of money, although they may serve as mediums of exchange, lack sufficient durability and transportability. There is no established and recognized standard of value in commodity monies.

2. *Odd* or *curious money,* such as fish hooks, precious stones, etc. This kind of money also lacks many of the qualities of the contemporary form of money.

3. *Full-bodied money,* a type of commodity money mostly in the form of metals, such as gold and silver, which do not lose their value when used for nonmonetary purposes. Full-bodied money's monetary value is equal to its commodity value. Gold coins circulated until 1933 in the U.S. are examples of full-bodied money.

4. *Representative full-bodied money,* a paper currency fully backed by a commodity, such as gold or silver. The face value of the currency is equal to the commodity value.

5. *Credit* or *debt money,* a kind of money indicating a promise to pay (debt) and a right to receive (credit). It constitutes contemporary money, which may appear in the form of demand deposits (checks) and currency. In the U.S., nearly 80 percent of the money is in the form of demand deposits.

Whatever the form of money, it has basically four uses: as a medium of exchange, as a store of value, as a standard of value, and as a standard for deferred payments. As a medium of exchange, money acts as an intermediary to effectuate exchange between goods and services. Its store of value involves saving and shifting of purchasing power over time and space. Its standard of value involves a measure of the relative value or worth of a good or service expressed in monetary terms. As a standard for deferred payments, money allows debts to be paid at a later date without having to preserve or store the goods and services involved in the transaction.

All forms of money perform these functions in varying degrees. For example, commodity money seriously lacks as a standard of value and as a store of value. The medium-of-exchange function of money is the pivotal role of any money regardless of its primitivism or modernity. The extent to which an object serves as a medium of exchange depends upon the confidence of the people in it; and of course the confidence is a function of the stability of its monetary value and the viability of the government.

Besides these direct functions of money, the monetizing of transactions enhances trade, specialization, and production efficiencies. Regions and societies that monetized their transactions earlier in history have experienced higher economic growth rates.

With increasing economic specialization and considerations of economies of scale and agglomeration effects in industrial location, the role of money in location decisions may escalate to the degree that it becomes as important as transportation factors.

The nature and structure of any banking system are a result of social and political influences. All banking systems are involved in controlling and influencing the money supply, facilitating exchange, and serving as clearinghouses for savers and investors. The supply of money has important bearing on the level of economic activity and on inflation. The clearinghouse role of banking systems may permit an efficient use of resources as bankers attempt to screen out loan requests for risky and inefficient undertakings.

Although different societies have different banking systems, space does not permit treating them individually. The discussion of the U.S. Federal Reserve system should provide an adequate understanding of the role of a banking system.

FEDERAL RESERVE SYSTEM

The need for centralization of banking in the U.S. was recognized as early as 1781 during constitutional debates. No legislation was passed until the National Banking Act of 1863 because Congress was concerned that centralized banking would create a concentration of monetary power in the federal government. The banking act allowed anyone to open a bank if a certain percentage of the deposits were not loaned out. This reserve requirement was intended to minimize the bankruptcy of banks and to enhance public confidence in banking institutions. Decentralized banking fostered inconvenience and heterogeneous currency, monetary mismanagement, and an inflexible supply of money. Recognizing that a growing economy needs a flexible and strong currency, Congress passed the historic Federal Reserve Act in 1913, which provides a system for effective money supply and control.

The Federal Reserve system is an integrated quasi-public structure headed by a board of governors that is linked to the Federal Open Market Committee, Federal Advisory Council, the twelve Federal Reserve district banks, the member banks, and the public. (Figure 23–1 shows the organization of the Federal Reserve system.) The Federal Reserve board consists of seven members appointed by the president and confirmed by the Senate for terms of fourteen years; their terms are arranged so that one expires every two years. No two members of the board may reside in the same Federal Reserve district.

One of the board's duties is to supervise the operations of the system. It appoints three of the nine directors of each Federal Reserve bank, including the chairman and the deputy chairman, and appointments of the president and first vice-president of each Federal Reserve bank are subject to the board's approval. The board also issues regulations that interpret and apply the provisions of laws relating to Federal Reserve bank operations. It directs Federal Reserve bank activities of examining and supervising member banks and develops and executes national monetary policy.

Monetary policy involves regulating the reserve ratio, i.e., the percent of demand deposits not loaned out; the discount rate, i.e., the rate at which member banks borrow money from Federal Reserve banks; the buying and selling of government bonds and securities; and the general money supply (see Figure 23–2).

The Federal Open Market Committee is comprised of the seven members of the Federal Reserve Board of Governors and presidents of five of the Federal Reserve banks—from the New York, Bos-

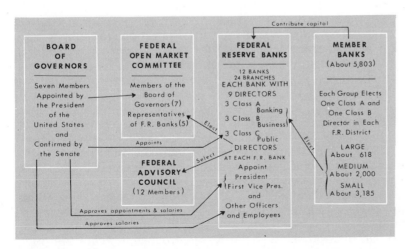

FIGURE 23–1 *The Organization of the Federal Reserve System*

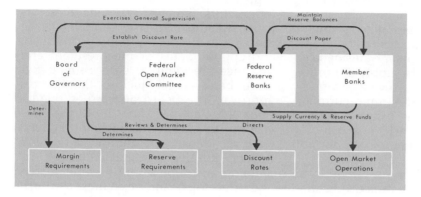

FIGURE 23–2   *Federal Reserve System of Organization for Monetary Policy*

ton-Philadelphia-Richmond, Cleveland-Chicago, Atlanta-Dallas-St. Louis, and Minneapolis-Kansas-San Francisco district banks. The committee is responsible for deciding changes to be made in the system's portfolio of domestic securities and bonds and holdings of foreign currencies. Federal Reserve banks, in their operations in the open-stock market, are required by law to carry out the decisions of the committee.

The Federal Advisory Council, consisting of twelve members, one from each Federal Reserve bank, is another channel of communication between the board and representatives of the banking and the business community. The council frequently meets at the board's office in Washington, D.C., to appraise the board of business conditions in respective districts and to make appropriate recommendations.

So that the Federal Reserve system would effectively serve the large area and diverse resources of the United States, the Federal Reserve Act provided that the system be divided into twelve districts. The boundaries of the Federal Reserve districts do not always follow state lines; in many instances part of a state is in one district and part in another (see Figure 23–3).

In each district there is a Federal Reserve bank, most of which have branch banks (see Table 23–1).

Decentralization is an important characteristic of the Federal Reserve system. Each Federal Reserve bank and each branch office is a regional and local institution, as well as part of a nationwide system, and its transactions are with regional and local banks and businesses. It gives effective representation to the views and interests of its particular region and at the same time helps to administer nationwide banking and credit policies.

Each of the twelve Federal Reserve banks is a corporation organized and operated for public service. The Federal Reserve banks differ from privately managed banks in that profits are not the object of their operations and in that their shareholders, the member banks of the Federal Reserve system, do not have the proprietorship rights, powers, and privileges that customarily belong to stockholders of privately managed corporations.

The provisions of law circumscribing the selection of Federal Reserve bank directors and the management of the Federal Reserve banks indicate the public nature of these banks. Each Federal

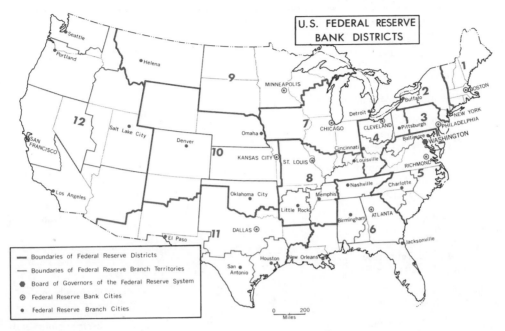

U.S. FEDERAL RESERVE BANK DISTRICTS

— Boundaries of Federal Reserve Districts
— Boundaries of Federal Reserve Branch Territories
● Board of Governors of the Federal Reserve System
◉ Federal Reserve Bank Cities
• Federal Reserve Branch Cities

FIGURE 23-3

Reserve bank has nine directors, three of whom are known as Class A directors, three as Class B directors, and three as Class C directors. Class A and Class B directors are elected by member banks, one director of each class being elected by small banks, one of each class by banks of medium size, and one of each class by large banks.

The three Class A directors may be bankers. The three Class B directors must be actively engaged in the district in commerce, agriculture, or some other industrial pursuit and must not be officers, directors, or employees of any bank. The three Class C directors are designated by the Board of Governors of the Federal Reserve system. They must not be officers, directors, employees, or stockholders of any bank. One of them is designated by the Board of Governors as chairman of the Federal Reserve bank's board of directors and one as deputy chairman. The chairman, by statute, is designated Federal Reserve

Agent and has special responsibilities on behalf of the Board of Governors in Washington.

Under these arrangements, businessmen and others who are not bankers constitute a majority of the directors of each Federal Reserve bank. The directors are responsible for the conduct of the affairs of the Federal Reserve bank in the public interest, subject to supervision of the Board of Governors. They appoint the Federal Reserve bank officers, but the law requires that their choice of president and first vice-president, whose terms are for five years, be approved by the Board of Governors.

Each branch of a Federal Reserve bank also has its own board of directors. A majority are selected by the specific Federal Reserve bank, and the remainder by the Board of Governors in Washington.

The board approves the budget for each district bank. In addition to the annual examination by the board's

411

TABLE 23–1   Federal Reserve Banks and Branch Banks

Federal Reserve Bank of Boston	District Number 1
Federal Reserve Bank of New York Branch at Buffalo, New York	District Number 2
Federal Reserve Bank of Philadelphia	District Number 3

Federal Reserve Bank of Cleveland
   Branches: Cincinnati, Ohio
                 Pittsburgh, Pennsylvania
	District Number 4

Federal Reserve Bank of Richmond
   Branches: Baltimore, Maryland
                 Charlotte, North Carolina
	District Number 5

Federal Reserve Bank of Atlanta
   Branches: Birmingham, Alabama
                 Jacksonville, Florida
                 Nashville, Tennessee
                 New Orleans, Louisiana
	District Number 6

Federal Reserve Bank of Chicago Branch at Detroit, Michigan	District Number 7

Federal Reserve Bank of St. Louis
   Branches: Little Rock, Arkansas
                 Louisville, Kentucky
                 Memphis, Tennessee
	District Number 8

Federal Reserve Bank of Minneapolis Branch at Helena, Montana	District Number 9

Federal Reserve Bank of Kansas City[1]
   Branches: Denver, Colorado
                 Oklahoma City, Oklahoma
                 Omaha, Nebraska
	District Number 10

Federal Reserve Bank of Dallas
   Branches: El Paso, Texas
                 Houston, Texas
                 San Antonio, Texas
	District Number 11

Federal Reserve Bank of San Francisco[2]
   Branches: Los Angeles, California
                 Portland, Oregon
                 Salt Lake City, Utah
                 Seattle, Washington
	District Number 12

[1] Kansas City, Missouri.

[2] Alaska is part of the Seattle branch territory, and Hawaii is part of the head office territory of the district.

examiners, the operations of each district bank are audited by the district bank's internal auditing staff. The district banks perform the functions of check clearance, execution of the monetary policy, and supervision of the member banks for solvency and compliance with monetary policy. They act as a fiscal agent for the federal government.

While somewhat less than one-half

the banks in the U.S. belong to the system, these banks hold nearly 80 percent of the country's total bank deposits, which, along with currency, serve as the medium of exchange. Consequently, Federal Reserve policies have a direct influence on institutions holding nearly 90 percent of the bank deposits.

Every member bank is required to subscribe to the capital of its district Federal Reserve bank. Its paid-in subscription is an amount equal to 3 percent of its capital and surplus, and another 3 percent is subject to recall.

In return, member banks are entitled to the following principal privileges:

1. To borrow from the Federal Reserve banks when temporarily in need of additional funds, subject to criteria for such borrowing (customarily called discounting) set by statute and regulation

2. To use Federal Reserve facilities for collecting checks, settling clearing balances, and transferring funds to other cities

3. To obtain currency whenever required

4. To share in the information facilities provided by the system

5. To participate in the election of six of the nine directors of the Federal Reserve bank for their district

6. To receive a cumulative statutory dividend of 6 percent on the paid-in capital stock of the Federal Reserve Bank

Use of these privileges by member banks throughout the country enables the nation's banking system to operate more effectively in providing the credit and banking facilities needed in a growing and diverse economy.

The blending of private and public and regional and national interests in the Federal Reserve system has created an organization well adapted to a dynamic U.S. economy. The viability of the economic system depends on the Federal Reserve's monetary policies; Federal Reserve policies must provide an adequate money supply for economic growth, and they must maintain stability of the value of the currency.

FINANCIAL INTERMEDIARIES

These are the operational ends of the U.S. banking system; not all intermediaries are members of the Federal reserve system. They are called intermediaries because they are institutions serving consumers, savers, and investors under the direct and indirect control of the federal reserve system. Major types of financial intermediaries are: commercial banks, savings and loan associations, mutual savings banks, insurance companies, finance companies, investment banks, trust companies, stock exchanges, and holding companies. Each intermediary specializes in certain functions, thus contributing to the overall efficiency of the banking system.

Considerations for location of these activities primarily relate to the location of the customers of the services.

INSURANCE SERVICES

Insurance is a means of protection against risks and insecurity inherent in certain economic systems, of which the United States is an example. The risks and insecurity might be voluntary or involuntary; private insurance services are offered mostly against involuntary risks and insecurity. Insurance services are characterized by:

1. A large number of customers to permit a smaller ratio of claims paid to premiums collected

2. Chances of possible risks and insecurities for all customers largely independent of each other

3. Risks and insecurities uncertain or unplanned beyond the control of the insured

4. Insurance claims tending to pay only up to the present market value of insured objects

Factors affecting the location of insurance services are the same as for banking, with the following additions:

1. The type of economic system (e.g., capitalistic economies would require more insurance services)

2. Tax advantages

3. Family bond and mutual responsibility

4. Church responsibility and attitudes toward helping the destitute

5. Degree of government involvement in welfare assistance

6. Incidence of casualties

The location patterns of insurance services may follow those that are insured, the offices of the agents, and the central headquarters. The latter follows a hierarchical pattern starting from the central offices located in large population centers, down to single insurance agents in small towns. There appears to be an agglomeration pattern with insurance agencies.

REAL ESTATE SERVICES

Real estate brokers serve as a clearinghouse between buyers and sellers of real estate. In the clearinghouse function, the listing of property for sale, appraisal, and other functions are associated with the transfer of real estate.

The location of real estate services is strictly demand oriented. They also tend to locate independently of each other. It seems that the intensity of real estate services varies with levels of education and training of a society, more educated or trained people tending to move more frequently because they are more fully acquainted with the job

market; with population mobility; with shifts in economic activity; temporary but expanding economic activities attracting a higher level of real estate services; and with zoning regulations.

references

1. Aliber, Robert A. *The International Money Game.* New York: Basic Books, 1973.

2. Baker, James C., and Bradford, M. Gerald. *American Banks Abroad: Edge Act Companies and Multinational Banking.* New York: Frederick A. Praeger, 1974.

3. Baum, Daniel Jay. *The Banks of Canada in the Commonwealth Caribbean: Economic Nationalism and Multinational Enterprises of a Medium Power.* New York: Frederick A. Praeger, 1974.

4. Beaton, W. Patrick, ed. *Municipal Needs, Services, and Financing: Readings on Municipal Expenditures.* New Brunswick: Rutgers University Center for Urban Policy Research, 1974.

5. Board of Governors. *The Federal Reserve System: Purposes and Function.* Washington, D.C.: Board of Governors, 1969.

6. Brown, Alan A.; Licari, Joseph A.; and Neuberger, Egon. *Urban and Social Economies in Market and Planned Economies: Policy Planning and Development,* vol. I. New York: Frederick A. Praeger, 1974.

7. Chandler, Lester V. *The Economics of Money and Banking.* New York: Harper & Row, 1973.

8. Crawford, Roger J. "A Comparison of the Internal Urban Spatial Pattern of Unit and Branch Bank Offices." *The Professional Geographer* 25 (November 1973): 353–56.

9. Davidson, Paul. *Money and the Real World.* New York: John Wiley and Sons, 1972.

10. Flechner, Harvey L. *Land Banking in the Control of Urban Development.* New York: Frederick A. Praeger, 1974.

11. Friedman, Milton. *Dollars and Deficits-Inflation: Monetary Policy and the Balance of Payments.* Englewood Cliffs, N.J.: Prentice-Hall, 1968.

12. Goldsmith, Raymond. *Financial Institutions*. New York: Random House, 1968.

13. Greenberg, Michael R., ed. *Readings in Urban Economics and Spatial Patterns*. New Brunswick, N.J.: Rutgers University, Center for Urban Policy Research, 1974.

14. Johnson, H. G., and Nobay, A. R., eds. *Issues in Monetary Economics*. London: Oxford University Press, 1974.

15. Klein, Philip A. *The Management of Market-Oriented Economies: A Comparative Perspective*. Belmont, Calif.: Wadsworth Publishing Co., 1973.

16. Nadler, Paul S. *Commercial Banking in the Economy*. New York: Random House, 1968.

17. Prather, Charles L. *Money and Banking*. Homewood, Ill.: Richard D. Irwin, 1969.

18. Stevens, Robert W. *A Primer on the Dollar in the World Economy*. New York: Random House, 1972.

19. Wessel, Robert H. *Principles of Financial Analysis: A Study of Financial Management*. New York: Macmillan, 1961.

government
services

24

24

Government services vary greatly between countries and change over a period of years within countries. There is a strong contrast, for example, between present government services of the USSR and those of the United States and between policies followed in the U.S. today and those operating during the 19th century. Contemporary changes in government policies for example, those designed to regulate foreign exchange—are so complicated that they can be understood only by a specialist. The role of government in economic activity has become so crucial that it must be a part of the study of economic geography. In chapter 5, political variables were approached as influences on the level and location of economic activity. In this chapter, government services are analyzed as a set of activities with an important impact on the economy.

The role government should play in influencing the economic activities of a nation and the policies it should adopt toward that end have long been subjects of political conflict. A controversy of long standing is that between the advocates of laissez-faire and those who favor government regulation. Laissez-faire policy no longer refers to the complete absence of all regulation and of all government activity in economic affairs. The protection of life and property, the promulgation of a legal system that upholds the sanctity of contracts, and the maintenance of a currency system are all government activities of vital interest to all people. Even the most extreme advocate of laissez-faire economic policy would consider them desirable and, indeed, necessary. A laissez-faire economist would also favor a certain amount of regulation of business activities where the selfish interests of individuals and the interests of society at large are in conflict; for instance, he would approve restrictions on opium trade. Conversely, all those opposed to a laissez-faire philosophy do not desire complete government regulation of all economic activities. The difference between the two points of view is one of degree: How much government regulation and how much economic activity by government? The theoretical argument largely centers on the relative interests of the individual versus those of the society as a whole.

These two groups also differ in the extent to which they rely on automatic adjustment of economic forces. The laissez-faire advocate argues that if the production of a commodity is so greatly increased that the price falls below the cost of production, producers will reduce their output, and, ultimately, the maladjustment between price and cost will be automatically rectified. It is claimed that such an automatic adjustment will ordinarily take place in all parts of the economic system. The advocate of government regulation contends that economic adjustment does not take place smoothly and automatically and that it is necessary to have government controls to speed and to rectify the process.

Many nations have experienced growing economic regulation, especially since World War II. This trend has arisen from the belief of an increasing number of persons that the interests of the individual and those of society are not identical and that we cannot expect automatic adjustment to correct the serious maladjustments of depression, trade imbalance, or inflation. Many government regulations and economic activities of the past have not been followed consistently over a period of years. They have not always proved consistent with one another, and often they have been largely opportunistic.

GOVERNMENT PARTICIPATION IN ECONOMIC ACTIVITY

For a variety of reasons, all levels of government—federal, state, and local—have entered the business sphere in one form or another. The main reasons for government involvement in business appear to be the following:

1. To overcome the inadequacies of government regulation of public utility enterprises by substituting full government ownership and operation for mere control of utility rates.

2. To provide a service for which there is a public need but which private enterprise is unable or unwilling to provide, e.g., defense, law enforcement, administration of justice, postal services, public health services, education, social security, etc.

3. To control more effectively business that involves special social problems, such as drug and alcoholic beverage businesses.

4. To sell goods acquired by the government for a certain purpose but which for one reason or another are no longer needed.

5. To enhance the achievement of nationally expressed goals of minimum unemployment, reasonable economic growth, stability of currency, favorable balance of payments, equitable distribution of income, and a cleaner environment.

Table 24–1 presents an analysis of expenditures of seventeen developed and developing nations of the world and shows the varying degrees of government participation in economic activities in these nations. Of the nations examined, government expenditures range from a low of about 5 percent in Mexico to a high of about 55 percent in the USSR. These figures would be considerably higher if state and local government expenditures of decentralized governments were included.

The system of government has a direct bearing on the percentage of government expenditures. Under a communist or totalitarian form of government, the state controls all segments of the economy, directly or indirectly. Virtually all economic expenditures in the USSR are government-directed and theoretically would total 100 percent. However, even under this rigid structure, there is a small measure of carefully monitored free enterprise.

DEFENSE EXPENDITURES

The United States and Israel spent about 34 percent of their national budgets on defense in 1972, representing the largest proportions spent on national defense in the world. However, if one carefully examines total Soviet government expenditures, the actual dollar amount spent for defense equals or surpasses the dollar value budgeted for defense by the United States. The USSR controls all factors of production and produces essential defense goods at low cost. The U.S., on the other hand, contracts with private industry and has less control over the final cost of defense products.

Israel uses slightly more than one third of its national budget for defense purposes. This relatively new nation is not only surrounded by hostile Arab states but also occupies a highly strategic land mass in the Middle East, historically a powder keg. Hostility between Arabs and Israelis frequently leads to violence, so military expenditures are high and probably will remain so.

Japan, on the other hand, spends only about 6 percent of its national budget for defense. Once a dominant military power, Japan now enjoys the military security offered by her strong alliance with the United States.

France, West Germany, and the United Kingdom also enjoy a measure of U.S. military security through the North Atlantic Treaty Organization (NATO). They are anchor pins of the

TABLE 24–1 Government Expenditures As Percent of Gross Domestic Product (GDP) in Respective National Currencies, 1972

	GDP (in thousand millions)	NATIONAL BUDGET (in millions)	NATIONAL BUDGET AS A PERCENT OF GDP	DEFENSE AS PERCENT OF NATIONAL BUDGET
Australia[1]	36.0	7,774.0	21.59%	13.75%
Brazil	302.3	32,176.8	10.64	20.25
Canada	104.0	20,035.0	19.26	9.80
Chile[1]	120.4	64,950.5	53.95	9.72
France	997.1	198,521.0	19.91	16.52
India[3]	368.2	46,580.0	12.65	22.18
Israel[2]	19,285.0	8,148.9	42.26	33.81
Japan	90,677.0	11,602.0	12.80	5.98
Mexico	513.7	24,221.0	4.72	9.43
New Zealand[1]	6,335.0	1,346.6	21.26	9.12
Philippines	56.7	5,588.2	9.86	10.77
Rep. of S.Af.	15,404.0	3,452.9	22.42	9.17
Spain[2]	2,264.0	304,993.6	13.47	13.79
United Kingdom	16.1	22,371.0	36.61	13.88
USSR	313.2	173,200.0	55.30	10.33
U.S.	1,159.0	231,876.0	20.00	33.78
W.Germany	829.4	191,220.0	23.06	12.80

[1] 1971 figure.
[2] 1970 figure.
[3] 1969 figure.

Source: Based on the *United Nations Statistical Yearbook, 1973* (New York: United Nations, 1974), pp. 553–56, 629–708.

noncommunist states in Europe, and their peace and security are vital to U.S. survival. Huge U.S. defense expenditures help to free the NATO nations from this burden and, consequently, they can use more money for capital investments and goods and services.

Mexico and Canada also allocate relatively low percentages of their national budgets to defense. Again, they rely on U.S. protection, for any attack on them would also be a major threat to Americans.

GOODS AND SERVICES

Government purchases of goods and services are primarily purchases of commodities and wage and salary payments. The expending government decides the use of tax revenue and therefore the uses of the resources that they purchase.

Of the seventeen countries examined in Table 24–1, the Philippines spent the highest percentage on goods and services—about 65 percent of government expenditures. This would suggest that the government has a large payroll and that it also is the major purchaser of commodities.

In Soviet society, where public ownership prevails and the authority of the Communist Party of the Soviet Union (CPSU) is supreme, the basic economic task of allocating scarce resources for competing ends is accomplished primarily by a centrally directed planning bureaucracy, rather than by the interplay of market forces. Based on general CPSU directives concerning major economic goals, the planning authorities formulate long-term and short-term plans to achieve specific targets in virtually all spheres of economic activity, although primary emphasis is on production and investment in heavy industry.

Production plans are supplemented by comprehensive plans for the supply of materials, equipment, labor, and finances to the producing sector, the procurement of farm products by the state; and the distribution of food and manufactured products to the population. Soviet economic plans have the force of law. They are worked out in great detail down to the level of the individual economic enterprise, where they are reflected in a set of output goals and performance indicators that management is expected to attain.

Adherence by enterprise management to the major plan directives is generally assured by manifold inspection procedures and through a system of incentives and sanctions. Aside from honors and opportunities for professional advancement, incentives are in the form of financial bonuses for performance equal to or better than that called for by the plan. Poor performance entails penalties ranging from reprimand and a reduction of income to loss of position and criminal prosecution. The rigidity of the system is mitigated to some extent by a provision for plan adjustments and by opportunities for limited maneuvers by management; within the confines of the plan, secondary targets can be sacrificed to attain a major objective.

SOCIAL SECURITY

Government expenditures for social security vary greatly from one nation to another, as do the financing and implementation of such programs. Japan, which spends about 29 percent of its revenue on social security, has the highest percentage rate in this category; it is followed by the United States (about 28 percent), the United Kingdom (about 25 percent), the USSR (about 15 percent), and West Germany (about 12 percent). Israel has the lowest percentage of the countries examined, spending only about 2 percent on social security.

In Japan, the state, the employer,

and the employee share the cost of four types of social insurance that are legally compulsory for employers: health insurance, welfare pensions, unemployment insurance, and workmen's accident compensation. The state's contribution to the health insurance plan goes toward administrative costs, rather than toward the direct payment of benefits, the cost of which is borne jointly by the employer and employee. The state also pays administrative costs of the welfare pension plan, but in this cast contributes from 10 to 20 percent of the cost of benefits as well. In the case of unemployment insurance, the state not only pays the entire administrative cost but contributes a full third of the benefit costs; the remainder is contributed by employers and employees. Management, on the other hand, bears the entire cost of administration and benefits accruing under the Workmen's Accident Compensation Plan in Japan.

The United States government enacted a Social Security Law in 1935; the program established by this act has since been extended by amendment. Social Security programs primarily: (1) provide old-age insurance and disability benefits; (2) unemployment compensation; (3) public assistance; and (4) medicare. They also contribute to workmen's compensation programs for industrial accidents, which are administered by state governments, and establish a variety of welfare programs, administered by state and local governments but financed in large part by federal grants-in-aid.

The U.S. social security system is a complex of measures designed to protect people in some degree against certain major hazards, such as (1) indigent old age, (2) involuntary unemployment, (3) inability to work, and (4) lack of parental support for children. The first two of these are the most important from the standpoint of the numbers of people affected and the money costs to the government. Special taxes are imposed to finance old-age pensions and unemployment compensations.

EDUCATION

Federal expenditures for educational purposes vary greatly among nations cited in Table 24–1. Expenditures range from a high of 25.12 percent of the GDP in the Republic of the Philippines to a low of 1.09 percent in the Republic of Indonesia.

The U.S. budgets 3.90 percent of its GDP for education, although federal education expenditures are not too meaningful because the primary obligation for education is delegated to the states in the U.S. In 1972, the amount spent by state governments for education exceeded 86 billion dollars, which is more than 37 percent of the national budget. Education is always the largest item in every state budget in the U.S. Federal support is only a token of the full cost of education in the U.S.; grants-in-aid do not support, but rather supplement, state and local expenditures. The total expenditure of federal, state, and local governments on education in the U.S. exceeds that of any other budgetary item, except that of national defense.

Although all states except Mississippi require that children attend school, state laws vary as to the ages and circumstances of compulsory attendance. In the majority of states, the laws require that formal schooling begin by age 7 and continue to age 16.

The Soviet educational system, with over 73 million students in 1972, consists of preschool nurseries and kindergartens, primary schools, secondary schools, special schools, vocational and technical schools, institutes and universities, correspondence schools, adult and parttime schools, and nondegree schools.

421

Compulsory attendance is required of all children between the ages of 5 and 15. Preschool facilities are not sufficiently developed to accommodate all children in that age group, but primary and secondary facilities enroll between 93 and 95 percent of all school-age children.

With over 4 million students, most institutions of higher learning in the USSR have concentrated on training engineers, scientists, and technicians needed in the Soviet economy. Of the more than 750 institutions of higher learning, only about 40 are universities; the remainder are institutes with highly specialized curriculums for training professionals in fields ranging from agriculture to medicine to teaching. The number of pedagogical institutes has increased rapidly with the ever-increasing number of new schools.

Universities and institutes of higher learning are open to all who pass the highly competitive entrance examinations, but only one in four graduates of secondary schools continues to a higher level. Choice of study is determined by priorities established by the State Planning Committee and its counterparts at lower government levels.

U.S. FEDERAL BUDGET AND ECONOMIC ACTIVITY

The composition of federal expenditures greatly influences the allocation of the nation's resources and the distribution of national income. Although it is less generally realized, the composition of federal expenditures can also have a powerful effect on efforts to stabilize prices and to maintain full employment.

GOVERNMENT EXPENDITURES

One common approach in studying priorities is to break down federal expenditures into basically two categories —transfer payments and purchases of goods and services. In either case, the government spends money. The two categories, however, have substantially different economic effects.

Transfer Payments. Where transfer payments are involved, the government acts essentially as a funnel. For example, a major transfer expenditure is social security payments. Social Security taxes are collected from the younger, employed members of society. Social Security benefits, however, are paid to older members of the society. Essentially, the role of government here is to transfer purchasing power from the young to the elderly. The government itself does not determine the final disposition of the funds; that is, it does not determine which goods and services are purchased with the funds. It does not tell the recipients of benefits that they must spend their money on rent or automobiles or clothing or anything else. Consequently, the government does not exercise direct command over the nation's resources in making social security payments. Although the fundamental nature of these expenditures is to transfer purchasing power, they also have effects on stabilization policies.

Similarly, federal grants-in-aid to states and local governments transfer purchasing power from taxpayers to state and local governments. There is, however, an important difference. Usually, grants-in-aid are accompanied by restrictions on how the funds are to be spent. Thus, the federal government retains some control of the use of these funds and, therefore, of the uses of national resources. In addition, it influences the uses of any matching funds. Of course, to the extent that grants-in-aid are not accompanied by restrictions, they do not increase the influence of the federal government over the use of the nation's

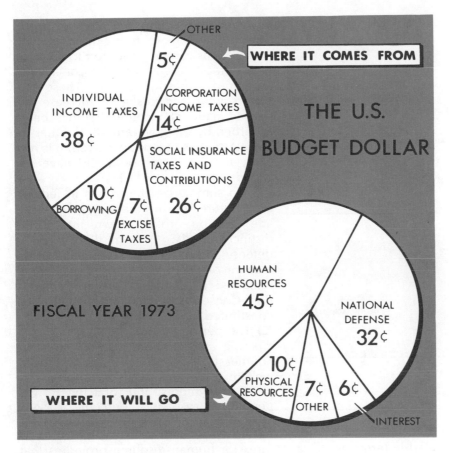

WHERE IT COMES FROM

THE U.S. BUDGET DOLLAR

OTHER
5¢

INDIVIDUAL INCOME TAXES
38¢

CORPORATION INCOME TAXES
14¢

SOCIAL INSURANCE TAXES AND CONTRIBUTIONS
26¢

BORROWING
10¢

EXCISE TAXES
7¢

FISCAL YEAR 1973

HUMAN RESOURCES
45¢

NATIONAL DEFENSE
32¢

PHYSICAL RESOURCES
10¢

OTHER
7¢

6¢

INTEREST

WHERE IT WILL GO

FIGURE 24–1

resources. Instead, the state or local government receiving the funds exercises the control. Here, again, the federal government essentially acts as a funnel.

Purchases of Goods and Services. Government purchases of goods and services are a different story. These expenditures are comprised primarily of purchases of commodities and wage and salary payments. The expending government decides the uses of these funds and, therefore, the uses of the resources that they purchase. The government has a direct effect on the allocation of the economy's resources. For example, the government might decide to reduce expenditures for military aircraft and to increase expenditures for pollution control, either directly through purchases of equipment or indirectly through restricted grants-in-aid. This policy would obviously represent a significantly different use of resources. The effects on the economy are obvious and intractable. On one hand, many workers in aircraft and related industries would no doubt lose their jobs. On the other hand, new jobs would be created in pollution-control industries.

This is not a simple problem, however. Aircraft workers could not simply apply for a new job in the pollution-control factory. Aircraft workers might not be qualified, or they might find that

423

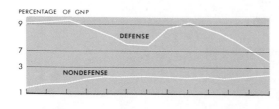

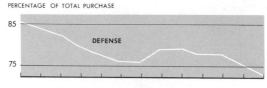

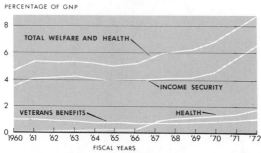

FIGURE 24–2 *Transfer Payments and Federal Expenditures in the U.S.*

they are overqualified in terms of education and skills. These are difficult, but hopefully temporary, effects of a government decision to reallocate resources. It might even be argued that the change in resource allocation gives rise to another high-priority need for use of federal government tax revenues; that is, the expenditures of funds to help displaced aircraft workers find new jobs that match their skills or to obtain new skills to match other available jobs.

Trends of the 1960s. During the first half of the 1960s, total federal expenditures absorbed a declining part of our gross national product (GNP). From 1965 to 1968, federal expenditures rose rapidly as a percentage of the GNP, reaching a high of 21 percent in 1968. Since 1968,

however, a leveling off has occurred. Most of the increase during the latter half of the 1960s can be attributed to the war in Southeast Asia and to the concurrent growth of domestic programs. These two factors combined to slightly increase the part of national income that has been absorbed by the government. If either of these activities had not occurred, it is not likely that any increase would have resulted.

To summarize the trends in federal expenditures during the 1960s, the decade may be broken down into three distinct periods: (1) From 1960 to 1965, defense and other purchases declined as a share of GNP, and transfer payments remained a relatively constant proportion. Consequently, federal expenditures constituted a declining share of GNP. (2) The period 1965 to 1968 saw an increasing commitment to the war in Southeast Asia and to domestic social welfare programs. Defense purchases, transfer payments, and total federal expenditures rose as a percent of GNP. Since 1968, declining defense purchases have been offset by increasing expenditures for human-resource programs that necessitated transfer payments, so total federal expenditures have constituted a fairly steady share of GNP (see Figure 24–2). Adjustments to a "peace economy" have not been easy. The U.S. has been suffering from a deepening recession since late 1973. Antirecession economic policies are likely to increase the ratio of government spending to gross national product during the mid-1970s.

Implications of Federal Spending in the 1960s. Clearly, the 1960s witnessed changing priorities in federal expenditures. Had the war in Southeast Asia not occurred, these changes would have been more pronounced. It is important to ask if these trends will continue and, if so, what some of the effects and implications for future economic policies will be.

The upward trend in federal transfers and grants is likely to continue. Current debate and discussion strongly indicate that the needs of the future will probably lie in areas, such as income security, welfare reform, education, urban problems, housing, and medical services and facilities. In that event, these areas will probably be assigned high priority in future federal budgets and could easily absorb even more of the nation's output than at the present.

The form of federal expenditures would almost certainly be increased transfer payments and grants, rather than purchases of goods and services. The growing fiscal crises among state and local governments may also lead to new grants from the federal government, such as some form of revenue sharing, or federal assumption of some of state government's transfer activities. In addition, federal assistance for urban and rural development problems will probably be in the form of grants-in-aid and other transfers involving fewer restrictions than in the past. Thus, as defense purchases fall relatively, transfers and less restricted grants are likely to continue to rise in importance. This would also mean that the federal government would tend to exercise less direct control over the allocation of the nation's economic resources. It is not clear, however, that federal expenditures as a percentage of GNP will fall in the light of deepening recession of the 1970s.

The future role of the federal government in the economy will be determined primarily by the needs and demands for public services. The flexibility of the government in responding to future requirements, however, has almost surely been constrained by the shift from defense to nondefense and from purchases to transfers. Increased social programs and transfer payments

often tend to involve uncontrollable expenditures. Under existing statutes, the government is committed to these expenditures.

There are at least two aspects to federal expenditures. First, to the extent that these expenditures rise as the economy slows down (or vice versa), such expenditures automatically provide a stabilizing effect on the economy. This could relieve, but not eliminate, the need for aggregate fiscal and monetary stimulation. Second, these expenditures could reduce the flexibility of fiscal policy for stabilizing the economy. For example, an overheated economy might require restrictive fiscal measures. As defense expenditures approach a minimum safe level and as nondefense, uncontrollable expenditures become a larger part of the budget, the federal government's latitude to make substantial expenditure cuts or slowdowns will be reduced. The government could still control fiscal policy but primarily through taxation policies.

UNEMPLOYMENT

The shift from federal defense purchases to nondefense purchases and transfers has resulted in fairly persistent and high unemployment in industries that were heavy suppliers of defense and related goods, such as the aerospace industry. This unemployment is primarily structural in nature, rather than cyclical. It may not respond quickly to even the most stimulating general monetary and fiscal policies. Skilled and highly trained unemployed persons may not only need another job, they may need additional training to meet the requirements of a new job. Plants and equipment will have to be converted to other uses. These transitions may require time and measures other than normal, countercyclical policies.

In the 1970s, cyclical unemployment

425

has developed and persisted because of lagging aggregate demand and has compounded problems of structural unemployment. Monetary and fiscal policies are attempting to stimulate aggregate demand in order to reduce unemployment. Although these policies may succeed in eliminating cyclical unemployment, they may be ineffective or even undesirable cures for structural unemployment.

If continued after cyclical unemployment is eliminated, monetary and fiscal policies to stimulate demand might eventually relieve structural unemployment in defense and aerospace sectors of the economy. But it would probably do so by creating or heightening inflationary pressures on prices in the nondefense sector; this phenomenon might be termed "structural inflationary pressure" in the nondefense sector. The relative rise in prices of the nondefense sector would provide a signal and incentive for unemployed defense resources to shift to nondefense production, although the shift would probably be slow and perhaps incomplete. Although restrictive aggregate monetary and fiscal policies might counter price pressures in the nondefense sector, they would do little to relieve structural unemployment. In short, there is little that countercyclical policy measures can do to offset structural disorders in the economy.

Therefore, it appears that one result of the shift in federal expenditure priorities will be a growing search for additional policy actions. Temporary measures may be required to shorten the transition period necessary to shift resources formerly employed in defense and defense-related activities to other productive uses. Additional federal programs may be called for to retrain workers. Tax breaks or subsidies could speed the conversion of plants and equipment. In other words, more structural policy measures may be required in addition to countercyclical measures.

Substantial changes have taken place in the pattern of federal expenditures. The altered priorities that these changes reflect will not go unnoticed in the private sector of the economy. But before the transition is complete, some new, but probably temporary, measures will be required to achieve a more orderly and rapid shift in the nation's priorities.

references

1. Allworth, Edward, ed. *Soviet Nationality Problem*. New York: Columbia University Press, 1971.

2. Armstrong, John A. *The Soviet Union: Toward Confrontation or Coexistence?* New York: Foreign Policy Association, 1970.

3. Berry, Brian J. L., and Marble, Duane F. *Spatial Analysis; A Reader in Statistical Geography*. Englewood Cliffs, N.J.: Prentice-Hall, 1968.

4. Boal, Frederick W. "Urban Growth and Land Value Patterns: Government Influences." *The Professional Geographer* 22 (March 1970): 79–82.

5. Bewhirst, Martin, and Farrell, Robert. *Censorship*. Metuchen, New Jersey: Scare Crow Press, 1973.

6. Green, Mark J., ed. *The Closed Enterprise System*. New York: Grossman Publishers, 1972.

7. Gustav, Ranis, ed. *Government and Economic Development*. New Haven: Yale University Press, 1971.

8. Hutchings, Raymond. *Soviet Economic Development*. New York: Barnes and Noble, 1971.

9. James, Peter N. *Soviet Conquest From Space*. New Rochelle. N.Y.: Arlington House, 1974.

10. Kaplan, Eugene J. *Japan: The Government-Business Relationship*. Washington, D.C.: U.S. Government Printing Office, 1972.

11. Kulski, Wladyslaw, W., ed. *The Soviet Union in World Affairs*. Syracuse, N.Y.: Syracuse University Press, 1973.

12. Okun, Arthur M. *The Political Economy of Prosperity*. New York: W. W. Norton & Co., 1970.

13. Pickles, Dorothy M. *The Government and Politics of France*. London: Methuen, 1972.

14. Samuelson, Paul A. *Economics*. 9th ed. New York: McGraw-Hill, 1973, pp. 147–77.

15. ———. *Reading In Economics*. 7th ed. New York: McGraw-Hill, 1973.

16. Shaffer, Harry G. *The Soviet Economy*. New York: Appleton-Century-Crofts, 1969.

17. Sontheimer, Kurt. *The Government and Politics of West Germany*. London: Hutchinson, 1972.

18. U.S. Bureau of the Census. *Statistical Abstract of the United States, 1974*. Washington, D.C.: U.S. Government Printing Office, 1974.

19. Waller, D. J. *The Government and Politics of Communist China*. London: Hutchinson, 1970.

20. Wesson, Robert G. *The Soviet State: An Aging Revolution*. New York: John Wiley and Sons, 1972.

21. Weston, J. Frederick, and Peltzman, Sam, ed. *Public Policy Toward Mergers*. Pacific Palisades, Calif.: Goodyear Publishing Co., 1968.

communication
services

25

25

Man is an occupant of social and geographic niches. He lives in, reconstructs, and adapts to a diverse range of environments. Because of a complex division of labor, man's performances are seldom isolated actions; he must communicate with other people throughout life. The more sophisticated his habitat, the greater his need for contact with other human beings.

Urbanization, industrialization, and modernization have created social conditions conducive to the development of mass communications. In turn, these processes of social change produce societies that are highly dependent on mass communication. Mass communications comprise the institutions and techniques by which specialized social groups employ technological devices (press, radio, television, films, etc.) to disseminate symbolic content to large, heterogeneous, and widely dispersed audiences.

Activities involved with gathering, handling, managing, and diffusing information are frequently classified as quaternary activities.

THEORETICAL CONSIDERATIONS

Communication services tend to increase with the size of central places in a positive and linear relationship. The information explosion, made possible by new ways to record, store, retrieve, and transmit data, has created a hierarchical clustering of communication services. This has been encouraged by the advantages of economies of scale and agglomeration effects.

These clusters may be termed *communication hubs.* The relative importance of a hub is defined by the size of population, the degree of industrialization, and its location. The influence of population is easily observed from the communication hubs of New York, Chicago, London, Tokyo, Moscow, Peking, Delhi, Paris, etc. A hierarchy of hubs appears within a country. Business concerns place a great deal of emphasis on communication facilities, as evidenced by the location of their headquarters. New York and Chicago, for example, host a predominant share of headquarters of large U.S. corporations. The development of Chicago as a major communication hub is primarily due to its location, which permits efficient and convenient marketing in eastern, western, and southern parts of the U.S.

Communication activities range from person-to-person contact to mass transactions. Exchanges and transactions between individuals, groups, institutions, and many social groups tend to increase with the size of the communication hub, where the opportunity for personal contact increases. The resulting overload of communication flow does not necessarily mean that the urbanite, having been overwhelmed by the flood of information, "succumbs" and is "turned off"; rather, he is likely to respond to the situation in one or a combination of the following ways:

1. Devise and use ways to allocate time more efficiently for each transaction or contact

2. Establish priorities for transactions, disregarding low-priority items

3. Reduce the intensity and number of communications by filtering out non-functional associations and contacts

4. Consciously block off entry of images and messages

Frequency of contact between people, their mobility or use of space, and the intensity of their communication are determined by age, occupation, culture, education, income, ability to overcome

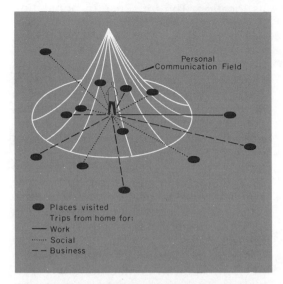

Personal
Communication Field

Places visited
Trips from home for:
—— Work
······ Social
– – Business

FIGURE 25–1 *Personal Communication Field (After John F. Kolars and John D. Nystuen, Geography: The Study of Location, Culture, and Environment [New York: McGraw-Hill, 1974]).*

friction of distance, and cost and availability of the means of communication. Given these variables, a person's communication space, the *personal communication field* (PCF) in Figure 25–1, is defined by the communication activities associated with work, visitations, meetings, shopping, etc. Each person has his own PCF, the size and shape of which are determined by individual patterns of communication activities.

Distance and communication have a relationship similar to that observed between distance and rent in chapter 7. Although a person's ability to communicate across space depends upon the variables mentioned above, the distance defines the frequency of these communications. The farther a person is located from another person the less likely are the chances that communication will occur. Thus the actual shape of a PCF looks like a cone, with the peak close to

one's residence and rising toward outer space (*see* Figure 25–1). (The communication space may be reduced to a conal base by averaging out various directional distances).

Since personal communication fields vary, it is necessary to aggregate such fields in order to show the communication behavior of a particular central place; such an aggregation is termed a *mean information field* (MIF). It would be useful to develop MIF pyramids or cones for central places to compare the extent and frequency of their communication activities. Unfortunately, communication information is not readily available or is very expensive to gather, so we can only use surrogate measures to serve as indicators of communication activities.

A CLASSIFICATION OF COMMUNICATION SERVICES

Communication services can be grouped into three levels: dense, moderately dense, and sparse.

Dense Pattern. A dense pattern of communication services includes complete coverage of an area by radio and television reception. A web of telephone and telegraph lines are present, as well as an abundance of newspapers, magazines, books, libraries, and daily postal services.

Dense communication services have been developed east of the Rocky Mountains in the United States, in southern Canada, western Europe, Japan, northern India, the Pampa of Argentina, industrialized areas of the USSR, and around large urban districts nearly everywhere.

Moderately Dense Pattern. A moderately dense communication service pattern consists of a thin grid of telegraph and telephone facilities. Parts of an area may not be served by radio and television broadcasting stations. Although postal services are well developed, newspapers are published in only a few cities in these regions.

A moderately dense communication service pattern covers the western interior United States, the Iberian Peninsula, the Balkan countries of Europe, much of the USSR, Chile, and southern India.

Sparse Pattern. Many regions of the world with the most primitive surface transportation facilities have a moderately well-developed network of airways. Postal service is casual and newspapers are rare. Radio and television are conspicuously absent.

A sparse pattern covers much of Amazonia, tropical Africa, the Old World desert areas, Borneo and New Guinea, the tundra and taiga of the USSR, Canada and Alaska, Tibet, Mongolia, and parts of China, Burma, Laos, Cambodia, and North and South Vietnam.

POSTAL SERVICE

Postal services involve the receipt and delivery of letters, postcards, and small packages by a government agency for a small fee paid for each item by the sender. In highly industrialized countries, the post office uses a complex network of communications extending to all parts of the country and to foreign lands in order to provide fast, dependable, and inexpensive postal service. In such countries, the post office achieves the status of a big business and makes an important contribution to economic and cultural life of the nation. Because post offices exist in every town and city, many governments have assigned to post offices a variety of miscellaneous functions, such as banking; selling licenses, revenue stamps, and government stock; and handling special payments of welfare programs.

Table 25–1 indicates the volume of mail traffic in highly industrialized na-

TABLE 25–1   Mail Traffic in Selected Countries

	1963	1972	PERCENT CHANGE
United States			
Domestic[2]	65,764M[1]	86,240M	+31.14%
Foreign[2]	529,000	916,000	+73.16
Japan			
Domestic	8,491M	12,297M	+44.82
Foreign	73,178	106,703	+45.81
United Kingdom			
Domestic	10,473M	10,206M	− 2.55
Foreign	414,030	551,902	+33.30
West Germany			
Domestic	8,208M	9,944M	+21.15
Foreign	341,900	595,100	+74.06
USSR			
Domestic	4,537M	8,532M	+88.05

[1] "M" signifies millions.

[2] "Domestic" refers to mail sent within a specific country, and "foreign" refers to mail received within a specific country.

Source: Based on *United Nations Statistical Yearbook, 1973* (New York: United Nations, 1974), pp. 485–90.

tions. In each nation, the volume of business generated by the postal service is astronomical. The decline in mail traffic in the U.K. is associated with its depressed economy. For the same reason, a small reduction in U.S. mail traffic was noted in 1974 and 1975.

There is a direct relationship between the technology of a country and the size and amount of business carried on through the mail (see Figure 25–2). A good example of the importance of mail in selling is illustrated by the Direct Mail Advertising Association, the world's largest and oldest international trade association, representing firms involved in direct mailing, such as IBM, Xerox, CBS Columbia House, American Express, McGraw-Hill Publications, Dow-Jones, Kimberly-Clark, Time Inc., Christian Science Monitor, and Procter and Gamble. Among DMAA's 1,600 member firms are manufacturers, advertisers, publishers, insurance companies, fund raisers, financial services and many other enterprises, large and small, which depend on the reliability of selling through the mails.

TELEGRAPH SERVICES

The telegraph communicates over a long distance with electromagnetic instruments through which information is conveyed in written, printed, or pictorial form. Development of the telegraph in the mid-19th century provided the public with the only rapid means of communication until the advent of the telephone, which led to a continuous decline of public telegraph traffic during the 20th century.

However, the continued development of telegraphic techniques, evinced particularly by the teleprinter and other improved transmission methods has maintained the operation of telegraphic communication in certain fields. Many organizations, commercial, transportation, press, and government, operate private networks for their internal business traffic. The high information density that can be carried telegraphically and the overwhelming value of the printed record provide a service that cannot be given by the telephone.

Despite a decline in the use of the telegraph, seventeen countries send and receive less than 10 million telegrams annually. Of these countries, six have a volume that ranges from 22 million in Italy to over 387 million in the USSR (see Table 25–2). However, the development of more sophisticated transmission equipment and substitution of telephones in nations, such as Japan, the U.S., and Italy, has resulted in a steady decline in telegraphy. Some countries, such as the USSR, India, Mexico, Czechoslovakia, and Colombia, have increased their use of the system because private telephones and other means of communication are not available on a mass scale.

TELEPHONE SERVICES

There were 313 million telephones in the world in 1972, representing an increase of 32 percent since 1968. The U.S. has 131 million telephones and its telephone system is capable of reaching 97.2 per-

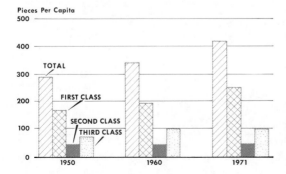

FIGURE 25–2 *Pieces of Mail Per Capita*

TABLE 25–2   Domestic Telegraph Service in Selected Countries

	1963	1972	PERCENT CHANGE
USSR	254,000	386,532	+52.18%
Japan	98,072	55,895	−43.01
U.S.	92,231	27,983	−69.66
Mexico	41,266	52,875	+28.13
India	34,142	58,400	+71.05
Italy	41,392	22,049	−46.73
Spain	20,195	17,921	−11.26
France	14,100	15,328	+ 8.71
Colombia	14,184	17,517	+23.50
Czechoslovakia	12,309	14,035	+14.02
W.Germany	18,656	8,166	−56.23

Source: Based on the *United Nations Statistical Yearbook, 1973* (New York: United Nations, 1974), pp. 491–94.

cent of the telephones in the rest of the world.

Countries with more than 5 million telephones include Canada, West Germany, Japan, the U.K., Italy, France, and the USSR (*see* Table 25–3). International

TABLE 25–3   Telephone Service in Selected Countries, 1972

	TELE-PHONES IN USE	PER 100 INHAB-ITANTS
U.S.	131,108	62.8
Japan	34,021	31.5
United Kingdom	17,572	31.4
West Germany	16,521	26.8
USSR	13,198	5.3
Canada	10,979	49.9
Italy	11,345	20.6
France	10,338	19.9
Sweden	4,680	57.6
Spain	5,713	16.4
Australia	4,400	34.0
Netherlands	4,003	29.9
Switzerland	3,404	53.5
Poland	2,087	6.3
Argentina	1,952	8.1
World	312,902	8.2

Source: Based on the *United Nations Statistical Yearbook, 1973* (New York: United Nations, 1974), pp. 495–98.

telephone service is expected to increase in the next ten years, especially in countries that recently have acquired direct access to other countries via satellite communication.

Of the highly industrialized states, the USSR makes the least use of the telephone. Vast distances between population centers, difficulties of maintenance due to severe weather conditions, and Soviet reluctance to provide free access to telephone service for the masses of people account for its low ranking.

PRINTING AND PUBLISHING

NEWSPAPERS

Writing enables an individual to communicate with others much more exactly than can be done by speech and to communicate with others who are distant. The written message can be sent great distances, and it can also be preserved for later generations. The tiny trickles of man's early writing have grown to great floods of communication through the invention of printing by movable type, followed by the introduction of the power driven press, the

433

TABLE 25–4 Daily and Non-Daily General Interest Newspapers in Selected Countries

| | | DAILIES | | | | NON-DAILIES | | | |
		NUMBER	CIRCU-LATION	PER 1,000 INHAB-ITANTS		NUMBER	CIRCU-LATION (1–3 times a week)	TOTAL	NON-DAILIES PER 1,000 INHABITANTS
Japan	1972	172	5,845	519	1972	—	—	—	—
West Germany	1970	1,093[1]	19,701[1]	319[1]	1970	93	93	4,918	80
United Kingdom	1972	109	29,557	528	1966	1,223[2]	1,223[2]	40,400[2]	668[2]
USSR	1971	647	84,953	347	1971	7,216	—	60,510	247
U.S.	1972	1,761[3]	62,510[3]	297[3]	1967	10,109[4]	—	79,834[4]	401[4]

[1] Including 700 regional editions of German-language dailies.

[2] Including 13 Sunday newspapers with a total circulation of 26,600,000.

[3] English language dailies only.

[4] In addition there were 598 Sunday newspapers of which an indeterminate number have separate legal status or staff.

Source: Based on the *United Nations Statistical Yearbook, 1973* (New York: United Nations, 1974), pp. 805–08.

linotype and montotype typesetting machines, and offset printing.

Newspapers (*see* Table 25–4) and magazines are essential communication media; books convey ideas, knowledge, and experience. Information needs of business are well-served by many printed materials, including financial reports, catalogs, directories, checks, and business forms. Advertising materials stimulate economic growth.

BOOKS

Table 25–5 shows the number of books produced in selected countries. The United States leads the world in book production, with over 81,000 titles produced in 1972; over 20 percent of these titles were in social sciences and literature. The USSR, ranking second in book production, allocates over 35 percent of its titles to social sciences and literature; about 50 percent of Soviet titles are devoted to pure and applied sciences. West Germany produces the largest number of religious titles, as shown in Table 25–5.

RADIO AND TELEVISION BROADCASTING

The United States leads the world in the total number of radio and television receivers and in the number of receivers used per 1,000 inhabitants (*see* Table 25–6). India has 23 radio receivers per 1,000 inhabitants compared to 1,695 in the U.S. However, the community listening stations in India serve a much larger audience than the figures show.

There is a wide gap between nations as to the use of radio and television communications systems. These means of communication tend to widen the MIF for central places and thereby to enhance competition between trade centers.

COMMUNICATIONS IN THE U.S.

Employing just under 1.1 million persons, printing and publishing ranks ninth among all manufacturing industries in total employment. Competition in the industry takes many forms. The quest for new or expanded markets, larger advertising revenues, utilization of new technology, and exploration of new communication formats exert considerable pressure on printing and publishing management.

Markets for small- and medium-sized printers tend to be local, while large printers or establishments with highly specialized product lines serve national markets. Since only one printer in five has more than twenty employees,

TABLE 25–5 Book Production by Selected Subject Groups in Selected Countries

		SOCIAL SCIENCE	PURE SCIENCES	RELIGION	OTHERS	TOTAL
Australia	1971	2,019	373	190	2,042	4,624
France	1972	5,176	1,573	922	16,826	24,497
India	1972	5,728	974	887	7,586	15,175
Japan	1972	6,994	1,788	691	21,601	31,074
USSR	1972	20,269	7,706	181	52,399	80,555
United Kingdom	1972	6,308	3,667	1,128	22,006	33,109
U.S.	1972	8,994	2,667	1,864	67,599	81,124
West Germany	1971	11,453	2,619	2,106	24,176	40,354

Source: Based on the *United Nations Statistical Yearbook, 1973* (New York: United Nations, 1974), pp. 793–95.

TABLE 25–6   Radio and Television Broadcasting in Selected Countries, 1972

	RADIO RECEIVERS	PER 1,000 INHABITANTS	TELEVISION RECEIVERS	PER 1,000 INHABITANTS
U.S.	354,000	1,695	99,000	474
Canada	17,932	821	7,610	349
Argentina[2]	9,000	370	3,711	155
India	12,772	23	49[1]	.08[1]
Japan	70,794	658	24,194	225
France	17,034	329	12,279	237
West Germany	20,290	329	18,064	293
Italy	12,488	230	10,951	202
Sweden	283	35	2,701	333
United Kingdom	37,500	672	16,999	305
Australia	2,758	213	2,939	227
USSR	100,000	404	40,000	162

[1] 1971
[2] 1970

Source: Based on the *United Nations Statistical Yearbook, 1973* (New York: United Nations, 1974), pp. 815–19.

industry competition facing the average printer is essentially local. In contrast, publishers of books, periodicals, music, and other publications generally serve national audiences, although newspapers and some greeting card publishers compete primarily on a local basis. The large number of U.S. printing and publishing establishments creates a highly competitive atmosphere for individual products and markets.

Total U.S. advertising expenditures amount to over $20 billion, and several segments of the industry compete among themselves and against communications media for increasing slices of this pie. Newspapers receive 29 percent of total U.S. advertising expenditures, direct mail 14 percent, and magazines 11 percent. Television's command of 19 percent of all U.S. advertising expenditures has resulted in a lag in magazine advertising over the past two decades.

U.S. NEWSPAPER INDUSTRY

Despite increases in newspaper prices, circulation of more than 62 million was achieved by daily newspapers in 1971, a gain of 50,000 over 1970 sales. Sunday circulation dropped, but weeklies gained a healthy 5 percent, so that total daily, Sunday, and weekly circulation was well over 1 million above 1969 sales (see Figure 25–3). The stable growth rate that has existed for more than a decade, should continue in the decade ahead. The close relationship of newspaper circulation to all economic growth factors, because of newspapers' advertising reflections, will boost receipts by this industry to an estimated $11 billion in 1980, reflecting an annual growth rate of 5 percent (see Table 25–7).

There are about 1,800 daily and 8,600 weekly newspapers, all privately owned. In the United States, newspapers may support political parties but they are not owned or supported by the parties or by the government.

PERIODICAL PUBLISHING IN U.S.

The periodical publishing industry serves three distinct markets: (1) the general population, through consumer or specialized magazines; (2) businessmen,

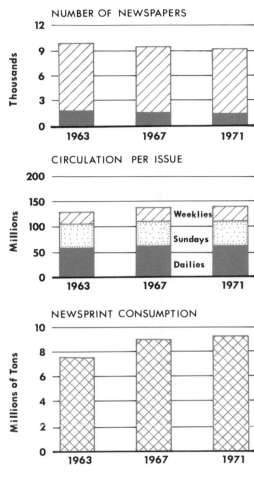

NUMBER OF NEWSPAPERS

CIRCULATION PER ISSUE

Weeklies

Sundays

Dailies

NEWSPRINT CONSUMPTION

FIGURE 25–3 *Newspaper Circulation in the United States*

ities and special interests of the population have spawned a diversity of periodicals whose competition for readers and advertising is intense. Recent trends point to new publications dealing with the environment, consumer affairs, women's liberation, sports, and the many hobbies and activities encouraged by increases in leisure time and discretionary income. In the last decade, circulation revenue of consumer magazines advanced at a rate of about 6 percent per year.

U.S. industry's information needs are served by the nation's business press. About 2,400 business periodicals cover the gamut of business activities, with distribution extending to over 62 million readers per year. Close to half of all business magazines are geared to many industrial segments to the economy. Men and women in merchandising, financial, medical, and education sectors keep informed via more than 100 publications reaching each of these sectors. The business periodical publisher relies on the sale of advertising space for more than $7 of every $10 of total publishing receipts.

A recent study of the business press indicates that in the last decade paper costs have increased by 7 percent, printing costs by 35 percent, and payroll expenses by 60 percent. Rates on second class subscription publications have increased by 119 percent, while postage on controlled circulation publications (distributed free to individuals based on their occupational title) have risen 36 percent.

Receipts from farm publications, the smallest segment of the magazine publishing industry, accounts for barely 3 percent of the entire periodical industry. A declining farm population has kept publishers' receipts from newsstand and subscription sales at a virtual standstill for many years. Increases in advertising

via trade publications; and (3) the farmer.

Consumer magazines serve the general population's multiplicity of information and entertainment needs through a variety of specialized publications. While the popularity of television has caused the withdrawal of a few mass circulation publications, other magazines with readership in the millions continue to grow and prosper. Leisure time activ-

437

TABLE 25–7 Value of Shipments of Selected U.S. Printing and Publishing Industries with Projections (in millions of dollars)

	1971	PERCENT INCREASE 1970–1971	1972	PERCENT INCREASE 1971–1972	1975	PERCENT INCREASE 1971–1975[1]	1980	PERCENT INCREASE 1971–1980[1]
Newspaper publishing and printing	$7,360	5%	$7,654	4%	$ 8,610	4 %	$11,418	5.0%
Periodical publishing and printing	3,210	2	3,435	7	4,200	7	5,650	6.5
Book publishing	2,560	5	2,715	6	3,230	6	4,500	6.5
Book printing	1,021	6	1,082	6	1,288	6	1,724	6
Commercial printing	8,410	8	9,209	10	11,650	8.5	17,118	8.2
Manifold business forms	1,311	5	1,525	9	1,851	9	2,848	9
Typesetting	491	6	530	8	667	8	980	8

[1] Compound annual rate of growth.

Source: U.S. Department of Commerce, Bureau of Domestic Commerce (Washington, D.C.: U.S. Government Printing Office, 1972), p. 59.

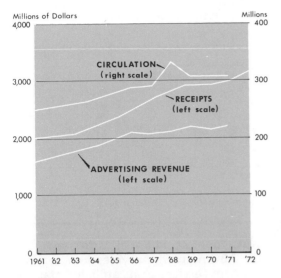

FIGURE 25–4 *U.S. Magazine Receipts*

revenue have come essentially from higher advertising rates and not from gains in the number of advertising pages. However, there have been notable publishing successes of individual farm magazines. Although some farm publishers reach national markets, many others are oriented to geographic regions. The content of farm periodicals has changed along with the farmer; articles on seed, grain, and livestock are supplemented with information on management techniques and business administration (see Figure 25–4).

BOOK INDUSTRY IN U.S.

Current demographic trends have favorably affected the book publishing industry. The percent of high school graduates in the total population continues to rise and graduates increasingly continue their education at colleges or career institutes. Rising income levels and additional time and interest in leisure activities have also expanded the book market. Gains in paperback sales

and books sold through book clubs have been especially high (see Table 25–7).

Although educational spending continues to rise, publishers are aware that declining birth rates of the late 1960s will result in smaller educational markets in coming decades. Projected lower enrollments may be offset, however, by gains in student expenditures on instructional materials.

Growth of shipments by the book printing industry of nearly 8 percent a year during the past decade can be attributed to an expanding population with higher levels of education, federal and state support for education, improved economic conditions, increased leisure time, and broader, more varied interests of the public. Although these influences will continue to support book printing growth in the 1970s, the industry's value of shipments are expected to increase at a slower rate (see Figure 25–5).

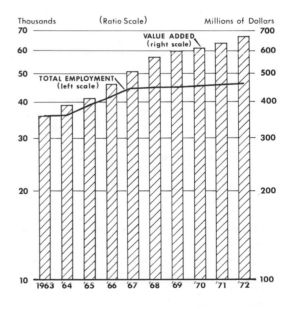

**TABLE 25–8   U.S. Radio Broadcasting: Trends and Projections
(in millions of dollars)**

	1967	1971	PERCENT INCREASE
Broadcast revenues[1]	$907	$1,203	5.8%
Income before taxes	$ 81	$ 97	4.3
Gross investment in tangible property	$671	$ 864	5.3
Depreciated value	$362	$ 432	2.2
Employment (number)[2]	67,210	72,120	1.5
AM stations, commercial (number)[2]	4,138	4,330	0.8
FM stations, commercial (number)[2]	1,719	2,304	5.7

[1] Net time sales, plus talent, program, and other sundry revenues.

[2] As of December 31.

Source: U.S. Department of Commerce, Bureau of Domestic Commerce (Washington, D.C.: U.S. Government Printing Office, 1972), p. 343.

RADIO BROADCASTING IN U.S.

The United States leads the world in the total number of radio receivers and in the number of receivers available per 1,000 inhabitants.

Radio continues as an effective advertising medium despite the popularity of television. Its comparatively low cost, flexibility, quick response, and ability to focus on specialized markets assure it a significant share of the total advertising dollar (see Table 25–8).

Radio is now primarily a local medium with some 68 percent of its revenues coming from local sources. National advertising sales have always been a steady source of revenue, and now account for about 28 percent of the total. Network radio has declined steadily as national advertisers have shifted to television; it now accounts for only about 4 percent of total radio time advertising sales.

Some 4,330 commercial AM stations and 2,304 commercial FM stations were in operation at the end of 1971. In addition, 25 AM and 479 FM educational stations were operating. The American Broadcasting Company (ABC), the Columbia Broadcasting System (CBS), the Mutual Broadcasting System (MBS), and the National Broadcasting Company (NBC) operate national radio networks. The ABC network provides four separate program services to its affiliated stations. ABC and CBS each own seven AM and FM stations and NBC owns six (see Figure 25–6).

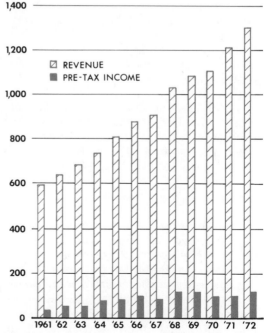

FIGURE 25–6   *U.S. Radio Broadcasting Revenue and Pre-Tax Income*

440

TABLE 25–9 U.S. Television Broadcasting: Trends and Projections (in millions of dollars)

	1967	1971	PERCENT INCREASE 1970–1971	1972	PERCENT INCREASE 1971–1972
Broadcast revenues[1]	2,275	2,740	− 2%	3,000	10%
Income before taxes	415	390	−14	510	31
Gross investment in tangible property	1,185	1,550	4	1,700	10
Depreciated value	661	760	3	830	9
Employment (number)[2]	51,718	58,500	0.1	59,100	1
TV stations, commercial (number)[2]	633	699	2		
TV stations, educational (number)[2]	154	205	0.5		
TV receivers in use (in millions)[3]	79	96.5	4	100.5	4

[1] Net time sales, plus talent, program, and other sundry revenues.
[2] As of December 31.
[3] Estimated number as of December 31.
Source: U.S. Department of Commerce, Bureau of Domestic Commerce, FCC *Television Factbook*, p. 346.

Radio networks are regulated by the Federal Communications Commission, which licenses stations and monitors them to protect the public. Radio will continue to provide advertisers with a very flexible medium at low cost that is capable of a broad or a selective reach. Market research and innovative programming will continue to be keys to maintaining the competitive effectiveness of radio as an advertising and entertainment medium.

TELEVISION INDUSTRY IN THE U.S.

The United States has more television receivers (99,000), sets available per 1,000 inhabitants (474), and variety of programs televised to the public than any other nation (see Table 25–9). The U.S. television industry is regulated by the Federal Communication Commission. Legislative and regulatory developments in Washington have always had an impact on the telecasting industry.

License renewal policy, cable television (CATV), access to the broadcast media, and fairness in handling controversial subjects are regulatory issues of prime concern to television broadcasters.

Three national networks, the American Broadcasting Company (ABC), the Columbia Broadcasting System (CBS), and the National Broadcasting Company (NBC) operate 699 commercial television stations. In addition, there are 205 independent educational television sta-

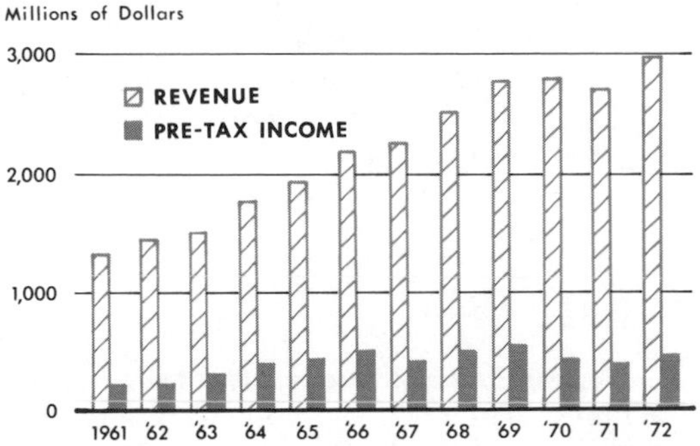

FIGURE 25–7 *U.S. TV Broadcasting Revenues*

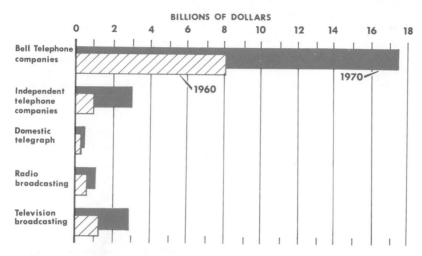

FIGURE 25–8 *Operating Revenues of Selected Communications Media, 1960 and 1970*

tions. The commercial stations employ 58,500 full-time workers and have a gross investment of $1,550 million in tangible property. Figure 25–7 shows TV broadcasting revenues and pretax income from 1961 to 1972.

The television broadcasting company can look forward to a resumption of growth in the decade of the 1970s, averaging about 7 percent per year; this is a slower rate than that of the mid-1960s, indicating some maturing of the industry. Net revenues should pass the $5.2 billion mark by 1980. Gross earnings should rise somewhat more rapidly, approaching $750 million in 1980.

Figure 25–8 compares operating revenues of selected communications media for 1960 and 1970.

references

1. Bagdikiun, Ben H. *The Information Machines: Their Impact On Men and the Media.* New York: Harper & Row, 1971.

2. Brucker, Herbert. *Communication Is Power: Unchanging Values in a Changing Journalism.* New York: Oxford University Press, 1973.

3. Cherry, Colin. *World Communication: Threat or Promise? A Sociotechnical Approach.* London: Wiley-Interscience, 1971.

4. DeVito, Joseph A. *Language Concepts and Processes.* Englewood Cliffs, N.J.: Prentice-Hall, 1973.

5. Girard, Chester; Garrison, Garnet R.; and Willis, Edigar E. *Television and Radio.* 4th ed. New York: Appleton-Century-Crofts, 1971.

6. Hamilton, Edward A. *Graphic Design for the Computer Age: Visual Communication for All Media.* New York: Van Nostrand Reinhold, 1970.

7. Lui, Alan P. *Communications and National Integration in Communist China.* Berkeley: University of California Press, 1971.

8. Mayer, Martin. *About Television.* New York: Harper & Row, 1972.

9. Mortensen, C. David. *Communication: The Study of Human Interaction.* New York: McGraw-Hill Book Co., 1972.

10. ———. *Basic Readings in Communication Theory.* New York: Harper & Row, 1973.

11. Mosher, Frederick C. *Democracy and the Public Service*. New York: Oxford University Press, 1968.

12. Padellaro, Giuseppe. *Italy Documents and Notes* 21 (July–August 1972): 313–46.

13. Pred, Alan R. "Communication Urban Systems Development and the Long-Distance Flow of Information Through Pre-electronic U.S. Newspapers." *Economic Geography* 47 (October 1971): 498–523.

14. Read, Hadley. *Communication: Methods for All Media*. Urbana: University of Illinois Press.

15. Riegel, Oscar W. *Mobilizing For Chaos: The Story of the New Propaganda*. New York: Arno Press, 1972.

16. Rogers, Everett M., and Shoemaker, F. Floyd. *Communication of Innovations: A Cross-Cultural Approach*. 2nd. ed. New York: Free Press, 1971.

17. Shreirogel, Paul A. *Communication in Crisis*. Nashville, Tenn.: T. Nelson, 1971.

18. Trent, Jimmie D.; Trent, Judith S.; and O'Neill, Daniel J. *Concepts in Communication*. Boston: Allyn and Bacon, 1973.

19. U.S. Bureau of the Census. *Statistical Abstract of the United States, 1974*. Washington, D.C.: U.S. Government Printing Office, 1974.

20. Wilkie, Bernard. *The Technique of Special Effects in Television*. London: Focal Press, 1971.

recreation
services

26

26

Recreation services provide opportunities for satisfying human wants and for relaxation which emerge from leisure or time not devoted to earning a living or performing daily chores.[1] There are two types of recreational services: direct and indirect. Direct services include services in which the recreationist is directly involved in the experience of recreation. Indirect services include the production or manufacturing processes that cater to the recreation services with little meaningful or direct involvement in recreation. Discussion here is concerned with the former.

Direct recreation services may be divided into: (1) indoor–outdoor activities occurring in and around residential quarters; (2) indoor–outdoor entertainment, such as theaters, symphonies, sidewalk shows or performances (3) indoor–outdoor athletic activities, such as local game leagues, fishing, hiking, golf, swimming, surfing, tennis, football, soccer, baseball, basketball, track, bowling, camping, horseback riding, etc.

Recreation services are basically quaternary in nature. Their variety, incidence, and frequency over a given space are determined by a multiplicity of factors. These factors and their resulting patterns are discussed in this chapter.

DEMAND FOR RECREATIONAL SERVICES

Engagement in a particular type of recreational activity at a particular place is a function of the availability and length of leisure time, taste and preference, income, education, sex, and age, as well as the presence of competing recreation facilities. These factors suggest that the location of recreation facilities is demand oriented; further evidence from findings of the U.S. Outdoor Recreation Resources Review Commission (ORRRC) support the thesis that the availability of recreation resources, particularly those for outdoor recreation, play a dominant role in the location patterns of recreation activities.[2] The ORRRC further asserts:

> Natural endowment is relevant and *may* be important, but it needs to be considered in relation to other relevant aspects of the location problem to be given its proper weight in analysis bearing on outdoor recreation development.
>
> The implications of natural endowment for location are brought into sharper focus by recognizing again one important distinction between outdoor recreation services produced at a site and the more usual type of good or service produced in an economy. This is, that the final outdoor recreation product is not transportable. Final consumers of outdoor recreation services must consume those services at the site of production. The large bulk of ordinary goods produced has incorporated in its production a certain amount of transportation, and cost of transportation becomes an essential component of cost of production. Ordinary goods are, on the whole, transported to consumers. In outdoor recreation, on the other hand, consumers transport themselves to the product. This distinction takes on some

[1] Recreation is very subjective and personal, varying from one individual to another; thus, a general definition is not possible.

[2] Created in 1958, the U.S. Outdoor Recreation Resources Review Commission has attempted to study the wants and needs of Americans now, with projections for 2000; the available resources to fill those needs; and policies and programs to ensure that the recreation needs of the future are adequately and efficiently met. The commission's findings, conclusions, and recommendations, contained in a series of reports submitted to the president and Congress, highlight the ever-increasing participation in recreation, the shortage of resources, and the steps to eliminate this imbalance.

importance with reference to measurement of demand for recreation. (9)

Various studies (3, 6, 9) measuring the demand for outdoor recreation in terms of participation of visitor days confirm the relevance of the ORRRC's stated influences on the location of outdoor recreation activities.

The demand for entertainment is heavily influenced by population thresholds. Given the location of a recreation site and the demand for it, the demand would be graphically represented in the shape of a cone; the shorter the distance from the site to population centers, the greater the frequency and intensity of participation, and vice versa. Unlike the mean information field (MIF), the demand cone is likely to be much wider at the base, reflecting recreation participation during vacations.

Difficulties in the specification and measurement of demand for recreation basically stem from the contention that values of recreation cannot be adequately measured in monetary terms. For example, who can estimate the value of a walk through majestic and serene woods, the sight of a sunset at the ocean, or the thrill of catching a fifteen-pound fish? Despite the difficulty of placing a true monetary value on recreation, many state agencies and the U.S. Bureau of Outdoor Recreation have collected expenditure data. These data, along with employment and participation rates, may be used for detailed analyses of outdoor recreation.

INTERNATIONAL TOURIST TRAVEL

Table 26–1 records the number of tourists who traveled abroad to twenty-one countries and the money they spent in the host country. Tourists include persons traveling for pleasure, domestic

TABLE 26–1 International Tourist Travel, 1972

COUNTRY OF ARRIVAL	NUMBER OF TOURISTS	TOURIST RECEIPTS (in millions of U.S. $)
Australia	426.4	$ 159
Austria	10,252.5	1,667
Belgium	6,952.7	435
Canada	37,148.2	1,344
Czechoslovakia	11,498.5	149[1]
France	14,700.0	1,920
West Germany	7,565.0	1,854
Hungary	3,616.7	138
Ireland[2]	1,692.0	185
Italy	10,977.7	2,178
Japan	723.7	201
Mexico[3]	2,250.2	1,132
Netherlands	2,594.3	762
Poland	8,339.1	96
Portugal	3,925.3	391
Scandinavia	14,800.1	1,105
Spain	32,506.6	2,511
Switzerland	7,131.1	1,062
USSR[3]	2,059.3	—
United Kingdom	7,255.0	1,380
U.S.	12,884.8	2,706

[1] Estimated
[2] Figures for 1971
[3] Figures for 1970

Source: Based on the *United Nations Statistical Yearbook, 1973* (New York: United Nations, 1974), pp. 467–68.

reasons, health, meetings, business, study, etc., and stopping for a period of twenty-four hours or more in a country other than that in which they usually reside. The figures do not include immigrants, residents in a frontier zone, persons domiciled in one country and working in an adjoining country, transport crews or troops and travelers passing through a country without stopping. The data are based on frontier checks. In the absence of frontier-check figures, data based on hotel reservations are given, but these are not strictly comparable with frontier-check data as they exclude certain types of tourists, such as campers and tourists staying in private houses, and as they may contain some duplication when a tourist moves from one hotel to another.

The volume of international travel soared to unprecedented heights in 1972, reaching a total of over 200 million world tourists. The amount of money generated by travel is difficult to measure because not all of it is spent directly on recreation services. However, any traveler in a foreign land spends money for goods and services he needs. Whether his trip is for business, pleasure, or health, he is contributing to the economy of the host country.

Travel gives rise to a wide variety of businesses directly related to it, as people traveling generate business. Travel has become so much a way of life among the affluent nations of the world that it is responsible for a significant portion of the income of many countries.

The tourist receipts for 1972 in Table 26–1, clearly substantiate the importance of travel to an economy. Eleven countries received $1 billion each in 1972 from international tourism. Of the twenty-one countries listed in Table 26–1, income from tourist receipts varied from a high of $2.7 billion for the U.S. to a low of $96 million for Poland. Canada and Spain attracted the largest number of international tourists—37.1 and 32.5 million, respectively.

U.S. TOURISTS ABROAD

In 1972, despite a business recession and rising unemployment, about 5 million U.S. residents traveled abroad (excluding Canada and Mexico); about 8 million Americans visited Canada or Mexico in 1972. U.S. travelers abroad spent over $5 billion in 1972 (excluding fares paid to U.S. carriers), a 16 percent increase from 1971, compared with a 14 percent rise in 1969 (see Figure 26–1).

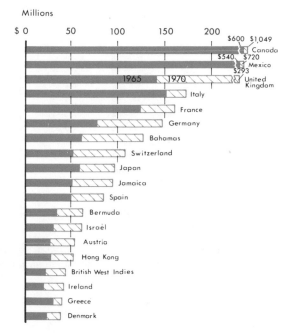

FIGURE 26–1 *Where Americans Spent Their Money: 1965 and 1970*

(Foreign visitors to the U.S. numbered over 13 million in 1972 and spent over $2.7 billion.)

About 98 percent of Americans traveling overseas went by air; only 120,000 went by sea, although cruise travel increased by 25,000. Almost all cruise travel is by foreign vessels, and these vessels received more from Americans in 1972 than in 1971.

Reduced air fares and the introduction of the 747 jet aircraft with its larger seating capacity contributed to a 22 percent increase in the number of Americans visiting Europe and the Mediterranean area and to a 22 percent increase in expenditures there. U.S. travelers to these areas spent over $900 per trip and remained in the area an average of 25 days in 1972, two days less than in 1971, continuing the downward trend of the recent past. (*See* figures 26–2 and 26–3.)

447

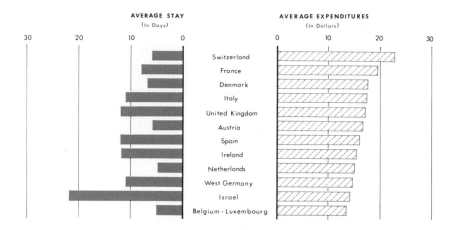

FIGURE 26–2 *Average Stay and Expenditures Per Day of U.S. Tourists in Selected European and Mediterranean Countries, 1970*

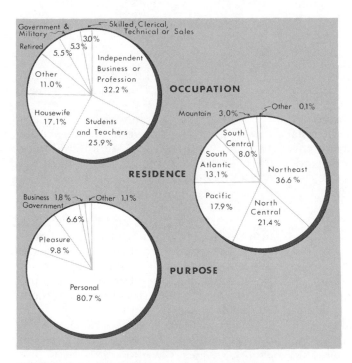

FIGURE 26–3 *Characteristics of U.S. Travelers Abroad*

448

As in the past, Americans spent more in Canada than in any other foreign country. The United Kingdom remained the leading overseas attraction to Americans, receiving nearly 1.4 million U.S. travelers. In the past five years, travel expenditures by Americans there have increased 106 percent. Growth of travel outlays by Americans in the West Indies slowed, apparently reflecting the U.S. business recession and dollar devaluation. An abrupt increase in the prices of Caribbean tourist services and price competition of lower transatlantic fares also contributed to slowing the growth of tourism in that area.

TOURIST ECONOMY IN SPAIN

Spain ranks second to the United States in dollar income from tourists. The tourist industry contributed $2.5 billion to the Spanish economy by attracting more than 32.5 million tourists in 1972. Of these tourists, over 63 percent came from four countries: France supplied 38.96 percent; the United Kingdom, 11.32 percent; West Germany, 9.16 percent; and the United States, 4.55 percent.

The number of foreign visitors to Spain has risen spectacularly during the past few years. This phenomenon is due to the rise in the standard of living in many European countries and to Spain's extraordinarily beautiful scenery, the courtesy and hospitality of Spaniards, the mild climate, a relatively low cost of living, and artistic treasures, epitomized by the Prado Museum.

Of course, the tourist influx also has an effect on Spaniards and a decided influence on their outlook and habits, contributing to the modernization of the country. Hotel capacity has more than doubled in the past five years; there are more than a thousand hotels, for example, in the Balearics, Gerona, and Barcelona. Tourism has a favorable effect on the balance of payments, serving to finance more than one-half of Spanish imports that generally consist of necessary equipment for industrialization of the country.

ITALY

Foreigners flock to Italy all year. It is second to Spain in Europe as a tourist attraction; more than 10.9 million visitors went there in 1972, spending over $2.1 billion. Its attractions are almost too numerous to list: the Italian Riviera along the northern Mediterranean coast, where beaches and scenic fishing towns rival those of the adjoining French Riviera; the art galleries of Florence, Genoa, and Milan; the Leaning Tower of Pisa; and the canals of Venice.

Rome offers the Colosseum, Forum, and other ancient structures still more or less intact, plus some magnificent cathedrals. Within the borders of Italy are two tiny independent countries with great tourist appeal: Vatican City, home of the Pope and world headquarters of the Roman Catholic Church and mountainous San Marino.

TOURIST ECONOMY IN MEXICO

Tourism also plays a vital role in the economy of Mexico, where new luxury hotels, motels, and restaurants are springing up all over the country. Various government agencies are encouraging operators of older tourist establishments to raise their standards, and federal control of room rates is rigorously enforced. Some authorities estimate that purchases by tourists account for one-third of the country's income.

Over 90 percent of Mexico's tourist trade comes from the United States and Canada. The tourism sector of the economy catered to 2.3 million visitors who spent $1.13 billion in 1972.

449

RECREATIONAL PATTERNS ABROAD

Tourism is a major form of recreation that typically involves a considerable outlay of money, allowing only the more affluent to travel. But how do the vast majority of the world's peoples spend their leisure time? Traditionally experienced, leisure requires little or nothing in the way of expenditure; it is more a matter of the spirit and the intellect. After having allocated the day between work, traveling to and from work, eating, and sleeping, people are left with what is commonly described as free time; part of this time is allotted to a variety of chores, such as shopping, getting haircuts, going to the bank, paying bills, etc., which are neither vocational nor recreational activities.

UNITED KINGDOM

A considerable proportion of people's free time and money in Britain is spent in their own homes. On a weekday evening, roughly seven out of eight adults are at home. About four out of five families do most of their own home decorating. In spite of the high proportion of the population living in urban areas, at least half the families in Britain have some garden, and the standard of both town and country gardens is high. Other home pursuits include entertaining friends, looking after pets (nearly one household in two has a pet, usually a cat or a dog), and pursuing hobbies. Probably the most popular hobby in terms of money spent is photography, which has had a striking increase in popular interest in recent years.

Outside the home, increasing prosperity, leisure time, and the influence of television have affected interest in playing or watching outdoor and indoor sports, especially soccer and cricket. Golf, tennis, riding, angling, bowling, rugby, skiing, and sailing are extremely popular. Camping, swimming, and picnicking are favorite family activities, often reserved for holiday outings. Cinema remains the most popular form of indoor entertainment outside the home.

WEST GERMANY

The German people share in large measure social values that are common to Western civilization and, more specifically, to continental Western Europe. They place a high value on the natural and the unspoiled, bodily fitness, and the great outdoors. Reverence toward nature is deeply rooted. Germans spend much time at the lakes and in the mountains and woods, which are easily accessible by a widespread system of well-kept trails, inns, and shelters. Hiking, sunbathing, boating, and skiing are very popular.

Much leisure time is spent reading; visiting museums of art, science and technology, and history; traveling. The movies, opera, and plays also attract large numbers of people, as do sporting events.

ITALY

Italian forms of entertainment include dancing, pin-ball machines, juke boxes, itinerant entertainers, fairs and expositions, circuses, radio and television in cafes and other public places, concerts of light music, zoos, go-carts, and bowling.

FRANCE

Only during the last few years have Frenchmen, particularly young Frenchmen, begun to travel a great deal throughout Europe for their summer holidays. The development of the Common Market, easing of border formalities, a rising standard of living, the development of low-cost vacation clubs, and a desire to see other places and peoples are reasons why Frenchmen have become more interested in foreign travel.

In France there are as many youth organizations and centers for adult education as there are tastes and interests. For example, there are youth clubs with facilities for meetings, games, arts and crafts, record concerts, reading, etc. The French Educational League groups all organizations devoted to after-school activities.

Sports play a significant role in French life. There are more than 20,000 sports clubs with about two million members. State aid is given in many different forms, from subsidies to reductions in rail fares to sporting events and the provision of facilities and equipment.

USSR

Consumption and traditional ways of life for an average urban Soviet family have changed substantially since World War II. Although still a widely accepted principle, paternal authoritarianism has given way to more freedom of action and thought among family members. Through schools, newspapers, radio, and television, people have learned about the rest of the country, but little about the rest of the world.

Leisure-time activities that Soviet officials consider to be most desirable are those that are held to contribute to the construction of society according to the principles of communism. Such activities include study to improve employment qualifications, self-improvement and self-education, civic and social work, hobbies, and sports.

Reading is the most important form of leisure-time educational activity. It has been accorded much respect in

Soviet society as a true indication of personal intellectualism. Books are both extremely inexpensive and available in great quantities.

Sports and physical activity are important in Soviet society, and both sexes and all ages are urged to keep physically fit. Individual or informal sport activities do not exist; the state organizes all sport activities and provides the necessary facilities.

The theater and motion picture are popular. Motion picture attendance is greater because cinemas are more numerous, and lower priced. Foreign films, rarely seen outside the large cities of European Russia, are most popular with young people.

Young people spend much free time in restaurants and cafes, which provide a place to relax, drink alcoholic beverages, eat, and dance. The state views this activity with disdain and has consequently attempted, without complete success, to draw youths from these activities by building youth centers.

JAPAN

Baseball is the favorite sport in Japan, and boxing, wrestling, and karate share popularity with baseball. Lawn tennis, golf, skating, and skiing attract thousands more enthusiasts.

Tokyo and Osaka have the largest amusement quarters of any large city. The Ginza district of Tokyo is more brightly lit than Times Square, and here one can enjoy a meal in one of the more than 30,000 restaurants or drinks in an equal number of drinking establishments. Dance halls, cabarets, night clubs, and coffee houses accommodate customers of varying means by the thousands; musical entertainment ranges from Bach to Beethoven to the latest in jazz.

Devotees of the more sophisticated arts spend their leisure time painting, sculpturing, playing music, or visiting numerous galleries, theaters, and concert halls. One can see and hear an amazing range of plays and concerts; Kabuki and Noh, the old classical plays, are performed and enjoyed as much as Shakespeare and modern plays. Musical events range from traditional Japanese to classical Western compositions. Available motion pictures include some from Japan, the United States, France, Italy, and the Soviet Union. Leisure time and a little extra money have helped to revive some traditional Japanese arts, such as flower arrangement (*ikebana*), the tea ceremony (*cha no yu*), raising dwarf trees (*bonsai*), brush painting, pottery, and lacquer work.

AMERICA AT PLAY

An increasing number of Americans are taking part in leisure and recreational activities; an estimated 14 percent of total personal consumption expenditure (PCE) is spent on goods and services related to recreation activities in the U.S. While growth in spending on recreation fluctuates considerably as new tastes and habits develop and old ones fade, the overall rise has been faster than that of total personal spending. Most forecasters of consumer expenditures project spending for recreation to grow faster than PCE in the 1970s.

The recreation industry has been expanding in all directions. From snorkeling to snowmobiling and television to tourism, recreation is a major manufacturing and service industry today. The boom in recreation is a natural outgrowth of mounting affluence and free time. People have more and more money and the time to spend it. How it is spent depends on the costs of different leisure pursuits, the availability of facilities, and the whims of fad and fashion.

Recreational activities in the United States range from professional and amateur team sports, such as baseball, basketball, and football, to professional and amateur individual sports, such as boxing, golf, fishing, swimming, etc. Professional baseball, basketball, and football are excellent examples of Christaller's central place theory; the population thresholds to support them are provided by large metropolises. All major league franchises are in cities with metropolitan populations exceeding 1 million. Only core cities such as these have the financial support and threshold to build enormous amphitheaters or astrodomes to attract the vast crowds, without which no professional team could survive.

Professional boxing, although quite ubiquitous, is also closely affiliated with the large population centers. Attendance at prize fights is a key to its financial success. Bowling, golf, the movies, boating, and sailing also attract people all over the nation.

Table 26–2 gives a regional picture of the number of people 12 years old and over who spent $7.50 or more and reported 3 or more fishing and hunting recreation days during the year; the study from which the table was derived was based on samples of approximately 18,000 households. Unlike recreational activities, such as baseball, basketball, and football, which rely heavily on large populations in metropolitan areas to support them, the activities in Table 26–2 require more remote and sparsely populated locations. Most people who hunt and fish are largely from small cities, suburbs, towns and rural areas, not from big cities.

Further analysis of Table 26–2 reveals that there is no significant per-capita differential of fishing and hunting; rather, the per-capita fishing and hunting days show a distinct inverse relationship with per-capita income. For instance, per-capita income of the east south-central region is the lowest among all

TABLE 26–2 Sport Fishermen and Hunters, 1970

	TOTAL PERSONS	TOTAL WHO FISHED AND/OR HUNTED	TOTAL WHO FISHED AND HUNTED	TOTAL WHO FISHED	TOTAL WHO HUNTED	TOTAL NUMBER OF RECREATION DAYS	
						FISHING	HUNTING
Male	73,601	26,928	10,612	24,073	13,467	555,465	195,386
Female	81,629	9,349	608	9,085	869	150,722	8,303
Big cities	24,222	3,212	670	2,984	898	48,512	7,841
Small cities and suburbs	57,643	12,142	2,999	11,433	3,708	245,413	41,976
Towns and rural areas	73,365	20,923	7,549	18,741	9,731	412,262	153,872
New England	8,652	1,579	433	1,430	582	29,534	7,234
Middle Atlantic	28,244	4,539	1,246	4,054	1,731	82,063	25,004
East North Central	31,550	7,284	2,227	6,699	2,812	137,317	35,279
West North Central	12,904	4,000	1,362	3,579	1,783	66,448	24,020
South Atlantic	23,539	5,461	1,572	5,129	1,904	137,036	29,568
East South Central	9,862	2,660	966	2,464	1,162	62,343	20,043
West South Central	14,624	4,380	1,544	4,006	1,918	86,823	30,206
Mountain	5,656	2,044	705	1,769	980	25,476	10,392
Pacific	20,199	4,332	1,164	4,030	1,466	79,148	21,943
Total	155,230	36,277	11,217	33,158	14,336	706,187	203,689

Source: U.S. Bureau of the Census, *Statistical Abstract of the United States, 1971* (Washington, D.C.: U.S. Government Printing Office), 1971, p. 200.

TABLE 26–3   Participation in Selected Outdoor Activities in U.S., 1970

	PARTICIPANTS (in millions)	AVERAGE DAYS PER PARTICIPANT[1]	TOTAL DAYS OF PARTICIPATION (in millions)	POPULATION PARTICIPATING				
				NORTHEAST[2] 4,881	NORTH CENTRAL[2] 4,370	SOUTH[2] 3,811	WEST[2] 4,524	TOTAL
Picnicking	82.1	6.6	542	49%	56%	40%	54%	49%
Swimming	77.3	22.3	1,722	52	47	40	49	46
Playing outdoor games and sports	60.0	44.6	2,673	37	40	30	38	36
Attending outdoor sports events and concerts	59.4	10.6	628	33	39	33	38	35
Walking for pleasure, 30 minutes or more	50.3	37.0	1,861	33	31	25	35	30
Fishing	49.4	11.4	562	21	32	32	32	29
Boating (canoeing, sailing, other)	41.1	10.2	422	23	29	21	26	24
Bicycling	37.1	46.8	1,736	21	26	18	25	22
Camping	35.2	11.3	397	14	22	18	34	21
Nature walks	30.5	12.3	374	18	21	14	23	18
Hunting	20.9	10.4	217	8	14	15	13	12
Horseback riding	16.1	12.9	208	7	11	9	13	10
Bird watching	7.5	58.0	433	5	5	4	4	4
Wildlife and bird photography	4.9	8.2	40	3	4	2	4	3

[1] Data refer to number of days that individuals participated regardless of amount of time spent in participation.

[2] Average income

Source: U.S. Bureau of Outdoor Recreation, *The 1970 Survey of Outdoor Recreation Activities,* 1972.

regions in Table 26–2, but the per-capita recreation days for fishing and hunting in this region are the highest.

Table 26–3 shows participation in selected outdoor activities based on a nationwide survey conducted by the Bureau of the Census in 1970; the bureau sampled outdoor recreation participation of 46,500 persons 9 years old and over. Leisure time and recreation play a larger role than per-capita income in determining the extent of recreation involvement, according to this study.

Over the years leisure activities requiring modest outlays and relatively few specialized skills have enjoyed the greatest popularity. Driving for pleasure, picnicking, swimming, and walking for pleasure were and still are most popular, measured not only by the number of participants, but also by aggregate hours devoted to these activities.

The highest rates of growth during the past ten years belong, however, to activities such as bicycling, camping, skiing, and hockey.

Bicycling is another activity which has recently found great favor with Americans, spirited by energy and environmental considerations. Estimated sales of 9.6 million bicycles in 1972 constituted an increase of 13 percent over the previous year. The current concern with environmental protection, as well as the health benefits associated with this sport, are partly responsible for its popularity.

The popularity of camping has also increased rapidly, and probably is largely responsible for the spectacular growth in recreational vehicles. There are about 4 million campers, motor homes, trailers, and related vehicles in the U.S. Pressures of urban living have contributed to a steadily increasing interest in second homes, of which about 150,000 are built annually. Travel trailers, truck camps, camping trailers, and motor homes are among the most rapidly expanding leisure product-lines in this country. About 450,000 recreational vehicles are sold annually, creating retail sales of $1.6 billion. While the number of units shipped rose 700 percent during the 1960s, spending on these units soared 1,700 percent as more equipment was purchased with each unit.

Motorcycles and minibike sales are booming. Cycle registrations have tripled since 1960. Minibikes, which do not need licensed operators and are mostly used by adolescents, have over $100 million in sales.

The popularity of skiing has increased greatly since 1960 and has a favorable outlook for the 1970s. In 1957 there were slightly over 100 ski resorts in the United States; today there are close to 1,000. The average income from each of these ski areas more than doubled between 1968 and 1973. Estimates vary, but it is generally assumed that no more than 50,000 people skied in this country in the late 1940s; today over 4.25 million persons participate in the sport, spending an estimated annual amount of $1.3 billion for products and services ranging from equipment to entertainment (see Figure 26–4).

Basic demographics and economics suggest favorable expansion for air travel, although foreign travel may decline due to recent dollar devaluations and increases in international fares. Propelled by rising incomes and a desire for increased mobility, five times as many people travel by air today as did ten years ago. The 25 to 44 age group will grow by 30 percent by 1980; a larger proportion of this group will be college-educated, and they are typically four times more mobile than the rest of the population.

The rapid expansion of recreation activities since 1960 can be traced to rising incomes and amounts of free time. Spending on leisure pursuits is relatively discretionary, i.e., it can be easily post-

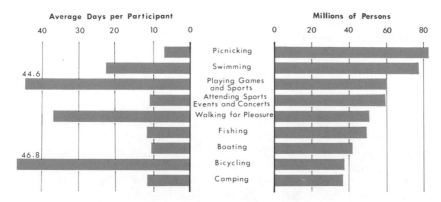

Average Days per Participant

40   30   20   10   0

44.6

46.8

Millions of Persons

0   20   40   60   80

Picnicking

Swimming

Playing Games and Sports

Attending Sports Events and Concerts

Walking for Pleasure

Fishing

Boating

Bicycling

Camping

FIGURE 26–4   *Participation in Selected Outdoor Activities, 1970*

poned or cancelled. Recreation is more sensitive to income fluctuations than to price changes. The general economic climate strongly influences discretionary and, therefore, leisure spending. Discretionary purchasing power, which is income left after paying for life's necessities, is divided among savings, leisure pursuits, and other luxuries. When income expansion slows, as in periods of sluggish business activity, people initially dip into savings rather than retrench their life styles. After a lag of about one year, though, families begin to protect remaining savings at the expense of discretionary items.

The spatial pattern of recreational activities is most likely to follow central place patterns as the importance of distance continues to increase with mounting costs of energy.

A steady increase in real family income makes expenditures on recreational activities possible. Today almost 25 percent of all U.S. families have incomes of

$15,000 and over; moreover, these families account for almost half of aggregate family income. Families in the 25-to-34 age group earning over $15,000 spend proportionately more on recreational activities, and the number of families in this group is increasing rapidly (see

Because recreation requires time as well as money, the increase in continuous, uninterrupted periods of free time is an important development. Compressed work weeks, three-day weekends, and longer paid vacations have led to substantial gains in the length of leisure time. Since 1960, for example, the amount of time spent on vacation increased about 50 percent to 2.2 weeks per fulltime worker. Legislation enacted in 1968 moved some holidays from midweek to extend the length of the weekend, thereby creating longer uninterrupted periods of leisure time. In addition, the rapidly rising number of women entering the labor force, coupled with steep declines in the birthrate, has

456

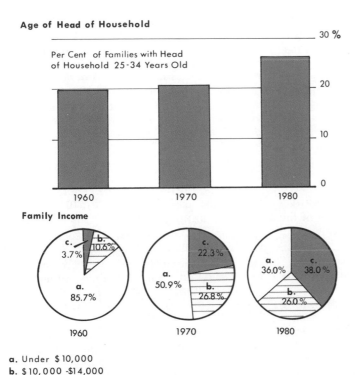

Age of Head of Household

Per Cent of Families with Head
of Household 25-34 Years Old

Family Income

a. Under $10,000
b. $10,000 -$14,000
c. $15,000 and Over

FIGURE 26–5 *Influences on Recreation Expenditures*

a double-barreled economic effect: it accelerates the increase in household income levels and shifts consumption patterns away from necessity items toward discretionary purchases.

Patterns of leisure spending may have to be modified over the next decade because of environmental concerns and urban pressures. Noisy equipment—snowmobiles, minibikes, motorcycles, etc.—and environmental and safety problems posed by this equipment, have prompted some states to legislate against these all-terrain vehicles. Laws restricting snowmobiles have caused snowmobile sales, which had increased at a 60 percent average annual rate until 1970, to decline.

Skiing will experience a slowing down from its explosive gains as suitable land becomes increasingly scarce. Skiing is becoming costly as it becomes more popular. Crowded slopes are detracting from its appeal. Competition from an increasing array of sports will be another limiting factor. Crosscountry skiing is cutting into the downhill market since it is easier to master, less expensive, and eliminates long waits at crowded ski lifts. New Englanders who are opening their property to crosscountry skiers are simultaneously closing out the snowmobiles.

Overcrowding may prove to be the chief restriction on the leisure industry. As more people reach comfortable income levels and participate in hobbies and recreation activities, they will spend more time queuing up in lines and sharing facilities. This is especially true of pursuits that use large land masses, such

457

as national parks and golf courses. Low entrance fees have made parks, seashores, and historical sites popular vacation spots for families unable to afford more costly vacations. Park facilities are straining from overpopularity. Officials are being forced to raise entrance fees or institute reservation requirements.

references

1. Bechter, Dan M. "Congested Parks: A Pricing Dilemma." *Monthly Review* of the Federal Reserve Bank of Kansas City (June 1971): 3–11.

2. ———. "Outdoor Recreation." *Monthly Review* of the Federal Reserve Bank of Kansas City (November 1970): 15–20.

3. Clawson, M. *Methods of Measuring Demand for the Value of Outdoor Recreation*. Washington, D.C.: The Resources for the Future, 1962.

4. Craig, William. "Recreational Activity in a Small Negro Urban Community: The Role of the Cultural Base." *Economic Geography* 48 (January 1972): 107–15.

5. Deasy, George F., and Griess, Phyllis R. "Impact of a Tourist Facility on Its Hinterland." *Annals of the Association of American Geographers* 56 (June 1966): 290–306.

6. Gillespie, G. A., and Brewer, D. "Effects of Nonprice Variables upon Participation in Water-oriented Outdoor Recreation." *American Journal of Agricultural Economics* 50 (February 1968): 82–95.

7. Lee, Ronald F. *Public Use of the National Park Service*. Washington, D.C.: Department of the Interior, National Park Service, U.S. Government Printing Office, 1968.

8. O'Brien, Bob R. "The Future Road System of Yellowstone National Park." *Annals of the Association of American Geographers* 56 (September 1966): 385–407.

9. Outdoor Recreation Resources Review Commission. *Economic Studies of Outdoor Recreation*. Study Report 24. Washington, D.C., 1962, p. 24.

10. Pickett, Margaret S., and Bechter, Dan M. "Skiers: Their Local Economic Impact." *Monthly Review* of the Federal Reserve Bank of Kansas City (June 1972): 10–16.

11. Robinson, G. W. S. "The Recreation Geography of South Asia." *Geographical Review* 62 (October 1972): 561–72.

12. Rooney, John F., Jr. "Up from the Mines and Out from the Prairies: Some Geographical Implications of Football in the United States." *Geographical Review* 59 (October 1969): 471–92.

13. Stillwell, H. Daniel. "National Parks of Brazil: A Study in Recreational Geography." *Annals of the Association of American Geographers* 53 (September 1963): 391–406.

14. The President's Council on Recreation and Natural Beauty. *From Sea to Shining Sea*. Washington, D.C.: U.S. Government Printing Office, 1968.

15. Williams, Anthony V., and Zelinsky, Wilbur. "On Some Patterns in International Tourist Flows." *Economic Geography* 46 (October 1970): 549–67.

16. Wolfe, R. I. "Perspective on Outdoor Recreation: A Bibliographical Survey." *Geographical Review* 54 (April 1964): 203–38.

VI

POLICY AND PLANNING

CHAPTERS

27 Regional Planning

28 Man, Environment, and
Economic Activity

29 Prospects

introduction

In Part I we dealt with the influences of culture on resources and economic activity. In Part II we differentiated and discussed these influences as frameworks in order to set the stage for parts III through V, which demonstrated by selected examples the principles established in earlier parts.

In Part VI, the student is given an opportunity to examine policy issues through various planning procedures. Given the kaleidoscopic nature of economic phenomena, spatial disequilibrium is more a rule than an exception. In order to maximize the achievement of material goals that are satisfied by primary, secondary, and tertiary goods and services, man seeks to devise various mechanisms, of which planning is one.

In chapter 27 we are concerned with regional planning as it relates to attempts to formulate ideas that directly improve man's utilization of the space he occupies. Chapter 28 continues the focus begun in chapter 27 on environmental problems and discusses how these problems affect the spatial equilibrium of man and his economic activities. In chapter 29, we look ahead to indicate trends, future research, and scholarly orientations for students of the spatial analysis of economic activity.

regional planning

27

27

The previous chapters of this text provided an understanding of the theoretical and substantive aspects of economic activities in the space economy. This chapter affords the student an opportunity to become a practitioner in one of the many areas—planning—toward which the material in this book may be applied.

HISTORICAL ANTECEDENTS

Long before the United States was formed, the tiny Atlantic Coast colonial settlements were adopting measures to restrain people from using their land in ways that would cause injury to others or to the community. The earliest measures grew out of experiences with explosions and fires and were simple regulations to keep gunpowder mills and storehouses outside the settlements. Market towns like Boston were authorized to assign locations for slaughterhouses, stillhouses, and buildings in which tallow was melted and leather was tanned.

The early laws were passed in the interest of people's health, comfort, and safety. No more restraint was placed on the use of private property than was deemed necessary to protect the rights of others. As the country grew, cities and problems arose. The way that people used their land sometimes harmed others. Areas with mixtures of homes, stores, and factories often became slums, hazards to health, safety, morals, and the general welfare.

Vexing land-use problems resulted in corrective measures. Separate zoning districts were created for homes, for business, and for industry. Conflicting land uses were thus set apart. Other zoning regulations were shaped to prevent overcrowding by limiting the height and size of buildings. The same object was attained by regulating the size of building tracts and residential acreage; larger lots on ample acreage allow for fewer houses in an area and fewer persons per acre.

A bursting of city boundaries in the booming 1920s brought unguided growth to the fringes of cities, but was gentle compared to what was to come later. Urban expansion really gained momentum after World War II. In the United States, new forces restructured rural communities. Good roads and automobiles permitted city dwellers to spread over the countryside. Rural people in great numbers found employment and new homes in and around urban centers. Trade areas and daily commuting distances came to be measured in travel time rather than in miles. Millions of people began to make hour-long morning and evening trips between home and work. Expressways and higher speed limits brought outlying areas within commuting zones. New suburbs burgeoned beyond suburbs, and scattered subdivisions soon were extended farther from the central city.

New communities took shape in forms that could not have been foreseen. Urban expansion meant the building of many well-planned business and industrial districts and attractive residential suburbs, but it also brought ugly areas of haphazard growth and mixed-use districts of roadside blight, dreary miles of honky-tonks, billboards, gas stations, junkyards, shops, and homes. Older residential areas began to look like untended orphan tracts. In places there was a helter-skelter peppering of nonfarm dwellings on small rural tracts, premature subdivisions that were not sold, and scattered housing strung out along country roads.

Mushrooming communities developed fiscal ailments. Many improvements—roads, streets, schools, libraries, water and sewage facilities—were all needed at once. Many citizens encountered unexpected increases in assessments and taxes to pay for the necessary public services. Crowded highways and road hazards presented dangers.

Some farmers faced new problems as subdivisions engulfed their lands. A few moved away with windfall profits from the sale of their farms at high prices; those who remained had higher taxes for public improvements and services that they did not need or want. Their farm plants were damaged, and their operating costs had increased.

As in colonial days, the problems stem from unwise relationships in the uses of neighboring tracts of land. In colonial days, however, the problems were obvious, and the corrective restraints were simple. Today's problems are a complex mixture of fiscal matters, public services, use and changing values of land, health, pollution, safety, and public attitudes. Planning is needed to solve these problems.

REGIONAL DEVELOPMENT

Before we discuss the concept of planning, it is imperative that we understand the forces and developments that necessitate the use of the planning process.

There is a growing body of knowledge of spatial and economic development with currency in several social science disciplines, particularly in economics and geography. Commonly known as regional economic development, this body of knowledge traces the evolutionary process of growth and identifies situations that require planning.

Most scholars agree with the Swedish economist, Gunnar Myrdal, that the location, intensity, and direction of the *initial trigger* or *initial kick*[1] to an evolutionary process yields substantial understanding of subsequent events in the development of an economy. The internal economic momentum of the initial trigger causes *cumulative growth* and exerts a powerful influence on the location over time.

Cumulative growth involves the *multiplier and accelerator mechanism* by which the economic base becomes large enough to develop backward and forward linkages called a growth center. *Backward linkage* refers to industries and spatial locations that supply inputs; *forward linkage* points to the industries and location that utilize the output of the growth center. (The concepts of multiplier and accelerator are spending, respending, and investment process that multiply the starting levels of the economy).[2]

Growth centers (sometimes loosely referred to as *growth poles*) refer to large centers and sometimes to specific industrial complexes, activities, or to a specific large plant, that play strategic roles in sparking new development. The influence of the center is on the bases of shopping and commuting distances and its central-place activities. The growth center develops further and is intensified by Weber's agglomeration effects.

The survival of the growth centers depends upon exports outside the region or the center. The effects of exports from the center are termed *spread effects*. The economic momentum of the center loses its impact with increasing distance from

[1] The origin of the initial trigger is frequently hard to disentangle. Historically, it emerges from special innovations and discoveries, political advantages, cultural challenges, or chance.

[2] These are very technical concepts, and space does not permit a full discussion of them here. Interested students may consult a standard principles of economics textbook, e.g., Paul A. Samuelson, *Economics*, 9th ed. (New York: McGraw-Hill, 1973).

463

the growth center. This relationship is particularly noticeable in a central-place hierarchy where a growth center tends to discriminate against lower-order centers. Spread effects are for the most part limited to the immediate vicinity of growth centers. *Peripheral centers,* or areas outside the influence of the growth center, may actually experience a counterpoised decline in growth, resulting from continued inflow of inputs and preferred migration to the growth centers by a young, educated, active, and aggressive labor force.[3] Trade patterns similarly favor growth centers. Thus the landscape reflects an array of spatial disequilibriums.

After reaching a certain threshold, growth centers may exert considerable influence on peripheral centers in terms of the location and growth of economic activity there. This threshold may be reached when congestion, pollution, overspecialization, shortages, cumbersome administrative structures, problems of waste disposal, crime, housing, transportation problems, diseconomies of scale, etc., begin to characterize the growth centers. Business concerns faced with these problems are likely to become conscious of survival and of the increasing social costs. The social costs are costs that are not directly born by the producers but are passed on to the community in the form of pollutants and other social problems.

Since the increasing social costs of pollution, waste disposal is not borne by the businessman but by the community at large, and some equitable system of allocating these costs to proper sources needs to be improvised.

As growth centers, which are complex socioeconomic systems involving gigantic transportation and communication networks, seek to survive, they force

clarification of social objectives of the community in ordering activities in supra-urban space. (Students may wish to review Rostow's stages of growth, presented in chapter 5, to provide a historical perspective of economic activities before proceeding to the next section.)

PLANNING PROCESS

One of the first principles of law is that land is a unique sort of property. Unlike money or most other physical objects, no two pieces of real estate are exactly the same. Each piece of land has its own relative advantages and disadvantages. In areas of human habitation, parcels of land take on unique characteristics and advantages, depending on their relative relationship to other buildings and facilities in the community.

In light of this, it seems only rational that land uses should be coordinated to secure the greatest possible well-being of the community because once land is committed to use, it is difficult to revise its use.

The concept of planning concerns:

1. Assessment of regional resources and clarification and/or definition of social goals in ordering activities in space.

2. Evaluation of comparative effectiveness of alternative land-use patterns.

3. Coordination or synchronization of resources and goals for the present and the future.

WHAT IS A REGION?

Definitions of *region* vary, depending on the objectives and criteria chosen for delineation. Nevertheless, a region basically has four characteristics:

1. Territorial extensions of contiguous space.[4]

---

[3] This phenomenon is particularly true of the "brain-drain" from the developing countries to the developed countries.

[4] The condition of contiguity may not apply in some cases; for example, regions delineated on

2.   Complementation and reciprocity of some activities between the component areas of the region.

3.   Some degree of uniformity and homogeneity invoked by the chosen criteria.

4.   Existence over a certain period of time, although interrelationships continuously change and suggest adjustments in the boundary lines.

The relative degree and importance of these characteristics differ for varying purposes of study and type of region. For example, geographical regional boundaries are more durable than economic boundaries. Regional boundaries involving multinational sovereignty exhibit a restricted form of complementation and reciprocity, as in the case of the European Economic Community (ECC) region. Multipurpose regions are larger than single-purpose regions; homogeneous regions representing direct recognition of the spatial distribution of economic activity have been most successfully used for economic analysis, while the concept of regionalism embodying a metropolitan system has often been used by demographers, sociologists, planners, and others.

Region may be generally defined as: An area containing an observable series of resources and commodity flows of specified internal consistency, subject to observation and measurement. A region exhibits a marked internal interdependence and linkage of elements through flow phenomena. Often, the data necessary to measure flow phenomena are not available. Although data availability places constraints on the precise definition of study areas, there is some latitude of choice. Efforts have been made to delineate regions using standard sources of data. Such efforts are discussed in the following section.

Another aspect of attempting to define a region is the choice of criteria used to determine the type and scope of regions. These are various types of regions: geographic regions, labor-market areas, nodal regions, Standard Metropolitan Statistical Areas (SMSA)[5] and State Economic Areas (SEA), resource regions, trade regions, climatic regions, agricultural regions, manufacturing regions, political and administrative regions, planning regions, soil regions, drainage areas, and regions based on standard of living, race, international political ideologies, trade, demographic factors, etc. The category of region reflects different reasons and purposes for divisions and groupings that are used for research, control, communication, and administrative purposes.

Each set of criteria for a given period of time may or may not satisfy more than one purpose; it depends upon the individual situation, the quality of results desired, and the added cost of defining the regions. Building on earlier works of McKenzie (18) and the National Resources Committee (21), Donald J. Bogue (1, 2) attempted to present a multipurpose standardized system of regions. It resulted in the division of the United States into 506 "State Economic Areas." These consist of one or more counties with similar economic and social characteristics, including a special class of "Metropolitan State Economic Areas," which, with some exceptions, are equivalent to the SMSAs defined by the U.S. Bureau of Census.

The need to improve regional delineation stems from several considerations. First, traditional divisions and boundaries are too small or too large to manifest meaningful analytical relation-

the basis of international political ideologies may be noncontiguous.

[5] The SMSA system of regions does not exhaust a whole geographic area, but rather delineates selective units. SMSAs use a central city or cities, with boundaries encompassing the economic integration of working and living in the central city or cities and its environs.

ships; this is especially true of smaller units. For example, counties, which are arbitrary units and generally too small to be of economic or geographic significance, seldom reflect lucid impacts of the broader forces affecting social and economic change in an area. Only in larger aggregations are relationships manifest. However, too large an area may offer a great many impracticalities. It is difficult to construct an econometric model of the world economy, even if the system of equations is saturated with statistics and data; its validity is always questionable. Resources are less diversified for smaller areas within a nation; hence the economies of these areas, taken as units, tend to be more specialized. In other words, some forms of economic activity represent specialized production located at certain sporadically distributed points.[6] These points tend to become pivots for society, as concentration of industry, people, and institutions conform to a regional character. For most metropolitan areas, the varying degrees of specialization, economic interdependence, and the proportion of local output exported tend to regionalize the location of economic phenomena. Finally, varying standards of living and economic prosperity suggest regionalization for effective analysis and policy.

Although greatly influenced by study objectives, the task of regional delineation requires judgment in the selection of criteria and method. Four major classifications have been used in various regional studies:

1. Homogeneous regions
2. Nodal regions
3. Trade regions
4. Political or administrative regions

[6] Sporadic locations of economic phenomena contrast with industries that are present in all localities. For example, in a given locality a grocery store may be called an ubiquitous type of economic activity, while the shipbuilding may be considered a sporadic industry.

Regions based on homogeneous criteria cover areas with the similar primary characteristics and with approximately the same degree of intensity; for example, the central city is a focus and the surrounding area with its environs is tied to the focus by various interdependencies. A nodal region is created by the geographical movement of people, resources, and goods. A trade region is a special case of nodal arrangements of habitat and economic activities, since trade is a process involving interdependence between the city and its hinterland. A political region is based on administrative, legislative, and social considerations. Ordinarily, there is a spatial hierarchy of at least three or four levels of these divisions—state, county, city, township, section, district, and neighborhood. Thus the definition of a region is oriented to the object. The word "local" generally refers to areas, such as city, county, and Standard Metropolitan Statistical Area (SMSA).

PLANNING GOALS

The establishment of a goal or goals, which are related to time and activity-related targets, is a necessary step in planning. How goals are arrived at and who determines them varies from and depends on the planning approach followed.

The process of establishing goals generally involves deriving general or broad titles—full employment of the labor force, social cohesion, clean environment, economic progress, etc.—through public concensus or government officials. Generally a government body, commonly called a planning commission, initiates this process. Once the general goals are identified, the subgoals can be expressed in terms of activity levels and targets; number of residential units at a specific place and time; the jobs needed to absorb the labor force at specific times; and the level of increase in the productivity and economic progress of the region.

The goals, subgoals, and objectives serve as guideposts to identify the level, structure, and performance of economic activities.

RESOURCE INVENTORY

The task of resource inventory is a routine but complex, expensive, and time-consuming chore, involving collection of relevant data about almost every aspect of the environment. The amount of detail in the data depends on the objectives. Data about demography, housing, utilities, transportation, economic structure, political structure and process, health, spatial patterns, trade, and education often form the basic set of required information. These data may be available in published form, so every effort is made to secure material that is already collected or published. However, data gaps common to published data must be judiciously resolved to achieve internal consistency in the data. Original data collection is an expensive part of the research.

COORDINATION

This aspect of planning deals with communication and resolution between goals and resources. Various tools, such as systems and input-output analyses, are used to find interrelations between activities.

Planners also use a technique called Program Evaluation Review Technique (PERT) to plan effectively. PERT is a diagrammatical representation of the flow, sequence, and interdependency of operations needed to produce a plan, product, or event, showing estimated completion time and cost figures for the activities in the flow (*see* Figure 27–1). The usefulness of PERT is not limited to

planning; it also is being used extensively by the National Aeronautics and Space Administration (NASA) and by industry to enhance achievement of goals.

Numerous other operations, such as projections, trend analysis, overlays, and statistical correlations, can also be used. The process of coordination is highly technical and requires knowledge of advanced statistics, operations research, and other tools previously mentioned.

Planning in totalitarian societies involves government participation not only in the development of a plan, but also in its execution. However, in a society like that of the United States, the underlying motivation behind planning is the coordination of privately run activities toward the achievement of collectively agreed-upon goals. This involves the determination of specific recommendations, which are translated into policy through law. Planning is sterile without policy, so any plan must lend itself to policy consideration and application.

The process of planning is dynamic. As times change, so do resources and goals. Consequently, a plan must be capable of adapting to changing circumstances.

Besides coordination within the planning process, it is essential to coordinate regional, urban, rural, and local plans. Coordination is an important task of all planning units, but it must be exercised in a way that encourages maximum participation of those affected by the plan.

PLANNING APPROACHES

The literature affords at least four identifiable approaches in planning. The first approach, which may be called *goal-oriented planning*, seeks to maximize benefits through rational choice of means from available alternatives. The

467

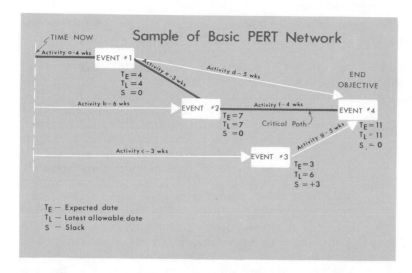

FIGURE 27–1

second approach focuses on resources and defines goals by the deterministic virtues of resources and seeks to optimize benefits from available resources; it may be called *resource-oriented planning*. In theory both of these approaches provide perspective, comprehensiveness, and internal consistency.

The third approach may be called *piecemeal planning*. Although the theoretical rationale for piecemeal planning is not the same as that of the first two approaches, it has attracted substantially more practitioners because of its sociopolitical acceptability and its effects causing the slowest change in the existing fabric of location.

The fourth approach may be classified *problem-oriented planning*, it completes the plan formulation process with highly specific objectives derived from the problems to be solved. Major types of planning processes are summarized in Figure 27–2.

The steps in the planning process followed by problem-oriented planning approaches are almost a complete reversal of the steps followed by the conventional planning approaches. This reversal of the planning process is largely due to the confusion over the definitions of goals and problems. Goals are generally broader in scope and perspective while problems are frequently specific. Professor Albert Waterson (29) argues that when the planning process begins by setting objectives that are only indirectly aimed at specific social problems, it is uncertain whether the realization of the objectives will in fact meliorate these problems. Any indirect means of resolving problems runs this risk. But there is no sense in trying to solve critical social and economic problems indirectly solely because traditional planning tools of analysis require it. This way of solving problems makes needs serve planning, when planning should serve needs. Furthermore, a direct approach is available with the problem-oriented approach, which has been tried and found to be responsive to the solution of social problems.

If the planning process begins with a rigorous evaluation of all pertinent information about the environment, without regard to disciplinary boundaries, it becomes possible to select means ap-

STEPS IN THE PLANNING PROCESS

CONVENTIONAL PLANNING: Goal-oriented, Resource-oriented, and Piecemeal Planning	PROBLEM-ORIENTED PLANNING
1. Setting goals.	1. Identifying the socio-economic problems to be resolved.
2. Transformation of goals into operational objectives.	2. Reconciliation between constraints, resources, and problems.
3. Devising a strategy showing the flow of events and activities.	3. Selecting projects to be undertaken.
4. Project operation.	4. Devising a strategy showing the flow of events and activities.
5. Reconciliation between constraints, resources, and objectives.	5. Setting operational objectives.
6. Solving socio-economic problems.	6. Choosing goals based on the problems to be resolved.

FIGURE 27–2

propriate to the resolution of the problems. The process by which these means are determined requires an evaluation of the real and financial resources and the identification of economic, social, political, institutional, administrative, physical, ecological, informational, and other constraints. Because the means selected to solve planning problems are keyed to the environment in which implementation will occur, they do not suffer from incompatibility between means and environment encountered in conventional plans. After the means for dealing with problems are selected, it becomes feasible to set realistic targets and objectives within a fixed period.

As Figure 27–2 indicates, the problem-oriented approach follows a sequence which is the reverse of the conventional one. A problem-oriented approach to planning starts as it were, from the bottom up, and ends the process with highly specific objectives derived from the problems to be solved. (For example, at the national level an objective might be raising per-capita income of people earning incomes below the national average to the national average). This is in considerable contrast to the objectives of traditional plans, which are usually too highly aggregated to meet varying needs of different constituencies. An objetcive of traditional planning processes might be to increase national income by a fixed percentage annually, for example. Over-aggregation is almost inevitable in plans made at the center of government since planners there cannot possibly be well enough informed to identify varying high-priority problems of different localities, as well as the resources available for dealing with these problems.

A problem-finding and problem-solving approach to plan formulation is also more promising than other planning approaches because it is purposively multidisciplinary in orientation. This orientation makes it easier to deal more effectively with social, economic, political, institutional, physical, and ecological facets of problems than a unidisciplinary approach allows. While the intrinsically

469

amorphous nature of many planning problems makes the proposed approach more heuristic and unstructured than traditional planning, there is no reason why projects chosen for execution in constituencies cannot and should not be integrated into programs for economic and social sectors. Projects can then be integrated into comprehensive short-term and long-term plans for an entire economy, a region, or an urban or rural area. The suggested approach also provides manifold opportunities to use sophisticated planning techniques, including cost-beneft calculations, systems analysis, and program and performance budgeting to directly identify and solve high-priority social problems.

In contrast to the use of these techniques to help achieve global objectives of planning from the top down, the use of these techniques in conjunction with planning from the bottom up increases their relevance for resolving specific social problems. Because of this and because of its multidisciplinary nature, the suggested approach can be more comprehensive than the traditional one.

STATE PLANNING

Besides providing state-level coordination, state planning may help in a number of ways to assist local communities to coordinate their efforts and to avoid conflicts. It can also provide planning services for rural areas that lack trained personnel. In most states, planning agencies have not been given sufficient funds or power to do an effective job, although they are currently being revived and strengthened. Hawaii, California, Tennessee, and Oregon are good cases in point.

The state planning agency is not a substitute for local government responsibility for local development plans. State planning helps in the creation of local and regional agencies, coordination of local plans, and establishment of liaisons between local planning agencies and state planning agencies. The process of state planning follows almost the same approaches as outlined earlier.

The same need to look at the problem, rather than at the political boundary, will produce cooperative planning arrangements among states to deal with regions that straddle state lines. Such arrangements have been put to effective use in joint operations for a variety of interstate services. Interstate compacts, agreements, and parallel legislation adopted in adjacent states have brought together an accumulation of experience and fostered cooperative work on transportation, recreation, water resources, and other functions.

Some cooperative interstate planning has also been accomplished, but it has been limited to planning for one or another specialized activity. Although presently largely unused, interstate arrangements are available for joint comprehensive planning by states or by local governments. Local governments can undertake joint efforts with neighbors across a state line on their own initiative, provided there are statutes that permit it.

Another responsibility of state-planning programs may be realized in the balanced development of urban and rural areas. Urban areas are increasingly dependent on rural activities, and urban residents will want the conservation of farmland, open space, forests, or well-tended but lightly developed countryside. Rural areas are increasingly dependent on urban areas, and rural residents will want to see their urban centers prosper to create jobs and markets. Both are concerned with the form of cities and the edges of urban development, where rural and urban land-use problems become most vividly one problem. A narrowly urban view of land-use problems can be tempered by the comprehensive view of a state planning agency.

REGIONAL PLANNING

Axiomatic to the concept of a need for local planning is a realization that local communities do not live or exist in a vacuum. They are constantly operating and relating with a host of other communities, districts, and organizational entities. They are constantly drawing on and in turn supplying a multitude of resources within an areal expanse. Awareness of the interrelationships of all resources—animal, vegetable, and mineral—within a region leads to the realization that utilizing the regional planning approach will improve the process of intergovernment action and better integrate urban and resource planning. Regional planning will coordinate local or statewide planning and will in turn be coordinated by national planning endeavors. The regional levels are complementary.

The term *regional planning,* particularly as it is used in the United States, has a variety of connotations because there have been several separate streams of professional thought on the subject over the last thirty years.

One concept of regional planning arose during the Great Depression and was oriented initially to the development problems of the South. It perceived a region as relatively united geographically and distinctive in that it possessed the largest possible degree of homogeneity measured by the largest possible number of economic, cultural, administrative, and functional indices for the largest possible number of objectives. The focus was on rural, relatively underdeveloped areas. This concept of regional planning was basic to the work of the National Resources Planning Board and to most of the river basin development agencies, such as the Tennessee Valley Authority (TVA). It was fundamentally economic in nature and emphasized resource development. A current and somewhat modified expression of this concept is represented by the Appalachian Regional Commission.

A second stream of thought in regional planning is based on land-control activities of city planners; it resulted from increasing urbanization of the U.S. population. Interest in this type of regional planning grew very rapidly in the post-world War II period when U.S. urban areas grew at an unprecedented rate. Its primary concern has been the physical use of space, and its action programs have involved spatial planning and use controls, such as zoning. In recent years, the focus of this thinking has tended toward metropolitan regions rather than cities because city limits have, for many purposes, lost their meaning. Although it has been suggested by Freidman that the emphasis of planning in the future may shift increasingly to the relations among metropolitan regions, planning for total economic development of rural and remote areas will continue to demand the attention of geographers and other land-resource specialists. Friedmann states:

> Although as much as 90 percent of the total population of the country may eventually reside within city regions, there will be large areas of sparsely settled land that fall outside the immediate influence of central cities. Such areas as the Cumberland Plateau, the Blue Ridge Mountains, the Ozarks, the Great Lakes cut-over regions, parts of northern New England, and large sections of the Southwest and West fall in this category. They pose special planning problems due to the poverty of their population and their limited resources. An extensive type of development through recreation, forestry, or grazing will often form the basic approach to these areas. They are

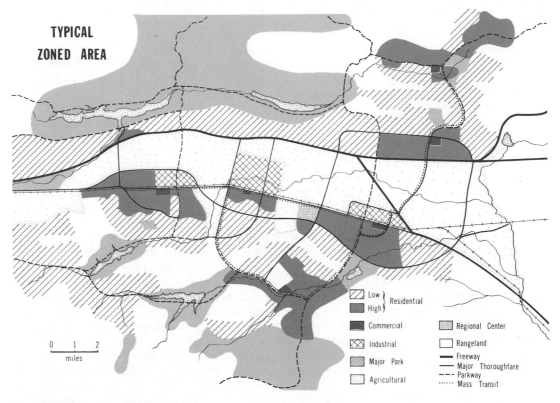

TYPICAL ZONED AREA

0   1   2
miles

▨ Low ⎰	Residential	
▨ High ⎱		
▨ Commercial	░ Regional Center	
▩ Industrial	▢ Rangeland	
▤ Major Park	━ Freeway	
░ Agricultural	── Major Thoroughfare	
	┅ Parkway	
	┈ Mass Transit	

FIGURE 27–3 *A Typical Zoned Area*

regions characterized by special physical disadvantage for more intensive development. They may be called "functional regions" when public policy addresses itself specifically to problems related to the development of their resources.[7]

Areas within a planning region are linked by common problems or common opportunities. The people of the region are economically and socially interdependent, do business with each other, often read the same newspaper, perhaps use the same hospital, and decline or prosper together. With widely diverse careers, people nevertheless share in some measure a single regional destiny.

To achieve a destiny that will be of our choosing, we have come to accept the need to plan our environment. We are beginning to accept social planning, despite an ingrained urge to decide individually how each plot of ground is used. We find it less possible to realize individual decisions. Many changes in employment and technology have diminished the individual power of decision. Regional planning attempts to regain control over the way land resources will work for society.

Land uses today are judged by more

[7] John Friedmann, and William Alonso (eds.), *Regional Development and Planning: A Reader* (Cambridge, Mass.: M.I.T. Press, 1964), p. 000.

472

demanding standards. For example, Robert M. Reser of Ohio State University, applying present development standards to the future development of Ohio, found that by the year 2000 a projected population of 22 million people in Ohio would require more than 33.5 million acres for agriculture, industry, houses, roads, recreation, shops, and other land uses. This is 7.25 million more acres than there are in Ohio.

Will we reduce our future population? Lower standards of land use? Invent new ways to get along with less land? Eliminate some uses of land? Change our forecasts? Events will yield an answer if we let the future just happen. If we prefer to exercise choice among the possible answers and work for a combination of alternatives that suit us, we will undertake to design and execute regional plans.

LOCAL PLANNING

The function of local planning is to promote the orderly renovation and development of community resources and activities to meet the needs of local people. A planning commission commonly serves in an advisory capacity to a local county or city governing body. The commission is usually armed with statutory authority to identify developmental and environmental problems and to develop plans for the common good of the entire community. In the U.S., local planning commissions tend to operationalize their plans first by developing zoned areas (see Figure 27–3). Maps of zoning areas, available from city or county offices, indicate current zoning of land deemed suitable for industrial, residential, and agricultural use. Current zoning indicates the type of neighboring development that may be expected in the future.

references

1. Bogue, D. J. *The Structure of the Metropolitan Community: A Study of Dominance and Subdominance.* Ann Arbor: University of Michigan, Horace H. Rockham School of Graduate Studies, 1949.

2. ———, and Beale, Calvin J. *Economic Subregions of the United States Farm Population.* Series Census BAE, no. 19. Washington, D.C.: U.S. Government Printing Office, 1953.

3. Borchert, John R. "America's Changing Metropolitan Regions." *Annals of the Association of American Geographers* 62 (June 1972): 352–73.

4. Brodsky, Harold. "Land Development and the Expanding City." *Annals of the Association of American Geographers* 63 (June 1973): 159–66.

5. Casetti, Emilio. "Equilibrium Land Values and Population Densities in an Urban Setting." *Economic Geography* 47 (January 1971): 16–20.

6. Clawson, Marion, and Hall, Peter. *Planning and Urban Growth: An Anglo-American Comparison.* Baltimore: Johns Hopkins University Press, 1973.

7. Friedmann, John, and Alonso, William, eds. *Regional Development and Planning: A Reader.* Cambridge, Mass.: M.I.T. Press, 1964.

8. Goheen, Peter G. "Interpreting the American City: Some Historical Perspectives." *Geographical Review* 64 (July 1974): 326–84.

9. Haake, John H. "Do Cities Grow in Isolation? Metropolitan Population." *The Professional Geographer* 25 (February 1973): 1–6.

10. Harries, Keith D. "Spatial Aspects of Violence and Metropolitan Population." *The Professional Geographer* 25 (February 1973): 1–6.

11. Hartshorn, Truman A. "Industrial/Office Parks: A New Look For the City." *The Journal of Geography* 72 (March 1973): 33–45.

12. Haynes, Kingsley E., and Rube, Milton, I. "Directional Bias in Urban Population

Density." *Annals of the Association of American Geographers* 63 (March 1973): 40–47.

13. Hudson, John. "Density and Pattern in Suburban Fringes." *Annals of the Association of American Geographers* 63 (March 1973): 28–29.

14. Lankford, Philip M. "Physical Location Factors and Public Policy." *Economic Geography* 50 (July 1974): 244–55.

15. Ley, David, and Cybriwsky, Roman. "Urban Graffiti as Territorial Markers." *Annals of the Association of American Geographers* 64 (December 1974): 491–505.

16. Liang, Chi-sen. *Urban Land Use Analysis: A Case Study on Hong Kong*. Hong Kong: Ernest Publications, 1973.

17. Lloyd E. Peter, and Dickens, Peter. *Location in Space: A Theoretical Approach to Economic Geography*. New York: Harper & Row, 1972.

18. McKenzie, R. D. *The Metropolitan Community*. New York: McGraw-Hill Book Co., 1933.

19. McNee, Robert B. "Regional Planning, Bureaucracy and Geography." *Economic Geography* 46 (April 1970): 190–98.

20. Myrdal, Gunnar. *Rich Land and Poor Land*. New York: Harper & Row, 1957.

21. National Resources Committee. *Regional Factors in Planning*. Washington, D.C.: U.S. Government Printing Office, 1935.

22. Natoli, Salvatore J. "Zoning and the Development of Urban Land Use Patterns." *Economic Geography* 47 (April 1971).

23. Pannell, Clifton W. "Urbanization and City Growth in Taiwan." *The Journal of Geography* 72 (January 1973): 11–20.

24. Porteous, J. Douglas. "Urban Transplantation in Chile." *Geographical Review* 62 (October 1972): 455–78.

25. Rees, Peter W. "Sources for the Study of Mexican Urbanism." *The Professional Geographer* 62 (December 1972): 591–98.

26. Ritter, Frederic A. "An Appraisal of Measures of Residential Land Value." *Economic Geography* 47 (April 1971): 185–91.

27. Semple, R. Keith; Gauthier, Howard L.; and Youngmann, Carl E. "Growth Poles in Sao Paulo, Brazil." *Annals of the Association of American Geographers* 62 (December 1972): 591–98.

28. Stutz, Frederick P. "Distance and Network Effects on Urban Social Travel Fields." *Economic Geography* 49 (April 1973): 134–43.

29. Waterson, Albert. *Planning 1971*. O'Harrow Memorial Lecture. Delivered at the 1971 Meeting of the American Society of Planning Officials.

30. Wilson, A. G. *Urban and Regional Models in Geography and Planning*. New York: John Wiley and Sons, 1974.

31. Wolpert, Julian. "Departures from the Usual Environment in Locational Analysis." *Annals of the Association of American Geographers* 60 (June 1970): 220–29.

474

man, environment, and economic activity

28

28

The health, well-being, and continued survival of man at any level of existence are directly dependent upon the economic systems which he has created to extract, transport, modify, and consume resources. Since people are not content in any cultural or socioeconomic system —whether Oriental, Occidental, modern, or primitive—to live a "natural" existence within a "natural" environment, the operation of economic systems inevitably involves some alteration of environments.

The ability and tendency of socio-economic systems to alter local, regional, or global components of their environments has recently re-emerged as a comprehensive social issue. This issue is not confined solely to Western industrial societies; it is also expressed in developing and pre-industrial societies, but for entirely different reasons. Contemporary environmental issues are relatively complex and compounded by diverse lay and scholarly opinion over causes, characteristics, and solutions. The following discussion is not intended to be pessimistic or optimistic; it is a presentation of the dominant thinking of outstanding contemporary scholars.

CONCEPTS AND CHARACTERISTICS OF ENVIRONMENT

The concept of *environment* has numerous interpretations. In a general context, it is defined as the entire set of external conditions, processes, and objects that influence the behavior of an organism.

We may narrow this general context to the "perceptual" environment, which is the set of relationships that an individual creates between himself and external phenomena. The perceptual environment is in flux to a certain degree, but it is constrained, moment by moment, to the space through which one's senses perceive external conditions and processes. The limit of the perceptual environment is often referred to as the sensory frontier and is constantly changing. (34) The perceptual environment is personalized in that it is unique to an individual. The continuing relationships that the individual has with this environment are stored as experience or memory and form the basis on which future relationships are sought and interpreted. One's stored experiences thus acts as both cause and effect in future environmental interactions. Although conceived in a theoretical context, the conceptual differentiation of the perceptual and the cultural environment has its counterpart in reality and may represent one obstacle to a united effort on environmental programs.

The data Table 28–1, based on a random sample of 300 heads of households in Cincinnati, Ohio, give an explicit example of the difference between images of the limited perceptual environment and the larger urban cultural environment. Each group considered its own neighborhood cleaner than the city as whole. The two male groups perceived their local environments as cleaner than either of the female groups perceived their environments. Neighborhood environment and city environment were perceived differently by blacks than by whites. All percentages for perception of the local environment as "unclean" are below 50 percent, but those for the larger urban environment are very near or over 50 percent. De Groot tentatively concludes that the major determinant of the responses was the place of residence of the respondents: whites generally reside in suburban areas and blacks in the central city.

TABLE 28–1 Perceptual Images of the Environment

RESPONDENTS' RACE AND SEX	PERCENT SEEING OWN NEIGHBORHOOD AS UNCLEAN	PERCENT SEEING CITY AS UNCLEAN
White males	31.4%	48.5%
White females	44.0	47.5
Black males	30.5	52.8
Black females	43.5	72.5

Source: Ido de Groot, "Aesthetic Aspects of Air Pollution," in *Man and His Environment: The Effects of Pollution on Man*, Tom Vickery, ed. (Syracuse, N.Y.: Division of the Summer Sessions, Syracuse University, 1972), p. 145. Reprinted with permission of the publisher.

The respondents perceived their local environment as significantly cleaner than the larger urban environment. A portion of the dilemma thus is suggested by this attitude that "other places are less clean than mine."

ENVIRONMENTAL DETERIORATION

AS A SOCIAL ISSUE

An operational definition of environmental deterioration is any undesirable modification in the physical, chemical, or biological characteristics of air, land, and water that may harmfully affect aspirations and abilities of the human condition or that of any other desirable species or industrial processes, or that may decrease the utility of any material resource.

Environmental deterioration has all the ingredients of a political, governmental, scientific, economic, and citizen controversy; it is a comprehensive social issue.

All social issues share a similar emergence process. The recognition that social objectives are not being met occurs in the perceptual environment. By discussion or by similar perceptions shared by other individuals, initial perceptual differences merge and are externalized into the larger cultural environment. If accepted by a sufficient number of people to cause decisive action, the issue then emerges to the comprehensive stage. In the process, it becomes political as it enters the phase where laws are sought for resolution. It becomes economic as the costs of resolution are tallied and allocated to the "causers." The environmental issue has been through this process more than once in this and in other societies. (25)

We offer the following as examples of a persistent concern with environmental alteration.

> The Great [Persian] King blocked up all the passages between the hills with dykes and flood-gates, and so prevented the water from flowing out. Then the plain within the hills became a sea, for the river kept rising, and the water could find no outlet. From that time the five nations which were wont formerly to have use of the stream . . . have been in great distress. In winter . . . they have rain, but in summer, after sowing their millet and their sesame, they always stood in need of water from the river.[1]

Herodotus was describing the damming of the River Aces in Asia Minor almost 3,000 years ago. A more contemporary description is provided by Wagner in

[1] Blakeney, E. H. (ed.), G. Rawlinson, trans., *The Histories of Herodotus*, vol. 1; (London: Dent and Sons, 1963), pp. 265–66.

477

describing what happens to the environment in the United States, where the Corps of Engineers represents the Great King.

> Imagine, for example, a narrow rural valley with a stream flowing through it year round. One day a bulldozer appears on the hillside above the valley and intensive development begins. . . . Then the Corps of Engineers is only too happy to build . . . a dam, which in turn permanently floods much valuable bottom land behind the dam. What is left of the stream alternates between feast and famine, flooding one season, dry the next.[2]

The environment as an issue has been expressed in other ways. Over 500 years ago the first sanitary acts in the Statutes of the Realm were enacted in Great Britain under Richard II. These statutes were created in order that ". . . much Dung and Filth of the Garbage . . . shall be removed, avoided and carried away [because] the Air is greatly corrupt and infect[ious], and many Maladies and other Intolerable Diseases do daily happen."[3]

The condition of the atmosphere in London, however, was not satisfactorily restored to the tolerance of Charles Dickens' perceptual environment:

> Fog everywhere . . . up the river [Thames] . . . down the river, where it rolls defiled among the tiers of shipping and the waterside pollutions of a great city. Fog of the Essex marshes, fog on the Kentish heights. Fog lying out on the yards and hovering on the rigs of great ships . . . and fog in the eyes and throats of ancient Greenwich pensioners, wheezing by the firesides.[4]

[2] Richard Wagner, *Environment and Man* (New York: W. W. Norton Co., 1971), p. 376.
[3] Charles Creighton, *A History of Epidemics in Britain,* 2 volumes, 2nd ed. (London: Frank Case and Co., 1965), p. 324.
[4] Charles Dickens, *Bleak House.*

This is the same fog that for several decades was considered by climatologists to be a natural part of the northwest European climate. Recently, however, Garnett has suggested that the famed London fog is due to water droplets that become coated with an admixture of tarry soot derived from imperfect combustion of bituminous coal. (11)

In 1860, Samuel Taylor Coleridge offered this characterization of Cologne, Germany:

> In Kolhn, a town of monks and bones,
> And pavements fangid with murderous stones
> And rags, and hags, and hideous wenches;
> I counted two and seventy stenches,
> All well defined and several stinks!
> Ye nymphs that reign o'er sewers and sinks,
> The River Rhine, it is well known,
> Doth wash your city of Cologne;
> But tell, nymphs, what power divine
> Shall henceforth wash the River Rhine?[5]

Oriental societies, although often praised for an environmentally sound attitude, have had environmental conditions rise to the level of major issues. The annual floods that have plagued North China for over two thousand years are directly due to the deforestation of steep slopes. (9) Yi-Fu Tuan suggested that one of the greater calamities the world has known occurred in this region. During the widespread flooding of the rivers from 1887 to 1889, over 2 million people perished from hunger, disease, and drowning. (41) Yi-Fu Tuan also lists six reasons for the widespread deforestation in China; most of these, as with many pre-industrial societies, center upon the use of fire in environmental modification or deterioration:

[5] Helen B. Morrison, *The Golden Age of Travel* (New York: Twayne Publishers, 1951), p. 305.

1.	Demand for wood fuel for heating and cooking

2.	Demand for wood for caskets and cremation of corpses, especially in Buddhist societies

3.	Utilization of wood to construct cities and to rebuild cities after a fire

4.	Use of timber for shipbuilding, especially during the Southern Sung dynasty, when reportedly on one occasion 17,000 men were sent to fell trees at one time

5.	Demand for charcoal, used for writing and drawing

6.	Engagement in the immemorial practice of setting the forest on fire to deprive dangerous animals of hiding places and to clear the land for cultivation

The outstanding achievement of early 20th-century ecologists in the United States was the White House Conference of 1908. At this meeting, plans were organized for national environmental protection activities associated with all aspects of the environment. In attendance were President Theodore Roosevelt, his Vice-President, members of the Supreme Court, Cabinet, Congress, governors or representatives of the forty-six states, and many representatives of industry, education, and the public. Never before had such an assemblage of powerful and influential people gathered to discuss and plan for this topic.

For a time, the results were highly successful. In addition to the national commission, each state had its own conservation agency and numerous local, urban- and rural-based organizations. The North American Conservation Conference with representatives from Canada, Mexico, and the United States grew out of this effort. The same U.S. group also arranged what would have been the First International Symposium on the Environment, but World War I cut short those plans.

The continuing interest of the U.S. in environmental protection is partly explained by the relatively high levels of energy consumption by American industry and households.

The high energy consumption per capita in the United States that was part of an overall increase in mobility, consumer and producer goods and services, and leisure time may indeed be the human support process that allows societies to turn attention to environmental issues. If a society must forage or scrounge for its livelihood directly from the environment in a context close to a natural one, with extremely limited resources, the society is not likely to be concerned with the impact it is making on its environment; to the contrary, that society will be concerned with the impact its environment makes on it. The following is illuminating in this respect:

> We must not embark on any environmental protection programs without placing a priority on maintaining income and consumption. Otherwise, the poorest people will be further depressed in their condition and have little opportunity to exercise their right to live decently and in expectation of improving their condition.[6]

In any context, the contemporary issue should be viewed at least as a partial outgrowth or continuation of an issue that has been expressed by other generations; environmental health is not unique to this generation. Earth Day, the International Symposium on Environmental Disruption and the United Nations Conference on the Human Environment represent formal expressions of a continuing issue, whose resolution has been postponed.

[6] Paraphrase of a statement by George Wiley, chairman of the National Welfare Rights Organization, "Ecology and the Poor." *Earth Day: The Beginning* (New York: Bantam Books, 1970), pp. 213–16.

CAUSES OF ENVIRONMENTAL DETERIORATION

Environmental deterioration has and is occurring within the general context of the cultural expansion of the environment, at the expense of the natural environment.

Less general causes of environmental deterioration have been suggested by numerous individuals from political, government, and academic spheres. The suggestions offered in the contemporary context often bear striking resemblance to those offered by earlier generations. (35)

CULTURAL AND ECONOMIC VALUES

An historian in the humanist tradition suggests that the source of environmental deterioration resides within the merger of the Judeo-Christian ethic with modern scientific thought. (40) This merger gave Western culture a powerful ethnocentric, amoral attitude toward the natural environment, the result being that instead of reverence toward nature, Western man was spiritually and intellectually divorced from nature.

ECONOMIC SYSTEMS

Scholars point to the modern corporation and capitalism as institutions that promote deterioration of the environment, outweighing other socioeconomic benefits they may provide. A socialist economist, suggests that the major reason for the despoliation of the environment and for poverty in the Third World (the states and former colonies whose national per-capita income is less than about $500 per year) is the imperialist practices of capitalist societies. (31) This argument is supported, by the geographer, Eliot Hurst (30), and in part, by Baran and Sweezy. (4)

An economist offers a different response to the question of the role different types of economic systems play in environmental deterioration. Limiting his attention to industrialized socialist and capitalist societies and to environmental decay directly affecting human well-being, Dahmén states that "there is no evidence whatsoever" to suggest that one form of economic system has contributed more to environmental deterioration than another. "Also, it should be added . . . that neither the political organization, whether democratic or totalitarian, nor the political color of the government appear to have been significant. Moreover, state-owned companies have been no different from privately owned companies in the extent to which they have damaged the environment."[7]

The corporate structure of industrial giants, such as General Motors, Du Pont, Phelps-Dodge, and Texaco make a significant impact on natural and cultural environments. There is also substantial impact on the environment caused by the consumption of goods and services produced by such firms.

One of the reasons why capitalist economies are more frequently condemned as prime contributors to environmental deterioration is that in these societies data are more easily obtained and travel is freer.

POPULATION GROWTH

Another group of individuals cites overpopulation as the cause of environmental deterioration.[8] Ehrlich, for example,

---

[7] Erick E. Dahmén, "Environmental Control and Economic Systems," *The Swedish Journal of Economics* 73 (March 1971).

[8] This theme has as its principal originator Robert T. Malthus, in his *Essay on the Principles of Population, 1798. See also,* Louise B. Young, *Population in Perspective* (New York: Oxford University Press, 1968), especially pp. 3–29 and *Popula-*

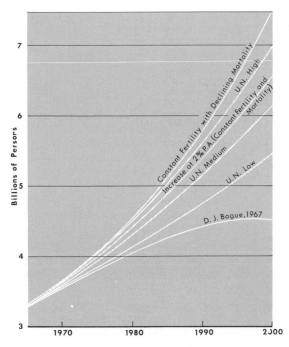

FIGURE 28–1 *Estimates of World Population*

states that the "causal chain of the deterioration is easily followed to its source. Too many cars, too many factories, too much detergent, too much pesticide, multiplying contrails, inadequate sewage-treatment plants, too much carbon dioxide—all can be traced easily to too many people."[9] Ehrlich also suggests that the overabundance of people has persisted for so long that "the capacity of the planet to support human life has been permanently impaired."[10]

The basic argument of those sup-

tion: A Challenge to Environment, Report number 13 (Washington, D.C.: Victor-Bostrom Fund Report, 1970).

[9] Paul R. Ehrlich, *The Population Bomb* (New York: Ballantine, 1968), p. 66.

[10] Paul R. Ehrlich and Anne Ehrlich, "What Can Be Done," in Q. Stanford (ed.), *The World's Population* (London: Oxford University Press, 1972), p. 319.

porting this resides on the usually projected ratios of population increase, resource availability, and consumption, and the resulting waste discharged into the natural environment. Figure 28–1 indicates six population estimates which have been made to the year 2000. Each one is based on a slightly different set of assumptions. Only one projects a decline in population. Figure 28–2 indicates that projected population growth has at least two significant directions: The less developed countries are expected to continue to increase their population more rapidly than the developed countries.

Paradoxically, it is the rapid increase in economic development and the associated increased per-capita consumption that has allowed developed countries to alleviate disease, hunger, and, to a great extent, to minimize the hazards of natural calamities.

During this period of rapid change there were corresponding increases, and later decreases, in the rate of population

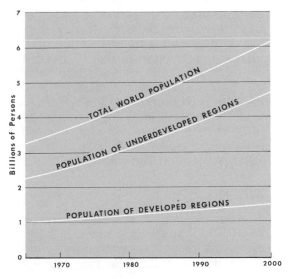

FIGURE 28–2 *Population and Development, 1970–2000*

481

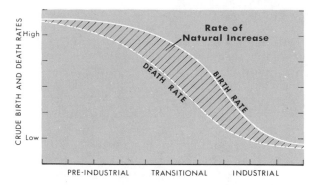

FIGURE 28–3 *Model of Demographic Transition Illustrating a Generalized Version of Trends in Vital Rates in Northwestern Europe during Industrialization*

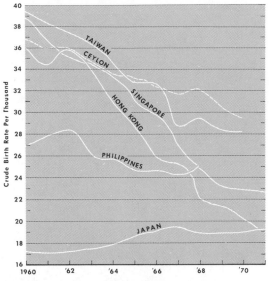

FIGURE 28–4 *Declining Birth Rates in Selected Asian Countries, 1960–1971*

growth. Schnell has labeled this transformation as the "demographic process" (see Figure 28–3), but suggests that it is not applicable to the developing countries because their rates of increase are already far in excess of those in industrial countries when they were developing into industrial nations. (36) There is evidence, however, to suggest that birth rates in some of these countries are diminishing, at least on a short-term basis (see Figure 28–4).

Ehrlich suggests that attempts to increase production further will accelerate environmental deterioration which, in turn, will reduce the capacity of the earth to provide food. (19) Keyfitz, takes a different tack and argues that "the only escape, . . . is through the economic development of the countries of Asia, Africa, and Latin America."[11]

TECHNOLOGY

The technological framework also has come under attack as the principal cause of environmental deterioration. A leading politician makes the point directly:

[11] Nathan Keyfitz, "United States and World Population," in *Resources and Man*, pp. 43–63.

for years, "a runaway technology has . . . poisoned our air, ravaged our soil, stripped our forests bare, and corrupted our water resources!"[12] Ellul suggests that "technique" has fashioned an omnivorous world which obeys its own laws and has progressively "mastered all elements of civilization [until] . . . man himself is overpowered by technique and becomes its object."[13]

Commoner (13), perhaps the leading spokesman for this view, suggests that environmental deterioration occurs in a definite, identifiable sequence: A desire to modify the environment prompts analysis of the process by which such a modification is to occur. A new technology is created to satisfy the desire and it then begins to modify the environment in the process of satisfying the need.

[12] Senator Vance Hartke, Indiana, whose Earth Day speech is reprinted in *Earth Day: The Beginning* (New York: Bantam Books, 1970), p. 134.
[13] Jacques J. Ellul, *The Technological Society* (New York: Alfred Knopf, 1964), p. 14.

482

When tested against stated aims, the new technology is not a failure: synthetic pesticides do kill pests, gasoline does fuel an automobile, plastic jugs do last a long time; nitrogen fertilizer does increase crop yields; and people do live longer and consume more. It is the overwhelming success of the new technology that promotes environmental deterioration, not the failure of that technology.

The basic flaw, then, is in the process of creating the technology; the environment is reduced to objectified, isolated, discrete components and is not seen as an organic whole, which functions only with fragile connections. (17)

The proponents of this view do not see an inevitable deterioration of the environment due to economic activity or economic growth. It is not necessary to abandon modern technology. Instead, it is incumbent on society to create a technology that is responsive to the natural environment into which it intrudes. One of the major solutions offered is recycling goods, not only within an economic system but to and from the natural environment. We must re-evaluate the relative merits of "engineering" the natural environment.

EXTERNALITIES

Thus far, the causes of environmental deterioration have centered essentially on components and processes that occur within socioeconomic systems. The form of ownership or type of economic framework, the number of people and their consumption rates, and the technological framework are contrived features that are imposed onto the environment.

Externalities refer to collective and cumulative effects that are external to socioeconomic systems and that result from these systems' internal operations. Externalities can be positive or negative. The removal of an old building to use its space for a park may considerably benefit adjacent residences. The benefit, which involves no direct expense or cost to those who benefit, is not considered a part of the initial purchase contract and thus is a positive externality. A firm that uses a stream to discharge its waste products and creates pollution downstream in a domestic water supply represents a negative externality to a municipality. The polluting firm will cause the municipality to incur additional costs, over and above the actual acquisition and pumping, by having to purify the water. In the long term, the externality to the municipality will feedback to the discharging plant and overall costs will rise for everyone.

Net negative externalities are deposited in the perceptual and cultural environments of those who are responsible for them. Because of the interdependency of externalities with the natural environment, they also affect the national environment, as well as other cultural environments.

In the first major work involving externalities, Kapp suggested that if the costs of negative externalities were included in a system's costs, in many cases they might well exceed the total benefits as determined by the conventional cost-benefit analysis. (32)

From this perspective, of the source of environmental deterioration, all socioeconomic systems are in "debt" to the environment.

SOLUTIONS TO ENVIRONMENTAL DETERIORATION

Societies are not awaiting doom or even tomorrow to commence action policies designed to improve the human and natural condition by creating better cultural and natural environmental relations. Actual and potential policies and

483

actions to solve environmental problems are diverse in scope and character, ranging from actions, such as "don't litter," to actions, such as revamping metropolitan sewage treatment and disposal systems. Some are asking whether "particulate and gaseous matter from the atmosphere be removed by stimulating the natural atmospheric circulation?"[14]

POLICIES AND PROGRAMS

Population-control programs are now underway in approximately 140 nations. Some of these programs had an early start; others have been initiated only within the past twelve years. For example, over 45 non-industrial countries have initiated such policies since 1960 (see Table 28–2). A decrease in the rate of population growth often associated with such programs is already being realized in several countries, including Taiwan, Singapore, Ceylon, Hong Kong, and the Philippines (see Table 28–2 and Figure 28–4). Each country instituted family-planning programs between 1964 and 1970. Population control received vigorous government support in India only after 1965. Although strenuously resisted, especially in rural areas, it is having a measurable impact on the rate of population growth predicted *prior* to birth-control programs. Resistance to controlling population by controlling the birth rate is still very strong among most less developed nations. In 1970, twenty such countries still had no official program associated for family planning; populations of these countries constitute about 13 percent of the world's population. (7, 27)

Although the United States experienced a significant population increase

[14] S. Frederick Singer, *Global Effects of Environmental Pollution* (New York: Springer-Verlag, 1970), p. 204.

following the depression and World War II (the "war baby boom"), the rate of growth now is estimated to be not only lower than at any other time, but only slightly higher than zero population growth.

Population increase, decrease, or equilibrium is invariably tied to food availability and technology to continue food production. The Nobel Peace Prize in 1970 was awarded to Norman Borlaug for his discovery of a "miracle" wheat, an integral part of the Green Revolution that has been underway for two decades. (9) It is debatable whether these food-production innovations would increase or decrease population growth rates in poor nations considering their level of economic development.

Paradoxically, realization of a better food supply has been instrumental in resistance to population control. What some scholars see as the best prospect for humanity to diminish hunger on a global scale could be lost if the gains in food production divert attention away from the immediate and continuing need to control population growth. (29)

Efforts to control discharges into the environment, especially into air and water, have also been implemented in several societies. Major federal legislation relating to water-pollution control in the United States is listed in Table 28–3. The development of water control was initiated slowly, with weak enforcement. Since 1965, however, permissive laws have been restructured to more stringent ones. In 1965 federal and state governments were authorized to set standards for the purity of water discharged from metropolitan systems. The Clean Water Restoration Act extended control authorization to all waste-water discharge processes.

Laws to control emissions into the atmosphere were initiated in 1955 in the U.S., which put the federal government in the business of researching air stand-

TABLE 28–2   Family-Planning Programs in Non-industrial Nations

POPULATION (in millions)	OFFICIAL POLICY TO REDUCE POPULATION GROWTH RATE	OFFICIAL SUPPORT OF FAMILY-PLANNING ACTIVITIES FOR OTHER REASONS	NEITHER POLICY NOR SUPPORT
400 and over	China (1962) India (1952)		
100–400	Indonesia (1968)		Brazil
50–100	Bangladesh (1971) Pakistan (1960)	Nigeria (1970) Mexico (1972)	
25–50	Egypt (1965) Iran (1967) South Korea (1961) Philippines (1970) Thailand (1970) Turkey (1965)		Ethiopia Burma
15–25	Morocco (1968) Taiwan (1968) Colombia (1970)	Algeria (1971) South Africa (1966) Sudan (1970) Afghanistan (1970) North Vietnam (1962) South Vietnam (1971) Zaire (1973)	North Korea
10–15	Kenya (1966) West Malaysia (1966) Nepal (1966) Sri Lanka (Ceylon) (1965)	Tanzania (1970) Uganda (1972) Iraq (1972) Chile (1966) Venezuela (1968)	Peru
10 and under	Botswana (1970) Ghana (1969) Mauritius (1965) Tunisia (1964) Laos (1972) Singapore (1965) Barbados (1967) Dominican Republic (1968) Jamaica (1966) Puerto Rico (1970) Trinidad & Tobago (1967) Fiji (1962) Gilbert & Ellice Islands (1970)	Dahomey (1969) Gambia (1969) Rhodesia (1968) Hong Kong (1956) Bolivia (1968) Costa Rica (1968) Cuba (early 1960s) Ecuador (1968) El Salvador (1968) Guatemala (1969) Haiti (1971) Honduras (1966) Nicaragua (1967) Panama (1969) Paraguay (1972)	Asia, 8 countries; North Africa & Middle East, 12; Sub-Saharan Africa, 28; Latin America, 5

Source: Based on Dorothy Nortman, "Population and Family Planning Programs: A Factbook," *Reports on Population Family Planning*, no. 2 (5th ed.), September 1973. Reprinted with the permission of the Population Council from "World Population: Status Report 1974," by Bernard Berelson, in *Reports on Population Family Planning*, no. 15 (January 1974): 24.

TABLE 28–3   Major Water-Pollution Control Legislation and Expenditures in the U.S., 1948–1971

		ENFORCEMENT	FINANCIAL	OTHER
1948	Water Pollution Control Act	Federally weak, mostly dependent on State governments, which were dis-interested	Construction loans for treatment plants	Temporary authorization
1956	Water Pollution Control Act Amendments	Interstate waters subject to Federal court action	Grants for treatment plants, $50 million annually	Permanent authority
1961	P.L. 87–88 (no title), amendment to 1948 act	Federal jurisdiction extended to pollution control in all navigable waters	$80–$100 million per year, to 1967	Research on urban sewage treatment, field labs established
1965	Water Quality Act	Previous enforcement processes tightened and streamlined; Federal and State levels authorized to set standards for discharged waters	$150 million in 1966 and 1967	Grants for research on combined, multiple sewage treatment plants
1966	Clean Water Restoration Act	Control and oil discharges transferred to Department of Interior	$450 million in 1968, $1 billion in 1970; Federal government to pay 55% of local costs	Research and construction extended to metropolitan sewage and industrial wastes
1970	Water Quality Improvement Act	Federal jurisdiction extended and tightened on pipelines, vessels, vehicles, transporting hazardous materials; increased standards for water quality and discharge, especially those Federally licensed and/or subsidized	$4 billion authorized	To be matched with state and local funds

ards and sources of emission. (37) The Clean Air Act (1963), the Motor Vehicle Air Pollution Control Act (1965), and the Air Quality Act (1967) gave grants directly to local governments, began research of vehicle emissions, especially sulphur oxides, and created 57 air-quality control regions; by 1971, these regions had been increased to 235. They are associated with areas experiencing moderate to severe pollution conditions.

Perhaps the major piece of enabling legislation that will shape the future environmental policy of the United States is the National Environmental Policy Act of 1969. The major purposes of this law are to encourage productive and enjoyable harmony between man and his environment; to promote efforts to prevent or eliminate damages to the environment; and to enrich the understanding of the environmental system.

The promise of this policy in great part rests with the cooperation of state and local governments in implementation and control. (38) Leaders in this endeavor are the states of Oregon, Illinois, Washington, and California. In Oregon, state and local legislation and enforcement have in some cases been far ahead of other states and the federal government. Illinois was the first state to comply fully with the provision of the Air Quality Act of 1967. Water-control legislation has been vigorously enforced in Washington, and California has been the leader in vehicle emission controls.[15]

Other states are also pursuing broad policies designed to control undesirable emissions into the air and water. Japan, West Germany, and the United Kingdom,

three of the more heavily polluted industrial states, have or are creating national environmental protection policies. The widespread deforestation of China has received critical attention also. In 1955 the government mounted programs to reforest over 258,000,000 acres of land and to establish fire-control stations. Perhaps the Hwang (Yellow) Ho (River), long known for its yellowish color from erosion along its banks, will be clear. (41)

These operational programs, even if successful, do not herald the end of environmental deterioration. Now that environmental deterioration has become a major social issue, it must receive continuing priority in terms of assessing its changing character, magnitude, and costs of alleviation. Most of the programs presently in operation are designed for politically bounded spaces, whether county, municipal, state, or sovereign. Global assessment and beneficial management necessitate a global perspective in objectives and policies.

SUGGESTED PROGRAMS

In the literature dealing with this topic one of the major recurrent conclusions is that mankind does not have sufficient information on which to base reasoned, prudent decisions about the extent and magnitude of environmental deterioration and its potential solutions. (12) The information gap is in our knowledge of specifically how the natural system operates and how it is connected to the cultural system. Thus, the acquisition of global data represents an initial step. Such data should not be susceptible to manipulation.[16] Data should be collected

---

[15] The smog over Los Angeles has received more attention than London fog. In 1940, approximately 2,100 tons per day of hydrocarbons were being emitted into the Los Angeles Basin by the petroleum industry. In 1957, this had decreased to about 250 tons per day, but the smog remained. Thus, the automobile was identified as the leading source of this now famous smog.

[16] Conventional means of gathering and reporting data are extremely slow and susceptible to great error. Inaccurate reporting of data in order to improve chances of obtaining an international loan or grant, to show rapid or potential growth in order to secure international investment, or for

simultaneously and continuously for the entire world. The technology for such an undertaking is now available with satellite communication; the daily weather satellite picture flashed on the screens of millions of TV sets is one form of this technology. The same technology that allows men to travel to the moon and to propel remote sensing devices to outer planets can be used for vital data-collecting tasks.

Scientists now can detect whether a forest is diseased and the nature of the disease from an altitude of many miles in a matter of minutes. Remote sensing devices can scan a wheat field in Iowa or a tropical rainforest in Malaysia and determine very closely environmental conditions of stage of maturity, soil moisture, heat content, sites of potential decay, and intrusion elements. Pollution of water—from the individual farmer's stockpond to the Pacific Ocean—can be detected. This type of environmental detection is presently in use on a limited scale. With additional research, it can be installed permanently on a global scale.

In order to gather and analyze data in a short time, the remote sensing devices must be used in conjunction with high-speed computers, which are also within the present reach of technology. They offer rapid receipt, assimilation, and retrieval abilities. It will no longer be necessary to wait 6 months to 5 years for data on various types of conditions. Technology in this task will create a much shorter interval between the initiation of deterioration and the possession of data about it.

The analysis of data over a period of time would also allow for the creation of holistic experiences not only between the components and the process of the natural environment, but also in connec-

tions of the natural environment with the cultural environment. This in turn would facilitate the creation of more elaborate models of the entire system. Such models, similar perhaps to those now being constructed of the atmosphere and river basins, would be programmed to perform in the same manner as the cultural and natural environments perform. By linking such a model with real data collected almost instantaneously, the computerized model might then reflect the "reality" of the earth's total environmental system, or at least that of its major components. Changes in regional or local ecosystems could be pinpointed by the model.

The Committee on Resources and Man offers the following recommendations for designing methods and establishing directions to cope with environmental problems.

1. Early action: A detailed inventory and assessment of the world's actual and potential agricultural and forest lands and mineral deposits. The creation of a comprehensive electronic system to monitor any major changes, including the appearance of radioactive materials.

2. General policy and research: Initiation of programs to reduce the rate of population growth; to ignite an intensive search for innovations to enhance benefits from all consumption patterns; and to intensify the development and use of nuclear reactors, especially breeder reactors.

3. Organization and action: Organizational context should include a broadly qualified set of resource specialists who will maintain a continuing surveillance of all resource production and distribution patterns; make public any changes that might result in general or specific environmental deterioration; and publicly recommend optimum courses of action in times of real or potential emergency.

A quote from Pascal provides an appropriate ending to this chapter:

---

political gain can occur too easily using conventional means of data collection and compilation.

In term of space, the universe enfolds me
In terms of thought, I encompass it.

references

1.   Abler, Ronald; Adams, John; and Gould, Peter. *Spatial Organization: The Geographer's View of the World.* Englewood Cliffs, N.J.: Prentice-Hall, 1971.

2.   Albaum, Melvin, *Geography and Contemporary Issues: Studies of Relevant Problems.* New York: John Wiley and Sons, 1973.

3.   *Bain, J. S. Environmental Decay: Economic Causes and Remedies.* Boston: Little, Brown and Co., 1973.

4.   Baran, Paul A., and Sweezy, Paul M. *Monopoly Capital.* New York: Monthly Press, 1966.

5.   Barkley, Paul W., and Seckler, David W. *Economic Growth and Environmental Decay: The Solution Becomes the Problem.* New York: Harcourt, Brace Jovanovich, 1972.

6.   Barrows, H. "Geography as Human Ecology." *Annals of the Association of American Geographers* 13 (1923).

7.   Berelson, B., et al., eds. *Family Planning and Population Programs: A Review of World Development.* Chicago: University of Chicago Press, 1966.

8.   Bernade, Melvin A. *Our Precarious Habitat.* New York: W. W. Norton and Co., 1970.

9.   Brown, Lester R. *Seeds of Change: The Green Revolution and Development in the 1970s.* New York: Frederick A. Praeger, 1970.

10.   Brunhes, J. *Human Geography.* Chicago: Rand McNally, 1952. Originally published in France in 1918.

11.   Bryson, Reid, and Kutzbach, John E. *Air Pollution.* Commission on College Geography, Resource Paper No. 2. Washington, D.C.: Association of American Geographers, 1968.

12.   Committee on Resources and Man. *Resources and Man.* National Academy of Sciences–National Research Council, 1969.

13.   Commoner, Barry. *The Closing Circle.* New York: Bantam, 1971.

14.   Crocker, Thomas D., and Rogers, Augustus James. *Environmental Economics.* Hinsdale, Ill.: The Dryden Press, 1971.

15.   Detwyler, Thomas R., and Marcus, Melvin G. *Urbanization and Environment.* North Scituate, Mass.: Duxbury Press, 1972.

16.   Dolan, Edwin G. *Tanstaafl: The Economic Strategy for Environmental Crisis.* New York: Holt, Rinehart, and Winston, 1971.

17.   Dubos, René. *Man Adapting.* New Haven: Yale University Press, 1965.

18.   Ehrlich, Paul. *The Population Bomb.* New York: Ballantine, 1968.

19.   Ehrlich, Paul, and Ehrlich, Anne. "What Can Be Done?" In Q. Stanford, ed. *The World's Population.* London: Oxford University Press, 1972.

20.   ———. *Population, Resources, and Environment: Issues in Human Ecology.* 2nd ed. San Francisco: W. H. Freeman, 1972.

21.   Enthoven, Alain C., and Freeman, A. Myrick, eds. *Pollution, Resources, and the Environment: An Introduction to a Current Issue of Public Policy.* New York: W. W. Norton and Co., 1973.

22.   Fabricant, Neil, and Hallman, Robert M. *Toward a Rational Power Policy: Energy, Politics, and Pollution.* New York: George Braziller, 1971.

23.   Freeman, A. Myrick. *The Economics of Pollution Control and Environmental Quality.* New York: General Learning Press, 1971.

24.   Garvey, Gerald. *Energy, Ecology, and Economy.* New York: W. W. Norton and Co., 1972.

25.   Glacken, C. *Traces on the Rhodian Shore.* Berkeley: University of California Press, 1967.

26.   Goodwin, Irwin, ed. *Energy and Environment: A Collusion of Crisis.* Acton, Mass.: Publishing Sciences Group, 1974.

27.   Hardin, Garrett, ed. *Population, Evolution, and Birth Control: A Collage of Controversial Readings.* San Francisco: W. H. Freeman and Co., 1969.

28.   Heller, Walter W. *Economic Growth and Environmental Control: Collusion or Co-*

Existence. New York: General Learning Press, 1973.

29.   Hines, Lawrence G. *Environmental Issues: Population, Pollution, and Economics.* New York: W. W. Norton and Co., 1973.

30.   Hurst, Eliot. *A Geography of Economic Behavior.* North Scituate, Mass.: Duxbury Press, 1972.

31.   Jalée, Pierre. *The Pillage of the Third World.* New York: Modern Reader, 1968.

32.   Kapp, Karl William. *The Social Costs of Business Enterprises.* Bombay: Asian Publishing House, 1963.

33.   Manson, Peter F. "The Distribution of Air Pollution in California: A Study of Spatial Interaction." *The Journal of Geography* 73 (December 1974): 30–37.

34.   Margenau, H. *Open Vistas.* New Haven: Yale University Press, 1961.

35.   Pascal, A. H. "Where Will All the People Go? How Much Will They Dump When They Get There? Population Distribution, Environmental Damage, and the Quality of Life." *The Annals of the Regional Science Association* (June 1971): 1–5.

36.   Schnell, George A. "Demographic Transition: Threat to Developing Nations." *Journal of Geography* 69 (March 1970): 164–171.

37.   Singer, S. Fred. "Our Universe: The Known and The Unknown." *American Scientist* (Spring 1968): 1–20.

38.   Thompson, Dennis, ed. *Politics, Policy, and Natural Resources.* New York: The Free Press, 1972.

39.   Wagner, Richard H. *Environment and Man.* New York: W. W. Norton and Co., 1971.

40.   White, Lynn. "Historical Roots of Our Ecological Crisis." In W. Anderson, ed. *Politics and Environment.* Pacific Palisades, Calif.: Goodyear Publishing Co., 1970.

41.   Yi-Fu Tuan. *China.* Chicago: Aldine Publishing Co., 1969.

prospects

29

29

Throughout this text man has been depicted as a powerful force influencing and determining the type, level, and location of economic activity. Aspects of culture were analyzed within material, economic, social, political, and technological frameworks. The influence of these frameworks upon the location of particular economic activities was demonstrated.

Analyses and discussion of economic activities were made with reference to distance. Distance, a function of time and space, has traditionally been viewed by geographers as a basic fabric over which the spatial variation of economic phenomena was analyzed. Some, seeing distance shrinking as a result of ever-improving means of transportation, express fear that the fabric might be deteriorating, and that it might be reduced in scope. Improved transportation actually builds a stronger fabric for economic activity.

A more extensive transportation network carries with it higher levels of trade and specialization. These in turn tend to produce a greater degree of spatial variability in economic phenomena and mean greater productivity, income, and leisure through the cumulative growth processes. Increasing income and leisure are likely to result in more service activities. However, the type and level of service activity will depend on the technological advances in providing "do-it-yourself" conveniences as substitutes for the many commercial service activities.

The location of service activities tend to follow population and central-place hierarchical patterns. Today, however, newer patterns are emerging, for example, crossroad complexes away from residential areas, recreation facilities, shopping centers, etc. One of the most logical and practical applications of economic geography is in the fields of industry location and planning. These topics were included to orient the student toward the practical and policy aspects of the field.

The spatial location of man's economic and noneconomic activities has become a more crucial concern to him than ever before for several reasons: Man's landing on the moon has added a vertical dimension to the concept of space, which previously was perceived horizontally as far as economic phenomena were concerned. Increasing population pressures, the drastic variation in land-population ratios, and vulnerability to complete devastation by nuclear attack place higher demands on our understanding of location patterns and on the arrangement of economic activities. Human needs and goals must be met with the greatest level of efficiency.

To obtain the maximum level of efficiency and safety, the economic geographer is presented with this dilemma: on the one hand, a concentrated and specialized effort by geographers is required to gain adequate insight into the problem; on the other, by virtue of the complexity of the problem, a broader treatment involving many other disciplines is also needed. One resolution that has been suggested is called an "orchestration approach." This approach recognizes each discipline's contribution and requires that it interrelate harmoniously with other disciplines to achieve a common goal of effectively satisfying human wants, whatever their structure.

The goal of a better society implies that economic development must yield affluence. Today affluence is known in only about one-third of the world. As Figure 29–1 indicates, the United States, the USSR, the European Economic Community, and Japan produce and consume

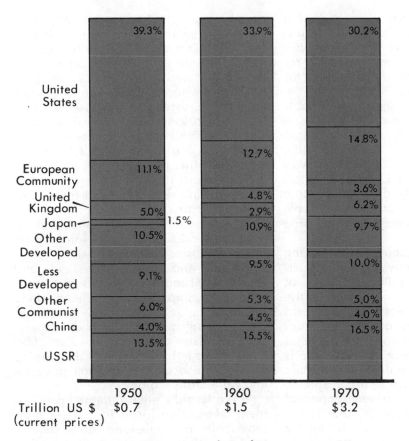

FIGURE 29–1 *World Gross National Product, 1950–1970*

over 80 percent of the world's production. Besides the size of this output, trends in the structure of production mean substantial changes in research and curriculums of economic geography. For example, the continuous trend toward the substitution of carbohydrate foods with protein-rich foods affects regional specialization and location patterns.

The ever-expanding services sector is providing job opportunities in government, recreation, distribution of goods and services, banking and credit institutions, healthcare, and repair services. (In the U.S., the service sector accounts for over 55 percent of human-resource employment.) The increasing share of the service sector is accompanied by the increasing productivities, specialization, and concentration in the primary and secondary activities.

These trends of economic growth and the changing structure of growth have caused and will continue to cause strains on regional balances of demand and supply of raw materials. The affluent nations can no longer enjoy their present rates of growth without recycling material resources, substantially substituting traditional energy sources and harnessing

493

environmental pollution. Local resources are being depleted quickly and the less developed nations have increasingly become conscious of their material resources, interests, and opportunities for economic development.

Historians of this century will doubtless record technological man's increasingly damaging impact on the natural environment and the quality of life. Some of the miracles of technology, with all their unquestioned benefits, have proved to be two-edged. Through some lack of guidance or control, they have produced unanticipated, harmful side effects.

Many citizen organizations are being formed to advocate environmental quality in the face of conflicting claims of economic growth. Major upsets of the balance of nature began to face stern questioning in courts of law and from the public. New laws and new agencies have imposed unprecedented controls on air and water pollution, automobile exhaust, municipal dumps, urban sprawl, noise, and other forms of environmental hazards. In the decade of the 1960s, higher environmental quality became a major social goal of the United States and of most of the industrial world.

The pressures of growing population and rising economic aspirations on a finite base of resources virtually assure that environmental issues are not transitory but will rank higher in decision-making priorities of future generations. Environmental challenges we now perceive will extend through all foreseeable time.

Equally striking is the extension of these concerns over the surface of the globe. Where the human environment is involved, all nations are neighbors sharing only one earth. The oceans, the atmosphere, fields, forests, and marine plankton, all chemical elements and life forms on earth are parts of one vast living organism, supplied by the virtually limitless fuel of solar energy. As technological man harnesses and redirects this energy in a multitude of new ways on an ever-growing scale, he is also acquiring a capacity he never sought—to unbalance an intricate system upon whose functioning his own long-term survival depends.

Winds and ocean currents that move ceaselessly across the face of the globe carry with them an immense and growing burden of noxious wastes generated by industrial-urban life. Lead from automobile exhaust has been found in the Greenland ice cap. DDT is spread all over the world. Sulphurous smoke from British factories blows with the prevailing winds and pollutes the fields and forests of Scandinavia. Fleets of tankers and cargo ships spill petroleum along the world's sea lanes and coastlines. Ever-growing quantities of chemical and animal waste produced on land find their way to the world's final dumping ground, the oceans, with their priceless and vulnerable ecology.

The world's environmental predicament takes other forms too. Major non-renewable minerals and fuels, whose total quantity on earth is unknown but is obviously limited, are being consumed at such accelerating rates as to raise serious questions about what will remain for future generations. The trend toward carteling by energy- and mineral-rich nations is likely to continue to cause newer and greater spatial disequilibriums and substitution of economic activities, challenging technology to discover new sources of energy and minerals.

Many living species have been extinguished for lack of adequate protection and countless others are in danger of extinction. Topsoil, on which future world food supplies largely depend, washes into rivers and estuaries of the world at rates equivalent to tens of millions of fertile acres every year.

All these disturbances of nature, together with complex global connections of trade, investment, technology, and travel have created specific operational needs for environmental collaboration among nations. Countries must cooperate to acquire and share an immense amount of environmental knowledge from scientific research, monitoring, information exchange, education, and training. They need to cooperate to control pollution of the oceans that lie beyond any nation's jurisdiction. They need new international agreements and programs for conservation of resources of world significance, especially living species. They need to concert their policies on the economic effects of environmental protection on trade, investment, and development.

A particularly active lead has been taken by the largest producer, consumer, and polluter of all, the United States. This leadership reflects a policy established in 1969 when the Congress, in the groundbreaking National Environmental Policy Act, directed the federal government to put its own environmental house in order and to recognize the worldwide and long-range character of environmental problems by joining in steps to minimize international decline in the quality of the environment. To that end, early in 1970 the Department of State created in its Bureau of International Scientific and Technological Affairs a new Office of Environmental Affairs. This office is to act as a focal point for information on and coordination of the government's growing collaboration with the rest of the world in this area.

THE ENERGY CRISIS

Probably no single event in human history has influenced our existence on this planet as much as the discovery of fossil fuels and the use of concentrated forms of energy. Over the last 150 years, human and animal labor have been increasingly replaced by inanimate sources of energy. This "energy subsidy" has increased the standard of living and the amount of leisure time for a sizable fraction of mankind.

In turn, the accumulation of capital and the availability of free time have allowed men to divert resources from basic necessities, such as food and shelter, in order to make investments in science and technology. The results of these investments have been spectacular. Technological progress also occurs at a greatly increased rate. Within the life span of most of us, we have developed television, computers, and atomic energy; man has landed on the moon; the genetic code has been broken; and many diseases have been eradicated.

In addition to improving our well-being, new developments, especially in medicine and agriculture, have led to an immense explosion of population throughout the world. To further complicate the situation, the adequacy of energy supplies is seriously being questioned. Worldwide geological, technical, economic, and political problems are pressing upon us, in addition to environmental and ecological problems.

Using conservative estimates, energy demand will more than double by 1985 and definitely will quadruple by the end of this century. Today, 90 percent of the world's energy comes from the fossil fuel of oil, gas, and coal, and only 18 percent comes from other sources (see Figure 29–2). By 1985, fossil fuels will almost certainly still provide three-quarters of the world's energy, and by the year 2000 about the same. During the decade of the 1970s, the world will consume more oil than it has since the dawn of history. The lesson is simple and stark: the world's energy will more than likely

495

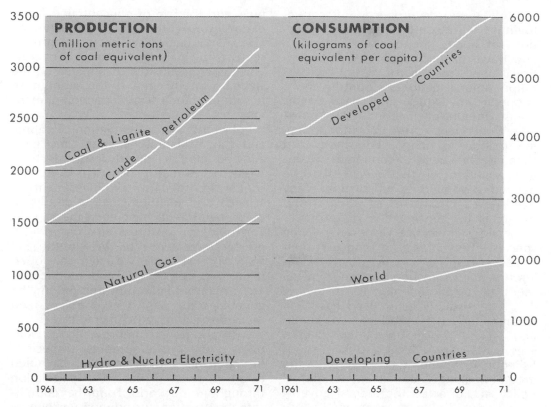

FIGURE 29–2 *World Energy Sources and Uses*

come from fossil fuels for the next two generations.

Although fossil fuel sources are abundant, a number of problems inhibit their development and use:

1. Distance between producing and consuming areas, which are often separated by an ocean

2. Topographic and economic feasibility considerations relating to transport facilities and transformation arrangements

3. Financing for the huge investments required

4. Feasible substitutes, such as nuclear, solar, geothermal, and other sources of energy

5. Pollution considerations—clean air and water and public fears and pressures

6. Cost of converting raw materials for use by consumers

Despite the abundance of hydrocarbon fuels, supply dislocations and constraints on energy use are possible and indeed probable. The U.S. has peaked out as an oil producer. Gas shortages in several areas already loom. Electric-power generating capacity is falling behind demand. Domestic refinery capacity is barely adequate.

Each year the world's largest energy consumers, the U.S., Europe, and Japan, grow more dependent on imported oil and gas, on the long chain of jumbo tankers carrying the fuel, and on the economic arrangements negotiated between producing regions and oil companies.

Japan and Europe have long since become dependent on Middle Eastern and North African oil. If present trends continue, by 1985 the U.S. will be importing 15 million barrels of crude oil daily; this amounts to half our oil consumption.

The cost of energy will rise. The bargain rates for all kinds of energy which Americans have enjoyed for 40 years cannot endure much longer. Recent consumer-price increases averaging about 30 percent are only the beginning. In the aggregate, they will be staggering and far greater than the 8 to 10 percent of the U.S. gross national product spent for energy. Without these increases, which must be paid by the consumers as the ultimate users of energy, new reserves will not be developed, pollution will not be kept at tolerable levels, substitute energy sources will not evolve, and some *real* crises will face us.

THE OTHER ENERGY CRISIS

Food is the basic energy source for man and animal. The sun generates the energy that green plants capture and convert this energy to consumable units. Livestock raised for meat are energy converters, too, because they are "fueled" on plant products. Certain basic food shortages present another "energy crisis" that is perhaps of more fundamental concern to mankind.

This is a worldwide energy crisis, and that was not expected to surface in this country so dramatically or so soon. Population growth, unfavorable weather, and expanding international markets all converged to eliminate our food surpluses and cause a new energy crisis.

We see grim reports that half the world's people go to bed hungry every night, and that vast populations exist on protein-deficient diets. We see new reports of famine in widespread areas. Suddenly the nation with the highest level of food productivity in the world is faced with empty meat shelves and a mounting domestic and foreign demand for food that is outrunning supplies (see Figure 29–3).

We need new sources of protein, as animals and fish alone cannot supply the world's present and predicted needs. We must develop plants to supplement the protein supply, improve the efficiency of producing meat, and reduce losses that diminish food supplies already produced. We need major discoveries to boost the productive capacity of prime food sources.

Solutions to these problems will not be achieved easily or quickly. They require an understanding of the basic processes of growth and reproduction. Solution of these problems is unmistakably in the public interest, and the research required to achieve them necessitates support by public funds. It is essential that the agricultural research developed in this nation be maintained and sustained as a public resource available to solve food problems.

The dramatic "food crisis" is a jolting reminder that the abundant food supply we have enjoyed is not guaranteed, not permanent, and not possible without constant and vigilant attention to the processes of food production and delivery systems. Human resource programs could have no higher goal than alleviation of human hunger on a worldwide scale.

ENVIRONMENTAL POLLUTION

Not long ago in every industrial nation's experience, smoke belching from factory stacks was a bright omen of progress. So it is today in most of the world, where the highest priority now goes to conquering poverty through development.

Yet the gospel of "growth at any cost" has begun to be questioned in

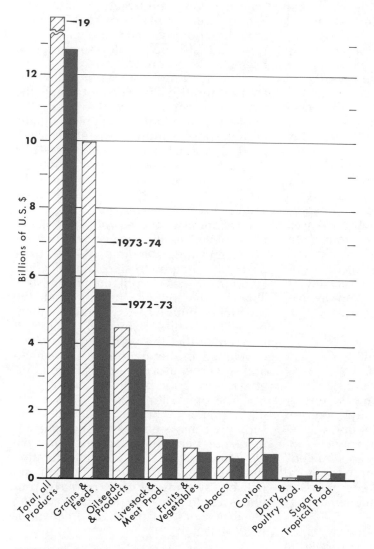

FIGURE 29–3 *U.S. Farm Exports, 1974*

many developing nations. There is a new awareness of the need to plan not only for quantity but also for quality; for such social needs as employment, housing, health, and education; and for environmental quality.

Perhaps it is time for the economic geographer and the ecologist to move out of the separate, cramped intellectual quarters they still inhabit, and take up residence together in a larger house of ideas.

In this larger house, the economic geographer will take full account of what formerly were called "external diseconomies"—pollution and resource depletion —and he will assign meaningful values to the purity of air and water and the

498

simple amenities we once took for granted. He will develop measures of well-being based on values other than those reflected by gross national product. The ecologist in turn will extend his attention beyond the balance of nature to include all activities of man's mind and hand that improve civilized life. Economic geographer and ecologist will collaborate to advise planners and decision makers to improve cities and the countryside in a manner that will promote the harmonious interaction of man with man and of man with nature; to preserve resources for future generations; and to ensure that development will lead not just to greater production of goods but also to a higher quality of life.

references

1. Brooks, Reuben H. "Drought and Public Policy in Northeastern Brazil: Alternatives to Starvation." *The Professional Geographer* 25 (November 1973): 338–46.

2. Bunge, William W. "The Geography of Human Survival." *Annals of the Association of American Geographers* 63 (September 1973): 275–95.

3. Caruso, Douglas, and Palm, Risa. "Social Space and Social Place." *The Professional Geographer* 25 (August 1973): 221–25.

4. Chakravarti, A. K. "Green Revolution in India." *Annals of the Association of American Geographers* 63 (September 1973): 319–30.

5. Cook, Earl. "The Flow of Energy in an Industrial Society," *Scientific American* 225 (March 1971): 135–44.

6. Eyre, John D. "Development Trends in the Japanese Electric Power Industry." *The Professional Geographer* 22 (January 1970): 26–30.

7. Haynes, James B. "North Slope Oil: Physical and Political Problems." *The Professional Geographer* 24 (February 1972): 17–22.

8. Hidore, John J. "Water, Water Resources, and Water Problems." *The Professional Geographer* 22 (May 1970): 117–19.

9. Hubbert, M. King. "The Energy Resources of the Earth." *Scientific American* 25 (March 1971): 61–70.

10. King, L.; Casetti; E.; Odland J.; and Semple, K. "Optimal Transportation Patterns of Coal in the Great Lakes Region." *Economic Geography* 4 (July 1971): 401–13.

11. Luten, Daniel B. "The Economic Geography of Energy." *Scientific American* 225 (March 1971): 165–75.

12. Mason, Peter F. "Some Spatial Implications of a Massive Industrial Accident: The Case of Nuclear Power." *The Professional Geographer* 24 (August 1972): 233–36.

13. Peet, Richard. "Poor, Hungry America." *The Professional Geographer* 23 (April 1971): 99–104.

14. Terjung, Werner H., and Louie, Stella. "Solar Radiation and Urban Heat Islands." *Annals of the Association of American Geographers* 63 (June 1973): 181–207.

15. Thomas, Trevor M. "World Energy Resources: Survey and Review." *Geographical Review* 63 (April 1973): 246–58.

499

INDEX

A

Accessibility, 12
Activities, 360
  marketing, 297–404
  recreational, 455
  research and development, 402–04
  spatial patterns of, 456
Activity. *See* Economic activity.
Aerospace industry, 303–08
Africa
  arable crop land, 34
  area, 34
  drainage, 54
  energy sources, 38
  forests and forest products, 34, 191, 193, 194
  fresh water fisheries, 185
  livestock ranching, 153
  petroleum reserves, 211
  population, 34, 36 (*table*)
  rubber, production of, 199
  rudimentary and sedentary tillage, 166
  shifting cultivation, 168
  urbanization, 36
Agglomeration, 362–463
  theory of, 263
Agriculture, 140–73
  and climate, 142
  dairy farming, 143–44, 144 (*table*)
  grain farming, 149–52
  horticulture, 145–47
  intensive subsistence,
    rice dominant, 159–61
    rice unimportant, 161–63
  livestock and crop farming, 147–49
  livestock ranching, 152–53
  Mediterranean, 154–57, 156 (*table*)
  nomadic herding, 169–71
  origin and dispersion, 140–41
  plantation, 157–58
  regions of, 136

  rudimentary and sedentary tillage, 165–66
  shifting cultivation, 166–69, 168 (*table*)
  spatial dynamics of, 132
  subsistence crop and livestock farming, 164–65
  systems of, 140, 142–43
  techniques of, 168
Air conditioning, 346–47
Aircraft industry, 303–07, 305 (*map*)
  airframes, 303–06
  location factors, 304–05
Air Quality Act, 59, 487
Airways, 391–93, 391 (*map*)
Alabama, 274
Alaska
  fishing industry, 179, 180, 185
  petroleum, 211–12
Algeria
  agriculture, 157
  petroleum reserves, 211
  truck farming, 147
Allegheny River, 264
Alumina, 274, 276
Aluminum, 274–75
Amazon River, 55
Amazon Valley, 168
American Manufacturing Belt, 277
American Public Works Association, 57
American Statistical Association, 98
American Indians, 169
Ammonia, 331
Amur River, 55
Amur Valley, 148
Animal husbandry, 169
Anshan (People's Republic of China), 272
Antarctica, 50, 183-84
Anthracite coal, 216
Appalachian Mountains, 134
Appalachian Regional Commission, 471
Arabian Gulf, 213

Aral Sea, 277
Arctic Ocean, 297
Areal differentiation, 383
Argentina
  agriculture, 154–55
  cattle, 148, 153 (*table*)
  cotton, 147
  grain farming, 152
  livestock and crop farming, 148 (*table*)
  livestock ranching, 153
  Pampa, 152
  radio and television broadcasting, 436 (*table*)
  tertiary activities in, 374
  wheat production, 149
Arkansas, petroleum in, 211
Asia
  arable cropland, 33
  drainage, 54
  energy, 38
  fish culture, 186
  forest products, 194
  grain farming, 152
  nomads, 171
  subsistence crop and livestock farming, 164
  urbanization, 36
Australia
  agriculture, 155
  aluminum, 276 (*table*)
  bauxite, 209
  coal reserves, 222–23
  copper ore, 208 (*table*)
  dairy farming, 146
  drainage, 54
  forests, 193
  government expenditures, 419 (*table*)
  iron ore reserves, 205
  livestock, 148 (*table*)
    and crop farming, 148
    ranching, 153
  mining, 217
  pearl fisheries, 184
  radio and television broadcasting, 436 (*table*)
  tertiary activities in, 374
  uranium reserves, 223

Austria, television-receiver
production in, 350
(*table*)
Automotive industry, 297–303
history, 299–300
location, 298–99
production, 297 (*table*)

B

Baffin Bay, 177
Bakhra-Nangal dam, 54
Baku, 212
Balsa, 195
Bamboo production, 197
Banana production, 157, 168,
158 (*table*)
Bangledesh, agriculture in, 160,
151, (*table*) 319
Barents Sea, 182
Barley, 155, 166
Barter, 22
Basic oxygen furnace, 266
Bauxite, 209, 273
Beans, 168
Belgium
coal, 221
textile machinery, 289
Bering Sea, 184
Bioculture, 155
Biotic pyramid, 176
Birmingham (Alabama), 80,
253, 269
Bituminous coal, 216
Black Sea, 170, 277, 297
Bogue, Donald J., 465
Boilers, power, 345
Bolivia
antimony, 48 (*table*)
tin, 49 (*table*)
Books, production of, 435
(*table*)
Borneo, fishing in, 178
Bottomfish, 183
Brahmaputra River, 55 (*table*)
Brazil
agriculture, 153
Amazon River, 55 (*table*)
bananas, 158 (*table*)
corn, 151 (*table*)
forests and forest products,
192, 194 (*table*)
government expenditures,
419 (*table*)
iron ore reserves, 204, 205
(*table*)
livestock and crop farming,
48 (*table*)

livestock ranching, 148
(*table*), 153 (*table*)
orange production, 156
(*table*)
São Francisco River, 55
(*table*)
sugarcane, 158 (*table*)
titanium, 280
Breadfruit, 168
British thermal units (B.T.U.),
36
Broadleaf forests, 193
Brown's Bank, 187
Brown, Harrison, 99
Bureau of the Census, 465
Bureau of Outdoor Recreation,
446
Buryats, 165
Bushman, hunting-gathering
culture of, 8
Butadiene, 339

C

Cacao, 157, 160, 168
Calcutta (India), 319
California, 193, 236, 238, 287–
88, 487
aerospace industry, 305
Central Valley, 288
citrus fruits, 155
dairying, 157
fishing, 177, 179–80
livestock grazing, 156
farming, 157
meat-packing, 157
natural gas reserves, 215
petroleum reserves, 211
potatoes, 157
San Joaquin Valley, 157
sheep, 156
sugar beets, 157
truck farming, 147
vegetables, 157
wine, 155
Cameroon, 209
Canada
agricultural implements industry, 288
aluminum, 277–78, 276
(*table*)
arable land, 34 (*table*)
asbestos, 49 (*table*)
automotive industry, 297
(*table*), 300
cobalt, 48 (*table*)
copper, 48 (*table*), 208
dairy farming, 144

defense expenditures, 419
(*table*)
energy resources, 38
fisheries, 180–81
forests and forest products,
34 (*table*), 192, 194
grain farming, 151
gold, 48 (*table*)
iron ore reserves, 204–05
lead, 48 (*table*)
livestock ranching, 153
minerals, 48–49
molybdenum, 48 (*table*)
natural gas reserves, 215
petrochemical industry, 337
petroleum reserves, 211
population, 34 (*table*)
potash, 49 (*table*)
radio-receiver production,
351 (*table*)
radio and television broadcasting, 436 (*table*)
silver, 49 (*table*)
sulfur, 49 (*table*)
television-receiver production, 350 (*table*)
tertiary activities in, 374
titanium, 280
uranium, 49 (*table*), 223
vegetables, 146
wheat production, 149, 151
(*table*)
zinc, 49 (*table*)
Cantril, Hadley, 108
Cape Horn, 182
Cape of Good Hope, 385
Capital, 20, 230
Capitalism, 93
Carbon[14] datings, 141
Caribbean, 47, 276
Carlyle, Thomas, 116
Carpathian Mountains, 164,
214
Carrying capacity, 153
Caspian Sea, 170, 213
Cassava, 168
Cattle, 152, 153 (*table*), 156,
159, 171
Caucasus, 213
Caustic soda, 331, 332 (*table*)
Central America
agriculture, 157
bananas, 157
forests and forest products,
193
shifting cultivation, 168
Central Business District (CBD),
362, 364

Central places, tertiary
    activities in, 375
Central place theory, 360–61
    modification of, 364
Ceylon. *See* Sri Lanka.
Change, 15–16, 118–19
Cheese, 157
Chelyabinsk (U.S.S.R.), 270, 285
Chemical industries, 328–42
    location factors, 329–30
Chemicals
    agricultural, 335–37
    industrial, 329–34
    petroleum-based, 337–38
Chesapeake Bay, and lobster
    fishing, 184
Chicago (Illinois), 104, 236,
    268, 284, 287, 298
Chicle, 197
Chile, 193
    agriculture, 154–55
    copper-ore production, 208
    defense expenditures, 419
        (*table*)
    fishing, 182
    iron ore reserves, 205
    livestock and crop farming,
        148
    lobster industry, 185
Chlorine, 322–33
Christaller, Walter, 360–61, 452
Chromium, 263
Chronite, 45
Chung-king (People's Republic
    of China), 272
Citrus fruits, 155, 157
Clean Air Act, 62, 487
Cleveland, 284, 299
Climate, 190
Coal, 216–23
    anthracite, 216
    bituminous, 216
    distribution, 218
    energy, 39 (*table*)
    mining, types of, 223
    production, 217 (*table*)
    reserves, 219
    transportation, 219
Cobalt, 45, 49 (*table*)
Cod, 176, 178, 181–82
Cologne (West Germany), 286
Colorado, 291
    coal deposits in, 219
Colorado Basin, 147
Columbium, 45
Command authority, 25–26
Commercial dairy farming, 143
Commercial fruit farming, 147

Commercial livestock and crop
    farming, 147
Commercial plantation, 157
Commercial printing, 438
    (*table*)
Commodity money, 407
Common Market, 338
Communication services, clas-
    sification of, 430–31
Communism, 93–94
Comparative advantage,
    concept of, 77, 84–85
Congo, The. *See* Zaire.
Congo Basin, 168
Coniferous forests, 192
Consolidated Edison Company,
    62
Continental shelf, 183
Copenhagen, 295
Copper, 207
    smelting, 48 (*table*), 253
Cork, 195, 197
Corn, 33, 153, 166, 168
Costa Rica, 158
Cotton, 157, 163, 310
Crab fisheries, 180, 184
Craft guilds, 247–48
Cuba, agriculture in, 108
    commercial plantation, 157
    crop tillage, 157
    sugarcane, 157, 158
Cultural man, 5
Culture
    and resources, 16
    and social traits, 11
Czechoslovakia
    coal reserves, 221
    dairy farming, 144
    linen industry, 318

D

Dairying, 143–44
Danube River, 55 (*table*)
Danube Valley, commercial
    livestock and crop
    farming in, 148
Davis, Kingsley, 35
Deccan Plateau, 163
Decentralized banking, 409
Deciduous forests, 192
Defense purchases, 424
DeForest, Lee, 347
Delhi (India), 429
Demand, 66, 71. *See also* Price.
    schedule, 67
Democratic Republic of
    Germany, 144

Denmark
    dairy farming, 143–44
    shipbuilding, 295
Department of Health, Educa-
    tion, and Welfare, 98
Depreciation, 79
Deterioration, environmental,
    477–79
Detroit, 236, 284, 287, 298
Devaluation, of dollar, 44
Diamonds, 45, 51
Direct Mail Advertising Asso-
    ciation, 432
Discount houses, 401
Discretionary purchasing
    power, 456
Disposal taxes, 61
Dnepropetrovsk (U.S.S.R.), 270
Dnieper River, 185, 279
Dogger Banks, 176, 182
Dollar devaluation, 44
Domestic system, development
    of, 248
Dominican Republic, 108
Donets Basin, 269
Donetsk, 219
Don River, 185
Dravidians, 107

E

Earth boundedness, 11–12
Eastern Europe, 38
Ebro River, 170
Economic activity, 4
    agglomeration of, 362
    classification of, 6–7
    cultural factors, 90
    government participation in,
        418–22
    and religion, 104
    spatial location of, 492
    and U.S. federal budget,
        422–26
    and wants, 20–21
Economic framework, 66
Economic geography, 6, 7
Economic phenomena, spatial
    distribution of, 381
Economic rent, 128, 130–31,
    136
Economic systems, 480
    tertiarization of, 369–70
Ecuador
    bamboo, 197
    bananas, 157, 158
    fishing, 184
Edison, Thomas A., 347
Education, 106, 421–22

Egypt, 108
    nomads, 171
    truck farming, 147
Ehrlich, Paul R., 480–81
Einstein, Albert, 56
Elasticity (economic), 68
Electrical equipment, 344–45
Electric furnace method of
        steel production, 267
Electrical machinery and
        equipment, 344–56
Electronics
    consumer, 350–51
    systems equipment, 351–52
Energy, 36
    animate, 36
    coal, 216–24
    crisis, 40–44, 495–96
    fuel generated, 36
    geothermal, 37
    hydroelectric, 274
    inanimate, 36
    natural gas, 36, 215
    nuclear, 36, 223
    ocean, as source of, 36
    production and consump-
        tion, 36, 38 (table)
    in United States, 38
Engines and motors, 289–91
Environment
    concepts and characteristics
        of, 476–77
    perceptual images of, 477
        (table)
    physical, 124–25
Environmental deterioration
    causes of, 480
    as a social issue, 477–79
    solutions, 483–84
Environmental perception,
        477–78
Environmental pollution,
        497–98
Environmental protection, 455
Erie Canal, 264
Eskimos, 169
Eurasia
    grain farming, 152
    livestock and crop farming,
        148
    livestock ranching, 153
Europe
    fishing industry, 180
    forests and forest products,
        191
    garment manufacture,
        324–25
    linen industry, 318

lobsters, 185
petrochemicals, 338
population, 100 (table)
subsistence crop and live-
        stock farming, 164
textiles, 315
urbanization, 36
European Economic Com-
        munity (EEC), 465, 492
Exchange (economic), 7, 21
    rate, 83
Explosives, 334–35
Externalities, 483
    related to economies of
        scale, 70

F

Factory system, growth of,
        248–49
Faeroe Islands, 176
Family
    as a social unit, 107
    planning programs for, 485
        (table)
Far East
    energy resources, 39 (table)
    land use, 34 (table)
    population, 36 (table)
Federal Advisory Council, 409
Federal Aviation Administra-
        tion (FAA), 352
Federal Communications Com-
        mission, 441
Federal Open Market Com-
        mittee, 409
Federal Reserve System,
        408–13
Federal Trade Commission, 404
Ferroalloys, 206
Fertilizers
    nitrogen, 335
    potash, 336
    phosphate, 336
Fetter, F. A., 363
Fibers, manmade, 319–21
Financial intermediaries, 413
Finland
    forests and forest products,
        194, 200
    titanium, 280
Fish, 175–78
    declining stocks of, 186–87
    distribution and consump-
        tion, 176–78
    farming, 185
    for fertilizers, 178

meal, 51, 178, 183
    stock replenishment, 187
Fishing
    in Aleutian Islands, 178
    culture, 186
    inland, 185
    in Indonesia, 178
    national management of,
        187–88
    in northwest Atlantic,
        180–88
    in northwest Europe, 181–82
    ocean, 178
    in western North America,
        179–80
    in western South America,
        184
Fjords, 182
Flax, 318
Food, 497
    web, 175
Food and Drug Administration,
        404
Forests and forest products,
        190–201. *See also*
        specific commodities.
    broadleaf, 193
    commercial products of, 194
    coniferous, 192
    gums, 197
    international trade, 199–200
    latexes, 197
    lumber, 195
    natural environment of, 190
    nonwood forest products,
        197, 199
    ownership, 192
    production, 194 (table)
    resins, 197
    rubber, 197–99
    sawmilling, 195
    trends, 200–01
Fossil fuel, 209–23
    coal, 216–23
    natural gas, 215–16
    petroleum, 209–15
Frameworks, 45
    economic, 66–88
    materials–resource, 32–63
    sociopolitical, 90–109
    technological, 112–20
France
    aerospace industry, 307
    agriculture, 153, 157
    automotive industry, 297
        (table), 301
    chemical industries, 328,
        tables: 330, 331, 332,
        333, 339

France (*cont.*)
  coal
    production, 217
    reserves, 221
  dairy farming, 144
  defense expenditures, 419
    (*table*)
  fishing, 182
  iron ore production, 204
  land use, 34 (*table*)
  natural gas reserves, 216
  population, 34
  radio and television broad-
    casting, 436 (*table*)
  recreational patterns in,
    450–51
  shipbuilding, 295
  television-receiver produc-
    tion, 350 (*table*)
  textile machinery, 289
  uranium reserves, 223
  wheat production, 151
    (*table*)
Free Trade Association, 338
Fresh water resources, 52–56
Fresno (California), 288
Friedman, John, 471–72
Fruit, 166
Fuel. *See* Fossil fuel.

G

George's Bank, 187
Georgia (U.S.S.R.), 317
Ghent (Belgium), 318
Glasgow, 286
Gold, 48 (*table*)
Goods, 23
  government purchase of, 420
Government expenditures,
  422–26
  as percent of gross domestic
    product, 419 (*table*)
  transfer payments, 422
Government services, 417–27
  defense expenditures,
    418–19
  education, 421–22
  and federal budget, 422–23
  role in economic activity,
    418
  social security, 420–21
Great Britain
  agricultural implements
    industry, 288–89
  aircraft industry, 306
  coal reserves, 222
  engine and motor industry,
    290

  locomotives, electrical, 344
  natural gas reserves, 216
  textiles, 314–16
  textile machinery, 289
Great Depression, 471
Great Lakes, 259, 283–84, 289,
  296
Greece, agriculture in, 157
Greenland, ice caps, 50, 494
Gulf Coast (U.S.), 275, 337, 339
Gross Domestic Product
  (GDP), 387
Gross National Product (GNP),
  106, 424
Group of Ten, 83
Guava, 168
Guinea, bauxite in, 209 (*table*),
  277
Gulf of Alaska, fishing in, 180
Gulf coast, and lobster fishing,
  184–85
Gulf of Mexico
  oysters, 184
  shrimp, 184
Gulf Stream, 177, 181–82
Gums, 197
Guyana
  bauxite, 209
  aluminum, 274

H

Hangchow (People's Republic
  of China), 315–16
Hard-Coal-Equivalent (H.C.E.),
  36
Hauser, Philip, 99
Herring fishing, 178, 181–82
Highways, 389, 390 (*map*)
Hindus, 105
Hoe culture, 166
Hokkaido (Japan), 222
Honan (China), 163
Honduras, banana production
  in, 158 (*table*)
Hong Kong, 348
Honshu (Japan), 318
Hopei (China), 163
Horses, 169
Horticulture, specialized, 145
Hudson–Mohawk Valley, 298
Hudson River, 264
Humboldt Current, 183
Hungary
  bauxite, 209 (*table*)
  livestock and crop farming,
    148
Hunting-gathering culture, 6,
  167

Hunting, sport of, 453 (*table*)
Hurst, Eliot, 480
Husbandry, animal, 169
Hydrocarbons, as pollutants,
  60 (*table*)
Hydrologic cycle, 50
Hydropower, 39 (*table*)

I

Iceland, fishing industry in,
  176, 187
Illinois River, 287, 333, 338,
  487
Ilmenite, 280
Immobility, as factor of
  production, 71
India, 108, 160
  agriculture, 155, 161–63
  airways, 392
  banana production, 158
  coal reserves, 222
  cotton textiles, 313–14
  Deccan Plateau, 162
  defense expenditures, 419
    (*table*)
  forest land, 34 (*table*)
  government expenditures,
    419 (*table*)
  iron ore production, 204
  jute production, 311
  land use, 34 (*table*)
  livestock, 148 (*table*)
  natural rubber production,
    158
  nitrogenous fertilizers, 335
    (*table*)
  per-capita gross domestic
    product, 388 (*table*)
  population, 34 (*table*), 388
    (*table*)
  radio and television broad-
    casting, 436 (*table*)
  rice, 151 (*table*)
  shifting cultivation, 168
  sugarcane, 158
  telegraph services, 432, 433
    (*table*)
  textiles, 289, 313–14
  titanium, 280
  wheat production, 151
    (*table*), 162
Indiana, 338
Indians, American, 169
Indigo, 166
Indonesia
  forests and forest products,
    193

Indonesia (*cont.*)
  natural rubber production,
    158 (*table*)
  petroleum production, 211,
    214
  rice, 151 (*table*)
  shifting cultivation, 168
Industrial chemicals, 329–34
Industrial location. *See*
    industry location.
Industrial revolution, 249–50
Industries
  agricultural implements and
    farm machinery, 287–89
  agricultural machinery,
    287–89
  aircraft, 303–07
  aluminum, 274–79
  automotive, 297–303, 297
    (*table*)
  chemical, 328–42
  computer, 351–53
  electrical machinery and
    equipment, 344–56
  electronics, 347–56
  engine and motor, 289–91
  garment, 321, 324
  iron and steel, 264–74
  jute, 319
  oriented toward labor,
    255–56
  linen, 318
  man-made fiber, 319–21
  oriented toward markets,
    257–58
  market-based, 228
  metal-fabricating, 283–308
  mining, 203
  mining machinery and
    equipment, 291–92
  newspaper, 436
  petrochemical, 337–38
  oriented toward power
    sources, 254–55
  oriented toward raw
    materials, 252–54
  resource-based, 228
  shipbuilding, 292–97, 293
    (*table*)
  silk, 318–19
  tanning, 253
  television, 441–42
  textile and garment, 311–25
  textile machinery, 289
  oriented toward transporta-
    tion, 256–57
Industry
  and location advantages,
    258–59

and taxes, 233
and waste disposal, 234
and water, 234
Industry location
  factors of, 228
    behavioral, 231
    capital, 230
    climate, 231
    community attitudes, 235
    labor supply, 229–30
    markets, 229
    personal reasons, 234–35
    political influences,
      232–33
    raw materials, 228
    site, 231–32
    social, 231
    structural, 230
    technological, 231
  and transfer cost, 230
  trends in, 235–38
Inertia, industrial, 258
Inland fishing, 185
Inland waterways, 285
Insurance, 413–14
Intensive subsistence tillage
  rice dominant, 157–59
  rice unimportant, 161–65
Interaction, spatial, 12–13
International Bank for Recon-
    struction and Develop-
    ment, 82
International Commission for
    North Atlantic Fisheries,
    187
International Monetary Fund,
    and special drawing
    rights, 82
International trade, 82, 199–
    201, 386
Investment, U.S. overseas,
    354–55
Iran
  manufacturing, 259
  petroleum reserves, 211, 213
  subsistence crop and live-
    stock farming, 164
Iranian Plateau, 163
Iraq, petroleum reserves in,
    211
Ireland, 117
  linen production, 318
Iron and steel production,
    264–74
  location factors, 263–64
Iron smelting, 253
Irrawaddy River, 159, 160, 55
    (*table*)
Irrigation, 166

Isard, Walter, 243
Israel
  agriculture, 155
  defense expenditures, 419
    (*table*)
Italy, 146–47
  agriculture, 154–55, 157
  air conditioning, 347
  automotive industry, 297
    (*table*), 301
  barley, 154
  dairying, 144
  fertilizers, 335 (*table*)
  gross domestic product,
    per-capita, 388 (*table*)
  iron and steel production,
    272–73
  locomotives, electrical, 344
  natural gas reserves, 216
  nitric acid, 332 (*table*)
  plastic and resin production,
    333 (*table*)
  population density, 388
    (*table*)
  radio and television broad-
    casting, 436
  recreational patterns in, 450
  shipbuilding industry, 296
  soda ash production, 331
    (*table*)
  steel production, 270 (*table*)
  sulfuric acid production, 330
    (*table*)
  tertiary activities in, 374
  textiles, 289, 316
  tourist economy in, 449
  wheat production, 154
  yarn production, 316 (*table*)

J

Jamaica, bauxite production of,
    209 (*table*)
Japan, 160
  air conditioning, 347
  aluminum industry, 276
    (*table*), 279
  automotive industry, 297
    (*table*), 302
  coal reserves and produc-
    tion, 217, 222
  cotton textiles, 314
  electronics equipment, 348
  engine and motor industry,
    291
  fishing, 178–179
  forest products, 194
  government expenditures,
    419 (*table*)

Japan *(cont.)*
  gross domestic product, per-capita, 338 *(table)*
  industrial chemical production, 329
  international tourist travel, 446 *(table)*
  iron and steel production, 271–72
  manufacturing in, 259
  metal-fabricating industry, 286–87
  metalworking industries, 284
  motors and generators, 345
  national budget, 419 *(table)*
  nitrogenous fertilizers, 335 *(table)*
  nuclear reactors, 346
  plastic and resin production, 333 *(table)*
  population density, 388 *(table)*
  radio–receiver production, 351 *(table)*
  radio and television broadcasting, 436 *(table)*
  rayon industry, 320
  recreational patterns in, 451–52
  rice, 151 *(table)*, 160
  shipbuilding, 292–93
  silk industry, 318–19
  steel mills, 272
  production, 270 *(table)*
  synthetic rubber production, 339 *(table)*
  television–receiver production, 350 *(table)*
  tertiary activities in, 374
  textiles, 289, 314, 317
  whaling, 184
  yarn production, 316 *(table)*
Java
  fishing, 178
  rice cultivation, 160
Judeo-Christian ethic, 480
Jute, 319

K

Kalahari Bushmen, 169
Kaliningrad (U.S.S.R.), 297
Kansas
  natural gas reserves, 215
  petroleum reserves, 211
Kansk-Achinsk Basin, 220
Karaganda Basin, 220
Kazakhstan (U.S.S.R.), 152, 177, 277

Kentucky, 338
  coal distribution in, 218
Kharkov (U.S.S.R.), 285, 291
Klystron tube, 347
Knowledge, 112
Kobe (Japan), 286, 291, 293
Kola Peninsula, 204, 277
Krakow (Poland), 222
Kuala Lumpur, 198
Kurds, 165
Kuroshio, 178. *See also* Japan Current.
Kuwait, petroleum reserves in, 211
Kuznetsk Basin (U.S.S.R.), 269, 271, 277
Kyushu (Japan), 222

L

Labor, 263
  as resource, 19
Labrador Current, 177, 181
Laissez-faire, economic philosophy of, 417
Lake Baikal, 165
Lake Erie, 264
Land-based resources, 32–36
Land use, 34 *(table)*, 35 *(table)*
  zones of, 125–26
La Plata River, 55 *(table)*
Latin America
  energy resources, 38
  natural gas reserves, 216
  rudimentary and sedentary tillage, 166
  urbanization, 36
Latex, 197, 339
Law
  and the legal system, 96–97
  of comparative advantage, 77, 84, 86
  of demand, 67
  of diminishing returns, 76
  of one price, 72
Lead, production of, 48 *(table)*
Le Havre (France), 315
Leningrad (U.S.S.R.), 291, 297
Liberia
  iron ore production, 204–05
  natural rubber, 158 *(table)*
Libya, petroleum reserves in, 211
Lignite, 216, 222, 275
Lignumvitae, 196
Limestone, 263
Linen, 318
Livestock
  farming, 157

grazing, 156
ranching, 152
  carrying capacity, 152
  cultural environment, 152
  physical conditions, 152
  labor, 152
  market, 152
Lobster industry, 182–84
Location (of industry). *See* Industry Location.
Location theories
  Lösch, 242, 244
  of secondary economic activities, 238–39
  Weber, 239–42
Locomotives, electric, 344–45
Logging, 191
London, 286, 288
Los Angeles, 157, 288
Lösch, August, 75, 242
Louisiana
  natural gas reserves, 215
  petroleum reserves, 211
Lumber, 195
  plywood, 194

M

McClelland, D. C., 109
McCormick, Cyrus, 287
Machinery
  agricultural, 287–89
  industrial, 289
  metal-cutting, 285
  mining, 291–92
  nature of, 249–50
  textile, 289
Machines, business, 353 *(table)*
Mackenzie River, 55 *(table)*
Madagascar, shifting cultivation in, 168
Madhya Pradesh (India), 314
Magnesite, 206
Magnesium, 51, 279
Magnitogorsk (U.S.S.R.), 270
Maharashtra (India), 314
Malay Peninsula, 160
Malaysia, 198–99
  natural rubber, 158 *(table)*
Malthus, Thomas, 99, 116, 480
Man
  and behavior, 99
  classification of, 5, 6
  cultural, 5
  determinants of population growth, 100
  and earth boundedness, 11–12
  and economic activity, 6–7

507

Man (*cont.*)
  and family structure, 107–09
  fertility rate, 100
  marriage rate, 100
  and material resources, 18–20
  and nature, 16–17
  and religion, 103–06
  and society, 11, 13–14, 97–99
  and technology, 115–17
  and wants, 20–21
Manganese, 48 (*table*), 206, 263
Mangoes, 168
Manioc, 166
Manmade fibers, 319–21
Manufacturing, 236–37
  defined, 247
  general pattern of, 252
  eotechnic phase, 247–49
  neotechnic phase, 251–52
  paleotechnic phase, 249–51
  regions, 259–60
  systems, 247–60
Marginal substitution, 76
Market, 71
  competition, 72
  consumer, 236
  defined, 71
  range, 362
  spatial relations of, 73
  types, 72
  Von Thünen's model of, 74
Market gardening, 145
Marketing
  and consumerism, 402–03
  function of, 397–98
  location of, 389–99
  industries, 257–58
  problems of measuring, 399–402
  retailing, 400–01
  services, 397–405
  wholesaling, 400
Marshall, Alfred, 66
Marx, Karl, 116
Mass production, 251–52
Masu, 178
Mediterranean
  animal husbandry in, 154–55
  characteristics, 154
  climate, 154
  cultural environment, 155
  land-use, 155
  livestock farming, 155, 156–57
  natural vegetation of, 155
  physical environment, 154–55

viticulture, 154–55
  winter grains, 154–55
Mediterranean Basin, 157
Mekong River, 160
Mercury, production of, 48 (*table*)
Mesopotamia, 310
Metal-cutting tools, 285–87
Metal-fabricating, 283–86. *See also* Machinery.
Mexico
  agriculture, 141, 155
  defense expenditures, 419 (*table*)
  electronics industry, 348
  international travel, 446
  lemon and lime production, 156 (*table*)
  natural gas reserves, 215–16
  subsistence crop and livestock farming, 164
  sugarcane, 158 (*table*)
  titanium, 280
  tourist economy in, 449
Michigan, 204, 338
Middle East
  agriculture, 141
  energy resources, 38
  petroleum reserves, 213
Millet, 162, 168
Minerals. *See also* Mining.
  classification of, 144–45
  grades of, 45–46
  production, 48 (*table*)
  reserves, 45
Mining
  asbestos, 48
  bauxite, 279
  coal, 216–23
  copper, 207–08
  ferroalloys, 206
  fertilizer minerals, 48–49
  fossil fuels, 209–23
  iron ore, 203–06
  lead, 48
  location of, 203, 235
  machinery for, 291–92
  and manufacturing, 228
  methods, 203–04
  natural gas, 215–16
  nickel, 48
  nonferrous metals, 207–09
  nuclear fuels, 223
  petroleum, 209–15
  technology of, 203
  tin, 49
  zinc, 49
Minnesota, 204

Mississippi River, 55 (*table*), 276, 333
Missouri, 204
Missouri River, 55 (*table*), 333
Molybdenum, 48 (*table*), 206, 263
Money, 22, 90, 407–08
Mongolian People's Republic
  crop and livestock farming, 164
  subsistence farming, 164
Monongahela River, 264
Monopoly (in economics), 72
Morocco, fishing industry of, 177
Moscow, 219, 285
Moscow Basin, 270
Motor Vehicle Air Pollution Control Act, 487
Motorways. *See* Highways.
Mumford, Lewis, 119, 247
Murray-Darling River, 55 (*table*)
Myrdal, Gunnar, 463

N

Nagasaki (Japan), 293
National Aeronautics and Space Administration (NASA), 98, 352, 467
National Banking Act, 407
National Broadcasting Company, 440
National Environmental Policy Act, 487
National Industrial Conference Board, 62
National Petroleum Council
National Resources Committee, 465
National Resources Planning Board, 471
Nation-state, 91
Natural gas, 39 (*table*), 41, 215–16, 275
Natural rubber, 197–99
Navajo, 22
Neckako River, 278
Neotechnic phase (of manufacturing), 251
Netherlands
  coal production, 221
  natural gas reserves, 216
  plastics industry, 333 (*table*)
  whaling industry, 184
New England, 283
New Guinea, shifting cultivation in, 168
New Jersey, 238, 283

New Mexico
  coal reserves, 219
  natural gas reserves, 215
New Orleans, 337
Newspapers, 433–35
New York, 238, 287, 290
  garment industry, 321–24
New Zealand, 193
  dairy farming, 143
  defense expenditures, 419
    (*table*)
  geothermal power, 37
  government expenditures,
    419 (*table*)
  livestock ranching, 153
  milk production, 144 (*table*)
  tertiary activities in, 374
Nickel, 263
Niger, 56
Nigeria, 108
  petroleum reserves, 211
Nile River, 56
Nitric acid, production of, 332
  (*table*)
Nitrogen, production of, 335,
  49 (*table*)
Nitrogenous fertilizers, 335
  (*table*)
Nomadic herding, 169–70
Nomadism, 169–70
Nonferrous metals, 207–09
North Africa, 44, 171
North America
  agriculture, 149
  arable cropland, 33
  coal reserves of, 40 (*table*)
  dairy farming, 144
  energy sources, 38, 39
    (*table*)
  fishing industry, 178, 179
  forests and forest products,
    191, 193–94
  hydropower, 40 (*table*)
  livestock ranching, 151
  lobster industry, 184
  nuclear power sources, 40
    (*table*)
  petroleum reserves, 40
    (*table*)
  population, 40 (*table*), 100
  urbanization, 36
  wheat production, 151
North American Conservation
  Conference, 479
North Atlantic Drift, 177, 182
North Atlantic Treaty Organization (NATO), 418
North Dakota, coal reserves in,
  219

North Sea
  fishing, 182, 186
  natural gas reserves, 216
Northwest Pacific Ocean, as
  fishing ground, 178
Northwest Territories (Canada),
  215
Norway, 184
  aluminum production,
    278–79
  fishing industry, 176, 178,
    182
  forests and forest products,
    192
  shipbuilding, 295
  titanium production, 280
  whaling, 184
Novokuznetsk (U.S.S.R.), 271
Nuclear
  fuel, 223
  reactors, 345–46
  power, 39 (*table*)
Nutmeg, 157
Nylon, 320–21

O

Ob River, 54
Ocean
  as food source, 51
  as power source, 51
  productivity, 178
  resources, 50
Oceania
  dairy farming, 146
  energy sources of, 38, 39
    (*table*)
  forests and forest products,
    191, 194
  land use, 34 (*table*)
  population, 36 (*table*), 100
    (*table*)
Oceanways, 383–85
Odessa (U.S.S.R.), 297
Office machines, 353 (*table*)
Ohio, 219, 283, 287, 291, 338
Ohio River, 264, 277, 333
Ohio Valley, 277
Oil, 41–42
Okhotsk Current, 178
Oklahoma
  natural gas reserves, 215
  petroleum reserves, 211
Oligopoly, 67, 72
Olives, 155
Oman, petroleum reserves of,
  213, 214
Ontario (Canada), 215
Open hearth furnace, 265, 266

Oregon, 134, 487
  fishing industry, 180
Organization for Economic
  Development (OECD),
  116
Organization of Petroleum
  Exporting Countries
  (OPEC), 44, 213
Osaka (Japan), 286, 291
Oslo, 295

P

Pacific Northwest, aluminum
  production in, 276
Pakistan
  milk production, 144
  wheat production, 163
Paleolithic culture, 169
Palms, 199
Pampa, 153
Panama Canal, 333, 385
Paotow (People's Republic of
  China), 273
Paper products, 196
Paris, 324
Passaic River, 319
Pastoralism, 156
Patent law, 113
Peanuts, 163, 168
Pearl fisheries, 184
Peking, 272
Penki (Manchuria), 272
Pennsylvania, 283, 287, 291
People's Republic of China
  agriculture, 163
  coal production, 200, 217
  corn production, 151 (*table*),
    163
  cotton production, 163, 315
  crop tillage, 157
  fishing industry, 178–79
  flax production, 163
  livestock, 148 (*table*)
  iron production, 273
  iron ore production, 204–05
  nitrogenous fertilizer
    production, 335
  petroleum reserves, 211, 214
  rice production, 163
  silk industry, 319
  soybean production, 163
  steel production, 273
  textiles, 315–16
  urbanization, 36
  wheat, 151 (*table*)
Periodical publishing, 437–39
Perkin, W. H., 335

509

Persian Gulf, 213
  pearl fisheries, 184
Personality structure, and
      man's economic
      behavior, 108
Peru
  coastal current of, 182
  copper ore production, 208
  cotton production, 147
  fishing industry, 178, 182–83
  iron ore production, 205
Petrochemicals, 337–38
Petroleum, 39
  cost, 213
  demand, 212
  importance of, 212
  origin of, 209
  production, 211 (*table*)
  reserves, 211 (*table*)
  in United States, 211
Philadelphia, 284, 290
Philippines, 160
  copper ore production, 288
      (*table*)
  defense expenditures, 419
      (*table*)
  government expenditures,
      419 (*table*)
  shifting cultivation, 168
Phosphate, 49, 336
Phytoplankton, 175
Pipelines, 219, 393–94, 394
      (*map*)
Pittsburgh, 236, 264, 268, 284,
      290
Plankton, 175–76, 182
Planning
  approaches to, 467–68
  concept of, 464–65
  goals, 466–67
  historical antecedents, 462
  local, 473
  process, 464
  regional, 471–73
  resource inventory of, 467
  state, 470–71
Plantain, 168
Plantation agriculture, 157
Plastics, production of, 333
      (*table*)
Point Barrow (Alaska), 211
Poland
  coal reserves, 217, 222
  dairy farming, 144
  milk production, 144
  nitrogenous fertilizer
      production, 335 (*table*)
  steel production, 270 (*table*)

television-receiver produc-
      tion, 350 (*table*)
Political factors
  institutions, 96
  law and the legal system, 96
  nation-state, 90
  systems, 91
  variables, 97
Pollution. *See also* Environ-
      mental pollution.
  air, 56
  control of, 57, 59
  economic effect of, 56
  sources of, 56
Population, 99–102, 288
  control programs, 484–87
  determinants of, 100 (*table*)
  growth, 480–82
  in cities, 35
Portugal
  crop and livestock farming,
      147
  fishing, 181
Postal service, 431–32
Potash, as fertilizer, 49 (*table*)
      336–37
Poza Rica, natural gas field in,
      216
Pribilof Islands, and seals, 184
Price (in economics), 66, 79
  basing point, 80
  equilibrium, 73
  free on board (f.o.b.), 79
Primary activities, 4, 125–24
Printing industry, 433–35
Production. *See* specific
      commodities.
Program Evaluation Review
      Technique (PERT), 467
Public Health Service, 404
Publishing industry, 433–35
Puerto Rico, 232
Pulp and paper industry, 195
Pyrenees (mountains), 278

Q

Qatar, petroleum production
      in, 211 (*table*), 214
Quantitative analysis, 374
Queensland (Australia), 222
Quinine, 197

R

Radio broadcasting, 435
Railroad
  gauge, 387
  passengers, 388 (*table*)

Rain forest, tropical, 193, 195
Rajasthan (India), 162
Rattan, 199
Raw materials, and industrial
      location, 228
Rayon, 320–21
Real estate services, 414
Recreational activities, spatial
      pattern of, 456
Recreation services, 445–58
Redfield, Robert, 107
Red River, 160
Refrigeration, commercial and
      industrial, 346–47
Regional development, 463
Regional geography, 26
Regional planning, 462–74
Regional tertiary systems,
      373–75
Region, definition of, 464–65
Reilly, W. J., 363
Religion, 103–05
Rent, 73
  economic, 128–31
Republic of South Africa, 206
  defense expenditures, 419
      (*table*)
  government expenditures,
      419 (*table*)
  titanium production, 280
  uranium production, 223
Republic of Sudan, forests and
      forest products of, 192
Research process, 117–18
Resins, 197
Resource, 16–17
  and economic activity, 26
  and man, 488
  and culture, 17
  recycling of, 56, 61
Retail hierarchy, central place
      theory of, 377
Retailing, 400–03
Retail trade gravitation, law of,
      363–64
Rhine River, 54, 55 (*table*)
Rhodole Mountains, 164
Ricardo, David, 116
Rice, 155, 157, 159–61, 166,
      168
Riga (U.S.S.R.), 297
River Rouge (Michigan), 297
Rivers, 55 (*table*)
Rocky Mountains, petroleum
      reserves in, 211
Roman Catholic Church, 104
Romania
  corn production, 151 (*table*)

Romania (*cont.*)
  gross domestic product, per
    capita, 338 (*table*)
  livestock and crop farming,
    148
  petroleum reserves, 214
  population density, 338
    (*table*)
Rubber, 157, 166
  natural, 197, 339
  plantation, 98
  synthetic, 338–40, 339 (*table*)
Rudimentary and sedentary
  tillage, 165–66
Ruhr River, 221–22, 272, 286,
  291

S

Saar River, 221–22, 272
St. Lawrence Seaway, 334
St. Louis (Missouri), 324
St. Maurice River, 278
Salinas (Ecuador), 177
Salmon, 178–79, 185
Salween River, 159
Samuelson, Paul A., 463
San Francisco, 157, 269, 288,
  324
  crab fisheries, 185
San Joaquin Valley (California),
  157
Sardines, 183
Saudi Arabia
  nomads, 171
  petroleum reserves, 211–13
Sawmilling, 195
Scandinavia, international
    tourist travel in, 446
    (*table*)
Scotland, 319
Sea of Azov, 270
Sea of Cortez, 185
Seals, 181
Secondary activities, 288
  location theory of, 228–44,
    372 (*table*)
Services. *See also* Government
    services.
  banking, 408–13
  communication, 429–43
  financial, 407–14
  government, 417–27
  insurance, 413–14
  marketing, 397–405
  postal, 431–32
  real estate, 414
  recreation, 445–58
  spatial distribution of, 357

telegraph, 432
telephone, 432–33
transportation, 381–95
Severance taxes, 61
Shanghai, 272
Shantung (People's Republic of
    China), 221
  flax production, 163
Sheep husbandry, 152, 156–57,
    169, 171
Shellfish, 179, 181, 183
Shifting cultivation. *See*
    Agriculture, shifting
    cultivation.
Shipbuilding, 292–97, 293
    (*table*)
Shrimp industry, 182–83
  fisheries, 185
Siberia, 219
Sierra Leone, 206
Silica, 206
Silk, 318
Site conditions
  amenity factors and
      industrial location,
      233–34
  and industrial location, 232
Skiing, 455
Skills, 113
Slater, Samuel, 283
Slaughterhouses, 253
Social choices, 22, 25
Social factors, 97–98
  and industry location, 231
Socialism, framework of, 94
Social Science Research
    council, 98
Social Security, 420–21
Social values, 11, 14
Soda ash, 330, 331 (*table*)
Soda, caustic, 331, 332 (*table*)
Soil nutrients, 168–69
Solid Waste Disposal Act, 60
    (*table*), 62
Somali, nomads in, 171
Sorghum, 162
South Africa, 193
  agriculture, 155
  corn production, 151 (*table*)
  fishing industry, 177
  livestock and crop farming,
    148
  rivers, 55 (*table*)
South America
  drainage, 54
  equatorial rainforest, 195
  fishing industry, 182
  forests and forest products,
    192, 194

grain farming, 152
livestock and crop farming,
    148
livestock ranching, 153
population, 100 (*table*)
shifting cultivation, 168
Southeast Asia, 160
  bamboo production, 197
  fishing industry, 179
  ladang, 168
  migratory agriculture, 168
    (*table*)
  pearl fisheries, 184
  rubber industry, 198
  shifting cultivation, 168
Southern Hemisphere, 183
South Korea, radio-receiver
    production in, 351
South Pacific, whaling industry
    in, 184
Spain
  agriculture, 155, 157
  defense expenditures, 419
    (*table*)
  fish catches, 178 (*table*)
  grape production, 156
    (*table*)
  international tourist travel
    in, 446 (*table*)
Spatial arrangement, 13–14
Spatial dispersion, efficiency
    of, 87
Spatial distribution, 12, 67
Spatial interaction, 12, 13,
    382–83
Special drawing rights, 83
Specialization, 78
Sri Lanka
  agriculture, 157, 160
  pearl fisheries, 184
  rice, 160
Standard Metropolitan Statis-
    tical Area (SMSA), 363,
    465–66
State Economic Areas (S.E.A.),
    465
State planning, 470–71
Steel, 267 (*table*), 270. *See also*
    Iron and steel
    production.
  alloys, 263
Steelmaking
  basic oxygen process, 266
  electric furnace, 266–67
  open hearth, 265–66
Stock replenishment (in fishing
    industry), 187

Strait of Matucca, 214
Structural factors, and
    industrial location, 230
Stuttgart (West Germany), 286,
    363
Styrene, 339
Subsistence crop and livestock
    farming, 164–65
Substitution, 66, 76
Sugar beet production, 157
Sugarcane, 157, 166, 168
Sulfur production, 49 (*table*)
Sulfuric acid production, 330
    (*table*)
Sumatra
    fishing industry, 178
    petroleum reserves, 214
Super Region Marts (S.R.M.),
    365
Supply, 66, 70
    curve, 69
    schedule, 69
Surinam, bauxite production
    in, 209
Sweden
    fishing, 182
    forest products, 194
    gross domestic product, per
      capita, 338 (*table*)
    international tourist travel
      in, 446 (*table*)
    iron ore production, 204
      (*table*)
    population, 388 (*table*)
    railway passengers, 388
      (*table*)
    shipbuilding, 295
    telephone services, 433
      (*table*)
    titanium production, 280
Switzerland
    international tourist travel
      in, 446 (*table*)
    gross domestic product, per
      capita, 388 (*table*)
    population, 388 (*table*)
    railway passengers, 338
      (*table*)
    telephone services, 433
      (*table*)
    textile machinery, 289
Synthetic fibers, 320–21
Synthetic rubber, 338–40, 339
    (*table*)
Syria, agriculture in, 157
Systematic geography, 26
Systems of agricultural produc-
    tion, 142

T
Tai-yuan (People's Republic of
    China), 272
Taman (Japan), 293
Tannin production, 197
Tanzania
    forests and forest products,
      192
    nomads in, 171
Tatars, 171
Taurus Mountains, 213
Taxes
    disposal, 61
    severance, 61
Tea, 157
Teak, 195
Technological change, process
    of, 115–18
Technological factors, and
    manufacturing, 231
Technology, 54, 112, 482–83
    and economic activity,
      118–19
Telecommunications, 348, 350
Telegraph services, 432, 433
    (*table*)
Telephone services, 432, 433
    (*table*)
Television
    broadcasting, 435
    receivers, production of,
      350 (*table*)
Tennessee, 276, 320
Tennessee Valley Authority
    (TVA), 62, 471
Tertiarization of economic
    activity, 369–72
Tertiary economic activity,
    361–499
    location theory of, 362–64
    employment in, 373 (*table*)
Tertiary systems, 369, 373–75
Texas, 236, 275
    natural gas reserves, 215
Textiles, 311–26
    cotton, 310–15
    economic outlook for, 325
    garment manufacture, 321,
      324
    history, 311–13
    machinery, 289
    manmade fibers, 319–21
    wool, 316–19
Thailand, 160
    fish catches, 178 (*table*)
    natural rubber production,
      158
    rice production, 151 (*table*)

Thorium, 42
Tientsin (People's Republic of
    China), 272
Tigris-Euphrates Valley, 169,
    213
Tin production, 49 (*table*)
Titanium production, 279–80,
    49 (*table*)
Tokyo, 286, 291, 293
Tourism, 446 (*table*)
Trade
    international, 82, 199–201,
      386
    patterns of, 464
Tradition, 25
Transfer cost, and manufac-
    turing, 230
Transformers, power and
    distribution, 345
Transhumance, 156
Transportation. *See also*
    specific forms.
    accessibility, 387
    agriculture, 125
    air, 391–92
    costs, 125
    freight rates, 81, 228
    hinterland, 128
    marketing, 229
    motor, 389–90
    pipeline, 393–94
    rail, 386–89
    services, 381–95
    spatial interaction, 382–83
    technology of, 381
    transfer cost, 239
    water, 383–86
Travel
    air, 455
    of international tourists,
      446–47 (*table*)
Truck farming, 145–46
Tuan, Yi-Fu, 478
Tuna, 183
Tungsten, 263, 49 (*table*)
Tunisia, 147
Turbulence, 176–77
Turkey
    agriculture, 155, 157
    kurds, 165
    subsistence crop and live-
      stock farming, 164

U
Ukraine, 204, 269
Unemployment, 425–26
Union of Soviet Socialist
    Republics

Union of Soviet Socialist Republics (*cont.*)
agricultural implements industry, 289
agriculture, 154–55
aircraft industry, 306
aluminum production, 277, 276 (*table*)
arable crop land, 34 (*table*)
area, 34 (*table*)
automotive industry, 201–302, 297 (*table*)
bauxite production, 209 (*table*)
beef production, 153 (*table*)
book production, 435 (*table*)
coal production, 217 (*table*)
commercial plantation, crop tillage, 157
copper production, 208 (*table*)
corn production, 151 (*table*)
cotton production, 147
dairy farming, 144
defense expenditures, 419 (*table*)
education, 421–22
energy, 38
engine and motor industry, 291
fishing industry, 178 (*table*), 179, 181, 185
forests and forest products, 191, 194
grain farming, 152
international tourist travel, 446 (*table*)
iron ore production, 204 (*table*), 205
iron and steel production, 269–71, 270 (*table*)
livestock, 148 (*table*), 152
ranching, 152
locomotives, electrical, 344
machine tools, 283
metal fabricating, 285
natural gas reserves, 215
newspapers, 434 (*table*)
petroleum reserves, 211 (*table*), 212
plastics production, 333 (*table*)
population, 34 (*table*)
recreational patterns in, 451
rayon industry, 320
shipbuilding, 297
social security, 420
soda ash production, 331 (*table*)

steel production, 270 (*table*)
telegraph service, 433 (*table*)
telephone service, 433 (*table*)
television receiver production, 350 (*table*)
textiles, 289, 313, 317
titanium production, 280
tractor production, 287 (*table*)
urbanization, 36
whaling industry, 184
wheat production, 151 (*table*)
woolen industry, 316 (*table*), 317
United Arab Emirates, petroleum reserves in, 211
United Kingdom
aircraft industry, 306
arable cropland, 34 (*table*)
area, 34 (*table*)
automotive industry, 297 (*table*), 301
book production, 435 (*table*)
dairying, 144
defense expenditures, 419 (*table*)
fishing industry, 181–82
land use, 33
merchant vessel tonnage, 293 (*table*)
metal fabricating, 286
milk production, 144 (*table*)
plastics production, 333 (*table*)
population, 34 (*table*)
radio-receiver production, 351 (*table*)
rayon industry, 320
recreational patterns in, 450, 452–58
shipbuilding, 293–94
social security, 420
sulfuric acid production, 330 (*table*)
telephone service, 433 (*table*)
tractor production, 287 (*table*)
whaling industry, 184
wool production, 316 (*table*)
United Nations
Economic and Social Council, 86
Educational, Scientific, and Cultural Organization (UNESCO), 98

International Financial Corporation, 82
United States, 158
Agency for International Development, 82
agriculture, 143, 155
aircraft industry, 305–06
air pollution, 60 (*table*)
airports, 35 (*table*)
Air Quality Act, 59
aluminum, 275–77, 276 (*table*)
arable cropland, 34 (*table*)
area, 34 (*table*)
automotive industry, 297–300
balance of payments, 44
banking system, 413
bauxite production, 209 (*table*)
book industry, 439
Bureau of Outdoor Recreation, 446
Bureau of the Budget, 98
Bureau of the Census, 455, 465
caustic soda production, 332 (*table*)
coal production, 217 (*table*)
communications in, 435–36
copper production, 208 (*table*)
corn production, 148, 151 (*table*)
cotton production, 157
dairy farming, 143–44
defense expenditures, 418
Department of Agriculture, 404
Department of Health, Education, and Welfare, 98
diamonds, 52
electronics, 347–48, 349 (*table*)
employment structure in, 372 (*table*)
energy, 38, 43
engine and motor industry, 290
Federal Aviation Administration (FAA), 352
fish catches, 178, 178 (*table*)
Food and Drug Administration, 51, 404
forests, 134
forest products, 194
geothermal power, 37
grain farming, 150, 152

513

United States (*cont.*)
highways and roads, 35
(*table*)
industrial chemicals, 329
international tourist travel,
446 (*table*)
interstate highway system,
389
iron ore production, 69, 204
(*table*)
iron and steel production,
268–69
land use, 33, 34 (*table*)
livestock, 152
and crop farming, 147
machine tools, 283
magnesium, 279
mail traffic, 431 (*table*)
pollution control, legislation
and expenditures, 486
(*table*)
manufacturing, 236–37
marketing, 146, 147
merchant vessel tonnage,
293 (*table*)
metal fabricating, 283–85
milk production, 214 (*table*)
minerals, 46, 47
mining, machinery and
equipment, 291–92
National Aeronautics and
Space Administration,
98, 113, 352, 467
National Bureau of Stand-
ards, 404
national defense areas, 35
(*table*)
National Environmental
Policy Act, 487
National Industrial Conference Board, 62
National Petroleum Council,
42
National Resources Planning
Board, 471
natural gas reserves, 215
newspaper industry, 434, 436
nitric acid production, 332
(*table*)
nitrogenous fertilizer production, 335 (*table*)
Organization for Economic
Development, 116
petrochemicals, 337–38
petroleum reserves, 211
(*table*)
plastics production, 333
(*table*)
population, 34 (*table*)

precipitation, annual, 53
Public Health Service, 404
radio and television broadcasting, 436 (*table*), 440
radio-receiver production,
351 (*table*)
railway pasengers, 388
(*table*)
ranching, 152
rayon industry, 320
resin production, 333 (*table*)
shipbuilding, 296–97
silk industry, 319
Social Security, 420–21
soda ash production, 331
(*table*)
soybean production, 148
specialized horticulture, 145
Standard Metropolitan Statistical Areas (SMSA), 58
state and national parks, 35
(*table*)
steel production, 270 (*table*)
sulfuric acid production, 320
(*table*)
synthetic rubber production,
199, 339 (*table*)
telegraph service, 433 (*table*)
television-receiver production, 350 (*table*)
tertiary activities, 374
textile industry, 310–13, 317,
319–24
tractor production, 287
(*table*)
transportation services, 383–
394
truck farming, 146
uranium production, 223
urban areas, 35 (*table*)
urban living, pressures of,
455
water consumption, 53
wheat production, 151
(*table*)
wildlife areas, 35 (*table*)
woolen industry, 316 (*table*)
Ural Mountains, 212, 270, 277
Uranium production, 49 (*table*),
223
Urbanization, 35
Uruguay, livestock ranching in,
153
Utah, coal reserves in, 219

V

Vanadium production, 49
(*table*)

Vehicles, recreational, 455
Venezuela
iron ore production, 205
petroleum reserves, 211
Vietnam, 160
Virginia, 320
Viticulture, 155
Vladivostok (U.S.S.R.), 297
Volga River, 185, 212
Voluntary arrangements, 25–26
Von Thünen, 4, 130, 140
theory of, 124–25, 360–61
model, modification of, 126–
127

W

Wants, 20–21
Washington (state), 487
coal reserves, 219
fishing industry, 180
Washington, D.C., 238
Waste disposal, 234
Water Resource Planning Act,
62
Water resources, 50–56
Waterson, Albert, 468
Water, supply characteristics
of, 53–56
Waterways, 383–86
inland, 285
and international trade, 386
ocean, 383–85
Watt, James, 119
Weber, Alfred, 4
theory of location of industries, 239–42
Western Europe
coal reserves, 221–22
energy reserves, 38
fishing industry, 176
natural gas reserves, 216
petrochemicals, 338
West Germany
aluminum production, 276
(*table*), 278
automotive industry, 297
(*table*), 300–01
coal reserves, 217, 222
dairy farming, 144
defense expenditures, 419
(*table*)
engine and motor industry,
290–91
fishing industry, 182
fruit production, 147
iron and steel production,
272

West Germany (*cont.*)
  linen industry, 318
  locomotives, electrical, 344
  machine tools, 283
  metal fabricating in, 285–86
  milk production, 144
  natural gas, 216
  newspaper industry, 434
    (*table*)
  nitrogenous fertilizers, 335
    (*table*)
  nuclear reactors, 346
  radio and television broad-
    casting, 436 (*table*)
  radio-receiver production,
    351 (*table*)
  recreational patterns in, 450
  shipbuilding, 294–95
  Social Security, 420
  television-receiver produc-
    tion, 350 (*table*)
  textiles, 289, 317

  turbine generators, 346
West Indies, 184
West Virginia, 219, 338
  coal distribution in, 218
Whaling industry, 183–84
Wheat production, 155, 162
Whittlesey, Derwent, 142
Wholesaling, 400
Wickham, Henry A., 198
Wilkinson, John, 119
Wisconsin, 291
Wood products. *See also*
    Forest and forest prod-
    ucts.
  industrial, 200
  pulp, 196, 199, 200
  tropical, 196, 199, 200
Wool, 316 (*table*)
World Food Conference, 172
Wyoming
  coal reserves, 219
  petroleum reserves, 211

Y

Yak, 169
Yakuts, 165
Yangtze River, 160, 163, 205,
    272
Yangtze Valley, 163
Yaroslavl (U.S.S.R.), 285
Yellow River, 163
Yokohama (Japan), 286, 293
Yugoslavia, 147
  agriculture, 147

Z

Zaire, rudimentary and seden-
    tary tillage in, 166
Zambia, copper production in,
    208 (*table*)
Zande of Central Africa, 130
Zimmerman, Eric W., 37
Zinc production, 49 (*table*)
Zones of land use, 125–26
Zooplankton, 176